BOB BOOTHBY

Robert Rhodes James was born in India and educated at Sedburgh School and Oxford. In 1955 he was appointed a Clerk in the House of Commons and in 1963 was elected a Fellow of All Souls College, Oxford. From 1972 to 1976 he was Principal Officer to the Secretary-General of the UN, and in 1976 he was elected Conservative MP for Cambridge; in addition to other posts he is currently one of the Chairmen of the House of Commons.

He is the author of a biography of Lord Randolph Churchill and award winning books on the House of Commons, on Lord Rosebery and what is still considered to be the definitive history of the 1915 Gallipoli campaign. His biography of Churchill is recognized as the most successful analysis of Churchill the man and *The British Revolution, 1860–1939* and his authorized biographies of Prince Albert and Anthony Eden have added to his formidable reputation as a historian and biographer.

FOR WANDA

AS BOB WOULD HAVE WISHED

'In truth, there are some characters which nature
has so happily compounded that even vice is unable
wholly to degrade them; and there is a charm of
manner and temper which sometimes accompanies the
excesses of a strong animal nature that wins more
popularity in the world than the purest and the
most self-denying virtue.'

Lecky on Charles James Fox

Contents

Illustrations

(Unless otherwise stated, the photographs come from Lady Boothby's collection and are reprinted with her kind permission.)

Preface

The origins of this biography were entirely characteristic of the subject.

While I was engaged in the late 1960s in research for my study of Winston Churchill's career up to 1939, subsequently published as *Churchill – A Study in Failure* in 1970, I was given much kindness and assistance by several people who had played significant parts in Churchill's life and career, and whose estimates of him varied to a remarkable and fascinating extent. These included Lord Avon (Anthony Eden), Harold Macmillan, Lord Swinton, Duncan Sandys, Sir Desmond Morton and Sir John Colville. I also approached Bob Boothby, whom I had known when I was a Clerk of the House of Commons, and who responded with enthusiasm by inviting me to the first of a number of splendid lunches and convivial conversations.

As with the others, he was only too willing to speak about the past and his own role in great events, and was among the most enjoyable interviewees of them all. In 1967 I invited him for a weekend to my then College, All Souls, Oxford, of which I was a junior Research Fellow, to return his hospitality and, with a certain impishness, to get him to sit at what he had denounced in the context of pre-war appeasement of the dictators, and unfairly, as 'that disastrous dinner-table'. He was on top form, with many old friends, including Lord Salter, who had always considered that Boothby had been scurvily treated and grossly underestimated. The evening was a great success, as was indeed the whole weekend.

Not long after, in November, I was attending a NATO conference in Brussels. When we came to depart, a thick and impenetrable fog had descended upon the airport. In the agreeable company of Arthur Blenkinsop, a Labour MP of much charm and gentleness, I made a very slow progress by rail to Zeebrugge and thence by night ferry to Dover. We arrived at first light after a bleak crossing in freezing temperatures, Arthur desperately calculating whether he could get to a vital meeting in his South Shields constituency.

At Dover station, somewhat blearily, I bought a copy of *The Times*. To my astonishment I saw a photograph of myself in the *Diary* column and, even more amazed, read that Bob Boothby had appointed me his biographer, cheerfully announcing that 'I chose him because I think he is the best. I met him at All Souls [this was incorrect] and thought he was

11

absolutely first class.' There was more in the same jovial vein. This was the first I had heard of it. Indeed, it was the last; he only referred to the matter once again, and then vaguely, in a meeting before his death in July 1986. I had assumed that he had thought better of the idea, and my own political and literary concerns had long since taken me into other fields. When I saw him in the House of Lords not long before his death, although he was sadly shrunken, the old fire, cheerfulness and beaming smile were still there, but, again, there was no allusion whatever to my putative role as his biographer.

It was only after his death that I realised that he had been absolutely serious, and that this indeed was his desire. I was torn between emotions of gratitude and of concern. Having just been through the experience of combining a full-time political life and writing a major political biography – that of Eden – I was very reluctant to repeat it. This hesitation was compounded by the fact that I would once again, as in the case of Eden, be 'threading a living crowd', in Rosebery's phrase, and I knew enough about Boothby's private life to see the difficulties that this would cause. On the other hand it was his wish that I should undertake it; his widow, Wanda, was very keen; and I had always had a soft spot for a man of such spirit and love of life, who, on the big political issues, had, in Lord Salter's words, 'been uniformly right'. His judgment on many other matters may have been faulty, as he himself happily admitted, but on the major issues he had not only been brave to the point of political suicide on several occasions, but his opinions and conclusions have been vindicated.

The width, depth and warmth of his many and varied friendships also said much for his intellect and character; and although his latter-day sharpness against Churchill was sad, it was not as unbalanced nor as unfair as some have alleged, and, as will be seen, he had some cause for these emotions. Also, I like people who live full lives, do not give a damn about what others think of them, and fight hard for the causes they believe in. If, also, he was the object of dislike and dismay to generations of Conservative Whips, I do not regard this as being to his discredit – nor did his devoted and staunch constituents.

Moreover, Boothby was of a generation that wrote letters and, with the exception of those from Lady Dorothy Macmillan, which he destroyed, he kept them. Unfortunately from the point of view of a biographer he did not keep a diary, although he wrote frequent notes on particular episodes, but his papers are far more voluminous than I had expected.

Boothby did in fact start a detailed journal at the beginning of June 1949, which he maintained for less than seven months. However, he showed it to a particularly close friend, who said that she was 'aghast at its complacency' and added, 'It was incredible that anyone could be so sure of, and so pleased with, themselves.' This was somewhat harsh, but it clearly disconcerted Boothby, and he abandoned the journal in August, perhaps to the relief of many, but to the dismay of his biographer. Boothby later wrote in a footnote to the journal that he had done so

partly through laziness; but mainly because I could not stand the inevitable egotism, and criticism of others. The truth is I hate autobiographies and diaries, and find them almost unreadable. Biographies are the thing. One day, perhaps, I shall find a biographer. The stuff is all available; and by it I should much prefer to be judged than by personal ephemeral jottings, although some of them would have been funny.

The journal might also have given a false impression of his character, and those of others. For example, on one occasion he described a prominent Conservative:

He talked much nonsense, in a rather hysterical way. I have come to the conclusion, with reluctance, that he is no good. Superficial charm. Not much guts, and a rather unpleasing streak of snobbery underneath. His wife is worth ten of him.

But a week later he was writing of the same man that 'He could not have been nicer, or more modest, or more sensible. So, of course, I have revised my view about him.' One can see why Boothby's friend was dismayed by the journal, and also why he gave it up, but it is a severe loss. His engagement diaries are of value in setting out the hectic pattern of his life, but are an inadequate substitute.

Thus, I accepted Lady Boothby's kind invitation and her husband's wish to attempt this portrait of a man whom *The Times* described on his death as a 'political maverick of unfulfilled promise'. There was truth in this description, but it was not the whole, and I hope that this biography fulfils his good opinion of me, in whom, I suspect strongly, he discerned a kindred spirit – although, I must add, not in all respects!

In his own autobiographies – *I Fight to Live* (1947) and *Recollections of a Rebel* (1978) – Boothby was meticulously discreet about his private life, not for his own sake but out of consideration for others.

In 1962, when a collection of his speeches and essays was published under the title of *My Yesterday, Your Tomorrow*, his friends were startled to read that 'I have had no private life at all.' John Strachey, his oldest and closest friend, rightly wrote:

This is an exaggeration. Indeed it is almost the exact opposite of the truth. The fact is that Lord Boothby has had one of the richest, strangest, most various, at times most hilarious, at other times most sad, of the private lives of all the public men of our time.

It is always difficult for the political biographer to achieve the right balance between the public and the private life, but it has been notably difficult in Boothby's case. His long romance with Dorothy Macmillan had a profound political and personal significance; other affairs did not, and so I have been reticent about them. I know the circumstances, but have chosen not to reveal them, as this would cause quite unnecessary pain to several people; they are also not relevant to the story of Boothby's life. He, too, would have been shocked and distressed if these matters were broadcast. I have exercised a similar discretion in the past, for which I make no apology. One day all may be revealed, but not by me, and certainly not now.

As Boothby once wrote in a private letter, 'Letters that are intended for one pair of eyes only should not be seen by others,' and he was meticulous to honour this principle for the letters he received. He had, of course, no such control over those he wrote to others, many of which have survived. No doubt, more will emerge in due course. He had several loves before he met his second wife, Wanda, and those to whom I have spoken about him have not only been very frank and co-operative, but have invariably used two words to describe him – his kindness and his generosity. He would not have wanted his biographer to abuse these confidences or to hurt those whom he loved.

All memoirs, and particularly those of actors and politicians, should be treated with considerable caution, but Boothby's have stood up remarkably well to the test of contemporary evidence, and demonstrate that he was a far more serious, thoughtful and wise man than he was often given credit for. That he was also foolish on occasion, self-indulgent and irresponsible, should not mislead the historian or commentator as often it has done.

That Boothby's glittering early promise was not fulfilled is incontestable, and much, although not all, of the fault was his. His career is a kind of personal and political Gallipoli – just as it seemed that everything was going well and great opportunities loomed, something disastrous would happen. But he had an extraordinary capacity for bouncing back, cheerful and optimistic, warm-hearted and genial, as if nothing untoward had happened. He was adored in his East Aberdeenshire constituency and by a remarkable constellation of friends, ranging from Lloyd George to Thomas Beecham, Michael Foot to Somerset Maugham, Brendan Bracken to Compton Mackenzie. He was the first British politician to become a national star of radio and television, to the chagrin of his colleagues in the House of Commons, and to those who remember them there have never been programmes like the early *Any Questions?* on radio and television's *Free Speech* and *In the News*. Media fame is notoriously ephemeral, but it left its mark on a particular generation, who responded to Boothby's cheerful iconoclasm more readily than most grave politicians did, especially in the Conservative Party. In an age of rather grey politicians, Boothby shone out as an extrovert, independent spirit of charm, intelligence and exceptionally wide reading. So, all was not failure, and the last twenty years of his long life were supremely happy.

My principal gratitude is to Wanda, Lady Boothby, who not only put her husband's papers in order, but catalogued them meticulously, and who was unfailingly helpful and understanding throughout my researches and the writing of the book. At no point did she attempt to influence my judgments or opinions, and her role has been uniformly constructive.

So many others have assisted me that the list would be long indeed if I were to include them all. Also, some who have been particularly co-operative have asked that their names should not be mentioned. But I am especially indebted to Lady Gage, for her assistance and reminiscences of her former husband; Madame Legentilhomme, an old friend and former secretary of Boothby's; his cousins, Mrs Ann Carey and Mr Ludovic Kennedy; Mr Peter Strachan of the *Buchan Observer*, whose 'Vintage Boothby' file was invaluable; Mr Patrick Wolrige-Gordon, his successor as MP for East Aberdeenshire; Mr Nigel Nicolson, for permission to quote from his father's letters and diaries; Mr Myles Eckersley, for information on his father's business relations with Boothby; Lady Mosley; Mr Iain Sproat; the Duke of Devonshire; Sir John Junor; Lord Gladwyn; the late Lord Duncan-Sandys; Lord Home; Lord Beaverbrook, for his permission to quote from his grandfather's corres-pondence with Boothby; the University of Texas at Austin, for allowing me to see, and to quote from, the Compton Mackenzie papers; the Churchill Trustees, for a similar kindness over Sir Winston Churchill's papers; the Weizmann Institute, whose Director enabled me to see Boothby's letters to Chaim Weizmann and related correspondence; the Secretary and historian of the Royal and Ancient Golf Club, St Andrews; three of Boothby's colleagues on the Court of St Andrews, Sir John Carmichael, Mr John Thompson and Mr D. P. Dorward; Sir Isaiah Berlin; and many other friends, acquaintances and constituents of Boothby's who have been so helpful in their reminiscences. If I pay par-ticular tribute to my parliamentary colleague, political opponent and friend, Michael Foot, it is because his letters to Boothby, and the poetical contributions of his late brother, Dingle, have given me such special joy, as they did to Boothby himself.

A project that became unexpectedly rather more considerable than I had expected would not have been possible to complete without the wonderful support and practical assistance of my wife and Mrs Gillie Coutts, who once again did all the tedious chores, and my perfect and irreplaceable secretary, Mrs Polly Andrews. John Curtis and Linda Osband remain the best of editors, and best of friends.

To everyone who helped me, I can only express my most sincere thanks but I owe a special additional debt to the Librarians and staff of the House of Commons Library, who have been invariably helpful.

This biography began as a reluctant duty. It became an increasingly absorbing and refreshing change from the burdens of contemporary politics, and has given me more enjoyment than I had expected. For this alone, I am grateful to Bob Boothby.

Robert Rhodes James
November 1990

I

Childhood
1900–18

To begin at the beginning, quite factually. Robert John Graham Boothby was born in Edinburgh, on 12 February 1900, in a snowstorm, the son of Robert Tuite Boothby and his wife Mabel. He later took a somewhat irreverent view of his distant origins. In a speech in London in February 1938 to the London Scots Self-Government Committee – whose purposes he strongly opposed, as he was to do throughout his life – he described himself as a 'mongrel':

I am a rather rare type. I am an English émigré. I come from Denmark, via Lincolnshire and Derbyshire. When my family had succeeded in losing all its money, my grandfather did a thing few Englishmen had ever had the courage to do. He migrated to Scotland, married a girl from Perth, and settled down at St Andrews. He spent the rest of his life catching salmon, playing golf, and dining with the University professors. I cannot think of a more ideal form of existence this side of Heaven, but it was unremunerative. My father, who drove his first ball at the age of two, was an even better golfer. But he had to earn his living. Thank God, he went to Edinburgh to do it. And that was where I saw the light of day.

I may be a mongrel by breeding, but I am a native of the capital city of Scotland. And, whatever you may think of my politics, I am as good a Scottish patriot as anyone in this room. As a matter of fact, I often think I combine the best qualities of the two nations!

In fact, the name of Boothby and its early variations of Bobi, Boby and Botteby have been earnestly researched as far back as the reign of the Saxon King Egbert. It is true that the family came from Denmark, prospered, became eminent in Lincolnshire and built fine houses. There is an unverified claim that one of Boothby's ancestors 'took an active part in the signature of Magna Carta', which both he and his biographer regard with considerable scepticism.

Robert Tod Boothby (1830–97), of whom his grandson spoke so admiringly, and who had eight children, had been one of the few investors in the British railway boom to actually lose money. It is clear that he did not lose it all, as he lived in comfort and happiness in St Andrews until his death, his widow Madeleine surviving him until 1908. Educated at Eton and Cambridge University, he served in the 79th Queen's Own Cameron Highlanders, retiring as a colonel; however, he was always known at St Andrews as 'The Major'. An outstanding golfer, he came to the game late, but it was to become his passion. 'His fine, manly, commanding form was so well known,' one of his partners has written, 'and his gentleness and courtesy were unrivalled.' One of his daughters, Edith, married Lord Cunliffe, Chairman of the Bank of England, and lived until 1965. Thus, it was not a totally destitute inheritance.

In 1906 Robert and Mabel Boothby moved to Edinburgh and bought Beechwood, a large eighteenth-century house with additions and interior by the Adam brothers on the southern slopes of Corstophine Hill, with a walled garden, some twenty acres of land and splendid views of the Pentlands. The Boothbys soon gained a reputation for warm hospitality, and one close friend recalled a happy weekend at Beechwood many years later:

> Your father sang a lot of Scots songs – two of which I have brought my children up on, though I only heard them once. He also sang Mozart.
> Your mama was marvellous – she had such charm & she was so clever – we didn't realise she was the pivot of everything, she did it so well.

Beechwood was a very contented home, the centre of its firmament being Bob (as he was called by his parents and all others), on whom his parents doted, particularly as he was to be their only child. In an unusual metaphor Bob later remarked that it was 'like living in a lukewarm bath'. He was very spoilt, excessively admired, and life was rather too easy.

A major influence on the young Bob was his maternal grandmother, Margaret Lancaster. Her husband, Henry, had died young, after a beginning of such promise that Gladstone had proposed him for the post of Lord Advocate; he was Jowett's favourite pupil at Balliol, who wrote of him that there were few who knew 'what force of personality, perseverance, and public spirit lay concealed under that gay and joyous exterior', and a friend of Thackeray. Although he had been long dead before Bob's birth, his widow treasured his memory so deeply that Bob, who adored her, came to know him as a living influence.

Another major influence were the preachers. The child Boothby, like the man, had little interest in religion, and the adult agnostic – if not atheist – could be detected in the child, but he was fascinated by the great Scottish preachers, especially John Kelman of the United Free St George's, who 'held vast congregations, and for some years the bulk of the student body in Scotland, in the palm of his hand'. Boothby put him into the same class as a natural orator with Lloyd George 'on one of his good days', and no praise could be higher than that.

Boothby later recalled that

My earliest memory is of a German band which came to play outside the house once a week. Every effort was made to get me to sleep before it arrived. In vain. On each occasion I had to be carried, screaming and terror-stricken, to a back room. In retrospect, it shows remarkable prescience. I also remember sitting on my grandmother's knee in the large drawing-room before a flickering fire. She looked at me long and earnestly, and finally said: 'You're a queer little fish.'

In his two volumes of memoirs Boothby wrote little about his childhood or his parents, but he was quite willing to discuss the latter, and did so in interviews and personal notes. From these it is clear that although he loved them deeply – he once commented, 'Oh, how much we loved each other. Perhaps we loved each other too much' – he was always in some awe of them. His mother may have been a small woman, but she had a strong and determined character. His cousin Ludovic Kennedy has given a vivid portrait of the adult Bob arriving at Beechwood somewhat dishevelled and Falstaffian off the night train from London meekly obeying his mother's commands; she also kept a beady eye on his whisky intake when at home. But her loyalty and love for him, although on occasions sorely tested, never wavered.

The three Lancaster daughters – Cecil, Ethel and Mabel – all made excellent marriages. They had had a somewhat neglected childhood, as their mother, after the loss not only of her brilliant young husband but of her only son, who had predeceased his father by a year, and whose death, Jowett wrote of Lancaster, was 'the one great affliction of his otherwise bright and happy life',* seemed to resent the surviving daughters, who, as Cecil's daughter Ann later remarked, 'virtually brought themselves up'. One thing they developed in common was a deep love of Italy, which Mabel was to pass on to Bob.

Cecil Lancaster married Nevill Dundas, a Writer to the Signet and a

---

*Foreword to *Henry Lancaster: Essays and Reviews* (privately printed and published, 1876). An anonymous poet wrote of the event that

> . . . but ne'er again
> Returned to him the old exuberant fun
> That used to sparkle with the day's work
> done.

brilliant lawyer, and had a son, Henry, and two daughters. Ethel married Sir Ludovic Grant, the Professor of Public and International Law at Edinburgh University, and had one daughter, Rosalind, to whom Boothby was particularly devoted, and who married Captain Edward Kennedy, RN, in 1918. Kennedy was a brave and good man, who was forced out of the navy under circumstances that did him credit, and the navy none, and became a Conservative Party agent until he was recalled to the navy in 1939, destined to die a hero's death. But Boothby, until then, never took 'K' seriously.

As Bob and his cousins were almost exact contemporaries, he was brought up virtually as their brother and developed for each a deep affection. Henry Dundas was the oldest and the one for whom a great future was prophesied, and whom the young Bob revered. Each family had a large house with extensive grounds, and, if not exceptionally wealthy, was certainly to be counted among the more affluent members of Edinburgh society.

Of the Edinburgh of his childhood Boothby has written:

Those were spacious days before Europe began, and continued, to blow itself to pieces. Edinburgh was surrounded by ducal palaces, and large mansions designed and adorned by the Adam brothers, inhabited by the most part by baronets. My parents were far from affluent; but I remember no period before the second world war when we had less than six indoor servants, two gardeners and a chauffeur. And there were only three of us!

Rosalind's son, Ludovic, has written vividly of his own difficult relationship with his mother, and Bob clearly had similar problems with his own, who has been described by a member of the family as 'the firebrand' of the three sisters. She was also ultra-critical, could be very unkind and was prone to jealousy. She was a very dominant personality, highly intelligent, very musical,* an excellent gardener and manager of her large home. She was also somewhat eccentric, as when she sued the Edinburgh Zoo, which was adjacent to Beechwood, to either subdue or remove a sealion whose roaring kept her awake; rather surprisingly, she won. Another of her actions was to deliberately falsify her age in her passport; when she died in 1949, her son discovered that she was not seventy-four, as she had claimed, but eighty. She had no time for other people's birthdays, either, and never remembered or recognised those of her husband or son.

Ludovic Kennedy has painted a portrait of Mabel Boothby with much felicity:

---

* She was one of the founders of the Edinburgh Festival, which first took place in 1947.

Aunt Mabel was like a round ball of fluff whom I remember mostly in a lavender-coloured tweed skirt, carrying a chiffon lavender handkerchief, and wearing thick pebble glasses. But she had a great zest for life and laughter and was a truly wonderful listener. 'No!' she would say with seemingly genuine interest when one had imparted some faintly boring piece of information. *'Not really? Oh!'* Before lunch she would retire to what she would call her boudoir (a little box of a room between the drawing-room and the library) and through the closed door you could hear her saying, 'This is Pink Carnation speaking. I want half a crown each way on Have a Go in the two-thirty at Haydock and five shillings to win on Plumgarnet in the three o'clock.'*

A biographer should always be deeply cautious about parental influences, but Boothby was also to be a gambler, although never, unhappily, in terms of half a crown or five shillings.

Boothby always freely admitted to being a gambler, but it was only relatively late in life that he realised it was just as much fun playing for low stakes that he could afford as for large ones that he could not. The course of his fortunes – and not only financial – would have been very different if he had made this discovery at an earlier stage in his life. Boothby used to say, not at all convincingly, about his gambling that 'I have tried to fight it.' One of his few moments of luck occurred in 1946, when he found himself in Boulogne at the end of a holiday with only £2. On a whim he got himself to Le Touquet, booked himself into an expensive hotel and went to the casino. At the entrance he met a gypsy, who urged him to follow his advice totally, and they would share the winnings. Boothby did so, and they won £450 – a very large sum in 1946. After paying off the gypsy, Boothby was able to enjoy a splendid dinner and returned to England in triumph. Unhappily, this was an unusual occurrence, but, win or lose, on this he was incorrigible until his second wife took matters in hand. By then, alas, much had been lost. It was an aspect of his personality that made his friends despair, and his enemies even more censorious. Boothby apologised to the former, and did not worry about the latter.

Bob's father – known to all as Tom – was not a very enthusiastic man of business and, it was claimed, owed his appointment as Joint Secretary of the Scottish Provident in 1904 entirely to the fact that his brother-in-law, James Watson, was the Manager; when Watson retired in 1920, Tom Boothby succeeded him and held the position until his death in 1941. The Scottish Provident was his only employer throughout his life, although he was also a director of the Royal Bank of Scotland, and it has to be conceded that its affairs were not altogether in impressive shape by the time of his death. 'Boothby was the last of a tradition of gentleman-Managers,' the historian of the firm tactfully puts it, 'who in the more

* Ludovic Kennedy, *On My Way to the Club*, p. 65.

competitive years ahead were to be replaced by technically qualified professionals.'

Tom Boothby was over six feet tall and regarded as one of the most handsome men in Edinburgh. 'To meet him was to experience a glow of well-being,' a friend wrote of him. Although he could not read a note of music, he was a natural improviser, and composed and performed his own verses and songs, of which *Flat-Footed Jean* became something of a Scots classic.* When a maid at Beechwood gave notice because she was marrying a policeman, Tom Boothby composed a song in her honour for the occasion that ended:

> Maggie McGee, Maggie McGee,
> The sun's in your hair an' its lichts in your ee.
> Oh what's to become o' ma washin' an' me
> When you marry your polisman, Maggie McGee?

Born in St Andrews, and a graduate of the University, whose Rector he was to become, he inherited from his father an almost fanatical devotion to golf. He became one of the finest players in Scotland and was appointed Captain of the Royal and Ancient in succession to Lord Haig in 1921, in his eyes a far greater honour than being a member of the Royal Company of Archers, the sovereign's ceremonial bodyguard in Scotland, or even his knighthood, which he received in 1929. He was also an excellent and enthusiastic shot, who was warmly welcomed on any shoot and was particularly appreciated by the Roseberys, no mean judges on these matters. In politics, like most professional men in Edinburgh of his generation, he was a convinced Gladstonian Liberal, and rather more radical than most. He was also a keen, and very perceptive, collector of seventeenth-century Dutch paintings.

Although it is evident that Tom Boothby's real view of life was that it should be enjoyed, preferably on a golf course, or with a rod by a river, or with a gun at the shoulder, or in joyous renderings of his own songs – *Flat-Footed Jean* became almost the company anthem – he was not wholly inadequate as a businessman and was very comfortably off. His will in 1941 was proved at over £66,000, then a considerable fortune.

Bob once described himself in words that were uncharacteristically

---

* Did ye ever hear tell of Jean Jamieson's bonnet?
  It was no' the hat but the ornaments on it
  That made everyone keek at Jean Jamieson's bonnet.
  Jean, Jean, my bonny bonny Jean
  Come into ma arms once again.
  Though ye're feet are rather flat,
  Yet ye're nae the waur for that.
  Come into my arms, ma bonny Jean.

modest, but which could equally apply perfectly to his father: 'I love pleasure. I love enjoying myself. I have a certain sense of public duty, which I sometimes resent. There has always been a certain conflict between the two.' What Tom Boothby certainly lacked was any vestige of personal ambition. He had an agreeable, well-remunerated, interesting, but undemanding profession; he had his Edinburgh clubs and friends. He was tolerant, kind and easy-going, and had, like most Scots, a great respect for education and learning. Although he would have denied intellectual qualities himself, he was very well-read and could have developed into a scholar if he had tried. He led a civilised and happy life. Brendan Bracken described him as 'one of the nicest men I have ever known', and all other testimonies, including that of his future daughter-in-law, are of exceptional warmth and affection.

Bob thus grew up in the most agreeable of circumstances. He was never to be as good a golfer or shot as his father, although he was considerably above average at both; shooting birds did not interest him very much, but he had a deadly eye, and when he took the trouble could astonish more serious shooters with his accuracy. But his heart was not in it – nor in most traditional country pursuits. His dislike of cats and dogs, and most animals, was well known to his friends. However, his father inculcated into him a love of outdoor sports and music, which was to be deep and lifelong, an enjoyment of company and the good things of life, a sense of civic duty, a Liberal outlook on affairs, an independence of spirit and a view of life that was not excessively serious. Tom Boothby's lack of interest in money and his generosity to others, which resulted in his being less rich than he might have been, were also to be faithfully inherited, with disastrous consequences in Bob's case.

Bob once remarked that one of the reasons he became seriously interested in politics at Oxford and decided on a political career was that this was the only area in which he could hope to outshine his father, as it was a career that he had never contemplated for a moment. In 1949, in his briefly kept journal, Boothby regretted that he had not written more about his father in his autobiography:

This is what I would like to put in. My father was a very gifted man. John Buchan once described him as Scotland's only modern lyric poet. He wrote and composed a number of delightful songs, of which one, *Jean*, achieved world-wide fame; and played the piano with a lovely touch, although he could not read a note of music.

Starting from scratch, he reached the top of his profession; and held the affectionate regard of the banking and insurance world throughout his life.

He was an extremely good shot; and a first-class natural golfer, born and bred in the classical school of St Andrews. *Nihil tangit quod ornat* is a phrase that might well have been applied to him; and, as if that were not enough, he was the happy possessor of infinite charm and an invincible sense of humour.

He suffered from almost continuous ill-health, but few outside the family circle knew it. Everyone loved him. For twenty years he tried, without success, to let me beat him at some game. I now saw that my only hope of avoiding a permanent inferiority complex was to strike out a line of my own where I should be free from any threat of parental competition.

There was more to it than that, but there are several other indications that Bob felt inferior to his father, who seemed to achieve the highest levels at everything he did without apparent effort or stress. But, as Bob always said, he was not only a wonderful father, but a wonderful friend. And so he was to be to the end.

The extent of Bob's feeling for his father was demonstrated later in his life when he was asked his greatest achievements; he at once gave them as having been Rector of St Andrews and a Knight of the British Empire. These had also been his father's achievements; in fact, when he was offered an honour by Churchill, he deliberately chose the KBE, as it had been his father's honour. So, he equalled him in the end. There is something deeply moving in these ambitions, which speak volumes for Bob's feelings for his beloved, boisterous and relaxed father.

The only shadow over this otherwise very happy childhood – and it was a very heavy one – came when his parents sent him to St Aubyn's school, in Rottingdean in Sussex, at the age of ten. Why the Boothbys dispatched the little boy by whom they were both besotted to a school about as far away from Edinburgh as it was possible to achieve always puzzled Bob, especially as his father was a firm believer in the merits of all things Scottish, in particular education. It remains a mystery. He suspected, probably rightly, that his mother had ambitions for him that went beyond Scotland.

Even in his early childhood it was obvious that he was exceptionally precocious. His first surviving letter was written at the age of four to his grandmother, and the handwriting is remarkably good. He learnt to read very early, and his letters home from Epsom, when he was five, show that his writing had improved further. 'I love being at Hedley,' he wrote to his grandmother. 'I wish you were here too. I get a bit of your toffee every day.' At the age of six he was writing to her and his parents regularly:

Dear Granny Boo

   Thank you so much for the half-crown. I am going to spend it this morning. I loved hearing about St. Andrews. I would have loved to come to late dinner with you. I am going to write to Auntie Mary tomorrow. I had a lot of presents at Exmouth and lots of money.

                                                            Much love from Bob

And this to his father:

> Darling Dads
>   I wish you were coming abroad with us, it would be such fun. I am looking forward at going at eight. It's raining now and Mummy has gone to the shops. I went on the omnibus this morning and it was great fun. I will now right about the wedding it was lovely so pretty and lordly. I had too ices they were lovely. (I don't now anymore to say.)
>   Lots of love from your loving Bob

It is unusual, even in such a privileged family, for a child to be able to read and write with some fluency at the age of four. Bob also had a bubbly, charming personality, accompanied with much volubility, and his grandmother in particular was startled by how articulate he was at such an early age. He was also developing a quite beautiful treble voice. Being strikingly good-looking, Bob as a choirboy, as he mischievously noticed, brought tears to the eyes of old ladies: 'At the lovely parish church in Rottingdean I led the choir, and much enjoyed reducing the old girls in the pew to tears with *Oh! For the Wings of a Dove* before I went back to suck a bulls-eye.' The only gratitude he felt for St Aubyn's was that the music master, called Holmyard, himself a very gifted organist, realised that Boothby had a quite exceptional voice and an unusually acute musical ear; unlike his father, Bob found no difficulty whatever in reading a score (although the chances are high that his father could have if he had wanted to). Boothby later recalled that Holmyard added that, 'As you are both lazy and conceited, it all adds up to the fact that music will play a great part in your life.'

A beautiful, natural treble rarely survives the breaking of the voice in adolescence, with subsequent disappointment, but in Boothby's case it was to do so, to the point that at Oxford Boothby's close friend, Freddie Grisewood, asked him whether he would consider a singing career. At Eton he was to win the school singing prize, and his voice was to mature into one of the most memorable of his time – deep, powerful, with a slight rasp and the marvellous clarity of the natural musician and actor – in its way as unique and familiar to huge audiences as Winston Churchill's. His passion for music was to be a major feature of his life; and as a child he heard Paderewski play and Caruso sing. Of the latter he has written:

Beecham once said to me that there has never been a voice to approach Caruso's. As a boy I heard him singing *Che gelida manina*. It remains the most unforgettable experience of my life. The world stood still. I can hear it now: *Aspetti Signorina*. He had the sob in his voice that the Italians alone have.

Music was to give Boothby some of the greatest joys of his life and one of his greatest friendships, with Thomas Beecham. But at Rottingdean it was the only consolation for a life of loneliness and misery, not perceived at the time.

Throughout his stay there he was utterly miserable, and always described it as one of the truly unhappy periods of his life. What is clear is that it was a good school, with an excellent academic and sporting record, and a headmaster and his wife – Mr and Mrs Stanford – who cared very much about their charges. At the end, Boothby passed into Eton with ease.

Many people later write of their schooldays with such exaggerated horror and even bitterness that the biographer should be cautious, and particularly in Boothby's case, as his sense of the dramatic became more evident with the advancing years. When he once had a fearful row with his second wife, he wrote to her that 'I haven't cried as much since Rottingdean', but the flow of letters to his parents and grandmother reveal that this was, for once, not an exaggeration. He was deeply afflicted with homesickness and loneliness, and, most unusually for him, this was the only period of his life when he did not make any friends. Interestingly, the exceptions were the Stanfords and the fondly remembered Holmyard. When a boy has more in common with his teachers than his contemporaries, this is a clear sign of precocity and the result of being brought up as an only child in a home of adults who treat him like an adult, and who enjoys the experience. When he was eleven, Boothby had tea with Rudyard Kipling, who lived in Rottingdean, and wrote to his mother afterwards that 'He is a very strange little man – I think there is a savage dog in him trying to get out.' We may also surmise that the young Bob's precociousness and good opinion of himself, no doubt accompanied with a certain amount of contempt for his inferiors, led to a brisk response from the other boys.

His letters home are voluminous, but a few extracts give the authentic flavour of them all.

Darling, darling Mum,

This is a dreadful letter and I feel very ashamed to write it. I know I am a cad a fool a selfish and vile little boy, but I cannot help it.

I am ashamed to say that I must ask either you or Dad, or both together, to come down as soon as possible before Sunday if you can, and see me, and perhaps take me away.

I know that it is very wasteful of money, & *very* tiring to Dad. But I am pretty in fact *very* homesick.

Don't be worried about this letter don't be sad I shall have a long talk with you if you and Dad come. You will have got my other letter by now.

Yours Bob

P.S. It is nothing to worry about.

Another piteous letter begging his parents to take him away at once ends: 'Oh *come come come come.*'

The headmaster's wife wrote to a very concerned Mrs Boothby about Bob's homesickness:

> Your little son is very sad whenever a pause comes in which his mind is not kept filled with other things, to the exclusion of thoughts about you and home, and we are trying to make it our business to distract him as much as possible, as we know well from long & varied experience that this is the *only* cure for the suffering of homesickness. He looks quite bright and merry when actually occupied, and in a very short time he will be able to bear to think about you without breaking his poor little heart. My husband brought him to me yesterday, & he had a good cry, and a talk, and I tried to help him to see that this meant just as much unhappiness to you as to him, & that as you were helping him to bear it by being brave, so he must help you, but I don't know that he is old enough for this thought to appeal to him, and we have to be with him constantly, as he is quite evidently meditating on the possibility of making his way to you somehow. He has asked where his boots and cap are kept, and the way to the front door, and how long it would take to walk to Brighton and so on.

This was not an idle fear. He did escape and went a considerable distance, until he realised the hopelessness of it; he returned, as he described it, to 'an icy reception'.

On another occasion Mrs Stanford wrote to Mrs Boothby: 'I am afraid we are not succeeding in persuading Bob that there is anything happier to be done in life than writing letters home.' One of these letters reads:

> Darling darling Mum and Dad
>
> I am having a miserable time of it up here in bed. For *heaven's sake* one of you come down soon as you can. I don't wish to be selfish but here I am stuffed up here in bed with no work or games no company, all alone.
>
> I can scarcely see for tears it is awful. *Do* one of you please come down if you can.
>
> I have got to rest now (after being in bed all day) for an *hour* don't worry please but it is awful.

Gradually the letters get more cheerful, or less gloomy, and are remarkably informative and long for a little boy. There was then a welcome example of self-parody:

> I'm looking forward to my birthday letter tomorrow. I love getting your letters. Fancy! 12 tomorrow! It seems hard to believe it!!!
>
> I will only write 1 P.C. this week, unless anything worth telling about happens, because I see now how dull it must be to you, and what a waste of money, to send the same old repetition.

'Only 7 more weeks,
How I love you
How I love you
Only 7 more weeks.
How I love you.
Love from Bob!!!!!!!'
How I adore you.

Love from your *Loving, well,* and *happy* Bob

Another one, undated, reads:

Sunday
Darling darling Mum and Dad
The only thing that makes me the least unhappy is how selfish I have been to you and Dad, always through my life. When I *think* of my taking the *huff* at going in to see *Gladys first*! Then when I was down here writing all those *letters*! Dragging Dad down sending him back to Brighton unhappy and making you unhappy at home. And then on top of all HALF-TERM how I dragged you away and tired you out. *How* I wept!!!! and then the PASAGE and goodbyes. I can't speak of it, all I say is, I have disgraced myself and I am *sorry* for all I have done.

I have not a very nice report to send you, most likely the results of H.[alf] term. But I will be nearly top next week. I have made quite a lot of runs lately, which pleases me, although yesterday I was bowled second ball.

It *would* be ripping if I could travel up with Digges [his nanny] (how good you are to me).

It is obvious that Boothby was a sore trial to the Stanfords, for whom his biographer feels a mounting sympathy. In a letter to his cousin Henry Dundas he mentioned that one of the many boring aspects of the school was gardening, every boy having his little allotment. Dundas wrote back to say that gardening was an occupation for women and was 'cissy' for a boy. Boothby took his advice, slipped out one evening to the shed where the implements were kept and buried them in his allotment. All attempts to find the culprit were unavailing. But some fifty years later, when a new swimming-pool was being dug, they were discovered. Boothby's relative and godson, Richard Calvocoressi, was a pupil at the school and told him of the mystery. Rather late in the day, Boothby owned up to the outrage.

Boothby gradually became reconciled to Rottingdean, in those days a small village, where Sir Edward Carson lived and sallied forth to do battle for Ulster, with the St Aubyn boys, waving Union Jacks, cheering him on his departures and returns. The Burne-Jones family also lived there. It was at the school sports day in 1911 that Tom Boothby won the father's race by winding another parent, Stanley Baldwin, Kipling's cousin and an obscure Conservative MP. Boothby later recalled:

He took this with perfect equanimity, and I knew then what a nice man he was. . . . We lived in an atmosphere of health, simplicity and security which we were never to know again; and Baldwin's kindly smile and cherrywood pipe brought added strength to it.

The politics of Mr Stanford and his school were staunchly Conservative, pro-Ulster (Stanford was an Ulsterman) and patriotic, the high points of the school being Trafalgar Day and Empire Day, when 'we dressed in grey sweaters and grey felt caps with our colours round them, and shot off blank cartridges in tiny rifles, and sang the school song which began:

> "St Aubyn's boys are we, are we,
> And we live by the side of the sea, the sea." '

Things did get better, and when Boothby left the school to go to Eton, the kind and patient headmaster wrote to him:

My dear Buzz
    We missed you most woefully and shall do so next term. In fact I hardly dare contemplate the thought of the school without its 'Buzz'. I have given Mr. Kindersley a golden character of you and hope you will live up to it – I at least don't hope, I *know* you will.
    Good-bye dear boy. God bless you always.
    Affectionately your friend and at all times to command.

A. E. Stanford

Boothby entered Eton in September 1913 and was placed in the House of R. S. Kindersley, who was also his classical tutor. But Eton was not much better, although again he did well. He later said in an interview: 'I was a rebel at Eton. I hated Eton. I hated the masters and my house.'

Boothby was beaten for the first time on the day that war broke out and greatly disliked the experience. His House, like all others, was ruled by a small group of senior young men, called The Library, who tended to be excellent games players and who had the right to beat any boy for a wide variety of offences. However, Boothby discovered that every beating had to be by unanimous decision of The Library. Thus, when Kindersley unwisely promoted him to The Library, he exercised his veto on every occasion. In his view this made for a much happier House, but Kindersley and the other swells considered that discipline was collapsing and that this anarchy must stop. Boothby's veto was thus declared null and void, and his protest was reduced to his walking out whenever a boy was beaten. As he later remarked, 'even at that time I realised that more damage was being done to the beaters and the watchers than the beaten, because very soon you could see that they began to enjoy it'. He was to hold this highly unfashionable view – especially in the Conservative Party – for the rest of his life.

The crucial fact of Boothby's four years at Eton was that they coincided exactly with the war. As he later recalled:

As a boy of fourteen in 1914 I attended my first and last cricket match at Lord's in time of peace. It was a glittering scene. The ladies in the latest fashions. The men (including the boys) in top hats, and wearing carnations. The coaches of the aristocracy. Strawberries and cream. In my House we had a member of the eleven, of whom we were very proud. His name was C. S. Vane-Tempest. He went in first, and made 37. Like almost every other boy of his age he was soon to be killed. . . . On the second day of Lords my father introduced me to a small man, with alert and kindly eyes. 'Take a good look at him,' he said, 'because you will hear of him again.' It was Jellicoe. And a fortnight later he was Commander-in-Chief of the British Grand Fleet in war.

Boothby's time at Eton was dominated by the war. Each Sunday the names of the dead old Etonians were read out in College Chapel. It was a long and fearful list, which included two of the brothers of Anthony Eden, who himself left Eton to enter the army in 1915 and who was destined to emerge unscathed after some very narrow shaves; another, slightly older, old Etonian was Harold Macmillan, who was badly wounded but survived. Boothby later wrote:

As we saw all the heroes of our youth being killed, one by one, and not far away, our whole attitude to life changed. 'Eat and drink and try to be merry, for tomorrow you will surely die' became our motto. Neuve Chapelle, Loos, the Somme and Passchendaele bit deeply into our small souls. If early and bloody death was apparently an inevitable consequence of life, what was the point of it?

In his room the only photographs were of Jellicoe and Admiral Beatty, whose Battle-Cruiser Fleet was based at Rosyth, and to whose officers the hospitality of Beechwood was always available. As a result of these parties, the young Bob Boothby came to know many of the officers well, particularly Arthur Leveson, the former Director of Naval Operations, who had fallen out so badly with the mercurial First Lord of the Admiralty, Winston Churchill, that he told Boothby that he wanted to take him out and shoot him.

Gladwyn Jebb, a distant relation of Boothby's, has also testified to the increasing impact of the war on Eton, which included some serious questioning about the British social system. Led by Buck De La Warr and Clive Burt, they invited prominent Socialists and trade unionists to address the Etonians, and published articles and a magazine that reflected their views about an acutely divided society. Although not a particular

intimate, Boothby gave clear signs of individuality, as well as bumptious-
ness and rebellion.

Although Boothby was destined for the army and the Guards, these
meetings, and visits to the Fleet, fascinated him, and especially the Battle
of Jutland, in which many of his father's new friends took part. He later
wrote an account of it based on his conversations with Jellicoe, Beatty and
other participants, which deserves to be read as a contribution to the
considerable literature on that controversial engagement.

No one who has been a schoolboy during a war is likely to forget it,
especially if members of his own family are in the Services. In terms of
casualties the First World War was infinitely more terrible than the
Second, but Boothby's biographer, who had the same experience in
the latter as he did in the First, knows how dominant war becomes
to a wartime schoolboy. Everything else seems minor and petty, and a
distraction from the true realities.

Boothby later liked to say that 'no sensible person ever liked school',
but his time at Eton was scholastically above average, and he described
C. H. K. Marten, who taught him history and English, as the finest
teacher he had known, even better than his Oxford tutor, Lewis Namier.
His contemporaries and friends included Michael Llewellyn Davies, the
protégé of James Barrie; the future publisher Roger Senhouse; and –
above all – John Strachey.

Boothby was never to be an enthusiastic Old Etonian and recalled his
time there without much pleasure, but some of his most severe strictures
may be viewed with caution, and many of his Eton friendships were to be
remarkably enduring. So, it cannot all have been misery, faggings,
beatings and ice-cold rooms. It was certainly a vast improvement on
Rottingdean.

With the exception of his strong rebellion against beating, Boothby's
letters home concentrated almost entirely upon the war, and his own
training in the school Officer Training Corps and then in the Guards
Training Battalion at Bushey. Of all the losses, that of Henry Dundas was
the hardest to bear. Although there were three years' difference in their
ages, they had been brought up together in Scotland and regarded each
other as brothers. Dundas' Eton career had been spectacular, both
academically and athletically, and he was also, in Boothby's words,
'incomparable company'. He was a fine soldier, winning the Military
Cross and Bar before the virtually inevitable happened at the Canal du
Nord shortly before the end of the war, when yet another young man of
great promise died. What was particularly distressing to his family was
that the circumstances of his death were controversial. One account given
to them was that Dundas had become deeply depressed and, in despair,

had walked towards the German trenches, inviting himself to be shot, which he duly was. What was incontestable was that he was a brilliant and sensitive young man. His family and friends, and especially Bob, never forgot him.

The one quality Boothby, even as a boy, admired above all others was courage, and his heroes were men of valour and of action. He was not as indolent or as indifferent to his studies as he later implied, and he was becoming, like his father, very well-read, but he was obsessed by the war and longed to leave school to become a man in the Guards. He positively enjoyed his military training, reporting proudly to his parents that he was becoming 'rather efficient' with hand-grenades. In one characteristic letter he wrote:

> I am *mad* about the Army, and am *counting* the minutes to Bushey! Every day that passes is a joy, I am looking forward to going *frightfully*. I obviously have been put into the world to fight these devils (tho' I may end by frightening strikers in the north of England). So the sooner I begin the better. . . . I wish I had been born a year younger (this not mere bravado, but when *all* one's friends are either there or going one feels out of it doing nothing).

Boothby passed out of the Household Brigade Officers Cadet Battalion with some distinction and was offered a permanent commission, but then in November 1918 came the Armistice, which he described as

> a fearful anti-climax. By that time we had 'passed out' and were keyed up to a high pitch. With some of my fellow cadets I went up to London, and together we watched the cheering, hysterical crowds. Dutifully we took a taxi, and climbed on the roof, and waved flags and blew whistles. But life had suddenly become rather pointless; and I think that we all felt a bit forlorn. That night our tears were not entirely alcoholic.

Peacetime soldiering did not have much appeal. When he was offered a place at Oxford, he chose, and never regretted, to abandon a military career and to become an undergraduate at Magdalen College, where he arrived early in 1919.

2

Oxford and Politics
1918–24

Oxford immediately after the war was, as Boothby later wrote, 'a strange place'. Older undergraduates who had survived the war, like Anthony Eden and Edward Beddington-Behrens, took life very seriously and worked hard to catch up on the lost years; after their experiences, they were in no mood for frivolities. Others, like Boothby, who remarked to a new friend, Maurice Bowra, that 'this is too good to be true', proceeded to enjoy themselves enormously.

In 1919 Boothby, Roger Senhouse and Michael Llewellyn Davies attended the great victory parade in Paris to cheer the British contingents, as a respite from enjoying themselves not learning French in St Malo. After their exertions, they decided to celebrate, as Boothby described to his parents:

> We unanimously decided that a good dinner was the only thing to pull us together, so trekked to Voisin where we proceeded to eat soup crème celery, celery, quite wonderful, trout grilled in butter – excellent, veal, peas, new potatoes – marvellous, sweet raspberries and peaches with clotted cream and sugar!!!! Two bottles of Pol Roger 1906 – coffee: cigarettes: waited on by five men: bill 268 francs – well worth it.!
>
> Emerged between grovelling waiters feeling like Rockefeller – new men.

There is a special glow about Boothby's recollections of Oxford.* Food and drink at Magdalen were excellent and cheap; Roger Senhouse, John Strachey and Clive Burt were there; and many new friendships were

---

*In Ann Thwaite (ed.), *My Oxford*.

formed, which included another, but older, old Etonian Victor Cazalet, a young American, Henry 'Chips' Channon, and Lord David Cecil.

One friendship ended tragically when Michael Llewellyn Davies was drowned during a swimming party. Boothby felt this loss acutely, and it shattered Barrie, whose most famous creation – *Peter Pan* – began as stories told to amuse the Llewellyn Davies boys, and whose play was first produced in London in 1904. After their father died in 1907 and their mother in 1910, Barrie had adopted the five boys and had financed their education. Michael's death resulted in Barrie's famous speech on Courage at St Andrews in 1922, when he described himself as 'playing hide and seek with angels'. He continued to write plays, but the spark was gone – drowned on that hot Oxford summer afternoon.

Boothby's aunt Cecil – known in the family as 'Cass' – sent him a touching letter on Michael's death. In his reply Boothby wrote that

> Michael's death came as a great shock to me: he was the person who, after Henry, I most admired. . . . Now the two people for whom I had the greatest admiration have been taken, at 21 and 20 respectively. Who can doubt that they are wanted for finer & more exacting work elsewhere? . . . Horrible rumours float about that Rupert [Buxton] was unhinged & tried to drown himself, & that M. tried to stop him, in vain: what is the use of such speculation? We can never know. I am sorry for Barrie: he fainted 3 times when told.

Cyril Radcliffe, like Bowra, had served in the war and had published a volume of poems that had been well received. Another friend, Roy Harrod, had had the same experience as Boothby – 'saved by the bell' as he put it – and was at that time posing as a man of the Left, who considered that the war had been totally unnecessary and who supported the Bolshevik revolution. More important in Boothby's life was that Harrod and Lord Cunliffe were the instigators of his lifelong fascination with political economics, which John Maynard Keynes was to foster further. Leslie Hartley at Balliol, and Eddy Sackville-West and David Cecil brought literature and literary discussion more into his life. It was not all carousing.

More complicated, although beneficial, was the interest shown in Boothby by two famous Oxford history dons, F. F. Urquhart, known universally as 'Sligger' – said to be based on a corruption of 'the sleek one' – and R. H. Dundas, whom the students called 'D'. Dundas' interest in his young friends went rather further than the intellectual pleasure of their company. He remains the subject of many stories and the victim of a wickedly funny portrait by the anonymous author of *The Letters of Mercurius*. Once, when he and Boothby shared a railway sleeper, Dundas suggested a greater intimacy, which Boothby, on the top bunk, strongly and successfully resisted. But the influence of these two men on the undergraduates they befriended was a very positive one, and in later years they spoke and wrote of them with affection, amusement and gratitude. Those of their young friends who survived – for several were to die relatively young – rose to positions of considerable eminence. Their eye for talent was indeed remarkable, but it was a remarkable generation.

However, the overall picture is one of constant parties, expeditions, some rowing, much golf, and a climbing holiday in Switzerland in a party led by Urquhart, which convinced Boothby that mountains looked far better from the valleys. Boothby also created, with the assistance of Hall Brothers, a new and repulsive fashion: shirts of a bright hue with no stripes and voluminous trousers, quickly dubbed 'Oxford Bags'. As Boothby claimed this as his only achievement at Oxford, his biographer must, shudderingly, record the claim.

Why Boothby, in his own words, 'turned to politics' at Oxford is unclear. Strachey was in his youthful High Tory period, and together they became joint editors of the *Oxford Review*. Boothby later said that he learned everything about journalism from Strachey's father, St Loe, who had revived the *Spectator*'s fame and whom Boothby admired to the point of adulation. With David Cecil as literary editor and Eddy Sackville-West as music editor, they published William Gerhardie's first short story and thought well of themselves.

It was Edward Marjoribanks, a close friend of Michael Llewellyn Davies and the stepson of a future Lord Chancellor, Lord Hailsham, and the half-brother of another future Lord Hailsham, who persuaded Boothby to read a paper to the arch-Conservative Canning Club. He chose as his subject 'The Conduct of Naval Operations during the War of 1914–18'. He later wrote that 'I got away with it, and was later elected Secretary of the Canning Club.'

He decided to speak regularly in the Union and was coached by Freddie Grisewood in voice production, for which Boothby – and many others – was eternally grateful. The university political stars were Leslie Hore-Belisha and Beverley Nichols, although Marjoribanks was the most brilliant of them all. In Boothby's opinion he, like Barrie, never got over the death of Llewellyn Davies, and he was to take his own life after a meteoric start in the law and in politics.

These personal influences drew the liberal Boothby into quasi-Tory politics, because they all supported the Lloyd George coalition, elected in 1918 and seemingly invincible. It was to Lloyd George, Austen Chamberlain, Lord Birkenhead and Winston Churchill, as pillars of the coalition, that they looked.

It was in his capacity as Secretary of the Canning Club that Boothby first met Churchill. He and his closest friend, Lord Birkenhead – still, after all these years, obstinately better known as F. E. Smith – had come to speak at the Union, and Victor Cazalet gave a small dinner party for them in his rooms at Christ Church, to which Boothby was invited. As Boothby later related:

Churchill was in full spate, and harangued us all for about twenty minutes. Suddenly he paused for breath. In the ensuing silence Lord Birkenhead, who was sitting in a corner, said in sibilant tones: 'Shut up, Winston. It's not as if you had a *pretty* voice.' Churchill remained silent for the rest of the evening.

As Churchill frankly admitted in his moving essay on Birkenhead, his friend's intellectual powers, wit and scalding contempt frightened even him, but to undergraduates and young people generally he was immensely kind and hospitable.

Unhappily, much of this hospitality was disastrous, and not all survived it. Birkenhead's physique was such that he seemed able to burn the candle ferociously with no apparent ill-effects on his extraordinary physical and intellectual powers, and it was only towards the very end of his relatively short life that the dire consequences of this became apparent. In fact, as those close to him noticed wonderingly, he was at his most brilliant and incisive after a consumption that would have flattened most men. Bowra shrewdly commented that alcohol to Birkenhead was as important as petrol to a car. But he considered this consumption as a test of manhood, which was one of the many reasons why Clementine Churchill regarded him as a thoroughly bad influence on her husband and her son Randolph, in the latter case absolutely rightly. So he was on other undergraduates who were swept out to Charlton, his estate near Oxford, where they were mesmerised by his conversation and overwhelmed – in some cases literally – by his lavish hospitality.

But there was a positive side. Boothby later echoed many of his contemporaries when he wrote that: 'Lord Birkenhead was perhaps at his best with undergraduates. He always made us feel not only that he preferred our company to any other, but that he himself was still an undergraduate.'

It was unfortunate – and in some cases tragic – that this wonderful opportunity for young men to be exposed to so much that was exciting and valuable in this remarkable man was accompanied not only with the praise of alcohol and its substantial consumption, but also too often led them to try to emulate Birkenhead's buccaneering and basically amoral attitude to life. Harry d'Avigdor Goldsmid, one of the Charlton guests, later remarked that only Frank Pakenham (now Long Longford) and Maurice Bowra escaped totally unscathed from these influences.

In Boothby's case not much harm was done, and much benefit. Birkenhead took to him and encouraged his increasing interest in politics. He was also delightful and memorable company. As Boothby related:

He often came to Oxford. One day he arrived with a straw hat on the back of his head, and a large pink carnation in his button-hole, looking about thirty-five. He told me that when he asked for a glass of beer at Paddington at ten o'clock in the morning the barmaid had called him a saucy boy. 'I suppose', he said, 'that it is the first time the Lord Chancellor of England has been called a saucy boy.' I said that it was one of his greatest achievements.

On another occasion, when he was prevented from dining with the Canning Commitee by an unexpected summons to the Peace Conference in Paris, he offered to come to breakfast instead. I viewed this prospect with some misgiving; and my apprehensions seemed to be fully justified when he arrived and sat in sombre silence for several minutes. Finally, he turned to me with a visible effort and said: 'Except for one melancholy occasion at Ten Downing Street, this is the first time I have breakfasted in company for twenty years; and I hope to God it is the last.' I ordered a tankard of draught cider, which revived him, and he made the usual brilliant impromptu speech.

Birkenhead gave Boothby priceless advice about the need for a politician to build himself a strong local base. In his case it had been Liverpool; in Boothby's it was to be East Aberdeenshire. It was advice he took, and passed on to many others.

When Austen Chamberlain came to deliver a passionate speech in support of the coalition in the summer of 1922, he was enthusiastically received by the Canning Club. But the bulk of the Conservative Party thought otherwise and were to bring it down at the famous – or, in Boothby's view, infamous – Carlton Club meeting of October 1922. It was an early example of Boothby's independence of political opinion, but also a clear sign of how he could be dazzled by great men, of whom for him Lloyd George and Birkenhead were the greatest. The fact that they were also excellent company and political swashbucklers made their attraction all the greater. Boothby's ambivalence about the Conservative Party had early origins.

At Oxford, Strachey was also an active member of the Canning Club, and enjoyed the social life of Magdalen and Oxford as much as Boothby did. He also wrote plays in which Boothby and Gladwyn Jebb played starring roles, as did John Rothenstein, Edward Marjoribanks and Victor Cazalet. Another friend, and ardent actor, was a future Lord Chancellor, Gerald Gardiner, although a somewhat aloof and distant one.

Strachey was to have a surprising intellectual and political odyssey. He joined the Labour Party immediately after leaving Oxford and was for a time mesmerised by Oswald Mosley. He stood for Aston, in Birmingham, in 1924 and was elected in 1929. Then he foolishly flirted with Mosley's New Party, lost his seat, thought better of it and gravitated to Communism. By 1939 he was thinking differently and, like Boothby, spent much of the Second World War in the RAF before becoming a Labour minister in 1945. By the time of his death in 1963, he was gravitating back to the Right.

Boothby's devotion to him was to be lifelong. Years later, when they had fallen out politically, but never personally, Strachey wrote to him that 'You are one of the very few people in the world I have *felt* about . . . if you become king of the cannibal islands, I shall still have, until I die, the same depths of feeling toward you.'

Strachey had a powerful intellect, was fascinated by ideas and had at times a complicated private life. It is not surprising that he and Boothby had so much in common, as undergraduates and afterwards, and no political differences ever affected their friendship. His son was the only other boarder with me at a preparatory school in Sussex at the end of the war, and Strachey taught me to throw a boomerang. Years later, when I was Clerk to the Scottish Grand Committee, he and Boothby paired; they attended every meeting for a matter of minutes, so that they had – technically – a hundred-per-cent record of attendance. There was the element of the cynic in both of them, but romanticism was far more dominant, and they always vastly enjoyed each other's company.

Bowra has written of Boothby at the time:

At heart he cherished ambitions of political success but for the moment he was out to enjoy himself, and succeeded on a handsome scale. . . . Bob announced early 'This is so good that it can't last', and made the most of it. He had inexhaustible energy; he was very intelligent and perceptive, especially about people, but also about politics; he had a fine appearance with black hair and dark eyes, a beautiful voice and a natural gift for eloquence, a capacity for enlivening any conversation by his acute or reckless comments and a most winning generosity and warmth. Yet though he enjoyed himself to the full, he knew what he was doing. He wished to go into politics, and for this a good degree was not indispensable. On the other hand even undergraduate politics have their uses for the aspiring politician, and Bob made a name for himself at the Chatham Club [*sic*] and spoke with skill at dinners when Cabinet Ministers were present. He presented himself as a bit of a swashbuckler, but this deceived only those who did not know him. To them his political gifts were already obvious, nor was there any doubt of either his courage or his sincerity. His hatred of cant and his love of the good life had already made him an independent Conservative.*

Boothby was allegedly reading History, the shortened war course that was not classed, being marked either Pass or Fail. He attended a few

*C. M. Bowra, *Memories*, pp. 123–4.

lectures and did some general reading, but, as he cheerfully observed, 'there were far too many other things to do'. In addition to dabbling in politics, speaking at the Union, chatting to the mighty political figures of the day and enjoying himself with his friends, he took up rowing for a while, but then dropped it in favour of golf. His father became Captain of the Royal and Ancient in 1921, which did little to reduce his son's inferiority complex to him on this score. But he was a good player, who could have been even better if he had not decided to play simply for fun; and in Roger Wethered and Cyril Tolley, the two outstanding amateur players of the day, he had good advisers and friends. Golf is as bad for an undergraduate as rowing in its demands on time; Boothby did not begrudge it.

Things might have gone badly for Boothby in his meeting with the Examiners if he had not been saved by Lewis Namier, whom he met in Balliol Quad. Namier rebuked him for his idleness and hedonism and forecast that he would leave Oxford without a degree. 'It is too late for reading and writing,' Namier said mournfully. 'There is now only one hope. Talking.' Boothby had the sense to ask the President of Magdalen, Sir Herbert Warren, if he could be tutored by Namier; he agreed, and suggested that Gladwyn Jebb should go with him. 'It was one of the richest experiences of my life,' Boothby later wrote, and gave Namier all the credit for the fact that he got his degree.

Namier did more for Boothby than making him do some work. It was through him that he met Chaim Weizmann and his wife, Vera, and, like so many others, became an ardent admirer of this remarkable couple and, through them, a committed Zionist. Boothby later wrote of Weizmann that 'He was a prophet, a mystic, a scientist, philosopher and practical statesman, all mixed up in one compound of inspired clay.' Here was another hero for him to follow and another cause to be championed – which he did throughout his life, eventually becoming Chairman of the Anglo-Israel Association. Boothby was so enthralled by Weizmann's company that he was unusually silent in his presence: 'I just wanted to listen to the distilled wisdom which was his most priceless possession.' Hero-worship developed into a close and enduring friendship, and was to have a major effect on his political attitudes, although not always to his advantage.

Boothby's list of heroes was largely drawn up at Oxford – Baldwin, Birkenhead, Lloyd George and Weizmann. Significantly it did not include Churchill. As he noted, Birkenhead and Lloyd George were the two men by whom Churchill was palpably awed. Boothby also firmly believed that Namier was the greatest of all contemporary historians – a controversial view, but he had fallen under Namier's spell, as did many others, and he entered the Boothby Pantheon of heroes. It was not at all a bad list, and the fact that those on it responded warmly to him, and forecast great things for him and became close friends in spite of the large disparity in their ages, gives some indication of his outstanding talents, as well as his charm, already almost legendary, and zest for life.

One of Boothby's odder – and much older – friends was Archie Clark-Kerr, whom he had met while training at Bushey, and who had entered the diplomatic service. Clark-Kerr, who was a homosexual, had written to Boothby as early as 1919 to urge him to apply for the diplomatic service, and Boothby was tempted. Clark-Kerr was coming to the end of his time as Consul-General in Tangier, a hot-bed of intrigue and drama, and at the end of 1921 he invited Boothby to stay with him and to accompany him on a farewell tour of Morocco. Boothby thought it would be as good a way as any of filling one of his last Oxford vacations, and went.

The frequent, if whispered, allegation that Boothby was a homosexual himself has been ridiculed by a considerable number of his friends, and particularly by his women friends, of whom he had not a few. However, to one of the latter he confided that during one period, particularly at Eton and Oxford, he had a 'homosexual stage', but said that it was not physical, but emotional. She rather doubted this, and so do I, but what is clear from his correspondence, especially with Clark-Kerr and close friends, is that he was teasing rather than active. Certainly his eye for women was not in any way deterred by any deviations he might have had with men.

Boothby was always particularly sensitive to this charge. When he subsequently supported homosexual law reform, he was indignant that it was hinted that he had a personal interest to declare, which he had not. Michael Foot described him as 'a non-playing captain', which Boothby appreciated. My own view is that there were some flirtations and some involvements, but little more than that. What is certainly the case is that his relationships with women in the 1920s and subsequently were to cause him far greater difficulties than any affairs, if there were any, with men.

Many of his closest friends were homosexuals; many others were not. Boothby's sexual urge was exceptionally strong, but after this early stage it was overwhelmingly heterosexual. There were several ladies who can testify, happily, to this fact. When in later years the allegation was made, quite falsely, that Boothby was a homosexual, he was able to achieve a spectacular victory over his accusers.*

Boothby subsequently wrote that

I came down [from Oxford] with my mind in a turmoil. Oxford immediately after the First World War was, basically, a homosexual society. By this I do not mean

*See pp. 414–21.

40

that all the undergraduates slept with each other. I simply mean that, with the exception of one week in the summer when the Colleges gave balls, girls never impinged on our lives at all. . . . For my part, I detected the danger, and sheered away from it.

Whether he did so totally is doubtful, if Clark-Kerr's lecherously teasing letters to him are any guide. One letter in 1922, after the visit to Tangier, refers warningly to the case of Lewis 'Loulou' Harcourt, whose political career and life were wrecked by a homosexual scandal and who had recently committed suicide. Clark-Kerr wrote:

> There is only one cure, and the longer it is put off the harder it will be. I had hoped a little that you would perhaps let the case of old Loulou be a lesson to You (how dreary must be an Oxford summer without those Sunday jaunts to Nuneham [Courtney, Harcourt's home]). Do you suppose that he is now asking St John to go for a walk with him in the cool of the evening and regretting that cherubims hath but heads and wings? Don't be silly my dear. Leave Oxford. It is lamentably weak of You not to.

Writing from Cairo, his next posting, he urged Boothby to visit him:

> I will take You to Luxor and show You the phallic temples – dead cock stands – and to the Wasaa in Cairo & show you modern phallic worship & very quick cock stands and very live clitoris. Incredible things done just like the art, art at a moment's notice, perfectly naturally and without any false shame or even self-consciousness. There is none of the fuss that You are accustomed to of pressing people who do things well to do them. It is just down with your breeches (or up with your skirts) and at it. It is squalid, bestial and filthy, but it is interesting, and somehow or other supremely ridiculous and amusing.

Clark-Kerr's career was to have some spectacular failures and successes. He made an appalling error of judgment in Egypt by advising the High Commissioner, Allenby, to cut off the water supply in response to a quite minor difficulty, and was sent to Guatemala, where, somewhat unexpectedly, he married a Chilean woman called Tita, whom he subsequently divorced and then remarried. But of his ability there was no doubt, and he rebuilt his career with outstanding success, in Stockholm, Chungking, and as Ambassador in Moscow during the war. As Lord Inverchapel, he was head of the Allied Commission after the war that gave independence to Indonesia. He returned to London in triumph, to be urged by Ernest Bevin to become Ambassador in Washington. He was doubtful and consulted Boothby, who urged him strongly not to accept it, as his 'oriental' mind and understanding and experience would not only be useless but positively dangerous in the American context. But Inverchapel accepted, and the result was even worse than Boothby had feared.

It was not his fault that he had a nest of Russian agents in his Embassy, but his handling of American politicians and journalists was disastrous, and his career ended in lamentable anti-climax. But Boothby, never one to be ungenerous, wrote of him that 'I cherish his memory, because he was one of the best friends I ever had.' In fact, as he was so often abroad, he and Boothby saw very little of each other, although they maintained a long correspondence.

Many years later Harold Nicolson, who had known him very well, was invited to write Clark-Kerr's biography. Boothby thought this an excellent idea, but Nicolson declined, writing:

> Really, I am right about Tita and Archie. How could I, without hurting her feelings, deal with the early Archie (whom you never knew) alabaster-hued, passionate, sentimental, lecherous? How could I deal with the middle Archie whom you did know – snobbish, rather coarse, using arrogance to hide his diffidence? How with the reasons for his success with easterners and his failure with westerners? How with the collapse of Washington? How with the dim drab ending and the little wet house in the valley? How with Tita the humming-bird? As I said, the interesting thing about Archie was his contradictions. Archie the diplomatist was as dull as most diplomatists. I suppose he took to drink in the end like his Papa. Drinking alone there while the rain poured down upon the house, and Tita away in Chile flaunting her fan.

Another letter from Clark-Kerr to Boothby from Cairo in March 1922 contains a strong, and significant, reprimand. Boothby, who had opted for a legal career after leaving Oxford, had been offered a place by a barrister called Seagar in his Chambers, and wrote proudly to Clark-Kerr on the high opinion Mr Seagar had formed of his character and potential. Clark-Kerr, who still hoped to lure Boothby into the diplomatic service, and thought him ill-fitted for the Bar, was scathing:

> But, my child, as far as the rest of it is concerned I must confess that my heart is disposed a little to sink.
>
> It is clear, or at least it seems to be, that Seagar is not entirely in Your confidence. In this, thank God, You have been entirely wise. But at the same time his opinion as to Your moral health & vigour is indeed utterly worthless. He has been misled by Your engagingly manly exterior into believing that in matters of 'powder-puffs' You have the same rich measure of guts. But You haven't . . . all the many strings that pull You towards them You won't; You know You won't, because really You don't want to; You know in Your heart all this boisterous resistance & heartiness is in effect only the throwing of dust in Your own eyes, because when the temptation is really strong enough You yield to it. When it isn't You don't of course, because that would be contemptible, and You are never contemptible.

And so, my dear, when Seagar said that You have, in the face of many temptations, maintained a healthy & vigorous outlook on life You were, of course, pleased. You were pleased when You wrote it to me, but all the time there was a part of You that knew that the whole thing was hollow and based on an untruth and You did not think for a moment that You would take me in and yet You tried to take Yourself in. What is that but 'play-acting' to Yourself? I wish that I could think that it was the first beginnings of auto-suggestion on a quite different line of things, a new orientation, but I don't.

But enough of this pi-jaw – except perhaps to implore You to try and find some more completely male companionship than that of purely Sligger and Dundas. I fully appreciate the charm, the peace & comfort of it, but You are '*in a very dangerous state of mind*' & You want something which means fecundity (potentially I mean) rather than sterility. Please, Bob, at least try to leaven it with something else.

You realise that this is all out of a very affectionate heart, don't You? Please tell me that. If I weren't ridiculously fond of You I should not bother to scold so You mustn't mind. I am sure You won't. I promise not to scold You always.

This was a very odd letter indeed!

By warning Boothby, once again, off homosexual adventures, the clear implication is that he was going through this stage, which is far more common among young men, a fact rather better understood and tolerated in other societies outside Britain. It also adds serious doubts as to whether his friendship with Clark-Kerr had any sexual side to it – which is unlikely – not least because Boothby kept all Clark-Kerr's letters and expressed the hope that they would one day be published, whereas in other cases he fulfilled his purpose of destroying intimate letters and protecting not only himself but others.

When Boothby arrived in Morocco, he was disconcerted to find that his hosts had kindly arranged a week of pig-sticking and snipe-shooting. Boothby had not ridden a horse since he was a child on a pony, but, assured that Arab horses were trained only either to walk or to gallop, he decided to bluff it out, 'and – on the principle that if you are going to lie you may as well do it thoroughly – gave the impression that I was a rider of no ordinary attainments'. He was also advised to give his horse his head. 'I gave him more than that,' Boothby wrote feelingly in 1947. 'I delivered myself to that horse, body and soul; and never for an instant regretted it.' Then disaster struck:

We were walking slowly down a ravine behind a plump French major in uniform, when suddenly a distant horn sounded, denoting the discovery of a pig. The fat French major broke into a canter; the horn sounded again – nearer; my pony pricked his ears; and suddenly I found myself riding a whirlwind. The path was narrow, and the fat major, hearing thunder behind, held out a warning hand.

Vainly I tugged at the reins. As well try to stop an avalanche at the height of its flow. We stormed past the major, who disappeared with a shout over the edge of the path and down the steep bank. In my excitement I had forgotten all about my spear, which I carried at right angles. It removed his hat. I turned round to watch for a second, the whirling, gesticulating, bellowing cloud of dust that had so recently been an immaculate cavalry officer. He was separated from his horse, which had plunged further into the ravine. I sustained the impression that both were on their backs, and kicking. Clearly, neither was dead. I urged my steed to even greater heights of speed and fury. He needed no encouragement, and I had considerable difficulty in avoiding the pig. To my mingled apprehension and relief, an angry and bedraggled major, in a torn and dirty uniform, reappeared about half an hour later. He complained bitterly, and with every justification, to the Master; and steps were immediately taken to discover the perpetrator of so monstrous an outrage. Mercifully, they were unavailing.*

When his companions discovered that Boothby had never ridden properly before, they were considerably impressed, and Boothby wrote home to his parents:

Sunday night we dined at the American Legation – a good dinner, and the usual crowd, headed by the Robertsons: we sat down twelve: Mrs. R. such a darling – American: & he is able & so nice: loves me: & we discuss Life & Love: he recommends politics by any means (but preferably the Bar) for the former: & nothing the latter direction until over thirty, and I agree! . . . I can't resist blowing my own trumpet by telling you that yesterday, after the pig-sticking was over, they all said that they had watched me all through the week, & hadn't said anything for fear of putting me off, but now it was over they (Robertsons, Archie, Kirkpatrick, Codrington, and Hope-Gill) wld. tell me that for one who had scarcely ridden before, they thought my whole performance the pluckiest they had ever seen.

I was pretty bucked!

I do love *guts*: here is Christopher, fought for three years & desperately wounded twice, stomach & lungs: all through the Gallipoli landing: & Archie who ran away from Rome to fight & then join the Russian forces in Persia & was often under fire & never rested until he got to Bushey, tho he was offered a good intelligence job in Mesopotamia.

At least I can say for myself that I shld. have been trained by my nineteenth birthday & in my PROPER place for Foch's final offensive, planned for April 1st. 1919.

I don't think you ever realised how bitterly I felt the end of the war – cried on Armistice night not from emotion, but from sheer chagrin: I wish the war had gone on – if I cd. have fought for a month even: and yet one cannot say that.

And for you it was a relief.

* *I Fight to Live*, p. 20.

Yet in this atmosphere of heartiness & *doing* things, it makes one long to have done one's bit if only to avenge old days.

With the new Minister, Malcolm Robertson, they set off to tour the south, accompanied by Walter Harris, the eminent *Times* correspondent, who introduced them to 'various Moorish potentates and merchants'. Boothby's account continues:

> They gathered round us in a respectful and expectant circle. But when Mr. Robertson told them that the British entertained for them no feelings other than those of friendship and goodwill, which he hoped would be reciprocated, they showed unmistakeable signs of impatience. We turned to Harris for an explanation, but he had disappeared; and the Moors soon left us, with gestures denoting something suspiciously like contempt. Subsequently it transpired that he had told them that we were a famous troupe of English acrobats, who had graciously consented to give a special performance. Mr. Robertson was not pleased.

Boothby always had the happiest memories of these adventures, and Clark-Kerr wrote to Boothby's mother on 22 February:

> . . . There was never a moment, bad or good, either at Tangier or in the interior when he was not quite delightful and absolutely to be depended upon. His appreciation of everything made it a joy to do things for him. It sometimes even went as far as to show itself in that jumping up and down and flapping of hands tht must be well known to you. I like to see him do that.
>
> Everyone, old and young, expected & unexpected, that he came into contact with fell under his charm or rather his lovableness, a thing that will always be of value to him whatever he does, and I wish he was going to use it in diplomacy instead of at the Bar. But, because it is far more than skin deep, however he uses it, it will always help him. . . . Then with his gentleness there was an amazing physical courage. He only admitted he had hardly ever ridden before after he had performed prodigious feats on my ponies, and in addition to this in the midst of our constant travels he shared a fortitude, good temper and patience that did my heart good. For all these things and many many more I shall always be glad that he came to Tangier and shall thank you for letting him come.

'It was grand to be British; and it was tremendous fun to be alive,' Boothby later wrote of 1922. In April he and a new friend, Malcolm Bullock, went to Rome, the beginning of a lifetime's love of Italy. He wrote to his parents an ecstatic description: 'I feel that at any rate I know a city called Rome, & she will recognise me when I return – that I love her & that she rather likes me – and was that not worth forty pounds?' Again, to his parents from Rome:

I really have money to stay a little longer, but I have been so complimented, & the Ambassador, & Nellie & Lady Rodd all saying they look to me as the politician of to-morrow, that I am in a frenzy about my career, and anxious to finish Bar exams, & thus be ready for all eventualities.

I do enjoy things, and I have THROUGHOUT worshipped this place. Sometimes, I get quite overwhelmed & want to kneel down & give thanks, a curious feeling I have never had before, and am much too shy to give way to.

But Rome has done more than anything else to help me to have faith – one breathes the atmosphere, one looks down the ages, & one feels, I think, the guiding hand.

They returned, unwisely, by way of Monte Carlo, where the lure of the casino was – and always was – inevitable. They also lunched with the mysterious Sir Basil Zaharoff, the armaments magnate, who urged them to go into politics young, and to begin on the Left and move gradually to the Right – advice that Boothby most conspicuously was not destined to follow.

Later in the year, there was an instructive episode, when he attended a reading party at Urquhart's chalet in the High Savoy. Boothby was put in charge of the party's funds. Unfortunately he discovered a casino with a roulette wheel, 'and that was the end of the funds. The remainder of our journey was accomplished, somehow, on tick.' Boothby then joined Compton Mackenzie and his wife Faith on the island of Capri.

Mackenzie had met Boothby on a visit to his old college, Magdalen, in 1920, and the mutual attraction was immediate and enduring. He was at the height of his fame and revered as the author of *Sinister Street*, *Sylvia Scarlett* and *Carnival*; he was also the most marvellous company. As in the case of Churchill, Boothby once remarked that his conversation was even better than his writings. On one later occasion, when Boothby was staying with him at his home in Barra in the Outer Hebrides,

we fell into an argument one day after breakfast, until he suddenly remarked that we ought to be thinking about going out. 'There's not much point in doing that,' said Chrissie, his secretary. 'Supper will be on the table in ten minutes.'

Boothby's extensive correspondence with Mackenzie began with this visit to Capri, and with a good example of how to write a letter from a grateful, and much younger, guest:

Dear Mr. Compton (Monty) Mackenzie,
I apologise very humbly for not having written before, to thank you and your wife for being so kind to me in Capri.
One of my difficulties was that I didn't know how to address you. Every combination sounded either too stilted or too familiar, so I've put the lot in.
I took every train-de-luxe I could see till I got to Paris, & fell madly in

love with a beautiful American heiress, whose name alas! I failed to discover, between Florence & Paris.

On arrival in Paris I found I had enough money for a second-class ticket to London, with 2 francs over. I paced the streets until midnight, drinking coffee at 50 centimes a glass, & then took an 'omnibus' train to Calais – a terrible night. Tipping nobody, I arrived in London at 11 the next morning, a shattered wreck!

Here [St Andrews], in the intervals of playing golf, & lunching with the Prince of Wales, I have been dancing to a gramophone with fat married women who are all more appreciative of such assets as I possess, more attractive, & more amusing, than the debutantes. . . . Now I am going to bury myself in the north of Scotland to work for Bar exams. . . .

In 1973 Boothby wrote nostalgically to a particularly important and valued former girlfriend of that time:

You were my first love; and until, at long last, Wanda came to my rescue, I so often wished you had been the last.

I still remember, and often have, the tunes they played when we danced together.

And I can see, as if it were yesterday, the face of the violinist with the moustache.

What fun it was. We were still the greatest Empire in the world, and Lloyd George was still Prime Minister: Little did we realise what lay ahead of us.

It was during the stay in Capri that Boothby first met Somerset Maugham. Mackenzie, who introduced them, did not like Maugham very much; nor did many people, and some who were close friends, like Noël Coward and Beverley Nichols, later turned violently against him. But Boothby was to be a constant friend and admirer. In their long friendship there were no complications. Boothby once remarked in an interview about Maugham:

It was a strange thing. Willie had a terrible stammer, but when we were alone it would just disappear. I think the reason was that I wanted nothing from him and he, thank God, wanted nothing from me. Sex, you see, never came into our relationship. I was always aware of who he was surrounded by, but I never gave a damn. He taught me to see life as he saw it. The senselessness of it, coupled with a determination to see the bloody thing through. He did frighten a lot of people. He was a formidable little man. His face was like a mask, rather like a tortoise. He never frightened me, nor tried to, because he knew he couldn't.

Boothby always refused Maugham's invitations to stay with him at the Villa Mauresque in Cap Ferrat, while being a regular visitor. Maugham was a stickler for order and punctuality: 'Breakfast dead on nine, and God help you if you were late,' Boothby recorded with a shudder. 'Afterwards you were allowed out, but unless you asked special permission you had to be back dead on quarter to one for lunch. I certainly wasn't going to be told what to do, so I never stayed.' Boothby never became involved in the intrigue and gossip that surrounded Maugham's somewhat spooky court, and, unlike Compton Mackenzie, kept well clear of Maugham's disastrous marriage, trying to remain friends with both partners, which he did.

The bond was Boothby's unbounded admiration for Maugham as a story-teller, putting him in the same league as Dickens, but he was never one of the fawning group of largely, although not wholly, homosexuals that gathered around him. Maugham for his part was genuinely fond of Boothby, and enjoyed his intelligent and rumbustious company. In the last pathetic years of Maugham's life, when most of his former friends had fallen away, Boothby stuck by him; and after his death, when it became fashionable to belittle his work, Boothby stoutly defended his reputation as a writer, while frankly admitting the less agreeable aspects of his personality. But Maugham's utterly negative view on life, and the afterlife, left a serious and permanent mark on Boothby's otherwise buoyant and hopeful personality that was not beneficial.

In spite of Clark-Kerr's centreaties, Boothby, when he reluctantly left Oxford late in 1922, with a respectable degree and many friendships and happy memories, definitely decided against the diplomatic service. Instead, encouraged by Cyril Radcliffe, he chose the law, seeing himself as another Birkenhead or Marshall Hall. Also, the law in those days was much more attractive as a means of entering politics than it is now, and a considerable number of senior barristers were MPs and ministers, with the virtual certainty of becoming a judge and a peer at the end of the road. The financial rewards for the most famous and successful barristers, and the huge publicity given to sensational trials, were also great attractions to Boothby.

What had impressed Radcliffe and another new friend, Walter Monckton, about Boothby, in addition to his intelligence, was his speaking ability and his remarkable 'presence' for such a young man; they and others considered that he could develop into an outstanding advocate. Through practice at Eton and Oxford, and under the guidance of Grisewood, he could speak with great fluency and conviction on complicated subjects without any notes, and, apparently, without any preparation – although in this case they were wrong. He was a great impromptu speaker, but he took more trouble over preparing his speeches than he was willing to admit to, and always worked much harder than most people realised. Too often they saw the frivolous and pleasure-seeking side of his character. But Birkenhead was not the only person who saw through this façade and had high expectations for him. So Boothby enrolled in the chambers of Walter Monckton to read for the Bar, while keeping a close eye on the political scene.

This was, by the end of 1922, a curious, indeed chaotic, one.

The Lloyd George coalition, to Boothby's lasting regret, had fallen. At the decisive meeting at the Carlton Club on 19 October the speech of the day had been made by Stanley Baldwin, a hitherto minor figure, whose denunciation of Lloyd George as 'a dynamic force', which 'is a very terrible thing; it may crush you, but it is not necessarily right,' had made a deep impression. Lloyd George resigned that afternoon. Andrew Bonar Law, officially in retirement, had been persuaded by Beaverbrook, J. C. C. Davidson and other friends to attend and speak; he then sought, and received, unanimous election as Party leader before he accepted the premiership. With Austen Chamberlain, Birkenhead, Arthur Balfour and Sir Robert Horne standing aloof, somewhat overly contemptuous, the Law Government was difficult to form and was not impressive. Churchill, still a Liberal, derided it as 'a government of the second eleven', but it emerged from one of the most confused general elections in British history with a healthy majority; the unexpected novelty was that Labour, with over four million votes, won 142 seats and the divided Liberals fared very badly. Among the victims was Churchill at Dundee; he was to remain out of Parliament for two frustrating years, only returning in 1924 as virtually a Conservative again. Baldwin, as Chancellor of the Exchequer, continued his late but meteoric rise. By next May, with Law dying of cancer, he became Prime Minister.

Boothby, the budding lawyer, at least welcomed this development. Baldwin's friendship with his father had extended to the son, and Boothby thoroughly agreed with his speeches on social questions and his moderate attitudes. At that time he also approved of Neville Chamberlain, another late starter who had entered the Commons in 1918 at the age of fifty, and whose Housing Act of 1923 was, by the standards of the time, remarkably enlightened and progressive. But the economic situation remained grim, with unemployment officially rated at over eleven per cent, but in reality much worse than this, and with devastating social consequences.

What few had realised was a streak of recklessness in Baldwin's character. There was no need for a general election in 1923, or indeed for another four years, but he suddenly and dramatically raised the banner of Protection in October and reminded a startled Conservative Party of a pledge given by Law in the 1922 election that there would be no fundamental change in fiscal policy during the current Parliament. There were other, purely tactical, arguments for a snap election, and the decision to go to the country was made on 12 November.

As so often happens, Boothby's entry into national politics was a matter of sheer chance. He had the advantages of his father's prestige and friendship with Baldwin, and his Oxford record, but when, spurred on by his friend Noel Skelton, he offered his services to Colonel Patrick Blair at the Unionist headquarters in Edinburgh, he was startled to be told that Blair had received orders from London to contest every constituency in Scotland, including the Western Isles and Orkney and Shetland, Liberal strongholds which the Conservatives had not bothered to contest in decades. William Shakespeare Morrison, known to his friends as 'Shakes', a young Scottish advocate, had been sent to the Western Isles by Blair because he could speak Gaelic, and Blair offered Boothby Orkney and Shetland. Boothby's father, who thought him far too young to be a parliamentary candidate, gave his consent with considerable reluctance, not least because the question of who was to pay for this apparently forlorn venture had not been made totally clear.

Walter Monckton gave his permission for three weeks' leave from Chambers much more willingly, having recognised that Boothby was hypnotised more by politics than by the law. But he still had hopes of him as a barrister and sent him on his journey with enthusiastic encouragement. Neither guessed how remarkable that journey was to be.

There was no nonsense about a selection committee for the choice of the Unionist candidate. Indeed, there was no Unionist organisation at all in Orkney and Shetland, a Liberal fortress for so long that the Unionists had given up all hope. Blair simply told them that their candidate was on his way. Warned by friends about the northern climate, Boothby bought two huge Fair Isle sweaters, perhaps under the impression that this would give him a local tone; the Orcadians were amazed by the spectacle, and many years later told their MP, Jo Grimond, that this had been one of the major features and talking points of the campaign, still remembered in the 1970s. At least Boothby did not make the mistake of arriving in a kilt! Boothby has written:

So, next day I found myself in a train bound for Thurso, and the following day in a small boat crossing the Pentland Firth from Scrabster to Kirkwall. As usual, it was a rough voyage. On board was my Liberal opponent, and the sitting Member, Sir Robert Hamilton. He advised me to wear warm clothing (it was mid-winter); and, when we got to Kirkwall, introduced me to my own Agent, who was awaiting us on the pier. That night I looked out over the vast expanse of Scapa Flow. Last time I had seen it, the German High Seas Fleet was there. Now it was empty. I was pretty thoughtful when I went to bed.

Orkney and Shetland, with a population of just over 50,000 and with an electorate of 24,000, was very improbable Conservative territory, but as the Liberals had not faced a challenge this century, it was a difficult seat to gauge. Moreover, it did not look as though this was to be a Liberal year, even in Scotland, where the Liberals were already being caught in a tight squeeze between the Conservatives and Labour, as they were in England and Wales. But the Conservatives entered the 1923 general election in an over-confident mood, which made their subsequent defeat all the more painful.

By every account that has come down, Boothby was a superb candidate. His beautiful voice had not yet reached its maturity, but was impressive enough, and if he ran a highly personal and idiosyncratic campaign with great good humour and enthusiasm, this was greatly appreciated. He, for his part, despite the severe difficulties of electioneering by sea, on one occasion in a sailing boat in abominable weather, was enthralled by the discovery, as he put it, 'that I was among Scandinavians', and by the wonderful light. So, he campaigned with gusto and enjoyment, which must have communicated itself to his audiences.

Uncharacteristically, Boothby was subsequently rather modest in his account of the election and of his remarkable impact upon the constituency, for the electors of Orkney and Shetland were the first significant group to be exposed to the Boothby charm, good looks, superb voice and quick intelligence. In those days of public meetings he was in his element, and the press reports of his meetings were remarkably long and fulsome. The *Shetland Times* wrote of his opening meeting in Lerwick that

the very large audience which assembled in the Town Hall on Thursday evening to hear Mr Robert Boothby's views on the political situation came away with the feeling that he is a young man of great ability. From the opening sentence of his lengthy address he caught the ear of the audience, and riveted and sustained their universal attention to its close. A fluent, easy, and forceful speaker, with a personality that put him at once *en rapport* with his audience, he marshalled his facts and put forward his arguments in a manner which deeply impressed the vast majority of those present. His honesty, sincerity and conviction cannot be questioned.

To modern eyes his speech was remarkably long. He met the inevitable 'carpetbagger' charge head on by claiming, not at all truthfully, that he had personally asked the Unionist Central Office to let him stand for the constituency, and referred to his previous visit to Scapa Flow in 1918 'on a battleship', giving the impression without actually saying so that his role had been rather more active than in fact it had been. What should have alerted the rapt listeners was his lavish praise for Gladstone, 'the greatest statesman the country has ever produced', and the old Liberal Party, 'the greatest Party the country has ever known'. He was, he declared, 'not a Unionist, Conservative, or Tory of the old school. I was brought up in a Liberal family with Liberal traditions, and my native county is Midlothian, where the Liberal tradition is pretty strong.' He lavished warm praise on Baldwin, but then added: 'It does not matter what anyone thinks about Mr Baldwin's policies – he is honest, sincere, courageous, and that is something in these days.'

One can see why the independent-minded electors of the islands so quickly took to him. After speaking movingly about unemployment, he announced that tariff reform and protection were the only answer. He would help the farmers; the crofters, who would receive £1 per acre for all cultivated arable land; the elderly, with provisions that would 'secure the working-man against ill-health, unemployment and old age'; the fishermen; and the British Empire.

As election speeches go, it was a great improvement on most, and the subsequent questions and answers – reported in great detail – revealed that the young man did not lack courage, as when he described the newspaper magnate, Lord Rothermere, as 'one of the greatest menaces this country has to face'. A persistent, and unimpressed, questioner was a Mr W. Sinclair, who marred the occasion by proposing a motion that 'Mr Robert Boothby is not a fit and proper person to represent the constituency on the ground that he is a young lad.' Boothby retorted that 'better men than me have entered Parliament while still younger than I am, and have done well. Pitt was Prime Minister before he was my age. But the disqualification of youth is one that will soon be got over (*loud applause*).' Mr Sinclair's motion got 'about twenty votes', but when the main one to adopt Boothby as candidate was moved, this 'brought up hundreds of hands, and the Chairman intimated that the motion had been carried by an overwhelming majority amid loud applause'.

Boothby's surprising maturity was also demonstrated in his election address – again, rather longer than they are today – and in all his meetings. But these were also characterised by a style in answering questions that was somewhat unusual. At Holm West School he said that 'as he wanted to have a free and easy informal talk, he would, with the permission of the ladies, ask them all to light up their pipes'. His views on a capital levy were contained in one answer in Stromness: 'I should certainly shoot any person who brought in a capital levy.' He made much of the so-called 'bounty' to farmers, which would bring in £70,000 to the constituency, and which his opponent, not unreasonably, described as 'bribery'. When asked: 'Would you be in favour of doing away with the Board of Agriculture?', he cheerfully replied, 'I am rather inclined to think that I would,' not unaware of the fact that the abolition of a major government department was hardly a conspicuous feature of the Conservative manifesto. All reports of his meetings refer to the fact that they were either 'well-attended' or 'crowded', or that 'the accommodation was overtaxed'.

The local reporting was so extensive, and the interest so intense, that some of the excitement it generated can be recaptured in the faded records. The *Shetland Times*, a staunch Liberal organ, tartly remarked that Boothby, 'although glib of tongue, was very much less convincing' than Hamilton, but fully reported a letter from Baldwin on the farmers' subsidy. The *Glasgow Herald*, summing up the campaign, reported that

Much interest has been displayed by all sections of the community in the election, which on all hands is recognised as one standing by itself. . . . It is generally recognised that the fight will be a close one. For a young man Mr Boothby has made a most favourable impression, both in Orkney and Shetland, and his prospects are distinctly good. He has, however, a big fight to beat down Liberal traditions of more than half a century, even with the advantages he has to offer.

Hamilton found that he had to fight a far more vigorous and demanding campaign than he had expected, and as it reached its climax the travelling and meetings became intense. On the eve of poll Boothby addressed six crowded meetings, bringing his total to over fifty in less than two weeks. *The Times*' correspondent reported that the change since 1922 was remarkable: 'Mr Boothby, the young man with the sunny smile – for he is not yet 24 – seems everywhere to be reaching the hearts of the people.' But old Liberal traditions and distrust of Tories were to prove too strong to overcome.

Boothby was also discovered by Baillie Booth of Peterhead and his farmer friends. They were all East Aberdeenshire Unionists, who were in Orkney on business; as they had time on their hands, they decided to go to a meeting addressed by the young candidate about whom everyone was speaking. Although they were not in search of a parliamentary candidate, they were deeply impressed by his oratory, if not by his knowledge of agriculture and fishing, on which Boothby was cheerfully ignorant, although very eloquent. When they returned to Peterhead, they reported their discovery to the East Aberdeenshire Unionists, Booth saying that 'when he gets up to speak, he goes off like an alarm clock'.

Boothby, dodging storms and on two occasions having to make for the shore, knew nothing of this momentous development in his fortunes, and at one point seriously wondered if he was going to win, so excellent were his meetings and the response. In the event, to real surprise in Edinburgh, he actually won Orkney, but, as he later wrote, 'the incredulous crofters of Shetland could not bring themselves to believe that a beneficent Tory government would really give them a pound an acre, whether they grew anything or not'. The Party had told him that it would pay his expenses if he held his deposit, a fair guide of its estimate of Boothby's chances, but in the event he lost by only 811,* having given the Liberals a very bad fright and making his name in Scottish politics at the age of twenty-three.

Seldom can a defeated candidate have received such universal praise. As one commentator wrote,

> [Boothby] had come forward as a stranger, just on the threshold of his political career, and after a very brief campaign lasting less than five days in Shetland and about the same length of time in Orkney, had come within measurable distance of capturing what has generally been regarded as the stronghold of Liberalism. On every hand credit was given to the promising young Unionist for the splendid fight he put up.

With these praises ringing around him, and fêted as a hero by his parents and friends in Edinburgh, Boothby had his first direct experience of election politics in Scotland and had, most importantly, deeply enjoyed it. This fact is worthy of comment, as it is somewhat unusual for politicians actually to enjoy elections, but Boothby, despite some over-done grumblings in later years, never lost his zest for the hustings, and it showed. One of the features of his meetings was that they were always fun, and he already had the gift of answering questions frankly and often wittily. He had, also, the qualities of a natural actor, with the presence, good looks and voice to accompany a sense of theatre that had developed early, and that he was never to lose. 'Ye should've been an actor, nay a politician,' a voter once shouted at him. 'You're quite right,' Boothby shouted back, 'and I would have been a bloody good one, too.' But there was also a warmth and joviality that had the effect of cheering people up. It had been a very remarkable beginning.

So deep was the experience etched on Boothby that in later years, for all his love of East Aberdeenshire and its wonderful people, he often mused on how his life might have been different if he had won Orkney and Shetland, and could have lived in that wild but enthralling part of Scotland. Constituencies do not often make such a deep impression upon an unsuccessful candidate, and this manifest love of the area must have had at least some effect on his high vote and excellent result. For all his life he had an astonishing rapport with a Scottish audience of any size, an alchemy that some even compared with Rosebery in his prime, and it was in Scotland that he was always most appreciated and loved.

He certainly was by Baillie Booth and his friends. The East Aberdeenshire Unionist Association was looking for a new candidate, and, on

---

*The figures were: Sir R. W. Hamilton (Liberal) 5,129 (54.3 per cent); R. J. G. Boothby (Conservative) 4,318 (45.7 per cent).

the urgings of Booth, agreed to meet this young phenomenon. They immediately decided that they need look no further, and at once adopted him as their candidate. Even at a time when Conservative Associations were selecting remarkably young candidates, including Anthony Eden, Harold Macmillan and Duff Cooper, this was an extraordinary achievement. East Aberdeenshire was certainly not a safe seat, but was eminently winnable by the right candidate.

As in the case of Orkney and Shetland, it was for Boothby love at first sight. Again, he found himself among a people – especially in Buchan – 'more Scandinavian than Scottish', who spoke their own dialect, the Doric, which Boothby initially found incomprehensible, but which he determined to learn, and did. He also had to learn about the fishing industry, then at its zenith, not only a great industry but, in Boothby's eyes, a romantic one. 'The great summer fishing out of Fraserburgh and Peterhead and the great autumn fishing out of Yarmouth and Lowestoft, to which my girls came down to gut the fish, and which I never failed to visit, were always intensely exciting,' he later wrote. Buchan also had Boothby's beloved light, that was so important to him.

But he also found a great reserve among his future voters and constituents, and realised that he was being taken on trust until they got to know each other better. Sensibly, he did not try to hasten the process. 'It takes a long time to get to know them,' he was to write, 'and still longer to gain their affection. But, if you do, their loyalty is quite unshakeable. . . .' Having taken Birkenhead's advice to find a political base and stick with it, he realised that it would be hard work to establish it. That he did so was one of the great achievements of his life, but at the beginning there were many who viewed him not only as too young but as a rank outsider, which, of course, he was, and wisely did not pretend otherwise. As Jack Webster, born and brought up in Buchan, and later to become a warm friend and admirer of Boothby, has written, 'I doubt if there is a Party which can face a general election in Buchan with feelings of utter safety. Dogmatic doctrine does not exactly clink with the native character.' This was, and was to remain, Boothby's real attraction. In Webster's words, 'The men of East Aberdeenshire liked what they heard and judged rightly that he was a man of such independent thought and action that he would represent them with good sense and conviction, even if it ran against the grain of his Party, which happened to be the Conservative Party.'

Among those who had noted Boothby's fine performance in Orkney and Shetland with great approval was Baldwin, under intense criticism for calling an election at all, and then losing it. The Conservatives had lost nearly ninety seats and were reduced to 258, a minority in the event of a Liberal–Labour coalition. That unthinkable event occurred in January 1924, when Ramsay MacDonald formed the first Labour Government. Baldwin became Leader of the Opposition. One of his first actions was to invite Boothby to join his small Secretariat; Monckton let Boothby go, realising that his life was to be dominated by politics.

Here was another turning-point, and a decisive one. In the view of many of his friends, and his biographer, Boothby made a great mistake. He had some income from a family trust and had no serious money worries at this point, but a steady income from the Bar would have prevented his seeking a career in the City of London, for which he was totally unsuited by experience or temperament. It was his choice, and the wrong one.

He found working with Baldwin interesting and enjoyable. He later recalled:

[Baldwin] was an extraordinarily equable man. Nothing seemed to ruffle his composure. One day a gentleman arrived in the office for a chat. Mr. Baldwin talked freely and expansively to his agreeable visitor. A few days later the report of an 'interview' appeared in a Sunday newspaper, containing frank and often caustic comments on practically every one of his colleagues in the Shadow Cabinet! The Secretariat was in a flat spin. The only person who remained perfectly calm was Mr. Baldwin himself.

One railway journey to Edinburgh together began unfortunately when Boothby unwittingly ate Baldwin's sandwiches. However, as they travelled, Baldwin said to him that 'The main ambition of my life is to prevent the class war becoming a reality'; 'the only real hope for industry in this country is Protection'; and 'If and when I get back to power, there is one man I am going to have by my side – Churchill.' Boothby was so impressed that he noted these comments down. He was subsequently to be highly critical of many aspects of Baldwin's character and leadership, but, as will be seen, their friendship was never affected.

At that time Boothby saw Baldwin as the great hope of enlightened Conservatism, as did many other young men with political ambitions. They, like him, later felt badly let down by Baldwin, but their affection for him, and above all his role as 'the apostle of appeasement in the class war', in Boothby's words, was his major achievement that they honoured. Also, as Lloyd George shrewdly remarked, 'Baldwin is a Celt, like the rest of us. That is why he understands us so well.' The difficulty that Boothby faced, and it was to be an enduring one, was that he was developing an admiration for Lloyd George that was to grow into something very close to hero-worship, whereas his boss, Baldwin, was obsessed by Lloyd George for very different reasons. As Boothby later wrote, 'He never stopped thinking and talking about Lloyd George, of whom, as a man, he disapproved; of whom, as a "dynamic force", he was frightened; and by whom he was clearly fascinated, to the point of obsession.' In these emotions Baldwin was far from being alone in the Conservative Party; indeed, after their terror of Communism and Socialism – which to most Conservatives were synonymous – their greatest fear was of Lloyd George. In this, at least, the Leader and his Party were at one. Boothby thought then, and always after, that this was a great national tragedy, but the gulf was unbridgeable. What is interesting is that Boothby, at so early an age, could move so easily from one camp to the other, and be welcomed in both. Of each he was to write subsequently with deep affection and respect, although not uncritically of either.

Having entered politics almost at the top, with developing friendships and acquaintance with many of the major political figures, as a parliamentary candidate and close to the Leader of the Opposition, Boothby was already being noticed. What was essential was that he should win East Aberdeenshire. As the Labour Government tottered towards defeat in the summer of 1924, the divided Liberals – now deserted by Churchill, who, after narrowly losing a by-election in London, had been in effect, although not in name, adopted as Conservative candidate for the safe seat of Epping – still posed a threat to him, and his only hope lay in a divided opposition in the constituency. When the general election came in October, he found the contest considerably more nerve-racking than the enjoyable romp in Orkney and Shetland. If he had learnt much from that experience it did not affect his campaigning style, which was cheerful and extrovert, relishing in hecklers. Many years later an anonymous constituent wrote:

I remember the first time he visited Turriff to make a political speech. The meeting was held in the old Picture House. There wasn't a spare seat, as everyone wanted to see the young aspirant for political honours.

We were enthralled by his voice and impressed by his manner and the content of his speech. None of us had any doubt about his political future in East Aberdeenshire.

This was a Conservative year in Scotland as in England, and this movement, together with the divided Labour and Liberal vote, was sufficient to overcome serious doubts about Boothby's youth and inexperience of the constituency. On a minority vote, and with a majority of 2,683, Bob Boothby, at the age of twenty-four, became a Member of Parliament.

Boothby's eventual achievement in making his constituency a safe seat for himself was a notable personal triumph, and their long association gave him and his constituents much joy. He was deeply at home there, spiritually rather than physically, as he never bought a house in the constituency and never lived there, although he visited it far more frequently than did most MPs of that time. This was not at all unusual then, as very few MPs in any Party lived in their constituencies, or ever considered doing so. The post-1945 introduction of regular constituency 'surgeries', or advice bureaux, was undreamed of. The electors expected their MP to be active on their behalf in Parliament and to visit them from time to time. Boothby did much better than this, as he loved his constituents and found them endlessly fascinating, often exasperating, funny and lovable.

Boothby was also to be particularly fortunate in having a succession of agents who were equally devoted, the most famous of them being Archie Campbell, who achieved some renown in Scotland as well as in the constituency with regular newspaper articles under the byline 'The Buchan Farmer', by which title he became widely known. Boothby's English and Lowland Scots friends found Campbell's Aberdeenshire accent incomprehensible, as Boothby often did himself, but his goodwill and devotion to Boothby were total. A successful farmer himself, he was generous about payment for his wares and gave good credit – except at election time, when the many who owed him money would find Archie on their doorsteps, demanding not their money but their votes. 'An ye'll be voting Boothby?' was not a request. Few were unwise enough not to receive the message and to act accordingly. If the politics of East Aberdeenshire were by no means unique in Scotland, it was not surprising that Boothby's English friends were startled by them. Boothby loved it, and loved Archie, particularly when the language difficulty was gradually resolved.

His constituency base was to become Hatton Castle, the home of Colonel Garden Duff, the Chairman of the East Aberdeenshire Unionist Association. Boothby's friendship with 'Gardie' Duff and his wife was to be one of the closest and most important of his life. The Duffs, who adored him, allocated a suite of lovely rooms for his exclusive use, available for him whenever he wanted. It really was a home; to their great sadness the Duffs were destined to be childless, and Boothby became an important member of their family, someone closer than a friend who was always joyously welcomed when he bowled up in his current motor-car and bounded in, all youth and enthusiasm, with the latest London gossip and presents, invariably irresistible. He certainly repaid their kind hospitality and devotion with his warmth, wit, outrageous indiscretions and sheer fun. They even forgave him when he arrived once in the early hours of the morning with his then secretary, climbed in through an open window, and then completely forgot about the poor girl, who appeared at breakfast the following morning – Boothby having departed on constituency business – to the amazement of the Duffs. But they rapidly became reconciled to the entrancing vagaries of friendship with Boothby, and had no complaints. Nor, oddly, did the secretary, who later related this, and other episodes, with much appreciation. Life with Boothby was never dull. They admired him intensely and stuck by him with total loyalty through all vicissitudes, and Boothby was able to obtain a baronetcy for Gardie in 1952.

But, in those happy carefree 1920s, with 'laughter and apple blossom floating on the water', all this was far ahead.

One who knew Boothby very well, and who loved him, considered it an 'eccentric' constituency (she was not Scottish) that suited him perfectly – perhaps too perfectly. She saw how bogus was the professed East Aberdeenshire emphasis on Temperance, for example. 'The farmers were all drunk and the fishermen and their families were euphoric,' she remarked; and although this sweeping generalisation may be viewed with caution, it is not difficult to understand why the people of East Aberdeenshire appreciated Boothby, and he them. The fact that they had a marked tendency to work hard and play hard, and loved a good time when they could afford it, while nodding dutifully and insincerely in the direction of Temperance and the Kirk, struck a very real chord in Boothby. Also, as the same observer shrewdly noted, there was virtually no middle-class Conservatism in East Aberdeenshire; indeed, from what she could see, there was no middle class at all. Not that anyone was at all interested in the subject, or thought about it. The assumption of social equality, which is the most wonderful of all the Scottish qualities, whatever one's job or whatever one's income, had an immense and natural appeal to Boothby. He never bothered whether someone was an earl or a fisherman; he either liked them or did not. The people of East Aberdeenshire took exactly the same view. Boothby often overlooked the fact that the English usually do not. He never understood the English, and never comprehended the importance of humbug and appearances which are so important to them. 'Think of what would have happened if Bob had represented somewhere like Cheltenham?' this friend asked. One can only hazard that the relationship would have been loveless and brief, on both sides. The Scots can recognise and appreciate a warm-hearted, cultivated and gregarious buccaneer better than any.

The fact was that Boothby quite quickly came to love the people of East

Aberdeenshire, and to care for them very deeply. For all their cheerfulness and good humour, there was real poverty, not only in Peterhead and Fraserburgh, but also in the country. He had never been exposed to poverty himself and was shocked by it. He became a passionate supporter of the herring industry and soon became almost a bore on the subject in the Commons. One day Baldwin walked into the Chamber when Boothby was in full flood and muttered, 'Herrings, *again*!', but the fishermen and their families loved it. Fifty years later he was still battling on for the protection of Scottish – and especially East Coast – fishing in the House of Lords. In old age he wrote nostalgically:

From a personal point of view, I not only worked harder for [the herring industry] than for any other, but I have now been deprived of my favourite food – the young *matje* herring. Caught in the spring, gutted, lightly salted and eaten raw, they are a delicacy beyond compare, far surpassing caviar, *foie gras* or smoked salmon. No wonder that for two centuries the Dutch, who caught most of them, put out flags and played bands when they arrived in April. Now, together with the rest, they have almost disappeared.

He also became the champion of the farmers, whose company he enjoyed, and who were having a worse time than the fishermen. He made it his job to get them a better deal and, eventually, had some success. But what mattered to his constituents was that he always did his best for them, and, after some doubts, they liked his style and were impressed by his intelligence. The fact that he enjoyed a drink – and all the good things of life – did not worry them. Indeed, Boothby had what amounted to genius even as a very young man in making every function an Event. Here, the actor in him was played to full measure. Many years later I was with him at a dinner. He was in rather low spirits and somewhat grumpy beforehand, but as he walked into the room he became a different man – the flashing smile, the booming joviality, the laughter were at once switched on, and the transformation was total.

He also had a remarkable skill for self-publicity from the beginning. He had the rare advantage among politicians of actually liking journalists – although not all, and few proprietors – and particularly local ones. He knew from personal experience as a fledgling journalist that they are always avid for 'copy', which he lavishly supplied to them. Thus, the *Buchan Observer* and other local papers were informed of all his speeches and questions in the Commons and elsewhere, and given good notice of his regular visits to the constituency.

But what is so striking about this record was how hard he worked for his constituents. It is one of the curses of politics that people with first-rate minds, who can deal with matters relatively quickly and have the time to relax, are often accused of laziness by plodders, who sometimes assume, wrongly, that the cleverer ones are neglecting their duties. The English, also, as George Orwell once wrote with some bitterness, have a contempt and suspicion of brains. Boothby seemed to do everything effortlessly, and to enjoy himself so hugely in London Society and in Commons Smoking Room gossip, that this aroused not only resentment but led many to underestimate him seriously. However, the people of East Aberdeenshire, after their initial doubts, did not underestimate him, nor he them.

To an extent that those outside politics seldom appreciate sufficiently, MPs come to reflect their constituencies. A good MP may influence his constituents, but it is usually the other way around. Richard Crossman once, disarmingly, wrote that he would never have been as left wing as he became if he had not represented a Coventry seat; Harold Macmillan and Duff Cooper were greatly affected by their experience of representing impoverished Stockton and Oldham respectively; and surely matters would also have turned out differently for Boothby if he had represented a more conventional constituency, and a less easy-going one. Few MPs would have had such unswerving devotion in his many vicissitudes than he was to have; perhaps, if he had been compelled to have been less reckless for fear of the censure of his constituents, he might have been more cautious. I personally doubt it, but what his elders had already noted as his flagrant lack of self-discipline was not likely to be changed by his delightful constituents, to whom, including his opponents, after they had got to know him, he could do no wrong. 'Boothbyism' was to long survive his retirement from East Aberdeenshire, when canvassers at subsequent elections were disconcerted to be told that the household would, as usual, 'Vote Boothby'. They still talk of him with joy and love.

Many people thought that Boothby, who became increasingly prone to magnifying his achievements in old age – in which he was far from unique – exaggerated his hold on the affections of the people of East Aberdeenshire. If anything, he was unduly modest. His successor, Patrick Wolrige-Gordon, discovered this, as did his cousin Ludovic Kennedy, who considered standing for the seat in 1962 as a Liberal. He decided against it, but wrote to Boothby of his former constituents that 'They spoke of you as cricketers speak of W. G. Grace, or sailors of Nelson. I was really quite moved.'

Also, East Aberdeenshire was not really a Conservative seat and its Conservatism was, to say the least, untypical. It was of a fiercely local variety, that had as little to do with Edinburgh or Glasgow Unionism as it did with London Conservatism, or the 'Lairdism' that was then, and much later, to be the curse of Scottish Unionism and to encompass its downfall, and which Boothby despised. Anything less like an hereditary land-owning Laird or Clan Chief than Bob Boothby would be difficult to imagine. If East Aberdeenshire Unionism could be classified at all, which is almost an impossibility, it was a curious and unique mixture of relaxed Scottish nationalism, local pride, liberalism, and the type of Conservatism that regards change with deep suspicion. What Boothby gave them was not political philosophy but his dedication to their concerns.

On some aspects of his constituency he has written engagingly:

I found myself confronted with the problem of religion. I had the lot. The Established Church of Scotland, the Episcopal Church, the Wee Frees, the Roman Catholics, the Brethren, Jehovah's Witnesses – and all at daggers drawn. It was hardly an advertisement for Christianity. I solved it by never entering a church or a chapel of any kind for thirty-four years, except twice for funerals. There was also a strong Temperance Movement. From the outset they realised that, so far as I was concerned, there was nothing doing. But we got on well enough. They once asked me to attend one of their processions in Peterhead, and I did. The two fishermen carrying the banner in front were so drunk that they had to be held up by their wives. Afterwards I was able to say, with truth, that I had never enjoyed a procession so much in my life.

Organised religion not only never attracted Boothby, but increasingly repelled him, especially the Calvinist variety. Robert Burns was his hero, and John Knox the embodiment of evil. Wisely, he kept these views to himself until he was no longer a Member of Parliament, but his constituents were never under any illusion that he was a pillar of the Kirk. Characteristically, he made an exception for the Salvation Army, because its members actually helped people, especially the poor, but he had no time for the rest. As he once wrote to John Strachey,

The proletariat, the Red Flag, the Host, the Virgin and Child, unadulterated materialism, unadulterated spiritualism – I'll have nothing to do with any of it. I've always thought the Holy Roman Church with its fanaticism, its Inquisition, and its fundamental falsity, the most sinister organisation in the history of mankind.

He was to take the same attitude to the new religions of Fascism and Communism, but he was never to go through the hypocrisy of attending religious ceremonies and services, except on very special occasions.

Boothby's Burns Night speeches were to become famous, and that at St Andrews in January 1961 was to be the most celebrated of all.* Their interest lies not only in Boothby's mastery of Burns' work, but his

---

* This speech appears in full in *My Yesterday, Your Tomorrow*, pp. 229–46, under the title, 'Robert Burns: The Poet and the Man'.

admiration for his rebelliousness against 'the tyranny of dogma, the tyranny of machine, and the tyranny of the monolithic state'.

On this, as on other matters, the people of East Aberdeenshire quickly realised where he stood.

3

Rising Star
1924–9

Having reached the House of Commons so swiftly, Boothby was determined to enjoy it. Indeed, his first action as an MP was to join a delegation of the Empire Parliamentary Association to Jamaica led by the affable and popular former Labour Colonial Secretary J. H. Thomas. In those days, these things were done properly. The delegation was given a civic lunch in Bristol, with much national as well as local publicity, and although their ship, the *Changuinola*, was only a banana ship of 6,000 tons, and they immediately ran into a fierce storm – he telegraphed to his parents: 'Splendid trip. Stormy weather yesterday, was utterly unaffected to-day, warm, sunny, cheery party, jolly life. Tennis, Bridge. I win. Love' – they were greeted with much respect when they reached Jamaica, with a doting, and indeed fawning, local press. There were an inordinate amount of dances on visiting British warships, many splendid lunches and dinners, and a significant absence of work. 'I feel the delegation did not achieve much,' Boothby later conceded. There were many speeches, and on one occasion Boothby was unexpectedly asked to speak at the end of yet another banquet. It went well, and the local paper rhapsodised:

The streak of untainted idealism – the expectations of a better world in his own lifetime – the desire to defend the country of his birth – the love for fair play – were all conveyed by one of the babies of the House of Commons, Mr Boothby, who sits for Aberdeen, is 'very much Scotland'. Congratulations were showered upon him by surprised statesmen. The speech was brilliant – and though it was serious, it gripped and refreshed everybody. It was good to hear the call of youth, and to remember that, after all in youth lies the world's hope for a better state. At the age of twenty-four Mr Boothby, who only recently went down from one of the oldest of the great Universities, shows promise of a striking future.

Boothby was to become an inveterate traveller on parliamentary delegations, yet often lamented that there were not enough of them. This first experience of dazzling sunshine, pure enjoyment and deferential hosts in Jamaica certainly encouraged him to pursue this course, and he joined any organisation that could give him these opportunities.

But he was determined to make his mark in the Commons as well as in East Aberdeenshire, and Noel Skelton, who had been elected for Perth,* wrote admiringly, 'Right from the first he threw himself into the battle at Westminster, and he has developed a Lobby activity and House of Commons sense which some men take years to acquire.' This may have been over-generous, coming from a close friend (who, tragically, was to die young), but Boothby's maiden speech on 26 March 1925 was a success. 'Mr Boothby is a dark young man with an Eton and Oxford education and a manner which betokens at once a studious habit and a robust self-confidence,' one commentator observed. Although he was acutely nervous, the latter aspect was certainly evident in his speech.

It is conventional on such occasions for a government backbencher actually to support the Government, while being uncontroversial. Boothby chose a debate on unemployment, initiated by the Opposition, for his debut. The Liberal, Sir John Simon, opened the debate for the Opposition. Boothby, who spoke after Lloyd George, then proceeded to denounce Simon for making no constructive comments of any kind. This was the beginning of an enduring, and, for Boothby, a fatal, antipathy. Boothby then turned to the facts of international competition and the need for a new spirit of confidence in British industry. 'But what is the Government doing in order to attain this end? Not, I am afraid a very great deal.' He urged cuts in taxation, and the need to raise the status of employment and to remove the dangers of the class war. 'It would not matter in the least who won, because we would all go down to disaster together. . . . I am an optimist and an opportunist, and I believe in compromise.'

The Times and other national newspapers gave him considerable coverage, the former heading its account, 'A Promising Debut'. Another was even more enthusiastic.

---

* Boothby later wrote of Skelton that he was 'a superlative talker, with a tremendous gaity and zest for life; but in the more concentrated Edinburgh tradition. He stimulated every gathering he joined; and in a flash generated the sparks of animated and provocative talk by means of audacious sallies and improvisations, flung out with reckless prodigality. Among others, the phrase "property-owning democracy", which has now passed into general political currency, was originally coined by him.' It was Anthony Eden who remembered it best and was to make it his own, acknowledging his debt to his long-dead friend.

It was quite a remarkable debate altogether. And not the least distinguishing feature of it was the maiden speech of Mr Boothby, coming immediately on top of Mr Lloyd George. Mr Boothby made a striking success, and members were interested in hearing this young black-haired man with his earnest manner of easy confidence. It was intriguing to study the inner working of his mind as revealed by the subconscious stepping backwards and forwards, until at times he was nearly over the borderline of the mat beyond which speakers are not permitted to go. Starting in a quiet voice of pleasing modulation, he soon worked himself up into a rapid state of delivery, which grew faster and faster as his argument developed. But the biggest compliment to him was that such a large House waited to hear him. The Prime Minister himself came in just as Mr Boothby got up, and sat throughout the twenty-five minutes of his speech. At the end Mr Churchill rose from the Treasury bench, and went across the gangway to the front bench where Mr Boothby was sitting, and congratulated him . . . and Mr J. H. Thomas crossed from the other side of the House also to pay his personal tribute.

As Mr Boothby pointed out, Sir John Simon, in a very long speech, never gave utterance to a single constructive proposal. His great purpose was to declare that the 'dole is dope' and because of this chloroforming process, we had not realised the extent of unemployment on account of the absence of hunger-strikers, marchers, and the like.*

It was the first indication of his movement towards Keynesian policies, and his first clash with Churchill. The *Buchan Observer* commented admiringly on 'Mr Boothby's extraordinary energy, undoubted ability, and readiness to lay down the law upon any subject at any time savour of Chancellor Winston at his very best.' Whether 'Chancellor Winston' appreciated this was doubtful, for at the time he was locked in dispute with the Admiralty in an attempt to cut the cruiser-building programme, and Boothby had come out strongly in support of the navy and against the Chancellor of the Exchequer. In March, addressing the Aberdeen Chamber of Commerce shortly before Churchill's budget, Boothby painted a dark picture of the industrial situation,

with too many theorists and intellectuals and too much Government meddling. I would view with apprehension any precipitate return to the Gold Standard . . . the Chancellor of the Exchequer would be taking a rash and unnecessary step if he went back to the Gold Standard.

He also called for trade-union representatives to be on the boards of company directors 'throughout the country'.

---

*In his Radner Lectures in New York, at Colombia University in 1960, on 'The British Parliament', Boothby said of the speech that 'it must have sounded clever, because I read it the other day and couldn't understand a word of it'. This raised laughter, but should not be taken at all seriously. Much of his lifelong economic policy and philosophy was forecast in this speech.

In his budget Churchill duly announced the return to the Gold Standard; to make matters even worse, it was to be at the pre-war pound-dollar parity. Boothby, getting in first before Keynes published his devastating *The Economic Consequences of Mr Churchill*, although already deeply influenced by him, immediately denounced it in the Commons. Churchill said angrily in reply, 'The dogs bark, the caravan passes.'* In his constituency town of Maud on 9 April, he said that 'the people have absolutely got their backs to the wall and are living in conditions which no people in any civilised country ought to be living in'.

In East Aberdeen Boothby was fighting for the herring industry and agriculture, calling for protection of both industries, government subsidies and all possible assistance; this was not the policy of his Government. When changes were proposed for Summer Time, which would have been disastrous for Scotland, he spoke vehemently against them in the Commons, and divided the House – together with Skelton. He was defeated by 228 votes to 56. It was his first rebellion. This did no harm at all in his constituency; nor did an all-night voyage on a drifter out of Peterhead, when he had 'an unpleasant hour at the stern communing alone with the sea' at 4 a.m. In a moment of populist inspiration he announced that on his annual holiday with his parents in Italy he would take, and sell, a barrel of Scottish herring in Milan – which he did.

Under the heading 'Comrade Boothby', 'Onlooker' commented in the *Buchan Observer*:

> Now wasn't Boothby erring
> When thoughtlessly he spoke
> Thus of his quest for herring,
> Inviting jibe and joke?
>
> Sad ills may now befall him,
> Unless he will desist.
> From talk like this, they'll call him,
> A coming Communist!

Boothby's retort, in another constituency speech, was that 'I am a progressive Member of Parliament for a progressive constituency.' Both in the Commons and in East Aberdeenshire he constantly preached the Baldwinite message of co-operation in industry, the perils of the class war and, more controversially, the need to expand the economy.

It was not long after his election that Boothby acquired another hero and friend in Lloyd George, now emphatically in the political wilderness –

---

* Boothby later remarked that 'It only passed on to six million German unemployed, upon whose backs Hitler climbed to power.' This was also very ill-received.

and, as it turned out, for ever. It was an unlikely friendship, not only because of the large difference in their ages, but politically, as Boothby was very firmly a Baldwin supporter, and there was no love lost between Baldwin and Lloyd George. But Boothby was fascinated by the actor in Lloyd George and by the fact that he listened; in turn, Lloyd George quickly adopted Boothby and another new young Conservative MP, Harold Macmillan. Macmillan was not a good speaker and, as Lloyd George remarked to him, his speeches read well as essays but were not speeches; Lloyd George gave him valuable advice, which Macmillan was to put to great effect many years later.

Although Lloyd George was a lonely figure, who never visited the Smoking Room or was at all gregarious, he developed an almost paternal interest in these two bright young Conservatives, who relished his company, conversation and advice. It was largely through him that both became progressively less enthusiastic about the Baldwin Government, although they made an exception for Churchill, who at least had ideas and fire and compassion, which seemed so notably absent in the Party as a whole and in the Government. Neville Chamberlain was making a considerable reputation as Minister of Health, but Lloyd George despised him, having sacked him as Minister responsible for National Service before Chamberlain was even in the Commons; the feeling was keenly returned. Here, again, Lloyd George's influence on the two young men was considerable; when, as will be related, they published their first book together in 1927, Chamberlain surprised Macmillan by writing him a letter of congratulatory disagreement – and then never spoke to him again for the rest of the Parliament. Boothby's hostility to Chamberlain also began early.

Lloyd George had the additional attraction of being a brilliant mimic, Boothby later putting him in the same league as Compton Mackenzie and Peter Ustinov. At the end of a long lunch with Boothby on the Riviera many years later, after excellent conversation and reminiscence, Lloyd George said, "I will now give you my famous imitation of Asquith leaving a restaurant." As he staggered from table to table and pillar to post, leaving his hat behind, everyone there was convulsed with laughter.'

The association and friendship between Lloyd George, Boothby and Macmillan were noted by Baldwin and other Conservatives, and disapproved of. But then and thereafter they both publicly and privately expressed their indebtedness to him warmly.

Boothby always considered the 1920s to have been the happiest and most enjoyable period of his life. He rented a flat in Pall Mall from a friend at a very reasonable price; he found that, for a bachelor, his parliamentary salary of £400 was quite adequate if supplemented by income from his investments, which at that stage were doing fairly well. He became a director of the Standard Trust Company in 1925 and, as will be related, joined a firm of City stockbrokers in 1928. He loved being an MP and enjoyed his regular forays to East Aberdeenshire. He was making new friends and was an important part of Oswald Mosley's circle, which also included Harold Nicolson, still then in the diplomatic service and an elegant writer who seemed destined for major ambassadorships; Leslie Hore-Belisha, another MP and Oxford contemporary tipped for very high things; Esmond Harmsworth; and a very remarkable young Irish journalist-adventurer, Brendan Bracken, not yet in Parliament and a total Churchill devotee, although at this stage their relations were not cordial.

Boothby first met Bracken through his father. Bracken, very much on the make, virtually forced himself into Tom Boothby's Edinburgh office, quite uninvited and unknown, to introduce himself and talk business. 'My father,' Boothby later wrote in an affectionate review of Andrew Boyle's biography of Bracken, 'like so many others, immediately fell under the spell of his vital and somewhat reckless personality.' Tom Boothby was right in his assessment that Bracken and his son would get on well together.

Among his Scottish colleagues, Archibald Sinclair, although a leading Liberal, became a particular friend. Another was Walter Elliot, who was twelve years older than him, and who had studied medicine at Glasgow and served in the Royal Army Medical Corps in the war, in which he had won the Military Cross and bar. He had been elected for Lanark in 1918, was defeated in 1923, but was returned for the Glasgow constituency of Kelvingrove in a by-election in May 1924. Walter Elliot was regarded as a future prime minister – as was Shakes Morrison – and Boothby enjoyed his pawky humour, erudition and company. It was through Elliot that he met Colin Coote, who had been the coalition MP for the Isle of Ely until 1922, after which he began an eminent career in journalism and literature, and became one of Boothby's warmest friends and travelling companions.

Another new colleague was his friend Malcolm Bullock. He was ten years older than Boothby, and had served in the Scots Guards in the war and then at the Foreign Office. His wife, who was a daughter of Lord Derby, was the widow of Neil Primrose, the son of the former Prime Minister Lord Rosebery, whose exceptionally promising life and political career had been ended, as in so many cases, by a chance bullet in the Mesopotamia campaign. Destined to serve as an MP for Lancashire constituencies until 1953, Bullock was always an amusing companion and friend, whose abilities were to be inadequately rewarded. Neither he nor Boothby fully realised the developing power of the Party Machine, and its hostility towards individuality and a somewhat carefree approach to life.

Many years later, in a highly controversial – and badly received – speech in the Commons, Boothby described what it had been like to be an MP in the 1920s:

When I first entered the House in 1924, it was possible to live quite comfortably on one's parliamentary salary. Happy days those were. It was also possible to work in another profession, and many Members did. I should say that the majority did, and this was of great value to the House and to the country. In those days it was quite a thing to be a Member of Parliament. One had prestige and social *cachet*. The doors of a society which no longer exists were open to one; and, if one was so minded, one could eat and drink and spend one's holidays entirely at other people's expense. They were delighted and honoured to have you, and you were delighted and honoured to consume their food and drink.

Ministers were, of course, tremendous swells, occupying Olympian heights almost beyond the ken of ordinary mortals; and even Parliamentary Private Secretaries cut quite a dash.

We are gradually reaching a stage when membership of this House will be confined to company directors, trade-union officials, journalists, and the rapidly diminishing number of those who have inherited wealth. That is about all it will come to.

Oswald Mosley was the star. It is still difficult today to realise the impact that 'Tom' Mosley made on British politics and young politicians in the 1920s. A brilliant orator, a man of real physical and moral courage, bursting with energy and ideas, he stood in glittering and glamorous contrast to the old gangs in both Parties. Disgusted with the Conservatives, he had quit them to join Labour, where he seemed to be their one hope for the future. Also, although he was unfaithful to her, he had found a wonderful wife in Cynthia, the daughter of Lord Curzon, known to her friends as 'Cimmie', whose valour and devotion were legendary. She was also a wonderful friend, and Boothby revered her. Her early death after a minor operation in 1933 at the age of thirty-four was a catastrophe for Mosley, and also for Boothby, whose relationship with her was totally platonic and one of real friendship. But, as Mosley went on his hectic political course to eventual disaster, Boothby had the sense not to follow him. However, in the happy 1920s, when everything seemed possible, Mosley was a potent and exciting prospect, a bright light in an otherwise drab political firmament. Some of that atmosphere can be recaptured from Boothby's letters. In August 1925 he stayed with the Mosleys in Venice, and wrote to Cimmie:

How can I thank you as you ought to be thanked? An impossible task. I enjoyed – rapturously – every moment. No, there was one – at Faustino's entertainment – when I drank too little and too much – that which produces that 'grumpy' stage – and when I was a credit neither to you nor to myself.

But I withdrew once more to 'commune alone with the sea' and speedily remembered myself & recovered. For that lapse which I trust you never saw (John [Strachey] – wretched man – had to bear the brunt) I apologise.

I hope there were no others.

For I can truthfully say that never in my life have I experienced such sustained enjoyment at so high a pitch. It was MARVELLOUS. Thank you a thousand times. It is impossible not to come back. And sweet of you to ask me.

And then, in November:

Your speeches affected even 'Unionist women', than whom there are no worse, if that is any satisfaction to you!

All being well I return to vote against communists on Tuesday. In my present condition, it is a matter of total indifference to me whether this country is ruled by communists, or, for that matter, tigers.

Venice seems like a glorious & quite incredible dream now. What a life – when sunburn and mosquitoes were all that troubled.

May those days – or some very like them – return.

DON'T go to America.

I don't know which is worse – it, or the people in it.

Love to Tom.

There was much travelling abroad and entertainment at home, as it was the age of the great London hostesses and houses, and long and luxurious country-house weekends had not passed into history. Boothby was a regular recipient of the generous hospitality of Mrs Ronald Greville, Lady Astor, Lady Cunard, Lady Londonderry and Lady Colefax, of whom he later wrote with much affection. There were some qualifications – there was never enough to drink at Cliveden, the teetotal Astors' beautiful Buckinghamshire palace, but he and the Mosleys brought reinforcements. It was thanks to Lady Cunard that Boothby first met the love of her life, Thomas Beecham, and began another deep and happy friendship.

Another dominating personality was Sir Philip Sassoon, described by Boothby as 'the greatest host and the greatest gardener I have ever known, and, in the right mood, the best company. For ten years he shaped my life.' Boothby was a constant visitor to his celebrated weekend parties at Trent and Lympne in Kent, and in the 1930s Sassoon rented him The French House at Lympne, a large Tudor farmhouse that he had restored, so that Boothby could entertain his friends properly. Many years later Boothby wrote:

To-day it all seems like the dream of another world – the white-coated footmen, Winston Churchill arguing over the tea-cups with Bernard Shaw, Rex Whistler painting alone, an immaculate Sir Samuel Hoare playing tennis with the professional, Osbert Sitwell and Malcolm Bullock laughing in a corner while Philip himself flitted from group to group, an alert, watchful, influential, but unobtrusive stage director.

Boothby thought then, as well as later, that he was in Paradise, but he also knew that there was another side to British society and life than this round of experiences of luxury, which made him very different to the wealthy hedonists of the time. But that did not stop him hugely enjoying himself, as he openly and frankly admitted. It was even better than Oxford. Admirers of the contemporary writing of P. G. Wodehouse can capture the atmosphere of the life of the affluent at that time. Not all the friendships were to last, including that with Sassoon, and virtually all the great houses fell upon hard times, but it was certainly fun while it lasted, and Boothby relished it to the full.

In 1972, to a particularly close friend, Boothby wrote:

> Never mind. The Twenties were well worth a visit to this planet. I enjoyed them too much. Particularly my friends – LG, Beecham, Compton Mackenzie, Willie Maugham, Malcolm Sargent, John Strachey, Colin Coote, Arnold Bennett, Noël Coward. With the Thirties the shadows began to fall.

At this point Boothby discovered another hero, whose influence upon him was to be deep and permanent.

Keynes had become famous overnight with his polemic *The Economic Consequences of the Peace*, principally for the brilliant and cruel personal portraits of Lloyd George, Georges Clemenceau and, most of all, President Wilson. Boothby disapproved of this work and later regarded it as disastrous, but was to agree with almost everything Keynes later wrote, especially his insistence that the effects of deflation are no less dire than those of inflation, and that the remedy for industrial depression is to be found in the expansion of demand rather than in a reduction of costs, including wages. Keynes' *A Treatise on Money* (1930) and his *General Theory* (1936) became Boothby's economic bibles, and he devoured his pamphlets and articles with reverence. He was also fascinated by Keynes' astonishing breadth of friends and interests. 'A brilliant and stimulating conversationalist,' he wrote admiringly of Keynes, 'equally at home and at ease with politicians, civil servants, bank directors, *littérateurs*, land agents, actors, artists, dons, Bloomsbury intellectuals, college porters, farm labourers, and professors, to all of whom he could talk on level terms.' To Boothby, his company was on a par with that of Lloyd George and Weizmann, which was praise indeed. He wrote of Keynes:

Hunched in his chair, with soft voice and glittering eye, he played every note of the huge keyboard at his command with unerring touch. If you were in doubt and perplexity, he made everything seem simple and clear. And even when, instinctively, you disagreed with him, the sorcerer's magic enforced a final, if reluctant, submission.

Boothby was particularly impressed by Keynes' concern about the impact of economic matters on the lives of individuals and society as a whole, rather than theoretical economics, and his hatred of unemployment and poverty, which he also considered unnecessary as well as evil. He rejected *laissez-faire* and set out alternatives, and his expansionist theories fitted in perfectly with Boothby's character. This was anathema not only to the Tory Party but to Labour, as Mosley was to find to his cost in 1929–31. When Lloyd George took up the arguments of Keynes and Hubert Henderson and advocated their remedies, the political as well as the financial Establishment *knew* that it was dangerous nonsense.

But Boothby and his new friend Harold Macmillan were captivated by Keynes' basic message:

Half the copybook wisdom of our statesmen is based on assumptions which were at one time true, or partly true, but are now less and less true day by day. We have to invent new wisdom for a new age. And in the meantime we must, if we are to do any good, appear unorthodox, troublesome, dangerous, disobedient to them that begat us. In the economic field this means, first of all, that we must find new policies and new instruments to adapt and control the working of economic forces, so that they do not intolerably interfere with contemporary ideas as to what is fit and proper in the interests of social stability and social justice.

This was to become one of Boothby's favourite quotations and his economic credo.

As usually happened with Boothby, admiration was accompanied by personal friendship. Boothby totally agreed with Keynes' diagnosis, was warmed by his humanity, and supported his denunciation of the return to the Gold Standard and the Baldwin Government's handling of the miners' strike, but he was never an unthinking disciple, and on several occasions disputed the arguments of The Master. These must have been lively occasions, and Boothby later lamented that

It is maddening that, without the miracle of a Boswell, the conversation of the great must always be lost to posterity. So often they surpass themselves in small and intimate gatherings where caution may be set aside, and ideas tossed into the air on the unpinioned wing. Maynard Keynes was no exception.

Another enduring result of Boothby's exposure to Keynes was a detestation amounting to contempt for The Treasury Mind; on several occasions he remarked in speeches that the supreme triumph of the British people was not winning two world wars but surviving the British Treasury. He was quickly to become a sharp and painful critic of successive Chancellors of the Exchequer, regardless of Party. They did not like it and made their displeasure clearly known, publicly and privately. Keynes made no impression at all upon the Bank of England, or on Churchill, to whom economics was a firmly closed book and who, unlike Lloyd George, was temperamentally ambivalent about large changes in social reform.

The fact that Boothby and Macmillan were the champions of Keynes on the Tory backbenches in the 1920s and 1930s did nothing whatever to improve their standing in the Tory Party, which came to regard Macmillan as a boring crank, Boothby as an interesting pestilential nuisance, and Keynes as a perilous Socialist, or even a Communist. To their eternal credit they battled on, and some of the best speeches they made in their long careers were in economic debates during the inter-war period.

Boothby's speeches on these matters, in the Commons, in his constituency and elsewhere, are so numerous that it would hardly be possible in a reasonable compass to include them all. However, their common purpose was not to adumbrate a new economic model or to give answers to all questions, but to demonstrate the appalling consequences of *laissez-faire*, to advocate expansionism, and to denounce deflationary policies and the declared helplessness of government to relieve the terrible blight of recession and unemployment and human tragedy on ordinary people. They read excellently today, but at the time no one was listening. When Mosley took up the same cudgels with courage and flair, and then crashed to foolish and unnecessary disaster, their political cause was fatally compromised. But they persevered.

Boothby found that he had a far more receptive audience in his constituency, the Commons and in the country than he did in the Conservative Party and the Conservative-dominated press. In East Aberdeenshire he concentrated on the practical effects on farming and fishing and on the families of his destitute constituents in terms that they could well understand. His rather grand friends in the constituency were often puzzled, and even alarmed, by what he was saying, but one of the principal reasons that Socialism never caught on in East Aberdeenshire was that the electors realised that they had their own champion. In the Tory hierarchy in London he was regarded with increasing distaste, and in many cases with real aversion. Boothby did not care and continued his assaults upon their orthodoxy, stupidity and lack of concern for those who were paying the price for it.

This was the same Boothby, serious, thoughtful, concerned and brave, as the Stock Exchange gambler, *bon viveur* and cheerful socialite, with a chaotic private life. It is this dichotomy throughout his life that so baffled his contemporaries and is so infuriating for his biographer. It was not the case, as some have suggested, that he took subjects up and then dropped them in order to hit Monte Carlo or Venice. He certainly did the latter, but his output in speeches, articles and public letters was prodigious, and was to remain so. There was The Good Boothby, but The Bad Boothby had its attractions as well. He was bubbling with enjoyment of life, public and private, and hurled into both of them an energy and spirit that many found attractive; more staid personalities did not. This explains why he was so widely and deeply loved and admired by many, and loathed by others.

As we have seen, Boothby has himself commented on how difficult it is, in the absence of a Boswell, to recapture the great conversationalists. Fortunately in Boothby's case his reputation as one of the best of all was later demonstrated frequently to millions of people on radio and television, but the private records are meagre. One can state with confidence that a man who more than held his own with Lloyd George, Churchill, Beecham, Maugham, Keynes and Noël Coward had something to offer, and, even as an older man, when I got to know him, he was the best company in London. His cousin, Ludovic Kennedy, has described him as 'one of the funniest men I have ever known, though often coarse in the extreme'. This genuinely surprised me, as this was one aspect of his talk that I never experienced. He certainly loved gossip, but it was seldom malicious, and his staunchness to his friends was total and legendary – and not only to his friends. One example may suffice.

His relations with General Edward Louis Spears cooled into virtual enmity in 1940 when Spears' previous Francophilia swung into violent Francophobia. However, when his wife, the writer Mary Borden, died many years later, Spears asked Boothby to make the address at her memorial service. Boothby declined, as he had not known her at all well and had never been on particularly good terms with her. But Spears insisted, almost tearfully, and after a sleepless night Boothby relented to his pleas. It was, like all his addresses on such occasions, beautifully prepared and delivered, and few realised the emotional difficulties that lay behind it.

It was the fact that he touched life in such an astonishing variety of ways that always made his talk so interesting and vivid. Although he could be very funny, and his delivery of a good story was incomparable, he could also be deeply serious, even grave. There were certain political subjects that were not at all humorous to him; he was quite remarkably well-read; he had his father's eye for art; and his knowledge of music was really profound. And he was as good value in a crowd of congenial friends as he was in a one-to-one conversation, which is unusual. Any act of meanness, unworthiness or betrayal made him angry, and his face would almost physically darken; he could spit out a contemptuous epithet with a venom that could be alarming, but these moods tended to pass quite quickly, and the sun would shine again. I have known no one who could see the comical aspects of great disasters, particularly those affecting himself, as swiftly as he, and he had the true journalist's eye for the significant detail that brought men and events to life, a gift he shared with Beaverbrook.

Although he loved life, he was never a hedonist, and was capable of hard and sustained work as well as a formidable capacity for enjoying himself. Gambling was always his greatest and worst vice, and one he never fully cured. It cost him dearly financially, but it gave him intense pleasure and excitement. If ever the phrase 'a born gambler' applied to anyone's character, it applied to Boothby – and not only at the gaming-tables.

Having come, quite early on, to an essentially sombre view of one's brief existence on this planet, and its ultimate futility, his philosophy of life was that it was to be lived to the full while it lasted, and that there was no point in bothering oneself with theories or doubts about destiny, the divinity or the afterlife. He thought that all of them were self-evident nonsense, and was genuinely puzzled when any of his friends 'got religion'. His own rules of conduct were, however, surprisingly severe. Excessively generous himself, in time as well as in money, he despised its absence in others and applauded its presence. As a private letter-writer he was meticulous in the social courtesies, and was upset when others were more casual; in this he was strikingly old-fashioned and could take serious offence when a relative or friend let him down, about which they would be rapidly informed in very clear and unambiguous terms. This was in marked contrast to his own casualness on money matters. He was honest, but feckless, and too ready to gamble. Until Edward Beddington-Behrens took matters in hand, and not before time, this aspect of his life was a shambles. The fact was that he did not care.

Above all, it was his voracious appetite for life in all aspects and in all countries that made him an exceptionally interesting and well-informed conversationalist and companion on almost every subject. Nor, as some have suggested, was it all about the past. Until his final illness his interest in contemporary events, and not only in politics, was intense, and his opinions were always worth listening to. He did not expect agreement, nor did he impose his views and prejudices, as too many politicians do. Indeed, he enjoyed a good argument on level terms, and winning it even more. Many people liked this, but there were others who did not.

The English fascinated him, and he was to live his entire adult life in London, but he not only never really understood them, he never really liked them. His spiritual home was in Scotland, where his style and very real erudition and wit were much more appreciated. He occasionally toyed with the idea of settling there, but London was where 'the great game' was being played, so that was where he stayed.

He was also an urban person. Although he loved the Aberdeenshire countryside and the farmers, it was as a visitor as well as an MP; country life, except at the highest levels of luxury, did not greatly appeal to him. The French House at Lympne was his country retreat for many years, but when it went he made no serious attempt to find another. He was a lifelong flat-dweller, and conspicuously lacked that urge to own a house of one's own that is supposed to be so deeply ingrained in the British psyche. He preferred to be on the move and enjoyed the restless flexibility of his life. The idea of 'settling down' with wife, family and home, so constantly urged by his mother, had little appeal in practice, although there were occasions when it temporarily attracted him. But he then shrank from the grim realities of such heavy commitments. He wanted to travel light, with the maximum enjoyment and comfort. Many tried to ween him away from this almost nomadic existence, but it was a major, and very important, part of his personality and approach to life. Brendan Bracken's was very similar, it might be noted; like Boothby he never owned a house in his life, nor did he want to.

There was, however, an interesting difference. Bracken regarded marriage with real aversion, having no wish to have encumbrances like a wife and children, not only hostages to fortune but also shackling his independence. But Boothby's attitude was more complex – and ultimately tragic. He feared the confines and obligations of marriage, yet craved love and companionship. These conflicting emotions were to cause him, and others, much anguish, but at this time these problems had not begun to haunt him. He was young, happy, successful and carefree, without commitments, except to his friends and constituents.

On one matter he was never casual. Boothby's journalism began at an early age and was to become a major part of his life. He was meticulous in meeting deadlines and undertaking assignments, and his beautifully written articles and reviews and telephoned reports made him a great favourite among editors. His output was enormous, and of high quality, and he never overlooked the needs of his local newspapers in East Aberdeenshire, who were never short of excellent 'copy' from their MP.

In this he was totally professional from the beginning, and was to remain so – something he shared with Churchill.

Another of Boothby's mentors was the formidable niece and biographer of Arthur Balfour, 'Baffy' Dugdale, so-called because of her attempt as a child to pronounce her family name. The great love of her life was Boothby's friend, Walter Elliot; it was Boothby's unhappy task to inform her of Elliot's engagement to another lady, upon which she dramatically fainted. Colin Coote has described her as 'Tense and tenacious, of a ruthless loyalty to friends and causes, polished, prejudiced and persistent'; she was also excellent and amusing company. She thought highly of the young Boothby politically and personally, but deplored his deficiencies – while recognising that when he put his mind to anything he worked very hard indeed – and his recklessness, particularly in his private life. As will be seen, she was to be a staunch friend and critic at Boothby's darkest hour.

Boothby's first experience of the United States was in the autumn of 1925, when he was attending the annual conference of the Inter-Parliamentary Union in Washington. Baldwin wrote to him that

> In common with Lloyd George and Baillie Hamilton, I have asked our Ambassador in Washington to get you in touch with anyone you desire, so call on him and boldly make your wants known. Whether it is Rockefeller, or Fatty Arbuckle, or Pussyfoot Johnson or the President, all doors will fly open for you.

In his memoirs, Boothby concentrated on the impact upon him of American music and of the feeling of confidence and prosperity in the country. He discovered Irving Berlin, Jerome Kern and George Gershwin, but was also deeply impressed by American employer–employee relations, which were in such marked contrast with those in Britain. He made a speech at the conference on the need for greater European co-operation and an end to 'the fever of nationalism'. When the IPU meeting moved to Ottawa, Boothby spoke again, and a friend of his mother, A. H. Grant, reported to her a lunch he had with the former Canadian Prime Minister, Sir Robert Borden:

> They were full of enthusiasm about a young British MP who had made a great impression there. Sir Richard [sic] dwelt on the excellence of his choice of words and delivery and the thoughtful good sense of all he said – and predicted a great political future for him. When I asked who this young man was I found that, as I had anticipated, it was your son Bob. I thought it might interest you to hear of this accidental testimonial from an ex-Premier of some note.

Boothby returned inspired by the American experience of worker participation and benefit and welfare schemes, on which he spoke at a meeting attended by Baldwin in Aberdeen on 6 November. If the Americans could achieve this, he argued, so could the entire British Empire. This was not exactly conventional Conservative thought at the time, but Baldwin was enthusiastic about the speaker personally, declaring, 'With such young men coming forward I have no fear for the future.'

Boothby had enthusiastically supported Baldwin's vision of social unity, and particularly an understanding attitude towards trade unions, especially the miners, which put him at odds with the bulk of the Conservative Party, but not in the company of his 1924 colleagues, who were beginning to be denounced by the hardline Conservative press as the YMCA.

Their doubts about Boothby were greatly augmented by his attitude towards Russia. Ever since the 1917 Revolution, the Soviet Union had been an object of total revulsion and fear to the Conservatives, and all actions of militant trade unionists in Britain had been ascribed to the activities of international Bolshevism. Boothby, perhaps influenced by Harrod, was more questioning about this assumption. There was also the fact that Russia had been a heavy purchaser of herrings, which, for constituency reasons, Boothby wished to restore. But there was more to it than that. Boothby already believed, as did Macmillan, that membership of the League of Nations should be universal, although they accepted that there were, for the present, difficulties over Germany, and said so in the Commons and in a joint letter to *The Times*, their first public collaboration. Boothby, for whom the travel bug was always intense, as was his curiosity about other countries, secured himself an invitation to Russia as a member of an entirely unofficial, and frowned upon, Conservative delegation, the other members being Sir Frank Nelson, Thomas Moore and his cousin Bobby Bourne, the MPs for Stroud, Ayr and Oxford respectively.

The visit to Russia took place in April 1926. 'I am most anxious', Boothby told the *Evening Standard*, 'to make a thorough investigation, if I can, of the whole machinery of government in Russia', for which task he and his colleagues had allocated five weeks! In the event they only got two, but this did not diminish Boothby's clear perceptions of the situation.

They travelled to Moscow by way of Berlin and Warsaw, and Boothby immediately recorded his impressions for the *Spectator*:

The first glimpse of the crowded streets – of strange people jostling each other in their efforts to avoid annihilation by motor-cars which dashed along at a pace calculated to turn the most intrepid Parisian taxi-driver green with envy, to accompaniment of ear-splitting hoots exceeding in pungency and horror anything the Italians can produce – was exciting. . . . Luxurious taxis for foreigners, uncomfortable taxis for Bolshevik officials, filthy *droshkies* driven by filthy old men, peasant carts carrying their produce to market, with here and there the Rolls-Royce of a Commissar – of such is the traffic. There are shops – rather rich shops – but nobody ever seems to buy anything in them. Perhaps they are just for show.

Boothby's developing capacity as a descriptive journalist was well revealed in this piece, although he did not foresee the future horrors of Stalinism. When they visited the Kremlin, they stood upon a terrace overlooking the river, winding its way through the city and beyond.

Moscow lay at our feet, and over Moscow a haze shimmered in the afternoon sun. A bell rang out; then another; and suddenly the whole air seemed to be filled with the sound of many bells merging themselves into a single vibrant note. The effect was memorable, and the city resembled Fez in the poignancy of its beauty.

Boothby was convinced that 'the campaign against Christianity has failed. The priests may have been killed. The churches remain. Once more the choirs sing, the candles are lit, the devout pray. Religion, the Bolsheviks have found, is a force to be reckoned with.'

The delegation witnessed the great May Day political parade, far more military than political, with 15,000 troops taking part and aircraft roaring overhead ('one wondered what would have been the effect of it all upon some of our Labour pacifists'), which went on all day with a crowd 'ruthlessly controlled by military police'. Boothby doubted whether many took part of their own free will and noted that they looked 'bored to distraction. But the children at least seemed to be enjoying themselves.' The Russian love of music made an immense impression on him, as did a lengthy meeting with Karl Radek in the Kremlin. Radek was then in eclipse after Lenin's death, but he was still a man of some influence and much knowledge. From these experiences Boothby returned convinced, as were his colleagues, that for all its evident inadequacies, the Soviet system was stable and that its leaders genuinely wanted better relations with the West.

The MPs had to return hurriedly because of the British General Strike, but when they got back it was already over. Although their report was realistic about the Communist regime, which they described as 'nothing more or less than an extremely efficient dictatorship over the proletariat', they called for 'a diplomatic and commercial settlement' between Britain and Russia. The timing could hardly have been worse. The General

Strike had collapsed, and people allegedly faced with the terrors of a Red Revolution in Britain were hardly likely to commend such sentiments, particularly in the Conservative Party. The report had, as Boothby noted, 'a cold reception'. It confirmed in certain quarters growing doubts about Boothby's Conservative credentials.

One person who did not note Boothby's attitude and speeches with approval for their content was Churchill, but, a natural rebel himself, he was attracted by this intelligent and self-confident young man who had a mind of his own and was refreshingly unpredictable. The fact that the Tory Right was already becoming restless with him was an additional bonus, and he enjoyed his company. Churchill's first letter to Boothby was on 10 August 1926, written from Chartwell:

> My Dear Boothby
>
> How very kind of you to send me the article which you wrote to the *Spectator* about my book [*The World Crisis*]. I read it with the greatest pleasure, all the more because it was written before we were friends – before we even knew each other – & when you might, as so many other people have done, have formed unfavourable views of my character & performance.
>
> You must not mind my chaff about the Bolsheviks. It has a serious underside however. I do not want to see you get mixed up with these snakes or their servitors in this country, just for the sake of herrings, & so prejudice what I dare say will be a prosperous political career.
>
> With good wishes
Yours sincerely
Winston S. Churchill

After the General Strike Baldwin had retreated to Aix-les-Bains, leaving Churchill to deal with the continuing miners' strike, an episode of misery in British social and political history from which only Churchill and the miners emerge with any credit. The most vociferous against the unions during the General Strike, he was anxious to meet the grievances of the miners in their confrontation with the private owners; he lost, but at least he tried.

While he was engaged in this thankless and fruitless task, he received an immensely long letter from Boothby, written at the Carlton Club on 9 October, setting out his concerns and his political philosophy, which made a deep impression upon him and was to greatly affect Boothby's life.

> Dear Mr. Churchill
>
> I must apologise for writing to you. But I am so troubled about the present trend of affairs that I would beg you to consider one or two aspects of the situation as they have struck me of late in Scotland. We are losing ground at a rate that is alarming, and the reason is not far to seek.

It is the impression, growing every day, that the Government has now divested itself of all responsibility for the conduct of our national industries in the interest of the country as a whole; that it has capitulated to the demands of one of the parties engaged in industry, and is now preparing legislative action at their behest, in order to encompass the destruction of the other. In short that, despite the promise of the first months, it has become what the people of Scotland have never tolerated, and will never tolerate – a government of reaction.

You know far better than I do, the mind of the average Scottish elector when it is not confused by side issues.

It is imbued with a spirit of true Liberalism. At the last election thousands of life-long members of the Liberal party voted for us for the first time. There are also those 'wise men who gaze without self-deception at the failings and follies of both parties; of brave and earnest men who find in neither faction fair scope for the effort that is in them; of poor men who increasingly doubt the sincerity of party philanthropy'.* They, too, voted for us.

It would be difficult to exaggerate the effect of your vigorous intervention in the mining dispute last month upon the moderate average-minded person in Scotland; or the disappointment which attended the failure of your effort. There are many who consider (I can really answer for this) that at the time you wrote to the Prime Minister the letter which you quoted in the House of Commons, you were resolved to go forward, and to compel the owners (not necessarily the MINING ASSOCIATION) to meet the executive of the federation, using if necessary the threat of suspension of the Eight Hours Act; but that you subsequently succumbed to pressure from many quarters.

Moreover the miners' leaders assert in speech after speech that you gave them positive assurances that if they made such an offer as their last one 'the whole force and authority of His Majesty's Government' would be brought into action in their support. This has never been publicly contradicted.

To put it quite frankly, there is a widespread feeling even amongst those who strongly disapprove of the policy and performance of the miners' federation, that you made a great attempt to obtain a fair and reasonable peace in the interests of the nation; that the miners went a long way to meet you; but that the owners, supported by a section of the Conservative party, contemptuously declined even to negotiate, and that you did not feel yourself strong enough to hold on the right course. Great hope has been replaced by great disillusionment.

Who are the owners that they should decide what is in the national interests, in opposition to the Government and elected representatives of the people? . . .

Meanwhile, the miners in the exporting districts are observed doggedly

* Churchill's concluding sentence in his biography of his father.

awaiting their fate. Obstinate, stubborn, and stupid. Misled by their leaders, abandoned by the Government. But loyal according to their lights, peaceable, and, despite increasing hunger, resisting (in Scotland almost to a man) what is to them the temptation to return to work. Is it to be wondered at that, with the cold weather now rapidly approaching, such a spectacle has attracted widespread sympathy?

It is generally recognised that there are certain abuses in connection with the Trades Unions which it is the duty of the Government to remedy, but the Scarborough conference has given rise to an uneasy feeling that a massed attack on Trade Unionism is now contemplated.

I apologise for writing at such length. My only excuse is my anxiety, and please do not think I want a written reply.

A Scottish owner observed to me the other day, 'The sooner you bloody politicians realise that there is only one tougher set of men in the country than the miners' federation, and that's the owners, the better.'

How, in the face of that sort of thing, can the Government, having placed the weapon in the hands of the owners, stand by and allow the miners to be bludgeoned and battered back, district by district?

Bludgeoned and battered they will be, in parts of Scotland at any rate. And the instruments? Longer legal hours, cold, and starvation. No. As Lord Hermiston once observed, 'There is a kind of decency to be obsirvit.'

If this is to be followed by legislative action calculated to convey the impression that the Conservative party has utilised the power given to it by the electors to plunder the funds of the principal opposition party, and smash the Trade Unions, then, in Scotland at least, a terrible retribution awaits it at the polls.

I cannot help concluding with a quotation [by Lord Randolph Churchill] which will be familiar to you.

'Labour in this modern movement has against it the prejudices of poverty, the resources of capital, and all the numerous forces – social, professional, and journalist – which those prejudices and resources can influence. It is our business, as Tory politicians, to uphold the Constitution. If under the Constitution, and as we wish to see it preserved, the Labour interest finds that it can obtain its objects and secure its own advantage, then that interest will be reconciled to the Constitution, will find faith in it, and will maintain it. But if it should unfortunately occur that the Constitutional party, to which you and I belong, are deaf to hear and slow to meet the demands of Labour, are stubborn in opposition to those demands, and are persistent in ranging themselves in unreasoning and short-sighted support of all the present rights of property and capital, the result may be that the Labour interest may identify what it will take to be defects in the Constitutional with the Constitution itself, and in a moment of indiscriminate impulse may use its power to sweep both away.'

Written by one who, in the year 1892, regarded the miners' Eight Hours

Bill as of greater importance than 'the Monarchy, the Church, the House of Lords, or the Union'.

> Yours very sincerely
> Robert Boothby

Churchill replied sympathetically to this remarkable letter on 16 October, saying that the situation had reached a point where there was no choice for the Government but to see the thing through. He added:

> The issue is not one between Govt. & Opposition but what are good laws for the community. Intimidatory picketing, privileged immunity, political levies under pain of boycott, are not – once the issue is raised – compatible with any form of good government.
>
> The GENERAL STRIKE constituted a direct challenge, & is a milestone in British politics.
>
> I quite understand your pangs & anxieties. But don't let them draw you from a coherent view. Let me know when you are in London & we can have a talk.

Boothby had not appreciated that Churchill was discontented with his Parliamentary Private Secretary, Sir Clive Morrison-Bell, and was looking for a replacement. In those days ministers appointed their own PPS, and only the most senior were entitled to them. Boothby was therefore genuinely astonished when Churchill asked to see him and cried out to him as he entered, 'You are my new PPS!'

The announcement caused delight in East Aberdeenshire, at Beechwood and among his friends, and, no doubt, much jealousy elsewhere. One political commentator wrote that

> the Chancellor of the Exchequer is youthful, if not young, and travels fast. He would not permit his speed-wagon to be retarded by trailing a bath-chair behind it. Sir Clive was sacked and Robert Boothby, the brilliant young Tory from Aberdeen, takes his place.

Boothby later wrote: 'This was my first great mistake. I was a little conceited. I entered his service, but could not carry out his terms. I got off on the wrong foot with him.' Another real problem was, as Boothby noted, 'all [Churchill's] emotions were involved in politics, the signature tune of a great man of action,' whereas Boothby's emotions were much more widely dispersed. He was a far more serious politician than he often appeared, but politics were never his whole life, as they were in Churchill's. Their relationship was to be turbulent, and ultimately sad, but it played a significant part in both their lives. Clark-Kerr wrote:

> Yes, Bob, I feel sure You are a coming man *dans tout l'exception du mot*. So am I still. When You see Winston commend me to him. . . .Oddly enough,

Bob, I believe in You – seriously I do – and I often think that You are a very jolly fellow.

Churchill, in 1926, was at the height of his physical and intellectual powers. In addition to being Chancellor of the Exchequer, he was writing the concluding – and greatest – volume of *The World Crisis* and was beginning his classic of autobiography, *My Early Life*. Chartwell was being virtually rebuilt, and he had vast projects for the house and grounds. As Boothby wrote, admiringly, 'He was also painting pictures and laying bricks; yet he always found time, plenty of time, to talk.' Boothby was dazzled by Churchill, who showed him great kindness and friendship, invited him to Chartwell, took him out to dinner in London and, the supreme accolade, made him a member of The Other Club, the most famous and illustrious of modern political dining clubs, which he and Birkenhead had founded in 1911. Boothby also, literally, shared the limelight with his master on budget days, walking just behind the Chancellor as he made his well-publicised walk to the Commons from 11 Downing Street. Working with Churchill in any capacity was never a sinecure, and the preparation of any speech, however minor the occasion, was a major enterprise in itself. Churchill was never a natural orator and all his speeches had to be drafted, and endlessly redrafted, before he was satisfied. And, all the time, he was thinking aloud and talking incessantly. It was highly stimulating, but also highly demanding.

However, their friendship, although very strong, never fully developed into a real closeness. As Lady Violet Bonham Carter later wrote of Churchill, 'He demanded partisanship from a friend, or, at the worst, acquiescence.' Desmond Morton, who also knew him well, remarked that 'the full truth, I believe, is that Winston's "friends" must be persons who were of use to him. The idea of having a friend who was of no practical use to him, but being a friend because he liked him, had no place.' Boothby later wrote of Churchill that '"Thou shalt have none other gods but me" has always been the first, and the most significant, of his Commandments.' The trouble was that Boothby was not cast by nature for this subservient role. 'God may have intended him to be a knight-errant,' as Robert Bruce Lockhart observed of Boothby, 'but surely never a disciple.' This was the fundamental difficulty. Boothby admired and liked Churchill, and marvelled at his astounding energy, but he was independent-minded and had his own life and political ambitions to pursue. He also liked to talk and hold forth with his own views on men and events, and found Lloyd George a far better listener. Indeed, as he came to know Lloyd George better, he was even more fascinated by him, and felt a much closer affinity with him that he ever really did with Churchill.

Even Churchill's greatest admirers have never denied that he was inordinately egotistical and was a difficult colleague. 'He saw and lived life in terms of himself,' Boothby later wrote of him. Also, the Treasury was the one department in his career that Churchill did not adorn, and where he felt uneasy. He once remarked to Boothby of his officials that 'I wish they were admirals or generals. I speak their language, but these fellows talk Persian.' Matters were not improved by the fact that Boothby was developing strong views of his own on economic matters, and he and Churchill continued to disagree on Russia.

There was a woman who was particularly close to Boothby at that time – although not in a sexual sense, being happily married and Boothby a friend of her husband – who took the view that Boothby not only disliked Churchill but actively hated him. There is no evidence whatever for this. Boothby liked him very much, and his brilliance and versatility awed him; it was also clear to him that Churchill was touched by genius, an opinion he never changed. Even in his old age, when his feelings towards Churchill occasionally turned to the malevolent, he always differentiated between Churchill the statesman and war leader and Churchill the man. The former he admired immensely; on the latter he had reservations. It has to be said that he was not alone in this assessment. Boothby was not the only person in Britain who, looking at Churchill's political record since his dramatic arrival on the national stage in 1900, had misgivings about his stability and judgment. This formidable assemblage included not only Baldwin, but Birkenhead, whom Boothby saw often, and who, rightly or wrongly, he considered to be the greater man.

There was also the problem of Mrs Churchill, described by the same lady friend of Boothby's at the time as 'the coldest woman I have ever met'. She frowned upon almost all of her husband's political friends, denouncing the 'three Bs' – Birkenhead, Beaverbrook and Bracken – to which could have been added a fourth, Boothby. She appreciated his friendship and good company, and he was welcomed at Chartwell as one of Winston's friends, but Boothby was always aware of more than a hint of disapproval – as was Bracken. But in fact Clementine Churchill, whose definition of political soundness was loyalty to Winston, was prepared to forgive Boothby much, and was to be his defender when things went grievously wrong, for which Boothby was profoundly grateful. Although caustic about Winston, he would never tolerate any criticism of his wife. He remembered those happy days at Chartwell.

What was remarkable was that Churchill gave Boothby so much freedom of action and speech for a PPS. In February and March 1927 Boothby made powerful speeches in the Commons on unemployment and the folly of the return to the Gold Standard, urged government subsidies for wheat and meat, declaring 'What does it matter whether it is Socialism or not, so long as the object is gained?', and called repeatedly for the restoration of trade with Russia. He wrote to another new friend, Lord Beaverbrook, on 25 May about his disagreements with Churchill and the Government on the break with the Soviet Union:

> . . . I propose to abstain from voting tomorrow as I profoundly disapprove of & fear the diplomatic breach, but I am not going to resign and maroon myself on this issue.
>
> I apologise for writing at such length, but you were so kind on Friday that I thought I would let you know how I felt about it.
>
> I propose to take your advice about reviewing my independence, & to leave Winston at the end of the session, but not on any specific issue. It is a much nicer way of doing it, and I should hate ever to quarrel with him.

Then, in April, *Industry and the State – A Conservative View* was published, the work of Boothby, Macmillan, Oliver Stanley and John Loder.

This production from the leading members of the 'YMCA' was greeted with astonishment. Their arguments were strongly interventionist and anti-*laissez-faire*. They denounced 'the present chaotic condition of the great industries. Whatever may be the risks of a policy of intervention the risks to the whole national fabric of a purely negative policy are greater still.' Conservatives read with amazement their proposals for 'an economic General Staff', the nationalisation of education and the police, an enquiry into the financial credit system, an international conference to develop continuous co-operation between banks, an imperial wheat insurance scheme, an import board, labour co-partnership with employers, and national wage boards for every industry.

Objective reviewers were kind, the *Spectator* hailing the book as 'courageous and profoundly interesting. . . . The authors have a genuine vision: the removal of the present psychological conditions of discontent and suspicion by knocking down the barriers that divide managers from men and Haves from Have-Nots.'

Conservative reactions, however, were violent, and the authors were denounced as 'cranks and theorists [who] must be disposed of'. Under the heading 'Socialists in Conservative Disguise', the *Daily Mail* railed against their 'half-baked sentimentalism' and 'crude and hasty theories characteristic of modern Socialism', particularly noting that the authors recommended increased taxes to cut local rates, and compulsory arbitration in industrial disputes which 'would play into the hands of the Communists and extremists'. The *Sunday Pictorial* thundered that 'the suspicion long entertained by many of us that the Consevative Party is honey-combed with Socialism has been proved up to the hilt. . . . The Party must be purged of its woolly-minded semi-Socialists. These Kerenskys will, unless they are hauled up, only prepare the way for Lenin.' There was much more in the same vein in the national press, but the *Buchan Observer* warmly praised the authors: 'We believe that they are the salt of their Party. On them depends the future of Conservatism.' Utterly unrepentant, within days of this furore, Boothby was denouncing 'the politics of tranquillity' in a major article in the *Graphic*, and repeating his appeals for better relations with Russia, Germany and France.

Nor did he conceal his strong differences with his political master on other matters. On 12 July he startled the Commons again by strong criticisms of Churchill's hostile attitude to defence expenditure: 'Our army is now hardly large enough for police purposes, our air forces are hardly sufficient for the defence of London alone, and our navy has also been largely curtailed, especially in battleships and cruisers.'

This was certainly not the attitude of a disciple, nor even of the usual PPS, but Churchill shared the widespread view that Boothby was a rapidly rising young man of exceptional talent and promise, and on three occasions refused his offer to resign if his independence was causing his master any embarrassment. In April, when Churchill introduced his budget, Malcolm Bullock cheerfuly cabled to Mrs Boothby: 'Boothby enters House unshaved sensation two minutes later Chancellor enters unnoticed.' It is very doubtful that Mabel Boothby would have been pleased by this unusual information.

Boothby was enjoying himself, and his celebrity. Asked if he was contemplating joining the Labour Party in view of his close friendship with the Mosleys, he replied, 'No, there is no truth in these rumours. Although', he added with a twinkle, 'I fear I shall always be a bad Party man, being of a restless and somewhat obstinate disposition.' In response, the *Patriot* declared that 'The East Aberdeen Conservative Association should investigate the state of mind and direction of travel of its Member', and the *Sunday Pictorial* urged that the entire 'YMCA' group should be 'flung out of the Party forthwith'. A more shrewd observer commented that 'If Duff Cooper is to be the Balfour of the future, and Harold Macmillan the Baldwin, Bob Boothby may even be the Winston Churchill of 1937.'

The real impact of *Industry and the State* was on Churchill himself, who was immensely taken by the proposal, of which Macmillan was the principal author, to re-rate industry. The Minister of Health, Neville Chamberlain, whose own star was rising rapidly, was hostile, but Churchill prevailed. The Derating Bill of 1929 was a major achievement for the 'YMCA', and further augmented the friendship between Boothby, Macmillan and Churchill.

Boothby's pleasure in his intimacy with the great is reflected in this letter to his parents on 11 November:

Darlings

How extraordinarily busy I have been! Hence moderate letters for which I apologise.

It is curious to be back once more in the H of C and I have been leading a stirring life.

Winston in very great form & more talkative than ever – hours & hours & hours on Bolsheviks and Armageddon & industry & finance & pyramids & taxation & life.

A remarkable fellow.

I enjoyed the Astor dinner.

Sat next to [Geoffrey] Dawson [editor of *The Times*] who was fulminating against the Govt. and P.M., & wanted to attack them now on seven grounds in the *Times* & would I lead (in the H of C) a band of rebels? I would get all his support.

I said the time was not yet.

Dame Lyttelton on my other side gloomy about slums and socialism. And Nancy [Astor] in grand form after dinner.

There is genuine dissatisfaction with the supineness of the Govt. & so far from being an unpopular figure I find myself greeted with shouts of approval in the Smoking Room & they have been to their constituencies & are beginning to be frightened.

I have always said the Tory party is only possible when terrified.

Dawson highly indignant about the personnel of the Indian Commission (except Simon) & Baldwin's general treatment of the young men.

I think he is rather silly about this because you can't sack all over the place.

But there is no *doubt* that S. B. *loathes* ideas, & still more anyone who expresses them, & that he has lost all grip on the machine.

As Dawson truly said, 'All I ask is that the chauffeur should have some idea where he *wants* to go. It is safer to take a wrong road than to have no idea where you are driving. And he doesn't even seem to *care*.'

All this is private.

But I am quite certain that it is not any particular mistake or bill that is the cause of the Govt's growing unpopularity, but its general aimlessness & lack of purpose & drive.

. . . Dined with Sir Abe Bailey.

A most swagger affair – thirty guests all men.

Dukes galore – Sutherland, Abercorn, etc. Winston, Kipling, Kylsant, Beaverbrook, Louis Greig, Jellicoe, [Laming] Worthington-Evans, & a dozen more 'stars'.

Max [Beaverbrook] very cordial to me! . . .

Sat next to Gwynne, editor of the *Morning Post*.

'Phew!' Winston shouted down the table. 'Be gentle with each other!'

Gwynne as amusing as really able diehards are. Especially about Russia. It admires Trotsky most! Said that they must be discredited at all costs as if they made *anything* of a success of it all the workers would begin wanting a 'workers republic'.

He said Austen Chamberlain was by far the stupidest man he ever met & continued in that vein.

He opened the conversation by saying, 'We have never met but I deplore you!'

In the end we made great friends.

He said Bolshevism and graft in public life were the two things he feared most: but admitted that MacDonald had done nothing as P.M. to lower the standards of public life.

He too is uneasy about Baldwin's lack of grip, but said he had always supported him, for he had cleaned up Downing Street.

True enough.

A dinner of appalling length. Oysters, soup, fish, beef, quails, ham, asparagus, ice, & savoury.

Ten courses with dessert stout, sherry, champagne, port, madeira, & three liqueurs.

I did all but ham.

But it was far too much. . . .

At the time the sheer fun of working with Churchill overjoyed Boothby. In January 1927 they travelled together to Rome by way of Malta, on which occasion Churchill became, to his subsequent embarrassment, seriously impressed by Mussolini. Boothby cabled to his parents: 'Spent all day with Winston Vatican morning lunched Embassy we walked Appian Way afternoon.' There were state balls at Buckingham Palace, at one of which Churchill, to his horror, had to shake hands with Admiral de Robeck, who in his view had lost the naval attack on the Dardanelles in March 1915, and ordered Boothby to get him a stiff whisky, 'and quick'; an evening with the megalomaniac American tycoon William Randolph Hearst and his mistress, the film star Marion Davies, who greatly took to Boothby, to the disapproval of both Hearst and Churchill; lunches and dinners at Chartwell, one with Charles Chaplin; and what was clearly a disastrous meeting between Churchill and Lloyd George, which Boothby, at Churchill's request, had arranged. When Boothby asked Churchill how it had gone, he replied: 'Within five minutes the old relationship between us was completely re-established. The relationship between Master and Servant. And I was the Servant.' This was an episode that Boothby should have recalled in 1940.

In 1928, in the debate on the Finance Bill, Churchill had influenza, as had Boothby, and the Financial Secretary, Arthur Michael Samuel, took charge. One evening he casually accepted a Conservative amendment to reduce the duty on British cigarette lighters. It seemed a trivial matter, but he had unwittingly raised the whole question of Protection. There was a stormy debate. 'Churchill kept ringing me up from his sick-bed to ask me what was happening,' Boothby related, 'and became angrier and angrier as the night wore on.'

On the following morning Boothby reported to his enraged master:

Dear Chancellor

I am so sorry I cannot come and see you, but the doctor is firm.

I reproach myself for not having been on the second bench last night, as I might have been able to dissuade the Financial Secretary from granting the concession. At any rate I could have had a shot at stopping him. But it was the dinner hour, the Chamber was practically empty, and there was no reason to suppose a hitch would occur.

Apparently the only people he consulted were [Leo] Amery & Williams, who misled him about the trade agreement.

Some of our people were irritated about the whole affair last night & there was a good deal of caustic comment in the Smoking Room, but to-day they are disposed to regard it as a joke, although rather a bad one.

It certainly was an astonishing performance.

I am not sure that the keynote of the evening was not struck by the gentleman in the Gallery, who called the Speaker a bastard, told Arthur Michael Samuel to shut up, and threw an old hat at Colonel Woodcock.

I have talked to – or rather been talked to by – many people to-day, and I am sure that no serious harm has been done. But anything like a repetition of yesterday's incidents would be very damaging. . . .

Not one but twenty Members have observed, in varying terms, how instructive it has been to see a difficult and almost dangerous parliamentary situation superbly dealt with on Tuesday, and a perfectly straightforward and easy one reduced to a shambles last night.

I am afraid poor old Arthur Michael is in great distress, and one is very sorry for him.

But he made a sad hash of it.

Yours ever so sincerely
R. B.

That was the end of poor Arthur Michael, who had to go. 'But he took it all with perfect equanimity and characteristic good humour,' Boothby related.

The experience of the Treasury had a somewhat negative effect on Boothby. He admired Churchill's Principal Private Secretary, P. J. Grigg – whom Churchill was later to make Secretary of State for War – but had already formed a hostile opinion of Montagu Norman, the all-powerful Governor of the Bank of England; his uncle, Lord Cunliffe, had warned him about Norman many years before, and closer inspection confirmed his views, and those of Keynes. He also considered that the sum total of Churchill's achievements was meagre, and that he was wrong in persisting with his own post-war ten-year rule, whereby military expenditure was based on the assumption that there would be no war for ten years. He had particularly opposed Churchill's attempted assault on the cruiser-building programme, which had ended in a most unsatisfactory compromise. Most historians have concurred with Boothby's views, which were, it must be emphasised again, forcefully and publicly expressed at the time, and not only in his memoirs.

Boothby was also beginning to develop his undoubted talents as a journalist. He had always written with an exceptional fluency and liveliness, and began to achieve a reputation as a serious journalist which attracted the attention, among others, of Beaverbrook. Their long friendship was to have its difficult moments in later years, but was to survive.

Boothby had been deeply impressed by two pieces of advice. The first was Birkenhead's that he should build up his base in his constituency, which he did, marvellously supported by Gardie Duff. The second came from an experienced MP, Sir Alfred Hopkinson, which he later described as:

Never hope to get on. Never have a career. If you do, you will always be miserable. The only way to have a happy life in the House of Commons is to have no ambition for office whatever; then you are not torn by jealousy as other people get office, and you can keep a single-minded desire to serve your constituents.

Boothby considered this 'the wisest advice ever tendered to those about to embark upon the stormy sea of politics'. It also fitted in exactly with his temperament, and those of his closest political friends, who lacked the dedicated ambition of Eden and Hore-Belisha. Duff Cooper did have ambition, but never let it get in the way of pleasure; Skelton was as fiercely independent as Boothby; and no one could possibly have foreseen in the young idealistic intellectual Macmillan the hard and cunning politician of his later years.

It was not that the young Boothby was indolent, which he certainly was not. The trouble was that his interests were so wide. This made him an especially attractive personality and won him many friends and admirers, but gave his political life little personal purpose except to be an independent gadfly, speaking his mind on most subjects. Accordingly, he was not taken as seriously as he would have been had he been an obvious candidate for office.

There was, however, the problem of money.

* * *

Boothby had soon found that his parliamentary salary, which had appeared so generous, was not adequate for his tastes, which had become notably more expensive. Surrounded as he was by rich and glamorous people, he aspired to be both. The City of London, then enjoying great prosperity, and making some people very rich very quickly, seemed to be the answer. He did not use his position as Churchill's PPS as a method of entry into this imagined Aladdin's Cave; indeed, when in 1928 he was offered a position, that later became a partnership, by the City brokers Chase, Henderson and Tennant, he at once offered to resign, but Churchill refused to accept his resignation. There was no conflict of interest between being a PPS and a City broker, and he asked Boothby to stay on.

Both decisions were, as Boothby later realised, mistakes. He was hopelessly unqualified, by temperament or experience, to be a major figure in the City of London. He regarded it as another Monte Carlo, a glorious gambling den in which he was bound to make a vast fortune. The law would also have been a gamble, but a far less perilous one. Boothby found British banking, and also most bankers, boring, but City speculation was considerably more exciting.

He was now a very self-confident young man, and with good cause. Churchill had picked him out personally; Lloyd George, Keynes and many others thought well of him; and with monotonous regularity – although not to him – he was being referred to as 'the coming man'. He was also developing a considerable, and justified, reputation as an intelligent and enlightened student of national and international finance. He had been right on the Gold Standard decision, and was to be remarkably correct on the big economic issues throughout his life. But he was to prove a lamentable businessman, essentially because he was not much interested in it. His purpose was to make a lot of money as rapidly as he could, so that he could concentrate on politics. Many others have done the same. Indeed, in a country that still refuses to pay its Members of Parliament salaries comparable to other professions carrying similar responsibilities, this course is essential for the majority.

One of Boothby's greatest coups was to recruit Nicholas Davenport, a disillusioned young stockbroker who was also an admirer of Keynes, to Chase, Henderson and Tennant. In addition to being an outstanding broker, he could write very well and had already caused a sensation with a book on the oil trusts and Anglo-American relations. As it condemned the oil imperialisation of British governments that had been started by Churchill and called for the present one to divest itself of the oil shares in the Middle East, it was perhaps not surprising that the book was hailed in left-wing journals and was translated into Russian and sold by the Soviet

War Ministry. But Davenport had been unhappy in his previous partnership, and was particularly depressed by the suicide of a close friend, for whom the City pressures had proved too great.

It was Brendan Bracken who, hearing of Davenport's distress, told Boothby of the situation. Boothby, 'exuding bonhomie and confidence',* and with 'his usual gaiety, wit and cock-sureness', suggested that Davenport should quit Rowe and Pitman forthwith and become a partner in Chase, Henderson and Tennant. 'I accepted Bob Boothby's offer, and have regretted it ever since,' he was to write many years later, tongue slightly in cheek.

An initiatory blow was when he had to pay his share of Boothby's debts after he had over-speculated,

as he loved to do, and lost his shirt. That was not too upsetting, because my share was small and it was worth paying something to have the constant pleasure of Bob's witty and exhilarating conversation. Like me, he felt like a fish out of water in the City, and really had nothing in common with his partners. They particularly seemed to resent my arrival and to harbour a suspicion of intellectuals and especially writers of the radical type like myself.

As Davenport's columns in the *Nation* and other journals constantly denounced the stupidity and deflationist lunacy of the Bank of England and the leading banks, this was not altogether surprising.

H. P. Chase, the senior partner, was both highly intelligent and highly emotional, and somewhat excessively addicted to whisky. Boothby fascinated him, and after he had been introduced to Churchill by Boothby, he became obsessed with the Nazi menace and a fervent anti-appeaser. His strong support for Boothby's political career and views was very helpful at the time, but, as will be seen, he was to render Boothby a terrible, if unintentional, disservice in the winter of 1939–40.

Another introduction by Boothby had more lasting consequences. John Tennant, in complete contrast with Chase's mercurial temperament and violent temper, had a gentler nature, was the nephew of Margot Asquith, was immensely rich, very snobbish and, in Davenport's words, 'intellectually a non-starter'; Tennant seems to have realised this, once commenting that at Dartmouth there were only two below his intellectual level – the future King Edward VIII and King George VI. Boothby introduced Tennant's intelligent and attractive wife Antonia to Cyril Radcliffe. A divorce followed, and she married Radcliffe, Boothby later remarking that their introduction was the one noble act in his life. Tennant's views are not recorded, but by then Boothby was no longer his partner.

'As for Henderson,' Davenport has written, 'he was a dour Scot who

*Nicholas Davenport, *Memoirs of a City Radical*, pp. 38–9.

made me feel that all Scots were distant foreigners suspicious and distrustful of the native English.' The gloomy and dark offices in New Broad Street in 'a hideous provincial-style building with the arms of some northern cities worked in stained glass' did not help, but Davenport delighted in Boothby's company and has written of him during this period:

I was fascinated by Bob Boothby's extraordinary character. His gaiety and wit reminded me of happy Oxford days. He had adored Oxford, where he had been immensely popular, and in some ways he remained an undergraduate. His charm and good looks certainly allowed him to get away with some outrageous undergraduate behaviour. He was a born gambler in both love and money, and it clearly gave him a kick to live dangerously. He would sooner gamble than do the hard work necessary for making money in the City. In fact the City bored him stiff. His real passion was politics. While the devil might be driving him on in his personal affairs he was invariably on the side of the angels in his politics.

Of course, it is not always right to be opposed to an occasional deflation, but Bob was a perpetual expansionist. Expansion suited his temperament, and particularly his portfolio of equity and gold shares which he was always buying for a rise.

As Davenport quickly realised, Boothby's only interest was to make money, and a lot of it, very quickly to give him financial independence for his political career. He found this aspect of the City much more fascinating than Davenport realised. When he saw the Stock Market in terms of a gigantic casino, even more fun than Monte Carlo, he hurled himself into it with a new gusto. It was his own money he was gambling with, but, although he had his triumphs, the fact was that he was, overall, a bad gambler whose casual attitudes and often outrageous risk-taking did not fit in at all well with the more staid traditions of the City.

Davenport left Chase, Henderson and Tennant at the first opportunity, going on to be one of the most consistently sparkling protagonists of Keynes, particularly in the *New Statesman* (which took over the *Nation* in 1930); he was also a highly successful financial adviser and a director of the National Mutual Life Assurance Company, to whose board he was nominated by Keynes in 1930, and of which he became Deputy Chairman, retiring in 1969. His influence on Boothby was itself considerable. His first marriage ended tragically, but his second was wonderfully happy. He bought and restored Hinton Manor, near Oxford, which became one of the passions of his life, and the Sunday lunches which he and his wife Olga gave were very memorable affairs. He always remained a radical and was always devoted to Boothby, sharing his political and economic views, and coming publicly to his support in his darkest hour. Both had an ineradicable contempt for 'the Treasury hierarchs', as Davenport dubbed them. 'They were like a lot of old-fashioned doctors desperately applying leeches to a raving lunatic. We alas! are the lunatic driven mad by their stop-go policies,' he wrote in 1962, to Boothby's strong, and public, approval, but it could have been written at almost any time during his career. And when Boothby wrote to him in 1966 denouncing 'the dear old Treasury, who have fucked this country up for forty years,' that letter could also have been written in 1925.

In December 1928 the difference in views between Boothby and Churchill over government policy towards Russia reached the point when, after a long discussion on the evening of 6 December, which appears to have been very heated, Boothby offered his resignation as his PPS. Writing to Churchill he said:

> Our talk last night convinced me that we are not likely to agree in the near future about our policy towards Russia, both economic and political. And it would certainly be fatal to me personally to fight the next election on an anti-Bolshevik ticket.
>
> If I thought that the interests of my constituents were contrary to the national interests, it would be a very different matter. But I do not. So far as I know we have never had a disagreement of any kind. And I want to avoid one now at all costs.
>
> I must therefore ask you to allow me to resign my position as Parliamentary Private Secretary at the earliest moment convenient to yourself.
>
> I hope on some occasion to be able adequately to express my gratitude to you for all you have done for me.
>
> I have now been with you for over two years, & I have not the slightest doubt that I shall look back on them as by far the happiest years of my political life – and the most interesting.
>
> We are now entering troubled waters, and it is due to you as well as to myself that, holding a curious constituency and perhaps some curious opinions on some subjects, I should be able to speak with freedom & without official responsibility.

This offer was again rejected by Churchill.

Boothby suffered from tonsilitis during the summer and had to have an operation to remove his tonsils, which he described, somewhat dramatically, as 'my ordeal'. Afterwards, he went on holiday with the Mosleys to Cap d'Antibes. On his return to London he received this letter from John Strachey:

> Dear Bob
>
> Your letter, found on coming home this evening; and awakening all those things which alone I think matter. But one thing, especially about Cim, and also me sometimes and often in the future I dare say. Please remember that we are all jealous of you, that our hearts are full of envy of you: that every upper-class socialist is a neurotic, on edge, 'up against it', and so shitty.

This is no particular excuse for us. But 'tu comprends'. . . .

You don't know how much Cim liked having you at Antibes. I came just after you left and know. Also she is really very shaken and worried about Tom's health at the moment, I think unnecessarily: but still one can see that it must be pretty stiff for her.

As to politics: you serve it up very well. I have faith. You have not. I am very sorry – not for you – for us. It is alright now – but some day it may be pretty terrible for us. All the more reason to live now to the best degree.

As to being an opportunist. God knows you are far less one than most. As you say you have your 'outbursts'.

But you must – if you care – forgive our outbursts too. After all you do serve, more skilfully than most, the British bourgeoisie; what to my mind is a very filthy master. Indeed you don't seem altogether to care for it yourself.

But thank you many times for writing that letter. You did – oh hell – you are alive. And that's pretty well unique.

You have 'embraced no faith'. How about that? Are you quite satisfied? What is your bit? 'Selfish, superficial, cowardly, self-centred, dishonest, egoist?' Well yes of course you are all that and more, and so am I and Cim and some forty-five million others. But I rather think that is no excuse for any of us, while you think it is a perfect excuse.

John

P.S. No danger of my telling anyone about your show. Although I have found that some people I met to-day know you had some sort of row on. I merely contented myself with denying that you had any row with Winston, and by saying that all successful young men had to start off by making themselves unpopular with their party.

P.P.S. You know how I think we feel about you at the bottom. At least I do. That at a pinch you would always and necessarily fail one. That you and your family and public opinion would always be against us. Don't think that is in any way a complaint. I have realised this fully for some time now. But inevitably it has some effect upon us.

Although their friendship was never to be affected, Boothby and Strachey were marching in different directions politically. By 1929 it appeared that Boothby's prospects were far brighter than Strachey's, but life and politics were to prove more complicated.

4

Political Rebel
1929–31

*T*he Conservative Government drifted towards the general election in May 1929 with little apparent purpose, enthusiasm or policies. Churchill, to Boothby's dismay, favoured a full-blooded assault on the 'Bolshevism' of the Left; Amery and Neville Chamberlain wanted to raise the banner of Protection again; Baldwin settled, rather desultorily, for the slogan 'Safety First' dreamt up by Conservative Central Office. Labour was bereft of ideas. The only economic policies of any originality and intellectual respectability came from the Liberals, advised by Keynes and Hubert Henderson, but which had little political impact.

This time, East Aberdeenshire put on Boothby's liveliest campaign. Labour had convinced themselves that he was vulnerable and chose as their candidate the Rev. J. E. Hamilton, an ordained minister of the Church of Scotland, who opened his campaign by declaring that 'I love abuse. I thrive on abuse.' He was to prove as good as his word. He was also the only election opponent that Boothby disliked. In response Boothby, at his adoption meeting, said that a Labour victory would be worse for the Empire than if the Germans had won the war. This set the tone. The Labour charges against Boothby included those that he had neglected his constituency, had bribed the fishermen and committed a wide range of political felonies. His meetings were noisy and often chaotic. 'Mr Boothby's meeting in Fraserburgh', it was reported, 'was unfortunately greatly disturbed by howling hooligans devoid of political intelligence.' This was a remarkable occasion, with an audience estimated at one thousand, which ended in tumult; another meeting at Peterhead was no better. By 17 May Boothby was complaining of a sore throat, and Labour was complaining about drunken Tories at their meetings. The Tories denounced 'Red Rowdies', and the Labour daily pamphlets attacked Boothby personally, who retorted that 'I call them all Boy Scouts – they do me a good turn every day.' His final meeting, again in Peterhead, was better than some of the others, but the Labour hecklers were again out in force. Lady Astor and Churchill sent warm wishes, Churchill writing of 'the barbaric fallacies of Socialism' and its 'moral and intellectual bankruptcy'. The *Aberdeen Press and Journal* could not recall so bitter an election, with red flags flying and Labour claims that Hamilton had been jostled, molested and intimidated by furious Conservatives.

What saved the day for Boothby was that the Liberals, declaring their respect for him, did not contest the seat where they had taken 4,680 votes in 1924; as a result, his majority actually went up, to 3,244 (13,354 to 10,110). Boothby's result was particularly notable, as elsewhere – and especially in Scotland – the Conservatives had fared badly, coming back with 261 seats to Labour's 287 and the Liberals' 59. MacDonald became Prime Minister for the second time, again with Liberal support.

Boothby's achievement was widely hailed as a personal triumph, made even sweeter to him by the fact that Hamilton had had to resign his position in the Church in the middle of the campaign as the result of protests about his performance and doubts about the legality of his position if he were elected. Boothby returned to London cheered by delighted telegrams from Baldwin, Churchill, Nancy Astor and Cimmie Mosley – 'Grand fight. Cannot help being pleased. Cim' – and hoarse, as he had spoken at over eighty meetings, usually amid uproar. There was a celebratory dinner at Turriff, where every speaker described him as a future prime minister, to which Boothby modestly replied that 'when that occurred, his first meeting with the President of the United States would be at Hatton Castle (*loud applause*)'. There were similar occasions at Fraserburgh and Peterhead. The *Buchan Observer* wrote that

Mr Boothby's triumph was a triumph of personality. Before his appearance at the opening of the campaign his position seemed hopeless. He had to face what was probably the most formidable opposition ever directed against any candidate in East Aberdeenshire; and he beat it down by sheer courage, indomitable willpower, and force of character.

The Conservatives had not expected to lose the 1929 election, and in their dismay turned on Baldwin and the Party Chairman, J. C. C. Davidson, the author of 'Safety First'. The Party was, as Austen Chamberlain noted, 'divided, disgruntled and confused'. Macmillan had lost his seat and was writing fiercely about the Party leadership. Beaverbrook, who had been politically quiescent for some time, suddenly re-emerged at the head of a campaign for Empire Free Trade, warmly supported by the Rothermere press, but not by Baldwin. Meanwhile, Churchill and Birkenhead were seething about India, suspicious of the Labour Government's attitude to the Raj, and even more about Baldwin's position. Davidson had to be sacrificed, but the hostility to Baldwin's leadership was not placated. When Birkenhead, to Boothby's sorrow, died early in 1930, Churchill led the opposition to the proposal to grant India limited Dominion Status. Boothby did not agree with him and warned that the kind of Conservative who would join him would not be his kind of Conservative. However, Churchill, convinced that he had a major populist cause, pressed on, with disastrous results for himself and his country. Their friendship remained, but Boothby's refusal to join him in this crusade – which was to last for six years – resulted in a cooling of relations.

Boothby opened the new Parliament in a highly unconventional manner by writing in the *National Review* that it was 'eminently desirable that the Government should remain in office for at least two years, and that it is the business of the Unionist party to keep them there, and even to assist them'. Then he voted with the Government on the issue of the resumption of diplomatic relations with the Soviet Union. Most interestingly, in his first radio broadcast, he not only denounced the idea of home rule for Scotland but advocated giving 'every child at school a free glass of milk every day'; he also declared his support for the new Secretary of State for Scotland, Tom Johnston. He then came out in Beaverbrook's *Evening Standard* in favour of Empire Free Trade; Beaverbrook was delighted and described him publicly as 'one of the most brilliant of the younger Conservatives'.

Boothby's summer holiday in 1929 consisted of taking his mother to Munich to listen to music, and then to Aix-les-Bains, where he at once received a short note: 'Dear Bob. Come over and talk to me. S. B.' There is no record of their conversation, but it was obvious to both that they were drifting apart. While Boothby never publicly joined the 'Baldwin Must Go' campaign, and detested Rothermere and most of Baldwin's critics from the Right, he had been disappointed by the overall performance of the previous Government and, in a remarkably prescient article in *The Times* on 5 August, had warned of the dangers in the international markets. He then joined the British delegation to the League in Geneva in a minor capacity.

Boothby later wrote that it was during a walk beside the river at Salzburg at that time, 'drenched with music', that he realised

so clearly that our efforts to build a rational society had failed. Under the impetus of American expansion, the world had reached a position of considerable material prosperity. But everywhere there was a sense of futility and frustration. Like patriotism, pleasure was not enough.

His account continued:

All of a sudden I knew that life itself, the quarry which for ten years I had tracked with such gay enthusiasm, had turned huntress; and that, together with my generation, I had become her captive. In that moment I contemplated flight. But where? There is only one escape from destiny; and it is better to die outright than to deny the living life. . . . It was in a mood of grim apprehension that I returned to England. A wave of speculative madness was sweeping the world, and it required no prophet to see that an economic system which lacked any solid foundation, and had now got completely out of control, was on the brink of collapse. Within a fortnight came panic. Tied by the gold standard and five billion dollars on loan from Wall Street, Europe accompanied the United States headlong into the Abyss.

In a series of speeches in his constituency he spelt out his philosophy of expansion, while Philip Snowden, the Chancellor of the Exchequer, continued grimly along exactly the opposite course, with the results that Boothby had foreseen.

It was at this time that Boothby, sad at the fact that his friend Harold Macmillan had lost his seat, invited him and his wife Dorothy to join his father's annual shooting party. They accepted, with momentous – and tragic – results, which will be subsequently related, as the love between Boothby and Lady Dorothy Macmillan merits a chapter of its own. But Boothby's political activities during this period – and, indeed, for many years – must be seen in the context of a very profound personal turmoil and much anguish and distraction.

One of Boothby's greatest Scots friends was Marjorie Macrae, whom he had first met in 1921. She shared his devotion to music, but her immensely promising professional career as a pianist was ended when, contrary to all advice and common sense, she went on a skiing holiday in Switzerland, had a terrible fall and broke all her fingers. Boothby persuaded her to take a secretarial course, and between 1929 and 1932 she was, as she puts it, his 'on and off' secretary, an experience that ended when she and her naval submariner husband were posted to China.

Her most vivid memories of that time are of Lady Boothby's frantic attempts to enlist her assistance to stop the Dorothy Macmillan imbroglio – in which she absolutely refused to become involved at all, very understandably – and the nightmare of the 1929 Wall Street crash and its aftermath. Her secretarial duties related entirely to Boothby's political and constituency concerns, and not to his banking responsibilities, but she clearly recalls what a desperate time it was, and how distraught and worried Boothby was. It was, from every point of view, a wretched period.

The 1929–31 Labour Government would have had a good claim to being the least distinguished in modern British history, were it not for its successors. MacDonald himself was fading, and the years of exhaustion and strain had left their mark. Snowden was even more Victorian than Churchill and, as Boothby later wrote, 'To every outworn shibboleth of nineteenth-century economics he clung with fanatic tenacity. Economy, Free Trade, Gold – these were the keynotes of his political philosophy; and deflation the path he trod with almost ghoulish enthusiasm.' The Minister allegedly responsible for dealing with unemployment was the garrulous and indolent J. H. Thomas. As Robert Skidelsky has rightly written of him, 'Totally devoid of constructive ideas, intimate with the City and big business, the boon companion of half the House of Commons, the jingoistic upholder of imperial and national unity, his appointment gladdened the conservatives and dismayed the radicals.' Among a trio of ministers supposed to be assisting him was Mosley, as Chancellor of the Duchy of Lancaster. Mosley was in a tearing hurry and in February 1930, in the immediate aftermath of the collapse of the American Stock Market, and with British unemployment rising to two million, he produced what he believed to be the answer. Its key features were a dramatic programme of increased pensions and allowances; protection of home industries by tariffs, import restrictions and bulk purchase agreements; a far more extensive use of public money for development; and the rationalisation of industry under central control.

How Mosley thought that Snowden would accept any of this, let alone the whole, is explicable only in his restless, impatient, arrogant personality. He was indeed surrounded by fools, but it would have been wiser not to make this knowledge so clear. Also, his following in the Labour Party was nothing like as substantial as he believed, and his natural self-esteem was increased by the huge audiences that he could command. The Cabinet rejected the memorandum in full.

Boothby's judgment could be variable, but in the events that followed he was absolutely right throughout. First, he attempted, unavailingly, to persuade Mosley not to carry his disagreement with his colleagues to the point of resignation, writing urgently on 18 May:

My dear Tom
    From France I have been contemplating the state of politics with a jaundiced but more or less unbiased mind: and I beg of you not to resign.
    I cannot see that you would achieve anything; and you might well do

yourself irreparable damage. It is God's mercy that the existence of your memorandum is known to the public.

That was essential, but for the moment it is surely enough.

I care about your political future far more than about any other single factor in public affairs, because I know that you are the ONLY ONE of my generation – of the post-war school of thought – who is capable of translating into action any of the ideas in which I genuinely believe.

Consequently I can conceive of no greater tragedy than that you should take a step which might wreck your chances, or at any rate postpone the opportunity of carrying through constructive work.

If you stay where you are that opportunity is bound to come soon.

Go, and where are you?

The example of [Lord] Randolph Churchill is significant and appalling. You deliver yourself into the hands of every enemy, and they are not few. Your own front bench will heave a sigh of relief, consign you to the Mountain, and take no more risks.

They will point to their own life-long services in the Labour cause, and contrast them with yours. They will regret that they are apparently unable to proceed at a pace sufficient to satisfy the desires and ambitions of a wealthy young 'aristocrat' in a hurry.

Picture the Parliamentary scene.

You will make your case against the government – a formidable one, but nine-tenths of the audience will be hostile. Snowden will reply with all the venom at his command. (I am sure that his recent outburst against me was an oblique thrust at you.) He will quote from your speeches at Harrow ten years ago.

All the pent-up fury which you have deliberately, and I think rightly, roused in so many breasts will simultaneously be released.

The Tories will cheer vociferously and savagely.

Your own orthodox back-benchers will be against you because they will feel that you have delivered a fierce blow at the government which may well involve their defeat at the next election.

The Mountain itself – traditionally impossible to work with – will suspect you of personal motives.

Lloyd George will certainly not hurry to your defence.

Finally, the Machine will be mobilised and put into operation against you, with all its power and strength.

The cumulative effect of so many hostile forces would overwhelm Napoleon himself.

I don't see how you could hope to stand up against them.

You can't return to us.

And however impelled you may feel to work once more with the 'gentry', you will be wretched if you did.

I know to my cost the limitations of the existing young Conservatives. They are charming and sympathetic and intelligent at dinner. But there is not one of them with either the character or the courage to do anything big.

Walter Elliot is the best, and his mind is the most interesting – and he will never take a step that might even remotely prejudice his political or Parliamentary position.

Where, then, can you go?

To [James] Maxton & Fenner Brockway [Left-wing Labour politicians]?

[John] Wheatley's death has removed the one commanding figure from that lot, and you know better than I do how futile they will be without him.

No. You would be marooned, and for perhaps too long.

What is the alternative?

Surely to remain within the official fold and by making yourself increasingly oppressive and uncomfortable to what Ellen Wilkinson so aptly described as the 'Bright Old Things', consolidate & strengthen your power.

The forces economic & political now at work must assist you.

With every increase in the unemployment figures the position which *you are known* to have taken up becomes more impregnable and easier to justify.

The Conservatives are now committed to food taxes. I doubt if this policy can enjoy any but the most transient success. In any case a Lib-Lab rapprochement is inevitable, paving the way for that left-centre government which is what a majority of the British electorate appears consistently tó desire.

The extreme Left-Wing will be squeezed out. But why should you lot work with, and ultimately direct, a moderate Government of the left?

You will get more constructive work put through that way than ever you will with Maxton, Brockway, or even [Roy] Wise (who, incidentally, would jump at a job in such an administration).

It is distribution that requires to be controlled and socialised first. And there are many of the younger Liberals who wouldn't jib at that.

Same with the policy of National development.

Same with monetary reform.

Same with state ownership of land and minerals.

There are fifteen years of valuable work ahead, all of which could be made to command Liberal support.

You occupy a key position at the moment. For God's sake don't chuck it away.

Incidentally, if you have a moment to spare you might modify the divorce laws.

My own difficulties do not diminish with the passage of time and the march of events.

I could have always managed a pretty hectic political existence. But I haven't the temperament for a desperate private life, and I don't know how long I can sustain it at this pressure.

If and when conditions become too hard to bear, there is really only one thing to do, and that is radically to alter them (I was always at heart a revolutionary). But I agree that gigantic efforts must first be made to render them endurable on a basis of compromise.

Good luck to you.

Don't think of answering this.

Yrs
Bob

Mosley totally ignored this wise advice, while sympathising on the personal aspects. When the Government confirmed the rejection of his programme in May, he duly resigned, and when he took the issue to a full meeting of the Parliamentary Labour Party, against all advice, including Boothby's, he was defeated by 202 votes to 29. By October, when unemployment was rising to three million, he put the programme to the Labour Party annual conference and was only narrowly defeated. This encouraged him to publish his own personal manifesto, which was supported by seventeen Labour MPs, including Strachey and Aneurin Bevan, the newly elected Member for Ebbw Vale.

Although Boothby's advice had been rejected by Mosley, he was appalled to learn that Mosley was prepared to form his own party on the basis of this very limited support, which now included Harold Nicolson, whose knowledge of politics was, and was going to remain, delightfully negligible. Horrified, Boothby wrote to Mosley:

My dear Tom

If I ever signed on the dotted line I would have played to the end – and beyond.

I think you know that.

But *in the meantime* I don't think the game is practical politics, and for the following reasons.

(1) Our chaps won't play, and it's no use deluding yourself that they will. You saw Oliver's [Stanley] reactions last night.

Of the whole lot Walter [Elliot] and I would be the most useful, because we have a territorial base, and between us we could shake up Scotland. But Walter has spent the last twelve months consolidating his position in the Conservative Party. He has won for himself a good deal of rank and file support.

He won't give it up unless he is sure he is going to win.

He doesn't think this will win.

As for Oliver, his influence could, and almost certainly would, be countered by Edward Stanley [Conservative MP and son of Lord Derby].

And, so far as the Conservatives are concerned, Harold [Macmillan] would be a definite liability. I know you think I am prejudiced against him. I am not. But even on the assumption that he decided to play (a large one), how many votes can he swing?

Not two.

Who is left?

Lloyd George, generally regarded as the 'Super-Diehard'; and rightly or wrongly regarded in many quarters as a shit.

And this brings me to my second point about our chaps, which is that they simply aren't good enough for the job (I include myself, with becoming modesty).

(2) Now what about your side?

I agree you can sway more votes than any other contemporary politician.

But I don't believe, at present, that you can bring over any substantial sections of organised Trade Unionism.

And, as for the parliamentary party, do you really think that you can send Aneurin Bevan to the Admiralty to lay down more cruisers, and John Strachey to spank the blacks?

I confess I doubt it.

Who else is there? The mugwumps who comprise 95% of your party will be solidly arraigned against you. The intelligentsia of the Dalton–Baker school will be actively & venomously hostile.

(3) We come now to the main sort of strength – Beaverbrook, with the dubious support of Rothermere.

The latter I regard as quite beyond the pale.

In any decently organised community his papers would be suppressed; and he would be executed.

Beaverbrook's qualities are sufficiently obvious.

I don't know him as well as you do. But I have long since come to the conclusion that he will be very nearly impossible to work with. And, as Oliver pointed out, he is in the impregnable position (which we are not & never can be) of being able to double-cross and let down the side at a moment's notice, without loss of power or even prestige.

If he were to do that we should be marooned, and ultimately sunk politically.

One other point.

What is going to be the reaction of the great British public to a Beaverbrook–Mosley–Rothermere–[George] Lloyd–Macmillan–Stanley–Boothby combination?

I don't know. But they might conceivably say, 'By God now all the shits have climbed into the same basket, so we know where we are.' Would they be so far out?

(4) Lastly, don't underestimate the power of the political machines. I believe that in the long run it far exceeds that of the press. And in this connection I had a long talk yesterday with Dr. Hunter, probably the shrewdest electioneer in this country.

He thinks the Liberals are done. And that the Tories will get back entirely owing to the vast power of their machine, which has not been weakened by the press to anything like the extent that the failure of your government has weakened your machine.

This is an interesting view.

He is absolutely convinced that two machines – and two only – right & left, will wield political power in this country in the years that lie ahead.

On this assumption the only game worth playing is to try & collar one or other of the machines, & not ruin yourself by beating against them with a tool which will almost certainly break in yr hand.

To all this I make one qualification & one only.

If there is really a serious economic crisis this winter, there may be a widespread demand for a National Government, new men & new measures.

It must come from the country & be *interpreted* by the press.

And if it does come, then the situation will be fundamentally changed, and a game of a kind we cannot yet envisage may yet open out.

Failing that it seems to me that you have a choice of (1) staying where you are, consolidating & strengthening your hold on the Labour movement in the country, and persuading the workers that they will not always be betrayed; or (2) making another speech or two along recent lines, and crossing the floor in the autumn. You would be amazed at the welcome you wd get.

The former is the 'long-term policy', and involves a further bleak period in the wilderness. That you would win through in the end I have not the slightest doubt.

Number (2) assures power at an early date. But power limited by the Tory machine, and the knowledge that you can't change again.

The choice lies of course entirely with you. Either way I believe you can render immense services to this country.

You have a great political position now. And my only concern is that you don't throw it away by trying to bite off more than any man can chew.

Well, my dear Tom, I have been very frank. I always will be with you, and I hope you don't mind.

I happen to think you can do more for us than anyone else now alive – a view I have held, & from which I have never deviated, for six years.

Only for God's sake remember that this country is old – obsolete – and tradition-ridden, & no one – not even you – can break all the rules at once.

And do take care of the company you keep. Real shits are so apt to trip you up when you aren't looking. And flat-catchers who want to be hauled along are only an encumbrance.

No answer.

> Yours ever
> Bob

Then, early in 1931, Boothby discovered that Mosley was raising funds in the City of London for his own political party, upon which he wrote to him on 30 January:

If it be true that you are trying to raise money in the City, then I feel I must say once more – and for the last time – that I believe this to be madness from your own point of view, and leave it at that. . . . You will remember that I left the dinner party given by Colonel Portal at the Garrick Club because I so heartily disapproved of it.

You are, of course, right to pursue the course you think best.

But I too am entitled to my opinions, which in this case are very decided. . . . You have persistently disregarded every piece of advice or suggestion that I have ever ventured to offer. And so, my dear Tom, I cannot feel that you have greatly missed the benefit of a judgement which you obviously do not value highly!

Again, Mosley took no notice at all and proceeded towards the formation of the New Party in February 1931; he was immediately expelled from the Labour Party. Thus began the lamentable march towards the formation of the British Union of Fascists, and oblivion. Boothby could at least claim with justice that he had done his best to prevent the calamity, and would have nothing to do with either the New Party or the BUF, which he abhorred. Then, after Cimmie's death in 1933, the last reason for having anything to do with his former friend had gone. But when Mosley and his second wife, Diana, were interned throughout the Second World War, for no discernible reason except deliberate malice, Boothby was one of the few former friends who took the trouble to visit him in prison, a courageous act that brought him much obloquy, but which he never regretted. He lamented Mosley's incredible folly, and worse, but he was never a fair-weather friend.

The year 1930 was a particularly difficult one for Boothby. His private life was in grievous agony, and the condition of the Conservative Party was not much better than that of the Labour Government. The economic situation was bad, and deteriorating, and Boothby's visions of making his personal fortune from the City of London, still reeling from the Wall Street crash, had proved illusory.

He was also without a leader, although Beaverbrook courted him eagerly. As this would have meant opposing Baldwin, who was in enough difficulties, Boothby was cautious. He could not understand Churchill's and Birkenhead's obsession with India, and did not follow their argument that the granting of Dominion Status meant the irrevocable end of the Raj. Although there was constant press speculation that he was to become the founder-member of a new political alliance – which became so persistent that Baldwin publicly criticised those 'who hunt in packs other than their own' – he was never seriously tempted. Nor was he much interested in opposition for opposition's sake, although he made the ritual denunciations of Labour in speeches and articles, on one occasion being on the receiving end of a speech of such personal vitriol from Snowden that Churchill, among others, protested. Boothby did not mind and considered it to be a compliment.

Not surprisingly, Boothby's themes were closely allied to those of Mosley and Strachey; and, although a protectionist and expansionist, he never took Empire Free Trade all that seriously. In effect it perished in the celebrated St George's Westminster by-election in March 1931, when Baldwin rounded memorably and devastatingly on the Beaverbrook–Rothermere coalition, and Duff Cooper easily defeated their Empire candidate. By this time Churchill had gone into the wilderness over India. He was also trying to recoup his losses in the American crash and had been seriously injured when he had been knocked down by a taxi in New York; consequently, he was largely out of action.

Remarkably, Boothby suffered the same fate. Driving between God-stone and Caterham in Surrey on a wet and slippery road – probably much too fast – the car skidded, left the road and overturned in a ditch. Boothby was able to crawl out and a passing car took him to Caterham Hospital, where severe back and head injuries were treated. In fact, they turned out to be less serious than they had first appeared, and he was discharged and driven to the small cottage near Brighton which he was then renting. He immediately cabled to his parents, who were in Biarritz: 'Skidded yesterday not my fault car overturned but quite unhurt except for small headcut already healed. Disregard press reports. No shock. Out and about and feeling grand. Bob.' Cimmie Mosley also cabled to them: 'Thought you would like to know press reports about Bob's accident grossly exaggerated. He is none the worse. Very fit. Out and about and staying put for weekend. Cynthia Mosley.'

Boothby was surprised and touched that one of the first letters of condolence he received came from Snowden, who wrote that 'I was very sorry to hear of the terrible experience you have had but I am very glad you escaped so miraculously. I hope you are little the worse for it.' From Beaverbrook there came good advice:

May 3rd 1930

My dear Bob

I am so sorry to see of your motor accident. It seems to me from the newspaper account that you received a very bad shaking, and I would like to hear now that everything is alright again.

May I be allowed to give you advice from middle age to youth, from experience to one now entering on the period of experience.

You will feel the accident a week after it. If you take things very very easily you will get plenty of relief. A failure to do so is quite certain to place you under an obvious or subconscious strain.

So do decide to stay away from town and take a complete rest for the next couple of weeks, no matter how well you feel.

Yours ever

Max

Politically still rather lost, Boothby's flirtation with Empire Free Trade continued in speeches and letters, including one to the Corstophine Unionists at a garden party at Beechwood in June. But his speeches concentrated on unemployment and the 'palsied incompetence' of government: 'We have a government today of old men, who, in the hour of danger, have buried their heads in the sand and instructed the Civil Service to buy off with other people's money anyone who seems likely to disturb their repose' may be taken as a fair example. There was much press and political flurry when Lloyd George was discovered with Boothby at a private dinner at the Hotel Metropole in Brighton. 'It is no use talking about co-operation in industry when we are making no attempt to co-operate in politics,' Boothby retorted, adding that if friends could not meet for dinner, 'life for an MP would be unendurable'. But it was taken seriously in some quarters, and not least by Baldwin.

5

Dorothy

The profession of politics tends to be regarded by those not involved in it as a matter almost exclusively of public concerns. The reality is totally different, and the intermingling of public and private life is so complex and so variable, but always so real and so important, that generalisations are perilous. But the only valid one is that there are very few exceptions indeed to the rule that the fortunes and misfortunes in private lives markedly shape, distort and affect the public ones.

There are few more remarkable, and melancholy, examples than those of Bob Boothby and Harold Macmillan.

As has been related, one of Boothby's less likely friendships since he had been elected to Parliament had been with the bookish and un-prepossessing Macmillan, who seemed to many to have drifted into politics by mistake as an accompaniment to publishing. But Boothby knew that he had a brave war record and a first-class mind, and was as dissatisfied and rebellious with the Tory Right as he was. Their work on *Industry and the State* had brought them close together. They represented different constituencies in many respects, but both constituencies were poor – Macmillan's even more so than Boothby's; they abhorred unemployment, and had something more than sympathy for Lloyd George's and Mosley's efforts to resolve it; and, being Celts, they had an emotional sympathy for the poor and underprivileged for which they found little echo in the Conservative Party. They were, economically, expansionists and Keynesians, and, politically, far more in agreement with Baldwin's social conscience and Lloyd George's radicalism than with the anti-trade-union reactionary Tories who surrounded them on the back-benches. They had gradually discovered that they had much in common politically and had become personal friends, Macmillan admiring Boothby's extrovert style, booming self-confidence and excellent company, and Boothby respecting Macmillan's courage and intellect. They both enjoyed London clubland and fulfilled Dr Johnson's description of being very 'clubbable', as did their mutual friend Duff Cooper.

This was in marked contrast with their contemporary Anthony Eden, who loathed men's clubs, refused Churchill's invitation to join The Other Club, was never seen in the Smoking Room of the House of Commons – in those days, and until relatively recently, the hub of the Commons – and, even when he became Prime Minister, refused the offer of honorary membership of the Athenaeum. Boothby had several clubs, as did Macmillan, but White's was to become his favourite.

This mutual enjoyment of masculine company and long conversations, often late into the night – a habit that remained with both into their old age, often to the exhaustion of others – was not matched in Macmillan's case with as much consumption of alcohol as in those of Duff Cooper and Boothby. Of the two, Duff Cooper was by far the more serious drinker, who had a formidable and well-deserved reputation as a successful pursuer of women, although he was happily and successfully married to the former Lady Diana Manners, whose beauty and engaging eccentricity* were accompanied by a remarkable degree of tolerance for Duff's excesses. Duff Cooper also represented a poor constituency, Oldham, and his easily aroused anger had been fired by what he saw around him in the mean streets and closed factories of Lancashire. Like the others, he was emphatically a Baldwinite and a caustic enemy of the Tory Right. The shy, untidy and reserved Macmillan, relatively abstemious and totally uninterested in food, would have been regarded as an unexpected companion of these two serious roisterers had it not been for his having so much in common with them politically.

It is difficult to realise, in the light of later events, how insignificant a personality Macmillan then appeared to others, or how tedious. He had married Lady Dorothy Cavendish, the daughter of the Duke of Devonshire, in 1920, by whom he had three children, but his Cavendish in-laws so disliked him, and were so bored by him, that there was intense family competition not to sit next to him at meals. His teeth were malformed, his clothes were scruffy and poor, he had a moustache that was in sore need of attention, but, above all, he was rated by them and many others – although not by Boothby – as the most stupendously boring

*Some of whose qualities were immortalised by Evelyn Waugh as 'Mrs Stitch' in *Scoop*.

man they had ever met, and they could not understand why the vivacious and attractive Dorothy had ever married him. By 1929 she was wondering why also. She had problems with her fierce American mother-in-law at Birch Grove, the family Edwardian mansion and estate in Sussex, and a husband whom she now regarded as unsatisfactory in most respects. She was bored. She was also exceptionally selfish and emotional, and craved excitement and drama. Macmillan, through no fault of his own, could supply few of her requirements.

Boothby knew nothing of this situation in 1929. Indeed, he had never met his new friend's wife until the Macmillans stayed at Beechwood in 1928 and they played golf together; but he was saddened by Macmillan's defeat in the 1929 election and, quite casually, invited him and Dorothy to stay at Beechwood again for some shooting, a pastime that was, somewhat improbably, one of Macmillan's enthusiasms. One of Baldwin's last acts as Prime Minister had been to recommend Tom Boothby for a knighthood, and the new Sir Robert and Lady Boothby were delighted to have their son's friend and his wife as their guests.

It was on the second day on the moors, when Boothby was waiting his turn to shoot, that he was startled to find his hand being squeezed affectionately, and turned to see a beaming Dorothy beside him. That was when it all began. It is true that she was later enchanted by him at a weekend at Bowood, when Lady Henry Bentinck lost her spectacles and Boothby, who had trodden on them, sent them to Dorothy with a merry note, but the damage was really done at that disastrous and kindly-meant shooting holiday in Scotland.

Although it was all so long ago, and the principals are dead and have destroyed so much of their intense and lengthy correspondence over so many years, enough remains to make the sad story very clear. It has been told by Alistair Horne from Macmillan's side, but Boothby's is no less melancholy and has often been misunderstood. Also, documents exist and records of conversations that were not available to Macmillan's biographer, nor to others. I have used my discretion, but this is, I believe, the authentic account of what happened.

Boothby had many qualities, but he was weak in matters of the flesh. Also, he did not have Duff Cooper's rather cavalier attitude towards his many conquests. If Duff Cooper saw a woman who attracted him, he laid siege with every device, and his success rate was very high, but he always returned to Diana, his only real love. He was a very passionate man of great and genuine warmth, and his many lovers never considered that they had been used or treated badly. He gave as much pleasure as he received, and we may safely discard the somewhat shocked tones in which his sexual appetites and escapades have been related.*

Although Boothby had had his adventures – and was to have some more – he was not by nature a philanderer and was sensitive to the feelings of others. In theory, he also wanted to marry and have a family, although he shrank from the reality. As one who was in an exceptionally good position to know has remarked, 'He was for ever falling in love and asking women to marry him.' This was not simply as the result of the frequent exhortations of his mother, but because he also believed that life was incomplete without a great passion. Unhappily, it was to come to him under impossible circumstances.

Dorothy was not beautiful, but she was highly sexed, seeking adventure and eager. However, what began as a casual affair initiated by her, and not by Boothby, very rapidly developed into something very serious on both sides. The portrayal of Boothby as 'a bounder' seducing a friend's wife is very far from the mark. In fact, it was Dorothy who seduced Boothby and who dominated him. He not only fulfilled her sexually, but gave her the fun, glamour and exciting company that her husband was unable to do. Also, Boothby was clearly a rising and successful politician, whereas Macmillan was evidently a failure, in this as in so many things. Nor is it the case that, as has been suggested, she wanted the best of both worlds – a husband and children at home, a lover in London and long holidays in Europe with him. What she wanted was to divorce Macmillan and to marry Boothby, which is quite contrary to the other version, but which is the truth.

The trouble was that Macmillan would not agree. Boothby and Dorothy became lovers either very late in 1929 or early in 1930, and for the next five years virtually lived together publicly. Their liaison was very well known, especially at Westminster, but this was a very different era in the history of the British press, and not a word of the fact was mentioned outside London Society. Indeed, it was generally unknown until long after Dorothy's death.

That they truly loved each other is unquestionable. So is the fact that it was Macmillan who adamantly refused to give Dorothy a divorce. He had done nothing wrong and would not cite his wife for adultery. In this situation the lovers were helpless and miserable.

Although their very large correspondence was destroyed, they wrote to others, and particularly to their mutual confidante Cynthia Mosley. Two

---

* In particular by Philip Ziegler in *Diana Cooper* (1981) and in John Charmley's biography of Duff Cooper (1986). In all other respects both are admirable books, but on this aspect of his character they seem to me to be excessively censorious.

letters to her, both in 1932, give a sad but totally truthful portrait of their position.

Darling Cimmie

I do feel so ashamed never having answered your very kind letter. It was delicious of you to write & horrid of me not to. As a matter of fact I did write pages [but] before I finished it it was all out of date & quite pointless. We seem to be in a hopeless impasse. Bob is back in London now so you will probably hear all about everything from him.

I wish to God I knew what was the best thing to do. Bolt at the moment does seem pretty hopeless. It may well happen in the end. I have not entirely given up hope of getting Harold into a more reasonable frame of mind about divorce, but at present he is hopeless.

I am afraid Bob must have led an awful time away. I should think he is sick of everything. He still wants to marry me, but if I don't come to him he probably won't go on waiting and wanting to. The future looks pretty grim.

With my love
Dorothy

The full misery of the situation was most graphically related by Boothby, who wrote on 14 September from the Hotel Claridge in Paris:

Darling Cim

Forgive me for not writing from Portugal. I wrote to no one.

Thank you for your letter. Venice must have been astonishing after I left. But I doubt if you have had a more extraordinary time than I have.

As soon as I got home I told Dorothy that I thought I had found a possible way through, and that in any case I couldn't go on with the life we had been leading.

Indeed, it has become unendurable. No basis & no meaning for me. Just an interminable series of agonising 'goodbyes' with nothing to go back to. Living always for the 'next time'. Work to hell. Nerves to hell.

No one can ever persuade me that a 'liaison' is anything but misery (with glorious, but oh so transitory, reprieves) if you care.

Then I have had the worst 3 days of my life yet.

One never realises, until one comes slam up against it, that when Byron wrote 'tis women's whole existence' he was stating the cold sober truth.

She just crumpled.

I had doubted the wisdom of Portugal, but she begged for it – as a last mercy.

So off we went, and of course it was marvellous, we had never had more than three days before; and now a whole fortnight.

We discussed the future sporadically & wildly, but for most of the time just let everything go & enjoyed ourselves.

Magnificent scenery, & the loveliest sub-tropical garden in Europe all to ourselves, & a little car to expedition in, and one lovely deserted beach after another to bathe from. On the hottest & calmest day great breakers about six feet high came and picked you up and turned you over and hurled you down & rolled you over & over until you couldn't see or breathe.

We climbed a mountain & looked at a monastery and photographed funny little Moorish villages & lay on the sand with nothing on.

One evening we went into Lisbon and saw a bull fight (Portuguese so nothing was killed) and another to the casino & lost thirty pounds between us and didn't care a damn.

But the funniest thing of all was that we spent three days running with —.

We used to arrive at their villa in time to bathe, go down to the market to buy food (have you ever tried fried *fresh* sardines?), lunch with them & siesta with them.

One day we all motored off to the roughest beach of all and — lost first of all his courage (such as it is), then his feet & then finally his head; while—, in the middle of teasing baby, was caught from behind by a whacking breaker, & knocked flat on her face.

Afterwards we all dressed on the beach (can you see — getting off with Dorothy, & saying in the car afterwards that they were as snug as bugs in a rug?)

& — produced port.

I must say I have never seen the old trout in such consistently good form, or the girls so happy.

And Dorothy. It was a new world for her. It was like taking a thrilled child to a play for the first time.

She brushed her hair back behind her ears, & actually put lipstick on, & got more radiant every day.

And now I have shipped her back to Birch Grove as Mrs. Macmillan. And dined last night with Miss Louise Iselin.*

. . . What to do? Go for the high jump, chuck politics, smash up that household, and marry Dorothy? Or cross the Atlantic and marry Iselin? Or try to stagger on alone? An impossible feat this last, I think, which increases the sheer desperation of this situation.

I like this girl. And I love Dorothy. As much as I have ever loved her. But can any marriage survive such crushing initial handicaps as a smashed political career (for I could never get back to the House of Commons), and four children† in more or less of a mess? Dorothy would do it now. Because she feels if I go out of it her life is broken. And, as you can imagine, Portugal, with all that it opened up, has made that infinitely worse.

She (Dorothy) said to me tragically yesterday, 'Why did you ever wake me? I never want to see any of my family again. And, without you, life for me is going to be nothing but one big hurt.'

On the other hand, Louise observed at dinner that some men were made

---

* One of Boothby's American 'fiancées'.
† By then Dorothy had had another child, see p. 120.

for careers, and some women were made to have children; and any marriage which jeopardised both could only end in misery. For which view, there is something to be said.

Naturally happy myself, I always want to make other people happy too if I can. It sounds priggish, but it's true. What keeps me awake is the knowledge that over this business someone is going to be very unhappy.

Perhaps more than one.

And that in struggling to keep things going all round for as long as possible, one may only end by increasing the sum total of misery.

Phew! I wish life wasn't so like a novel. And a Russian one at that.

Boothby felt that he was trapped. A very difficult situation was made even worse when Macmillan won back Stockton in 1931 and became a parliamentary colleague again. Macmillan accepted that his marriage was over, but would not countenance a divorce; even if he had, Boothby reckoned that the resultant scandal would have profoundly shocked even the tolerant electors of East Aberdeenshire, although, as events were to prove, perhaps not quite as strongly as Boothby feared. He cared deeply about his political career; so did Macmillan, who was striking out in a highly individualistic direction over the handling of the economy to the point of actually resigning the Party Whip in 1936 over unemployment, and who was developing into a surprisingly formidable political writer and speaker. Alistair Horne is surely right to detect in this activity an antidote to his private, deep unhappiness. When rearmament became a major issue, Macmillan, like Boothby, gravitated towards Churchill and away from the Government and the bulk of the Conservative Party. Indeed, politically, he and Boothby were in agreement for virtually their entire lives, and their personal relationship was quite extraordinarily good, and was to remain so.

One cause of this remarkable fact was that Macmillan was in the far stronger position. He at least had a wife, children, a large home for them, and a prosperous family business as well as his political interests and career; Boothby had only the latter.

On 7 November 1933 Boothby poured out his feelings to John Strachey from New York:

I envy you your present position. You have got your faith, your life, your girl, and your medium of expression. You are a brilliant writer (I do not exaggerate).

And, whatever happens, you are at home.

Whether you are destined to influence the course of events by ideas or by actions, or first one and then the other, it is uncertain and almost irrelevant.

The point is that the obvious power spreads out before you – the path to self-fulfilment. . . .

My position, on the other hand, is desperate and critical.

The Power urge and the Love urge waging this terrific hellish battle within me. The apparent necessity for sacrificing one or the other. And the agony of the choice.

Last night I stood on the end of the pier in front of this house rocking and swaying in the struggle – until I began to laugh at it, and at myself.

But it's bloody.

You see, assuming that communism is not the immediately next phase, and holding the views I do hold, I've got a hell of a part to play.

God knows I don't overrate my intelligence. But it's luminous in comparison with that of my 'rivals' – whether in politics or in the City – always excepting Walter Elliot who wants me with him.

Now I know also that the only way I can 'fulfil myself' (tiresome phrase) in the larger sphere is through contacts and action. On the other hand, there stands Dorothy.

The most formidable thing in the world – a possessive single-track woman. She wants me, completely, and she wants my children, and she wants practically nothing else. At every crucial moment she acts instinctively and overwhelmingly. And when the final choice is to be made she will, I am convinced, come to me. From the point of view of fulfilling *herself*, she would be mad to do anything else.

I am passionately in love with her.

But if I take her, it's goodbye to everything else.

Damn it all, she has completely immobilised me for the last three years.

Sometimes I long for her so much that I feel like getting straight back and taking her off to the country and sending everything and everyone else to hell. And then that bloody Power urge comes uppermost and says, 'fool, if you do that you will never forgive yourself or her. The country is alright for a month or for a year or ten years. But what then? The Stracheys were happy in Sussex and are happy now. And for why? Because he was doing creative work. You can't do that in the country. Are you then going to sell yourself to a woman and to your children? Chuck it. Be ruthless, as you tried and failed to be ignominiously ruthless last August. Romantic love is an illusion anyway. Go and do the work you can do. Get out and fulfil your destiny.'

Probably I will do that, and curse myself for ever afterwards. And if I do, Dorothy remains a permanent menace to my peace of mind, and to any marriage I may make.

It's a jolly predicament.

What, then, is the solution?

I can hear you answer: 'There is no solution.'

Still, I think you will have to tell me what to do. Meanwhile, the enclosed girl [Louise Iselin] wants to marry me. And, in ordinary circumstances what an admirable wife she would be. Good sort, intelligent, sophisticated without being bloody, sympathetic, ambitious for *me*, affectionate, loyal.

Prepared even to abandon the Holy Roman church, at any rate as far as the children are concerned.

I am not going to get engaged, no fear.

But if Dorothy and I decide to chuck it (somehow) next January, then if there is to be any chance of translating the decision into effective action, I'll have to marry her sometime.

The risk, even in 1934, would be unspeakable.

But what is the alternative? To drag along, illicitly, indefinitely. The worst of all.

What a rigmarole. . . .

I get on very well with these people [the New Yorkers]. They have no reserve, an initial bond in common. I like talking to the taxi drivers and exchanging with them the tragic stories of our lives. . . . Even in the most desperate moments the curious feeling of exaltation which is always latent, sometimes surges up inside me; and I want to throw up my arms and shout for the sheer joy of living. It's very odd.

But that's how I am made. And it seems to me that the best – perhaps the only – service that I can render to my fellow creatures is to establish contacts with them, which I can do very quickly.

For most people life is a constant flight from loneliness. Ultimately we all have to live – and die – alone. But if anyone with whom I am in sympathy cares to come and warm themselves even in a short time at my fire, and derives any comfort from it, on the journey, then I am happy.

Too few people live at all today. Almost no-one is gay. I don't see that any useful purpose is served by making life sadder and drearier than it need be, even in the decline of capitalism. And, disagreeing with you, I believe that capitalism has been brought to its present pass by deliberate acts of folly on the part of those who are running it.

Boothby wrote to the sympathetic and understanding Strachey again on 11 November:

All my bravery has evaporated since I wrote.

Where is the 'power urge' now? All I know is that I am half dead most of the time, very nearly took the *Bremen* home last night.

Any hell would be better than the sort of numbed existence that appears to me to be almost inevitable if she hasn't begun to do something about me. Meanwhile Iselin has to be told that marriage to anyone else for me is – and probably always will be – out of the question. A sticky business. But I think she realises it very well already. It removes one remote complication. However, there are plenty left to be going on with.

One way out of this morass was for Boothby himself to get married, and he made several attempts to escape from Dorothy. He was particularly attracted by American women, preferably with money, but then thought better of it – or, to be more precise, Dorothy made him think better of it. There were several expensive crossings of the Atlantic to disengage himself – when a friend asked him why he simply didn't write a letter or telephone, he replied that 'these matters must always be resolved face to face' – and on one occasion Dorothy pursued him across Europe, until she finally found him, to break off yet another engagement. If the situation had not been so tragic, these episodes would have had their farcical aspects.

What had not been comical at all was when Dorothy became pregnant and gave birth to a daughter, Sarah, in 1930. Dorothy said that she was Boothby's child, and, given the fraught situation at Birch Grove and the general imbroglio, this was quite possible. But Boothby himself had considerable doubts, as the child bore remarkably little likeness to him and seemed to have Macmillan eyes. There was also an episode, too sensitive to relate, when Sarah was an adult, that greatly increased these doubts. The dates, also, arouse suspicions, as Sarah was born so soon after the affair had really begun. It is very difficult to avoid the thought that Dorothy's claim was designed to persuade Macmillan to grant her her longed-for divorce. But although Boothby was very doubtful about Dorothy's claim, as are others, he accepted responsibility for Sarah and, as will be seen, was generous and helpful towards her and, eventually, her step-children, a fact which Macmillan greatly appreciated, and which goes some way to explain why their relationship remained so civilised and friendly, a fact which so mystified their contemporaries – and some members of Macmillan's family.

Indeed, it was the fact that Boothby liked and respected Macmillan that made his personal anguish even worse. Dorothy, whenever she was not with him, telephoned him constantly, often in the earshot of her children and husband, and deluged him with letters; she also had the unfeeling absent-mindedness to leave Boothby's letters to her lying around at Birch Grove. After her death in 1966, Boothby remarked that whenever the telephone rang he expected to hear her familiar voice saying, 'It's me,' her invariable beginning. If she could not have him as her husband, she was totally determined to keep him as her lover and constant companion, in which she succeeded up to her death. Boothby, try as he could, never really escaped from her. As he wrote in 1977 to Nigel Fisher, then writing a biography of Macmillan:

What Dorothy wanted and needed was emotion, on the scale of Isolde. This Harold could not give her, and I did. She was, on the whole, the most selfish and most possessive woman I have ever known. Once, when I got engaged to an American heiress, she pursued me from Chatsworth to Paris, and from Paris to Lisbon. But we loved each other. And there is really nothing you can do about this, except die. Wagner was right.

Another consequence of this lamentable state of affairs was that it caused acute, and often bitter, divisions in the Cavendish and Macmillan families, as individuals took sides. Some blamed Boothby, others Dorothy, and some had depressingly little sympathy for Macmillan, particularly some of the Cavendish girls, who strongly sympathised with Dorothy for taking a lover. As the relationship was destined to last so long, some of these rifts became permanent, adding another wretched dimension to the already dismal saga.

There was also to be a political dimension to these family feuds. James Stuart, the Conservative MP for Moray and Nairn, who was destined for the Whips' Office and to be Churchill's Chief Whip in 1941 and, later, Secretary of State for Scotland, was married to Dorothy's sister, Rachel, who was emphatically anti-Boothby; so was David Balniel, the future Earl of Crawford and Balcarres, who also married a Cavendish. Apart from the fact that he had been at Eton, was a Conservative MP and a Scot, Stuart had nothing in common with Boothby. The third son of the Earl of Moray, and a good representative of the Conservative Lairdism in Scotland that Boothby so detested, his political career since his election in 1923 had been so inconspicuous as to be virtually invisible. In 1935 he was made Scottish Whip and became Deputy Chief Whip in 1937 under David Margesson. He thus came to occupy a position of real political importance. This was bad news for Boothby, and also for Churchill and Eden, whom Stuart also cordially disliked: the feeling was keenly reciprocated. An additional cause of bad feeling between Boothby and Stuart was that the latter's own private life did not, in the former's view, give him a high moral platform from which to censure others. They hated each other. In his memoirs* Stuart was vicious about Boothby, without mentioning him by name; Boothby retaliated by publicly pointing out that Stuart had been cited as co-respondent in a divorce case.

Just to make matters even more complicated than they were, Boothby had also fallen very much for another of Dorothy's cousins, Diana Cavendish, the fourth daughter of Lord Richard Cavendish, and she for him. Indeed, Boothby seemed for most of his adult life to be surrounded by Cavendishes, some of whom loved him and others who loathed him. In later years, unhappily, he had rather more vivid memories of the latter than the former, with the exception of Diana and Dorothy. 'Once you get into the clutches of that family, by God, you haven't a hope,' he told an interviewer in 1973. 'They are the most tenacious family in Britain.'†

---

* Stuart's autobiography, *Within the Fringe* (1967), is unusual in another respect: there are only two, cursory, references to his wife, who is also omitted in the list of acknowledgments and in Lord Home's Introduction.

† Interview with Susan Barnes (Crosland), *Sunday Times*, 1 April 1973.

Boothby had met Diana in 1929 at her first dance, given by Lady Astor at 4 St James's Square, in her own words, 'with immediate affinity'. She had met his friends Peter Rodd and Patrick Kinross, who moved with Boothby in what she considered 'a slightly raffish circle', but bursting with vitality and fun. She knew all about Dorothy, of course, but patiently waited for the passions to abate and for Boothby to wrench himself free. By 1935 it at last appeared that he had succeeded, as the nervous exhaustion had got him down; it also looked as though Dorothy had accepted that for everyone's sake some degree of normality should enter their lives. No doubt she meant it at the time, but she did not release Boothby willingly. Indeed, she did not release him at all.

As he later remarked, everything would have been all right between him and Diana if they had never married. According to his version, he proposed on impulse after rather too good a dinner and when he thought about it again in the cold light of morning it was too late, as her mother, Lady Moyra Cavendish, had announced the news to the world and congratulations were pouring in from family, friends – including a delighted Churchill – and constituents. Diana strongly disputes this version. She was convinced that the Bob–Dorothy affair was truly over, and she loved him; she also believed – rightly – that he loved her, and that it would all work out. As by the time of the engagement they knew each other very well, her optimism seemed entirely justified. Both her parents disapproved of the marriage, but accepted how devoted Diana was to him. It seemed that the nightmare was over.

But Boothby had exceptionally serious pre-marriage qualms, particularly as he was genuinely deeply fond of Diana as a trusted and loved friend. Boothby's former secretary, Marjorie Macrae, now Marjorie Brooks, was returning by sea with her husband and and baby son from their China posting when she received an agitated telegram from Boothby asking her to return to Britain as fast as possible, and suggesting that she disembark at Marseilles and come to London by train, as he was in the worst possible trouble. She cabled back that this was impossible, but when she reached London she telephoned Peter Rodd to ask what was going on. Rodd told her that Boothby was going to be married in two days' time and was in a state of alcoholic despair. She contacted Boothby, who begged her to extricate him from this looming disaster. Very sensibly she told him that as he had got himself into this mess, it was his affair and not hers, that it was much too late to back out, and that he should at least turn up at the altar sober. This was exactly Rodd's advice, to which Boothby unhappily acceded. Boothby later wrote of Diana in a private letter: 'She has been one of the oldest, the closest, and certainly the most valued friends in my whole life.' He was worried whether this would be enough.

For the rest of his life he blamed himself very deeply for not having had the courage to tell his fiancée about these grievous doubts – not about her, but about himself.

They were married on 21 March 1935 at St Bartholomew-the-Great. The service was conducted by the Bishop of Exeter; Cyril Radcliffe was due to be the best man, but was called away on an urgent legal case and was substituted by another close friend, Richard Bazell. Boothby's presents to his bride were a car and a diamond and sapphire ring, and among the imposing list of gifts was a handsome cheque from his constituents and 'a magnificent silver ink-stand and pot' from the Churchills. As he later wrote, sadly, 'I was then still his blue-eyed boy.'

There are elements of real sadness in what was to prove a short-lived marriage. The couple were devoted to each other, and always remained so, but it was not long before Diana realised that her husband's many qualities did not include those normally associated with a successful husband. Although he was only thirty-five, he had been a wayward bachelor too long to be able to change into a dutiful and conventional husband, and, although he tried, it became quickly clear that this was not a natural state for him. Love, friendship and fun, which he supplied in full measure, were compensations rather than a substitute for an ordered and happy settled married life. Boothby gave little indication of being ready for the latter, and every sign of rebelling against it. These strains, which Diana had anticipated, might not have been important and might have been resolved, had it not been for the fact that Dorothy reappeared on the scene.

Boothby had assured Diana that the affair was over and had meant it sincerely. Dorothy, however, had not taken the same view and, when they met, Boothby realised that she was right. As he later said, 'It is impossible to be happily married when you love someone else.' It was when Diana discovered that her husband was seeing Dorothy again that she realised that the situation was impossible and that their marriage had been a dreadful mistake. He had also come to the same conclusion, and they decided that divorce was inevitable. Their parting was amicable and affectionate, and they remained close for the rest of Boothby's life.

When a friend, who, like many others, was rather shocked by the brevity of the marriage and its ending, asked him about it, Boothby wrote:

> I married Diana because we were old friends, and she was a first cousin of Dorothy, and we were both unhappy. It was a damned silly thing to do . . . The reason I was unhappy was because, deep down, I was dissatisfied. And the reason I was dissatisfied deep down was because I passionately wanted a home and children of my own.

In those days divorce was not easily procured, and in public life was virtually unknown, politicians still shuddering at the memory of what it had done to the Irish Nationalist leader, Charles Stewart Parnell; and, in 1937, the recent experience of public outrage at the King wanting to marry a twice-divorced woman was all too vivid. As A. J. P. Taylor has written of the situation in 1936, 'England was a laxer country than she had been thirty years before. But appearances were kept up in public. Divorce still carried a moral stigma and still drove men from public life.' Even in the late 1940s Eden's divorce was considered by many to be a fatal barrier to his becoming prime minister. What was even more worrying to Boothby was the reaction of his constituents. In the event, as Jack Webster has written,

the folk of East Aberdeenshire winced but granted that his private life was his own, even if divorce was hardly known among the farming fraternity of Buchan at that time. Irreconcilable couples tended to thole each other, no matter how deep and interminable the misery, rather than be dragged into the shame and prominence of the Court of Sessions.

Boothby wrote to Beaverbrook on 31 December 1936:

Dear Max

My marriage crumbled into ruins six months ago, and there is only one thing I can honourably do now.

I realise that there must be a good deal of publicity. But don't let your boys hunt me down.

Because I am not going to let go of public life; and still believe that one day I may do something.

What a hell of an autumn this has been.

Don't bother to answer this, but please accept my very best wishes for the New Year.

Yours ever
Bob

Beaverbrook was understanding.

Before Alan Herbert almost single-handedly made the divorce laws more humane, in effect the only way was to prove adultery, usually accomplished by a professional agency with an arranged visit by the husband and a paid woman to an hotel, with witnesses also paid and arranged in advance. It was a sordid method, but it satisfied the courts, and this was the course that Boothby was recommended to take, and did.

The public mood towards divorce was changing, as the passage of Herbert's Matrimonial Causes Act in 1937 showed, and the Archdeacon of Coventry, speaking to the Diocesan Conference, said that

The limitation of the grounds of divorce to the one ground of adultery has resulted in a state of affairs which is disastrously prejudicial to public morality. As the law stands at present those who wish to bring an end to the marriage are forced to take one of two alternatives – either one must commit adultery or one must commit perjury.

But such progressive views still ran some way ahead of the general opinion, especially in Scotland. The fact that Boothby's constituents accepted that it was a matter for him and not for them shows how strongly he had captured their affections. But it was a miserable experience, which he did not care to dwell upon or wish to remember, and over which there is no need for his biographer to linger.*

One result Boothby did not expect was the wrath of the Cavendishes, who now had two causes of anger towards him. He came to believe that they were determined to make him pay a heavy political price for his affair with Dorothy and his failed marriage to Diana. He felt very strongly that they had led a conspiracy to discredit and defame him, and later often expressed the wish, and not only in private, that he had never met 'that bloody family', while carefully excluding both Dorothy and Diana from any involvement in the alleged conspiracy. As Boothby's character was refreshingly free from malice and vindictiveness, this particular obsession should be taken with some seriousness by his biographer, especially in view of later events. Also, it did not help his strained relations with the Churchills, particularly Clementine, who had very strong views on marital fidelity and abhorred scandal. 'Churchill bitterly resented my divorce,' Boothby later said. 'He was fond of Diana. He thought I had behaved badly. I hadn't . . . I acted with good intentions. In fact, behaved like a gentleman. But Winston disapproved.' The Boothby–Dorothy affair had been condoned in London political and Society circles, but public involvement in what appeared to be a squalid and scandalous divorce case was different. Boothby's real friends rallied round; others fell away; his enemies gloated. Boothby quickly sensed an even more hostile atmosphere than usual towards him in the House of Commons, in his clubs and in London Society generally. The early failure of his marriage depressed Boothby deeply, and he felt that he was suffering from disappointment and melancholia. He confided in Harold Nicolson, who replied on 22 December 1936, in a wonderful letter, so characteristic of a true and sensitive friend, who had himself been through the furnace:

I have had much experience of that sort of thing. Some people say it is entirely due to circumstances. Other people say it is entirely due to health. I think it is due to temperament. Yet I observe that all the people I like go through a phase of melancholia, and that all the people I dislike do not know what that black poison means. It is no good assuring my black and

*Diana Boothby subsequently married Colonel Ian Campbell-Gray in 1942, who died of leukaemia in 1946. When she became engaged in 1970 to Boothby's Oxford contemporary, Lord Gage, Boothby was asked for a comment and said, 'She is the closest and dearest friend I have. The one mistake we made was to get married.'

beloved melancholics that the phase is charming and inevitable; they do not believe it. They think they are finished and damned – AND THROUGH THEIR OWN FAULT.

Now much can be done in this by Messrs. Boots. There is a thing called exercise, there are things called cold baths in the morning, and there are several small and immensely volatile things called little liver pills.

These things help in a way; but it is not the vital way. The best thing is 'time, passage of'. For in truth, if one is intelligent, these black moods pass. One imagines that they are wholly due to circumstances and that one's own circumstances are such that no lip can utter or ear comprehend. . . . But that is not always the case – the mood comes from a far deeper cause.

I think it comes, it stalks upon one, at that phase in one's life when the first fine careless rapture has been spent, and when one feels that middle age is approaching, and that never can one recapture that particular and far-flung gesture of youth. One feels that one's fling was superb; and has missed that fling. I have felt that six or seven times in my life. I have felt 'My God! How sad! How unutterably sad!!!! Such talent, such ambition, such force (in a way) and all lavished on false causes and unpaid impulses.'

One feels that one has thrown into life the surfeit of one's energies; that people have been impressed for a moment by one's initial energy; but all this is a sham; that people have found one out; that one is a dud, a failure and a middle-aged person capable only at leering at the success, or the waistline, of other and more aspirant souls.

. . . What is your inconvenience is that you appear an objective person, while being really subjective. You are a fighter with delicate nerves. For the moment the delicacy of your nerves has got the better of your combative faculties. Yet, were it not for this ebb and flow of tides in your being, you would be a stagnant lagoon . . . Your melancholy is a proof of your value. You have reached the stage when you can no longer hope to be impudently promising. You have reached the stage when you must integrate and cease analysing. And you will do it. I should welcome your melancholia as a symptom of a second wind. And in active life that second wind carries one on to eighty-six years of age.*

As time passed and physical passion faded, Boothby and Dorothy saw a great deal of each other up to her death in 1966. When Boothby and Macmillan discussed the matter many years later, Boothby lamented that it had cost him much, and especially his friendship with Macmillan; but, as their correspondence and their discussions show, this was not really the case, and Boothby's relationship with Maurice Macmillan was a particularly warm and close one, especially when Maurice went through a terrible period of what one member of the family frankly called 'the Cavendish disease', acute alcoholism. The manner in which Maurice and his wonderful wife Katie overcame this grim burden was an epic of its

* As it did.

kind, and Boothby was one of those friends whose kindness in his ordeal Maurice never forgot. Nor did his father.

Macmillan also knew of Boothby's generosity to Sarah, who had become a cause of deep concern to them both. To Boothby's horror, she had had an abortion on her mother's orders, had married unhappily and had also succumbed to 'the Cavendish disease', going into clinics regularly, but without lasting success. Her two adopted sons were an additional source of concern, and Boothby contributed £10,000 to the trust fund that he and Macmillan set up for them. The doubts about who was her father were reflected in the trust deed, where Boothby's status is described as 'Friend' and not 'Father'. She saw him frequently, and he tried to help, but Sarah's tragic decline was inexorable, and she died in March 1970.

It had also been demonstrated, as Boothby himself fully admitted, that in matters of the heart he was not only impetuous but very weak. To be fair to him, the one thing that emerges with special clarity is how strong and dominant and utterly selfish a character Dorothy Macmillan was. But, to an extent that he only later realised, the matter demoralised Boothby and did lasting damage to his self-confidence, to the point that in old age he often pondered on whether his weakness over Dorothy and the failure of his first marriage had not revealed some fundamental flaw that made him unsuitable for high office. This was going much too far. There were no signs whatever of personal or political modesty or lack of confidence in the Boothby of the 1930s, nor later. But it left scars on a personality that was far more sensitive and emotional than was generally realised by his contemporaries.

His mother, who desperately tried to extricate her son from a position which she rightly regarded as totally disastrous for him, was distraught, and begged him and his really close friends to persuade him to end this catastrophic liaison. Many tried, and Boothby often promised to follow their advice, but it took only one letter or telephone call to bring him back to Dorothy's arms. The simple fact was that he loved her, and she loved him. Their love had its turbulent moments, Boothby once writing in his short-lived journal: 'Dined with Dorothy. Her garden is really lovely. She made me frightfully cross at dinner; and then I couldn't remember why. She is the only person who can make me frightfully cross.'

'The truth of Bob's life', one who knew him specially well has said, 'was that he had many lovers, but until Wanda [Boothby's second wife] only one true love – Dorothy.' The other lovers were aware of this, although very reluctantly and unhappily. They were loved, but were ephemeral; Dorothy was permanent. They knew it, Dorothy knew it, and so did Harold Macmillan. There was an understanding. It does not make it any the less sad.

The Macmillan–Boothby affair, recorded maliciously by Maurice Bowra in his privately circulated *A Statesman's Tragedy*, badly affected Boothby's reputation among many of his colleagues. They did not know how deep was their love, or indeed much about it except that here was a Conservative MP virtually living openly with the wife not only of another Conservative MP but of someone who was supposed to be a close friend. They drew the conclusion, not at all surprisingly, that Boothby was an unspeakable cad, who drank too deep, lived too well, gambled too heavily and stole other men's wives. (The same could be said, much more justifiably, and was, about Duff Cooper.) There was, unfortunately, just enough truth in this grotesquely harsh caricature to do Boothby's reputation real and lasting harm.

The other, and very ironical, aspect of the story is that if it played some part in damaging Boothby's political career, it was the making of Macmillan's. In his personal unhappiness and loneliness, and he was, throughout his life, basically a very lonely and withdrawn man, he turned his mind and energies almost exclusively to politics. Although Macmillan was never close to Churchill, and certainly not as close as Boothby then was – indeed, he always disliked Churchill, even more than Boothby did, describing him to Boothby many years later as 'ruthless . . . [with] a large touch of megalomania and slightly crazy, totally egotistical. He was good to me, but only because it was in his interests' – he became convinced that he was right, and the Chamberlainites wrong, about the European situation. He made common cause with Boothby and his friends on this issue and became one of the Government's most trenchant and effective critics in Parliament and outside. With almost suicidal political reckless-ness, which not even Churchill or Boothby dared to do, he was to hurl himself into the post-Munich Oxford by-election in 1938 to support the anti-Government candidate against the Conservative, Quintin Hogg. He was an avowed opponent of the Chamberlain Government until its downfall. If his appointment as special Minister in North Africa in 1941 seemed at the time a poor reward, he was to make it the taking of his long-awaited opportunity. He was to pay a heavy personal price in his children for this total concentration, but the tragedy of his marriage was to him a goad, much as had been Lord Randolph Churchill's celebrated quarrel with the Prince of Wales in 1876 and his exclusion from London Society and banishment to Ireland. Such are the vagaries of life, and of politics.

What Macmillan always appreciated, after his initial hopes, was that the love affair between his wife and Boothby was absolutely genuine, and no casual mating. Although this would have made it even more hateful for a proud and sensitive man, it did give him some fellow-feeling for Boothby, caught as they were in the same trap that was essentially of her making.

Macmillan, many years later, when they were reconciled, remarked to her that she had been the chief beneficiary, with husband, lover, children and home, and it would not be difficult to cast her as the villainess of the piece, as many did. But it was, again, much more complex than that. An unhappy marriage – for such it was when she met Boothby and fell so swiftly and totally in love with him, and remained so for the rest of her life – cannot be blamed on one partner alone, and Macmillan had his own causes for remorse and self-criticism.

The final chapter in this sad, but for both men vitally important, saga, had its mixture, again, of tragedy and comedy, as was perhaps appropriate and fitting.

Before Dorothy's unexpected death, which hit Boothby much harder than he expected and plunged him into a bad period of his life, he had gathered together all her letters to him, which he counted at over seven hundred, and taken them to the incinerator in the basement of his flat at 1, Eaton Square, and burnt them.* After Dorothy's death, Macmillan found a huge number of Boothby's letters to his wife at Birch Grove and also decided to burn them. As he afterwards assured Boothby, he had not read them. He also noticed that there had been no attempt to conceal them, as they were easily found in her room. One suspects that she, as Boothby did, frequently reread their letters and recaptured their happiness and their anguish.

But Macmillan discovered that the one fireplace at Birch Grove, in the library, was inadequate. As he told Boothby, 'I didn't want some Arizonan professor writing a thesis about you and me,' so he took the letters to the garden incinerator. Given the nature of his task he did not want any assistance or witnesses. He had never lit an incinerator in his life and found it a difficult business. Then, the wind got up, and the letters, only partly burned, started flying around, with Macmillan chasing them. It took some time for the task to be accomplished, and, characteristically, Macmillan saw both the comical and the poignant aspects of this remarkable scene of an elderly and now poor-sighted former British prime minister frantically chasing the letters of his wife's lover across the grounds of his home.

Macmillan's own sardonic account to Boothby of this half-melancholy, half-comical, destruction of Boothby's letters to his wife was pricelessly funny, but both knew it was not. There was a long silence and then Macmillan said, 'And so it all ended.' After another long silence, Boothby said, 'And so it all ended.'

*Dorothy was apparently enraged when Boothby told her that he had burnt her letters, saying, 'They were *my* letters, you had no right to burn them.'

6

Towards War
1931-7

*B*oothby's own fortunes in 1931 were decidedly mixed. There was the usual running battle over herrings. The Labour Government discouraged the export of herrings to Russia in February; Boothby denounced this 'do-nothing policy' and made a point of making a well-publicised visit to the head of the Soviet Trade Delegation on 17 February. On the 22nd there was a public debate at the Scottish Arts Club in Edinburgh with Compton Mackenzie and Moray McLaren, when he declared that 'I hate the English. I hate them for their moral cowardice, their lack of humour, their lack of imagination and their incredible snobbery. And I hate them for their bovine stupidity.' This nonsense caused a disproportionate amount of comment, criticism and support.

Equally controversial was a speech he made in the Commons on 24 February advocating free first-class travel for MPs, as 'travelling third class to Aberdeen is the nearest thing to hell I know'. 'A loud burst of laughter greeted this outspoken declaration,' one report read. He also 'seriously wondered whether the conditions that are being imposed on people in public life are not becoming so unendurable that nobody will go into public life at all. There is nothing to be got out of being an MP, yet they have very onerous duties to perform.'

On the storm that his anti-English remarks had caused, the *Glasgow Herald* sagely observed that 'Mr Boothby is well able to look after himself in this matter.' The Directors of the London Midland and Scottish Railway were indignant at the criticism of their admirable third-class sleeper service to Aberdeen, which, they pointed out, left Euston promptly at 7.30 p.m. for a journey that only took twelve hours and twenty minutes. Other users of their service rallied strongly to Boothby's support. As usual, Boothby had the last word. He told the *Manchester Guardian*:

The moral to be drawn from all the commotion is that it is inadvisable for those engaged in public life to attempt any form of witticism. And perhaps the best way of ensuring this is to compel all Members of Parliament to make up their speeches in railway carriages which contain not less than six other people.

One reaction came in a Sunday paper:

I mean to tell the first fat-headed ass
Who annoys me with his blether
On the subject of the weather
To '*Go to Aberdeen – Third Class!*'

In the middle of this innocent fun, the Labour Government's difficulties grew deeper. Having rejected Mosley, and with no ideas of its own, it had retreated into a cloud of commissions and committees. In February 1931 it virtually abdicated its responsibilities by announcing the appointment of a committee on national expenditure to be chaired by Sir George May, while what Churchill called 'the economic blizzard' still raged and unemployment increased. On 23 February, in the Commons, Boothby denounced the decision as another example of the impotence not only of the Government but of Parliament in these grave matters. One commentator on this speech wrote of Boothby's general style at that time:

He has no genius for phrasing. His language is entirely ordinary. It might even be called slipshod. Nor is his manner of the grand kind. He practises none of the arts dear to it, and he is deficient in the capacity of conveying in the most impressive way the ideas with which he is filled. For form, in all its aspects, he has, so far, shown no regard.

But it is to his practical thinking that Mr. Boothby owes his Parliamentary position. It gives his speaking an unusual amount of power to compel attention. His appearance, too, is attractive, and he has a hint of the artistic. He is also a personality, and his personality shines through the severity of his topics.

On 30 April Boothby was invited to address the Primrose League at Caxton Hall with Churchill, Eden and Oliver Stanley, where he described Snowden as 'a hoary-minded and dyed-in-the-wool old Radical of the 1860 school'. One who was present wrote:

Mr. Boothby is rather a dark-skinned young man, with a mop of unruly black hair. Every word that falls from his lips is hard, delivered with fierce intensity, and gives the impression of war to the death. Captain R. A. Eden has a quiet manner which suggests the professor lecturing his students. . . . Of the four [speakers]

Mr. Boothby is the man who can most easily – and even naturally – sway a large audience of voters.

This was his first public appearance after the influenza he had contracted early in March had been followed by jaundice, which had required a recuperative holiday in Rome. He was in fact quite seriously ill and had not fully shaken off the effects of his car accident. But Italy, as always, restored his spirits.

He returned not only to the political crisis, but also to his personal one. He denounced the budget in the Commons and his constituency, urged the total abandonment of reparations and – at the British–Russian Chamber of Commerce dinner in London – a greater response from the Russians to British trade offers. On 25 June, in the Commons, he put forward a five-year plan of his own for Scottish agriculture.

But the political crisis of the summer took him totally by surprise. He was invited by Archie Sinclair for his annual shooting holiday in Caithness when Parliament went into recess in July, before a round of constituency meetings. Never one to ignore the possibilities of pleasure, he stayed with Compton Mackenzie on his way north, whom he had assured that 'Ramsay MacDonald has gone to Lossiemouth. All looks quite peaceful at the moment.' Like almost everyone else he was out of London when the crisis came. Lloyd George was ill, recovering from a serious prostate operation; Churchill was in the United States; and Baldwin was at Aix-les-Bains, as usual.

When May reported, after Parliament had risen, his conclusion and recommendations, which included a huge reduction in unemployment payments and other benefits, caused panic and a run on sterling. MacDonald had to return hurriedly from Lossiemouth to meet the ferocious terms of the bankers and a Labour Party crisis. The Cabinet tottered towards collapse, and Baldwin was, with difficulty, recalled to London. The role of the King became crucial: he urged the formation of a national government. MacDonald, with a totally split Cabinet, was in favour; so was Herbert Samuel for the Liberals; Baldwin, the last consulted, felt that he had no choice. Thus was formed, under MacDonald's leadership, as it was announced, 'not a coalition in the ordinary sense of the term, but a co-operation of individuals'.

These astounding events wrecked Boothby's shooting holiday, and he and Sinclair very reluctantly decided to give it up and travel south. In Boothby's account:

At Dingwall we heard the news that the Labour Government had resigned; 'You will be a minister tomorrow,' said Archie. At Perth we were told that MacDonald had once again kissed hands as Prime Minister – this time of a 'National'

Government. 'It is not I but you who will be the minister,' I said to him. And so it proved. But he did not seem elated.

Sinclair became Secretary for Scotland in this extraordinary new administration, from which Churchill, Amery and Lloyd George were excluded, as was Boothby. The *Buchan Observer* found this 'astonishing', but as Snowden was still Chancellor of the Exchequer Boothby was not surprised. As soon as Parliament reassembled, Snowden introduced yet another deflationary budget, described by Keynes as 'replete with folly and injustice'. Boothby attacked it in the Commons. 'The tone was conversational,' one report reads, 'but intensely sincere; the argument was direct and concrete; there were few cheers, but that sudden silence which is the greatest of all compliments to a speaker.'

Boothby always lamented the advent of the so-called 'National' Government, and history has strongly endorsed his view. It certainly dashed his own hopes, because if Baldwin had held firm for a Conservative Government after the disintegration of the MacDonald administration, it is virtually certain that he would have received office, by some accounts that of President of the Board of Trade. Baldwin held him in particular regard and affection, and no serious shadows had yet appeared between them. Sinclair had made his confident assurance to Boothby in the belief that it would be a Conservative Government; being a coalition of three Parties meant that the number of Conservatives who would be favoured was greatly reduced, and one of the victims was Boothby. At the time he shrugged his shoulders at the vagaries of politics and of life. Only much later did it become so clear that the events of September 1931 were not only a disaster for Britain but for himself. He was unquestionably on the verge of office, but had been denied it. From this many consequences were to flow.

One fundamental problem that was becoming evident, and was to become increasingly clear, was that Boothby did not like, and was not liked by, the majority of his Conservative colleagues. He was in good company, as they also disliked and distrusted Churchill and Macmillan, and considered Amery an out-of-date bore. Eden was more skilful in concealing his detestation of the bulk of the Tory Party by immersing himself in foreign affairs and treating the House of Commons simply as a place where he made the occasional speech. Duff Cooper's great ambition also made him less outspoken in public than he was in private. It was ambition, also, that dominated Boothby's friends Walter Elliot and Shakes Morrison, but they were far more natural Conservatives than Boothby ever was.

It was this fact that won him great and genuine respect on the Labour benches. He followed Baldwin's wise advice in never condescending to them, but there was more to it than that. His denunciations of the follies of Socialism were genuine, and he never contemplated changing Parties, but the romantic, even sentimental, aspect of the Scots character was very strong in him, and all his sympathies were with the unfortunate. There was, accordingly, a far closer affinity on social matters between him and Labour than with the Conservatives, whose collective social conscience in the inter-war years was difficult to discern. On foreign affairs, in contrast, there was no affinity at all, and Boothby's scorn at Labour's pacifism and woolly thinking throughout the 1930s was as strongly expressed as by any Tory. There was also a strong anti-Semitic element in the Conservative Party, and Boothby's espousal of the Jews and Zionism also put him – and Churchill and Victor Cazalet – beyond the pale.

The trouble was that Boothby had no particular objective in life, except to fulfil himself. He had no political ambition for office – indeed, apart from wanting to continue to be an MP, no political ambition at all. He enjoyed being a well-known MP and seeing his name frequently in the papers, and made no bones about it. He was a natural self-publicist, with an eye for the headlines. He was wholly uninterested in those aspects of politics, such as sitting on boring, if worthy, committees, that are part of the job. Those who had to undertake the necessary chores greatly resented Boothby's cavalier dismissal of their endeavours, judging, quite rightly, that he considered such things as being beneath him. Besides, they did not achieve much publicity or attention, and Boothby craved both. Thus the myth that he was lazy was created, and became established as fact.

His charm, humour and friendliness, combined with his independence of mind, greatly attracted the Labour Party, and, significantly, the Scottish Labour MPs most of all. Boothby loved Jimmy Maxton, with his flowing hair, gaunt face and passionate oratory, while deploring his laziness, and Emmanuel Shinwell and David Kirkwood were other close friends. Kirkwood, indeed, once told James Margach, when the latter was a young lobby correspondent, that he had high hopes that Boothby would join Labour, and he certainly tried to bring him over on several occasions. Years later he told Margach that if he had succeeded, he was convinced that Boothby would have risen to the leadership of the Party, which is one of the more improbable possibilities of Boothby's life. He was, and always remained, a Radical Tory.

Years later Margach posed to Boothby the question: 'Why did the Tories never take to you in the sense that most of the Labour MPs did?' There is no record of Boothby's reply, but it would have been on the familiar lines that Tories cannot abide rebels, and that he was a natural rebel. He would probably have added that they hated the fact that he was usually right. The real reason was that politicians and political observers like to 'place' MPs in categories and are bewildered when one of them defies such categorisation. Boothby had clear views on economic and social policies, on foreign affairs, and on the protection of the interests of his constituents. For the rest, he made it up as he went along, on almost a daily basis. It was this unpredictability that confused people, and it was only a short step from the accusation of unreliability, which was as undeserved as that of laziness. His unconcealed admiration for Lloyd George, after Churchill the most widely distrusted politician in Britain, confirmed his colleagues' mistrust of him.

Boothby also lacked the advantage of a stable private life – indeed, he had all the disadvantages of a chaotic one. Only the gambling aspects of his work as a stockbroker, and later as a banker, interested him, and his judgments were notoriously hit-or-miss – usually the latter. His mother considered that his continuing and deepening love affair with Dorothy was wrecking his health, mental stability and political fortunes, and she was right, but the causes of Boothby's political loneliness lay much deeper. He was by temperament what the Americans call a 'loner', and an unusual combination of brash extrovert and sensitive introvert, as Richard Crossman once shrewdly noted, and which John Strachey and Roger Senhouse had seen since they were at Eton together. One of the keys to the Boothby of the 1930s was that he was very unhappy and very insecure. If he was seen by many Conservatives to be erratic politically, this was not to be wondered at. What was remarkable was that, in these dismal circumstances, he was so consistent on the big issues.

'Not for the first time', Boothby later remarked, 'Britain was saved by the Royal Navy.' Snowden's last budget* cut unemployment payments and the salaries of all paid by the state. For the sailors at Invergordon this was the last straw; whether it was a mutiny or simply an angry disturbance is immaterial. The Government's proposals had to be hastily revised, but not before Britain had been unceremoniously forced off the Gold Standard. The Conservatives now pressed for an immediate general election for 'a doctor's mandate'. They would campaign for a modest protectionist policy, the National Liberals for free trade, and the Mac-Donald National Labour for a review of these issues after the election. Mosley's New Party, which contested twenty-four seats, stood for Mosley.

---

* In November 1931 he went to the Lords and was replaced by Neville Chamberlain.

For Boothby, as for every other Conservative candidate, the 1931 general election was the easiest that any had experienced, or was ever to experience again.

He had so entrenched himself in the affections and admiration of his constituents, and was so warmly praised by his opponents, that he could afford a notably relaxed campaign. He took as his theme 'National Government or Collapse', of which he was not particularly proud, and concentrated on his record and local issues. His opponent this time was Fred Martin, who was brave, blind, and a superb example of the old Labour Party, which Boothby deeply respected. Boothby greatly admired Martin, who was a gallant and courteous opponent, but whose cause, in 1931, was hopeless. He courageously campaigned on the cry of 'Labour Government and Reconstruction'. Boothby's poster was a huge photograph of himself, declaring 'Vote Boothby. The Friend of All.' When asked about this somewhat succinct message he replied, 'Well, I don't have any policies.' His majority was 10,097. Everywhere, Labour was routed, as were Mosley and his New Party.

Early in 1932 a crucial episode in Boothby's life occurred.

He had visited Germany often in the 1920s, but had not been there since the great crash of 1930–1, which had been especially disastrous for the country and had given the once-derided Hitler his opportunity. But few, outside Germany, took Hitler seriously, and few outside the country had met him or had read *Mein Kampf.*

Towards the end of 1931 Boothby was invited to deliver lectures on the economic crisis in Hamburg and Berlin, as his speeches on reparations and his fame as *'Privatsekretar von Winston Churchill wahrend seiner Schatzamtstatigkeit im Kabinett'*, as he was hailed and billed, had been recognised in Germany. Also, as Boothby later wrote, 'they were desperate. I have never had bigger or better audiences.' One British press report of his visit added, inconsequentially, 'Mr Boothby also met Herr Hitler and Dr Brüning.'

When Boothby reached Berlin he took the advice of Harold Nicolson, formerly at the British Embassy, to go to the annual New Year's Eve ball. He later recalled:

We went to an enormous hall, where we found over a thousand people dancing, including some of the prettiest girls I have ever seen. The band was excellent, the food and drink both good, and the atmosphere gay. It was an enjoyable evening, which I have never forgotten. When my host took me back to the Adlon Hotel, and I thanked him for his kindness, he said: 'It may interest you to know that there was not a single girl there!' After I had gone to bed I found myself wondering whether this was symptomatic of the decadence of a great nation; and decided, rightly, that it was not.

The theme of Boothby's lectures was directly opposite to Brüning's policies of massive deflation and, consequently, of industrial paralysis. He called for the ending of reparations and war debts, for genuine co-operation between the banks, and for the restoration of the exchange system, which had totally broken down. 'To talk of over-production in present circumstances is ridiculous. The remedy lies in the restoration and stabilisation of prices and the expansion of credit.'

Immediately on his return Boothby wrote an article in the *Evening Standard*, which was published on 22 January:

> The visitor to Germany sustains an impression of terrific strain, resolutely born.
>
> Successive 'emergency decrees', drafted to maintain the mark at an artificially high level, have imposed enormous sacrifices and no inconsiderable suffering upon every section of the population. My own experience confirmed a long-held belief that the horrors of intensive deflation over a considerable period are hardly less great than the horrors of inflation itself.
>
> As the export trade has fallen, the number of the unemployed has risen. Today, a third of the population is out of work. And the whole standard of living has been sharply and ruthlessly reduced. Hamburg is like a dead city. Magnificent buildings, spacious highways and parks, the finest workers' houses in the world. But nothing doing.
>
> The houses are full of workmen without jobs. The Elbe is full of ships without crews.
>
> I was told that the condition of Hamburg is typical of provincial Germany. There is no unrest on the surface. No riots. But a mood of gradually increasing desperation, which finds political expression in 'Hitlerism'. The rise and growth of the Nazi movement is one of the most interesting phenomena of the post-war era.

Boothby's meeting with Brüning was a depressing experience: 'I took away with me the impression of a lonely man, upon whom the burden of supreme responsibility bore heavily; and of a tired man.'

One of Boothby's German friends was 'Putzi' Hanfstaengl, 'who was at that time Hitler's personal private secretary and court jester. He told me that the Führer had been reading my speeches with interest, and would like to see me at his headquarters in the Esplanade Hotel.' Hitler was not at that time *Führer*, except to his acolytes, and was generally underestimated and regarded – especially by the British – as an unbalanced nonentity. But Putzi was anxious to arrange a meeting between him and Boothby, and the latter, after a long and agreeable lunch, and 'feeling rather mellow', willingly agreed.

His report, written immediately afterwards, and published in the *Evening Standard* again, should have been more widely pondered upon than it was.

By way of contrast, Hitler . . . I saw him at his hotel on the evening that he had delivered his final memorandum to the Chancellor, breaking off all negotiations.

An enthusiastic secretary [Hanfstaengl] assured me that this was a 'masterpiece'; and when, a little later, we heard a chime of bells through the wide-open window he exclaimed: 'Listen. Our letter is being delivered now. The bells are ringing the knell of the old regime. They ring out the old and ring in the new.'

I was taken to an inner room where a short, dark, spare figure with a small moustache and limpid blue eyes, sprang to his feet, clicked his heels together, raised his arm and shouted 'Hitler!'. Momentarily I was taken aback,* but before I had time to feel embarrassed he was explaining that the events of the past few days had made his advent to power, within a measurable space of time, inevitable.

'And I am going on alone now,' he added. A secretary asked me to put questions, and I asked him for his views on the economic situation. 'You have been laying too much emphasis on the economic side,' he said. 'This is a political crisis. Political forces will carry me to power.'

I asked him if he wanted an election now, and if he thought he would win outright. His reply to both questions was a vehement affirmative.

And then suddenly, he burst into an impassioned harangue. 'How would you like', he demanded, with an indescribable emphasis, 'if your colonies and your fleet had been taken from you, and if a corridor had been driven between England and Scotland? What would you be? What would you do?'

I had no time to say that I wouldn't like it.† On he swept. . . .

About Hitler's intellectual ability I am not qualified to give an opinion. But this much I can say. He has youth. He has abundant vitality, and he has passion. It is, I know, the fashion among our intellectuals today to decry passion, to disparage its virtues and its forces. Nevertheless, I continue to believe that, even in the modern world, deeply felt passion retains the power to move men to heroic action and painful sacrifice.

Somehow Hitler has managed to communicate this passion of his to masses of rather desperate people. And therein lies his power. The cry 'Heil Hitler!' re-echoes through Germany to-day. We should not underestimate the strength of the movement of which he is the living embodiment.

It is impossible to forecast the future. No one knows whether the Nazis will be swept into power, or whether Dr. Brüning will manage to steer the ship of State

---

* Boothby's later version was that he had responded by clicking his heels and shouting 'Boothby!'. Ludovic Kennedy (*op. cit.*, p. 67) makes rather heavy weather of this, pointing out that the same story was attributed to Maurice Bowra, which Bowra, very regretfully, had to deny. Boothby was always emphatic about his version. It is a minor matter compared with the importance of the meeting and its impact upon Boothby.

† Boothby's later version was that he had replied, 'You forget, Herr Hitler, that I come from Scotland. We should have been delighted,' upon which Hitler crashed his fist on the desk and said, 'So! I had no idea that the hatred between the two peoples was so great' (*Recollections of a Rebel*, p. 110). Boothby in his old age believed that this was why Hitler 'sent Hess to Scotland, for I am sure that he did; and why he never bombed Edinburgh'. His own contemporary account belies these fantasies.

into calmer waters. From one point of view it scarcely matters. For if Hitler wins it is highly improbable that he himself will accept office.

There are men of the highest capacity who, although they have not openly joined his Party, are prepared to serve in a National Goverment formed under its auspices. For example, Dr. Schacht, one of the great central bankers of the world, is freely spoken of as a possible Finance Minister.

The points to bear in mind are two:

The first is that, whether it achieves power or not, the Nazi movement will profoundly influence German politics in the years that lie ahead.

The second is that if we want any more reparations we shall have to go to Berlin, with troops, to get them. As they won't be worth the paper they're printed on when we get there, it seems scarcely worthwhile.

This remarkable meeting lasted for over an hour. When Boothby asked Hitler about the Jews, 'I thought Hanfstaengl was going to faint, but only a flicker of irritation crossed his face. After a moment he said: "There will be no pogroms." I think, at the time, he probably meant it.'

Although Boothby was wrong about Hitler's immediate ambitions – and his later references to this crucial article carefully omitted the words 'For if Hitler wins it is highly improbable that he will himself accept office' – he was right on everything else, and particularly on Hitler's magnetic capacity to arouse passions; and in his article he quoted Rodin's comment on Bernard Shaw: '*M. Shaw ne parle très bien; mais il s'exprime avec une telle violence qu'il s'impose* [Mr Shaw does not speak very well; but he expresses himself with as much violence as is essential].'

This interview was in itself a personal coup, and one that impressed many people; his article was an example of Boothby's journalism at its best, and it was widely reported and quoted from. The *Buchan Observer* admiringly reproduced it in full. But in January 1932 public interest in Germany and in Hitler was not great in Britain, and Boothby's interview and article were quickly forgotten – but not by him.

On 22 January he also wrote to Churchill, who was convalescing in Nassau from his accident in New York:

Dear Winston

Many thanks for your cable. I am so relieved to hear you are now well on the road to recovery. But I fear it may be a tedious business, because you will not have begun to feel the full shock effects until quite recently.

I remember when I had my miserable little accident . . . I thought I had quite got over it until about three weeks later. I started not sleeping, and for a time my nerves went all to blazes.

The only thing to do is to take it easy for a bit, and I do hope you will. . . .

I have just got back from Germany, where I had a most interesting time.

They asked me to lecture in Hamburg and Berlin, and I had one audience of over eight hundred students, to whom I opened up on the values of democracy and personal liberty, as opposed to either Fascism, Communism, or the Roman Catholic Church!

They took it very well.

God intended them to be the docile and contented inhabitants of a series of bourgeois democratic states; but they were turned upside down by that filthy military clique and bogus Potsdam aristocracy.

Now they are in a hopeless mess. They have no flair for politics; and their parties are a mad jumble of conflicting forces and theories, based on institutions like the Trade Unions and the Catholic Church, which ought to be outside the business altogether.

But as a people they are tremendously formidable still, and I don't blame the French for being frightened.

· In Berlin I saw both Brüning and Hitler; and enclose an article I wrote for the *Evening Standard*, in case it should interest you. . . .

The two things that impressed me most were their workers' houses which are magnificent; and their orderly desperation.

I sat next to a very nice young chap at dinner – a partner in Wasserman's bank* – and he said the 'most hopeful' characteristic of the younger generation in Germany was their fundamental desperation. The older people were lost without a foothold. But his own generation had never known security. They were thankful for anything – especially a good meal – and ready for anything, because they never knew what the morrow would bring.

Another man, also at the dinner, was manager of a chemical factory which was going into liquidation. I asked him if he was depressed, and he said, 'I can never be depressed again. I was captured by the Russians in 1915. I spent nine months in Turkestan. Then I was sent to Siberia. I made enough money at woodwork to buy four horses and a sledge. I escaped and got to the Polish frontier in the winter of 1916/1917, where I was recaptured.

'Then I went to Vladivostok, and escaped again when the revolution came. I had to earn my living first under Kolchak, and under the Bolsheviks; and didn't get back here until 1920. After that I can't burst myself over liquidation of a chemical factory.' . . .

Brüning told me that he believed that the payment of reparations & international debts was fatal to the economic equilibrium of the world, and aggravated the currency difficulty: but that in any case no Chancellor who agreed to further payments would live for an hour in Germany. He pins his

---

*Wilhelm (Bill) Wasserman was a delightful German Jewish banker friend of Boothby's, who subsequently fled from Nazi Germany to the United States, where he established himself prosperously and was a regular host to Boothby. They remained close personal friends until Wasserman wrote his memoirs in the 1970s and sent a draft copy to Boothby, who was enraged by them, wrote a scalding letter of rebuke and contempt, and consigned his effusion to the incinerator. Wasserman had written at length about his own private life, which was not without incident, and Boothby's, but in the latter case got everything wrong. To be fair, Wasserman was a dying man when he wrote his lamentable and unpublished autobiography in his old age.

faith to a change in the French attitude after the election; and said he would
rather have the whole question shelved until the summer or autumn.

He seems to have succeeded in this.

But his outlook for the future is, on the face of it, unduly optimistic. . . .

Yours ever
Bob

Boothby returned from Germany 'depressed and oppressed by the
situation I found there, and also by the lunacy of our own financial policy'.
Having seen the appalling consequences of deflation in Germany, he
began to warn insistently of the perils of the same policies being urged on
ministers by the Bank of England. Boothby thought little of the Treasury
and even less of the Bank, and particularly Montagu Norman, in his view
the true author of Churchill's failure as Chancellor. On 25 April, in the
Commons, he denounced the Bank's strategy and the fact that it was
accountable to no one:

A statesman is judged by results. If his policy goes, he goes. It may be unfair, but
there is a kind of rough justice about it. Mr Montagu Norman, on the other hand,
is never called upon to explain or justify or defend his policy; and it is his policy
which has been carried on for the last ten years. Governments may come and
governments may go, but the Governor of the Bank of England goes on for ever.
It is a classic example of power without responsibility. . . . I do not ask for more,
at the moment, than an assurance that the policy of deflation which has brought
such terrible damage and brought such misery to this country is no longer to be
continued.

This was to be Boothby's principal theme not only in the 1930s – when
he ruefully saw the German economy transformed by Schacht exactly on
the lines he recommended – but for the rest of his life. At the time this
speech, again prominently reported, did not go down at all well in the City
of London, and there was much hostile comment about brash young men
impudently lecturing their elders. However, Beaverbrook, now a firm
friend and admirer, was much taken with it, writing on 1 May:

As a matter of history – when Bonar Law became Prime Minister he
inflated. Baldwin was his instrument, the Governor was his opponent. You
can see the process of inflation going on if you look at the Bank accounts of
that day. No Governor of the Bank dared oppose Bonar Law. He frightened Cunliffe's successors to death when he dismissed that nobleman from
his Governorship.

I think Cunliffe was your uncle perhaps. He was a hell of a bully.

Norman is consumed by vanity. He wants to get back to the GOLD
STANDARD in order to justify his past conduct.

Winston Churchill was Norman's tool. Churchill has a great brain. In

God's name why did he not use it when Norman persuaded him to bonus the City at the expense of the manufacturers and the working people? Why did he allow Norman to fling all those miners out of work?

Winston really did understand it. He asked me to talk it out one day with his Favourite in the Treasury, and in his presence. The Favourite told him that the Bank could not inflate. I explained at once the process of inflation to Winston. That genius understood. His Favourite should have been dismissed for deceiving him. He was not.

Boothby was so encouraged by being held so high in Beaverbrook's estimation that he asked him to give publicity to Baffy Dugdale's Zionist campaign, which he strongly supported, as did Churchill. However, Beaverbrook would not co-operate, writing to him on 30 June:

Thanks for your letter and enclosures.

But there is not a chance in the world. I would not even do it for Lady Diana Cooper.

All propaganda is kept out of the paper, except that put there by me, and as I have so much there is no room for anyone else. Mine is all on the Empire.

I don't give a damn for Austria; I hate France; I detested Germany as soon as they began attacking the equivalent of Presbyterianism. I never go abroad except with the purpose of renewing my hatred.

In June Boothby was commissioned by the *Sunday Dispatch* to cover the Lausanne international economic conference, whose only achievement was to confirm the death of reparations against Germany. By this time Brüning had been replaced by Franz von Papen, described by Boothby as 'looking like a well-groomed fox', Edouard Herriot represented France, and the British team consisted of MacDonald, Neville Chamberlain and Walter Runciman. Boothby's reports to his newspaper were lively, but nothing like as lively as his private reports to his mother and friends, in particular this one to Strachey:

My dear John

I had a good laugh out of this place. Arrived here on Thursday morning, and am leaving to-night. Ramsay commanded me to accompany him on one of his famous before breakfast lakeside walks. It was like taking Melba for a stroll after her farewell performance at Covent Garden.

I said – deliberately – that he looked very well, and this produced, immediately, the desired effect. 'To tell you the truth I am absolutely rotten.' Then a lot of stage work. Head in the hands, etc. Hardly ever slept without drugs. Awful strain. Especially having to do Chamberlain's work (a most frightful lie). Eyes giving way (they are much better). Heart giving way. Mind giving way. Doubted if he would carry on much longer.

He then proceeded to talk of the Hoover proposal [on reparations] as if it was done for the sole purpose of wiping his eye and of the French as if they had come for the sole purpose of teasing him.

He wailed and wailed about the Labour party and Conservative party and the Press and the weather and the House of Commons and the leakages from the French delegation (as if that was anything new), until I wondered whether to push him in the water and throw stones at him, or try to smother him with a handkerchief. What a man. Awful.

Breakfast followed with Ishbel [MacDonald]. 'Help yourself. . . .' At last Runciman arrived, pink, brisk, and competent.

'Runciman,' said MacDonald, 'the French leakages are worse than ever. I have three letters this morning from people prominent in the social world (I detected a gleam in Runciman's eye at this) which shows they have reached London. I am going to talk very seriously to Herriot about it.' I murmured 'give him a Georgic', but luckily it conveyed nothing.

The strange thing is that with all his vanity and pettiness and suspicion (he is now a *very* disagreeable man), he is amazingly good at this sort of show.

They all respect him, they are all rather frightened of him, and if this conference achieves anything at all (which I doubt), it will almost entirely be due to him. . . .

There was a grand incident over the Hoover proposal. All the journalists rushed over to Geneva, leaving MacDonald all alone here, without a limelight of any sort or kind.

Finally he could stand it no longer, and a telephone message was received in Geneva (where [Sir John] Simon was holding forth): 'Would the British press kindly return at once to Lausanne, as the Prime Minister had an important communication to make to them.' They wouldn't. Enough gossip for one letter.

. If I go into politics at all, I intend to model myself on Herriot. He is the real full bonhomme. A social democrat. Can't bear to see anyone unhappy. Cares chiefly for music and food. Is a funny man – tells funny stories funnily. Very sentimental. Cries on the slightest provocation. Is GIGANTIC. The most colossal stomach I have ever seen, with a watch chain a yard long across it. Dressed in a dirty old suit with a soft collar. Looks like a head waiter who has been out of a job for six months.

Believes in liberty and love.

My love to Celia.

> Yours ever
> Bob

He wrote, more decorously, to his mother:

After this talk [with MacDonald], I am more than ever thankful that I never had anything to do with this Government. It is a ramshackle concern, without character or theme. I must say that MacDonald has been very agreeable to me personally; and although I have said some things that he cannot have liked – among others that Snowden's speeches were noxious – he has taken it in good part. I am very sorry for him. He is melancholy and lonely. That is the fate of all suspicious people.

Before he went to Geneva, Boothby, in another strong denunciation of the Government and the Bank in the Commons on 9 May, echoing one he had just made in Fraserburgh, had said that 'Everyone knows that the chances of success at the Lausanne conference are so thin as to be negligible', and so it proved. He joined forces with Bracken and Aneurin Bevan to give the Finance Bill a rough time, and Walter Elliot, the Financial Secretary, was good-naturedly on the receiving end. Inevitably, there was a dramatic intervention about Russian purchases of Scottish herrings, ingeniously contrived and well received in East Aberdeenshire.

On his return Boothby attended a special dinner given by Churchill at Claridge's in honour of his American friend and adviser, Bernard Baruch. 'Mr Churchill', it was noted, 'was supported by his young henchmen Mr Brendan Bracken and Mr Robert Boothby.' It was at this dinner that Baruch suggested that Boothby should come to the United States, which he had only visited once, in 1925, to see the post-crash situation for himself and to observe the presidential campaign. Boothby accepted with alacrity and made plans to sail on 26 October, after completing his autumn constituency tour and speeches, which included one in Peterhead, where, in the presence of the Scottish Secretary, William Adamson, he denounced the English neglect of Scotland in the Commons and urged that the Scottish Grand Committee be moved to Edinburgh. This was hailed by the *Daily Express* as 'Mr Boothby Supports Devolution', which he certainly did not.

In 1925 the United States had been booming. Now, as Boothby wrote,

The wheels of industry had stopped; the banks had closed their doors; the Stock Exchange, having sold every share on the market, was like a morgue; and the number of unemployed was estimated (no one knew the exact figure) at twelve million. The collapse was total.

It was Germany all over again. Boothby found it intensely depressing, even frightening. But there was one remarkable moment:

On the evening of the Presidential election I dined in New York with Mr. Bernard Baruch. We were alone. As soon as dinner was over he put on his top hat and said, 'Now I think we will go and see Franklin.' We drove to the headquarters of the Democratic Party at the Hotel Biltmore. All was bustle and confusion. The tall, distinguished, and familiar figure of my host opened every door. We were at once taken up to a small room where Mr. Roosevelt sat at a table, smoking a cigarette, with Mrs. Roosevelt and about a dozen of his campaign managers. He greeted us warmly. I was astonished at his vigour and coolness. He looked as if he

Baby Bob with his mother

As a young child with
his father

Reluctant schoolboy

Undergraduate

Young politician

With Churchill on
budget day, 1927

M.P.s'. GOLFING HOLIDAY.—The Hon. Charles Baillie-Hamilton, Lady Dorothy Macmillan, Mr Robert Boothby, M.P., and Captain Harold Macmillan, M.P., on Gleneagles Golf Course.

A fatal meeting,
Gleneagles, 1928

Dorothy

Diana Boothby at
The French House,
1936

Boothby at The
French House, 1936

Noël Coward and Lady Boothby at The French House, 1936

Oswald Mosley (left) and John Strachey, c. 1930s

With Gardie and Lady Duff at Hatton Castle

Talking to East Aberdeenshire fishermen, 1940

had just returned from a holiday, instead of one of the most exhausting campaigns in electoral history. Suddenly the door was flung open. 'Greetings, Mr. President!' The Republicans had just conceded the victory. This was a moment. As I shook hands with him, the first foreigner to do so [as President], the smile that was to become famous throughout the civilised globe lit up his extraordinarily handsome features. There was no trace of apprehension. 'Well, gentlemen,' he said, 'everything seems to have gone according to plan.' Nothing was certain, except that we had entered a new era.

This account, written in 1946, is only marginally different to the one he cabled home at the time to the *Daily Express* in an article that was surprisingly optimistic:

I came over here expecting to find apprehension and dismay on all sides, but I have found a great deal of faith and optimism, and a wonderful readiness to scrap obsolete methods and ideas and adopt new ones. The American people yesterday gave a free hand to the party which they believe will do this.

Roosevelt made this impression on many people, but on reflection Boothby recognised the sheer scale of Roosevelt's problems and sent a somewhat gloomy account to Beaverbrook, who responded:

Thank you very much for your postcard and for the copy of your letter.

The postcard was a masterpiece of journalism. You put more misery into fewer words with greater effect than I have ever known before. The fellow who copied the New Testament on to the back of a postage stamp was only slightly your superior.

I find it all extremely interesting, and from my own knowledge of what is going on, I am convinced you are correct in your reading of things.

You think we must not default on the Debt. I wonder if you still think so. We have had some revelations in the last few days here. The Treasury says we can't pay – impossible. Chamberlain, MacDonald and Runciman all agreed. We were going to refuse. Even Norman was convinced. What do you say to that?

But that was all last week's stuff; what has happened since? MacDonald has lost his memory again. Norman has changed his mind. Chamberlain has lost his resolution. Thomas can't contemplate anyone not meeting his just obligations. These are the voices that prevail.

The Elder Statesmen (I mean Churchill and that lot) strike attitudes. They are determined that the young shall pay for the war, though they didn't have the luck to fight at Antwerp.

As for the press, the 'Times' and the 'Daily Herald' shudder at the consequences if we don't pay. The 'News Chronicle' is terrified by what will happen if we do pay. The 'Express' says we can't pay. It said that first, and I expect it will be left to say it last.

You say Roosevelt has no guts. Come over here, and tell me what you think about the innards of *our* great men!

Boothby's warming friendship with Beaverbrook was important to him at this time. When he became a full partner at Chase, Henderson and Tennant, Beaverbrook wrote delightedly that

I congratulate you on emerging now as a man of business. I am very glad. You will stand in the market place for a time. When you go to the Government you will have the experience behind you which has not been possessed by any Chancellor of the Exchequer in my time, excepting Bonar Law. Without exception, these ex-Chancellors became Ministers and afterwards sat in the market place. In other words, they got their City jobs as a result of their Westminster triumphs. I am hoping to see you soon. You know you are always welcome at Stornaway House.

However, Boothby's relations with Churchill were cooling. Churchill was hard at work on his biography of Marlborough and was obsessed with India, on which Boothby supported the Government. Boothby, with his emotional life increasingly fraught and complicated, was considerably more interested in national and international economic affairs, in which Churchill took no interest whatever. They shared a mutual contempt for the MacDonald Government, Churchill denouncing its Indian policy and Boothby its economic one, but although they remained close friends and much enjoyed each other's company, politically they were divergent. It took Hitler to bring them together again.

Boothby was a regular visitor to Germany. He later wrote:

I got the impression of a demoralised society, desperately trying to find a way out. Among the youth, homosexuality was rampant; and, as I was very good-looking in my twenties, I was chased all over the place, and rather enjoyed it. I used to go to the *Oktoberfest* in Munich every October to listen to operas, drink tankards of foaming *Lowenbrau* beer, sing in the beer-cellars with burly Bavarians in *lederhosen* and Tyrolese hats with what looked like shaving-brushes, eat one of the thousand chickens roasting in the open on spits, and ride on the Big Dipper. I loved it all. The cold sparkling air; the lakes, especially Stahnberg; Ludwig's castles; a walk in the Englische Garten; a visit to Nymphenberg. Not until 1932 did the shadow of Hitler begin to make its presence felt. I pushed it aside.

Boothby had been virtually the first politician from any country who had publicly warned about Hitler. Also, in 1928, after a dinner with the Thyssen brothers, he had been greatly attracted by their proposal of the formation of a European coal, iron and steel cartel in which Britain and Germany would take a leading part – the brainchild of the assassinated Walter Rathenau – and had advocated it in a speech in the Commons and in an article entitled 'An Economic Locarno'. Although the press, particularly Beaverbrook, who had not yet turned against Europe in favour of his quest for the Utopia of Empire Free Trade, praised Boothby's initiative, it was greeted with hostility by the British coal-owners, and neither Baldwin nor Churchill demonstrated much interest. Rebuffed, the Thyssens turned elsewhere – and found Hitler.

During his 1933 visit, after Hitler had come to power and taken Germany out of the League of Nations, Boothby found a new and unpleasant atmosphere. As he drove round the country he saw more and more signs outside villages reading 'Jews forbidden here', and swastikas everywhere. Even the music was appropriated and, in Boothby's words 'Bayreuth was turned, or distorted, into a Nazi shrine.'

In his old age, in one of the most vivid passages in his second volume of memoirs, Boothby tried to recapture that atmosphere:

In order to understand the Germany of the 1930s, you had to go there often, love it, hate it, live it and *feel it*. All this I did. You had to know a great deal about Wagner, homosexuality, racism and anti-semitism, and the connection between them; and to realise the magnitude of the ferment to which, in combination, they gave rise. The way in which Hitler managed to impart his own hysteria to the vast audiences he addressed was not only miraculous but terrifying. . . . As the fibre of the German people strengthened, under the impetus of Hitler, that of the French weakened. Lloyd George once said to me that the life-blood of France had been drained at Verdun. Churchill failed to realise that it had not been restored. Laval did.

Thoroughly alarmed by what he had seen and heard, Boothby returned to London to impart his concerns, but no one, not even Churchill or Lloyd George, was much interested. The mood of the country was strongly pacifist, especially the slowly reviving Labour Party under George Lansbury; a sensational Labour victory in East Fulham had been interpreted, probably wrongly as most by-elections are, as a strong endorsement of this policy and a clear warning against rearmament. What particularly appalled Boothby was the sheer ignorance of the major British politicians about what was actually going on in Germany. Churchill only gradually began to take an interest, but this was when the Germans began to rearm seriously, and his dominant concern was less about the character of the Nazi regime than air superiority. He overrated both the French army and the Royal Navy, and was still preoccupied with India.

In November 1933 Boothby sailed again for the United States, as usual mixing business with pleasure, once again in the process of becoming engaged to a beautiful heiress and having second thoughts – particularly when Dorothy heard of it. He paid for the visit with a number of newspaper articles, which were, as usual, very shrewd and prescient –

The Good Boothby at its best. After seeing the situation at first hand in Washington, Boothby expressed serious doubts about the way Roosevelt was beginning the New Deal:

It is impossible not to admire his courage. He assumed power in an hour of crisis and collapse. Everything was thrown into his lap. Every section of the community, not excepting Wall Street, turned to him for guidance, leadership, for salvation. He shouldered every burden with a smile, and has been shouldering them, with an avidity that is almost disquieting, ever since.

It was this concentration of power and influence, which for most of the New Dealers was a time of unparalleled excitement, that worried him. 'As far as I can see,' he wrote, 'the inevitable result must be an experiment in state capitalism on an unprecedented scale.' Under the National Recovery Act passed by a frightened and bemused Congress, Roosevelt had given himself almost dictatorial powers and, contrary to his pre-election promises, was centralising virtually every activity in Washington. Also, the results were bound to be inflationary. 'The dangers of the situation are obvious. On the credit side there is the immense natural wealth of the country, the abundant vitality of the people, a faith in Mr. Roosevelt which is not yet on the wane, and a rising export trade.'

Roosevelt was never one of Boothby's heroes, particularly when the policy was abruptly reversed in 1937 and the deflationists took over again, which resulted in a European panic about gold and a major slump – except in Germany. He did not think much of his foreign policy – such as it was – either. His closest American friends – particularly Harrison and Mona Williams, with whom he regularly stayed in their mansion on Long Island – viewed Roosevelt with scepticism, and so did Boothby, who once asked a leading Democrat if Roosevelt had any deep sense of purpose about anything, to which he got the reply, 'Only one; to remain in office.' Boothby found this not only immoral but incomprehensible. In public life he was a man of principle, genuinely uninterested in office. This gave him so much of his attraction, but it was another profound character difference with Churchill, who, like Roosevelt, craved power and was bitterly frustrated at being deprived of it.

Boothby's reputation, and it was becoming a considerable one, was based upon his economic writings and speeches, and their effect was beginning to be seen. Under Chamberlain the first, if tentative, steps were being taken towards a more expansionist economic policy; Boothby wanted more of it, especially in housing and agriculture. On this front he had clearly won the intellectual battle, and events in Germany and America were proving him right. The fact that huge housing schemes in Germany were being financed with British money was a further infuriating fact to which he often drew attention, and very effectively. He kept

up his battles on behalf of his beloved herring fishermen and still wrote
extensively on economic questions. But these now became subsidiary to a
new obsession.

He returned from America in a mood of considerable depression. In
October 1933 he had made the first of many speeches to his constituents
warning them of the perils of pacifism and military weakness. It was
received politely, but in East Aberdeenshire, as everywhere in Britain,
local concerns came first.

Although Boothby had travelled considerably since his election to the
House of Commons, and had a far better personal knowledge of the
situation in Europe – and particularly in Germany, France and Italy – than
most MPS, including Churchill, he had not intervened seriously in foreign
affairs debates. Therefore, when he wrote to Baldwin in January 1934
to complain about the Government, it was confined to the domestic
economic situation:

Dear Mr. Baldwin

I don't want to bother you with a long letter, but I am so troubled by the
present course of events that I feel bound to tell you, as leader, of my
uneasiness & apprehension.

I occupy a more or less detached position in Scottish politics these days,
and have had many recent opportunities of estimating public opinion at
gatherings of a non-partisan character.

There is little enthusiasm for the national government; and I am firmly
convinced we are now moving towards a very considerable electoral
debacle.

This seems to be due

1. To the absence of any political philosophy, or theme, or policy
adequate to the needs of the times; and

2. To the lack of constructive measures, and a reactionary tendency on
the part of the Government which has become apparent lately.

E.G. Ineffective housing policy; continued and unwarranted retardation
of public works; and, last but not least, the financial provisions of the
Unemployment Insurance Bill.

I don't share the views of some regarding the necessity for state
'planning' of industry, although I think that some guiding principles have to
be laid down to enable us to deal with certain industries of national
importance along modern scientific lines.

But I do jib at starving the unemployed.

And that is what it amounts to in some districts at the present time.

If the Government is to prosper, the people *must* be given something in
which to believe.

But my immediate purpose in writing to you is simply to say that if something isn't done to mitigate the sufferings of the unemployed either on this Bill or in the Budget I personally could not go on supporting the Government.

It isn't fair to ask people to vote down the proposal to give an extra shilling to the first two dependent children, and vote for the purchase of a Bible which no one can read.

I have written in this sense to the Prime Minister; and apologise for the outburst.

Yours sincerely
Robert Boothby

There is no record of any reply; this would have been characteristic.

The trouble with Boothby's position was that, with a few exceptions, he considered the Conservative Party as 'rotten to the core', terrified of the possibility that the Communists would seize their properties and wealth, and applauding Hitler and Mussolini as bastions against this menace. Under the grip of the Government Chief Whip, David Margesson, no dissent was tolerated, and the Party as a whole was united in its deep distrust of Churchill – a sentiment encouraged by Churchill's prolonged India campaign, one of the greatest misjudgments of his career. Boothby's contempt for the majority of his colleagues was fully merited. 'You have no idea how awful they were,' Eden, whose own star was rapidly rising at the Foreign Office, once remarked of the pre-war Conservative Party to his PPS, Robert Carr, in the early 1950s. Boothby may have had glowing notices in the press and was becoming revered in his constituency, and seen by many – perhaps too many – as a future prime minister, but the general estimate of him in the Parliamentary Party was low.

So far as the bulk of the Party was concerned, Boothby was not only a maverick but he kept bad political company. It was characteristic of Boothby to see a kindred spirit in the fiery young Aneurin Bevan and his future wife, Jennie Lee, with whom he became close friends. After Bevan's death in 1960, Jennie wrote to Boothby that 'Nye truly loved you', and the feeling was warmly reciprocated. Indeed, when one looked at the list of Boothby's political friends, it was in the view of the Political Faithful a litany of the Unsound – Lloyd George, Churchill, Keynes, Leo Amery, Harold Nicolson (who had recovered from his New Party madness, as had Strachey), Brendan Bracken and that Welsh Communist Bevan! Boothby still believed that Baldwin was the only hope, but Baldwin was now a shadow of his former self; although on special occasions he could, and did, rouse himself, the old energy had gone for ever. MacDonald drifted around in a haze; only Neville Chamberlain seemed to have any ideas and dynamism, but expenditure on rearmament featured low in his priorities and his experience of foreign affairs was virtually nil.

Boothby's first major intervention in foreign affairs in the Commons was on 21 December 1933, and was not designed to enhance his position in the Party. He said that British influence on the Continent was negligible 'because we have not got a foreign policy':

Society is not likely to abandon the use of force in our time. If we concede the necessity for the use of force in a society of individuals, it is surely logical to concede the use of force to a society of nations. But we must arm the law, and not the litigants. Are we prepared to use force on behalf of the collective organisation of peace? The alternative seems to me to be the final collapse of the League of Nations, followed by individual rearmament, and ultimate war. I doubt whether Germany would ever attack the democracies of the world if she knew that, if she had recourse to war and aggression, she would have them marshalled against her. But do not let us minimise the dangers.

Early in 1934 Boothby revisited Russia. Contrary to his 1926 hopes, Stalin's ferocious control was seen everywhere. Boothby tried to sell Scottish herrings to the Commissar of Trade without success. He found the situation ghastly and depressing, and had to endure another long and boring military procession in Red Square. To his mother he wrote that 'If I lived in this country I should be on Stalin's side – if only to survive.' Most of the Russian leaders he met thought they were on his side, but virtually all were later killed by him. Boothby still believed that, for all the horrors of the Stalinist terror, it was politically dangerous to treat the Soviet Union as a pariah, on which subject he found Churchill still obdurately hostile.

After a cheerful visit to the Clark-Kerrs in Stockholm, Boothby returned to a still complacent Britain, but Churchill was beginning to stir uneasily. He had many sources of information about the alarming increases in German rearmament and the nature of the Nazi regime, but he did not forget that it was Boothby who had first sounded the alarm about Hitler when he had been distracted by his futile campaign against the Government of India Bill, which was, mercifully, now approaching its conclusion. Bracken was also convinced from his sources that Britain was frighteningly weak militarily, and that the Government was blindly indifferent to what was happening. In fact, although they did not know it, concern was rising, particularly in the Service Ministries, although not in the House of Commons or in the Conservative Party. As Churchill reached the final stages of his lamentable Indian misadventure, and cast his eyes upon Europe, and especially Germany, his relationship with Boothby warmed again. Politically, they became inseparable and saw a great deal of each other. Sadly, neither kept a diary, and Bracken's papers were destroyed on his orders after his death. Their actual correspondence was not great, but Boothby has told me that hardly a day passed without telephone calls or discussions in the House, or in Bracken's house in North Street (later called, on his initiative, Lord North Street), or in Churchill's London flat. Amery and Austen Chamberlain, who fully shared Churchill's concern, although his half-brother Neville did not, were also part of this wholly informal Conservative group, which Macmillan was shortly to join.

Boothby was watching the air pageant at Hendon with Philip Sassoon on 30 June 1934 when word came to them of momentous and terrible events in Germany. Hitler had struck ferociously at his enemies, and the Röhm massacre was the only topic of conversation at Trent that evening. As Boothby later wrote:

One thing, we all agreed, had emerged from the shocking and squalid events of the day. The Nazis had been shown up for what in fact they were – unscrupulous and bloodthirsty gangsters. In future they should be treated as such. How true; and how right were our conclusions. Alas! in other and more influential quarters, a different view was taken.

On 7 February Churchill had made the first of his Commons speeches on the European situation on air defences, what he later described as an 'unavailing protest', and on the 17th he made another, which concluded, 'The Romans had a maxim, "Shorten your weapons and lengthen your frontiers." But our maxim seems to be "Diminish your weapons and increase your obligations." Aye, and diminish the weapons of your friends.' The Air Estimates introduced in March 1934 contained provision for only four more squadrons, involving a cost of £130,000 in the first year; the total estimate was for £20 million. Churchill protested at this inadequacy, and Baldwin assured him and the House that the Government 'will see to it that in air strength and air power this country shall no longer be in a position inferior to any country within striking distance of these shores'. The Labour and Liberal Parties, however, after the Röhm purges, moved a motion of censure on the Government denouncing even these modest proposals, Attlee stating that 'We deny the proposition that an increased British air force will make for the peace of the world, and we reject altogether the claim to parity.' This was the sort of thing that Churchill and his few friends were up against, and which was to continue until virtually the eve of the catastrophe in 1940.

Baldwin, noticing that Boothby and Churchill were again seeing a great deal of each other and making speeches on European matters that were becoming markedly similar, took the occasion to warn his old friend, Sir Robert Boothby, that Churchill was 'a bad guide for youth', a warning that he duly passed on to his son, who ignored it.

In the *Daily Mail* in particular Boothby called for strong British rearmament ('we are a third-rate military power, and every nation knows it'), denounced pacifism and wishful thinking, and emphasised what the new German realities were. By September he was writing that

War will come in two or three years if certain problems are not tackled, if Germany is ready for it, and if the world remains as bankrupt of real statesmanship as it has been since the war . . . wholesale political butchery without trial and the bombardment of working men, women and children in tenement houses – these are terrible and shocking events. If for a moment we give the impression that we are indifferent to them then civilisation will indeed tremble.

In October he made his regular visit to Germany. The situation was even more grim than in the previous year, and Boothby was haunted by the continuing beauty of the country and the oppressive atmosphere. 'Why,' he wrote, 'when life could be so delicious, should humanity, with masochistic perverseness, deliberately turn it into hell?' On his return he wrote a detailed account which he circulated to selected friends, including Churchill, drawing attention to the fact that 'a new and formidable figure has arisen. This is [Heinrich] Himmler, the head of the Secret Police.' While he noted that Hitler personally did not appear to be popular, his real power was greater than before as the army backed him. 'No attempt is made to deny or conceal the fact that Germany is rearming on a very large scale. . . . But I don't want to paint too sombre a picture. For the next three years at least there is, in my opinion, no real danger of war. That gives us all a breathing space.'

But what he had seen – including Hermann Göring devour an enormous amount of food and drink at an adjoining table that 'made me feel, for the first and last time in my life, an ascetic' – had further alarmed him, and on 24 October, at Strichen, he again spelt out his concern to his constituents. The issue, he told them, was whether Britain was prepared to fight for freedom and liberty, or to submit to tyranny and force.

This did not come as a surprise to his constituents, but then Boothby took on an audience outside East Aberdeenshire. He was invited to address the annual Armistice Day rally of ex-servicemen in Corstophine, in recognition of his strong Edinburgh family connection, and in the presence not only of his parents but of the widow of Lord Haig. They expected 'a nice innocuous sermon', on the usual lines, but what they got was this:

Those who gave their lives in the war did so to save freedom and to gain peace. But today tyranny has regained the upper hand in Europe, and the danger of war is as great as in 1914.

The cream of Britain's manhood was killed in the last war, and those who survived were never allowed to play any part in the rebuilding of Europe. The result is that there is little but brute force left.

Today Germany is governed by a group of able and ruthless men, who have persuaded the German people that they can never become great again except through armed force.

I tell you they are rearming. And I say this – that if we go on as we are today, in a year or eighteen months' time they will be in a position to strike a vital blow at the very heart of the British Empire.

It is not too late to save the situation if only we learn the lessons of the past. The British Empire still stands for the things those men died to win – freedom and peace. But I would not care to share the responsibility of those who today are exposing us to mortal peril.

In relation to the facts of the present situation our air force is pitifully inadequate. If we are strong and resolute, and if we pursue a wise and constructive foreign policy, we can still save the world from war. But if we simply drift along, never taking the lead, and exposing the heart of our Empire to an attack that might pulverise it in a few hours, then everything that makes life worth living will be swept away, and then indeed we shall have finally broken faith with those who lie dead in the fields of Flanders.

This was received in shocked silence, 'except for faint cries of "No! No!" from Lady Haig, who was sitting behind me'. The five clergymen, who represented different denominations and who were on the platform, were visibly upset. Boothby received virtually no applause, and no one wanted to talk to him, let alone shake hands with him. The audience of nearly two thousand was appalled. Boothby later wrote that, 'As I walked [to Beechwood] in sombre solitude, I said to myself, "We are going to betray them all." We did.'

One who agreed with him – as few did – was Noël Coward, about whom Boothby wrote many years later in a letter to Coward's close friend and biographer, Cole Lesley:

> I myself only touched a small segment of his life; but it was one that cut pretty deep. He cared about the political policies we pursued in the Thirties more passionately than anything else. Not unnaturally this bored the theatrical world. But he used to come over to The French House quite often and talk with me, alone, into the deep watches of the night. He knew, as I did, that it was the finish.

However, Boothby's tenth anniversary as MP for East Aberdeenshire was celebrated in fine style in Maud, with Walter Elliot slyly remarking that 'Mr Boothby's able and independent criticisms are respected on both sides of the House, and more than once his support has been of the utmost importance to the Government.' This went down well in Maud, who appreciated the jest, as did Boothby.

There was also some relevance in the tribute paid by Mr A. J. Irvine, the prospective Liberal candidate for Kincardine and West Aberdeen, who told his executive that Liberals should 'think twice' before contesting East Aberdeenshire. 'Of course', said Mr Irvine, 'the situation is complicated by the fact that Mr Boothby might join the forces of the Left at any moment. He obviously would like to. Mr Boothby has more ideas in his head than all the other Aberdeen MPs put together.'

When Parliament reassembled on 28 November, Churchill moved an amendment to the Loyal Address – also signed by Amery, Admiral Sir Roger Keyes, Lord Winterton and Boothby – that 'the strength of our national defences, and especially of our air defences, is no longer adequate to secure the peace, safety and freedom of Your Majesty's faithful subjects'. In a full and attentive House Churchill claimed that Germany was rapidly approaching parity in air power with Britian and that by 1936 it would have superiority. This Baldwin strongly denied, to general relief. Churchill was unconvinced, as was Boothby, who strongly supported Churchill and denounced Labour and Liberal pacifists, declaring that 'we are not war-mongers. We are trying as best as we can to secure the peace of Europe and the world.' Turning on the Chancellor of the Exchequer, Neville Chamberlain, who had just made a gloomy major speech in Manchester on the nation's financial difficulties, Boothby urged that

consideration of finance should not stand in the way of a cautious, moderate and unhysterical rearmament programme. It is quite obviously the duty of any British Government, in face of the present situation, to secure the safety and security, so far as it lies in their power, of this crowded island. It is no good telling me or anyone else in the House that to leave this island defenceless in the face of Europe in its present condition is conducive to the maintenance of peace. It is not. It is one of the greatest menaces to the peace of the world. . . . If the people of Britain in the next ten years who believe in freedom are not prepared in the last resort to defend it, freedom will assuredly perish in this world at the hands of those who do not believe in it.

But the almost universal judgment was that, although Churchill and Boothby had made impressive and powerful speeches, Baldwin's assurances had eclipsed their alarmist warnings. There was general agreement that there was nothing much to worry about, although Churchill, Amery, Boothby and Bracken continued to worry about it a great deal, virtually to the exclusion of other political concerns.

After Christmas Boothby held public meetings at Rosehearty, Fraserburgh and Peterhead. Fishing, agriculture and unemployment benefit were the main topics. He urged the supply of cheap fresh milk for children, criticised the Government for not adopting a bold policy of capital development, and called for a strong and constructive foreign policy to prevent war. His meeting in the Rescue Hall, Peterhead, was standing-room only. One commentator reported that

The heckling was prolonged and intensive. It was good-humoured and not in any sense hostile to Mr. Boothby as an individual; but its chief characteristic was the persistent and logical way in which most of the questioners directed their inquiries to practical issues, affecting legislation past, present, and to come. Needless to say Mr Boothby kept his end up, but so also did the hecklers, and at the close of the evening honours were even. . . . He has never been a keen Party man, and during the life of the National Government he has maintained an attitude of independence and critical detachment, while working hard and incessantly for the special needs of his own constituents. His breadth of mind, and readiness to face both sides of an issue, is respected by his opponents, and when the various election programmes have been outlined he can be depended upon to take a frank and fearless personal line, at whatever cost may be involved to his own political future.

In *The Times* on 15 January 1935 Boothby again deplored the over-cautious attitude of the Government on public works, particularly in the north, and especially on housing. Their policies and statements were incoherent:

Sir Kingsley Wood obviously believes in and practises constructive expenditure. Mr [Neville] Chamberlain does not. Mr Runciman continues to extol the merits of expanding production and international trade. But Mr Elliot tells us that the only hope for the future lies in the limitation of production and 'economic autarcky'. Now Mr Baldwin, with Mr Runciman's ardent support, informs us that the next election is to be 'a fight against Socialism'. I hope not. It will be a worse slogan than 'Safety First' from the point of view of winning votes. Incidentally, what does the Prime Minister [MacDonald] think of this clarion call on the part of his colleagues to action against Socialism? It is a subject in which at one time he took quite a keen interest.

The only hope to my mind lies in the production of a courageous and constructive economic policy. And the most alarming feature of the present situation is that nobody appears to be even thinking about it. For the country is demanding action. And if the people do not get it from the present Government they will turn elsewhere, with results both disastrous and unnecessary.

On 29 January in the House Boothby denounced the 'terrible poverty' among fishermen and their wives, and said that the Government was destroying the fishing population of Scotland. 'The Prime Minister used to make political capital out of the fact that he was brought up among these poor fisher people of Scotland. He has never raised a finger on their behalf.' The *Daily Telegraph* reported his 'scathing language' prominently:

Mr Boothby, young, dark, and indignant, flashed into the already heated atmosphere and declared trenchantly that in parts of his constituency there had been an average reduction in allowances of 6s 11d per household per week. . . . Reductions, he said, in the neighbourhood of which he spoke, ranged from 2s 6d to 18s 6d per week. 'That kind of thing cannot be tolerated.'

After his assault on MacDonald, Labour MPs called for him to come, on which Boothby said, 'I think the Prime Minister should be here. On the facts as I have received them the new administration is brutal. I can use no other words.' The press reported his speech very prominently, nationally and locally.

In a Labour motion of censure on 14 February, he called for national leadership: 'The country has not had the leadership it deserves.' One report said that 'Mr Boothby's speech was one of the best in the debate, and incidentally one of the best in his parliamentary career. He created a fine impression on the crowded House.' The Conservatives were, once again, incensed.

Randolph Churchill, Winston's wayward son, convulsed the Conservative hierarchy by standing as an Independent, anti-Government Conservative in a by-election in Wavertree, Liverpool. It was a fairly mad venture, and it ensured a Conservative defeat, but his father supported him and Boothby described Randolph's large vote as evidence of a widespread demand for 'a definite and coherent line of policy. If this demand remains for much longer unanswered, apathy and disruption in the ranks of the Government's supporters can scarcely be avoided. Because there will be nothing tangible to support.'

On 12 March, immediately after the announcement of conscription in Germany, Boothby spoke in the Commons in the debate on the Defence White Paper. He quoted Stresemann's words to Robert Bruce Lockhart: 'The youth of Germany, that we might both have won for peace, we have lost. That is my tragedy and your crime.' In a strong defence of the League, and an attack on Labour and Liberals, he said that

If those who believe in collective security through the League of Nations, and in the freedom of the individual, are not prepared in the last resort to defend their belief with force, assuredly they will be overwhelmed by those who do not believe in those things, and who do believe in force: and then the civilisation that we have known, for what it is worth, will be swept away.

MacDonald, for so long the object of Boothby's scorn and despair, made way for Baldwin as Prime Minister, once again. But this was no longer the Baldwin that Boothby had once admired, although he still liked him. 'He was too old, too tired, too bored,' Boothby later remarked. It was not at all an inaccurate portrait.

Boothby had married Diana Cavendish in March, and his new wife made her first visit as Mrs Boothby to the constituency in May, when they stayed at Hatton Castle. 'By her grace and charm of manner Mrs Boothby has quite won over the slow-to-praise folks of Buchan,' the *Buchan Observer* enthused.

She thought the circumstances hilarious, because the principal purpose was for Boothby to address the Salvation Army's meeting at the Rescue Hall in Peterhead on the occasion of the Jubilee of King George V. The editor of the *Buchan Observer* knew his man when he solemnly remarked on Boothby's courage in presiding over such a gathering: 'One of Mr Boothby's most admirable traits is his willingness to undergo new experiences for the sake of increasing his first-hand knowledge of men and affairs,' rating this one even braver than his night aboard a Peterhead drifter. Boothby first told his audience how much he loathed night travel from London and that

the only organisation in the world for which I would do that is the Salvation Army (*applause*). I have long believed it to be the greatest single institution in the world. When the time comes, as assuredly it will come, when I am absolutely down and out, I shall come to the Salvation Army and I know that I shall not turn to them in vain (*laughter and applause*).

His theme was freedom and liberty:

Tyranny is abroad. We have seen the rise in other countries – the mushroom rise, I might say – of governments that do not believe at any point in the value of the individual and individual liberty. . . . We must be prepared to defend and fight for the things we most passionately believe in.

On 15 October, at Rothienorman, he said that

If the peace of the world is to be preserved Britain should rearm intensively during the next two or three years. . . . The real problem to be solved is whether the world is to be governed by law or by force. I hate force in any shape or form, and that is why I hate Fascism and Communism, because they depend for their existence upon force. That is why I hate what Italy is doing today. If Italy was to get away with what she is doing, it would mean the end of the reign of international law and the end of the League of Nations. . . . But Italy is not the only problem. There is the problem of Germany. They are arming, and have been rearming for the last two years on a gigantic scale. So far as an air force is concerned they are far ahead of this country. Tomorrow they could blow London to hell and we could not stop them. So long as this country is in a position of virtually defenceless impotence against such a formidable menace as the mighty armed German nation will be in the next two years, there is cause for the gravest possible anxiety. It is imperative that at the next general election there should be returned to power a National Government that will build up a strong navy and air force, which is vital if peace is to be preserved – otherwise, we might find ourselves involved in a war which would finally shatter and destroy civilisation.

One of the problems of those Conservatives who were becoming deeply concerned about the European situation in the summer of 1935 was the ambivalence of many of them about Mussolini. There were those, who included the vehemently anti-German Sir Robert Vansittart, the Permanent Under-Secretary at the Foreign Office, who regarded Nazi Germany as the real threat and thought that nothing serious should be done to alienate the Italians, whose large modern navy was causing the Admiralty considerable concern in the Mediterranean. Churchill, who had been impressed by Mussolini, shared this view, and Boothby's love of Italy coloured his attitudes also, but not as badly. Both were far more indignant about the Anglo-German Naval Agreement, which, as Boothby bitterly remarked, 'set the seal of British approval upon the German denunciation of Versailles'. It also greatly angered the French and the Russians, who were not consulted.

With a general election approaching, which was clearly going to be a considerably more difficult one for the Conservatives than the rout of 1931, a wholly unexpected event was a speech by the new Foreign Secretary, Samuel Hoare, to the League in Geneva in September pledging a policy of 'ready and collective resistance to all acts of unprovoked aggression'. Mussolini responded in October by attacking Abyssinia; the British retaliated by advocating economic sanctions. At this point Baldwin called the general election.

Boothby was again opposed by the gallant Fred Martin. In his election address he wrote:

My views on foreign affairs are, I think, very well known in the constituency. I am a strong supporter of the League of Nations.

I believe in the collective application of economic, but not military, sanctions to an aggressor. And I think that in the present state of the world our own country should have adequate defensive forces.

I am amazed at the truculence of so many so-called 'pacifists' who are always howling for the disarmament of this country, and then, when a crisis arises, demanding the most extreme measures. They are the people who land you in a war with inadequate forces.

For my part, I would never go to war except in self-defence. And I believe that if we are reasonably strong no one will dare to attack us.

This was an exceptionally lively campaign, with Boothby suffering the experience of being howled down again in Peterhead, which was entirely his fault: he had unwisely said at Strichen that there was not enough heckling. Diana had even had to have a police escort to the meeting. The key moment in Peterhead was when Boothby roared above the tumult that 'every vote cast for a Socialist means one for war' and then continued: 'Shout me down if you like. It will only do me good. We are fighting for democracy, and you are the scum who make democracy impossible.' He later said that he had only been referring to the hecklers, but the audience was enraged and the meeting was abandoned. Boothby said that he would return to Peterhead, and Martin made an urgent public appeal for calm, saying that 'Mr Boothby, whose gifts and qualities I personally admire, is entitled to a courteous hearing.' He had one on the 13th before an audience, with overflows, of over a thousand. One reporter wrote that 'for an hour and a half he gave a demonstration of fierce concentration which bordered on the uncanny'. But his majority was reduced to 3,121 (12,748 to 9,627), a tribute to two exceptionally popular and respected candidates.

Overall, the Conservatives had a comfortable victory. Two unexpected, but to Boothby very welcome, new colleagues were Harold Nicolson and Alan Herbert, Nicolson being elected as National Labour Member for Leicester, and Herbert as an Independent for the two-member Oxford University, both bringing a welcome addition of wit and erudition to the House of Commons. In 1937 Herbert was joined by Arthur Salter, a former national and international civil servant and university professor, who would develop into one of the Government's most trenchant critics, and an admirer and close friend of Boothby's. Macmillan, safely returned for Stockton again, was entering his period of most acute disagreement with the Government's economic policies and current Conservative philosophy, culminating in the publication of *The Middle Way*, a powerful Keynesian polemic which took forward the arguments of *Industry and the State*, and in his resignation of the Conservative Whip in protest at the Government's seeming indifference to unemployment. He was also developing profound misgivings about defence and foreign policy, on which, again, he was very much on Boothby's side, although not as publicly identified as Boothby was with Churchill.

Of their generation, the careers of Eden at the Foreign Office and Duff Cooper as Secretary of State for War prospered, and they were far ahead of Boothby and Macmillan in position and prominence. Boothby was never quite sure about Eden, who seemed rather too good to be true, but his intelligence and knowledge of foreign affairs were obvious. Duff Cooper was an exceptional speaker, always delivering his Army Estimates without a note, but his reputation was affected when he wrote and published an admiring biography of Haig, which had a mixed reception and was savaged by Basil Liddell Hart in *The Times*. No one seems to have thought it odd that a Cabinet minister in a key post – or what should have been – had the time to research and write a major lengthy biography.

What worried Boothby and Macmillan most of all was Baldwin. MacDonald's last premiership would have been laughable were it not for the national and international situation. When Baldwin had taken over the premiership in May 1935, it had seemed a significant improvement; it was, but Baldwin's total lack of interest in foreign affairs was now combined with the lethargy of advancing years. He had won the election principally because he reassured people. He gave no indication that he had any strategy, either at home or abroad; like the vast majority of his countrymen, all he asked for was a quiet life.

Hardly had the new ministerial arrangements been announced – with Churchill, Amery, Boothby and the other critics studiously omitted – than the Government was plunged into a major crisis. Hoare went to Paris to see the French Foreign Minister, Pierre Laval, and the resultant Hoare–Laval Pact in effect consigned the greatly suffering Abyssinians, whose ordeal was arousing intense sympathy in Britain, to their aggressors. The news leaked, there was a storm of outrage, and Hoare was swiftly sacrificed, being replaced by Eden.

Churchill was abroad, and his friends – including Boothby – advised him not to return. In any event, the crisis itself was so short that the dissidents did not have to do very much. And they were still divided among themselves as to whether it was wise to do or say anything that would make a German–Italian Axis more likely. Appeasement was not then a word in common use, but it was already becoming clear that there was a significant number of foreign affairs specialists and politicians who were prepared to appease Mussolini, and that Hoare's venture had not been an aberration, as his speedy political resurrection was to demonstrate.

Boothby's public reactions to the Hoare–Laval Pact were much stronger than Churchill's, describing it as 'one of the most discreditable documents ever issued in the name of the British people'. Writing in the *New Statesman* on 4 January 1936, he pointed out that the lesson was to strengthen the economic and military strength of the League

with overpowering international force. The only alternative seems to me to be a war of final destruction within the next five years. To abandon Abyssinia at this juncture would be to destroy the League, and to give the 'All Clear' signal to Hitler for 1937. It was infernal impudence and hypocrisy on our part (especially after the moral song-and-dance we had put up for four months) suddenly to urge the Emperor to dismember his country for the exclusive benefit of Italy.

The *Manchester Guardian* commented that 'To new Members this may have seemed a surprising contribution from the Conservative benches, but they will soon learn that Mr Boothby cannot abide ready-to-wear

Party garments.' What was interesting was that Boothby was one of the first to appreciate that it was not possible to differentiate between dictators who were also aggressors, and that it was the authority of the League and the principle of collective security which were being fatally eroded. He argued that to reward Mussolini's aggression and the brutality of his methods would send the clearest of signals to others – as it duly did. He also argued, in the Commons – most notably in a speech on 25 February, which was highly critical of both Baldwin and Eden – and in the press, that feeble economic sanctions were worse than none at all, and that the key would be oil sanctions. From this, in spite of Eden's efforts, the French shrank; so did others.

One factor in Boothby's outspokenness at this time, and Churchill's total quiescence, was that the latter had not given up hope of a return to the Government, now that the India issue was out of the way. In this course he was fully justified. Fine speeches from the backbenches are no substitute for the reality of power, and few politicians craved power as avidly as Churchill did. Boothby not only understood this, but actively urged Churchill to be cautious, also believing that his return was inevitable.

Boothby's concerns were different. A Canon Wilkinson wrote of him in the *Glasgow Evening News* warmly praising him, but stating, truthfully, that 'his intellectual vision is too keen, his sympathies too wide, his honesty too sensitive to be welded to half-truths, to obtain office'. In that Conservative Government, this was only too true.

During the spring and summer of 1936 Boothby found nothing that the Government did was of any worth. Its agricultural, fishing and housing policies were lamentable, and it was scandalous that the Scottish death rate was so high. On 19 May he accused the Government of doing more for the colonies than for the British people, and that the new housing projects in Scotland had 'a hideous monotony and drab ugliness', particularly in Edinburgh. He was, again, absolutely right, but on 18 July, after another assault on the Government's agricultural policies, Walter Elliot turned on him in the House, saying that he 'has never fed a beast, never bought a beast, never sold a beast'. Boothby retorted: 'May I ask if the breeding of beasts has been the Minister's sole concern in life?' 'The Hon. Member', Elliot replied, 'has never put his hand to the plough, never forked a load of hay, never pulled a turnip.' Boothby advised him to ask his constituents 'and they will answer. They have answered for twelve years.' This exchange was widely reported in the Scottish press, greatly to Boothby's advantage, the National Farmers' Union of Scotland greeting him warmly as their recognised champion. Elliot, a warm friend, quickly regretted his jibes.

Churchill, denied office, returned to the front line on defence and resumed his alliance with Boothby and Bracken. On 6 May, in a debate on the Abyssinian fiasco, Churchill attacked Baldwin personally, to the fury of loyal Conservatives. Two weeks later he and Boothby, together with other Tory dissidents, were the guests of Lord Winterton at his country home; this was given great prominence in the press as clear evidence of a cabal, and Baldwin said in the Commons that it was 'the time of year when midges come out of dirty ditches'. In a private meeting with a Conservative delegation on rearmament led by Churchill in July, Baldwin said that 'I am not going to get this country into a war with anybody for the League of Nations or anybody else or for anything else.' It was generally remarked that Baldwin looked unwell and had lost his grip after a dreadful period since the election. Churchill publicly denounced Baldwin and Mac-Donald in a memorable article on 13 July, writing that they 'excelled in the art of minimising political issues, of frustrating large schemes of change, of depressing the national temperature, and reducing Parliament to a humdrum level'. Boothby and Bracken cheered him on; few other Conservatives did. It was destined to be the high point of their personal and political friendship.

Years later, on a holiday in the South of France, Churchill said to Boothby of that time that 'You were on the right side then.' As there was almost a tone of reproach in his voice, Boothby could have retorted that on these matters he had always been on 'the right side'. But he did not, although his biographer can.

When the House rose for the summer recess at the end of July, it was clear that Baldwin's previous mastery over the Commons was wavering, and Churchill and Boothby were convinced that they were winning the rearmament battle. Speaking in Peterhead early in August, Boothby caused a flurry when he described himself as 'a completely independent Member of Parliament', and, given the Government's arrogant attitude to its backbenchers, added that he was 'very doubtful whether I will submit myself again for re-election'. He also specifically referred to Churchill's continued exclusion from the Government.

Boothby professed himself very surprised that this was taken so seriously nationally and locally, but his constituents were genuinely alarmed that he meant to retire. At Gardie Duff's urgent request he issued a statement that he would stand again, which had an excellent response in East Aberdeenshire, but not in the hostile Beaverbrook newspapers, Peter Howard commenting that 'It is a pity to see a man who might one day be Prime Minister steering such a zig-zag course towards his goal.' It was not, as it happened, his goal at all.

One political commentator noted

the growing similarities between Mr R. G. Boothby and Mr Harold Macmillan. Both represent North-East constituencies, both are loyal to the Conservative Party, but both strike out boldly for themselves and believe in what they think. Both, too, frequently earn the displeasure of their Conservative colleagues.

When Boothby described the British industrial cities as 'a dirty, squalid desert, like Abyssinia after an air-raid,' the commentator understated the Tory reaction.

The Arms and the Covenant all-Party group was attracting a large membership, with Churchill and Violet Bonham Carter the key figures; other leading members included Sinclair, Boothby, Macmillan, Bracken, Lord Cecil, Professor Gilbert Murray and Kingsley Martin. When the World Anti-Nazi Council was created in London, it was chaired by Walter Citrine, the General Secretary of the TUC, a clear sign that at least some members of the Labour movement were becoming alerted to the gravity of the European situation, although the attitude of the Parliamentary Labour Party remained dispiritingly pacifist and unhelpful. All the omens were that Churchill's campaign in the wilderness was attracting increasingly significant adherents.

When it was announced that Baldwin was fatigued – he was in fact close to a nervous breakdown – and was taking a complete rest, Boothby caustically said in a speech in Fraserburgh on 18 September that

Whether we like it or not, we have already entered rough seas, and the storm signals are up. Under such conditions, there is only one place for the captain, and that is on the bridge. Stalin has recently given forcible evidence to the world that he has not left Moscow. Mussolini has not ceased to preside over his own cabinet; and we have not read in the newspapers that Hitler was too tired to attend the Nuremberg Congress.

A number of Conservative MPs were guests of the Nazis at the Berlin Olympic Games; Boothby and Churchill were not in their number.

Boothby was passing through his period of deep sadness over the collapse of his marriage, but seldom in his life were his political activities being more warmly praised. One commentator wrote that

It seems incredible that a young man with the brains and ability of Robert Boothby should not have been utilised long ago – especially looking at some of the oddities that have been promoted to the Front Bench. Boothby has two fatal (political) defects – an insistence on thinking for himself, and announcing the results; and a constant loyalty to a fallen leader. But if the Churchill star should start to rise again, Robert Boothby will rise with it.

That star was indeed rising again, but was about to fall.

Throughout the summer there was speculation by those in the know – which included everyone in London Society – about the future of the young King Edward VIII and his virtually open affair with Mrs Wallis Simpson, an American lady with an English husband, whom she divorced on 27 October. Through a self-denying ordinance among the newspaper proprietors, the British public was totally unaware of the feverish interest being shown in their sovereign by American and European reporters and photographers. But even those who knew about the liaison, including the King's close friend and adviser Walter Monckton, never thought that the King would actually marry her. For the head of the Church of England to marry a twice-divorced American was unthinkable. When the King had told Baldwin of his intentions as early as February, both Baldwin and J. C. C. Davidson had considered it literally unbelievable. In retrospect, it would have been better if Baldwin had made this point emphatically at an earlier stage. On 16 November the King told him of his determination to marry the now free Mrs Simpson.

The crisis that followed has often been described. The storm broke on 3 December, when the press ended its silence. By this time the King had ignored all the advice given to him that his decision was incompatible with his position. That evening there was the first meeting of Arms and the Covenant at the Albert Hall. Churchill had just seen the draft of a broadcast that the King wanted to make and was obsessed with the matter. He told the other speakers that he wanted to refer to the royal crisis, but they told him that if he did they would walk off the platform. Churchill was taken aback by the intensity of feeling, but, dominated by his loyalty to the King, he did not realise that his views were far from being universally shared.

Indeed, the general reaction, after one of astonishment, was overwhelmingly hostile to the King. Boothby's sympathies were with the King, but he recognised, as Churchill did not, that so long as he insisted on marriage, his position was untenable, particularly as Queen Mary and other members of the royal family – especially the Duchess of York – were outraged by his behaviour.

Churchill, unhappily, did not agree. He tried to talk the King out of his decision, urging him at least to reflect further on an action that could only lead to abdication. He issued public statements calling for delay, and strongly implied that Baldwin and the Cabinet were acting unconstitutionally by trying to 'extort' abdication from the King. This inflamed matters further, as Rothermere, Beaverbrook and their newspapers took the same line.

Although the crisis was brief, it aroused intense emotions. Churchill did not consult his friends, but went roaring off on his own, crashing around angrily with fierce feelings. His enemies said that it was a Churchill/Beaverbrook plot to bring down the Government; his friends, most of whom disagreed with him, were dismayed.

Churchill, Sinclair and Boothby thought that they saw a way out of the impasse. Together at Chartwell on the evening of 6 December they prepared a declaration by the King promising not to contract a marriage against the advice of his ministers. This was conveyed urgently to a close friend of Boothby's, the King's Private Secretary, Godfrey Thomas, at Buckingham Palace. Walter Monckton was at once in touch with Boothby and asked him to come to see him; for a very short while Boothby clutched at the hope that this intervention might have saved the day, particularly when Mrs Simpson issued a statement that appeared to be a complete renunciation of the marriage proposal.

As we now know, Boothby's optimism foundered on the rock of the King's determination to marry even if it meant abdicating the throne, but it was his view at the time that he, Churchill and Sinclair had found the magic formula, which Churchill then proceeded to wreck. It was this that precipitated the fiercest row they had yet had, and from which their relations never really recovered.

On the following day, 7 December, disaster struck. Churchill came down to the Commons to hear another statement by Baldwin – who was handling the situation in a masterly manner – not only in a highly emotional state but after rather too good a lunch at the Anglo-French Association. Boothby remarked after Churchill's death that it was the only occasion he had ever seen Churchill the worse for drink in public. He did not appear even to be listening to Baldwin; when Churchill rose to plead again for delay, the House turned on him in fury and shouted him down. Amery thought that 'he was completely staggered by the unanimous hostility of the House', and he eventually stormed out of the Chamber, with only Bracken joining him. Winterton has described this episode as 'one of the angriest manifestations I have ever heard directed against any man in the House of Commons'.

Among them was Boothby, who, in an angry mood, wrote what he later came to believe was a fatal letter to Churchill.

Dear Winston

I understood last night that we had *agreed* upon a formula, and a course, designed to save the King from abdication, if that is possible.

I thought that you were going to use all your powers – decisive, as I believe, in the present circumstances – to secure a happy issue, on the lines that were suggested.

But this afternoon you have delivered a blow to the King, both in the

House and in the country, far harder than any that Baldwin ever conceived of.

You have reduced the number of potential supporters to the minimum possible – I shld. think now about seven in all.

And you have done it without any consultation with your best friends and supporters.

I have never in my life said anything to you that I did not sincerely believe.

And I never will.

What happened this afternoon makes me feel that it is almost impossible for those who are most devoted to you personally to follow you blindly (as they wd. like to do) in politics.

Because they cannot be sure where the hell they are going to be landed next.

I am afraid this letter will make you very angry.

But not, I hope, irretrievably angry.

I could not leave what I feel unsaid.

Yours ever
Bob

Seldom has there been such a dramatic reversal of political fortunes. Churchill's reputation fell to its nadir, Baldwin's rose to its zenith. The King abdicated and Churchill's allies were seething. 'He has undone in five minutes the patient reconstruction work of two years,' Nicolson noted, and Macmillan has written that 'All the effect of the Albert Hall meeting was destroyed – first by the Abdication and secondly by the catastrophic fall in Churchill's prestige. It was not possible to restore the situation.' Churchill himself later admitted that 'I was myself so smitten in public opinion that it was the almost universal view that my political life was at last ended.' He told Boothby and Bracken in the Smoking Room that he was sure it was ended. Boothby wrote to him again on the 11th:

Dear Winston

I am sorry I wrote that letter.

We were all, I think, strung up at the time.

And you can imagine how bitterly disappointed I was that our talk the night before seemed to have borne no fruit.

Even now, I don't quite understand what happened. When I said Good-night to you at Chartwell you were resolved to try and persuade the King to accept the formula which we had all helped to devise.

Next morning, quite by chance, I received a letter from Godfrey Thomas: and in my reply which – again by chance – I sent by hand, I told him of our hopes; and added that it was essential that the King should be shown the words of the formula and, if possible, see you, at the earliest moment.

When I reached the House of Commons you would not speak to me; and Archie told me that when you came down at Chartwell that morning your 'mood had changed'.

I was dismayed, and feared the worst; and, at Question Time, the worst seemed to have happened.

Afterwards in the smoking room I found several members of the particular group you always imagine are your most loyal supporters, roundly abusing you, & accusing you of 'playing your own hand'. And I wrote to you, in a ferment of indignation and disappointment, the letter which I now wish I had not sent.

And at that particular moment the tension was very great; and I am sure you will make due allowances.

The aftermath was extraordinary.

I got a message from Walter Monckton asking me to dine with him. He came straight from Fort Belvedere, and told me he was afraid the game was up.

The King remained obdurate, and the Duke of York was dining with him.

I showed him the formula, *which he had not seen before.* He became quite excited, and telephoned the King in the middle of dinner, asking him to hold his hand, as he had a new suggestion to make.

The King agreed; and Walter left for Fort Belvedere immediately after dinner, saying there was hope once more.

What happened afterwards I know not. At least further delay. But can you blame me for thinking, at the time, that if you had done what you said you intended to do the night before, and pressed the King to accept the formula that morning, the result might have been different?

I am now convinced that no human effort could have altered the course of events.

The one thing I regret is that your intervention at Question Time last Monday may have temporarily diminished your power and authority in the House, which prior to that had seldom been greater, and certainly had never been so necessary for the country.

But this raises an old issue between us.

I have made many mistakes in my life, and paid for them; but I still don't think my political judgement is altogether bad, although you have never attached any value to it.

For ten years, as one of your most devoted followers, I have fought a losing battle against the influence of the die-hards, the Press Lords, and Brendan.

Because I believe that the die-hards are not fundamentally loyal to you, that the Press Lords (and especially one of them) are your most dangerous enemies, and that Brendan is the best friend and the worst counsellor in the world. (For instance, only this morning Clive Baillieu told me he thanked God he had refused to send a series of cables to friends of his in the

Australian government at Brendan's instigation, but under the aegis of your authority, which were not only wild and mischievous, but bore no relation to any of the facts which had since been made public.)

All these people give you advice which is immediately the most alluring, and ultimately the most fatal. I cannot help feeling that one of them got at you last Monday morning.

It is only when you rely on the power of clear disinterested advice, based on your unrivalled intellect and experience, with *the solid central mass of the House of Commons*, that you rise to the position of commanding authority which you should always occupy.

You have done it during recent weeks & months.

You can, and must, do it again.

I believe passionately that you are the only man who can save this country, and the world during the next two critical years.

And that must be my excuse for writing this letter.

Yours ever
Bob

Churchill replied somewhat contritely on 12 December to Boothby's violent letter:

My dear Bob

Thank you so much for your letter. Even if you had not written it, our old relations would have been unchanged.

I reached the House on Monday rather prepared in my mind to be attacked for what I had written over the weekend, and addressing myself rather too attentively to that possibility, I did not sufficiently realise how far the Prime Minister had gone to meet the views I had expressed. I ought of course to have welcomed what he said. But I cannot however think it was wrong to repeat the request that no irrevocable decision should be taken.

I made careful enquiries yesterday at Belvedere and I am absolutely satisfied that the point was to be put to the King most fully, Archie's name and mine being used; and that he turned it aside on the grounds that it would not be honourable to play for time when his fundamental resolve was unchanged, and as he declared unchangeable. It was certainly this very strict point of honour which cost him his Crown. Whether I could have prevailed upon him personally, I do not know. It is however certain that I should not have been allowed access to him, as the Ministers were already angry with Baldwin for having given him permission to see me on Friday, and he had been made aware of this fact. Therefore I feel that you are right in saying that no human effort could have altered the course of events.

The only thing now to do is to make it easy for him to live in this country quietly as a private gentleman, as soon as possible, and to that we must bend our efforts by discouraging noisy controversy (apart from quasi-historical investigation) and refusing to take part in it. The more firmly the new King is established, the more easy it will be for the old one to come back to his house.

Yours ever

W

Although Churchill had said that their friendship would not be impaired, the fact that he took five days to reply was in itself ominous. Boothby had already personally apologised, but he felt instinctively that Churchill had been deeply wounded by the fact that one of his few close allies had written and acted as he did, and that the wound would fester. Unhappily, his judgment proved to be correct. The old intimacy was never to return. Boothby, for his part, again questioned Churchill's judgment in a crisis, as did many others. He also feared that Churchill had destroyed himself and was a spent political force.

Boothby thankfully left London with his parents to spend Christmas in Monte Carlo. He has related the sequel:

Maugham rang me up to ask me to lunch at the Villa Mauresque on Christmas Day. I told him I was with my parents, and he said: 'You can dine with them. You are very g-g-greedy and I have got a s-s-s-sucking pig. Also I need you. I will send a car to fetch you.' When I arrived I found a small party; and was offered one of his excellent cocktails. 'Have another,' he said. I said: 'No thanks.' He replied: 'You'd b-b-better.' At that moment the door opened, and Mrs Simpson and her aunt Mrs Merryman were announced. I just had time to say to Willie: 'How dare you!' before I was introduced. At lunch I found myself sitting next to Mrs Merryman, the famous Aunt Bessie. She opened the conversation by saying: 'You know, Wallis and I have been having a very tough time lately.' All I could think of to say was: 'I seem to have read something about it in the newspapers.' After lunch we played bridge. I cannot remember who my partner was, but we were playing against Mrs Simpson and Maugham. When the first hand was dealt, Mrs Simpson declared one no trump, my partner said no, Maugham said three no trumps, and I said no. As he put down his hand he said: 'I'm afraid I am not a very good partner. I've only got a couple of k-k-kings.' Never able to resist a wisecrack, Mrs Simpson flashed back: 'What's the use of them? They only abdicate.' Maugham said: 'I d-d-don't think that's in v-v-very good t-t-taste.'

Thus ended 1936.

7

The Years of Disaster
1937–8

*B*oothby opened 1937 with a series of public meetings in his constituency, complaining good-humouredly that whenever he attacked the Government – which he conceded he did often – it was assumed that he was leaving the Conservative Party. The *Buchan Observer* stated that his constituents

know their Boothby. They realise that he will never be content to become one of those monuments of dull consistency who so often receive recognition as heaven-sent statesmen, only to be discovered later as survivals of an earlier political age. His is that divine inconsistency which is constantly seeking to adapt general principles to the changing needs of the time.

As always, his speeches and question-and-answer sessions ranged from local issues to foreign affairs, and particularly the German threat. 'His series of meetings have been a triumphant success', the *Fraserburgh Advertiser* enthused, 'and must be highly gratifying for himself and his constituents.' As this was a dark period in his private life, this was indeed the case.

Politically, he was certainly living dangerously, being a platform speaker at the first rally of the 'People's Front' at Friends House, Euston Road, attended by an audience of some two thousand. He had accepted because John Strachey had asked him to speak, and did so on the familiar lines of friendship with Russia and on the German menace. When he tried to justify British non-intervention in the Spanish Civil War, which had erupted into a major new element of international tension, with the Germans and the Soviet Union taking different sides, this did not go down well with an overwhelmingly left-wing audience. Fortunately for Boothby the historian and Socialist firebrand, G. D. H. Cole, called for the Front to bring down the Government, thereby enabling Boothby to walk off the platform, in either real or feigned dudgeon. What he was doing on it in the first place is explicable only for one who enjoyed excitement.

Nineteen thirty-seven was destined to be, politically, a quiet year abroad – the last one before the storms. At home it was dominated by the Coronation of the Duke and Duchess of York as King George VI and Queen Elizabeth, and, immediately following it, by the retirement of Baldwin and the unopposed succession of Neville Chamberlain. At the time, this again seemed a distinct improvement, and both Churchill, who formally proposed Chamberlain to be Leader of the Party, and Boothby were initially optimistic; so was Eden. It appeared that Chamberlain's energy and keen new interest in international affairs, in contrast to Baldwin's lethargy and total lack of interest, would be beneficial. It was not long before they realised how wrong they were.

It was also the year of Boothby's divorce, and the painful publicity that accompanied it, but his activity in the Commons, the press and his constituency was as considerable as ever. He was particularly critical of the first budget of the new Chancellor, the greatly disliked Sir John Simon, for whom Boothby had a special aversion. But his sensible criticisms of a proposed profits tax – which the Government withdrew – and the proposed national defence contribution – which, again, had to be dropped under fire from all sides – prompted one political observer to write that 'this is proving to be the most successful session for Mr Boothby since he entered Parliament'.

Abroad, with the terrible exception of Spain, Europe seemed quiet, and even Churchill began to believe that the peril was passing; Boothby's speeches became notably more optimistic. Even the economic situation was improving, and although Boothby's criticisms continued, they were now more muted and more thoughtful. He had the doubtful satisfaction of being warmly praised both by Chamberlain and Simon in the House, and a speech on foreign affairs praising Eden was rewarded by a pencilled handwritten note: 'My dear Bob, Warmest congratulations & Thank you, yours ever Anthony', which is one of the very few letters from Eden in Boothby's papers. Boothby's views on the international economic situation, and particularly what he regarded as Roosevelt's disastrous policies, were now being prominently reported in the American press. 'What is the point of making a trade agreement or attempting to co-operate with a government which seems determined to sabotage the economic system under which we live – without any alternative system to put in its place?' he asked in the Commons in another widely reported speech, in which he strongly criticised Roosevelt's new policies of lowering commodity prices and actively discouraging investment in American industry. 'As a result of that, at a very critical moment, the underlying strength of democratic countries has been greatly diminished and the danger of war sensibly increased.' This made the front page of the *New York Times*, amongst others. Some of his British – but not American – critics accused him of using the Commons to attack personally the head of a friendly state, but it was not a personal attack at all.

By the end of the year he had become convinced that the threat of war had definitely receded. 'The main danger to be guarded against in 1938', he wrote in the *Evening Express*, 'is not a military explosion. The theoretical arguments and the practical checks against any large-scale military adventures in Europe are too convincing. The main danger – and until recently it was a very real one – is sustained economic depression, culminating in a slump.' He was wrong.

Boothby opened 1938, which he later called 'The Year of Disaster', by using the Burns Dinner at Turriff on 28 January to call for compulsory training colleges including military instruction, skilfully quoting from Burns' writings during the Napoleonic Wars. The speech caused a considerable amount of comment, much of it from Labour spokesmen and MPs, who strongly denounced it as calling for camouflaged military conscription, but the reactions in East Aberdeenshire were calmer; the local newspapers were unenthusiastic, but when Chamberlain asked Boothby at the House what the response had been, he said that he had not received a single letter on the subject that was hostile to his argument.

The next major shock, in what was destined to be a year of shocks, was the resignation of Eden and his Minister of State, Lord Cranborne, on 20 February. It was in effect an enforced resignation, in which Eden had been skilfully outmanoeuvred by a prime minister whose authoritarian approach to his office was only just being realised. The blow to Churchill was intense, and it was from this point that definite anti-appeasement elements emerged on the Conservative benches. Unhappily they did not coalesce. Boothby and Bracken stood by Churchill, Amery led another group whose meetings Boothby attended, and now Eden led a much larger, but more cautious, group of Conservative MPs, derided by the faithful as 'The Glamour Boys', who took good care to keep well away from Churchill. Personalities as well as tactical attitudes, and the lack of a single decisive leader, made these groups far less effective than they could have been, and they were easily contained by the Whips.

None the less, in the debate following Eden's resignation, in which Eden's speech left most Members bewildered about the real cause of his departure, twenty Conservatives refused to support the Government, including Macmillan, who had only recently taken the Whip again. Boothby spoke in the debate on 22 February. He did not mince his words and attacked Churchill's own role since 1918 and his silence over the Rhineland in 1936: 'It is a story of muddle and disaster without parallel in history, caused by the incorrigible reluctance of the people of this country to face at any period the realities of the European situation.' But he also gave Chamberlain the benefit of the doubt and praised his 'high courage', while warning that he was playing for very high stakes by gambling on Mussolini's good faith. He also abstained. Bracken was incensed by his criticisms of Churchill, and it is reasonable to assume that Churchill was as well. Boothby had succeeded in offending both sides.

Boothby, like many others of his friends, had welcomed Chamberlain's energy and drive after Baldwin's lethargy, and at this time concentrated principally on the rearmament aspect of the situation. On 12 March, Boothby wrote to Chamberlain urging him to double the production of front-line aircraft. On the next day Hitler annexed Austria. It was another bloodless coup, warmly welcomed by the bulk of the Austrian population.

For the hapless Austrian Jews it was the herald of total disaster. Many were able to flee to the West; those who could not or did not were subjected first to brutal persecution, and subsequently to much worse. A then unknown sociologist, philanthropist and businessman, Sir Frederick Marquis, was one of those who realised what had happened. He was a respected figure in banking and business in Liverpool, and had no involvement in politics, but in a speech in Leicester he announced that the firm in which he was principally involved, John Lewis's, would no longer buy or sell German products, and urged other companies to do the same. This caused fury both in Berlin and London, and Marquis was summoned to 10 Downing Street to receive the full measure of Chamberlain's disapproval. This was the first that Churchill, Boothby and many others had heard of the future Lord Woolton.

Churchill also realised what had happened and made one of his greatest speeches on 24 March:

I have watched this famous island descending incontinently, fecklessly, the stairway that leads to a dark gulf. It is a fine broad stairway at the beginning, but after a bit the carpet ends. A little further on there are only flagstones, and a little further on still these break beneath your feet.

Boothby wrote to him: 'Your speech was *magnificent* – from the first word to the last. It makes me very proud to have been associated with you in public life.' But, as the American journalist Virginia Cowles, watching from the public gallery, noted, the impact was short-lived and the Conservatives were unconvinced.

Like many other people, including Churchill, Boothby was bewildered by the contrasts in Chamberlain's character. Writing of him many years later, he mused on the dichotomy:

In private life Chamberlain was affectionate and sensitive, with a great love and knowledge of country pursuits and the music of Beethoven. These are endearing qualities which were rewarded by the complete devotion of a small and intimate family circle. In public life he was aloof, arrogant, obstinate and limited. He was also a failure. . . . He was a first-class municipal administrator, who well understood and radically changed the structure of British local government; and he was the first prominent politician to grasp the power of the political machines in the modern age, which he re-animated and subsequently used for his own purposes. There it ended.

Boothby frankly admitted that he himself 'fell under the spell' of Lord Halifax, who had succeeded Eden, and whom he liked and admired. However, he actively and fiercely distrusted Geoffrey Dawson, editor of *The Times* and, as Boothby later described him, 'the Secretary-General of the Establishment, and fervent advocate of Appeasement'. Characteristically, he also saw his virtues, but could never forgive him for his craven attitude towards Hitler and the Nazis, and especially his brutal editing of the reports of Norman Ebbutt from Berlin to ensure that nothing would appear 'that might hurt their [German] susceptibilities'.

As we have seen, Noël Coward was a frequent visitor to The French House, where he would often bring his theatrical friends; Boothby responded by bringing 'some drab and wild-eyed politicians' to Coward's house. As Cole Lesley later wrote, 'Laughter predominated at both their houses,'* and Boothby saw to it that the Coward household was as plentifully supplied with herrings as The French House. But as 1938 progressed Coward, one of the most deeply patriotic of men, developed a passionate hatred of Neville Chamberlain that was far more ferocious than the attitudes of Churchill and Boothby. Coward always said that he had never hated anyone in his life except Chamberlain, and Lesley wrote that 'he never felt so strongly about anything before or after'. In *Cavalcade* in 1931 he had warned of the dangers of national decline; he had seen it happen and was convulsed with fury and contempt for its authors. He was, naturally, a total supporter of Churchill, Eden and Boothby.

Churchill – and Boothby and Bracken, not to mention Coward – were anathema to people like Chamberlain, Dawson, Halifax and Philip Lothian, whose collective role in the politics of the 1930s was so crucial. This was on personal as well as political grounds. Boothby recognised that

*Cole Lesley, *Noël Coward*, pp. 197–9.

In themselves, they were the antithesis of decadence; high-minded, self-effacing, hard-working, acutely conscious of their own moral rectitude and intellectual superiority. . . . Round they hopped, like birds in an enormous cage, from shoot to shoot, from Cliveden to All Souls, to the Athenaeum, to the Travellers' [Club], to Grillions dining club, to Round Table 'moots', and back again; with the result that they were out of touch with ordinary people, with all that was happening in Europe, and finally with reality.

Boothby thought it significant that Margot Asquith compared Neville Chamberlain's 'spare figure and keen eye' with 'Winston's self-indulgent rotundity'. This was another charge against Boothby himself in the ruling circles, asceticism and moral rectitude not being exactly his strong suits.

Margot Asquith regularly telephoned Boothby early in the morning to rail against Churchill. Her step-daughter, Violet Bonham Carter, emphatically took Boothby's side, writing to him consolingly on 22 March that

> You must *never* be 'disheartened' by early morning hiccoughs from Margot! I get screeds (sent by car) on the same theme. I wrote one strongly worded reply, to which she replied, 'I agree with *every word* you say', but the spate continues. I can't imagine what made her take 'the wrong turning' over this issue – for tho' her politics are *quite* incoherent (& always have been) she is usually to be found in the right lobby for the wrong reason. Now both are wrong. But *how* disheartened I feel by the general recession of feeling I am somehow aware of feeling in the last 3 days. Is it only my imagination & the tied Press? Or is everything we thought had been roused settling off comfortably to sleep again? I wish I could do *anything* to help except argue myself hoarse at meals on the telephone! 'Self-destruction' is the word – we are committing inglorious suicide.

This was exactly Boothby's view, and he fully shared her intense frustration and forebodings, but at least both he and Churchill had a public platform in the Commons and in the press. The trouble was that their audience was almost totally unreceptive; indeed, they often wondered whether anyone was listening at all.

Boothby's admiration for Lloyd George did not improve Margot Asquith's temper, and she wrote pages to 'My dearest Bob' vilifying him, 'an *ungrateful, unprincipled*, little hound' being one of her milder descriptions of her husband's successor; more congenial to Boothby was her loathing for Simon.

Churchill and Boothby were now certain that Czechoslovakia would be next on Hitler's list, and on 15 March Boothby appealed in the *Daily Telegraph* for 'a clear-cut foreign policy which commands the general support of all Parties'; he called for 'a pact of mutual assistance between those Powers which are resolved to offer effective resistance to further aggression in Europe', specifically naming Czechoslovakia, and the need for full co-operation with France. A week later, in the same newspaper, he again urged national military service and a foreign policy that would convince Mussolini that he should move his forces out of Spain:

The real reason for the Berlin–Rome axis, and the present uncertainty in Eastern Europe, is the growing conviction on the part of Mussolini and of some of the smaller states that, as a nation, we are fundamentally decadent and can no longer be depended upon to resist aggression or even to defend our Empire.

On 21 April, at New Deer, he told his constituents that

Once again I am 'a voice crying in the wilderness', but if the people of this country imagine they are secure today they are living in a fool's paradise . . . at this rate [of aircraft production] the superiority of Germany in the air next year will be sufficiently overwhelming to bring the knock-out blow within the realms of practical possibility. Such a position cannot be tolerated. Either we must double our home production in the next six months or buy aeroplanes elsewhere. . . . I still think war can be averted by resolute, timely, and wise action on our part. But we must realise that the German national effort and leadership today can only be compared with our own supreme effort under the direction of Lloyd George.

The *Buchan Observer* remarked:

Mr Boothby does not pretend to bring the anodyne of complacency. Instead he administers the sharp and unpleasant medicine of warning. Of that we make no complaint whatever. But we do protest a little against the confusion and discouragement which may arise from the suggestion that Britain's case is if possible worse than her last.

The *Buchan Observer* criticised Boothby's inconsistency. There was further evidence of this on 8 May, when, after a visit to Holland, Belgium, Germany and France, he reported to his constituents supporting Chamberlain strongly and announcing that

the tension – in Western Europe at any rate – has greatly decreased during recent weeks, and Mr Chamberlain's realistic foreign policy commands universal admiration in each and all of these countries. But if we are to carry this policy to a successful conclusion it is essential that we should be strong. Our aircraft production *must* be speeded up during the next four months.

'We rejoice that Mr Boothby is solidly behind the National Government's foreign policy,' declared the *Buchan Observer*.

On 17 May he submitted a long memorandum to the President of the Board of Trade, R. S. Hudson, on the perils of German economic penetration in Central and Eastern Europe, and the urgent need to counter its tactics. On 31 May he wrote in the *Daily Telegraph* that

Czechoslovakia has been, and still is, the acid test. . . . If Germany were allowed to annex, or even to establish complete political and economic control over Czechoslovakia, the way would at once be open for her to establish a similar control over Hungary and Romania. Before we realised what had happened she would be on the Black Sea, and her writ would run from the Baltic to the Dardanelles. The balance of power in Europe would be hopelessly and irretrievably upset. Germany would dominate all.

The Berlin correspondent of the *Telegraph* reported that Boothby's article 'has aroused unfavourable comment here'. It was officially described by the German Government as 'a typical contribution from the school of politicians whose whole attention is concentrated on the imaginary danger of a German drive for hegemony over the whole Continent'. Undeterred, on 15 June, in the Commons, he publicly reiterated his memorandum to ministers on the danger of Central and Eastern Europe becoming 'part of a Reichsmark empire'.

These speeches, letters and articles had little effect. Nor did what Boothby described as Eden's 'frigid disapproval of government policy and the tremendous salvoes from Churchill's heavy guns'.* Meanwhile, Chamberlain had got rid of the energetic Secretary for Air, Lord Swinton, and appointed a convenient nonentity, Kingsley Wood, in his place. Appeasement was now well into its stride, and was moving from a policy into almost a religion. It was also apparently achieving widespread support in Britain and the Conservative Party – and in the *Buchan Observer*.

The German campaign of vilification against the alleged Czech oppression of the Sudeten Germans had increased in May after President Beneš mobilised the Czech army, one of the most formidable in Europe. But the respite was only temporary, and the episode caused considerable alarm in London and Paris. Lord Runciman was dispatched to lead a mediatory mission whose purposes seemed unclear.

At this stage Boothby's relations with Chamberlain were good. As he wrote frankly in 1947,

Unlike his predecessor, he was intensely interested in foreign affairs, and encouraged one to speak one's mind. The fact that on no single issue or occasion did he ever agree with the conclusions I had reached made no difference to our

---

*In May Eden stayed with Boothby at The French House, and, during a convivial dinner, concocted a government of national safety, of which Eden would be Prime Minister, Sinclair Foreign Secretary and Churchill Minister of Supply. It was harmless fun, but the low priority given to Churchill's role was not without its significance (Norman Rose (ed.), *Baffy – The Diaries of Blanche Dugdale, 1936–47*, pp. 90–1).

very agreeable personal relationship, the memory of which I cherish. People who say they don't like being written or talked to by Prime Ministers are either great fools or great frauds.

Boothby, for all his protestations to the contrary, did not lack either ambition or vanity. His relations with Churchill were now more political than personal, and those with Eden remained cool. If he had a mentor at all it was Amery. He was flattered by Chamberlain's apparent interest in his opinions, and thought that he could influence events and policies. It was to prove a major miscalculation.

Boothby decided that there would be value in seeing the Czechoslovak situation for himself while enjoying a holiday, and in the agreeable company of Gardie Duff motored to Marienbad, where 'we soon found ourselves subjected to an intensive flood of Sudeten German propaganda'. They attended a huge rally at Eger addressed by Konrad Henlein, the Nazi Sudeten leader; on the platform, Boothby noted with amazement, was one of the famous Mitford sisters, Unity, 'with a swastika brooch pinned to her bosom'.

They were equally surprised by the intense poverty of the Sudeten areas. As he reported to Chamberlain, 'there is great, and visible, poverty, accompanied by widespread dissatisfaction,' but found no evidence whatever of 'intolerable political pressure' by the Czech Government on the Sudetens, as Hitler was claiming daily. But he was, then, convinced that a compromise solution could be reached. Boothby also reported to the Prime Minister on 27 July a long meeting he had had with Beneš in Prague at the Hradschin Castle. Beneš' message was that the legitimate grievances of the Sudetens were being, and would be, met, but added, 'Don't forget I am also responsible for nine million Czechs, who value their freedom, and will die to the last man to defend it.' Chamberlain replied in his own hand that he had read his 'extremely interesting letter' and had passed it to Runciman. Boothby met Runciman and his Mission in Prague and Carlsbad, but remained baffled by their purpose. Before he left Czechoslovakia he visited the great Skoda armaments works at Pilsen 'and watched, with considerable satisfaction, the vast works in full blast', as it produced tanks, guns and munitions that were to be used, as it happened, with devastating effect by the Germans in the 1940 *Blitzkrieg*.

Boothby returned to England by way of Bayreuth to attend the Festival. The city, and even the churches, were plastered with huge swastikas. 'To understand this Germany', he later wrote, 'you had to feel Wagner in your blood and bones, and then realise how skilfully and wickedly he had been distorted by the Nazis for their own monstrous purposes.' He and Duff returned from their holiday, profoundly disconcerted by their experience, and Boothby decided to see Chamberlain personally, which he did on 24 August.

Chamberlain told Boothby that he would not commit Britain in advance to war in the event of a German invasion of Czechoslovakia, but he gave Boothby the clear impression that he was going to take a firmer line and emphasise to Berlin that he could not answer for the consequences if it took such action. Simon was about to make a major speech at Lanark, and Boothby assumed that he would be instructed to say exactly this. In the event, Simon said nothing of the sort, as Vansittart had warned Boothby. This was an important moment of disillusionment in Boothby's attitude towards Chamberlain.

There was another warning. On 28 August Boothby reported to Chamberlain that he had attended a private dinner in London with a group of German industrialists, who told him that

The [Nazi] plan is to continue a ferocious press campaign against Czechoslovakia, to arm the Sudeten Germans, to turn down all offers of concession, to work up to a climax at Nuremberg, then to stage an incident, and invade with five army corps between the middle and end of September. They estimate that Prague can be captured and Bohemia occupied within three weeks and bargain on our persuading the French to remain neutral.

This information was to prove remarkably accurate. The industrialists also urged a firm British and French public line 'to enable the moderate elements, and particularly the General Staff, to make effective use of the warnings'.

The letter was read out to the Cabinet. The opinion was taken that 'it took an unduly alarmist view of the situation'. Boothby then circulated to eight chosen Cabinet ministers a memorandum reiterating his points, and turned to the press for support. 'There was not much available,' he noted later, the great exception being Seymour Berry, who gave him a platform again in the *Daily Telegraph*. On 30 August Boothby, now convinced that the Sudeten Germans were being urged to intransigence by the Nazis, wrote his strongest public warning so far; but in counselling firmness and clarity, he also wrote that 'If the Nazi leaders are counting on French and British inaction in the face of German aggression against Czechoslovakia, they are making a terrible miscalculation which must be corrected before it is too late.'

He also wrote to Walter Elliot and Oliver Stanley supporting Lloyd George's call for a clear British commitment to France to join it and its allies to resist aggression. 'This is what we are all saying,' Boothby wrote to them both. 'But it must be made to the world before Hitler speaks [at Nuremberg]. If you don't do it, war may still be averted by the resolution of others. If you don't do it, and war comes, then your responsibility will be unthinkable. There are no valid arguments against doing it.'

To Duff Cooper he wrote on 11 September:

> I make no excuse for writing again because I believe it is a matter of life or death to declare the attitude of this country in the face of naked aggression before Hitler speaks.
>
> We are morally committed, by the Runciman Mission, to support Czechoslovakia if she is now attacked.
>
> We are also morally committed – to the hilt – to France.
>
> But the issue cuts deeper than this. In its simplest, crudest, and ultimate form, it is the issue between REASON and FORCE, civilisation and barbarism.

It was now at last clear to Boothby that the real purpose of the Runciman Mission was to put the maximum British pressure upon the irresolute Beneš and none whatever on Henlein or Hitler. Writing again in the *Daily Telegraph* on 13 September, he said that

> we are morally bound to go to the support of Czechoslovakia if she is made the victim of naked aggression. We are also morally and practically committed to France. If war now breaks out on the Continent of Europe we are, therefore, bound to be involved; and it is far better to face up to that fact.

He then called for immediate military staff talks between Britain, France and Russia.

The hopelessness of this was made plain to Boothby on 19 September, when he went to Geneva on a brief business visit and met Maxim Litvinov, the Russian Foreign Minister, who was enraged by the fact that no British representative had even paid a courtesy call on him. Boothby asked him about his idea of staff talks. 'He laughed the idea to scorn. "How do you expect staff talks", he asked, "when we haven't even begun political talks?"' But he did say that if the French fulfilled their obligations to the Czechs, the Soviet Union would fight. Boothby flew back to London as soon as possible and saw Halifax to give him a verbal account of this conversation and its momentous implications. But it was all too late. Chamberlain had already flown to Berchtesgaden to see Hitler. The death of Czechoslovakia was at hand.

In later years Boothby often asked himself whether he could have done more to prevent this catastrophe. It is very doubtful; few, apart from Churchill, had done as much as he had to warn and to advise, publicly and privately, of the dangers of the situation, and, as has been related, his information from Germany had been remarkably accurate. But

Chamberlain had no intention whatever of involving Britain in a European war and, wholly wrongly, thought that it could only be prevented by the Czech concession of the Sudetenland. As he later frankly admitted, Boothby had totally underestimated his pacifism. The whole wretched story of the betrayal of the Czechs now moved to its ghastly climax. It gave Boothby no pleasure whatever, then or later, that on the main issue he had been right throughout.

Chamberlain's purpose when he flew to see Hitler was a straightforward Anglo-German deal for the surrender of the Sudeten German areas to Germany in return for the preservation of the rest of Czechoslovakia; indeed, he was prepared to go further to placate Hitler, but Hitler wanted even more than Chamberlain offered. The Cabinet rebelled when Hitler's terms at his meeting with Chamberlain at Godesberg on 22 September were revealed. Chamberlain returned to an unexpected new belligerence in the House of Commons and the normally pacifist and compliant British press. War seemed imminent. His response was a radio broadcast on the 27th in which he said, 'How horrible, fantastic, incredible it is that we should be digging trenches and trying on gas-masks here because of a quarrel in a far-away country between people of whom we know nothing.' The question was therefore put: Is Czechoslovakia worth a war?

On the following day the Commons met in considerable confusion. Chamberlain described his discussions, and it appeared that he was going to conclude that Britain would, most reluctantly, have to accept the failure of negotiation and to stand by France and Czechoslovakia. At the end of his speech he was handed a piece of paper. At once his melancholy demeanour changed. 'Herr Hitler', he announced, 'has just agreed to postpone his mobilisation for twenty-four hours and to meet me in conference with Signor Mussolini and Monsieur Daladier at Munich.' This was tumultuously greeted with a memorable standing ovation, in which Churchill, Eden, Amery, Nicolson and Boothby did not take part. They had serious apprehensions that something terrible was about to occur, but Boothby still clung to the hope that there would not be a total betrayal. In this he was, again, wrong.

Chamberlain went to Munich a national and international hero; even Duff Cooper joined the Cabinet members who saw him off at the airport. The cynical dismemberment of Czechoslovakia did not take long. The French were virtually ignored, and the Russians totally. The German occupation of the Sudeten territories would be spread over ten days. Chamberlain suggested to Hitler a statement that their agreement was 'symbolic of the desire of our two peoples never to go to war with one another again', which Hitler gladly signed.

Chamberlain returned to London from Munich to frenzied applause, declaring in Downing Street that he had brought back 'peace with honour. I believe it is peace in our time.' Boothby was appalled, declaring that 'This could only mean capitulation.' On the 24th he told Baffy Dugdale that 'this Cabinet must be hurled from power, whatever happens'.

Boothby's conviction that the Czech army would have given the Germans a very hard time was, unknown to him at the time, confirmed by the reports of the British Military Attaché, Brigadier Stronge, who informed the CIGS, Lord Gort, Hore-Belisha and Halifax in June that the training, equipment and morale of the Czech army were excellent. He later wrote to Boothby:

> I gained the impression, however, that Ld Halifax had expected a less favourable report on the army and that Ld Gort was more interested in secondary details than in the factors of greater import. Mr Hore-Belisha impressed me as the soundest man of the trio. No army in Europe was ready for war in 1938; the Czech was by far the most advanced towards that state.*

But Beneš was no Churchill and was a willing partner in capitulation. 'The man primarily responsible for Munich was Beneš,' Boothby wrote.

On the evening of 29 September The Other Club dined, as usual, at the Pinafore Room at the Savoy Hotel. Colin Coote, who was there, has described Churchill as being

in a towering rage and deepening gloom. . . . Hotly seconded by Archie Sinclair, he turned savagely on the two Ministers present, Duff Cooper and Walter Elliot. One could always tell when he was deeply moved, because a minor defect in his palate gave an echoing timbre to his voice. On this occasion it was not an echo, but a supersonic boom. How, he asked, could honourable men with wide experience and fine records in the Great War condone a policy so cowardly? It was sordid, squalid, sub-human, and suicidal.†

There was a lot more in the same vein. Duff Cooper felt obliged to defend his Prime Minister, but without conviction. 'The conversation was pretty rough,' Boothby noted. He was a major contributor to the rising tide of anger. J. L. Garvin defended himself by saying that he had written a

---

* Stronge's detailed memorandum on 'The state of morale and general readiness for war of the Czechoslovakian Republic at the time of the Munich crisis in September 1938 and the period immediately preceding it' was sent by him to Boothby, and it is in his papers. There are copies also in the Bodleian Library, Oxford, and the Imperial War Museum. It should be read by the Munich revisionists.

† Colin Coote, The Other Club, pp. 88–9.

strong article in the *Observer* the previous Sunday. 'What use is that', Boothby intervened, 'after forty flabby ones?' Garvin was incensed and left. Then, after midnight, someone realised that the first editions of the morning papers would be on sale and rushed out to buy them. They had the full, abject, Munich terms. Duff Cooper read them out 'with obvious anger and disgust', in Coote's account. 'His nose was wrinkled with horror already. There was a silence as if all had been stricken dumb. Duff rose, and exited without a word.' Boothby's account was that Duff said, 'I can't stomach this,' and, without a moment's hesitation, 'I shall resign.'

The next day he courageously and honourably did so, but Elliot did not. Boothby was devoted to Elliot, but he always considered that his friend never fully recovered, either psychologically or politically, from this failure. After Elliot's death Coote wrote his biography, about which Boothby commented, 'Munich broke the spring, and the watch never told the right time thereafter.' Of Duff Cooper Boothby wrote publicly on 2 October that his resignation 'has already brought a gleam of hope to thousands who have hitherto believed in the fundamental decency of British public life, and who were beginning to despair'.

On the following morning, at eight o'clock, Boothby received an unexpected delegation at his Pall Mall flat. It consisted of a Czech business friend, Richard Weininger, and Dr Victor Jansa, the Commercial Counsellor at the Czech Legation. 'They were both in great and visible distress,' Boothby recorded. They had come to see him to seek his assistance for a British loan to what was left of their country. 'After a mournful cup of coffee', Boothby telephoned Eden, Vansittart and other friends, all of whom were sympathetic. The sum requested was £30 million; in the event the British gave £10 million. Weininger and Jansa had not come to see Boothby as a banker, but as a prominent politician with an outstanding record of support for Czechoslovakia. He had no business or other interest in the matter. It was only much later that some chose to put a sinister interpretation upon his actions.*

On 1 October Boothby sent a despairing letter to Churchill, spelling out the enormity of what had been done and describing it as 'a complete victory for the gangsters'. But he also, correctly, warned him about the immense popularity of Chamberlain's alleged triumph. 'No conqueror returning from victory on the battlefield had come adorned with nobler laurels,' *The Times* declared; and when Churchill described Munich in the Commons as 'a total and unmitigated defeat', an angry hubbub broke

* See chapter 8.

out on the Government benches, and for several minutes it seemed that he was going to be shouted down again. It was one of his most moving speeches: 'All is over. Silent, mournful, abandoned, broken, Czechoslovakia recedes into the darkness.' Surprisingly, Attlee agreed with him, and Duff Cooper's resignation speech was the finest he had ever made, or was ever going to make. Over thirty Conservatives refused to vote for a motion of confidence in the Government. Boothby was one of them.

There was evidently some confusion about whether Boothby had actually abstained. Bracken thought that he had voted for the Government and angrily upbraided him. Boothby at once indignantly wrote to Churchill to inform him that he had indeed abstained with him, but Churchill's reply was remarkably cold: 'Of course, you were perfectly free to vote as you chose, and I am very glad to note that you abstained from voting on the government motion,' but he went on:

I do not understand the agitation which seizes you in these moments of what is, after all, only petty Parliamentary action. You get so distressed about these matters both at the beginning and at the end, and nearly all our friends thought that you had crumpled under the strain. You will certainly live to see many worse things than you have seen at present.

This was a harsh response to a friend and supporter, and Boothby replied with spirit that

I do not think that I have 'crumpled'; but I confess that I cannot regard the events of the past few days, which I sincerely believe portend the doom of at any rate my generation, without agitation. . . . I feel that the consequences of our defeat are incalculable; and that we may well have witnessed the first stage in the downfall of the British Empire. I certainly doubt that we can live to see any worse thing happen than military defeat at the hands of Germany.

This was a highly significant exchange. In the Abdication crisis Boothby had accused Churchill of acting emotionally and erratically; now the charge was reversed. Also Churchill and Bracken could not have failed to notice that Boothby was gravitating much more towards Amery and his circle. Everyone was under a heavy physical and emotional strain, and under such circumstances in the House of Commons even the most calm and level-headed of people may behave oddly and irrationally, but Churchill's rebuke goes beyond this and demonstrates a definite estrangement. Boothby thought that it was only a temporary misunderstanding. This is doubtful. There is a distinct note of exasperation in Churchill's letter at Boothby's temperamental volatility and excitability, but to describe the Munich debates as 'petty Parliamentary action' reads very oddly indeed, except in the context of something approaching contempt, which, for all his faults, Boothby did not merit.

On 9 October he received this telegram:

Executive Committee greatly perturbed over your non-support of Government and request you to meet them before addressing any meeting. Meanwhile we have instructed [Archie] Campbell to withhold notices of public meetings and we invite you to meet Executive on Saturday at 4 p.m.

Boothby's position in his constituency was so strong because of Gardie Duff's skill; the fact that he had been to Czechoslovakia with Gardie Duff; the record of consistency that he had shown; and his immense popularity. In his lengthy speech to his Association at Maud he emphasised that the Commons vote was not a vote of thanks to Chamberlain but a vote approving the policies that had resulted in Munich. He opened his speech by declaring that he came in no 'white sheet of repentance'; he described Munich as 'the greatest diplomatic defeat this country has suffered since the Treaty of Utrecht' and called for national unity, intensive rearmament and national service.

Duff had carefully prepared a motion that 'This meeting is of the opinion that Mr Boothby's actions have been consistent throughout the crisis and in the events leading up to it', which, after a meeting of an hour and a half, was carried unanimously. That evening he spoke to a packed meeting in Fraserburgh; there was some heckling and criticism, but this meeting, also, went well. 'By the time he was finished his critics were shaking him by the hand,' one commentator reported of the Association meeting. Of that in Fraserburgh, 'Again he won his audience. . . . Heckling was moderate and applied in good humour.' He then spoke in Peterhead, where the *Aberdeen Press and Journal* recorded another full hall and that he 'was given an enthusiastic reception'. On the 19th he spoke at two meetings in Turriff and had the same response.

The *Buchan Observer*, which disagreed with him so strongly on Munich, was characteristically generous:

Mr Robert Boothby, MP, has claimed more than once that he has a special hold upon the affections of his constituents; that they like him, enjoy heckling him, and would hate to turn him down.

This is true. If ever there was a time when he might have been expected to encounter hostility, that time is now. Instead, he receives a unanimous vote of confidence from his Executive, cordial hearings at all his meetings, and something that looks very like a general gesture of approval. . . . Why? Leaving personal considerations aside, we believe the explanation is that his constituents have learnt to take the long view of Mr Boothby, and on a long view he is sound.

The other 'rebels' were not so fortunate.

* * *

The fury of the Chamberlainites against the anti-Munich Conservatives carried them into excesses of zeal and conspiracy. The Party organisation, taking its lead from Downing Street, where press management under Chamberlain – in close co-operation with the German Embassy – had reached unprecedented skill and ruthlessness,* would not tolerate any more dissent. There were threats to withdraw the Whip, and immense pressure was put upon the constituency Associations of the anti-appeasers; Macmillan later recalled that it was the most intense period he ever experienced, and even Churchill was under severe threat in Epping.

A particularly well-organised and squalid campaign was launched by Patrick Blair in Kinross and West Perthshire against the Duchess of Atholl, who responded to the planned vote of no confidence by her Association by immediately resigning her seat and standing in the resulting by-election as an Independent. She was a controversial woman of great courage and character who had already rejected the Conservative Whip, but a poor speaker and notoriously humourless; Churchill and others had urged her not to make this precipitate step, but she had been greatly heartened by the fact that Vernon Bartlett had taken the same action and had been triumphantly re-elected at Bridgwater over the Government candidate.

Blair was determined that this humiliation would not be repeated, and he and James Stuart hurled themselves into defeating her. The Liberals ordered their candidate to withdraw, but she did so with ill grace and did not support the Duchess. The Conservatives poured senior ministers and MPs into the constituency, which was deluged with pro-Chamberlain literature; one pamphlet had the names of seventy Conservative MPs urging electors to vote for the Government candidate, one William McNair Snadden, a Perthshire farmer. The Duchess had no organisation and had good cause to be resentful of the discreditable methods employed against her.

One of these was to pressurise Boothby, who had at once offered to speak for her. One difficulty was that although Churchill had issued a letter of support, he had decided not to speak for her, recognising that to do so might well occasion a final dispute with his already highly critical Epping Conservatives. She was also, officially, no longer a Conservative. Stuart now told Boothby – as he did Churchill – that if he spoke for the Duchess, he would assuredly lose the Party Whip. It was characteristic of the tactics employed in one of the dirtiest by-election campaigns of modern times, from which only the Duchess emerged with any distinction,

*See Richard Cockett, *The Twilight of Truth*, for the full disclosure of this extraordinary, and very successful, manipulation of the press. It confirms totally what Churchill, Boothby and others strongly suspected at the time. It was despicable.

and which faithfully reflected one of the most disgraceful periods in the history of the Conservative Party, and Chamberlain's personal vindictiveness against anyone who stood against him.

In the post-Munich Oxford by-election, caused by the death of Bobby Bourne, of the Conservative dissidents only Macmillan publicly campaigned for the anti-Government candidate, A. D. Lindsay, the Master of Balliol, against the Conservative, Quintin Hogg. This was an act of outstanding political courage, which prompted Boothby to describe him as 'the bravest of us all'.

But Kinross and West Perthshire was a Scottish seat, and even Boothby buckled under the pressures. Gardie Duff told him in no uncertain terms that he had done his best to save him from the East Aberdeenshire Association's wrath, but that if he spoke for the Duchess he would resign as his Chairman. This was decisive. 'I could not face the possibility of your resignation,' he wrote to Duff. 'You may or may not be flattered by this!'

He wrote to the Duchess:

> A good deal has happened here since you went north! When it was announced in the press that I was going to speak for you I was given to understand that if I did so the authorities would take such a serious view that it would probably involve my being deprived of the Whip. I might have been prepared to leave the Party on this issue, although as you know it is a serious step to take. But the Chairman of my Association is Gardie Duff, whom I think you know. He is also Chairman this year of the Eastern Divisional Council. He is also my oldest and best friend. He told me that while he personally deplored the action of your Association, if I came out in open support of you he would feel obliged to resign. Frankly, I cannot face this.

There was also the important point that both Boothby and Churchill had tried to persuade the Duchess not to resign her seat, as they believed that opinion in the country and Party was moving in their direction. This may not have been true in terms of numbers, but the calibre of the rebellious Conservatives was formidable. Also the Duchess had made the major mistake of standing as an Independent, not as an Independent Unionist, as Bartlett had done, in spite of Churchill's advice to her to do so. Boothby courageously told her that he would be glad to write her a public letter of support, but she foolishly rejected this generous offer, tartly replying that his resignation of the Whip would have been more useful to her campaign. She was a difficult woman, as her biographer frankly concedes,* but I suspect that Boothby felt uncomfortable about succumbing to these intense Party pressures; significantly, he never referred to this dismal episode in his memoirs.

*S. J. Hetherington, *Katherine Atholl, Against the Tide*.

If the Liberals had been more active, and polling day on 21 December had not been in the middle of an unseasonable blizzard, which was to the great advantage of the Conservative machine with its fleets of cars, there might have been a different result. In a low poll – sixty-seven per cent – the Duchess was defeated by only 1,400 votes. In view of the massive Conservative investment in people and pressure – over fifty MPs having been dragooned into the campaign – this was hardly a triumph for the Government, although it was hailed as such. James Stuart's brother-in-law, Ivor Cobbold, charmingly telegraphed her: 'Am delighted you are out.' Stuart taunted Churchill over the result and challenged him to be the next to resign the Whip. 'I fear that this incident led to some harsh words, perhaps mostly on my part,' Stuart later wrote, 'and the wound took a long time to heal.'* When Churchill felt compelled to agree to Stuart's appointment as Chief Whip in January 1941, it was with deep reluctance. But Stuart was as adroit an operator and acolyte for Churchill as he had been for Baldwin and Chamberlain, and achieved his favour as a necessary link with the Conservative Establishment. His role in poisoning Churchill's relations with Boothby is difficult to overestimate.

When Churchill became Prime Minister in 1940, the Duchess applied to rejoin the Conservative Party, to which Churchill readily and enthusiastically agreed; however, although she continued to render notable public service, the death of her husband in 1942 was a heavy blow and her political career was at an end. Happily Mr Snadden's moment of fame was to prove very brief. He had served his purpose and duly returned to the obscurity from which he had unfortunately emerged. In 1951 Stuart made him Parliamentary Under-Secretary for Scotland. He had a long memory.†

Duff Cooper wrote to Boothby from the Travellers' Club in Paris on 26 October:

> What a bloody world it is. Situation here is worse than in England. In the Chamber Henri de Coalis stands alone for what at least a score of us represents in the House of Commons. To doubt the good faith of Hitler is to admit you are a Soviet agent. A friendly paragraph about me in the French press pointed out that as I was related to the Dukes of Fife and Rutland it was most improbable that I was in Soviet pay! I repeat, what a bloody world – frosty mornings golden trees misty evenings and great peace that one can forget the bloodiness for a few hours.

---

*Stuart, *op. cit.*, p. 95.

†Boothby, in spite of everything, came to like Snadden, remarking, in 1949, that 'he delivered his usual livestock speech, inaudibly, for about the seventh time'. Thus was he marked out for preferment.

Speaking in the Commons on 1 November Boothby said that

We have been continuously and grossly misled by ministers over a period of several years as to the true state of our defences. You cannot get away from that. To listen to the speeches of some ministers, at different periods, you might have thought that guns and aeroplanes were flowing in on them in such an avalanche, like rain, that it was almost a source of embarrassment. Indeed, there were moments when one felt quite sorry for the Germans.

His disillusionment with Chamberlain was made clear in this and other speeches when he called for courageous and effective leadership.On 8 November he said in the Commons:

His Majesty's Government does not yet realise the feeling in this country, the determination of the country to maintain at all costs its principles, its prestige, and its position as the centre of the greatest Empire in the world. . . . The people do not want to be soothed, humbugged and drugged any more. They want to have the truth; they want to face the realities of the modern world, however grim they may be. They also want imaginative and courageous leadership . . . if the people do not get the leadership from this Government they will find a government, as they have often done before, which will give them the leadership they require to save themselves before it is too late.

As the post-Munich euphoria subsided, people were beginning to listen more carefully to this reiterated message, but the Government did not. There was to be no Ministry of Supply and no urgency in rearmament. The Skoda works and *matériel* of the Czech army were now in German hands, a magnificent addition to their own already formidable military resources. The Chamberlainite revisionist argument that Munich bought Britain a year to rearm sufficiently is a total myth. Self-satisfied, over-confident and unaware of the even greater dangers, for which they were largely responsible, the Chamberlain Government drifted contentedly along, deaf to all warnings and entreaties, arrogant and intolerant. The Labour Party, with the exception of a few realists, was little better.

Shortly before Christmas Boothby wrote a public letter to Gardie Duff, lamenting the continuing failure of the Government to rearm or to recreate a Ministry of Supply, on which he had spoken and written so often:

The melancholy and inescapable fact remains that this Government have allowed Hitler to reverse the decision of the Great War. The people who were killed between 1914 and 1918 died in order to prevent the German domination of the continent of Europe, and to bring about a system of collective security which would end war. To-day, Germany is the undisputed master of Europe, and collective security does not exist. . . . My warning is a very simple one. It is that unless the Government demand a far greater effort from all classes of the community than they now contemplate, the end of the British Empire is in sight.

But there were some glimmers of hope. Even the *Daily Mail* commented on Chamberlain's intolerance of criticism and, referring to Eden, Churchill, Duff Cooper and Boothby, wrote that 'In their irascible independence old English Toryism is reborn significantly in the hour of crisis. Commented a fruity voice in the Carlton Club last week: "They are rogues, but by God we may need them yet."'

8

Czech Assets

*B*oothby spent the Christmas of 1938 with Oliver Stanley, now President of the Board of Trade, in his Westmoreland home. He found that although his host was troubled about the European situation, Stanley told him that the Prime Minister was supremely confident of the ultimate success of his policy, that the sense of mission was strong within him, and that this had greatly impressed the Cabinet. 'This looked like another dose of Appeasement,' Boothby glumly wrote.

Speaking at his regular public meetings in his constituency on 17 and 18 January 1939, he concentrated on local issues, notably herrings and farming, but struck a more optimistic note on British strength, particularly the navy, which, as he stressed, was essential to deter the Germans. The *Buchan Observer* continued its unqualified support for Chamberlain and Munich, but also reported Boothby's fears that the dictators,

now at the peak of their power and confronted with the prospect of waning predominance, may decide to gamble all on the chance of a great military triumph before it is too late. That is the danger spot, which makes preparedness the overwhelming concern of Britain, France and America. One year's uninterrupted devotion to national defence is not a heavy price to pay for that long future in which social reform will be able to function freely. Allow disaster to overtake democracy now, and there will be no future for free men. In that terrible thought there is the fullest justification for suspending all minor differences, and no purpose can be served by evading the issue.

The *Buchan Observer*, probably accurately reflecting Boothby's constituents, opened the New Year cheerfully, but carefully reported that

Boothby did not; it was certainly not enamoured of his proposals for compulsory national service.

The East Aberdeenshire Conservatives continued to proclaim their faith in the Prime Minister and all his works, but although Boothby expressed the hope that the Government's foreign policy would work, he gave another robust defence of his position in a long letter to the *Buchan Observer*, on which the editor commented:

One of the things which I have always admired about Mr Robert Boothby MP is the skill and force with which he defends himself when attacked, and maintains his viewpoint in the face of challenge. . . . Frankly I am so intensely pro-Chamberlain that I may be suspected of bias; but on great issues all points of view deserve respectful consideration.

Seldom has the importance of having a strong constituency base been more vividly emphasised. All the other Munich rebels, most conspicuously Churchill, had a very difficult time indeed in their constituencies and in the press, but although Boothby's press and Association were overwhelmingly pro-Chamberlain and Munich, he alone had very little trouble. As matters progressed even this evaporated as his constituents realised that he had been right all along, but even at this most difficult period they were staunch, particularly Gardie Duff. It says a great deal for them, and for him.

Taking the view that 'Russia was now the only hope', he spoke in Edinburgh on 4 March to urge the still very unfashionable view that 'Friendship and co-operation between Great Britain and the USSR would tip the European balance of power decisively in favour of the Western democracies; and the effect of this upon the countries of Central and Eastern Europe would be immediate.' Such expressions were ill-received in Downing Street, and Hoare was instructed to denounce these 'Jitter-bugs' and 'timid panic-mongers', and to announce the dawning of 'A Golden Age'. This was on 10 March. Five days later Hitler's forces occupied the remnants of Czechoslovakia; a day later he was himself personally in Prague, marvelling at its beauty. Chamberlain at first seemed to be prepared to condone this outrage, but the mood in the Commons and in the country had now definitely changed. When he spoke in Birmingham on 17 March, there was a new note; if this was a step in the direction of world domination, it would have to be resisted.

But how? On 19 March Boothby denounced appeasement again in a long and prominently featured letter in the *Daily Telegraph*:

What are the facts of the present situation? Let us face them at last. We began to rearm two years too late. The 'policy of appeasement' was a desperate gamble, out of weakness, on the good faith of the dictators. From some points of view it was a legitimate gamble. We did not mean business over Abyssinia, over Spain, or over Czechoslovakia. And, if you are so weak that you do not mean business, it is sometimes advisable to try to do business. The attempt has failed. The policy is in ashes.

What are the lessons of the past six months? That you cannot do business with the Nazis, because their signature is not worth the paper upon which it is written. To them treaties and agreements are simply instruments of policy. They are out for world domination, and can be checked only by superior strength and iron resolution.

He called for a Polish–Romanian–Balkan entente, fully backed by Britain, France and Russia. What he got from Chamberlain, to his astonishment, was a wholly unexpected British guarantee to Poland, which, without any alliance with Russia, struck Boothby as 'an act of insanity'; in this he was fully joined by Lloyd George. However, Churchill was impressed by the completely new tone of Chamberlain's Birmingham speech, and the Conservative dissidents decided to welcome the guarantee, Churchill remarking in the House, 'God helping we can do no other.' As he later wrote, 'Here was decision at last, taken at the worst possible moment and on the least satisfactory ground, which must surely lead to the slaughter of tens of millions of people.' It only made some sense if the alliance with Russia was pressed forward, but it was not. Chamberlain's dislike and distrust of both the United States and the Soviet Union were very deep, and the negotiations were conducted with exceptional dilatoriness.

Meanwhile, on 7 April the Italians invaded and swiftly occupied Albania. Speaking in the Commons Churchill declared that 'the dark bitter waters are rising fast on every side'. Indeed, they were.

On 27 April Chamberlain, with much reluctance, agreed to introduce military conscription. If it was, in the circumstances, little more than a symbolic gesture, it was welcomed by the dissident Conservatives; but, to their dismay, it was denounced by Attlee and Sinclair, who led their Parties into the lobby against it. This particularly upset them as Churchill and his friends were now calling for a national government and found support from Stafford Cripps; Oliver Stanley actually offered his post in the Cabinet if this would help matters, but he only got a formal acknowledgment. So much had the tide turned, and so swiftly, that a strong 'Churchill Must Come Back' campaign developed, with the *Daily Telegraph*, *Manchester Guardian* and *Daily Mirror* taking the lead. Posters urging this course began to appear, but little else seemed to be happening in that eerie and unreal summer, except that the British now agreed to guarantee Romania and Greece.

Among Boothby's friends was Virgil Tilea, the Romanian Ambassador, who fully shared his views on the perils of the Polish guarantee, and Boothby later claimed some involvement in the guarantee to Romania; he also urged a conference between Britain, France, Russia and the Balkan powers. The Romanians got their worthless guarantee, but the conference proposal was curtly rejected. Speaking to his constituents in Maud on 15 April, Boothby described the policy of guarantees as

in some respect a reckless, and even desperate, policy – but, if carried through ruthlessly to its logical conclusion, it may still succeed in saving the world from war. One thing is certain. A policy of collective security on a limited liability basis cannot hope to succeed. Abyssinia, Austria, Czechoslovakia, and now Albania, are melancholy witnesses of that fact. If we are now to have a pact of real security, and not a suicide pact, we must come in ourselves with all we have, and make sure that this Eastern Front is a reality, and that the forces behind it are adequate. The key to this is unquestionably Russia.

He urged a mutual assistance pact with military staff talks, and said that he had 'good reason to believe' that it would be accepted by the Soviets. His source was the Russian Ambassador Maisky, who told him that Litvinov was urging a six-power meeting in Bucharest; its rejection by the British was a major factor in Litvinov's downfall and his replacement by the evil Molotov. 'Let us save humanity from the final catastrophe by taking, at this eleventh hour, resolute action in time,' Boothby was declaring at Maud. He later wrote in 1947:

This was my last effort. It got a great deal of publicity; and had about as much effect as a wave breaking on the seashore. When Litvinov was dismissed, owing to the patent failure of his policy, I gave up hope; and resigned myself to the inevitability of another world war.

As he wrote in a detailed memorandum in September, after a long discussion with Maisky on the Anglo-Soviet negotiations, 'The whole story is one of muddle, bungle and blunder without parallel; and it fits in well enough with the rest of the policy which has landed us where we are.' This was only too true. Churchill's and Boothby's discontent with the Government was not confined to Europe.

At this point, when the Conservative dissidents were concentrating upon Europe, there came another British betrayal – this time of the Jews, when the Government published a White Paper on Palestine which was in fact a repudiation of the Balfour Declaration. The key proposal was that Jewish immigration of a maximum of 75,000 over five years could be stopped at the end of the period by majority decision of the population of Palestine. It was not difficult to anticipate what that result would be.

When the White Paper was debated in the Commons on 22 and 23 May, first Amery and then, most memorably, Churchill denounced the

Government for its perfidy, and especially the Minister responsible, Malcolm MacDonald. Churchill also quoted, with devastating effect, the repeated public pledges of Neville Chamberlain on behalf of the Declaration and the rights of the Jews to their own homeland. 'Well, they have answered his call. They have fulfilled his hopes. How can he find it in his heart to strike them this mortal blow?' The Zionists were outraged by this betrayal, and the Arabs were not placated. MacDonald and the Government had a terrible two days, and its majority in the vote slumped dramatically, Churchill, Boothby and Cazalet being the most prominent Conservatives who voted against the Government. Walter Elliot – Baffy Dugdale's source of vital Cabinet information – did not vote, nor did Hore-Belisha. But Elliot, to Dugdale's renewed despair, did not resign. His friends were becoming tired of his excuses; Boothby took the view that Munich had broken his political nerve, and he may well have been right. Churchill, certainly, had come to a hostile view of Elliot's political courage, which he did not forget when he formed his Government a year later. Nor did he forget MacDonald's performance, either.

Boothby wrote to Churchill:

> Long after the names of the miserable creatures who are now supposed to govern us have been lost in a merciful oblivion, the incredible services you have rendered this country will be remembered. . . . One of the few things in my life of which I am proud is that in all matters of major policy during the past five years I have hitched my waggon to your star.

But, in the course of these intense political activities, as the war clouds gathered blackly in the summer of 1939, Boothby had additional preoccupations.

It is not the task of a biographer to paint the portrait of his subject in false colours, and Bob Boothby would hardly have selected this one if he had sought such a result. He cheerfully admitted error and stupidity in his own lifetime, but believed that on the major incidents in his life he had nothing to fear from a totally objective examination of his actions, based on the facts. When his role in the events which will now be related came under question, he willingly and voluntarily handed over all his personal papers to the body investigating it, later remarking that 'This was hardly the action of a guilty man.' The papers are very substantial, and, based upon them, this is his biographer's account of what actually happened over the tangled affair of the Czech assets.

This narrative is based particularly upon the documents and evidence submitted to, and published by, the Select Committee of the House of

Commons set up in October 1940 to investigate Boothby's conduct.* The published letters and memoranda are quite exceptionally voluminous, and while the conclusions of the Committee were, as will be seen, controversial, the thoroughness of their search through Boothby's and Richard Weininger's papers cannot be questioned.

Few people at the time did more than read the actual Report, which is relatively brief, and most relied on the details in the press. As this episode is so crucial in Boothby's life, a new examination of the actual record is long overdue.

As has been emphasised, Boothby was impulsive, easy-going and remarkably casual about money. He was, throughout his life, absurdly generous to others, while enjoying the good things of life for himself. He was a natural gambler with his own money, although a scrupulous banker and broker for his clients and his company. He himself saw no dichotomy in all this, and it constantly puzzled him when others did. He was obsessed with politics, and being in politics, unhappily, meant making money in order to stay in them. His hero Lloyd George had often sailed very close to the wind to achieve the same purpose, as had many others, before, then and later. With a derisory parliamentary salary, no paid expenses, a far-flung constituency and no other source of income, his banking interests were vital to his survival.

After he left Chase, Henderson and Tennant in 1936, he had had to put up £25,000 when he became Managing Director of the First British-American Corporation. His personal resources were only £10,000, so he borrowed the remaining £15,000 against the security of his shares in the Corporation. In the context of 1936, this seemed a perfectly reasonable security. By the beginning of 1939 things looked very different. It was not a time for banking and business confidence, and as the Stock Exchanges of Europe and the United States slumped, so did the fortunes of investors and brokers.

Boothby kept his banking and political activities strictly separate, and his papers contain little or nothing on the former. There is nothing remotely suspicious about this because they were the property of his bank. However, at least one of his peripheral ventures was somewhat odd. This was Airtime Ltd, which in 1937 sought to exploit commercial broadcasting in Europe, and in which Mosley and one of his strongest supporters, Peter Eckersley, a former chief engineer in the BBC, were closely involved. Boothby represented Jack Buchanan Radio Corporation Ltd.

* *The Select Committee Report on the Conduct of a Member. With the Proceedings of the Committee, Minutes of Evidence and Appendices* (published 18 December 1940).

The only known success of Airtime Ltd was a part interest in a station in Heligoland, and there is no evidence that Boothby was involved. Indeed, all the evidence is that he was not. This seems to have been wholly a banking matter: they all wanted to make money and failed to do so.* Boothby certainly did not share Mosley's and Eckersley's political views, and subsequently broke all connections with Eckersley.

In the course of his business activities with the First British-American Corporation, Boothby had met and befriended Weininger. As Weininger later affectionately wrote,

We first met at the London Stock Exchange. Then, as now, Boothby was warm, gregarious, overweight, drinking heavily,† and loving every minute of his life. When a customs official once asked him if the bottles of whisky he was carrying were for resale, or gifts, or for his own personal use, Boothby said with a big smile, 'Look at me.' Bob Boothby's red complexion, his massive girth, left no question as to the eventual destination of the whisky.'‡

What began as a business relationship developed into one of the great and enduring friendships of Boothby's life, and of Weininger's.

Richard Weininger was born on 27 July 1887, in Baden, near Vienna, in the old Austro-Hungarian Empire. His father was an eminent goldsmith, or, as he called himself, a 'gold artifacteur', or gold-working man. His principal works were in the Vienna Museum of Fine Arts and his most beautiful were in the Hermitage of St Petersburg, now Leningrad, where they had been commissioned by Czar Alexander II. He had a deep dislike of Freud, commenting to his son that 'that man is so money hungry I want to tell you I don't want to have anything to do with him'. Richard's brother, Otto, who was seven years older than he, was a legend in Vienna. While he was still in his late teens he wrote a book called *Sex and Character*, which was not only an instantaneous best-seller, but was also remarkably durable and made a great impression. But, at the age of twenty-three, he took his own life, and his second book, entitled *About the Last Dreams in Life*, was published posthumously.

In spite of this tragedy the family's life was comfortable and successful, although austere. The family was strongly Anglophile and a supporter of the Emperor, Franz Joseph. Richard not only became devoted to music,

* I am most grateful to Mr Myles Eckersley and Lady Mosley for their detailed information on this curious episode. It appears to me to have been a wholly legitimate, and wholly unsuccessful, business enterprise, with no political implications at all.

† This was excessively harsh. Boothby's consumption of alcohol was, like Churchill's and other politicians of the time, considerably more than would be regarded as prudent, but he was, although overweight, remarkably fit and healthy, and an excellent golfer. He was also at this time working immensely hard, and Boothby's surprise at this reference was shared by others who knew him well.

‡ Richard Weininger, *Exciting Years*, p. 121.

but loved the theatre and was intimately involved in its development as he grew up.

As a young man he visited Germany – although not Berlin – Paris, London, the United States and Russia. When he reached America in 1905, he had a letter of introduction to Henry Goldman, the founder of the firm of Goldman Sachs, the investment bankers. The young Weininger was fascinated by America, and in particular the virtually undeveloped Florida; he was in San Francisco before the earthquake and 'was in Los Angeles before there was Los Angeles. This was all great, but I wanted to get back to New York. This is where I wanted to be.'

It was in New York that he met the businessman, Otto Kahn, and the composer, Gustav Mahler, whom he had previously met in Vienna. One day Kahn told him that the Union Pacific railway company intended to increase its dividend. He knew this in advance as he was a director of the company, and estimated that Union Pacific shares might well rise from 100 to 140, an increase of forty points. And on the New York Stock Exchange at that time it was possible to buy stock on ten-per-cent margins and at interest rates of three to three-and-a-half per cent. Kahn bought on margins for Weininger's account a very large amount of Union Pacific stock, which did indeed increase by forty points. The young Weininger, at eighteen years of age, found that he had a paper profit in excess of $1 million. As he put it,

So I moved out of my bachelor quarters on Morningside Heights and moved into the Waldorf Astoria, then still on 34th Street, the site of the Empire State Building. I had beautiful quarters, a bedroom and a drawing-room, and I set out for the next year or so to enjoy life in New York.

This idyllic period ended rather rapidly when he lost his paper profit of $1 million and, in fact, saved just enough to cover the cost of his hotel bill. He had ventured into the commodity market, had made an error of judgment and lost everything. In his words:

So I moved out of the Waldorf Astoria and moved in with another bachelor friend. We were both very poor. In fact, there was only one bed in the apartment, and we had to share it. But it did not matter to me. I knew my routine remittance from my family would soon be arriving from Vienna. It is strange, looking back on it, but I had almost a sporting feeling of festivity at the time. I never took my fortune seriously when I won it. I never took it seriously when I had it. So I did not take it seriously when I lost it. Irresponsible though it may seem, it was fun to win, and was fun to lose. I knew someday I would win again.

Weininger then returned to Vienna and became the manufacturer of a folding typewriter, from an idea that he and a friend had developed, which made their fortune again. Weininger personally, still only in his early twenties and a student, made more than $200,000 out of this particular project.

Meanwhile, he maintained and developed his passionate interest in music. He was now married with a small son, but was appalled when the First World War broke out. 'All I know is that I hated the Prussians and loved the English. In little more than a week, a summer holiday from the University had been changed into a world war, on the wrong side.'

He presented himself for military service in the late spring of 1915, but as he had been ill he was not considered fit for active duty. He joined a horse-drawn artillery regiment and was put to work in the War Ministry, where he spent the whole of the war. Afterwards, following a brief and extraordinary mission to buy animal skins from the Communist Béla Kun in Hungary, he resumed his strange entrepreneurial business career.

He was appalled by the collapse of the Austro-Hungarian Empire and became a friend of Thomas Masaryk, who had been his university professor in Vienna, and who became, somewhat reluctantly, the leader and first President of the new Czechoslovakia.

Weininger then began buying and selling the huge quantities of surplus clothing and equipment left by the Americans at the end of the war when they returned to the United States. 'Everything was completely legitimate, above board, and we made a small fortune.' He then bought a controlling interest in the Union Bank in Vienna, generally known as the Vienna Bank. In March 1923, having divorced his first wife, he married his second, Trude. He also decided, 'for reasons to consolidate our whole family on one passport', to become a Czech citizen.

There followed years of happiness in Munich and then in Berlin after 1923, which he described with such enthusiasm in his memoirs. He came to know almost everyone in the worlds of art and literature as well as in business, became a passionate and successful polo player, and a scholar as well as an extremely wealthy businessman. Like so many in Europe, he initially regarded Hitler, whom he first met at a railway station in 1930, as a joke: 'On our daily rounds, we simply did not meet people who voted for Hitler, and so we did not take him seriously. Similarly, many of our business dealings were conducted in the city of Hamburg and other anti-Nazi strongholds.' It was only in January 1933, when Hitler became Chancellor, that Weininger realised the reality of the Nazi threat.

But there then ensued, none the less, a strange co-existence of four years with the Nazis in which my friends and I continued to be victims of our own illusions. The Nazis outraged us, then mollified us. We thought the Nazis intractable, but hoped that their attitudes could be mitigated. In retrospect, the Nazis played the game of the nineteen-thirties brilliantly. We were fools.

Weininger gradually expanded his business interests, primarily in Czechoslovakia and England, but it was not until late 1937 and early 1938 that the full impact of the Nazi ambitions dawned upon him. He was particularly shocked, with his love of Vienna, to discover that

the Austrian Nazis seemed even worse than the German ones. There were Austrian officers and recruits in the SS at once. We were all so horrified, as were the good Germans of all origins, by the *Kristallnacht* purges of Jewish men, women and children throughout the Third Reich. As aliens, as non-Aryans, as people, we knew we had to leave Germany at once or risk certain death. So, holding our Czech passports, we simply travelled as a matter of routine from Berlin to Prague. We left everything we owned in Germany behind. We had saved very much, and lost very much.

One thing Boothby and Weininger had in common was an intense interest in developments in Czechoslovakia as that unhappy country approached its doom, and it was a subject on which Boothby felt passionately. When he made his visits in April and September 1938, it was in his capacity as an alarmed British politician; at the time he had no business relations with Weininger at all. His speeches and actions in 1938 over Czechoslovakia and Munich had no connection whatever with his quite separate City interests. These were going very badly, but he was not alone: Eden was in despair about his financial situation, and Churchill was seriously considering selling his beloved Chartwell.

So bad was Boothby's situation that in August 1938 he raised a temporary unsecured personal loan of £5,000 from Sir Alfred Butt, a former parliamentary colleague. This was a purely financial and business transaction, but it was a terrible mistake, from which everything flowed. Butt was not a pleasant man, and it remains a puzzle why Boothby did not seek another source for urgent finance. However, it was a straightforward arrangement – or so it seemed at the time.

By January 1939 Weininger was extremely anxious about his wife's personal assets in Czechoslovakia, which were blocked by the National Bank of Prague, the National Bank of Czechoslovakia and the Boehmische Union Bank. They were in the form of Czech Government bonds, worth over £200,000, which today would be equivalent to nearly $1 million. Weininger turned to Boothby and asked if he could negotiate the unfreezing of his wife's assets. This was wholly understandable. Boothby was not only a personal friend, but was so well known as a friend of Czechoslovakia that, as has been related, immediately after Munich the official Czech delegation seeking a loan from the British Government called on him in his City office to seek his advice and help, which he willingly gave. There was no question of any payment to Boothby being sought or given.

Weininger's new proposal was a personal transaction between a client and his banker. Boothby said that he would try, and it was agreed that he would receive ten per cent of the amount of any assets that he recovered. Weininger paid Boothby £1,000 for expenses for his trip to Prague. In order to facilitate the release of the funds, a British company, the Zota Company Ltd, was established, with Chase as Managing Director. The purpose was simple: to seek the transfer of the Weininger assets to Weininger personally, in the hope that this might be more acceptable to the Prague banks and, more importantly, to the Czech authorities. This was a calculated stratagem – 'to put a British flag on the claim', in Weininger's own words – but a perfectly justifiable and wholly legal one. It was Boothby's idea, as he later made clear to the House of Commons. The assets, once received, would be paid by the company to Mrs Weininger and her daughters. If these methods were unusual, the circumstances and the times were also very unusual. Chase, for all his limitations, was a man of the utmost probity and would never have agreed to be involved in anything remotely dishonest or dishonourable. Nor was he.

But on 15 March the Germans invaded and occupied the remainder of Czechoslovakia. This thunderclap event, the crucial incident on the road to war, made it obvious that there was no point in Boothby even attempting to go to Prague. He and Weininger agreed that their arrangement must come to an end, and Boothby returned the £1,000 he had received for his expenses. It seemed that his personal and business financial interest in the matter had, accordingly, ceased. There was no written record of the transaction apart from the documents establishing the Zota Company. With the Nazis now in control in Prague, it seemed that Weininger had lost everything, and the matter was, apparently, closed.

But, on the morning of 15 March, as soon as he reached the Treasury, S. D. Waley,* the Under-Secretary, on his own initiative – subsequently endorsed by the Chancellor of the Exchequer, Simon – ordered that payment of all Czech balances in Britain should be immediately blocked to prevent the Germans seizing them as they had in the case of the Austrian assets. It was a welcome change from appeasement, but it was not immediately made public.

This resulted in a major misunderstanding. On the 16th, Boothby and Weininger lunched together at the Carlton Grill, at which they agreed that the assets should be blocked at once. Boothby telephoned Waley to

* Sigismund David Waley, CB, MC, later Sir David Waley, head of the Foreign Finance Division of the Treasury, 1924–39.

urge this; he also alerted the Chief Whip, Margesson, and then spoke to Waley again. He did not know, nor was he told, that the action had already been taken.

Boothby had known Waley since he had been Churchill's PPS, and they had maintained personal contact as members of a small group interested in economic matters, who regularly lunched together as an informal club. Although it was Waley who had frozen the Czech assets, when Boothby telephoned him to urge him to take this course as no public announcement had been made, Waley, accordingly, was non-committal and merely said that he had taken note of Boothby's views. Boothby telephoned him several times during the day and had the same response. Margesson also did not know the situation, but, again, said he would take careful note of Boothby's arguments.

The announcement of the blocking of the assets was made on 17 March and it was confirmed by Act of Parliament on the 27th. Boothby believed for some time that his intervention had been decisive and that he personally had prevented another craven capitulation to Germany. This was, in the circumstances, understandable. As a senior civil servant Waley could not tell him what had been done, even as a friend. As he subsequently said,

the relation[ship] between a Civil Servant and a Member of Parliament is always a little delicate, and may be characterised either by great zeal or great discretion on the part of the Member of Parliament. I think it is in keeping with Mr Boothby's character that he showed great zeal in the [Czechoslovak] cause.

When he was later questioned, he robustly defended Boothby's actions, then and afterwards, as perfectly proper throughout. This fact has not been given its rightful prominence. Waley emerges from this, and later matters, with considerably more distinction than his Chancellor of the Exchequer. He did not deliberately deceive his friend on this occasion; as no public announcement had been made by the Government and the Bank of England, he had no choice as a civil servant but to be evasive. Boothby, when he learned the full truth, entirely accepted this, but at the time he was unintentionally misled as to how decisive his intervention had been.

The decision also reopened the question of the Weininger claim, as the Bank of England issued instructions to ascertain the amount of such claims by British holders of obligations from Czechoslovakia, including persons not of British nationality but ordinarily resident or carrying on business in Britain. Weininger's solicitors, on Treasury and Bank advice, advised him and Chase that claims could not be entered by the Zota Company, but only directly by Mrs Weininger and her daughters. This was duly done. The sum involved was £240,000. Again, there was no question of impropriety, let alone illegality. The Weininger claim was a perfectly valid one under the terms of the Bank of England's ruling and was, eventually, honoured. Mrs Weininger received £100,000, and her daughter Edith £50,000; the other daughter, Charlotte, who had gone to France, was judged not to be a Czech refugee resident in London and received nothing. The payments were made in 1941.

This was the situation when, on 22 March, the House of Commons debated the Czechoslovak (Banking, Accounts, etc.) Bill in an atmosphere of rare unanimity and in a totally different political atmosphere. Boothby spoke and congratulated Simon warmly on his action. One of his main points was that

There should be a single fund established as quickly as possible of all the Czech assets in London, in order to pay off those British creditors who either left funds in Czechoslovakia or invested funds in Czechoslovakia, relying on the assurances of the British Government and the other Governments signatory to the Munich pact. . . . Every person – and I would apply this to Czech residents in this country as well as to British residents – who can prove assets in Prague ought now to be paid out of the fund, at the last quoted rate of exchange prevailing prior to the seizure of Czechoslovakia. This applies particularly to Czech bonds. . . . I feel, and I am sure that the House as a whole feels, that there really is a great necessity for speed in this matter. We are rightly giving an indemnity to the Government and to the banks in respect of the wise, courageous and quick action they have taken. But it is very necessary . . . that the position arising out of the credits held at present by British citizens in Prague, and by other citizens resident in this country, should be cleared up at the earliest possible moment, and that the minimum of hardship should be involved. I beg of the Right Honourable Gentleman, if he contemplates, as I imagine he does, setting up a fund, that this should be done, and the fund distributed as quickly as possible.

These sanguine hopes were to be dashed. Had prompt action been taken on the lines Boothby had argued, the story – and Boothby's whole life – would have been very different. Having, for once, taken decisive action – significantly, not by ministers but by a senior official entirely on his own initiative – the sense of urgency passed. This was demonstrated by the fact that although Waley had blocked the Czech assets in Britain, some £6 million in Czech gold was transferred to the Germans by the Treasury and the Bank of England, an action that Boothby vehemently criticised, in terms 'which were not appreciated by the Chancellor of the Exchequer', as Boothby later noted.*

In spite of the guarantee to Poland and the introduction of conscrip-

*There was subsequently some confusion between the Czech gold and the Czech assets, and a myth has arisen that Boothby had an interest in the former. He had none at all, nor was he ever accused of having any.

tion, the Chamberlain Government did not accept the inevitability of war with Germany until it was virtually forced upon it in September. The Czech claims were proceeded with a dilatoriness that would seem extraordinary were it not for this background. Boothby believed that the problem was that Simon came to regret his endorsement of Waley's action, and that his heart was not in the matter. In this conclusion he was almost certainly right. It should also be emphasised that at this stage Boothby had in fact no interest to declare, nor, as it happened, any need to do so even if he had had; interestingly, not even his sternest subsequent critics made any reference to this particular speech, not least because the two references to Czechs resident in Britain were only in passing. He had no personal financial interest whatever in the transfer of the Czech gold.

Boothby, like most MPs, was very vague about what the parliamentary rules actually were on the declaration of a financial interest. This was not to be wondered at, as they themselves were vague.* In Erskine May, the 'Bible' of Parliament, it was stated:

In the Commons it is a rule that no Member who has a direct pecuniary interest in a question shall be allowed to vote on it. But, in order to operate as a disqualification [to vote] this interest must be immediate and personal, and not merely of a general or remote character.

At the time Boothby assumed that his 'interest', if any, had vanished, and on this occasion, as on 23 January 1940, the only other occasion on which he spoke in the House of Commons on the matter, there was no vote. Indeed, both debates were notable for their unanimity in support of the Government's actions, so it cannot even be claimed that Boothby's two brief speeches had any effect whatever on the opinion and judgment of the House of Commons.

Many years later, in the early 1950s, Mr Speaker Morrison – as Shakes was to become in 1951 – reiterated this ruling. There was no need to declare a financial interest in debate unless a vote was involved. Boothby was in the House at the time and immediately sought a meeting with Morrison. What he had in mind was to raise publicly the contention that he had not declared a personal interest in his two speeches. Morrison advised him against reviving the matter, and Boothby accepted his advice. He later regretted it. This having been said, Boothby's subsequent claim that he had been severely criticised, and wrongly, for a mere parliamentary technicality was not, as will be revealed, at all the whole story.

While there was no guarantee at all that his claim would be met, at Weininger's request Chase wrote Boothby a formal letter on 3 May to

---

* This was the situation then and for many years after. Only recently have they been revised and clarified.

state that the Zota Company had been authorised to pay him ten per cent of his assets when and if received. Both Boothby and Weininger insisted that in June the latter had offered Boothby a written contract, but that Boothby had torn up the paper. This was irrelevant. Both men had a real interest in the success of the claim.

Both emphasised, then and afterwards, that this was a simple business transaction that was quite normal between banker and client, and even Boothby's fiercest later critics could not cavil at that. But it was more complex. Boothby was now being very hard-pressed by Butt for immediate repayment of his loan and wrote to him on 30 June that,

> as a result, however, of certain events which I will recount to you, I am, at the moment, the possessor of assets amounting to approximately £20,000 in the form of cash and bonds in Prague. . . . Either way, it is a matter of days, but I cannot guarantee that I shall have the money by the 15th. I might be able to raise a loan against these assets, but it would be difficult to do without breach of confidence; as I have been taking part in the negotiations with the Treasury.

It was not to be 'a matter of days', but of years; however, the scale of the Treasury's dilatoriness was not yet apparent. Indeed, Boothby was receiving regular assurances from Simon and Treasury officials that matters were proceeding rapidly, which they were not.

Up to this point Boothby's actions had been perfectly proper and reasonable. One also has to recall that the summer of 1939 was a menacing and turbulent one politically, in which Boothby was especially active, with many other concerns apart from Czech assets and the Weiningers' increasingly desperate financial predicament. But the Butt loan and his own financial difficulties provided an additional private cloud as well as the infinitely more sombre ones now gathering over Europe. In these grim circumstances, when much that he had anticipated and warned against for so long was about to happen, he foolishly overstepped the invisible, difficult, but crucial borderline of public and private interest. He was not the first, and by no means the last, politician to do so, and very few have had to pay so heavy a price.

There was now the additional complication of the Boothby Committee.

On 18 April, on the initiative of an eminent solicitor, Colonel Harry Nathan, who had given advice to Czechs with business interests in Britain over a number of years and had many Czech clients, it had been agreed to set up a committee in London to represent claimants against the Czech assets. The meeting was held in Nathan's office. A number of Czechs were present, including Weininger, and Boothby was invited to become its Chairman, to which he agreed. Boothby was to become the driving force of the Committee as he was the natural leader, with an honourable and honoured record as a true friend of the Czechs, but his principal merit in their eyes was that he was a well-known and respected MP, with the access to ministers and people in high places that they lacked. None realised, apart from Weininger, his potential personal interest in the resolution of one of their claims; nor did he mention it. He should have. It was at this point that he crossed the invisible line.

Harry Louis Nathan was not only a solicitor but had been Liberal MP for Bethnal Green between 1929 and 1935, had joined the Labour Party in 1934 and had been elected for Bethnal Green again in 1937. He was subsequently to become Lord Nathan in 1940 and to be a senior minister in the post-war Labour Government. He spoke in the House of Commons on several occasions on Czech assets and was never accused of not declaring a personal interest.

The meeting was a small one with twelve people present, including Dr Victor Jansa, the former Commercial Counsellor at the Czech Legation who had sought Boothby's advice in January over the British loan; Dr Drucker, who was a Czech refugee to whom Nathan had given space in his firm, although he was not an employee of it; and the Chairman of the Czech Chamber of Commerce, Dr Curt Calmon.

It was agreed that it would be 'an informal voluntary committee'. Weininger proposed that the first priority should be given to the smaller claimants, and that after all claims were met there should be a contribution to the Czech National Committee, namely the Czech Government in Exile. It was also agreed that the existence of the Committee would be advertised in the newspapers so that the other claimants would be encouraged to join it. Contributions were sought for the cost of the advertisement, at £2 per claimant at the meeting, which raised £24. In the event the advertisement cost £30, so that Drucker, the 'treasurer', was £6 out of pocket. This was the only contribution sought or received by the Committee or its Chairman. At the second meeting of the Committee Calmon proposed that Boothby, as Chairman, should be remunerated for his work on behalf of the claimants, which Boothby refused. The only financial concerns of the Boothby Committee were Nathan's free use of his office, his kindness to Drucker, and the contribution to the advertisement announcing the existence of the Committee. Nathan also agreed to telephone Waley to ask whether the Treasury was opposed to the establishment of the Committee, and was told by him that 'it was quite a useful thing to do'.

One person who realised that Boothby was moving into potentially

dangerous waters was his old friend Peter Rodd, a brilliant mathe-
matician, who was then married to Nancy Mitford (whose sister, Diana,
had married Oswald Mosley), but Boothby did not heed his warnings. His
relationship with Weininger was not only one of friendship, but he was his
banker and, as such, fully entitled to his fee. This was technically
absolutely true, but it was as a Member of Parliament that he was of such
value to the other holders, who had no idea that Boothby had a particular
interest in one of their fellow-claimants. If they had known it, it is doubtful
whether they would have minded much. The only fee that Boothby
received for his chairmanship was a silver cigarette box presented to him
in gratitude for his work for them. None the less, rumours began to
circulate in the City, and then at Westminster, that Boothby's activities on
behalf of the Committee were being paid for. As this was completely
untrue, Boothby dismissed Rodd's concern with some impatience and
carried on naïvely, not appreciating how damaging these rumours were to
his professional and political reputation. Some, including the eminent
banker Sir Edward Reid, came to believe them, with catastrophic
consequences.

As Rodd knew, Boothby was doing nothing improper or dishonest, but
he was laying himself open to suspicions which were wholly unfounded,
and which he should have taken action to allay at once, as Rodd urged him
to do. His failure to act on Rodd's wise warnings before the rumour-
mongering became serious was his greatest single error, for which he was
to pay dearly. But at the time he had no qualms and pressed on with typical
fire and enthusiasm.

Boothby was already concerned that after the initial blocking of the
assets, the Chamberlain Government was again succumbing to its appeasement tendencies. He had evidence for his apprehensions. It was not
until early May that the Council of Foreign Bondholders was asked to
nominate an advisory committee to assist the Treasury in dealing with
claims of British bondholders against Czech assets in London. Two of
the largest claimants were two cousins and partners, Paul and Walter
Petschek, who had an alleged claim for £1 million, and the Weininger
ladies. This dilatoriness seemed ominous, and so it was.

Boothby wrote to Weininger on 1 April:

> I am staying the weekend with the Financial Secretary to the Treasury, so
> will be able to bring further pressure to bear in that quarter. And on
> Tuesday I propose to ask the Chancellor to give an assurance that no
> further monies will be paid out of the fund until existing claims have been
> met.
>
> This, together with my letter to Waley, pretty well exhausts the possi-

bilities of political effort on my part. And I think now that the sooner you get the Solicitors on to the job the better.

The solicitors concerned, Ashurst, Morris, Crisp and Co., wrote to Weininger on 3 April to confirm that

> your wife and your step-children are deemed to be British holders and they fall within the terms of the anticipated scheme. . . . I sincerely hope that the anticipated scheme of the Bank of England will prove beneficial and that you will receive some sum for your Czecho-Slovak assets.

Weininger at once wrote to 'My dear Mr Boothby' on the next day to point out that the Bank had not named any date for the presentation of the claims, and that 'I think I am right if I beg to state that, from all angles, speed in reaching a settlement would be productive of nothing but good.' On 5 April Boothby forwarded this letter to Simon, stating that he had received a number of communications since his speech in the Commons

> which I won't inflict upon you. They put forward no facts or considerations with which you are not already familiar. But the enclosed letter from Mr Weininger is in rather a different category, and seems to me to raise a point of some importance.

In his reply on 20 April Simon said that a new Notice would be issued shortly and that

> I think this will meet Mr. Weininger's point. I need hardly say that the absence of any fixed date for returning the claims did not mean that there could be any question of postponing a settlement a day longer than necesssary. It may be some time before a settlement can be reached but you may be sure that there will be no unnecessary delay.

On 1 May Boothby wrote to Simon again, this time as Chairman of the new Committee, to urge that

> British holders of balances in Prague, and other holders who can establish the necessary proof of residence in this country, and of the validity of their claims, should be compensated out of the corresponding assets we now hold with the least possible delay. . . . As holders of balances in Prague in the form of cash or bonds are now undergoing considerable hardship, we venture to express the earnest hope that any legislation which may be necessary in order that their claims as at March 14th last may be met, will be introduced as soon as possible.

On 3 May there was correspondence between Weininger and Chase, which put the arrangement in writing:

Private and Confidential
R. J. G. Boothby, Esq., MP   3rd May 1939
3 Lombard Street,
E.C.3.

Dear Bob,

Mr. Richard Weininger has authorised the Zota Company Limited, of which I am Governing Director, to pay out of the sterling proceeds of our Czech holdings the sum of ten per cent of the total amount.

These balances and holdings, which are comprised entirely of cash and Czech Government bonds, amounted on the 15th. March last to £242,000.

The sterling value of the balance in Prague which we now hold on your behalf, therefore, amounts to £24,200.

Yours sincerely
H. P. Chase

On the same day Boothby wrote again to Simon on behalf of his Committee, enclosing a letter from Weininger and stating that

I am authorised to say that we adhere to the view expressed in our previous letter that British holders of balances in Prague in the form of cash or bonds should be compensated out of the corresponding assets we now hold in London as soon as possible; and that any surplus assets should be held in escrow by His Majesty's Government.

He wrote again to Simon, in the name of his Committee, on the 31st: 'It has been represented to me that if the claims of British holders of balances in cash – including bona-fide Czech residents in the country – could be met at an early date, the position would be greatly alleviated.'

The unmentioned fact was that Boothby's own position would also have been greatly alleviated. As will be seen, he was to try Chase very hard in later months over the Butt debt, but the point was, as he admitted in a letter to Chase in May 1940, that

Weininger tells me that you apparently have some idea that I possess a trust fund, or some other fund in Scotland, from which I might have borrowed money. I can assure you that is not the case. Apart from the Czech assets, I have no assets of any sort or kind in the world. I hope we may be friends again some day.

The obvious person whom Boothby should have turned to was his father, who had the resources to resolve the Butt problem without much difficulty, and who was to do so later when he independently realised the situation. But, again, one detects Boothby's awe of his father, his sense of inferiority to him, his own personal pride, and fear of his mother's reactions to her beloved son's failure. The embarrassment and distress caused to his parents would have been intolerable – or so Boothby thought. All the evidence is that they would have come strongly and staunchly to his rescue, but he never told them. They fondly believed that their brilliant and wonderful son was enjoying a triumphant career not only in politics but in the City, and he did not disabuse them. When I once asked him about this, Boothby replied, simply and movingly,

I was ashamed of my failures. My marriage had failed, which upset them greatly, and now this. Also, I was an independent so-and-so, and for a son who was nearly forty to seek his parents' assistance would have been pretty unimpressive. They thought I was doing bloody well, when I wasn't.*

The attitude of the Petschek cousins increasingly infuriated Boothby. He had no interest in them, personal or financial, except that their refusal to have anything to do with him or his Committee undermined its significance for all the claimants.

One of the most redeeming, and honourable, aspects of Boothby's activities, which were considerable, as Chairman of his Committee was that both he and Weininger were as concerned about the other – smaller – claimants as they were about their own. If the Committee was to have the impact they wanted for all the claimants, the involvement of the Petscheks was vital. But they, playing their own game, were not willing to become involved. Also, they had their own, separate advisers, while remaining clients of Nathan. Their cunning and deviousness were indeed remarkable, and Boothby never began to appreciate their formidable measure. Their obduracy and capacity for intrigue were veiled by carefully prepared letters and equally calculated silences. They were never called to account for their actions, and silkily retained their fortunes by means that remain unclear, but which were certainly highly effective. They were cold-blooded and money-dominated professionals, whilst Boothby was a blundering amateur. Boothby was right in his estimation that whereas the Weiningers' claim was a strong one, the Petscheks' was not, and this was subsequently confirmed. Of all the ironies of this extraordinary episode, this was the greatest of all. The Weiningers received substantial sums on their claims and the Petscheks virtually nothing; nor did Boothby. He simply could not understand the Petscheks' game and wrote to Weininger on 23 July:

Dear Richard
The more I think about it, the more impregnable my case becomes.
(1) I got the Czech assets blocked at your request; and you can bring Chase to give evidence of this.

* I am always cautious about unrecorded memory, but this discussion – one of the few occasions on which I raised the matter – has particular vividness for me, and I believe that I have caught the essentials.

(2) I accepted the position of Chairman of the Committee of Czech holders, at their invitation.

(3) I received assurances from you that I would be compensated out of the larger holdings for what I had done and proposed to do.

(4) As Chairman of the Committee I conducted long and arduous negotiations with the Chancellor and Treasury officials on behalf of Czech holders, including the Petscheks; and was accepted by the Treasury as representing their interests. . . .

In these circumstances it is really incredible that the P's – whose case is by no means a cast-iron one, and *not yet* decided – should seek to evade the whole of their obligations.

Yours ever
Bob

On the 27th Boothby drew up a list of his activities on behalf of the Czech holders:

Points

(1) Action after Munich with a view to getting a loan for Czecho-slovakia.

(2) Subsequent speeches on the Loan Bill in the House of Commons.

(3) Action at the Treasury on the Friday following the annexation of Bohemia, and at Downing Street that night and the following morning, which resulted in the blocking of all Czech assets in this country.

(4) Subsequent speeches in the Debates on the Czech Assets (Restrictions) Bill.

(5) Appointment as Chairman of the Committee of Czech holders of Assets.

(6) Subsequent representations to the Chancellor, and negotiations with Waley, resulting in the decision of the Treasury to demand payment in full for holders of cash and bonds.

This document was subsequently held against him as evidence of his political activities on behalf of his interests with the Weininger family, and was to make a bad impression. In fact it was a straightforward summary of the reasons why the Petscheks and other claimants should have confidence in him. But it could be misinterpreted, and it was.

The Petscheks had a reputation in their own country and among the Czech émigrés in London of being hard and parsimonious men of business. Also, as later became clear, they had no intention of remaining in Britain, while Weininger did. On 24 July, as a result of Boothby's bitter complaints, Weininger wrote to Walter Petschek in German. It was a letter that was to have momentous consequences. Boothby did not see it, or know of its existence, until November 1940.

Weininger opened with long recollections of how he had helped Petschek buy a house in Cobham sixteen years earlier, had entertained him at the Stoke D'Abernon Polo Club, had arranged for him to be elected to an exclusive golf club and had introduced him to his friends at White's Club. Having reminded Petschek of all he had done in the past to assist him to meet influential people in Britain, he came to the point:

> Now please listen to me. You and I are the only genuine owners of London accounts. We are a class in itself. In order to get our wishes executed, certain machinery must function in our favour. Of course this machinery needs sacrifices on our part – very small sacrifices if the result is 100 per cent in our favour. I have agreed to that sacrifice. When I was asked if I thought you would agree to the same sacrifice I answered unconditionally in the affirmative. I had and I have no right to accept any obligation on your behalf, but as you did not show up in my office and as it was necessary that a certain work was done, I could do nothing else but express my belief in you that you would honour the work done on your behalf. I appeal to you in my own interest not to contradict or refuse me. If my own interests are damaged because you are going to contradict my belief in your fairness, you will suffer just as much as I shall. . . . Under the circumstances I can only emphasise again the importance for you not to make any mistakes which would be very unfavourable for you and me.

Petschek replied curtly on 31 July that while he had always liked Weininger's company,

> I am very sorry that the sympathy which I had for you was not returned by you and apparently you wanted my company only in order to derive some business profit. . . . I regret that I must refuse to accept your proposition and in connection therewith to accept responsibilities.

This was a complete misinterpretation of Weininger's letter. The reference to 'the only genuine owners of London accounts' was a simple statement of fact: they were the only claimants with 'Weininger London' and 'Petschek London' as well as Prague accounts. If the Petscheks had attended the Committee meetings, they would have realised what Weininger meant by 'sacrifices', but the inordinate suspicions of the Petscheks were aroused.

The second meeting of the Boothby Committee had been so well attended by claimants responding to the advertisement that Nathan's substantial office was filled. Calmon's account confirms that the question of 'sacrifices' by the larger claimants in favour of the smaller was discussed again, as well as the continued refusal of the Petscheks to co-operate. Boothby agreed to prepare a scheme for their consideration for submission to the Treasury, but there was a general consensus that the absence of the Petscheks was a major weakness in any such scheme. As Calmon later testified, the Czech pressure on the Petscheks to join came from many claimants, and not only from Boothby and Weininger, although those who knew the cousins were aware of their notorious meanness and selfishness. What was also made clear was that Boothby's scheme should be for compensation on a sliding scale, with the smaller claimants being paid in full and the principal ones to be satisfied with fifty per cent, and a contribution made to the Czech National Committee. There seems to have been general agreement on these principles, but everything depended on the participation of the Petscheks, whose claim for over £1 million was by far the largest. Weininger himself was strongly in favour of the sliding scale, even though his expectations would accordingly be considerably reduced. Although there were no formal Minutes, the accounts of all the participants are identical.

It can hardly be emphasised too strongly that Boothby assisted a considerable number of Czechs in many ways, and without any financial or other possible advantage to him. One typical letter of thanks may be quoted:

> It is hard to find adequate words to express my gratitude for literally saving my life and providing me with a chance to find lasting happiness in this country.
>
> Your extreme kindness towards somebody you had hardly met – at a time when you yourself were involved in a difficult political struggle – was to me the more wonderful when compared with the sudden aloofness of many who I thought were firm friends. I must say that the brief meeting at your flat gave me unshakable confidence in a happy ending throughout the most serious crisis of my life. Thank you from the bottom of my heart.

But the Petscheks would not even agree to see Boothby, Walter Petschek writing to Boothby on 10 July that

> I have retired from active business and feel that after the strenuous times that I have passed through during recent years, I need a good rest. Therefore I feel that it would not be fair to take up your valuable time in explaining your certainly very interesting ideas and then being obliged in the end to tell you what I have stated above.

Boothby replied that there was no question of discussing 'a business proposition', but that

> I only wished to consult with you about some very difficult negotiations which I am now conducting with the Treasury. Meanwhile I have got in touch with Nathan, who will be able to advise me on these matters which are causing me anxiety and would ask you to accept my apology for troubling you – even with the best intentions!

The Petscheks considered that they were being unduly pressured from all sides. A Mr Infield, who was an assistant secretary at the Ministry of Health, invited Walter Petschek to see him at the Ministry, where he urged the latter and his cousin to join the Boothby Committee. It turned out that his brother, an international lawyer, was representing a number of the smaller Czech claimants, and that the meeting was at Boothby's suggestion. Neither of the Infields had any connection whatever with the Weininger claim, but the action of the civil servant was subsequently censured and he was strongly reprimanded. The episode, however unusual, considerably strengthens Boothby's point that he was interested in *all* the claimants, not simply the Weiningers.

Nathan saw Walter Petschek on 21 July. Petschek, Nathan later related, said that 'he did not see what good Mr Boothby could be to him. . . . Undoubtedly there was a disinclination to join. . . . I think they probably thought themselves too big for the Committee.'*

On the next day Petschek wrote to Nathan that they had decided that 'not being British subjects, it would, for general reasons not be advisable to take the initiative, or make any active move. We feel, that being foreigners, we should be somewhat reticent. . . .' He carefully did not add that he and his cousin were being advised by Sir Edward Reid, a member of the official Treasury Advisory Committee on Czech assets, and a partner in Barings. Nor did Petschek reveal that he and his cousin had no intention of staying in Britain; indeed, one emigrated to Canada, and the other to Mexico. Neither died in penury. The reality was that they were not the slightest bit interested in 'sacrifices' for poorer claimants, in the Czech National Committee, nor in anyone but themselves. Boothby, as he freely admitted, was enraged by their attitude, particularly as an unexpected new factor had emerged.

In July a Herr Wohltart from Berlin had arrived in London, allegedly to discuss whaling problems on behalf of the Germans, but in fact to act on behalf of the German Government over the frozen Czech assets. Boothby saw him and was excited by the prospect of conducting the negotiations with the German Government, for which he would certainly have sought payment as a banker, just as others had; indeed, the contact with Wohltart and the Petscheks had been through Hambuechen, the Chairman of Boothby's First British-American Corporation. As he later told the Commons, as he had the Select Committee,

I want to tell the House frankly that I hoped to bring all the Czech claimants together, to produce a comprehensive scheme which would cover them all, and to be invited to represent their case in a professional capacity with the German

*Select Committee Evidence, Q 1333.

Government. Towards the end of July these hopes of mine crystallised into a strong expectation that this would happen.

Boothby poured out his vexations to Nathan on 1 August:

Thank you for your letter [of 28 July].

I've written a final letter to Weininger, setting out, precisely, the facts as I see them. For obvious reasons I shouldn't like it to fall into the hands of anyone who bore me ill-will; and therefore I think it would be advisable not to pass it 'intact' to Dr. Petschek, or anyone else.

At the same time I think they *ought* to realise the true facts of the situation – which I cannot believe they do at present – and the difficulty of my position.

Frankly I cannot understand their attitude. It is not as if I had put forward some unreasonable or fantastic claim – I have not in fact put forward any specific claim at all. But how can I represent the claims of the Czech Holders adequately, if the largest claimants of all disassociate themselves altogether from my actions, and from the Committee itself?

I would not in any circumstances do anything to prejudice their case. But it is by no means as cast-iron as (I suspect) they imagine,* and if I hear nothing from them, I am bound to assume that they are disinterested. If, on the strength of my letter to Weininger, you can persuade them to modify their attitude, I am still convinced it would be in the interests of all concerned. If not there is nothing more that I can do.

I am *very* grateful for all the trouble you have taken on my behalf.

On receipt of this, obviously delivered by hand, Nathan at once wrote a letter to Petschek that was also to have momentous consequences:

August 1st. 1939

Dear Dr. Petschek

It was a great pleasure to me to have that conversation with you the other day and I have since received your letter of the 22nd July. Naturally, I have passed on to my Client the purport of our conversation and your letter.

As the result, he takes the view that he seems to have been acting under a complete misapprehension. It seems to me that in everybody's interests it is very desirable to clear up the position, hence this letter.

The negotiations which my Client has conducted with the Treasury as Chairman of the Committee of Czech Holders have, of course, been protracted and arduous. It was assumed throughout by him and by the Treasury that he was acting on behalf of all the Czech claimants. Obviously, indeed, if the Treasury had not asumed this, he would not have been aware of your claim, which Herr Wohltart in a recent conversation with my Client also assumed that he was representing.

* This was right; their eventual payment was £120 from the British claims fund. But they had made other dispositions, which fully explains their activities with regard to the Boothby Committee. As they well knew, their claims were fraudulent.

If I correctly understand your letter as meaning that you do not wish him to act on your behalf, and you take the view that you do not wish to associate yourself with the Committee of Czech Holders or that my client should represent your interests, then he feels that he will, of course, be bound to make this clear to the Treasury.

I think, therefore, that I ought to write to ask you to let me know specifically whether or not this is, in fact, the position which you wish to adopt.

Perhaps you will be so kind to let me hear from you as to this at your earliest convenience, as the discussion between my Client and the Treasury will probably be resumed within a few days.

Yours sincerely
H. L. Nathan

As such a sinister interpretation has been placed on this letter Nathan's own account must be inserted at this point.* One of the confusions that arose, and from Boothby's point of view it was a very serious one, was Nathan's professional relationship with him and the Committee. In fact, as Nathan later testified, he never made any charge whatever to Boothby or the Committee:

Neither Mr Boothby nor the Committee have ever actually been entered as my clients at all from a purely accounting point of view . . . so far as Mr Boothby is concerned, he came to see me in matters arising out of a situation in which he was Chairman of this Committee. He was also a fellow Member of the House of Commons and, when I am approached by personal friends on matters which afford me very little trouble, it is not my habit to make them charges in that way.†

Nathan was acting for the Committee and Boothby in a wholly honorary way, and without payment, whereas the Petscheks were his real clients. This was a confusing situation and was to cause many difficulties. There is no question about Nathan's integrity and sincere desire to help his Czech friends and clients; the Committee had indeed been his idea, and he had wanted its membership to be wider than Czechs; he admired Boothby and wanted to help him, although he was not technically or professionally his client. His use of this word in his letter to Petschek was to cause additional confusion.

His firm, as has been recorded, had many Czech clients, who included the Petscheks, although until June Nathan had not actually met them personally. He was also the honorary, and unpaid, legal adviser to Boothby and the Committee, which created problems as to who were his 'clients'. He was not Boothby's personal solicitor. The purpose of his

---

* See his evidence in *The Select Committee Report on the Conduct of a Member.* . . .
† Select Committee Evidence, Q 1437 and 1439.

letter of 1 August, as he later explained to the Select Committee, was to convey Boothby's views to the Petscheks. When asked whether the letter could be regarded, as Simon did, as to 'bring any form of improper pressure to bear upon the Petscheks', he replied:

I should have thought it was quite impossible to read any such suggestion into the letter. Far from having any such intention, I thought it very desirable that everybody should know exactly where they stood. Indeed, may I say (I do not know whether it is proper for me to say this, but I think I am entitled to say this) that as a solicitor of very long standing and no inconsiderable practice (I would even say, important practice) I greatly resent any such suggestion.*

Nathan added that he had never heard any complaint from the Petscheks about the letter, and that they remained clients of his firm. He also confirmed that he had acted in the spirit of Boothby's complaint without showing him the letter first.

At this point the Petscheks approached Sir Edward Reid, showed him both Nathan's and Weininger's letters, and complained that they were being pressured by Boothby and Nathan. From this claim of theirs, which he accepted, and from Weininger's and Nathan's letters, Reid drew the erroneous conclusion that the Petscheks were being blackmailed. He was himself directly involved in the Treasury examination and was very much an established City of London personality. He was also an adviser to the Petscheks. But although he was a totally honourable man, he made a mistake.

It is also clear that he was activated by a personal antipathy towards Boothby. What Boothby never understood in his buccaneering financial adventures in the City was that he had, very understandably, developed a reputation in that very small circle of being an adventurer and a gambler who had failed. It was known that he had 'plunged' and was deeply in debt. When the Petscheks approached Reid, the latter drew the worst conclusions. It was a classic case of the adage that 'a man who is labelled is often libelled'. When the Petscheks presented Nathan's letter and the translation of Weininger's to him, Reid's suspicions of the real role of the Boothby Committee were confirmed. The fact that he was totally wrong was immaterial. He had access where Boothby had not. He was City Establishment, and Boothby was not. His memoranda initialled 'E. R.' were to have a potent influence on Waley and Simon. Reid told Waley that he had been concerned for some time about 'the activities of Boothby and his friends', and spoke to him on the telephone and then by letter, ending that

*Select Committee Evidence, Q 1461.

I agree with you entirely that these most improper activities of Boothby and his friends ought to be stopped at once. The steps you suggested yesterday seemed admirable, and if as you said you can keep my name and that of the Petscheks out of it, I should be grateful.

The steps Waley had in mind were to inform the Chancellor of the Exchequer, Simon, and particularly to show him the Weininger and Nathan letters.

Reid's action in sending Waley these two letters, and with his own interpretation of them, was then made far worse from Boothby's point of view when Waley referred the papers to Sir Horace Wilson, the head of the Civil Service and Chamberlain's confidant. If Boothby's relations with Simon were cold, they were arctic with Wilson, the high priest of appeasement. In referring the letters to Simon, Wilson wrote an extremely hostile covering note, saying that

They [the Petscheks] have registered their claims with the Bank and hope that when an Agreement is made it will be possible for them to benefit from it, but they do not wish to take part in any intrigue or agitation which has as its object the pressing of their or anybody else's claims.

This was a travesty of the situation, but when Simon read the letters and Wilson's note he considered the situation 'scandalous', and at once dictated his own notes for an immediate meeting with Boothby in his office, in which he stated that

In fact, the Committee is a business venture which expects to be rewarded for its activities. I do not know how many Czech claimants may have been induced to employ it for reward by similar representations. It may well be that others have not shown the resistance of Dr. Petschek.

As Simon later admitted, he and Wilson had come to this totally wrong conclusion on the basis of these two letters alone. There was no other evidence that the Boothby Committee was 'a business venture which expects to be rewarded for its activities', for the simple reason that it was not. Wilson and Simon detested Boothby and, like Reid, had come to a summary and hostile conclusion that was, in fact, wholly wrong.

Boothby was delighted by the summons to see Simon on 3 August, as he thought that he was going to be asked to conduct the negotiations with the Germans, for which he would certainly have expected remuneration, as other bankers had in the past. In the event, he was confronted by a glacial Simon presenting him with Nathan's letter, which Boothby had never seen. Nor had he seen Weininger's, but Simon did not show it to him or even reveal its existence; Boothby knew nothing of it until faced with it over a year later. Furthermore, as has been emphasised, the reference to 'sacrifices' did not have the sinister meaning that Reid, Wilson and Simon had put upon it, nor was there any attempt by Simon to elucidate the matter further by interviewing either Nathan or Weininger. Simon's subsequent evidence on this meeting, which was to prove so damaging and misleading, contained one major untruth when he said that 'I never for a moment suspected [Boothby] of having any sort of financial reward in prospect',* when in fact, as his own notes for the meeting show, this was exactly what he and Wilson believed was the case.

The meeting, whose importance was later to loom very large, was accordingly based on a total misunderstanding, overshadowed by mutual hostility. Until Simon showed him Nathan's letter – but not Weininger's – Boothby had no idea what the meeting was about, although it was quickly made clear that he definitely was not going to be invited to conduct the negotiations with the Germans. As he later told the House of Commons,

The sole topic under discussion was my position as Chairman of the Committee, and the allegation of the Chancellor of the Exchequer – for that was what it amounted to – was that I had been using that position for the purpose of making money. Indeed, that is the only question upon which the Chancellor of the Exchequer had at this time any interest in the matter.

Simon's record of this crucial meeting was not challenged by Boothby, except the opening exchanges, and may be accepted in full.

Simon opened by formally pointing out that the Boothby Committee was entirely unofficial and that it was no part of the offical organisation that the Treasury had established to examine the claims, and that no claimant would suffer if he did not use the Committee. This was obvious. 'To all this Mr Boothby accepted without qualifications.' Simon then produced Nathan's letter of 1 August to Petschek. Simon's report continues:

Every one of these statements was without any foundation at all. Boothby agreed and expressed the greatest astonishment.

I pointed out that the letter plainly conveyed (a) that Boothby is the authorised and recognised channel for negotiating Czech claims with the Treasury; (b) that the Treasury regarded him as speaking for all the claimants, with the consequence that if Dr Petschek refused to be represented by him his claim suffered; (c) that negotiations between Boothby and the Treasury were actively going on and were shortly being resumed.

All this, as Boothby agreed, is completely untrue.

Boothby said he would like to give an explanation which would explain the whole matter in two minutes. His explanation was to the effect that the Czechs who had joined this Committee (he said they were the whole body except

* Select Committee Evidence, Q 198.

Petschek) strongly felt that Petschek ought to join the Committee. It was not fair, in their opinion, for a principal claimant to stand outside and gain any advantage which might result from the efforts of those who joined. They felt very indignant about it. Weininger had been generous in helping many poor Czechs while Petschek had not contributed a farthing.

Boothby went on to assure me on his honour that he had no financial interest in the matter at all. I said that I had always regarded him as taking the matter up because he knew Czechoslovakia and had Czech friends. I could not understand why contributions (to the Committee) should be required from anybody. He suggested stationery and solicitor's fees.

Misunderstanding could hardly go further. Simon's assumption was that large sums were involved in this 'business venture'; Boothby was puzzled why there should be such a fuss over a 'budget' of £30. They were speaking at total cross-purposes, but it was clear enough to Boothby that Simon wanted his Committee wound up immediately.

There was also confusion about Boothby's negotiations with the Treasury, conducted principally with Waley, and both Nathan and Calmon later testified positively – as did Waley – to Boothby's warmth and application. 'Mr. Boothby took such an active interest in all these matters', Calmon said, 'that I wondered how he could afford to do it.' Nathan, strongly defending his letter to Petschek, for which *Boothby* and not he was later blamed, said, 'I had before me pages and pages of letters and memoranda which Mr Boothby had submitted to the Treasury with regard to this matter, which he had sent me in July. I had them before me at the time [he had written to Petschek].' When he had called Boothby his 'client', it was in the context of his own firm's unpaid connection with the Committee. If Simon had not already made up his mind about Boothby's venality, the matter could have been resolved immediately, but he had not been an outstanding prosecuting Counsel for nothing. The accounts of both stress that Simon did almost all of the talking, Simon recalling that 'I think he [Boothby] was very much distressed. At any rate he hardly spoke at all in the early part of the interview, except to say that he agreed with me: I think he was very much dejected.'* Boothby's recollection was that

I was extremely astonished. That was my main feeling. . . . I was absolutely dumbfounded when I heard from him that Dr Petschek had sent correspondence which I had not seen straight to the Treasury without informing me, and having refused to see me. If I may say so, I was rather indignant at the obvious implication – I will not say 'imputation' – which the Chancellor attached to the correspondence.†

---

* Select Committee Evidence, Q 170.
† *Ibid.*, Q 181.

When he had the time to look at Nathan's letter again in rather less fraught circumstances, Simon's wrath baffled him even more. He did not realise that he had been taking part in a trial by a judge who had sentenced him beforehand.

Boothby assured Simon that this was the first time he had seen Nathan's letter and that he was not his 'client'. Simon commented dryly:

I said this was very surprising. I told Boothby that I did not think he had realised the seriousness of Nathan's letter as affecting himself. It contained, as Boothby admitted, a series of statements which were utterly untrue. It professed to be written on his behalf. If anybody wrote a letter which professed to be on my behalf and without my authority telling a series of falsehoods and practically threatening a man that it would be all the worse for him if he did not do something which he was free to refuse to do, I should have a good deal more to say about it than Boothby had said. On this, Boothby looked at the letter again and said 'blackmail'. I said emphatically that I had never used the word nor implied the thing. All I pointed out was that the letter might be read as warning Dr Petschek that if he did not join the Committee his claim would be cancelled or would in some way suffer.

Boothby went on protesting that he had no financial interest in the business. I said my information was that Nathan's letter was not the first attempt to put pressure on Petschek to do what he did not want to do.

Simon then told Boothby that he had arranged for a parliamentary question to be tabled so that he could publicly state that Boothby's Committee had no official status and that all claimants would be treated equally. 'I pointed out to Boothby that if the matter was handled in this way his name or constituency would not be mentioned.' When Boothby asked for his advice, 'as a friend', Simon said that he should see Nathan at once and should realise that he was 'in a very false position'. Boothby said that he intended to wind up the Committee immediately, 'on which I made no comment'.

Boothby, who was by now very angry, went straight to the third meeting of his Committee in Nathan's office to tell it that it must be wound up immediately. When pressed by the startled, and in some cases angry, claimants, he replied simply that as they did not have Treasury support their claims would have to be pursued by other means. He wrote to Weininger on the 4th:

I'm afraid it will not now be possible for me to have an agreement of any kind with you or Zota, because legislation may be necessary, and, if I do, I shall be unable to take any further part. I think I must go on, because although the Committee has been disbanded, the Czechs are relying on me to put their case, and the House of Commons would think it very odd if I remained completely silent. Such is life!

In fact, Weininger did not cancel his instruction to Chase, and assured Boothby, knowing his serious financial position, that he still wanted to help him when circumstances permitted; his purpose was, as he said, 'to help a friend and put the man outside the danger zone of bankruptcy'.* Chase later testified that 'I was desperately anxious, not so much from the personal point of view, but from the national point of view. I felt that Mr Boothby had certain qualities by means of which tremendous service could be given to this country.'†

All that existed was that Boothby had expectation of at least some funds from his friend when and if they materialised. Neither had any inkling of the dark suspicions of Reid, Wilson and Simon; few others realised how deep and strong was their personal friendship, which was to last all their lives.

On 4 August Nathan wrote to Petschek fully accepting his position and saying that

> I have had a word with my client [Boothby], who tells me that he has made the position perfectly clear to the Treasury and wishes me to say that he greatly regrets that there should have been any misunderstanding, which he is sure would never have arisen had he had an opportunity of seeing Dr. Petschek personally.

On the same day Boothby wrote at length to Simon to tell him that it had been decided to wind up the Committee 'forthwith'. He added that

> I asked Nathan if he would be good enough to watch my interests professionally in any matters arising out of these negotiations, or of the activities of the Committee, in order to guard against precisely the kind of situation that subsequently arose.

He admitted that he had expressed himself very forcibly to Nathan on the subject of the Petscheks on 27 July.

> It was at this point that I made what I now recognise to have been a grave mistake. I should have let the matter drop. But my blood was up, and I'm afraid I expressed myself to Nathan on the subject of the Petscheks in no uncertain terms. I find in my file a letter to him, dated July 27, in which the following – significant – sentence occurs: 'Frankly I cannot understand the attitude of the Petscheks, which seems to me to be both discourteous and churlish. *It is not, after all, as if any specific financial demands were being made of them.*'
> I did not – and do not now – know the extent of their claim. But I know it was substantial; and it seemed to me intolerable that they should adopt a

---

* Select Committee Evidence, Q 657.
† *Ibid.*, Q 1218.

dog-in-the-manger attitude, when others had done so much, and worked so hard. Moreover Weininger, to whom Dr. Petschek had written in such insulting terms, is a very great friend of mine; and has, to my knowledge, rendered quite incalculable services to the Czech refugees. Not only has he poured out his own money on their behalf, but he spent the first two months of this year in Prague, helping them to get out, and assisting those who were left behind. His efforts, as any Czech Refugee Committee will gladly acknowledge, have been nothing short of heroic.

I apologise for the length of this letter, but as my personal honour is involved I feel I must put you in possession of the facts in so far as I know them. The long and the short of it is that I lost my temper; which is a foolish, but not a venal, thing to do.

With regard to Nathan's letter, I think it is a matter that can only be dealt with by himself and myself. But I may say that it is almost incredible to me that it could have been written by an experienced solicitor; and that if I had seen it it would certainly have never been sent.

In the light of events, I reproach myself for having allowed the apparent discourtesy of Dr. Petschek to nettle me to the point of saying to Nathan that I thought he ought to be pressed to join the Committee, or at least to meet me as Chairman. But this is my only sin.

In conclusion I would ask you to accept my personal assurance –

(1) that I never saw Nathan's letter to Dr. Petschek;

(2) that my sole purpose in agreeing to act as Chairman of the Committee of Czech Holders was to give them as much assistance as I could; and

(3) that I have received no remuneration, and have no financial interest of any sort or kind in the work of the Committee.

All this was absolutely true, and later verified. Also, Boothby's letter to Weininger of 4 August cancelling the agreement with Zota removed from his mind any question of an actual or potential conflict of interest. That indeed was the position on 4 August, but Weininger assured him later that in his eyes the agreement stood; as Boothby's financial difficulties remained, Boothby agreed. As he subsequently told the House of Commons,

It is easy to be wise after the event. But, looking back, I can now see that I was guilty of a tragic error of judgment. If I had even put a postscript to this letter [to Simon] to the effect that, although the Weininger claims were now technically British claims with which my Committee was not directly concerned, and although I had no legal or enforceable contract with him, nevertheless I had an expectation of financial assistance from him if and when the claims of his family were met, this case could never have been brought against me.

As has been recorded, Calmon had suggested at the second meeting of the Committee that Boothby should be remunerated, as he was doing so much on the claimants' behalf, but he had refused. No contributions beyond the £2 per head for the cost of the advertisement were ever sought. Nathan, Waley and others later testified that Boothby had indeed been very active in pressing for as early a settlement as possible for all the claimants; the only financial arrangements he had with Weininger were a personal loan which he repaid, and the expectation that he would get ten per cent of the received Weininger assets. It cannot be stressed too much that this had been at Weininger's initiative before the fall of Prague. It had not been formally cancelled by Weininger, who wanted to help his friend and who persuaded his brothers-in-law, Hans and Fritz Weinmann, to pay him five per cent if they received 100 per cent of their claims in sterling; this was also for Boothby, Weininger writing to Chase that 'this means about £3,000 to Bob in the first instance'. When this was later disclosed it looked bad, but Boothby had no knowledge of Weininger's proposal.

As Butt was now pressing very hard for his money, Boothby pledged to assign the £5,000 to him 'out of the Czech assets now held on my behalf by the Zota Company Limited'. When Chase learnt of this pledge, he was, briefly, very angry that Boothby had made such a commitment without informing him, but the misunderstanding was resolved when Chase appreciated the seriousness of Boothby's position after Butt threatened a writ and public action.

At this point, 24 April 1940, Sir Robert Boothby, whose sources of information are unclear, telephoned Chase 'to ask some very pertinent questions regarding his son'. Chase told him the full situation, as a result of which Sir Robert stepped in to settle the whole matter and to repay Butt in full, with interest, as well as all his legal costs. Had this course been followed earlier, instead of chasing the will-o'-the-wisp Weininger assets, much grief would have been avoided.

The most grievous result was that, because of Simon's total misunderstanding of the role of Boothby's Committee, Nathan's letter and the points Weininger was making in his letter to Petschek, he, Wilson and the senior Treasury officials had come to a wholly false and unfair conclusion about Boothby's activities as Chairman of the Committee. Boothby made no record of his meeting with Simon, but the latter had, and it, together with Wilson's memorandum and his own inaccurate notes, remained in the Treasury files.

Although the Butt problem had been resolved, Weininger's promise was still on record. When Boothby, still holding Butt at bay, asked for this to be confirmed in writing, Chase wrote to him on 1 November that

In reply to your letter of yesterday, I confirm the contents of my letter to you of 9th August to the effect that if and when the sterling equivalents of the various Czech holdings, to which this company is entitled, are paid, the percentage agreed upon will, immediately, be paid to you in full.

What is in fact noteworthy is how little Boothby did to press the Weininger claim after August 1939. On 23 January 1940 he spoke in the debate of the Second Reading of the Czechoslovakia (Financial Claims and Refugees) Bill, in which he urged that special consideration should be given to all claimants resident in Britain, a point which could not be to the advantage of the Weinmanns, or any putative interest he had in their claims. Again, there was no vote. On 4 March he saw Sir Stanley Wyatt, the newly appointed head of the Czechoslovakian Financial Claims Office, and repeated the points he had made in his January speech. He continued to raise, rather intermittently, the Czech claims for early settlement until August 1940.

What subsequently weighed so heavily with his critics was that at no point had he revealed in his discussions with the Treasury, Simon and the Claims Office that he had a personal interest, or, more precisely, expectation, that he would be a beneficiary from the successful settlement of the Weininger claim. Unquestionably he had no technical or legal reason to do so; also, unquestionably, he should have. As will be seen, the Select Committee investigating his conduct did him several injustices, and its principal conclusions were wrong, especially over the interview with Simon on 3 August, which effectively vitiates its Report. None the less, what is remarkable is that Boothby could never realise that a fatal misconstruction could be placed upon his actions, and was.

His defence was completely displayed in his final statement to the Committee about his speech of 23 January 1940:

Now what is it suggested that I might have done upon the occasion of that speech of mine at the Second Reading? Is it suggested that I should have opened my speech by saying 'Mr Speaker, I propose to make some general observations upon the subject of the Czech assets which have been blocked and the claims that should be met. But before doing so, I think it is my duty to make it plain that I am seriously in debt; that I have a friend who is a Czech, and whose family have a substantial claim against these assets; that this friend has promised me that he will help and assist me to repay my creditors whenever he receives money from any source; and of course if the claim of his family is met, he will be in a very much better position to do so than he is now.' I could not have said to the House of Commons that I had a more specific interest than that, because I do not believe that I had one.

In defiance of the rules of chronology Boothby's activities on behalf of the Czech claimants after the outbreak of war, in addition to his speech in the Commons on 23 January, were as follows.

He wrote a detailed letter to his colleague, H. Graham White, on 20 January 1940, pointing out that the Government's dilatoriness in payment was harmful to the claimants.

> Strong arguments can be advanced in favour of meeting *all* the claims of British holders. There is plenty of money available (£17 million) to do so. So far as *cash* claims are concerned, there can be no question that they ought to be met in full and at once. The Treasury propose to pay only one half of these claims, and in no case more than £50,000. Why?

Boothby asked him to speak in the debate on these lines.

On 24 May, after he had become a minister, he wrote to Sir Kingsley Wood, the new Chancellor, pointing out that the Claims Office had not made a single payment, in spite of repeated assurances of payment for claims that had been clearly established, and out of funds authorised by Parliament. The Financial Secretary to the Treasury, Harry Crookshank, replied on 25 May that there had been a very large increase in claims, but that 'it is the intention of the office to deal with the more straightforward cases as quickly as possible'. The difficulty had been that the prolongation of the period of claims had been extended to the end of January. Boothby replied on 27 May that 'I think I should therefore let you know that, according to my information, which comes from the best Czech official sources, all valid claims of a substantial amount were in fact lodged by April 30th last year.'

On 31 May Weininger wrote to the head of the Czechoslovakian Financial Claims Office, enclosing a letter from Boothby praising his services since the outbreak of war and supporting his proposed visit to the United States for the purchase of tanks and aeroplanes. Weininger asked that the claims of his family could be met 'at an early date'.

On 25 June Boothby saw Wyatt again. Wyatt's note of the meeting recorded that he wanted to know 'whether and when the claims of the Weininger family, in which he takes an interest, will be admitted, and when this Office will start payments generally'. Wyatt assured him that the Weininger claim 'is proceeding normally and no obstacle has arisen so far'. Boothby 'suggested that claims such as Petscheck, where the claimants leave this country, should be excluded'. Wyatt explained that nearly twenty-five per cent of claims had been dealt with already and that payments to 'small claimants in the more straightforward cases would start immediately'.

Weininger, through his solicitors, continued to press his claim. On

5 August Boothby wrote to Wyatt to say that Weininger might have to leave for the United States 'on a mission of very considerable importance in the course of the next few days'. In reply, Wyatt wrote that there were difficulties about Weininger's savings in Czechoslovakia and went on:

> Mr. Weininger's own small claim offers no difficulty and it will be paid during the next two or three days. I am not yet in a position to admit and pay the other family claims although they have been examined. I see no reason why they should not be left in the hands of Mr. Weininger's solicitor during his absence. Perhaps, instead of troubling you, it would be better and more normal for Mr. Weininger to communicate with me directly in future.

Boothby accepted the rebuke and wrote at once to apologise.

On 9 August Boothby gave £3,000 to Weininger in repayment of a loan of £6,300; it was agreed that no pressure would be placed on him to repay the balance

> for the duration of the war or for a period of three years, whichever is the shorter. . . . As you know, I am hoping to receive a substantial amount when the second half of the Czech assets is paid and if the amount I get from this source is sufficient, I pledge myself to clear the entire balance as soon as I receive it. Of course, if my share is insufficient to cover the balance I owe you I shall pay over whatever I do get out of it.

On 17 August Boothby again wrote to Wyatt complaining of the delay in settling claims, pointing out that it was over a year since Simon had assured him that they would be dealt with as quickly as possible, and that ministers had given assurances to the same effect in Parliament. This letter, like those of 5 and 7 August, was written on Ministry of Food notepaper, where Boothby was now Parliamentary Secretary to the Minister. Wyatt again said that everything was being done to settle the claims.

These were the sum total of Boothby's 'political services' to Weininger over a period of more than a year. Meanwhile, mightier and more terrible events bore down upon him and Britain, and Boothby forgot about the Czech assets.

9

The Fall of Chamberlain
1939–40

The key failure of the anti-Chamberlain Conservative dissidents continued to be their total inability to work together. The largest group was Eden's 'Glamour Boys', but Eden himself was cautious both in his speeches and actions, and his followers were especially careful not to be involved with Churchill, whose only real supporters were Boothby, Bracken, and his son-in-law Duncan Sandys. There was little contact between the Eden, Amery and Churchill groups, and no co-ordinated strategy. Some decided to lie low after their bruising experiences with their constituency Associations; others believed that they were winning the battle over rearmament; while others were in semi-despair. Few were as certain as Churchill and Boothby that war was inevitable, while the rest had exaggerated hopes of the new guarantees and the Anglo-Soviet talks.

Leo Amery wrote to Boothby on 7 June 1939:

> My dear Boothby
> I had a quiet evening yesterday and glanced through your past efforts to make our rulers see sense in time. One sometimes feels weary of playing the Cassandra part, but in the present issue it does look at least as if our warnings have born fruit. Possibly even in time.
>
> Yours sincerely
> Leo Amery

After the rape of Czechoslovakia in March, a new mood had been evident in the country and the House of Commons, but it was not one to which Chamberlain responded, or even believed in. Harold Nicolson noted on 11 April:

Harold Macmillan is enraged that Chamberlain should remain on. He thinks that we Edenites have been too soft and gentlemanlike. That we should have clamoured for Chamberlain's removal. That no man in history has made such persistent and bone-headed mistakes, and that we shall go on pretending that all is well. 'If Chamberlain says that black is white, the Tories applaud his brilliance. If a week later he says that black is after all black, they applaud his realism. Never has there been such servility.' That Chamberlain must go is the word that is passing through the country.*

But the fact was that this was not the declared aim of any of the groups, much though some individuals wanted it. And who was to succeed him? Churchill was certainly not the favourite of the Eden group, and his following in the Party remained obstinately minuscule, although his reputation outside was reviving rapidly. Boothby even attempted, quite unavailingly, to secure the assistance of Beaverbrook, whose newspapers slavishly followed the optimistic Chamberlain line. What neither Boothby nor anyone else realised was that a Cabinet Minister, Samuel Hoare, was on Beaverbrook's payroll. On 8 March Beaverbrook briskly rebuffed Boothby:

> I do not know whether we *must* give the Germans their colonies. Probably not. But I am sure that we should do so.
>
> If it is true, as you say, that the Germans are not very nice, it is also true that the colonies are not very valuable.

Boothby became increasingly critical of the cautious approach of the Eden and Amery groups, and upbraided Nicolson, who replied on 7 June with total, and disarming, honesty:

> Apart from that there is the fact that I have slipped out of gear in the House of Commons. I give all sorts of explanations of that but they are not real excuses. The real fact is that old queens like myself are capable of hysterical heroism but are not good at the constant fight. I lack (as do many of my kind – those of what we may call a literary temperament) a lust for battle. We have no combative qualities. Apart from that I try for financial reasons to do too much. I am always a trifle overworked. This leads to shortcuts and hard study and all sorts of softnesses.
>
> Then I am not ambitious. That would be all very well were it not for another thing. I really do not believe (one never knows oneself) that I have any ardent appetite for success. But I do know that failure makes me miserable. I love the House since I am a sociable person and much enjoy observing the oddities of my fellow beings. I find the House rather like one of those marine diving bells in which one can sit and watch the vagaries of the deep sea fish. Yet I am also conscious (otherwise your letter would not have made such an impression on me) that I ought to devote more time and

---

* Nigel Nicolson (ed.), *Harold Nicolson: Diaries and Letters*, vol. 1, p. 397.

will power to my Parliamentary career. I do an immense amount of constituency fuss. But that may be because it gives me the illusion of activity. What I ought to do is to concentrate my central energies upon the Chamber. But the one point where you are wrong for certain is the point of insincerity. You do not accuse me of that but you imply it. The real accusation would be that, having discovered that by being sincere I expose myself to awkward situations in my own constituency, I keep silent and cover up my silence by a rather silly pose of aloofness.

Anyhow your letter has given me a shake. I am not one of those who believe that one should be unduly grateful for purely material benefit. But for spiritual benefits one should never cease to be grateful. You have given me a great spiritual benefit in writing that highly disagreeable letter. Bless you Bob.

These discontents simmered throughout the summer, until they dramatically surfaced on 2 August, when Chamberlain announced that Parliament should adjourn as usual for the summer recess. Ronald Cartland turned on him in fury, and with dramatic effect. Some of the dissidents wanted to vote against the motion, but Eden persuaded them out of it. But forty Conservatives, including Boothby, did abstain. On 22 August, with Parliament scattered, the Nazi–Soviet Pact was signed, and Parliament had to be urgently recalled. Hitler now turned his maximum pressure upon Poland. However, as war moved rapidly closer, there seemed to be every indication that Chamberlain would seek another Munich rather than honour the Polish guarantee.

It was this possibility – and it was a very real one – that at last galvanised the Conservative dissidents into something approaching a fighting force. On 2 September the House had expected Chamberlain to announce a declaration of war. Poland had been invaded on the previous day and was suffering grievously, but, to universal amazement, Chamberlain made it clear to the House that no decision had been reached. In the absence of Attlee, who was ill, Arthur Greenwood rose from the Labour front bench, clearly as astounded as anyone. Nicolson, who was there, recorded in his diary that Boothby called out, 'You speak for Britain'; other accounts say that it was Amery who cried out, 'Speak for England.' It does not particularly matter, but the remarks drew a prolonged burst of cheering that temporarily disconcerted Greenwood, but he recovered and asked Chamberlain, with real passion, why there was this delay. Normally devoted Chamberlainites shouted their support. 'The front bench looked as if it had been struck in the face,' Nicolson recorded.

There then followed an evening of high drama, in a raging thunderstorm, which has often been related, when Chamberlain was told by his colleagues – even Simon – that if there was not an immediate ultimatum to Germany, the House of Commons and the Party would be out of control. With deep and obvious reluctance Chamberlain had to agree.

The principal Conservative rebels met in Churchill's flat in Westminster. Amery, Eden, Boothby, Duff Cooper, Bracken and Sandys urged Churchill to go to the House on the following day to denounce Chamberlain 'and take his place'. Churchill was in a particularly difficult position, as Chamberlain had asked him to return to the Admiralty: he had accepted, but had heard nothing more, which increased the suspicions of his friends that the Government was about to betray Poland as comprehensively as it had Czechoslovakia. The tension was very great, but then the telephone rang to inform Churchill that an ultimatum to Germany had been agreed and dispatched. It was decided to adjourn the meeting until the following morning.

At this meeting, at Ronald Tree's house, the main discussion was whether Eden, who was present, should rejoin the Government. Churchill's appointment had still not been confirmed, so he remained on the backbenches, from which he spoke, movingly, later in the day.

In spite of all the telephoning and meetings on the previous evening, confusion still reigned. After the dissidents had listened to Chamberlain's mournful radio broadcast announcing the declaration of war, they made their way to the House. As they walked across Parliament Square the air-raid sirens began their soon to be all-too-familiar wail, and they suddenly realised that this was the real thing (in fact, a British aircraft had been wrongly identified). Thus, with MPs, ministers, officials and cooks packed into one of the lower rooms of the House, did the war begin for Parliament. Lloyd George said to Boothby that the position of the country was far worse than it had been at even the worst moments of the last war. As Boothby later wrote: 'Thus we tumbled into Armageddon without heart, without songs, without an ally except France (and she lukewarm), without sufficient aircraft, without tanks, without guns, without rifles, without even a reserve of essential raw commodities and feeding stuffs.'

Later in the day it was announced that Churchill would return to the Admiralty and Eden would become Dominions Secretary; there were few other changes. Eden was reluctant to return at all, and particularly to a department that was so far distant from the really important decisions, but felt that he had no choice. Churchill took up his task with relish and ardour. Boothby, after a long talk with his Liberal friend, Clement Davies, decided to set up an all-Party successor to the Churchill group to monitor the progress of the war and to receive expert advice. It was the genesis of the forces that were to bring Churchill to the premiership, but at the beginning that was not its purpose.

As Poland, now invaded from the east by the Soviet Union, entered its long and terrible night, and German submarines began to take their toll of British shipping, the British Expeditionary Force safely crossed the Channel to France, where, together with the French, it merely took up defensive positions and did nothing. British bombers, at heavy loss, achieved little more than dropping leaflets on Germany. The Phoney War had begun.

The actual outbreak of war had put the anti-Chamberlain Conservatives in a dilemma, particularly now that Churchill and Eden were ministers. As the Amery and Eden groups had no formal existence, and now had no particular target, they were reduced to individual critics.

After Poland had been plundered by the Germans and the Russians, an eerie silence fell. On the Western Front there was virtual passivity. Children were evacuated from London, but the dreaded aerial bombardment did not materialise. Simon introduced a war budget of remarkable complacency and prudence. Armageddon had arrived, but nothing seemed to be happening.

The exception was the war at sea, which came home very personally when Boothby's cousin-in-law, 'K' Kennedy, went down with his armed converted liner *Rawalpindi* in November after an heroic and hopeless fight against the German warship *Deutschland*. Boothby had had little in common with 'K', but the manner of his death moved him to write a tribute in *The Times*. Kennedy's son, Ludovic, then aged twenty-one, wrote a poetical tribute to his father that was widely published, and which Boothby greatly admired.

Politically, he was increasingly critical of the dilatory and complacent peacetime inactivity of the Chamberlain Government. With the exception of Churchill, back in his element at the Admiralty, there was no sense of urgency. The Phoney War drifted along, the only real action being the attempted Russian invasion of Finland.

Boothby's speeches and articles in the winter and spring of 1939–40 concentrated on two themes: the need for a small War Cabinet on the Lloyd George pattern – in which he was deeply influenced by Lloyd George himself – and for a coherent economic policy. Influenced in this area by Keynes, he advocated higher taxation on unearned incomes, a large selected sales tax, post-war credits, and a compulsory savings plan. Looking further ahead, he also urged a federal Europe and an international economic organisation. Shocked by John Boyd-Orr's evidence that ten per cent of British families suffered from malnutrition, he also called for a substantial increase in family allowances. With some pleasure he informed the readers of the mass-circulation *Picture Post* that 'the days when large staffs of butlers, footmen, gamekeepers, gardeners, etc., can be maintained by the rich have gone, never to return'. None of this went down particularly well in government and Conservative circles.

It was a short step from this to advocating a War Cabinet coalition, and in March 1940, after Finland's resistance had at last been overwhelmed, this is what Boothby, Richard Law and Macmillan did when the Commons debated the matter, Law in particular coming very close indeed to demanding Chamberlain's resignation.

Very remarkably, with the surprising exception of *The Times*, the press reaction was to portray the debate as a triumph for Chamberlain. However, one political commentator, who was there, wrote that

The impression consistently conveyed to the general public is that the House of Commons, as a whole, is completely satisfied with the policy, performance and personnel of the present Government. It is a false impression; and one which, if allowed to prevail, may do considerable damage to the Allied cause.

Boothby now had a regular 1,000-word column in the *Sunday Chronicle*, in which he could elaborate his criticisms of the Government's conduct of the war. In denouncing the shambolic performance of the Ministry of Information he was careful not to blame his old friend Walter Monckton; and when Chamberlain did a modest reshuffle in April, following the political demise of Hore-Belisha as War Minister, the only appointment he welcomed was that of Lord Woolton as Minister of Food. It was difficult to keep the balance between attacking the Government in wartime and constructive criticism. Boothby's strictures were not as strong as those of Law and Macmillan, but with them, and Amery, he maintained a consistent theme that the situation was grimly reminiscent of the Asquith Government in 1914–16, and that the solution was a Lloyd Georgian coalition Cabinet.

Boothby's record on these matters was a long and honourable one, as was those of Churchill, Bracken and Macmillan, and, at a later stage, Eden and Duff Cooper; not many others in public life in the 1930s, and especially in the Conservative Party, could make a comparable claim. None of this had done him, politically, any good at all, and it had made his already bad relations with the Tory hierarchy even worse. The latter had to accept Churchill and Eden, and did so grudgingly, but there was to be nothing for the other dissidents, whom they blamed for having caused so much trouble. The fact that the rebels had been right made the Whips even angrier, and the formation of the new group made them even more vexed. Margesson rebuked Boothby in no uncertain terms. Boothby responded on 3 October with a splendid letter, which only served to reduce further the limited esteem in which he was held by the Whips:

> Dear David
>
> If the House of Commons has failed in its duty during recent months and years, it is largely due to the extremely effective control you have exercised over it.
>
> I have never concealed the fact that I have thought the policy of the Government prior to the outbreak of war disastrous from the national point of view. . . . The fact that nobody paid the faintest attention to anything I said is not conclusive proof that I was wrong. And in any case, I just ask you to believe that I have not attacked the Government for the last twelve months simply for the fun of the thing, but out of very genuine conviction.
>
> The inescapable truth, which will be noted with amazement by the historian of the future, is that, within the miraculously short period of five years, your Government reduced this country from a position of world supremacy and absolute security to one of mortal peril. It took the Roman Empire a hundred years of most enjoyable decadence to achieve the same result.
>
> I have no doubt we shall win through. But if we do, it will be mainly due to the man whom you kept out of office for seven critical years, whose character and judgement you continually derided, and to whose coat tails you are now desperately clinging.
>
> Yours, Bob

This particular episode was the result of one of Boothby's best speeches in the House, on 20 September, when, after a speech by Chamberlain which, as Nicolson described, could easily have come from 'the secretary of a firm of undertakers reading the minutes of the last meeting', Archie Sinclair had called for secret sessions. Boothby had strongly supported him, upon which Margesson had turned on him angrily and cried out, 'You would!' As Nicolson noted, 'tempers are becoming somewhat frayed'.

They were in Paris together on a parliamentary visit on 5 October and dined afterwards alone in the famous restaurant, Larue. At the end of their meal Boothby remarked to Nicolson, 'We shan't dine here again for a very long time,' upon which Nicolson said, 'Or in Paris.' Neither could identify the problem, but 'not even Noël Coward, who was running the gayest and least secretive secret service it has been my good fortune to encounter, could revive our drooping spirits,' Boothby later wrote.* He

---

* Described hilariously by Coward himself in *Future Indefinite* (1954), which includes an account of a dinner with Churchill at Chartwell, with Boothby present, when Churchill dramatically told Coward that his wartime role was 'to sing to them [Royal Navy sailors] when the guns are firing – that's your job!' to Coward's considerable indignation, as he saw himself, rightly, as being something more than a light entertainer. The evening was not a success. Nor was his extraordinary mission to Paris, for which failure he was not at all responsible. It was a characteristic shambles of that shambolic period.

saw Paul Reynaud, the French Minister of Finance, with whom he was impressed, and not least because he was contemptuous of Chamberlain. In a detailed account that Boothby wrote to the Clement Davies–Boothby Committee, he said of Reynaud that 'he is one of the very few dynamic figures in France'. It was only too true, but in London complacency reigned.

On 10 September Boothby wrote a despairing letter to Lloyd George from Beechwood expressing his deep anxieties about the current situation. He was particularly worried about feelings in Scotland, especially among the younger people, who referred to 'helping the Poles with confetti', 'the war of appeasement', 'the old gang being at it again', etc.; '. . . but for the inclusion of Winston in the Cabinet,' he wrote, 'the criticism would I think be more vocal and widespread. Meanwhile an atmosphere of uneasiness pervades the whole scene up here, which if it continues must affect the morale of the people.' He emphasised his view that there must be a genuine national government and added, 'This is the Asquith situation all over again, at double speed, and against heavy odds. And Chamberlain is nothing like the man that Asquith was.'

Boothby's despair at the prospects led him into a very odd initiative, about which he was subsequently, and understandably, very reticent. He wrote to Lloyd George on 29 September:

I feel very strongly that we are in no position to reject a Peace Conference out of hand.

What I am afraid is that Chamberlain's personal venom against Hitler, and hatred of Russia, may induce him to force this country into a long and bloody struggle, at the end of which victory may well be unobtainable. He has been out-manoeuvered at every point, and at every turn, for the last three years; and there is no reason to believe that this process will not continue.

We still have a few cards, if only we can get someone to play them. For example, we can, and should, insist upon the participation of the United States Government in any conference that may take place; and there commit them to any stand they may think we ought to take.

Much depends on the terms we are now offered. But whether we have to play for a peace that is at least endurable, or whether we have to adopt the dire alternative and fight for our existence, I cannot believe that the men who have landed us in this mess are capable of getting us out of it. You are, I believe, the only man in this country who can state the alternative plainly to the nation during the next few days; and I hope you will not hesitate to do so.

This suggestion, which did enthuse Lloyd George, was of very short duration, killed in the House of Commons by an impassioned speech by

Duff Cooper after Lloyd George had proposed it. Boothby also quickly changed his mind.

On his return from a five-day visit to France in October, Boothby submitted another detailed note to Lloyd George on the situation there, in which he concluded that

> . . . unless Hitler climbs down to a point which can fairly be represented as a partial triumph by the allies – e.g. the restoration of complete independence to Bohemia and Moravia – it will be suicidal for us to embark on a peace conference at this juncture. For one simple reason. In signing a truce we should unquestionably sign away the French army. We cannot afford to do that. It is still the best army in the world.

He added that 'I came away filled with admiration for the strength and for the spirit of the French nation.'

On 31 October Boothby wrote a substantial personal memorandum on the situation, which he showed, amongst others, to Lloyd George. It was a very shrewd assessment of the situation as it then was, and was highly critical of the military and political leadership of Britain. And he went on:

> The dominating figure is Churchill. His hold over the country is very great indeed, and his political position is therefore one of exceptional interest. Contrary to the general view, Churchill makes a fetish of personal loyalty. He was absolutely loyal to Asquith. Indeed if his advice had been taken in the spring of 1915, and Asquith had courted a debate in the House of Commons before submitting precipitately to Bonar Law's demands, he might never have been subsequently overthrown. He was loyal to Lloyd George throughout his premiership, and after. Until the split over India, which took place when they were out of office, he was loyal to Baldwin. Today he is fanatically loyal to Chamberlain, who has shown him every consideration in a Cabinet over which he presides with great competence.
>
> It is quite true that right up to the outbreak of warChurchill denounced the present Government as an 'outworn sham', and accused the Prime Minister of examining every problem through the wrong end of municipal drainpipes. But he is capable of rapid psychological and emotional changes, which makes it easier for him than for others to adapt himself to new conditions – especially when he finds himself in general agreement with a policy actually being pursued at a given moment. Those who are building their hopes on the advent to power of a genuine national government under Churchill are therefore, I think, under a delusion. He will take no action to displace the man who at the twelfth hour gave him his confidence, and who put him at the head of a department which absorbs all his interests and energies.

Early in 1940, under the pseudonym of 'Watchman', Samuel Adams published a collective portrait of those whom he considered the outstanding contemporary politicians, and, in addition to the obvious names of Chamberlain, Churchill and Eden, included Boothby. After stating that Boothby had 'most of the necessary endowments' for office, Adams wrote:

But for some reason he is deemed unsafe and too adventurous. . . . His standing is now sufficient to enable him to laugh at any gross extremes of party discipline; but he spares a good deal of laughter for himself. 'I know what they think of me, but why should I worry?'

However, he added that

As Boothby's deep voice rapidly delivers his fresh speeches you feel you are listening to someone who is intellectually out of training. His words reverberate with great and breathless emphasis but without any ordered rhythm. Yet he is worth criticising as, with more balance and less cynicism, he might attain the excellence which would attract a following. With such a start he may well become the Father of the House. May his prestige grow with his increasing ounces.

In March Boothby returned from a two-week visit to Belgium, Switzerland and France, extremely concerned by the situation, which he set out in a detailed letter to Lloyd George and to Chamberlain. He also regarded the atmosphere in Germany as extremely ominous, detecting a widespread confidence in victory, and a considerable contempt for the British, with the exception of Churchill.

Wagner is the prophet; and Hitler, in the role of Siegfried, is preparing to fight his way to Valhalla, armed with the unbreakable sword of his faithful German people, and sustained by the fire music.
   Underlying it all is the race theory, of which Himmler is the living exponent. He is the Dzerzhinsky [the dreaded head of Stalin's secret police] of the Nazi movement, and his policy in Poland – pursued with a cold impersonal fanaticism – is a policy of extermination. There the young men have been shot in droves, the young women sterilised and placed in the soldiers' brothels, and the old people driven out to die of hunger and exposure. It was related to me that only a few days ago a high German staff officer, when speaking to a friend of recent events in the Posnan district, completely broke down.
   This account may seem to be highly coloured. But in fact it is not so. For the first time in history the German people – with all their thoroughness, rigidity, administrative capacity, and underlying brutality – find themselves under the direction and control of a southerner and a madman, with a magnetic personality, and a genius for swift decision and flexible action. The resultant combination is formidable.

After a very accurate assessment of the wavering position of the neutrals, Boothby went on:

. . . I travelled through the night to Paris, and demoralisation is not too strong a word to describe the mood which prevailed in the French capital that evening.

The fact that, for the time being, Hitler has been successful in seizing and retaining the initiative is more upsetting to the French than it is to us. They are less phlegmatic, and are beginning to fret. Of one thing I am certain – and it is an element of real danger in our situation, which requires careful watching. The French army will find it increasingly difficult to sustain a prolonged period of total inactivity. The German military attack in the west remains 'mounted', but I very much doubt whether it will be attempted this year. They have plenty of political and economic plans to occupy their attention in the Balkans and in Russia. The apparatus and the façade alike are formidable, but not by any means invincible. Meanwhile I should doubt whether Hitler himself has made up his mind what he intends to do.

Chamberlain wrote to Boothby on 21 March, thanking him for his letter: 'You did, indeed, succeed in making very valuable use of the time at your disposal and I have read your memoranda with great interest. I shall arrange for it to be shown to the Foreign Secretary and others concerned.'

At this point Boothby became involved in one of the most remarkable episodes of his life. He was not allowed to relate it until after the war – in 1947, when his first account was published – and Weininger subsequently published his own description. Neither has been challenged; indeed, the 1947 version, published when most of the participants were still alive, was confirmed by them. There is no doubt of its authenticity.

Boothby's account opens dramatically:

On Sunday, April 14th, the Intelligence Division of the Admiralty was directed by the First Lord [Churchill] to get in touch with me immediately and find out whether I could go over to Belgium and Holland at once, on a private and secret mission, in order to get hold of arms for this country – above all, rifles. I asked a Belgian friend of mine, Louis Franck, who was partner in the firm of Samuel Montagu & Co., to go to Brussels first, in order to find out from the Belgian Government whether arrangements could be made for the necessary export licences. This he readily agreed to do.

On Monday, April 15th, I saw the Minister of Supply, Dr Burgin. He asked me to be 'precise'. I was rather nettled by this, and told him so in a letter the following day, adding, however, that I was very hopeful that Franck would succeed, and that I should then be able to bring him something definite and substantial. His reply was encouraging. 'Do not be angry,' he wrote. 'My words "be precise" were most friendly, and pointed simply to the fact that I wanted to find and secure these rifles.'

Franck's report was positive, provided that the goods were allegedly purchased in the first instance on behalf of neutral countries, about which there was no difficulty. Boothby asked Weininger to accompany him. Weininger later wrote:

He said he needed me as an interpreter, and he was aware of my exploit with Béla Kun and knew I enjoyed business negotiations of a rather hare-brained and slightly dangerous nature. At any rate, he told me, 'You speak French. My French is very bad.' I needed no documents, I was assured, as my role was known to the authorities. My Czech passport would still suffice. Of course, I jumped at the opportunity to go with my friend.

They flew to Brussels on 22 April to find that the entire British military and intelligence unit there consisted of two Military Attachés, a Colonel Blake and a Major Mckenzie, who were immensely helpful. The Belgians, also, co-operated fully, and at Liège Boothby negotiated successfully for 9,000 rifles, over 100 machine-guns and 1,000 light automatics, for immediate delivery.

Blake had found another contact in Amsterdam, and they went there to meet a man called Woolf, whom Boothby had known previously. Woolf took him and Weininger to a private room at the Amstel Hotel, where there were four Dutchmen waiting to see them. To Boothby's astonishment and excitement he was offered between 200,000 and 400,000 new German Mauser rifles, with 1,000 rounds of ammunition each, with delivery to start the following week and to be completed within three weeks.

Boothby later wrote:

I travelled back from Amsterdam to Brussels in a fever of excitement. I had no doubt that the rifles were of Krupp manufacture. Equally, I had no doubt (although I said only that I had come to negotiate on behalf of 'a foreign Government') that the Dutchmen were under no illusions regarding their ultimate destination. Finally, I had no doubt that the offer was genuine, for the very good reason that it was made through, and under the guarantee, of the Amsterdamsche Bank.

The sum proposed seemed to Boothby and Weininger to be reasonable, the key points being that payment must be made in American dollars, and that there was a four-day option. 'I had never seen Boothby so excited as we travelled back from Amsterdam to Brussels,' Weininger's account continued. What was specially exciting was the knowledge that the bulk of the rifles were in Germany, but could be swiftly moved over the border into Belgium. 'The combination of anti-Nazi sentiment among industrialists and army officers, and the need for American dollars on the part of corruptible Nazi officials, added up to quite a potent force,' Weininger wrote; 'Boothby was rhapsodic.'

When Boothby reached Brussels and reported to Blake, he, also, considered the offer genuine. He at once offered to drive Boothby to the British headquarters at Arras and to arrange for him to be flown back to London the next day, while Weininger remained in Brussels. Boothby dined at GHQ, where he sat next to the Director of Military Intelligence, General Mason Macfarlane, who knew of Boothby's enterprise, but startled him by saying that when he was Military Attaché in Berlin before the war, German arms were freely available, but any proposals to buy them had been vetoed by the War Office and the Treasury. He was also, rightly, gloomy about the Norway campaign and anticipated a massive German attack on France; 'in a very short time we shall be fighting for our lives here – here, in Arras,' he remarked.

Boothby was flown back to London on 28 April and immediately reported to Burgin on the success of his mission, emphasising the shortness of the option period. On the following day Burgin asked Boothby to cable for an extension of the option for three additional days; this Boothby did, and received a reply of acceptance. But on 7 May Burgin rang up again to tell him that the rifles were no longer required, and that, even if they were, Simon, the Chancellor of the Exchequer, would not provide the dollars. So that was that!

This was the morning of the two-day debate that was to bring down the Chamberlain Government, and was, for Boothby, the last straw. He wrote bitterly to Churchill:

> I was sent over to Belgium at the shortest notice, and as a matter of the greatest urgency, ten days ago, in order (in Burgin's written words) to 'find and secure rifles'. I found them. This morning I am told by Burgin that no rifles are required; and that, even if they were, the Treasury would not pay for them. It would be incredible if it were not true.

Churchill had other preoccupations that morning, and so did Boothby, but the matter rankled. Weininger, when he returned from Brussels, was equally amazed. He later wrote with generosity: 'As it was, speaking personally, I was permitted only to be grateful to serve a great man – Boothby – in one of his prime moments of national service. Otherwise, I am still angry.'

The choice of Boothby to undertake this startling mission had been Churchill's, and it was a wholly Churchillian enterprise, but when Weininger met Simon to talk about the mission the Chancellor preferred to talk about birds; when Weininger raised the matter of the rifles, 'there was no reaction'.

The fact was that ministers had no inkling of the storm that was about to erupt. The possibility that the British army would have to evacuate Europe and leave most of its precious equipment behind – including vast numbers of rifles – was undreamed of. When that reality occurred, the desperate shortage of rifles became only too evident and led to Churchill and Eden making frantic – and, fortunately, successful – appeals to Roosevelt for rifles and ammunition, not only for the newly formed Home Guard, proudly parading with broomsticks and farming implements, but even for the regular army. Some time later Boothby was told by Waley that they had made 'a serious mistake' in refusing to buy the rifles. 'It was a bit more than that,' was Boothby's comment.

This extraordinary episode finally convinced Boothby that the war was as good as lost so long as it was being managed by Chamberlain and his gang. The complacency of Chamberlain seemed to have no bounds, and when he had declared in April at the beginning of the disastrous Norway campaign that Hitler 'has missed the bus', he unwittingly wrote his political death-warrant. What worried Boothby, Clement Davies and the other dissidents was that it was clear that Churchill, their favoured candidate, bore a heavy responsibility for the Norwegian disaster; also, never a conspirator himself, Churchill was fiercely and honourably loyal to the Prime Minister. This may have been all very noble in principle, but it was evident that he would not reach for the crown.

Although in later life Boothby often tended to exaggerate his role on certain occasions (in which he is not alone in politicians' memoirs), on this occasion it was indeed crucial, as was that of Davies. On 7 May, on the motion for the adjournment of the House, the Commons debated the Norway campaign. It developed into one of the finest of all modern debates and still, after all these years, makes enthralling reading.

The result was very much in doubt. On the afternoon of 7 May Boothby gave tea to Dorothy Macmillan and Baffy Dugdale, who had been in the Ladies' Gallery watching the debate. The latter noted that

He repeated that there would be no change of Government, that Lloyd George and the Labour leaders were determined not to take charge of affairs at this juncture, that the mess is so great, and the disasters to be experienced in the next six weeks so terrible, that those who had sown the wind, reap the whirlwind.[*]

Lloyd George had not intended to speak at all, but on Davies' personal urgings he agreed to consider it and came to Westminster. Davies asked

[*] Dugdale, *op. cit.*, p. 168.

Boothby to organise a meeting of the dissident Conservatives and to name a chairman. Boothby suggested Amery, who willingly agreed. On the first evening of the debate Amery electrified the House by, for once, rising to the heights of oratory with a fierce attack on the Government, ending with Cromwell's denunciation of the Long Parliament: 'You have sat too long here for any good you have been doing. Depart, I say, and let us be done with you. In the name of God, go!'

At the meeting of the unhappy group of dissidents held immediately afterwards, the principal task was to ensure that sufficient, and chosen, speakers would be ready to be called on the next day; this was particularly necessary, as in the debate so far the Speaker had called on the Conservative side, until Amery, a collection of Government loyalists. Those at the meeting were still doubtful about the advisability of a division, as were the Labour leaders, but the effect of Amery's speech had been immense.

On the following morning Amery's own Watching Committee met at Lord Salisbury's house in Arlington Street, and the mood had definitely turned to the need to change the Government. But no decision actually to vote had been taken. But when Chamberlain responded in the House to Herbert Morrison's statement that Labour regarded the debate as a vote of confidence by appealing to his friends – 'and I have friends in this House', upon which Boothby growled, 'Not I,' and, as he later wrote, 'got a withering glance from the eyes of an arrogant blackbird' – Davies hurried to Lloyd George's room behind the Speaker's Chair to report this development and to repeat his request to intervene; Lloyd George hastened into the Chamber and, as a former prime minister, was called at once. It was, as Churchill later wrote, 'his last decisive intervention in the House of Commons', in which his deep personal loathing of Chamberlain came out in an eloquent and scornful denunciation, while taking care to exonerate Churchill.

As the debate raged, and the Conservative Whips were frantically trying to persuade Conservatives to vote for the Government, and making specious promises of mighty changes in the air, for the first time all the dissident groups met together in a committee room, with Amery in the chair. What particularly struck him, and others, was how many Conservatives were in military uniform. It was at this meeting that the fateful decision was taken to vote against the Government, or to abstain.

Churchill wound up the great debate, defending the Norway campaign and the Government's handling of the war with spirit, but without convincing the rebels. All day the pressure of the Whips had been relentless and lacking in subtlety, and it continued even after Churchill had sat down and the vote was taking place. There were angry scenes between the 'loyalist' and 'dissident' Conservatives as they moved towards the lobbies, a scene most vividly described by Chips Channon: '"Quislings," we shouted at them [the anti-Government Conservatives], "Rats". "Yes-men", they replied.'* Other accounts indicate that the language was considerably more vigorous than this; with Boothby, Duff Cooper and James Stuart around, it would have been.

When Margesson announced the result in the packed Chamber, in total silence, there was a universal gasp. The Conservative majority should have been 213. It was eighty-one. Forty-one Conservatives, including Boothby, Amery, Duff Cooper, Macmillan, Quintin Hogg, John Profumo and Ronald Tree, had voted against the Government, and a further sixty had abstained. Amidst cries of 'In the name of God, go!', Chamberlain left the Chamber alone, looking stunned. But he still refused to accept the verdict.

In his personal account of this occasion, written immediately afterwards, Boothby said:

I was standing beside the Speaker's Chair when the result of the division was announced. It clearly came as a surprise, and a great shock, to the Prime Minister. For a moment he blanched, but quickly recovered himself, and smiled at some of his supporters. Then he rose abruptly, and walked out alone. I watched his solitary figure going down the dark corridor behind the Speaker's Chair until it disappeared from sight. I thought of him standing in Downing Street, barely eighteen months before, with the cheering crowds surging around him. All is vanity, saith the preacher. I felt very sorry for him in the hour of his fall. God knows he had struggled, according to the light that was in him, for peace. But I called to mind a sentence in John Buchan's *History of the Great War*: 'If a man is determined not to fight, and his enemy knows this, it is unlikely that he will escape without finding himself in strangely undignified positions.'

Although he owed nothing to Chamberlain, and was one of the leading figures in the campaign to remove him from the premiership and to install Churchill in his place, it was not in Boothby's nature to kick a man when he was down, and he wrote of this poignant episode:

The last phase of [Chamberlain's] life, when he passed, within the space of months, from the dizziest heights of success, when he was acclaimed by the entire civilised world, to the depths of public and personal disaster, had something of the nobility of Greek tragedy.

Two days of immense confusion followed, well described by Amery in his diary. When the dissidents met next morning under Amery's chairmanship again in the House, the numbers had swelled significantly, including several who had voted for the Government on the previous

---

*Robert Rhodes James (ed.), *Chips, The Diaries of Sir Henry Channon*, pp. 246–7.

evening. They agreed that they would support any prime minister who would form a truly national government, 'appointing its men by merit and not on Whips' lines and making a real War Cabinet. The personal issue I carefully kept out of the picture in order to avoid waste of time discussing alternatives.'*

Davies and Boothby, very active behind the scenes in fomenting the 'Chamberlain Must Go' campaign, while Chamberlain obstinately refused to do so, also operated in public. On 9 May Davies moved that the House should not adjourn until 21 May, which, amazingly, was the Government's proposal, unaware of the imminent German onslaught on Holland and Belgium, which occurred early the following morning.

Davies' role had already been of supreme importance and now became crucial. As Boothby felt very strongly that his friend had never been given sufficient credit for his part in the fall of Chamberlain and the appointment of Churchill, a recorded interview he gave to Davies' biographer can be inserted at this point:

Much of it was done at my flat. When Chamberlain was still Prime Minister, he [Davies] and I formed a ginger group in the House of Commons. He was the Chairman and I was the Secretary of the group. It was a non-political discussion group which met about once a week over dinner. I remember Attlee frequently attended these meetings. This was of course the period of the Phoney War. Many people called it the Bore War. About a dozen MPs usually attended these meetings, although far more attended the final meeting on the eve of the vote in the Commons on the Norway debate. Herbert Morrison had eventually decided to press for a division, which inevitably meant a question of confidence as Chamberlain had appealed to his friends. After this our group met, and it was at this meeting that the fateful decision was taken to vote against Chamberlain. About thirty-three Conservative members, including myself, did vote against the Prime Minister. Many of them were young Conservative MPs too. Attlee and Greenwood were pretty sure that they would refuse to serve in a coalition government under Chamberlain, but it was Clem Davies who convinced them that they should not serve. He made sure that a new coalition was necessary, and under a new Prime Minister.

For a vital few days during and after the Norway debate, Clem Davies did much of his work at my flat in Pall Mall. From there he did a great deal of telephoning, mostly to Attlee and Greenwood in Bournemouth because they were attending the Labour Party Conference. He was in constant touch with them. He also spent a great deal of time at the Reform Club. He played a decisive part in these events: he was one of the architects of the advent to power of Churchill. It was a tragedy that Churchill never gave Clem Davies office. Amery asked Churchill for something for him, but he received nothing. But Churchill

*John Barnes and David Nicholson (eds), *Leo Amery Diaries; 1929-45*, p. 612.

did not treat his friends well. The fact was that Churchill depended upon the support of the Conservative Party – for the time being at any rate. He had to have the Party behind him. But Clem could have been given the Ministry of Education – he was offered this post some years later by Churchill.

But, strangely, Churchill never really forgave the men who had put him in power. Clem Davies should have had office; in fact he came away with nothing. He was a thoroughly charming man, but he talked too much. He was very nice, but he never made the top flight. He played a decisive part in an important period; he played a difficult role well.*

In seconding Davies' motion Boothby, who was ill-received on the Government benches, opened by declaring robustly that

The events of yesterday proved that the Government, as at present constituted, does not possess the confidence of the House and country (*ministerial cries of 'No! No!'*). It is common knowledge to every member of this House, if he faces the facts, that national unity can never be achieved under the present political leadership.

The motion failed, but the point had been registered.

On the evening of the 9th, Boothby wrote urgently to Churchill to keep him up with developments.

Dear Winston
I have been in the House all day. This is the situation, as I see it.
(1) The Labour Party won't touch Chamberlain at any price.
(2) Nor will Archie [Sinclair].
(3) Nor will our group.
Therefore it is inconceivable that Chamberlain can carry through a reconstruction of the Government.
A majority of the House is, nevertheless, determined on a *radical* reconstruction, which will involve (inter alia) the elimination of Simon and Hoare.
(4) Opinion is hardening against Halifax as Prime Minister. I am doing my best to foster this, because I cannot feel he is, in the circumstances, the right man.
At the moment of writing, our group would oppose his appointment, unless it commanded universal assent. It is quite a powerful group. It is now led by Amery; and includes Duff Cooper, Eddie Winterton, Belisha, Hammersley, Henderson Stewart, Emrys Evans, Mrs. Tate, R. Tree, Russell, Harold Nicolson, [Derrick] Gunston, Clem Davies, & [Stephen] King-Hall.

* When Davies died in 1963, Boothby was asked to speak at his memorial service. Mrs Davies wrote to him in gratitude: 'It was quite perfect. Thank you, thank you. Clem loved you, I love you. Jano.'

Boothby then set out his group's terms, which had been issued to the press, calling for a genuine national government, and went on:

> In fact I find a gathering consensus of opinion in all quarters that you are the necessary and inevitable Prime Minister – as I wrote to you some weeks ago.
>
> God knows it is a terrible prospect for you. But I don't see how you can avoid it.
>
> Yours, Bob

Boothby added a postscript, that Davies had told him that Attlee and Greenwood would not serve under Halifax, which was rather more wishful thinking than fact.

The German invasion of Holland and Belgium actually persuaded Chamberlain, now totally out of touch with reality, that this was another reason for him to stay on, despite the fact that Attlee and Greenwood had made it clear that Labour would not serve under him. The difficulty was that whereas Davies and Boothby were ardent for Churchill, the clear favourite, from the King downwards, was Halifax. Then, there came a wholly unexpected ally for Churchill in Kingsley Wood. Bracken was also hard at work, with his unique press contacts, especially with Beaverbrook. The tide against Chamberlain was now unstoppable, as he had begun to realise, and he asked Churchill and Halifax to see him on the morning of the 10th. On Bracken's urging, Churchill said nothing. Eventually, after a long silence, Halifax said that it would be impossible for a peer to be prime minister in wartime. 'It was clear', Churchill later wrote, 'that the duty would fall upon me – had in fact fallen upon me.' Chamberlain reluctantly resigned, and Churchill embarked upon his glorious premiership under dark circumstances that were rapidly to become even darker. There were mighty celebrations in Pall Mall.

10

Minister of Food
1940

Cabinet forming is a difficult, and usually messy, business at the best of times. Creating an all-Party coalition in wartime, in the midst of what Bracken rightly described to Boothby as a 'whizzing crisis', was even more difficult, especially as Churchill was determined to get on good terms with a still largely hostile Conservative Party. In this endeavour he went too far. His attempt to make Chamberlain Chancellor of the Exchequer was vetoed by Labour and the Tory dissidents, Lord Salisbury being deputed by them to convey to the new Prime Minister that this was absolutely impossible.

Eventually a small War Cabinet was announced, as well as the major appointments. Not very much seemed to have changed. Chamberlain would be Lord President of the Council, Halifax would remain Foreign Secretary, Kingsley Wood would become Chancellor of the Exchequer, and Simon, Lord Chancellor; for the Service Ministries Eden went to the War Office, A. V. Alexander to the Admiralty and Archie Sinclair to the Air Ministry. Beaverbrook would become Minister of Aircraft Production, Ernest Bevin Minister of Labour, Lord Woolton Minister of Food, Herbert Morrison Minister of Supply, Sir John Anderson Home Secretary, and Leo Amery Secretary of State for India. Attlee and Greenwood would be in the five-man War Cabinet.

This came as a severe disappointment to the Conservative dissidents, who felt, with good cause, that those who had put Churchill in Downing Street could reasonably expect some reward. There were few promotions from the Conservative backbenches, nothing for Clement Davies, and Amery had been effectively side-tracked. The infamous Whips Office remained in place, still led by Margesson and Stuart. Boothby and his friends felt that this was carrying magnanimity too far, and demonstrated a lack of loyalty to Churchill's real friends and allies. Even the devoted Bracken only became Churchill's informal Parliamentary Private Secretary,* the Whips having a real one up their sleeves in George Harvie-Watt, an impeccable nonentity who had said and done nothing except serve as a Whip in the nine years he had been in Parliament. The more the rebels saw, as the lists came out of Downing Street, the more it seemed the same mixture as before – as, indeed, it was. Even Eden was not in the War Cabinet.

So alarmed were Boothby and Macmillan that on 12 May they went to see Amery to ask him if they should join the Government. 'I said yes', Amery recorded in his diary, 'in order to be inside the fortress and help with the next change, for by now it was clear to me that this was only an interim government. Winston has not been nearly bold enough in his changes and much too afraid of the Party.' This remained the very strong view of Boothby and Macmillan, but they accepted Amery's wise advice, not least because they knew of his doubts whether he should accept the India Office.

Boothby was convinced that he, also, had been passed over until he had a telephone call from Beaverbrook to tell him that he was definitely 'on the list'. He hoped that he would be Beaverbrook's Parliamentary Secretary at Aircraft Production, and has described his meeting with Churchill when the summons came:

Churchill received me somewhat grumpily, and gave me one of his Graham Sutherland looks. 'I would have offered you Scotland,' he said, 'but I was advised that your divorce made that impossible.' (This was nonsense.)† As it is, I can offer you the post of Parliamentary Secretary to the Minister of Food. Your Minister [Lord Woolton] will be in the House of Lords, so you will be in charge in the House of Commons; and we will see how you get on.

Boothby was disconcerted by this somewhat graceless invitation, but Churchill also said to him that 'It took Armageddon to make me Prime Minister. But now I am here I am determined that power shall be in no other hands but mine. There will be no more Kitcheners, Fishers, or Haigs.' At the time, Boothby was pleased to hear this. It was not long before he was having doubts.

*This was at Bracken's own wish, which was not appreciated at the time. It was with considerable reluctance that the King agreed to Churchill's recommendation that he should be a Privy Councillor; the King was also deeply unhappy about Beaverbrook's appointment. In both cases Churchill firmly, but courteously, prevailed. Duff Cooper became Minister of Information, a post he did not adorn; Richard Law and Macmillan received minor office, but otherwise the dissidents did not do well.

†In another account of this meeting Boothby recorded that he had reminded Churchill that James Stuart had been a co-respondent in a divorce case.

It is clear that the meeting had not gone well. In his letter of acceptance Boothby wrote that 'I'm afraid I must have appeared ungracious yesterday, but it was one of the rare occasions in my life when I felt shy and I found great difficulty in saying anything.' The letter ended, rather oddly, '*au revoir*'.

There was much joy in East Aberdeenshire and ecstasy at Beechwood. The *Buchan Observer* celebrated with one of 'John Citizen's' almost incomprehensible but friendly doggerels, and the leading article declared that 'Mr Boothby has always been regarded as one of the most brilliant of the younger men in the Unionist Party, and his promotion to Government rank has always been accepted as a matter of time,' while tactfully refraining from pointing out that it had taken sixteen years in the Commons, of which fourteen had been under Conservative Governments.* As with Churchill and Eden, it had taken Hitler to overcome the hostility of the Whips Office.

Nicholas Davenport wrote a ferocious denunciation of Conservative ministers and MPs in the *New Statesman:*

Even now they strut about, trying to run this war like the last war – or the Crimean War. They are angry with people like Amery and Boothby who voted against Mr Chamberlain. Not cricket to vote against your own side and deprive a man of a comfortable job while the brave boys die in Flanders. . . . Some day I'd like to write a study of the Tory mind which has wasted mankind's opportunity between 1918 and 1940.

Unfortunately, he did not.

The appointment of 'Fred' Woolton as Minister of Food was to prove absolutely inspired. Although not a politician, and with no Party allegiance – or, perhaps, because of these alleged deficiencies – his exceptional knowledge of the food retail business was accompanied by a jovial and utterly convincing manner, particularly on the radio, whose crucial importance for public information and the maintenance of morale was now becoming recognised. Under his leadership, which amounted almost to genius, the British people as a whole not only never starved, or came

---

*Harold Macmillan, who had joined in the singing of *Rule Britannia* after voting against Chamberlain, became Parliamentary Secretary to the Minister of Supply. He and Boothby were mentioned together in the press as 'among the ablest men in the House'.

In 1979, a group of eager new Conservative MPs asked Macmillan for the secret of his political success. 'What you young men need', he said gravely, 'is sixteen years on the backbenches.' It was not the reply they had expected, or that they welcomed.

anywhere close to it, but poorer families were better fed than ever before. There were, of course, severe shortages and deprivations, particularly when the U-boat campaign got into its terrible stride in 1941–2, but food shortages never approached the depths that they were to reach in Germany and in most of Europe.

Woolton, for his part, was delighted by Boothby's appointment. They had not known each other before, but they got on famously from their first meeting and quickly established themselves as a formidable team.

Boothby's appointment was greeted with widespread approval. Margot Asquith wrote on 17 May, characteristically:

Dearest Bob
   I am *enchanted* that you are in the Government, *not* under your hero L.G.! but under Winston.

Very ever affectionately,
Margot

On his first appearance in the House as a minister Boothby received a memorable and prolonged ovation from both sides. In the Ministry he began pouring out ideas, of which the most important was his early project for a national milk scheme to provide free milk for poor children and nursing mothers on request, and without a means test; others would receive it for 2d a pint. He urged a new national bread formula containing Vitamin B1 and calcium salt, and a new food order against waste. He was fertile with ideas – most of which, like these three, were put through Parliament by him personally. He shared the radio duties with Woolton very shortly after his appointment, and for the first time a huge radio audience heard his incomparable voice. But, at the beginning of his ministerial career, he had difficulties with Churchill.

Woolton had intended to go to Edinburgh and Glasgow to launch what he called his 'Kitchen Front Campaign' against waste in the home, but could not afford the time. Therefore, at their first meeting together, he asked Boothby to deputise for him, which he did with relish. In the course of his widely reported speeches Boothby robustly condemned 'luxury eating' in hotels and restaurants, particularly in London. This rather startled his friends, but Boothby was genuinely shocked that, with the enemy at the door, the rich were still enjoying meals on pre-war scales. The providers and receivers of these luxuries were indignant and protested strongly. Churchill, who saw no harm in people enjoying themselves in wartime, shared their views and complained to Woolton about his Minister's 'indiscretion'.

Boothby was astounded, and with good cause, to receive such a strong rebuke from Churchill at such a time and replied on 20 May:

Dear Prime Minister

My Minister has shown me a copy of your minute. I should like you to know that, on the very day I took over my duties in this Department, he asked me to proceed immediately to Scotland and deputise for him, at two important meetings in Edinburgh and Glasgow, in launching the FOOD ECONOMY DRIVE.

I should have hesitated to assume so heavy a responsibility at the outset of my ministerial career, had the meetings not been held on my native heath, and had Lord Woolton himself not taken me so completely into his confidence. We had a meeting last Thursday afternoon at which the heads of the Department were present, which lasted for nearly two hours; and subsequently a brief was prepared for me, to which I strictly adhered. As a further precautionary measure, I went over the notes of my speech in Edinburgh next morning with the Minister's Private Secretary, who accompanied me to Scotland.

In these circumstances I do not think a charge of indiscretion lies against me. . . .

Yours sincerely
Robert Boothby

This episode demonstrated an aspect of Churchill's character to which his admirers have devoted inadequate attention. Beaverbrook, who knew him so well, had written of him many years before that 'he is the stuff of which tyrants are made', and it is the view of the author of the best essay written on him* that, had it not been for his wife, he might very well have actually become one. When Boothby, many years later, in an otherwise admiring portrait, referred to an 'element of cruelty' in Churchill's character,† there was much public uproar at this assault on such a revered figure, but the fact is that it was true. Boothby's personal opinion was that 'Winston was a shit; but we needed a shit to beat Hitler.' But his differences with Churchill never obscured the fact that, although he considered Lloyd George the greater man, Churchill was an incomparable wartime Prime Minister, to whom this nation largely owed its salvation. But this did not mean that he had to like him.

The fact was that, after so many years of frustration and impotence, Churchill seized his power voraciously. Nineteen forty saw him at his best, but also at his worst, particularly in human relationships, and especially towards those who had been his friends. Ruthlessness was indeed necessary, but instead of concentrating totally on the desperate military situation, he probed, hectored and enquired into every detail of government. Fierce, and often unfair, criticisms descended on ministers,

* Professor E. D. Williams in *The Dictionary of National Biography*.
† See pp. 439–40.

military commanders and officials, marked ACTION THIS DAY, and there was widespread resentment – and worse – among the many recipients. Also, he made copious use of the telephone. Matters got to such a lamentable point that Mrs Churchill, in a famous note to him, rebuked him lovingly but emphatically about his conduct.*

In this tiny matter, blown by Churchill into a wholly unnecessary row, Woolton strongly supported Boothby, and the silly storm passed over. But it further exacerbated relations between the two former allies.

The National Milk Scheme had been Woolton's idea, but he had passed it over to Boothby simply as a thought; within a week it was presented back to Woolton as a scheme by Boothby and his officials, was carried swiftly through the Cabinet and then through the Commons without debate. One of Boothby's first memoranda to Woolton set out his views on parliamentary tactics:

I feel very strongly that the announcement of the Milk Scheme should be made, in the first instance, to the House of Commons.

There is no other domestic subject about which the House feels so strongly. Two things must be borne in mind:

(1) that this has been a burning subject for several years past; and

(2) that the intentions of the House, as expressed in past Resolutions and Legislation, have never been given effect to.

The proposed scheme touches the House of Commons at several vital points, viz:

(a) malnutrition;

(b) the rationalisation of distribution;

(c) the welfare of the poorest class;

(d) distributive margins;

(e) the relationship between the Central Government and Local Authorities;

(f) the means test.

All these questions have been repeatedly raised on the floor of the House in recent years, and at one period the campaign for the supply of cheap milk to those who needed it was actually conducted for the Labour Party by Tom Johnston [now Regional Commissioner for Scotland], and for the Conservative Party by myself.

I can give you an unequivocal assurance that I do not wish to claim, or to obtain, any personal credit in this matter. At the same time it is my duty to express my absolute conviction, in the light of past experience, that an announcement of any scheme dealing with the provision of cheap milk to

---

* See Martin Gilbert, *Winston S. Churchill: Finest Hour 1939–41*, pp. 587–8.

those who require it most in another place would be deeply resented by the House of Commons, and would greatly increase my own difficulties in the days that are to come. This applies to no other aspect of food policy. I should not raise the slightest objection to the announcement of *any* other scheme either in the House of Lords or through the Press, should this be considered convenient or desirable. But I cannot exaggerate the importance which, in my opinion, attaches to the *announcement* of the Milk Scheme to the House of Commons, in the first instance.

I am quite sure that if this point were put to Lord Samuel, he would concur.

I attach a note by Mr. Harwood giving reasons why the announcement should not be deferred beyond next week, on purely practical grounds.

If the premature disclosure wh. he anticipates is made, I am apprehensive of real trouble in the H of C.

8 June 1940
R. J. G. BOOTHBY

P.S. I should, of course, only be able to announce the scheme to the House in the barest outline. . . .

Forgive me for pressing you on this matter, but I do feel most strongly about it. If the House of Commons – which is not at present in a very easy mood – feels that it has been well treated upon a subject which so vitally concerns it, it may well make all the difference to our success or failure in the future.

The scheme was widely praised at the time, and later, and its withdrawal by a Conservative Government in 1971 created such a national uproar – in which Boothby himself was involved – that for a time it was thought that the political career of the minister responsible, Margaret Thatcher, might never recover.

Boothby's 'indiscretion' in Edinburgh resulted in the introduction of the 'one main course only' rule in restaurants, which lasted throughout the war. As Boothby later remarked, 'it did not save much food, but it did allay the growing public irritation'. It was indeed ridiculous that those who could afford it could eat more in restaurants than they could at home under food rationing, and on this Woolton and Boothby were certainly right, and Churchill wrong.

Reading the Ministry of Food papers one is struck by Boothby's energy and enthusiasm, and when he introduced the Ministry of Food estimates in July his speech was hailed as a parliamentary triumph by the press and the House. But when Margesson told Churchill of this, he only replied, 'I am sorry to hear it.'

Churchill had swiftly developed an unreasonable dislike of the Ministry of Food. In a characteristic memorandum to Woolton on 14 July he wrote:

Almost all the food faddists I have ever known, nut-eaters and the like, have died young after a long period of senile decay. The British soldier is far more likely to be right than the scientists. All he cares about is beef. . . . The way to lose the war is to try to force the British public into a diet of milk, oatmeal, potatoes, etc., washed down on gala occasions with a little lime juice.*

On the following day he was complaining about the introduction of tea rationing. Although the Ministry was coping very successfully with its heavy national responsibilities, all it received from Downing Street were complaints and criticisms, which read well but did not address the real problems.

Apart from Churchill's interference, all seemed to be going well on the ministerial front. Clem Davies wrote ecstatically to Boothby about his Estimates speech:

Bob dear,
    Good Morning.
    I am sorry I was not in the House to hear you yesterday, but though I missed your speech, I had some compensation in hearing your praises sung on all lips. I have not heard for a long time such spontaneous and unanimous praise, and you can imagine how that pleased one who will always be anxious to be known as your admiring friend

Clem

Walter Elliot, back in the army, wrote delightedly from Chester to say how pleased the constituency would be by his speech, 'but still more your family, and particularly your Old Man. It is a Good Thing. Strength to your elbow.' There were many more similar messages. On 29 July Boothby broadcast again about fruit and vegetables, and managed to make these unlikely subjects interesting; and, by making the subjects simple, conveyed the message of the Government's policy. Woolton and others were delighted, and there was more praise – but no comment from Downing Street.

The fact was that Boothby was in deep disfavour with Churchill, for reasons that had nothing to do with the Ministry of Food.

To a degree that seems astonishing today, Churchill felt politically deeply insecure in the summer of 1940, and it was this fact, combined with the grim military position, that explains his irascibility, imperiousness and constant meddling in virtually every aspect of government and

* Gilbert, *op. cit.*, p. 663.

the Armed Services. It was only after the Battle of Britain had been won (and the victor, Hugh Dowding, promptly relieved of his command), and the peril of invasion had receded, that he began to relax. Also, the originally hostile mood in the Commons had by then been totally transformed by his unforgettable speeches and bearing. But in June and July Churchill was unsure about the reality of his support in the Conservative Party, and was particularly sensitive to the position and attitude of his old master, Lloyd George. Boothby, of all people, should have realised this, but his devotion to, and admiration for, Lloyd George took him on to a fatal collision course with Churchill.

Boothby, Lloyd George and many others were dismayed that so many of the appeasers remained in the Cabinet, particularly Chamberlain, Sir 'Snake' Simon, Halifax and Kingsley Wood. On 12 June Bracken wrote to Boothby, in a letter marked 'Really Private':

Dear Bob

The Boss knows that the campaign against the old gang does not come from any of your boys.

This is, of course, a stop-press government. It contains many glaring misfits. But most of the key jobs are in the hands of the right men. And when this whizzing crisis is over, I dare say some improvements can be made.

W has been making great efforts to enlist the aid of L.G. But that great man (for quite understandable reasons) is coy about sitting with some of the old gang. I dare say that he will see Winston's difficulties and will keep his black spots in cold storage. God knows they should be delivered. But this is no time for an assize.

I have great sympathy for L.G.'s views. And I know he feels acutely that some of the men still in the Government have brought this country to the edge of a precipice. And after all, he, above all other men, brought us victory in 1918. And he has seen that victory thrown away by conceited duds in the manger – men who do nothing, and who did everything in their power to prevent anybody else from obtaining a chance of doing their duty.

Yours
B. B.

Boothby's concerns were demonstrated in one of many letters to Lloyd George early in June:

Dear L.G.

I have had sleepless nights over our conversation at lunch last Tuesday.

I wrote that, if our situation ever became desperate, we should need you – and God knows it is desperate today. I cannot help feeling that the moment has now come when you should go into Government at all costs.

I don't think you should do this without making it plain that, in your view, the men whose criminal negligence in the past is mainly responsible for our present plight should now have the decency to resign. But their position in the country is so weak that I no longer believe that they are capable of being a menace. Once you are there, you can deal with them as they deserve. The vital thing is that you should be able to influence policy before final disaster overtakes us – and I cannot see how you can do this from outside.

In my view, the only government now capable of saving us is a dictatorial triumvirate consisting of Winston, yourself, and a representative of the Labour movement – be it Attlee or another. Personally I would like to see you go to the Foreign Office, because I believe you are the only living man who can still do something to restore our prestige in those countries we have not yet succeeded in bringing into the war against us – notably the USSR. If Lord Halifax can establish a liaison for us with the Almighty in a sinecure office, there can be no objection to it. But it is quite clear that where Russians, Italians, Spaniards, or Turks are concerned it is nothing short of a calamity.

Any moment now decisions of immense magnitude and fateful consequence may have to be taken. And I feel most strongly that your wisdom, your resources, and your experience, should be at the disposal of this country.

Meanwhile the tide of public opinion is rising steadily. At present it expresses itself in a savage hatred of Chamberlain and Simon on the part of those who supported them through thick and thin during the fatal years when they were engaged in throwing away the British Empire; and in a widespread – although probably mistaken – conviction that we were not doing enough to help the French. There are admittedly some bad patches in this administration. And my fear is that this tide, which may very easily assume a revolutionary character, will overwhelm Winston – and with him, all of us – if something drastic is not done NOW.

Nothing, in my opinion, could do more to restore confidence both at home and abroad than your entry into the Government.

Yours ever
Bob

Boothby later considered that his greatest single mistake was to respond to a request by Lloyd George to talk to him about food production by inviting him to lunch at White's. 'As I should have foreseen,' he later wrote, 'this caused a tremendous stir. Within the hour it had been reported to Churchill that I was plotting to make Lloyd George Prime Minister instead of himself. He may have believed it.'

What became regarded at 10 Downing Street as a conspiracy against Churchill in the middle of June was in fact nothing of the sort, but it certainly looked like one to the beleagured and apprehensive Prime Minister. The particularly foolish aspect of this so-called conspiracy was that Churchill, to the dismay of his wife and others, had offered Lloyd

George a senior government appointment and had suggested Agriculture, with keen memories of how close the U-boats had come in the last war to wrecking the British merchant fleet and vital food supplies; now, with all Europe in danger of falling to the enemy, Churchill put food production and distribution very high on his agenda. It was, therefore, much more than a symbolic appointment, and Churchill pressed Lloyd George hard. 'I was in an agony for fear he should accept,' Mrs Churchill later wrote.* But Lloyd George was not impressed by the new Government, either its personalities or its organisation, and was deeply despondent about the national prospects. Mrs Churchill's judgment was much better than that of her husband and Boothby.

Many years later, having consulted his diaries and papers, Amery described to Boothby his account of what happened on 17 June:

> I think, however, you must be mistaken in saying you were not at the meeting in my library on the morning of June 17th. My diary for the day certainly gives those who were present as Lloyd George, Clem Davies, Macmillan, Walter Elliot, yourself and Ian Horobin, who used to act as secretary for our group of stalwarts. My diary does not actually mention your coming on to Lloyd George's office with Salisbury and the others after lunch at White's. But it does go on to say that after that meeting you, Macmillan and Davies came round to see me (presumably at the India Office) to say that Bevin shared our general point of view but could take no step without consulting his party leaders.
>
> I think that there is no doubt that several of our Junior Ministers felt unhappy about the 'phoney war' atmosphere which still lingered on in the department, and did wish respectfully to put it to Winston that the whole machine needed further toning up. The main points as put to me by Macmillan were:
>
> A. Greater power of Ministers to deal with their civil servants, even to the point of sacking them;
>
> B. that members of the War Cabinet should have some sort of definite responsibility for groups of departments;
>
> C. (though this was a hope and not, I think, a definite suggestion) to be put to Winston that there were still too many of the old gang, viz. Neville and Halifax, in the War Cabinet.
>
> Lloyd George was brought along by Davies, not so much as directly taking part in anything we did, but as a paternal adviser which was also the case with Salisbury, while I, as leader of the group in the past, was asked to be spokesman. The issue of Lloyd George being invited into the Cabinet or not had already been dealt with by Winston after he had overcome Neville's objections. My recollection is of Lloyd George prancing up and down the

*Gilbert, op. cit., p. 332, fn. 2.

room in his office, waving the invitation from Winston and snorting at the idea of being allowed back by permission of 'that pinhead'.

There was no plot, certainly no plot to impose a charge on Winston, but certainly a serious desire to make some sort of representation to him as to what Junior Ministers were finding in their departments.

From whatever source, word of this 'cabal' got back to Churchill. That was bad enough, but on 19 June, on an idyllic summer morning, in a moment of madness, Boothby took it upon himself to write to Churchill as follows, sending a copy to Attlee:

Dear Prime Minister

1. As a Minister in your Government I claim the right to put my views before you for your consideration. With the exception of one individual – Mr. Lloyd George – I am not interested in questions of personnel. This letter deals only with policy as it affects the general situation.

2. The mood of the country is rapidly becoming revolutionary in a militant sense; and this force can, in my view, be directed into most advantageous channels, from the point of view of national security, by vigorous action taken now.

3. Information which reached me months ago in Switzerland leads me to believe that the impending German attack will be threefold, namely (1) an attempt at concerted landings on the east coast from sally ports stretching from Persazo to Le Havre, in medium-size craft, containing a proportion of amphibian tanks, under the protection of fighter aircraft; (2) parachute landings in the west; and (3) heavy aerial bombardment of the ports.

4. In the circumstances I submit that our present preparations to meet this attack are neither extensive enough nor quick enough. It is no fault of mine that we have not got enough rifles to train the new Defence Force. But this should be no deterrent to calling immediately for recruits for National Service in the largest possible numbers. A single announcement over the wireless would suffice to throw a vast civilian army – now doing nothing – into the vital task of constructing defences and obstructions for the protection of every strategic point, every town, and every village in this country. Every private motor-car should be commandeered. Surely every young man under thirty who is not indispensable should now be weeded out of the Universities and of reserved occupations, and embodied in properly constituted military training units. I had occasion to visit Oxford last Sunday, and was amazed at the number of young men of the age of twenty who thronged the pavements. The porter at my old College told me that the number of undergraduates up this last term was practically equal to the pre-war figure. And this does not apply to Oxford alone.

5. It seems to me that there is much truth in the following sentence from the first letter in to-day's *Times*: 'The bane of the form of government

which we are trying to preserve is lack of speed and capacity to put first things first.'

Immense improvements have been effected in the machinery of the administration of government during recent weeks. The workers have been mobilised under the direction of the Minister of Labour, the production of aircraft has been greatly accelerated. With respect I submit the arrangements made in this department for the distribution of food in an emergency will be found adequate. But there are still delays caused by a multiplicity of committees, of memoranda, and of minutes; by overlapping of functions; by departmental 'bottlenecks'; and, in certain spheres, an absence of effective personal direction.

This is not an implied criticism of men. It is a criticism of methods. In circumstances like the present, the Hun, the men will always beat the committees. You will remember the impetus given to naval construction by Fisher in 1915.

6. Speed is now the essence of the contracts.

In order to achieve speed, may I venture to make the following suggestions:

1. The War Cabinet should be replaced by a Committee of Public Safety in which absolute and omnipotent powers should be vested – and would be vested – by Parliament. Such power to be ruthlessly exercised.

2. Ministers should be given dictatorial powers over policy and over personnel in their departments subject only to the over-riding control of the Committee of Public Safety.

3. The authority of the Commander in Chief – who again would be subject only to the direction of the Committee of Public Safety – should be strengthened by a declaration of martial law.

4. Parliament should be summoned only as occasion requires for the purpose of hearing statements on behalf of the Government, of debating general policy in secret, and of granting the necessary supplies. The activities of the Select Committee of War Expenditure should be curtailed or suspended.

5. Private Members of Parliament, not otherwise engaged in national service, should be requested to assist in the organisation and direction of local effort in their constituencies.

There is one other aspect of the situation to which I beg of you to direct your attention; it is the question of age.

In a secret memorandum which I sent to the War Cabinet on the 20th March last I wrote: 'It is this incredible conception of a *movement* – young, virile, dynamic, and violent – which is advancing irresistibly to overthrow a decaying old world, that we must continually bear in mind; for it is the main source of the Nazi strength and power.'

Broadly speaking the German effort is based upon youth, and the main executive posts – both civil and military – are held by men in their forties. In our own effort the significance and importance of youth is not sufficiently emphasised, and the main executive posts (this applies more to the Services than to the political field) are held by men in their sixties. The climax has been reached in France, which has surrendered to Germany at the instance of men over seventy. Clemenceau and Lloyd George are simply phenomenal exceptions, which go to prove the general rule.

This is essentially a young man's war. And I can assure you from personal experience that the young men in the Services are becoming increasingly restless as the result of the grip on the machinery of an administration still exercised by men who have already worked themselves to a standstill, and who, by reason of this and their age, lack the imagination, the energy, the drive, and audacity which are now so urgently required.

It should not be forgotten that men of the calibre of Layton, Salter, Beveridge, Keynes, Blackett and Lothian were promoted to the highest posts during the last war; and that was over twenty years ago.

I hope you will forgive me for putting these considerations before you at this time. But I believe them to be of vital importance.

This was insane, and Boothby later related the sequel:

I was immediately summoned to Downing Street, where, in the Cabinet room, he [Churchill] went through my letter sentence by sentence, and scorched it. After this I went to the House of Commons and drank a quadruple whisky. Next day I received a red ink Minute from the Prime Minister: 'It would be very much better if you confined yourself to the work you have undertaken to do.' This marked a further deterioration in my relationship with Churchill.

Boothby, shaken, told Baffy Dugdale that Churchill had said to him that

if he did not mind his own business he would perhaps have no business to mind. He accused Bob of being one of the people 'intriguing' against Neville. He said, 'You went to Amery's house the other night. You had no business to go there.' Bob thinks Chamberlain flatters Winston.

As Boothby later remarked, 'I was arrogant, conceited. It wasn't the moment to tell him how to win the war.'

What Boothby did not mention in his account was that, in spite of this clear and devastating rebuke, he did not give up in his attempts to reform, indeed run, the Government and bring in Lloyd George. To the latter he wrote on 6 July:

Dear LG

I lunched with Brendan to-day, and gather that Winston increasingly feels the need of you.

He thinks you spurned his last invitation. . . .

If another reaches you in the course of the next few days, I beg of you to give it serious and – if possible – favourable consideration.

Yours ever
Bob Boothby

Then on 9 July he wrote to Bracken, enclosing a copy of a memorandum for Churchill:

Dear Brendan

I attach a memo of a very important conversation which I had with L.G. this evening. I leave it to your judgement whether to repeat the gist of it to the P.M. yourself, or whether to submit it to him direct.

I know I am prejudiced, but I was more than ever struck by the astonishing vigour of the old boy, and by the fertility of his mind.

I believe he wd. be a tower of strength to Winston in the coming weeks, if only he cd. be brought in.

Yours ever
Bob

This was Boothby's memorandum:

Mr. Lloyd George asked me to see him this afternoon, and I think it my duty to give you a brief account of our conversation.

He began by expressing approval of the action taken with regard to the French fleet, and went on to say that, in his opinion, we could win a long war, and that this would be by far the greatest of our achievements. He was inclined to the view that Hitler would content himself with intensive bombing of our ports and factories for the time being; but said it was obviously right to take every conceivable precaution against invasion. His general views were very robust; and he told me that he definitely refused to allow any of his grandchildren to be evacuated from this country.

Turning to the political side, he said he had no personal animus against Mr. Chamberlain, but considered that at the present juncture both he and Lord Halifax were a liability to the country. Evidence reached him from all quarters that the continued presence of Mr. Chamberlain in the War Cabinet was a source of mingled bewilderment and irritation to the working classes, with the result that at perhaps the most dangerous moment in our history it would be difficult to arouse the unrestrained enthusiasm of the workers, which was so necessary if we were to win through. He said he understood that all the Trade Unions would shortly pass resolutions [hostile to the Government] similar to that recently passed by the NUR, and that this was a very bad thing in time of war.

Continuing, he said that he personally took the view that Lord Halifax at the Foreign Office was a much greater liability than Mr. Chamberlain, for the reason that he is profoundly distrusted both in the United States and the USSR. He felt that if we were to achieve a decisive victory it would be necessary not only to build up the productive strength of the British Empire to the maximum during the next few months, but sooner rather than later both America and Russia should be – and could be – associated with us. So long as Mr. Chamberlain and Lord Halifax retained their present posts this would not be possible.

He then said that nothing would induce him to accept any responsibility for 'throwing them out'. It was up to them to go, if they felt it was their duty to do so. At the same time he did not feel able to join the present administration, not because he had a personal dislike either of Mr. Chamberlain or Lord Halifax, or because he thought that they would help or hinder him, or because he thought that they would adopt a hostile attitude towards him personally, but because he felt so strongly that any effort of the Government along the lines that he indicated would inevitably be stultified by their continuance in their present offices.

He said he could not understand why, in present circumstances, and in view of the continuous attacks being made upon him, which could be withstood in time of peace but not in time of war, Mr. Chamberlain would not agree to continue his leadership of the Conservative party in the House of Lords. This, coupled with the transference of Lord Halifax to another post, would, in fact, meet the views of the critics, and greatly contribute to the strength and unity of the country at a critical moment.

Meanwhile he has refrained from answering your invitation to join the War Cabinet for two reasons:

1. Because he did not wish to commit himself in writing to opinions which might put him in the position to force Mr. Chamberlain out of the Government against his will, and thus to a breach with the Conservative party and perhaps also with yourself which might prove irreconcilable; and

2. Because Max [Beaverbrook] had most strongly urged him not to answer for the time being. He had sustained the definite impression from Max – who motored down specially to see him at Churt – that Mr. Chamberlain contemplated resigning in the near future, and that premature action on his part would therefore do no good, and might do harm.

At the same time he said that he would not wish you to think that his failure to send a written reply was due to any sort of discourtesy on his part, and that if you wished to know his precise reasons for not joining the administration at the present juncture, he would send them to you immediately. He asked me to find out, on his behalf, what your desires were in regard to this matter.

The general impression I got was that 'au fond' he is not only anxious to serve; that he is *not* trying to play any political game, or to make any capital out of debates in the House of Commons, etc. He believes the situation to be far too serious for that, and the flame of his patriotism still burns high. But he is, I think, convinced that the foreign policy which he believes to be essential to our ultimate success cannot be successfully carried out unless certain changes are made.

R. B.

Although Bracken was sympathetic, Churchill definitely was not. He still feared Lloyd George, but it was obvious to everyone, except Boothby, that he was not the Lloyd George of 1914–18; indeed, he was becoming increasingly defeatist, to the point when, in a terrible moment in the Commons, Churchill compared him to Pétain. Also, being a realist, Churchill could not politically dispense with Chamberlain and the 'old gang' without causing a major rupture in the Conservative Party, whose leadership he coveted, having learnt the lesson of Lloyd George's ultimate failure – that he had been, in Beaverbrook's words, a 'Prime Minister without a Party'. Churchill had no love for the Tories – and his wife even less – but he was a pragmatic professional politician, who knew on reflection that having Lloyd George in his Government would have caused a Conservative explosion of fury. Few knew better than Churchill how enduring, deep and unforgiving are the Conservative Party's hatreds. He also knew that bringing in Lloyd George would mean resignations, starting with Chamberlain, who remained the Leader of the Party, and was to do so until his death, from cancer, in November. With the Battle of Britain beginning in earnest, and the British army virtually without *matériel* until desperately needed rifles, ammunition and artillery arrived from the United States, the proposal was not only dangerous, but utterly preposterous.

Boothby subsequently recognised that he had made 'a terrible mistake'. He later told friends that he had not enjoyed being a minister. This was not their impression at the time, but the fact was that he did not enjoy being a junior minister, and one dealing with relatively humdrum – if vital – matters when Armageddon was raging. Having been in the wilderness for so long, and used to his independence, he chafed at his comparatively lowly status in the Government, and at being expected to act as a loyal member of a team whose other members he did not like or respect very much. Also, wrongly, he thought that he had a special direct line to the Prime Minister, who would be interested in his views and his advice on great matters. He had not realised that when a friend becomes prime minister – and especially at such a time – the relationship changes, and very abruptly. Boothby was to learn this lesson the hard way.

When Amery saw Churchill on 18 June he realised that 'my young men' – particularly Macmillan and Boothby – 'had successfully frightened Attlee, Greenwood, and above all Neville, and roused Winston's authoritarian instincts. They had better resign themselves for the time being to doing their work, however acute their sense of the national danger.' To be fair to Boothby, his motives had been sincere and, in his eyes, in the national interest. He genuinely believed that Lloyd George's presence in the Government would be a national asset in this grim crisis, if only as a token of past glories. Also, Churchill himself did not handle the matter well. But once again, Boothby allowed his heart to rule his head. The Tory Establishment would not have Lloyd George at any price, and Boothby had forgotten Lloyd George's past praises of Hitler, which the press would assuredly have not. Of all the madcap ventures that Boothby engaged in this was perhaps the maddest of all, and Churchill's fury was wholly understandable – as Boothby later appreciated. What he did not recognise at the time was that the episode did not represent 'a further deterioration of my relations with Churchill'; it marked, so far as Churchill was concerned, the end of them for the time being. It was an act of much naïveté and folly, however honourable the motivation.

When the London Blitz began in earnest in September, Woolton suggested that Boothby should go down to the East End early in the mornings and see what could be done to help those who had spent the nights in the shelters, and, most urgently of all, those who had been bombed out of their homes. Boothby was amazed by the fortitude of the East Enders, who reminded him of the people of Buchan as a race apart, in his own words,

warm, affectionate, gay, rather reckless, and almost incredibly brave. Sometimes the language was pretty rough, but it was so natural and innocent that it never jarred. One day I came across a small boy crying. I asked him what the matter was, and he said:

'They burnt my mother yesterday.' Thinking it was in an air-raid, I said: 'Was she badly burned?' He looked up at me and said, through his tears: 'Oh yes. They don't fuck about in a crematorium.' I loved them, and I am glad to have been close to them in their hour of need.

Boothby's reaction to the plight of the East Enders was characteristic. On 19 September he reported to Woolton:

Dear Minister

I am sorry I was not able to see you again last night, but yesterday was a pretty hectic day for us both. . . .

Even two nights' experience of this performance has convinced me that a lot of drastic re-organisation – involving not only the location but also the habits of the population of Greater London – is necessary if people are going to be able to 'take it' during the Winter months.

I was talking to two air-raid wardens (West End) late last night, and they told me that transport for the ordinary 'daily breader' in and out of London had now almost completely broken down; and that they had the greatest difficulty in finding alternative accommodation for people who had been bombed out of their houses, owing to the lack of adequate powers to requisition empty buildings, flats, houses, etc.

Meanwhile I am sure you are dead right in insisting that the most important thing *of all* is to see that the people who are bombed out, and who are not casualties – particularly the poorer people in the East End – get a hot cup of tea or soup. My warden friend told me that, from their point of view, this would do more to restore the morale of people who are temporarily shattered than anything else.

If the Ministry of Health or the L.C.C. [London County Council] won't play on this, I think we ought to organise and run a service of mobile canteens ourselves. We might tread on some people's toes; but we should be acclaimed by public opinion on every side – and we should be on quite impregnable ground.

Yours ever, R. B.

The immediate result was the setting up of canteens in the East End, manned entirely by volunteers, including friends of Boothby like Kingsley Martin, the editor of the *New Statesman*, and Ritchie Calder, a left-wing journalist, academic and politician. In spite of the outstanding success of the canteens – 'What the people want', Boothby minuted, 'is a kiss and a cup of tea' – the presence of Calder proved to be a mixed blessing, as Boothby warned Woolton in a letter of 27 September, in which he took his views far beyond the remit of the Ministry of Food, and which demonstrates just how good a minister he was:

Private and Confidential

Dear Minister

I hear from two very reliable private sources of information that Fleet Street is prepared to launch a heavy and concerted attack upon the Government for the alleged inadequacy of its treatment of the problem of the refugees, the homeless, and those who are obliged to take shelter away from their homes in London.

I think the attack began with Calder's article in the 'Daily Herald' this morning (attached); and that the main barrage may open up on Monday next.

I am most anxious that this ministry should elude it – but I think it is a question now not of days but of hours.

I took the opportunity this morning of making a tour of the main shelters on the north bank of the river between 5 and 7 a.m. What struck me most was the pathetic gratitude of these people to anyone who seemed disposed to take an interest in them. Most of them had been in the shelters since the previous afternoon. None of them had had any food. All of them – including quite young children – were preparing to take a morning trek across the bridges of anything up to three miles, upon totally empty stomachs. Those whom I interrogated would have been only too glad to pay for a cup of hot soup or cocoa and some food if they had been given the chance to do so.

The other thing that struck me was the large number of people gathered together in comparatively few shelters. For instance, I was astonished to discover that there were nearly a thousand people in Thames House alone. It seems that a situation exists here which could be dealt with by this Ministry at once in a manner which would reflect great credit upon us, and exclude us altogether from any charges that may be made against the Government of culpable neglect. It isn't a case of 999 canteens. A dozen, even half a dozen, would be sufficient to deal with the immediate problem of giving these unfortunate people something hot to drink and something to eat before they start wandering back to their homes after their night's vigil. Canteens in factories, and the larger communal feeding centres in the industrial districts, can be developed over a period of time – although the sooner we announce that it is our intention to do this the better. But this question of the large shelters ought to be dealt with immediately – if possible this week-end. Personally I should like to see a fleet of mobile canteens organised simultaneously, which could be rushed at short notice to the areas which had been actually bombed.

I approached French on the subject, but I am afraid I found him wholly unresponsive. He said in terms, 'We really cannot be expected to undertake to feed these people.' But that is just what we *are* expected to do. And if the expectation is not realised very soon, it will become an imperious demand.

I found the press men in our Publicity Department just as concerned about Fleet Street as I was; and in the circumstances, acting on their advice, I took the responsibility of letting the press know that I had been round the shelters, and of having an informal chat about the situation with some of them this afternoon, at their request. I committed the Ministry to nothing definite, but I think the effect of this will be to hold the position so far as we are concerned for a few days longer. I asked them to relate my morning pilgrimage to your speech on communal feeding to-day.

There is another aspect of the situation which I believe to be of very great importance. These people are continually reading in the press about the intentions of the Government with regard to them. But it is all negative. Are the tubes going to be shut up? Are they going to be cleared out of the larger shelters? etc. It is high time they read about a Ministry which is prepared to take a positive interest in their welfare, and anxious to give them practical assistance.

Four points were raised in the course of my talk with the pressmen, which seemed to me worthy of immediate consideration on our part:

(1) The possibility of mobilising the coffee stalls, which have been driven off the streets by order of the police.

(2) The possibility of obtaining the help of the Army through the loan of a limited number of lorries and field kitchens.

(3) The possibility of obtaining a number of disused pullman and container cars from the railways for conversion into canteens; and

(4) The possibility of running one or two tube cars through the night containing hot drinks and light refreshments, which the refugees on the platforms could purchase for a reasonable sum.

Yours ever

Robert Boothby

His regular broadcasts were also becoming very popular, and their style can be shown from one example, which was transmitted on 20 August:

COMMON SENSE ABOUT FOOD

Common sense about food. It is a prosaic title to what sounds a prosaic subject in these tremendous days, when the most amazing events succeed each other with such bewildering rapidity that it is difficult for any of us to grasp their full significance.

Some of these events are sudden and spectacular, like the air battles which made last week one of the most dramatic in the history of the world. Others take time to develop, and their cumulative effect may not be felt for some months. For instance much of the work of the Royal Navy and the Merchant Service is necessarily performed outside the glare of publicity, in a kind of twilight. Yet sea power is no less essential than air power to the security of the British Empire.

And food, although one of the least spectacular aspects of security, is perhaps the most fundamental of all. What are our airmen and our sailors fighting for, and achieving, every day – and every night? That absolute supremacy at sea and in the air which alone can secure adequate supplies of food for the people of this country. In war food is a decisive factor. Without it, we can do nothing. With it, victory in the long run is certain.

The ultimate test of the Ministry of Food is going to be its ability to feed everyone in this country, in all circumstances.

It is a heavy responsibility. Today our stocks of food are high, but we must not be over-confident. Optimism is a good thing provided it is not acquired at the cost of vigilance. It is our duty to anticipate sustained attacks upon our ports and shipping in the immediate future, and to take the necessary precautionary measures. We must stock food, disperse it, and grow it as hard as we possibly can. And we must also see that those foods which are essential to the health, strength, and happiness of our people are made available to all.

But if we are to discharge this vital task efficiently, we must have the active assistance and co-operation of every housewife in the country upon what Lord Woolton has so well called the 'Kitchen Front'.

What can you do to help? I think the best thing you can do is to exercise your own common sense. For instance, I spoke just now about the desirability of dispersing our stocks of food as widely as possible. That is why we are encouraging not only wholesalers but also retail shops to stock up. Before the war housewives were asked to build up a small store of about a week's normal supply as a measure of security in case distribution should break down or be delayed in their neighbourhood. I hope all of you who can are maintaining this additional week's supply. If you take from it in any week a little extra of some commodity, be sure and replace it as soon as you can. Your store cupboard may, before the war is over, prove a great help not only to your own family but possibly to your neighbours. . . . We want to make quite sure that, in the event of a serious emergency, you all have enough food in your own district or village or home to keep going quite comfortably for a few days.

I said just now that it was our job to see that adequate supplies of essential foodstuffs were available to everybody. These were not empty words. It is the declared policy and intention of the Ministry of Food to keep the price of the basic foods – such as milk, bread, meat and potatoes – at a level within reach of the poorest section of the community. With regard to other articles of food, I must again ask you to use your common sense. There will undoubtedly be shortages of certain things from time to time. There was a severe, and un-expected, shortage of soft fruit a few weeks ago, owing to the dry weather. There is a shortage of eggs at the present, owing to what has happened on the Continent of Europe. On the other hand there is a very good plum crop. Therefore we must go easy on eggs for the time being, and I suggest to you that you should buy plums while they are plentiful and cheap, both for immediate consumption, and for preserving and making jam. With the co-operation of the Women's Institutes, we are doing everything we can to encourage the preservation of fruit in the country districts, and to demonstrate how it can be done.

Last but not least, I would beg of you to avoid waste. It is simply a matter of using your own good judgment. . . . Remember always that simple food and simple cooking produces the nicest and the most nourishing meals; and remember also that, although it may not earn you a decoration, good work on the 'Kitchen Front' is a powerful contribution to victory.

Boothby was in his element. He was rapidly becoming a national figure, who, in addition to his work in the office and in the House of Commons, where he was widely regarded as an outstanding minister in his deft handling of the House and in his responses to MPs' individual concerns, travelled the country to speak to large and appreciative audiences. In the East End of London he became a familiar and immensely popular regular arrival first thing in the morning after an air-raid, crunching jovially through the broken glass and debris, and cheering up his canteen workers, and indeed everyone. Woolton was lavish in his praises. Even his personal enemies on the Conservative benches in the Commons were, albeit reluctantly, impressed. His family and friends were proud of him. For the first time since his early years in politics he basked in general approval and even admiration. He had, at long last, arrived. Or so it seemed.

11

'A Terrible Injustice'

1940–1

In the fever of war common sense and justice are early victims, and, as happened in Britain in 1914 and in 1939 (and in America in 1941), xenophobia and a terror of spies and Fifth Columnists quickly made their appearance. Under the draconian powers of the Emergency Powers (Defence) Act thousands of innocent foreigners in Britain were arrested and interned without trial or any charge being laid against them, their only crime being that they were foreigners. It never occurred to either Boothby or Weininger that the latter would be interned, and Weininger was actually with Boothby in his flat when the police came to arrest him on 16 September. In fact, Weininger had already been interviewed at the hotel where he and his wife were staying, and the inspector had raised no objection when he asked if they could go to Boothby's flat first. 'There the inspector accepted a drink from Boothby and was politeness itself, but Boothby exploded.'* Weininger and his wife were then taken to their bank to open up her safe deposit box before he was driven to Brixton Prison. But, while Trude Weininger was not to be interned, her daughter Edith was, again with no charge or reason.

Boothby protested vehemently and angrily to Churchill, Attlee and the Home Secretary, Sir John Anderson, a stern, bleak man, of whom Boothby later wrote:

He came from Edinburgh, and was the type of Lowland Scot which I knew only too well, and never much liked. He will be remembered not only for his administrative capacity, but as the man who imprisoned more people without charge or trial than any other Minister in British history.

* Weininger, *op. cit.*, p. 142.

It is more than probable that Anderson's opinion of Boothby was equally bleak.* Certainly, he did not reply to Boothby's letter; Boothby therefore told his office that he intended to send a copy to Churchill. When the Under-Secretary, Osbert Peake, telephoned to ask him not to do so until he had seen Anderson, Boothby tried to stop the letter to Churchill, but it was too late.

Before Weininger had been taken to Brixton Prison he had authorised Boothby to be in charge of his papers, and had told his secretary this. Two days later she telephoned Boothby to say that the police wanted his papers and suggested that he should go through them himself first.

I asked her whether there were any love letters,† and she said no. I then said that I was very busy at the Ministry of Food, but would try to come round to have a look at them. Next day (the day before the CID arrived), I telephoned to her and told her to give them the lot. This was scarcely the act of a man with a guilt-laden conscience.

Boothby later believed that it was Anderson who alerted Churchill to his relationship with Weininger, but it appears that the papers initially went to the Claims Office, where Wyatt realised their significance. They were then sent to the Treasury Solicitor, who took a serious and hostile view of them. The matter thus came to the attention of Churchill, who immediately summoned Boothby to see him.

In a private memorandum written many years later, but attached to the contemporary letters and documents, Boothby recorded that he received Churchill's letter (which has not survived) on 9 October, saying that he had seen documents that disclosed a financial association with Weininger before the war and asking him what he proposed to do. 'I replied briefly, expecting a summons from him when I could have given him a full explanation.' Woolton wrote to him that 'I don't think you should do anything. You have presented your reply: it is up to the P.M. now; and I should "stay put" until he acts.'

Boothby had told Churchill that he would be glad to explain his business relations with Weininger, and had expected to find him alone.

Instead he was sitting at the Cabinet table with the Attorney-General on his right, and a number of civil servants. He did not ask me for any explanation. He simply said that he had decided to set up a Select Committee of the House of Commons

---

* Anderson's widow, Ava, whose first husband Ralph Wigram had been emphatically on the right side with Churchill and Boothby over appeasement, later made amends by telling Boothby that Anderson had come to regret his involvement in Boothby's arraignment, and had been deeply moved by Boothby's letter of congratulation when he received the Order of Merit, which, she wrote, he was holding in his hand when he died. As Lady Waverley (as she was by then) was capable of exaggeration and drama, her unverified (and unverifiable) claim can only be recorded. She certainly felt very unhappy about her husband's role in Boothby's misfortunes and Weininger's ordeal.

† This was a wise precaution. Weininger had a complicated private life.

to enquire into my conduct. Then I knew that, as Mosley had predicted, he was out for the kill.

This is very unlikely. What Churchill had before him was a prima facie case of allegedly discreditable behaviour by a Member of Parliament with an alien now interned under Regulation 18B. There was never any question of Boothby being prosecuted for any crime or serious misdemeanour, and this matter had nothing whatever to do with Weininger's internment. But Churchill had been told, or had seen, enough to impress him with the necessity of doing something, and a Select Committee of the House seemed the appropriate forum. How this can have occurred to him after his embittering experience of the pre-1914 Select Committee on the Marconi scandal, which had nearly ended Lloyd George's political career and before which Churchill himself had made an impassioned and memorable appearance, and his even more harrowing experience of the Dardanelles Commission in 1917, is difficult to comprehend. He and his official biographer have been totally silent on the matter. Indeed, apart from a brief footnote, Martin Gilbert does not refer to it at all, in spite of the fact that Boothby co-operated with him totally and willingly and gave him access to his papers. It is a very strange omission.

In the absence of conclusive evidence, the most reasonable interpretation of Churchill's attitude was his anger that Boothby, supposedly so close to him, had not told him of his 'interest'. Churchill had also spoken in the House on Czech assets and gold, and would have reasonably assumed that Boothby, like him, had been acting entirely in the public interest. Now it seemed that he had not. Some sense of a personal betrayal must have been in his mind, which, once implanted, could not be removed. To be fair to Boothby, he was not given a chance to remove it. In a sense, both were in the wrong. Boothby should have told Churchill long before of his close relationship with Weininger; Churchill should have asked him, as a friend, colleague and leader of the Government of which Boothby was a member, for a personal explanation. Instead he reached for the dubious machinery of a Select Committee.

On 17 October Churchill informed an astonished House of Commons of the proposed action and moved that a Select Committee be appointed

to investigate the conduct and activities of Mr Boothby in connection with the payment out of assets in this country of claims against the Government and institutions in the Republic of Czechoslovakia: to report generally on these matters and in particular to consider whether the conduct of the honourable Member was contrary to the usage or derogatory to the dignity of the House or inconsistent with the standards which Parliament is entitled to expect from its Members.

Boothby was not the only one to consider these terms of reference in themselves as being heavily loaded against him, as though the matter was already determined. Compton Mackenzie wrote supportively to him, saying that 'I could almost hear on Barra the sound of the rats scampering away.' Boothby cheerfully replied on 23 October that

> It is a bloody and ridiculous business. But I think I shall come through all right. If I don't I shall join you in Barra, and enjoy myself much more than I have done for a long time past. It is wonderful in this country how they go for anyone who looks like beginning to do a job well.

Boothby was not asked to resign his office, but was suspended from his ministerial duties while the Committee was considering the matter. This, also, looked bad. Woolton, ever generous and loyal, was utterly dismayed at the loss of his exceptionally able and dynamic junior and pledged his full faith and support. So did Beaverbrook. So did many others, as well as those who were astounded that at the height of national peril and a Europe convulsed by war, with nightly bombing raids on London, ten Members of Parliament assisted by the Attorney-General should devote months to examining such an apparently trivial pre-war matter while Britain was fighting for its very existence.

Harold Nicolson wrote at once:

> My dear Bob
> I was in the House this afternoon when the PM brought forward his statement. Never have I heard a House so friendly to the victim. When Winston said something about your energy and efficiency there was a strong sympathetic murmur and mainly among the Labour people. I bumfed (Oh my God how badly I type!) into the PM just after. I said, 'What a beastly thing.' He said, 'I hope it is going to be alright.'
> Anyhow Bob I wish I could help; my whole heart is with you and if in any way I can do anything (beyond bumbling about the Lobbies which I shall do in any case) you know you can trust me to do all I can.
> I never quite realised how seriously devoted I was to you until I felt my heart stand still when Winston sprang his surprise motion.
> You can count on me if I am any help. But what help can I be?' Damn!!!!
> Yours ever, Harold

Boothby was not comforted by the fact that the Chairman of the Committee was to be Colonel Gretton,* an elderly Tory die-hard over India but a passionate Chamberlainite and supporter of Munich. He also had a deserved reputation of being a thoroughly unpleasant man, whom

---

*Colonel Gretton (1867–1947) was MP for Derbyshire South, 1895–1906; Rutland, 1907–18; Division of Staffordshire, 1918–43. In 1944 he was created the first Baron of Stapleford.

Boothby – and many others – cordially detested. He detected in Gretton's appointment the hands of the Whips' Office, particularly that of Stuart, and he may well have been right. The fact was that the Chairman of the Committee was an implacable personal enemy, which was a deeply ominous beginning. Another important member, Spens,* was also no friend of Boothby's.

A Select Committee is not a court of law, and one of its fundamental problems in examining matters of this kind is that it is composed of backbench MPs who are in effect judge and jury. In this case they had the assistance of the Attorney-General, Donald Somervell, who was in effect, although not in title, the prosecuting counsel. Boothby was given permission to be represented by counsel 'if he think fit'. The Attorney-General's services, of course, came free; Boothby's counsel did not. Nor was any specific charge placed before him; indeed, he was given no information about what documents the Government had, or was choosing to put before the Committee. He was given the opportunity from his own records to write his own account, but until shortly before he was asked to give evidence he was completely in the dark as to what he was being accused of. It was the blatant injustice of these proceedings that subsequently caused such a surge of sympathy for him.

Nor was it subsequent. Beaverbrook wrote on the 18th:

My dear Bob

I am a Cabinet Minister.

For that reason I have no right to take part in issues which may, sooner or later, come before the Cabinet.

But an expression of my confidence in you will not interfere with my doing my duty.

I therefore express my belief that you are innocent.

And I will not believe you are guilty until I see the evidence of it.

Yours ever
Max

Boothby, deeply moved, replied to him on 23 October:

Dear Max

I would like you to know how very grateful I am for your letter, and how deeply I appreciate it.

For once my conscience is clear, and I do not think I am going to let my friends down. But I am always frightened of lawyers.

Yours ever
Bob

*William Patrick Spens, QC (1885–1973), was MP for Ashford, 1933–43; Chief Justice of India, 1943–7; and MP for South Kensington, 1950–9. He was created the first Baron Spens in 1959.

Woolton wrote to his beleagured junior:

My dear Bob
Just a line to tell you how often I am thinking about you in all this trouble
and perplexity you are in and wishing you well. Good luck to you.

Yours ever
Fred

There were many other such messages, from MPs, friends and constituents. Bracken reported a furious row at lunch at Downing Street when Mrs Churchill, Beaverbrook and he upbraided Churchill for his handling of the affair so strongly that he had angrily left the table.

This was all very well, and encouraging in its way, but the realities facing Boothby were now very daunting, and he entered unquestionably the darkest period of his life – 'almost as bad as Rottingdean', he once said.

Boothby later considered that Churchill had quite deliberately thrown him to the wolves. In his eyes their old relationship had soured; Churchill was politically in the hands of the Conservative machine, which, although Churchill was temporarily beyond its reach, was out for revenge against one of its most independent spirits; and he was quite prepared to sacrifice an old friend for his own interests. Boothby did not think so at the time, although he was shocked and upset by Churchill's hostile demeanour towards him and by his decision, but although his character was normally free from bitterness, that most lethal and corroding of all the political vices, he did eventually feel bitter about Churchill's failure to help him or even to listen to him.

But there are other interpretations, much more favourable to Churchill. Amery noted in his diary how distressed he was over the matter. Churchill knew what financial stringency was and had suffered it throughout his political career. He, also, had gambled on the Stock Exchanges as well as at Monte Carlo, and had also been badly burned. Few knew better than he what political isolation was like, and he had never regarded politics as an amateur sport. But although often sentimental and emotional, and a man of feeling, he had a hard element in his complex personality, and there are several instances of his indifference to loyal allies once their usefulness was over. During Boothby's ordeal he never once sent any direct message to him of friendship or reassurance, which Boothby interpreted as a sign of hostility, whereas it was much more probably one of disillusionment and embarrassment at a desperate moment in his and the nation's fortunes. It is very probable that he had personally become convinced that Boothby had in some way behaved badly by conducting a political campaign for personal gain, but did not have enough evidence on which to convict him and dismiss him from the Government; he was therefore giving Boothby the opportunity to clear his name and return in triumph to the Government. I much prefer the latter theory, but, as Churchill's papers are so silent and his biographer's references to the matter so minimal, this can only be conjecture.

Duncan Sandys, however, was almost certainly right when he told me in 1969 that the dominant concern of Churchill's was the position of the Government, and that if Boothby had still been a backbencher nothing more would have been heard of the matter. But to have a senior and very well-known minister virtually accused of corruption, even though the episode was long before he became a minister, might give to the Government's enemies within the Party a powerful weapon against Churchill himself if there were any attempt to cover up the actions of someone formerly so close to him, and which were subsequently disclosed. I was convinced then, and remain so, that herein lies the answer.

The Select Committee took detailed evidence from fifteen witnesses, including Weininger, who was brought up specially from Brixton Prison to face the awesome tribunal. With the exception of the Petscheks and Sir Edward Reid, all the principals gave evidence, and the Appendices of documents alone constituted 126 pages of closely printed material; the Report, evidence and the documents produced a volume of 289 pages. It was certainly an exceptionally exhaustive enquiry, pursued with great diligence, particularly by Gretton and Spens. They also had the advantage that they saw the material first and had the advice of the Attorney-General.

At this point Boothby's great friend, Cyril Radcliffe, let him down badly, for which he later expressed great remorse. He advised Boothby to have legal representation and suggested Mr Moelyn Hughes, QC. It was only some time later that Boothby discovered that the great Sir Norman Birkett was willing to undertake his case for no fee. Hughes turned out to be wholly inadequate and was quite out of his depth in these strange surroundings. He was also clearly in awe of the Committee and excessively deferential to its Chairman. In particular, his questioning of Simon was notably feeble. One suspects that he was as bewildered as others at the proceedings, when none of the usual rules of admissible and inadmissible evidence applied and there was no charge directed against his client. Boothby never blamed him, publicly or privately, and it did not affect his friendship with Radcliffe, but Hughes proved to be a disastrous choice.

The key witness turned out to be Simon, and it was here that Hughes' inadequacy as Boothby's advocate was most painfully revealed. Simon was by this stage Lord Chancellor, which cannot have increased Hughes' already limited self-confidence, and his version of events went unchallenged until Boothby himself effectively contested it later. Simon was disingenuous to the point of deceit, especially when he commented on his meeting of 3 August and Boothby's letter of the 4th:

If a man is acting disinterestedly and solely in the public interest without any thought of reward or any hope or expectation of payment, that is one thing; if he is doing the two things at once, it appears to me to be different; and it appears to me to be more different still if he conceals the fact that he has a private interest. But I am not pronouncing judgment. I do not know the facts.*

This was, of course, deadly, and was meant to be. He was not known as Sir 'Snake' Simon for nothing. Boothby did not help himself by his own frankness.

Mr Spens: Mr Boothby, I want, if I can, to see if I have got your case right. The implication, of course, is that you had a financial interest in a claim, a substantial financial interest, at a time when you were advocating the payment of that class of claims, both inside the House and at the Treasury?
Mr Boothby: Yes.†

Two questions later he emphasised that he had 'no personal interest beyond a general expectation of payment from Mr Weininger', but his laconic answer to Spens' hostile leading question had done him considerable damage, and may be seen as another turning-point in the case.

Nor did Boothby help himself by commenting on his meeting with Simon that

To be perfectly frank, my relationship with the Chancellor has never been a very good one, and the circumstances under which that interview took place, and the atmosphere in which it took place, did not lend themselves to any very confidential or frank talk on my part.‡

This, also, could have been expressed better.

Another major difficulty for both Weininger and Boothby was that the former was very anxious to tell the full story of the rifle-purchase mission to demonstrate his total commitment to the British cause and to the strength of his friendship with Boothby. He was utterly miserable and distraught in Brixton, bewildered and disheartened, and he was not only anxious to clear Boothby's name but his own, so that his personal

---

*Select Committee Evidence, Q 209.
†*Ibid.*, Q 256.
‡Select Committee Evidence, Q 326.

nightmare could be ended and his anti-Nazi credentials made publicly clear. He accordingly prepared, under very difficult circumstances, a full account for the Committee. In the event it was judged too sensitive for publication or cross-examination under war conditions, and, although formally submitted to the Committee, was silently received and suppressed.

The reasons are obvious, but Weininger took a sinister view of the decision, which he felt was deeply hurtful to his case and to Boothby's. The latter, however, although he considered that the memorandum was crucial, recognised that its revelations would certainly not help the Government and would be of considerable interest to the Germans. Thus, no hint was given in the Report or the evidence of Weininger's services. Boothby later claimed that this decision severely damaged his case and that of Weininger, and it is surprising that it could not have been the subject of evidence taken in secret and subsequently not published, a very frequent occurrence in Select Committees, in peace as well as in war. But Gretton, no doubt in consultation with Somervell, ruled otherwise. This is the background to Gretton's otherwise rather mysterious ruling when Weininger gave evidence that 'the memorandum is only for our convenience. It is not a document which is put in. I think we should proceed.'

It is fair to say that Weininger's solicitor and friend, J. H. Thorpe, the father of the future Liberal leader,* did not press the matter too hard. He put in only one copy, saying that

It is a full statement not only of Mr Weininger's connection with these immediate matters, but containing a certain amount relating to his personal life. While a great deal of that may be irrelevant to this Committee's proceedings, I do ask that we might be allowed to circulate that to such members of the Committee as would like to read it – and for this reason: I think it goes a long way – as indeed it is designed to do – to put forward the reliability of Mr Weininger as a witness.

Gretton then observed, 'You say that a great deal of it is irrelevant. So it is, for the purposes of our enquiry,' to which Thorpe replied, 'I quite appreciate that.' Neither Weininger nor Boothby was present for these exchanges, a fact of considerable ire to both of them, but it is difficult to see how the memorandum could have been published, and the rifles' episode was very far indeed from the Committee's remit.

In his private account of the Committee's proceedings Boothby later wrote that

---

*When Thorpe's son Jeremy was tried on exceptionally grave charges in 1978, Weininger was among those who contributed to the costs of his ultimately successful defence.

It was a farce. . . . I myself soon lost interest in the proceedings. I came to the conclusion, in total ignorance of the charge against me, that a number of Members of Parliament, armed with certain selected documents of which I had no prior knowledge, had been called together to decide whether I was a good chap or not; and that, with certain exceptions (notably Edward Cadogan),* they thought that I was not.

In fact, Boothby conducted his own defence – without much help from his counsel – with spirit, and his concluding statement on 5 December was not only convincing as to his conduct – 'I plead guilty to some folly and some carelessness' – and frank, but ended with a stringent denunciation of the Committee's procedures that can be read with advantage by every parliamentarian. If it was rather melodramatic on occasion ('I am on trial for my life'), it was one of his masterpieces, and infinitely superior to Hughes' final submission. But, with the exception of Cadogan, he was not among friends.

One of the problems of the documents placed before, and published by, the Committee was that they can be read as a relatively brief consecutive correspondence, but in fact cover a period of over eighteen months. They also give the quite false impression that Boothby was thinking of or doing little else than looking after his own interests in 1939 and 1940, when it was actually a period of intense political activity for him – and everyone else; and, particularly after his Committee was disbanded on 3 August 1939, the Czech assets occupied very little of his time or attention. After his father had settled the Butt matter and Weininger's loan of £3,000, his immediate financial crisis was over.

The whole matter resolved itself into one of interpretations. That Boothby had gambled on the Stock Exchange and lost and was in deep financial trouble in 1939 and early 1940 was uncontested. Nor could his March 1939 arrangement with Weininger be criticised. It is clear that Simon had been misled by Reid and by Nathan's and Weininger's letters and had reached an interpretation of the Boothby Committee that was entirely wrong. Boothby had made only two speeches in the Commons on the subject over a period of ten months, and had not exactly pestered colleagues or officials about it. Yes, he had an expectation of benefiting from Weininger's generosity, but was an expectation 'an interest'? And how had his conduct been incompatible with, or unworthy of, his duties as a Member of Parliament?

---

* MP for Reading, 1922–3; Finchley, 1924–35; and Bolton, 1940–8. When I was an undergraduate at Oxford, Cadogan showed me, and other history undergraduates, much kindness by allowing his house to be used for reading parties in the summer vacation. He was a fascinating and charming Conservative of the old school, and always believed that 'the Boothby affair' was a storm in a teacup, and that Boothby had been unfairly treated.

But the interpretation of the Committee, and particularly of Gretton and Spens, was different. To his dying day Weininger was convinced that his friend was the victim of a conspiracy engineered by his political enemies, and that they went through the documents looking for anything they could find that would be useful for their purposes, and either ignored or distorted contrary evidence. On the latter point he and Boothby certainly had a case, and a very strong one.

The 'conspiracy' theory may have had something in it, and Boothby and Weininger were not alone in their suspicions, but the hostility of the Committee was almost certainly more personal. Here Boothby's whole style as a banker, individual and politician counted against him in their eyes. Many years later, in a famous television *Face to Face* interview with John Freeman, Boothby said that the one thing he should have been censured for was his inept and disastrous speculations on the Stock Exchange, and the revelations of these were unlikely to increase his reputation. Also, in a moment of bitterness about not being told of the Butt loan, Chase had retired to the country to compose a harsh memorandum against Boothby's treatment of him. This was made available to the Committee and was published in full; it was not remotely relevant to their enquiry, but it added to the general impression of Boothby's untrustworthiness in money matters, whereas Chase's actual evidence to the Committee had been far more positive.

The majority of the Committee, led by Gretton and Spens, became censorious and suspicious of all Boothby's actions in the light of his general character and reputation. They deliberately drew the darkest conclusions. His entire personality was on trial and was found wanting. To them he was an adventurer, a maverick, a gambler and a cad. They all knew of his divorce, and some, almost certainly the Conservatives, must have known of his relationship with Dorothy Macmillan, the worst-kept secret in London. Boothby's friends saw all his weaknesses and despaired at his follies, but, knowing the real man, made lavish allowances. His enemies, and those who were not, but were easily shockable people leading sober and staid lives, saw only the former. Perhaps an element of jealousy also played its part.

Many years later Thomas Balogh, the eminent Hungarian-born economist, remarked with shrewdness that

Boothby was grossly misrepresented. In fact, he was enormously productive. He had a superb grasp of economics. He was full of courage on causes. But he got this image which misled people. In Britain, image and performance are farther apart than in any country in the world. . . . A terrible injustice has been perpetrated on him.

However, Boothby was totally confident. He spent Christmas with his parents at Beechwood, and eagerly responded to an invitation from Compton Mackenzie to spend a short holiday with him on Barra. In his letter of acceptance he added that

> The Almighty, who seems at long last to be veering over to my side, blew up the Report of the Select Committee the other day, together with all the typeset and the documents, with a well-directed bomb. So they have had to begin all over again. It is not easy to know what to do, and I want your advice. *For once* Right is on my side, and I shall emerge as the champion of Freedom and Justice – as against the Gestapo and the Star Chamber.

He asked whether he could bring an old friend, Araminta Balfour, who was in the process of a divorce. In case the letter did not reach Mackenzie in time, he also cabled, 'Can I come for ten days bringing Araminta?', but it reached Mackenzie with the word 'armaments' for 'Araminta', such an exotic name having baffled the telegraphist. Mackenzie cabled back enthusiastically, and alerted the islanders and their Home Guard to the imminent arrival of the arsenal. There was, accordingly, considerable surprise and disappointment when only Boothby and his pretty friend arrived. Luckily, all involved had a sense of humour, and Mackenzie was so enchanted by Araminta that he urged them to marry. This was obviously not possible at the time, but they evidently had a delightful holiday. Boothby wrote to him in gratitude:

> It was sheer joy from start to finish, and I feel a completely new man. Already I have a nostalgia for the Hebrides which is almost unbearable. They kept it up to the finish, and the beauty of the islands on Thursday morning could nowhere have been surpassed. . . . I thought, when I set out on my voyage to Barra, that it was going to be fun. But in my wildest dreams I never thought I could enjoy myself as I did. To live the Perfect Life is an experience granted to few these days. I can at any rate say that I made the most of it! Now I go south to meet my Fate – with more than a sneaking longing that it may carry me back to the Islands 'ere long, to write 'The Great Illusion'. . . . Araminta, who also enjoyed herself mast-high, characteristically took a train from Glasgow which went in the wrong direction, and didn't get home until ten. . . . Infinite gratitude to the best of friends, the best of hosts, and the best of companions.

Boothby's optimism, based on his total faith in his innocence, was swiftly and brutally shattered.

The conclusions of the Committee were heavily, and unfairly, loaded against Boothby.

There had been, for example, no evidence whatever, apart from the unverifiable and untrue allegations of Reid, Wilson and Simon, that Boothby had any expectation of payment for his work for his Committee, but the Select Committee found 'the evidence inconclusive'. In fact, it was non-existent. They stated, damningly, that there was no evidence that the Boothby Committee had even considered the proposal that the larger claimants should assist the smaller, which was in flat contradiction to the evidence not only of Boothby and Weininger, but also of Nathan, Jansa and Calmon. As has been related, this was a crucial point concerning the Petscheks. The Committee regarded the Boothby–Simon meeting, which had had nothing whatever to do with the real issue, as conclusive evidence against him. The two deadly paragraphs read:

Your Committee do not accept the plea that this interview occurred in an interval in Mr Boothby's affairs when his expectation of reward was of such a tenuous character as entitled him to deny it. . . . Your Committee equally do not accept the plea that Mr Boothby's disclaimer related only to the question of whether he was to receive special remuneration as Chairman of the Committee of Czech claimants. It was certainly not so understood by the Chancellor of the Exchequer, and the letter which Mr Boothby wrote on 4th August, 1939, using the words 'I have no financial interest of any sort or kind in the work of the Committee' was not likely to undeceive him. If Mr Boothby intended to delimit his disclaimer it was essential that he should have stated explicitly what his interest was and what it was not in the whole matter of the Czech assets.

On this, the Select Committee was on untenable ground and had got the matter wrong. It had in fact been deceived by Wilson and Simon. Where it was on stronger ground was when it stated that in view of Weininger's promise,

Mr Boothby took no steps at any time to disclose to the House of Commons as a whole or to those Members to whom he wrote urging particular action or to the Treasury that his private interests were in any way affected by what might be done about the Czech assets.

This was absolutely fair comment, but what was not were these paragraphs, which were a travesty of the real situation:

Your Committee are satisfied that, generous as Mr Weininger may have been and anxious as he was to help his friend whose political activities he admired, the promise to pay him [Boothby] such a considerable sum of money was given on the understanding that Mr Boothby would render services in return. Such services included political speeches and pressure on Ministers of the Crown and Treasury officials.

Mr Boothby could not fail to be influenced in his advocacy by this fact; and the knowledge that Mr Weininger might withdraw his promise or be unable to fulfil it would make Mr Boothby all the more anxious to get Mr Weininger his money and get it promptly. In all his speeches in Parliament, in his interviews with Treasury officials and in his letters to the Chancellor of the Exchequer, Mr Boothby did, in fact, urge early satisfaction in full of the class of claims to which that of the Weininger ladies belonged.

The conclusion was portentous, but devastating:

The finding of your Committee is that Mr Boothby's conduct was contrary to the usage and derogatory to the dignity of the House and inconsistent with the standards which Parliament is entitled to expect from its Members.

After his experience before the Committee Boothby had expected some criticism, but not this. It had consistently taken the bleakest interpretation, even describing his speech in the Commons of 23 January 1940 as 'very material'; as has been recorded, in the course of over a year Boothby had made only two, quite brief, speeches in the Commons on the subject, and in which no votes were involved, and yet the Committee referred to '*all* his speeches in Parliament . . . [when] Mr Boothby did, in fact, urge early satisfaction in full of the class of claims to which that of the Weininger ladies belonged', without adding that he had consistently urged settlement for all claimants. The Committee did not, and could not, directly, accuse him of venality, or indeed of any major offence, and, significantly, did not refer directly to the Declaration of Interest issue, on which it was on very thin ice, but the implications were clear enough. Having been through his private affairs over eighteen months with a remarkable assiduity and suspicion, this was all that they could come up with. But it was enough.

Boothby now had to rely upon the reactions of his friends, the press, the House of Commons and his constituents. Without their sympathy and support his political career was over, as, indeed, many thought it was, with different emotions of delight and dismay. It was clear to him that he would have to resign his office, but in his formal letter of resignation to Churchill he added that 'I have no intention whatever of resigning from the House of Commons'; he also refused to make any public statement until the Report was debated in the Commons.

The Times' political correspondent contented himself with the comment on the Report that it created 'a painful impression in political circles', but its Leader pronounced that it was 'a particularly unqualified condemnation':

It must in fairness be said for Mr Boothby that the cause which he was advocating was the same which he had advocated before he had any financial interest in it; and that it was also one which commanded the sympathy of all those rightly suspicious of German designs and anxious to do something for Germany's victims. But these considerations can have no real bearing upon the transaction in its later stages. . . . It is indeed a stern warning of the scrupulous care and candour which public life demands.

The first reaction from his constituency was one of total support, the *Scotsman* reporting 'a well-known businessman' in his constituency declaring that

We will stand by Mr Boothby because we have found that he is the best representative for such a constituency. He knows exactly what we want and what the needs of our industry are. Of course, we regret that anything should have occurred like this, but not only in Peterhead but in Fraserburgh and all through the constituency I am certain that we will stand staunchly by Mr Boothby.

Its leading article pointed out that the Committee was not a court of law but a censor of morals, and that it 'can only be regretted that a political career so full of promise should have had such an unfortunate termination'.

To the *Daily Express* Boothby said that he was 'astonished' at the findings of the Committee: 'Tell 'em I'm going to fight back.'

In fact, Boothby's resolution to stay in the Commons was not as immediate and decisive as this. On 25 January he wrote to Beaverbrook defending his actions, but asking him whether he should resign his seat as

I am receiving conflicting advice on this point. There are those who say that it would be the right and wise thing to do. And there are others – with whom I am inclined to agree – who say that I should certainly go away for a bit and render services in another sphere until time has had its inevitable effect; but that if I give up my seat now I will never come back. I don't know whether you can give me advice in your private capacity. But it would be very welcome.

Beaverbrook replied that while 'I feel deep sympathy with you in your trouble', he could not, as a Cabinet minister, attempt to give him advice on this matter, but that 'recent events would not interfere with my giving you any advice that might be useful to you on any other subject'. As Beaverbrook correctly divined, Boothby had decided to fight, and told the new Chief Whip, James Stuart, this, which did not greatly surprise him.*

To his dismayed parents he cabled:

* Churchill had not forgotten Stuart's threat to withdraw the Whip from him, and strongly resisted Margesson's recommendation that he should succeed him. Unfortunately, the alternative, Thomas Dugdale, was abroad on active service, and so, with deep reluctance, Churchill appointed Stuart. This was bad news for Boothby; it became even worse when Churchill and Stuart, to their mutual surprise, worked well together, and Stuart gained his confidence. Stuart's enmity against Boothby was implacable, and was warmly reciprocated.

Report is a surprise and disappointment and I cannot accept the findings or some of the evidence on which they are based but I am very satisfied with this morning's press. In many ways it is a relief to have the issue clear cut. Chase's evidence proved damaging as I thought. Much now depends on me and we are confident that my speech to the House will restore my personal position.

In further telegrams to them he said that he was 'taking infinite trouble [over his speech] and am very well advised'. He was also:

. . . receiving wise and encouraging advice from all quarters including the highest. One great satisfaction is that my old chief emerges in a different light to what I had supposed and his power is behind me although at present unseen.

Boothby later became convinced not only that Churchill could easily have prevented this débâcle, but that he had actually engineered it. However, it is clear that the latter was not the case. Boothby wrote that

Churchill held out no helping hand in this time of trouble, and I began to feel that he wanted to do me in. Sometimes I woke up in the night trembling. I could not understand why this mighty Titan, then at the zenith of his power, and carrying the main burden, whom I had known so well, and served for so long to the best of my capacity, should harbour such resentment against anyone as completely unimportant as myself.

This was grossly unfair. Even though it is an episode in Churchill's career that makes many of his admirers – and members of his family – uncomfortable, he had no choice but to accept Boothby's resignation. Also John Colville, no friend of Boothby's, has written that

Churchill, always sensitive to the misfortunes of those who had served him, deprecated the heat that was generated, calmed the Lord Chancellor [Simon] who was out for Boothby's blood without paying due heed to the arguments in his defence, and declared that there was nothing he disliked so much as a man-hunt.*

It may have been that Churchill felt some personal responsibility for Boothby's position and had no cause to think well of those Conservatives who were gleeful at his downfall. The message from Downing Street via Bracken was that the Prime Minister was deeply unhappy about it all and was in a very sympathetic frame of mind, but that everything would depend on Boothby's speech in the debate on the Report, which would be as soon as possible. Also, the motion itself would not be condemnatory of Boothby, but would merely seek agreement to the Report.

*John Colville, *The Churchillians*.

Meanwhile, press reporting was increasingly sympathetic. Davenport in the *New Statesman* got it absolutely right when he wrote:

Bob Boothby's great mistake in life has been to plunge too deeply in the City. Having a load of debt about his neck he looked for help from his friends, and was clearly not as candid as he should have been about his expectation of help from his friend Weininger. That he sincerely believed, and with good reason, that he was serving this country by this fight on the issue of Czech gold [*sic*] everyone will agree. They will also agree that he ought to have divulged his hope of benefiting from the campaign. At the Ministry of Food Boothby showed just that kind of drive and enthusiasm which government departments need. He is one of the most popular MPs, and one of the most delightful of companions. That the nation should have lost his services at such a time and on such an issue is a wretched business.

It was also increasingly the view of Boothby's colleagues, including members of the Cabinet and other ministers, and Boothby was very surprised to learn that one of his strongest champions was Kingsley Wood. Others included Walter Elliot, Ellen Wilkinson and Arthur Salter. Ellen Wilkinson wrote to say that

the feeling I meet everywhere is 'Why on earth couldn't this be settled by a private wigging if he had stepped over the line an inch, & anyway it was all over before the war, & we can't afford to lose a man like that from the M/Food!' Simon could give the Germans £8 million of Czech gold. And then there is all this fuss because apparently you let the poor Czechs have 2 1/2d of their own money. I suppose these remarks are lese-majesty, or contempt of court, but this is just what all the people I meet are saying.

The Weizmanns sent a telegram of warm support, to which Boothby replied that 'It is in adversity that one discovers true friends. And that is a great reward and consolation.' Lloyd George was absolutely incensed. As Boothby later recorded:

From him I received a peremptory message to come down at once to Churt, and I did. He greeted me by saying: 'Churchill has behaved to you like the cad he is. If I had been there, this would never have happened.' Then he paced up and down the room, with blazing eyes, shaking his head, and pausing at intervals to speak in terms of imperious authority. It was the only time I ever saw him in anger. And I must confess that, although I knew the anger was on my behalf, I was pretty frightened.

Lloyd George spoke of how reasonably Asquith had treated him over the Marconi scandal, and said if Churchill sought Boothby's removal from the House he would speak in opposition to it. He urged him to rely upon his constituents: 'If they stand by you, he won't be able to break you.'

Those who had actually read some of the key evidence realised how thin the case was against Boothby, and that everything depended upon Simon's and Boothby's interpretation of the notorious 3 August meeting. The Committee had favoured Simon's; others did not. Many simply could not comprehend why so minor a matter had caused such fearsome repercussions. Perhaps there were those who were thoughtfully considering their own past conduct, and the fact that although the Committee had taken such a high moral stance, it had left the whole issue of Declaration of Interest as vague as it had ever been. Boothby sensed a surge of sympathy for him in the Government and in the House, which was further manifested by a clear direction to the press from Downing Street that if there was a motion to expel him from Parliament or condemn him the Government would strongly oppose it. From his parents, friends and constituents came a giant flow of letters and messages of support.

If ever a man needed friends, it was then, and Boothby's own capacity for friendship and loyalty to those in difficulty was never better rewarded. Out of apparent disaster there loomed the possibility of a triumph. Weininger also, through his solicitors, was preparing a strong counter-attack, which was given considerable prominence when published in January. Sir Robert Boothby, who had caught a severe cold and had a bad cough and was confined to his bed, issued statements of support and faith in his son. His parents' confidence in him was total.

Some of the letters of support may be cited. Colin Coote wrote from *The Times* on 21 January to Lady Boothby:

> At the moment when all his friends are thinking of Bob, at least one of them is thinking of you. For you will, I fancy, feel the stab more keenly than anybody. You may therefore like to know that Bob is bearing up nobly to the – to him – unexpected condemnation with the greatest courage, and that all who really know him have never had the slightest doubt that he has nothing of which he need be in the least ashamed. To me, it would not make the slightest difference if he had deserved the Committee's censure, because his standards and his conduct are on so very much a higher level than those of the men who secured his condemnation; and it is far better to have got into trouble by courage, as he did, than to have brought trouble on millions by cowardice, as they did. Moreover you may like to know that he is by no means 'finished'. The worst feature of the whole affair seems to me to be that the country has lost his services at the moment when she needs men like him most. But she has not lost them permanently; he has not lost for a moment the affection and admiration of yours very sincerely
>
> Colin R. Coote

Woolton wrote on 22 January:

My dear Bob

I am terribly sorry.

Don't let this get you down: there is plenty of time for recovery if you can avoid being carried away by present emotions: and you have such great gifts to offer in public life. You mustn't get in a bad position now.

Don't think this impertinent advice.

Time really does heal and men will realise you have got into this jam through some spirit of recklessness: what will impress them more than the report is the way you handle it, and there is your chance of future political usefulness: be prepared to wait.

I shall always remember our association here and the way you helped us in the Ministry. We are all greatly sorry for this ending.

Yours ever,
Fred

His mother wrote to him on 23 January:

Darling

Thank you for your telegrams. There is no use offering advice as to the speech – you have other men at hand and I think you yourself have realised how much depends on your attitude, requiring frankness and dignity.

It might be the *turning* point of your life. . . .

D[addy] fairly well. . . .

The shock to him was great. I have borne less well as I *never* expected anything else – curious for me. Rather an optimist and 'hoper'. But now I *do* hope, and I feel so certain that you will triumph.

Two days later she wrote again:

Darling

Remember I am sending you a cheque for the trial and you need it in your account as soon as possible and square it all up.

Courage is the only thing left to us all and we must show the world what stuff we are made of.

I know you are going through icy waters, and I feel so sad for you – we were too optimistic. But out of evil good may come. . . .Well there is nothing, absolutely nothing, to say. You have wise counsellors in the south, but be moderate in your utterances in the House – you will gain nothing by vituperation. I love you always.

Mother

Thus, by the time the Report was debated in the Commons on 28 January, Boothby knew who his friends were and that he would get a sympathetic hearing, but he knew that everything depended upon his speech and demeanour. He felt strongly that his case had been inadequately listened to by the Committee, but he knew that he could not denounce a unanimous Report without antagonising the House. It was a very delicate balance.

One of Boothby's key difficulties as he prepared his speech remained the extent to which he could refer to the role Weininger had played in the rifles' affair. It was the same problem they had faced in the Select Committee, and the answer had to be the same. In the event the words he chose were:

Immediately after the outbreak of the war I asked him [Weininger] to co-operate with me in work of considerable potential importance and magnitude. I gave some account of this work to the Select Committee, but they decided that it would not be in the public interest to disclose it at present, and I bow to their decision. Some day the full story may be told.

Boothby spent the weekend at the home of his close friend, Simon Harcourt-Smith, where he worked on his papers and his speech. In London, Roger Senhouse and John Strachey came to his flat to take him to the House, but at the last moment Strachey said that he could not face it, and they left him with a bottle of sherry. Boothby found Walter Elliot, in his colonel's uniform, waiting for him, having travelled down specially overnight from Scotland to sit beside him. The House was packed and sombre.

Boothby's speech is one of those rarities – a Commons speech that reads as well as it sounded to its audience.

He went through the main issues – especially the Simon meeting – clearly, frankly and accurately; he drew attention to certain matters that the Committee had got wrong – particularly the question of the smaller claimants and the Weinmann matter – and strongly denied the principal charges, while admitting that he should have told Simon, in his letter of 4 August, that he did have expectations from the Weininger funds.

Looking back, the whole unfortunate business seems so unnecessary. A postscript in a letter, a sentence or two in a conversation or a speech – which could have altered neither the facts, nor the course of events, nor my conduct in relation to them – are all, it seems, that were required. But it never occurred to me that they were necessary. It may be that I was thoughtless. . . . The true picture of events is still so clear before my eyes that I am quite unable to comprehend how an interpretation could have been put on them which would make me seem unworthy of membership of this House. It is not true that I suddenly took an interest in Czechoslovakian affairs because I was given a financial interest. I helped the Czechs because I did not want them to be robbed by the Germans, not because I wanted to rob them myself. It is not true that I pressed the claims in which I might be held to have an interest as against others. On the contrary, I pressed in this House that the small claims, in which no one suggests that I had an interest, should be met in full. It is not true that I deliberately deceived the Chancellor or the House. I was answering his charge that I and my Committee were working for payment, and that I was being paid as Chairman. It is not true that I advocated any case on account of personal interest. . . .

Finally, it is not true that I have received one single penny for anything I said or did with regard to the Czech claims. Knowing all this, I cannot, of my own free will, take any action that might even imply an acknowledgment of guilt on my part. Folly I have admitted: guilt I cannot admit.

Senhouse was not the only observer who commented on Churchill's unease and lack of his usual exuberance or pugnacity. In advising the House to accept the Report, he deprecated any further comments on it. He also spoke with marked warmth of his distress and his long personal friendship for Boothby, and his ability as a minister, saying that 'We are none too fertile in talents of the order that have just been displayed to us.' He concluded:

Altogether, it is a heart-breaking business. The popularity of my Hon. Friend, his abilities, and the manner in which during his short term of office he has conducted himself, all add to the poignancy of our feelings, but I do not think they can influence our course of action. There we must leave this matter. We should accept the Report of the Committee, and that is all we have to do. As for my Hon. Friend, one can only say that there are paths of service open in wartime which are not open in times of peace; and some of these paths may be paths to honour.

Churchill wrote to his son Randolph on 31 January of Boothby's 'remarkable Parliamentary performance, that perceptibly affected the opinion of the House. I do not think that he will have to resign his seat.'

Walter Elliot also looked to the future: 'the past being the past, tomorrow is also a day, and great opportunities for service may still be open to him'.

Boothby, by custom, had left the Chamber when he had finished his speech, encouraged by

a subdued but sustained cheer from both sides; and Maxton gave one of his unforgettable smiles. In the Lobby outside Kingsley Wood came up to me and said: 'The Select Committee never heard anything like that.' I then went back to my flat with Roger Senhouse. We found John Strachey still sitting there, with the bottle empty. 'It's alright,' said Roger, 'he's saved himself.'

Lady Boothby telegraphed to her son: 'Darling I love you always and loved your speech, Mother.'

The speech made an immense impression. There are many contemporary accounts, but the most vivid is that of Roger Senhouse, who wrote immediately to Lady Boothby:

Dear Lady Boothby

I have not written to you all these weeks of what must have been bewildered and heart-rending anxiety and stupefaction, in the belief that no word of mine would do anything but set up some new vibration in your mind, which would be unnecessary, because I could not be certain that it would bring comfort or calm as coming from the past. I relied on the stronger and inevitably sympathetic bonds of friendship, and so did not write. I had hoped that I might catch Bob at Beechwood when I was staying with my sister Dorothy after Christmas, but he had already left for Barra – and again I did not trouble you.

Now however, when this ghastly drama has come to an end, I feel compelled to say something – not of my feelings, which have naturally remained constant throughout, but of my impressions of what took place in the Commons to-day.

Bob was as calm as I have ever known him when I called at 11 a.m. There were a few pieces of crumpled paper on the floor scrunched up and some thrown in the fire. I at once asked him whether he was going to read his speech. 'I now know every word by heart,' Bob said, 'but I shall of course take the speech with me.' . . .

Bob had arranged for a ticket for me, and St. John Hutchinson and I were in the gallery some minutes before he was called. He had come in and sat next to Walter Elliot some five minutes before speaking. He started with a full audience, never faltered once, and carried through the full thirty-five minutes without a break in his voice or a hesitation of any kind. As a rhetorical feat it was, in its complete execution, an unqualified success, as an exposition of his case I found it utterly convincing, dramatic, but with the proper humility, and varied according to the content. It was heard throughout in pin-dropping silence – not a cough, not an interruption of any sort.

I am not myself sufficiently conversant with the attitude of assembled M.P.s in listening to Bob – or indeed to any other Member – to say or give any critical opinion of the true effect of the speech; but he did with them whatever he wanted, there can be no doubt of that. I could not help comparing this 'set piece', given in such awe-inspiring circumstances, with some stage piece given in a theatre where the actor can gauge at any moment the exact reaction he may expect from his audience and play upon the mass emotion, as he alone has learnt how after many rehearsals and many other performances in the same theatre of the same words arranged in the same order.

Bob knew his limits, it is certain, and was familiar with his surroundings and was therefore able to control the periods of his speech, but he could never give full bent to his true feelings: such action would have been fatal; he could not even be judge of the temper of his audience, or test it. Comparatively, it must be mere child's play for an accomplished actor to be certain of his house on any given night and give them emotionally as much as they will appreciate, but in the House of Commons to-day Bob could rely only on that really very chilling cliché 'a sympathetic hearing'. It was clear to me after a very short wince that the assembly was giving him that and very much more. But he was perfectly correct in giving himself no extra rein. He was at all times interesting and therefore held their attention and the well-trained range of his voice carried him along as so many of his listeners would have failed miserably. His voice rang out and by its quality alone compelled attention. Hutchinson was riveted throughout I was always sure of that. My observation hardly extended across the floor as I did not wish to miss a word. Nor did I. Yet I found I could not always remain with my eyes fixed on the orator, for there were at least two reasons when I was not certain of my own emotional state or imminent reaction to whatever might come next.

There were, it seemed to me, two perorations, and the second was taken at a faster pace and therefore in a major key. The effect was terrific. He could not have given a better account of himself – or a truer. All must have been aware of his intention and on this speech history must judge him. The fourfold repetition of 'it is not true' was the highest point in the peroration to my mind, as no doubt it was intended by its author.

He carried himself so well throughout, his right hand sometimes in his jacket pocket, his papers usually in his left, and an occasional short dramatic gesture throwing sometimes into a wider sweep. There was a quiet and proper dignity in delivery and his departure and general bearing were really superb. Yet at no time could he be accused of acting – that is the very last impression I wish to convey – it was the very accomplished control and individual aplomb that gave him the great advantage of making this nightmarish ordeal appear so easy, when the whole House must have been keenly aware of the bleak and lonely apprehension with which such a cruelly shattering experience had to be tackled.

The whole tenor of his speech had been delivered with great confidence and, I would add for myself, consummate understatement. He had once mentioned his chief antagonist by name and left his listeners to draw their own conclusions. He accepted in principle the findings of the Committee but clearly stated his guilt lay in the folly of omission and nothing else. Those are the words by which history – and not only his fellow Members – will judge his conduct, and everyone of them rang out in the clearest tones.

Winston rose to his hateful task with every outward sign of constrained emotion and distaste. He began with short, staccato, hesitating utterances – shifting his position continuously in the limited space at his disposal, in his curious, delicate, almost pirouetting movement of first one foot, and then the other, such small feet so easily controlled under the rotund tummy – all eloquent of his unease at this 'heart-breaking business'. I found this unutterably moving. The impression given was one of grave doubt in the face of inexorable duty, and the expression of a sincere and lasting friendship to which he was determined to give full weight. 'It is at least the interruption of a career of high parliamentary promise' are words of high praise and encouragement. To follow these in almost the next sentence with references to the present personal friendship 'often a supporter in lonely and difficult moments' was a glowing tribute and his final words I take to be of high encouragement for the future. From any other man they would have rung quite differently – the mention of 'honour' even without 'glory' is dangerously close to claptrap and I felt certain that it was not the P.M.'s intention. . . . I do trust that all will now be well for you, for here was the great vindication of the victim of a vicious attack.

Yours ever
Roger Senhouse

Baffy Dugdale wrote to Lady Boothby on 28 January:

Dear Lady Boothby

I am sure that you will not mind my writing to give you some description of Bob's speech to-day – which I heard – for there are things you will be happy to know, which he cannot tell you himself – though I think he does know he spoke well. But he cannot know what an impression he made – not only on his friends, and on those of us who have always known that Bob could never have been guilty of what he was accused of – but on those who had not made up their minds or who had only read the findings of the Report, and had not looked for themselves at the evidence and these people of course made up the great majority of the House of Commons.

Bob's speech can only be described as a great speech. In matter it was most skilful – but, listening to him, one felt that for the audience *what* he said was almost less important than his manner of saying it. There was such perfect dignity – and he kept the very difficult middle way between defiance and undue humility. The House of Commons listened in absolute silence – in fact when someone sneezed there was a murmur of 'Order, Order' – and of course even a much less experienced Parliamentarian than Bob could not but feel that he *had* the House and no doubt he spoke the better for it. Then when he made his exit there was a murmur of cheering, and I am told by very experienced MP friends that such a thing is unprecedented on such an occasion, and they had never expected it however well Bob would acquit himself.

The PM's speech (as subsequent private remarks to someone I know) is also held to have shown that Bob's speech made a good deal of difference to his attitude.

All this is a *very* feeble description of a scene I am thankful not to have missed. I won't say any more, except that I have thought of you so often!

Bob has been through one of the toughest ordeals that any man can face – and he has to-day earned admiration for the way he has stood up to it – not only pity. Several people have said that to me.

Yours very sincerely
Baffy Dugdale

She also wrote to Boothby on the 30th:

Dear Bob

Only one more little bouquet for you reached my ears yesterday but I think it is from a source worth passing on.

Ernest Bevin and [Arthur] Creech-Jones lunched with one of my Zionist friends – and the latter expressed the *warmest* admiration of your speech, descanted on it apparently, and EB kept nodding his head and putting in words of agreement. CJ said he had seldom seen the House so influenced. I think their opinion is interesting?

. . . I wonder how you are – I shall be surprised if you are not beginning to feel very tired – for the nervous strain was terrific, and lasted so long. You have much in your past to be ashamed of – but *nothing* in the way you have stood up to this. In fact in some ways you have been, in the last few weeks, what my mother used to call 'a lesson to us all' though I think she would turn in her grave if she heard me apply these words to *you*!

I feel much more nervous about you in the next few weeks than I did while the whole thing was going on. For my sake don't play the fool in any of your usual ways.

Bless you!

Yours ever Baffy

Compton Mackenzie was among those who rallied totally to Boothby's side. In his letter of thanks Boothby wrote that

In the end they wouldn't believe that Weininger wd do what he did except on a £5,000-a-speech basis. So that was that. The Report was a travesty of the truth, but I think my speech did something to restore the balance. Now I am suffering from a bit of reaction. Before I fling myself into uniform – and therefore back into their power – I shall have to find out who has been doing all this Gestapo work against me. And whether it will stop.

Then, another heavier blow fell. Boothby's father still had a bad cold, but there were no serious apprehensions about his health. Boothby telegraphed to him on 31 January:

Interesting and important moves and consultations now going on regarding my immediate future and I think I should not come north until things are settled. I have of course placed myself in the hands of the person you suggest. No need despondency. My speech has secured recovery. Thanks for all your help. Love Bob.

On the same day Weininger's solicitors, Joynson Hicks, published a letter in *The Times* supporting his case and that of Boothby, and strongly denying any impropriety on either side. This letter was to get this eminent firm into difficulties with the Select Committee, but Boothby cabled to his father: 'Letter about Weininger published by Times on leader page this morning has caused considerable sensation here. I could ask for no better footnote to my speech. Love. Bob.'

He was due to go to Edinburgh the following weekend to stay with his parents before going on to his constituency, but early on the morning of 6 February Sir Robert suffered a sudden heart attack and died at the age of sixty-nine at Beechwood. His death was a complete surprise to his doctors, and a devastating blow to his wife and son. It would be excessive to claim, and Boothby never did, that this was the direct result of the furore over him, but it is the case that his father had been deeply shocked and upset, which certainly cannot have helped. Among the many letters Boothby received was a characteristic one from Bracken: 'You are indeed a man of sorrows. Your father was one of the nicest men I have ever known. Alas, he died before he could see your recovery. Your mother will.'

Many other tributes to this kind and cheerful man poured in, and several of his obituaries gave prominence to his publicly declared faith in his son's innocence and future. But there was no letter, or message of any kind, from Churchill. Boothby was surprised at the time, but later it was to rankle with him very deeply, and quite unreasonably, as Churchill had not known his father at all well and had much else on his mind. But it constituted another stage in Boothby's personal disillusionment with him. At the time, it was another tragic episode in his personal nightmare.

Violet Bonham Carter was one who understood Boothby's feelings, although she had always adored Churchill and would hear little against him. For when many years later her husband died, she was enraged that her close friend Harold Macmillan, then Prime Minister, only sent a formal letter of sympathy from his Private Secretary and did not write personally. 'Silence would have been preferable,' she wrote furiously to Boothby. 'These are the things that one remembers with one's heart. It destroyed him for me as a human being.' She never forgave Macmillan for his thoughtless insensitivity; with far less justification, Boothby never forgave Churchill, and his feelings reached the point when Violet had to rebuke him strongly for describing her hero as 'the most horrible man I have ever known'. Boothby kept her letter, and her phrase, 'These are the things that one remembers with one's heart', especially struck him, as it was also true in his case. The curious similarity is that these omissions were so out of character. But very busy and preoccupied prime ministers – and in January 1941 Churchill was desperately busy and preoccupied – cannot fairly be criticised for not sending a message of condolence to old friends on a family bereavement. The fact was that Boothby, and later Violet Bonham Carter, felt these omissions very deeply. One can only record the facts with sadness. But there were some glimmers of light in the darkness. Stanley Baldwin, himself in the shadows of public obloquy, wrote to Boothby from Astley Hall:

> Dear Bob
>
> If you feel it would be good to get away from the crowd, and just rest, and have only an old man to talk to, come down here. Whether you will or not I shall quite understand; do just as the spirit moves you. But if you do care to come you will be welcome. . . .
>
> Yours sincerely
>
> Baldwin of Bewdley (once known in a previous existence as S.B.).
>
> I don't want your visit to fall through.
>
> You will be coming to two people who have a real affection and regard for your parents, and who can realise what such a shock as you have suffered means to you at this time.

This deep act of kindness from a former prime minister whom he had so often criticised and opposed was in very marked contrast with his treatment from the one he had always supported, and moved Boothby greatly.

Strachey wrote:

> About you. Be as bitter as hell. It is far your best and healthiest reaction. It means that you are still fighting. And as long as that is so, you are not broken. Of course, it was plot and a purge. The fact that you were vulnerable and, in that sense, technically guilty (though not, at that, of many of the things which the report accuses you of) was utterly irrelevant to the blow they struck at you; though it was by no means irrelevant to the result. Certainly, never forgive. Why should you? But, especially as you will now be able to go on with your political life, if you can, look at the man at HQ [Churchill] objectively. The fact that he attempted a cold-blooded political murder of you (from whatever motives) should not blunt you to his startling historical appropriateness at this juncture; which makes him very strong.

Boothby found Churchill's attitude incomprehensible and wounding, and, although they were to come together again and Churchill was to make some amends, their old friendship had been irretrievably ended.

In spite of such comforting messages, the future seemed bleak, and at this especially dark moment in his fortunes Boothby travelled to his constituency to discuss his future with the Executive Committee of the East Aberdeenshire Unionist Association. The result was virtually a foregone conclusion, as 'a prominent member of the Association' – almost certainly Duff – had already told the press that 'the Unionists in the Association are almost unanimous in their desire for him to retain his seat. The main object of the meeting is to try and make it unanimous.'

Boothby's key point was that while he did not impugn the Select Committee,

I am reluctant to take any step which might appear to be an acknowledgment of a guilt which I do not feel and cannot admit. It has never been suggested in any quarter that I acted contrary to the national interest, and I was never at any time a party to an agreement by which I was to receive payment for political services of any kind.

He said that he would serve the country 'in another and humbler capacity if the Association approved my retention of the seat. This will involve no relaxation of the obligation to represent your interests.' He added that 'some day the whole story will be told'.

'Mr Boothby is personally popular, even with his opponents,' one commentator wrote, 'and after the findings of the Select Committee the predominant feeling was one of mingled regret and exasperation that a career of so much promise had been foolishly imperilled.' Although he did not ask for a vote of confidence, the Committee passed, by thirty-eight votes to six, a resolution that

having heard Mr Boothby's statement with interest, we are conscious of our deep sense of gratitude for his services in the past, and are glad to take this opportunity of thanking him further, and, in learning of his reasons for retaining his seat in Parliament, concur with his decision to do so until such time as he can make a full statement.

Boothby added that 'I shall continue to fight for justice for my friend, Mr Weininger.'

Even this caused trouble in the House of Commons, when the egregious Mr Mander, the MP for East Wolverhampton, who had challenged Boothby's evidence to the Select Committee, raised Boothby's speech as an issue of Privilege, as being critical of the Select Committee. By this stage the House had had enough of Mr Mander, who had an angry and critical reception. In contrast, Boothby was warmly received. He had intended no criticism of the Committee, but had wanted to point out that it was not the entire story, with which Gretton wholly agreed, stating that their terms of reference had been limited:

It was a painful enquiry, and no member of the Select Committee had feelings of vendetta or resentment or ill-will against my Honourable Friend, and they desired during the enquiry and now to give him every opportunity to re-establish himself in the good feeling of the House.

Churchill then intervened to move that 'The House be not called upon to proceed further in the matter', and to say that, as Boothby had made clear that he intended no disrespect or reflection on the integrity of the Committee, 'the House would do well to allow the matter to drop', to which the House thankfully agreed.

Thus, publicly, the matter rested. 'The universal hope', wrote the *Daily Telegraph*, 'is that no more will be heard about it.' The *New Statesman* reported that Boothby 'left the Chamber to the music of a sympathetic cheer'. But although many felt that he had been badly treated, and had conducted himself with skill and dignity, the fact remained that his ministerial career had been ended, at least temporarily. The problem now was how he was to restore a gravely, if unfairly, shadowed reputation.

12

The Paths to Honour
1941–5

*B*oothby later wrote about this period of his life:

> For my part I had to take a lot, and can only claim that I managed to stick it out. My stoical philosophy saw me through. I had no illusions about death, or luck – or indeed about Churchill. I knew, for certain, that the former was part of life, and therefore unavoidable: and that Churchill alone was the Man for the Hour.

It was James Stuart who later claimed that Churchill, when asked by Malcolm Bullock what Boothby should do for the war effort, growled that he should 'join a bomb-disposal squad'. Margesson, who despite past difficulties was genuinely sorry for Boothby, mentioned the case of another Conservative MP who had become a rear-gunner in the RAF; this inspiring example was somewhat marred by the fact that the poor man had promptly been killed. So had the much younger Ronald Cartland, and so were others to be. Boothby however quickly found that the army had no great demand for former subalterns of forty-one, particularly one who was not exactly the fittest and leanest.

So, with Margesson's rather unfortunate example in mind, he turned to Archie Sinclair, who promised him an RAF commission – a promise which Boothby later claimed that Churchill countermanded when he heard of it. 'In more ways than one it was a relief to get into the Royal Air Force. There at least one was in contact with the action,' he later wrote. At the time, he wrote to Peter Eckersley that

> Things are not so bad for me. I love this life – for which there is really a good deal to be said in time of war. At the moment I am on a course, but

when it is over hope to get the adjutantcy of one of the 'star' Bomber Squadrons in East Anglia, and that – from a psychological point of view alone – is fascinating work. I am not sorry to be out of politics at present. From what I hear, the 'goings-on' in the highest quarters are somewhat insanitary – & judging by the way they treated me, I can well believe it. However the constituency remained, & remains, staunch; & that – in the long run – is all that matters. Best of luck to you. And – who knows? – we may yet survive to rebuild our fortunes through the microphone.

In fact, Boothby achieved his commission after training at the RAF station in Loughborough and was subsequently posted to Malta. This was then changed, and he eventually found himself with the rank of flight lieutenant as Adjutant of Number 9 Bombing Squadron at Honington in Lincolnshire, which was flying Wellingtons. The motto of the Squadron was 'There's always bloody something.'

Of all the charges ever levelled against Boothby, the one that was the most monstrous was that he had deliberately evaded active service. In fact, he had sought it in the RAF, but had his orders like everyone else and did what he was told. He wanted a commission and asked Sinclair to assist him, while at no time seeking any special favours. He was not the only middle-aged politician who tried. Duff Cooper, in his wife's words,

had wound his puttees tightly round his elegant legs, filled his water-bottle, brushed up his kitbag, and packed it with his few troubles. He had marched off to a field-day, looking as portly as a Secretary of State, and jumping with surprise when the Generals called him 'Sir'. By evening he saw that the Army had no future for him.*

When Duff appealed to his old colonel of the Grenadier Guards, with whom he had served with such courage in the First World War, the answer was firmly in the negative. He was then forty-three, and that was judged too old for the army on active service for a non-professional; it was also the RAF's judgment on the forty-one-year-old Boothby. Stuart claims that Churchill commented that Boothby was 'all flight and no lieutenant'. If he did say this – and any anti-Boothby story from Stuart should be treated with much caution, and vice versa – it was grossly unfair, and certainly based on a wholly false assumption.† I prefer to believe that

*Diana Cooper, *Trumpets from the Steep*, p. 12.

† Stuart, *op. cit.*, p. 104. As on another occasion, Stuart wisely did not refer to Boothby by name, but it is quite obvious to whom he is referring. He wrote, meaningfully, that Boothby was 'of active service age'; Stuart himself was less than three years older than Boothby. The fact was that they were all too old to resume Service careers in wartime. At least Boothby, Duff Cooper and Eden tried, which Stuart did not. Churchill no doubt remembered that he had rejoined the army in 1915 at the same age as Boothby, and had seen active service on the Western Front, although not for very long. But circumstances had changed, and the highly professional RAF of 1941 was not the amateurish volunteer British army of 1915.

it was deliberate and malevolent calumny of Stuart's. As Churchill knew better than most, lack of courage was not one of Boothby's deficiencies.

Boothby reported to Compton Mackenzie from Loughborough on 11 May:

> Behold, I am a Pilot Officer, R.A.F., V.R.!
>
> I am on a pretty tough preliminary course – drill, lectures, P.T., from dawn to dewy eve.
>
> Last time I did it was in May 1918, which demonstrates the progress of humanity.
>
> For God's sake get an Air Station established in Barra, and then I can come as Adjutant.
>
> The great thing about this place is that one is kept so busy & made so tired that thought of any kind is absolutely out of the question.

And it was to Mackenzie again that he described what then transpired, in a letter from RAF Honington, close to Bury St Edmunds in Suffolk:

> . . . My position is as follows:
>
> I passed out top of my Training Course at Loughborough (including drill – not bad for a fat old politician of 40!).
>
> This has given me a good start.
>
> They then suggested I shld go to the Middle East immediately – it takes 2 months to get there. Thinking this might be an attempt to get me out of the (political) way, I protested to Archie Sinclair.
>
> I told him that I wd gladly go out there if there was a real job for me to do; but not otherwise, as I had very considerable obligations (a) to my constituents, and (b) to my Mother. (Actually, my constituents voted me back to the House of Commons on the understanding that I would occasionally go there.)
>
> It then appeared that there had been the inevitable muddle, and I was posted here as assistant to the Squadron-Leader in charge of administration.
>
> The man in charge of postings at the Air Ministry is Squadron-Leader Pearce. He still wants me to go to a Middle East Station in three months' time; and I have tentatively agreed to do this, although I can't see the point of sending me all the way out there *unless* to a very special intelligence job.
>
> Meanwhile I am learning a hell of a lot about how a Station should be run. We have one of the crack Bomber Squadrons. They go on operations almost every night, and I spend much of my time in the operations and intelligence rooms.
>
> In quite a short time I really shall know something about it, from practically every angle.
>
> Sorry to bore you with all these preliminaries, but I must give you the background.
>
> What I think they have in mind for me is a job first as Adjutant of a

Station, and ultimately as 'Squadron-Leader Admin'. This is alright, and I don't think I wd be bad at it. Moreover promotion shd be reasonably rapid, as they are frightfully short of administrative officers owing to the present rate of expansion. But of course it is on the dull side, and doesn't really give one very much scope. . . .

My God I'd like to be in Barra now!

It must be superb in this weather.

I have finished my 'magnum opus' & will be sending you a typed copy in due course. If you cd find time to glance through it, & criticise it ruthlessly, it wd be a very great help. There are, I think, some interesting bits. . . .

This was the early draft of what was to develop into his books *The New Economy*, and the much longer and more ambitious *I Fight to Live*. 'It is such an extraordinary & sorry tale, that many people will simply not believe it,' he wrote to Mackenzie, who had willingly agreed to help. 'Nevertheless, it is all true.'

Boothby's resilience and character were seldom better demonstrated. Although his RAF duties were an inadequate use of his talents, they were not light, and he undertook them seriously and conscientiously. Giving an outwardly jaunty impression, and a popular member of the Mess, he was in fact deeply depressed, still in serious financial difficulties, and with his political fortunes temporarily ruined. But in his spare time, instead of moping or drinking, he was hard at work on his comeback, with the only weapon he had at hand: his pen.

As he wrote to his mother from Honington on 15 July:

As for me I suppose in one sense that I have 'pitched things away'.

But in another I have reaped a rich harvest.

Long ago I decided that ambition was not worth the candle – at any rate for me. I watched what the world calls success come to people – and go.

And neither process seemed to me to bring them much happiness.

The grapes are not so *very* sweet; yet you miss them when they are taken away, and so get the worst of both worlds. Anyway I found a good deal of happiness, a good deal of pleasure, much affection and many friends – and I have lived an extraordinarily full & interesting life.

I don't think one can ask for more. . . .

I believe the only thing to do with life is to live it, and I have a certain gift for that. What that woman wrote about Tessa in *The Constant Nymph*–the others had a touch of music amounting to genius but her touch was a touch of life.

Years and years ago that strange Nancy Cunard who was something of an artist in her way wrote to me in Paris, 'You do things so *gaily* – that's rare'; and I remember that it pleased me.

I think you have to take people as they are.

It is my love of life & a certain natural gaiety and zest, that gives me what you call charm which amounts to a capacity for living, & for enjoyment.

If I was a brilliant surgeon, or a great businessman, or a teetotal Secretary of State, or an ascetic like Stafford Cripps, or valued success to the point that I strove to achieve it that would be very interesting, and very satisfactory from many points of view.

But it wouldn't be *me*.

It saddens me to see humanity as a whole suffering so desperately and so unnecessarily.

At this point two friends were crucial in the revival of his ambitions – Mackenzie and Victor Gollancz, who was not only one of the finest publishers but the finest of friends. They could understand his misery and were determined to help him. Mackenzie, with some courage, dedicated his latest book, *The Monarch of the Glen*, to Boothby, who was overwhelmed, writing on 26 June:

I am completely knocked out by your proposal to dedicate *The Monarch of the Glen* to me – and can truthfully say that I have never felt so pleased, proud and honoured in my life.

It is a superb gesture on your part, and I shall never forget it.

Noble friend!

. . . . Meanwhile this station has its points.

It is in the front line of all – and yet curiously remote and aloof from the main stream of events.

As I think I told you, there seems to be nothing between the local pub & Düsseldorf. But the drama of the nightly take-off, the operations room in the silent watches, and the return at dawn, never palls.

They may send me to Russia now it is the only country where my 'dossier' is first-rate. . . .

Gollancz also read the draft of Boothby's books with enthusiasm, and Strachey offered to help with the contract. Boothby wrote to Mackenzie:

One advantage of going to him [Gollancz] is that he automatically secures one an immense circulation in 'left' political circles – which might be a good thing for me later on, because I don't see myself returning to an orthodox Conservative Party. My Tory friends will read it anyhow.

Boothby, like most other servicemen, found the systems of postings and promotions somewhat bizarre, although he did not help himself, as he reported to Mackenzie on 31 July:

I dined with Archie Sinclair 10 days ago, and murmured something about Benbecula, and being of more use dealing with crofters than sheiks.

The horrifying thing was that 3 days later I was posted to Orkney!

My immediate boss was leaving 'instanter' for a course, & I was (now am) supposed to take his place; so the C.O. here nearly had a seizure. It took 48 hours of frantic string-pulling to cancel. Which goes to show that wangling must be done with immense caution, if at all!

Now I am here for at any rate another month. And I shall enjoy one crowded hour of glorious life as Acting Squadron-Leader Admin.

I cling to the hope that Benbecula will one day see me, in a slightly more exalted rank.

Till that day comes, au revoir.

And a thousand thanks for everything.

But Boothby's efforts were rewarded. He joyfully wrote to Mackenzie on 12 December:

After six months in labour, I've got the job I wanted most at the moment – the Adjutantcy of one of our star Squadrons. It is a relief to be doing work of real use once more; and a pleasing feature is that the Air Ministry had nothing to do with my getting it.

He wrote to Beaverbrook on 31 October:

I love my bomber chaps; but it is strange to be so completely out of the world I have known for so long. And being put on the shelf at the age of forty-one – and at this particular juncture – is apt to make one cynical, and even bitter.

I can't imagine a better tonic than five minutes' conversation with you, if you can spare them.

Yours ever
Bob (once quite a promising young politician!)

Beaverbrook replied at once inviting him to see him when he was in London and went on: 'I can well understand the sense of frustration which bothers you. But at forty-one a man is young. He has no just cause to feel that he is on the shelf. At sixty-two it might be different.'

Boothby subsequently wrote movingly of his 'brief but intense experience of the Royal Air Force ... with feelings of pride, emotion and profound admiration'. The bombing offensive against Germany was in its infancy, and the slow and vulnerable Wellington was not the aircraft to undertake it, but it was the only one then available, and the loss of brave crews was grim. 'Seeing the crews on most evenings at their dispersal station,' Boothby wrote, 'watching them take off with winking lights; and then the dawn vigil, wondering how many would return. Seven, eight, nine? Or only three or four? For the crews themselves the psychological strain was almost intolerable.' He himself confessed to working 'under considerable emotional stress'. He came deeply sceptical about the value of 'hurling the bomber crews into hell' at such heavy cost and little discernible advantage, but, recognising the morale-boosting importance of the offensive to the British people, kept his silence. His subsequent commanding officer, 'Turkey' Rainsford, jestingly described him as the worst adjutant in the RAF. Boothby was later made an honorary member of the Squadron's Association and an honoured guest at its reunions. But, whenever he recalled those who had not returned – too many of his friends – his feelings were mixed.

One of these was Percy Pickard, known universally as 'Pick', who was one of the true air aces of the war and, rightly, one of the most decorated; he was also star of the British documentary *Target for Tonight*. In 1944 he insisted on flying again, although he had been grounded after far exceeding the normal tours of duty, and was killed after he had led a totally successful strike on Amiens prison. Boothby later wrote:

The truth is that in those days the instruments for accurate navigation did not exist. There were high hopes for one gadget, which I did not begin to understand; and which was brought to us one day in a brand-new Wellington bomber. All the navigators in the Squadron went up to see how it worked. Five minutes after take-off a wing fell off the plane, and they were all killed. After that the Station Commander sent for me and said: 'I'm now going to give you the most difficult order you have ever received. You have got to be cheerful at lunch in the Mess.'

Rainsford's recollection of Boothby at this time was as

a breath of fresh air and his tales of Parliamentary life and his ready sense of humour combined to make our association a very happy one indeed. Bob was, and is, one of the kindest men I have ever met. On one occasion when things were a little slack he asked me if I would like to go and spend a weekend with him in Edinburgh. I agreed readily and since the Station Commander – another Irishman, Group Captain Rudolph Taafe – was willing to let us both go, Bob duly booked tickets for us on the main line to the north.

When we got on the train it appeared that my Adjutant, as a Member of Parliament, had the privilege of having a sleeping berth, which was a luxury in those days, while I, as a mere Wing Commander, was, of course, expected to travel hard arsed. This did not please Bob at all and when we had got on the train he insisted that in no circumstances should I, as his senior officer, be allowed to sit up while he languished in a bed.

We discussed this weighty matter at some length, and when we had reached a complete impasse Bob from somewhere or other produced a bottle of superb malt whisky which was a great treat in those spartan times. We had a long drink of that and wished each other excellent health, and then we had another, and I have to confess that my memory of the rest of that night is a little hazy, but to the best of my recollection we shared the Parliamentary berth in turns until we reached our destination, and we managed to arrive in Edinburgh in remarkably good shape. . . . The whole weekend was typical of Bob's warmth and generosity, and it made a very welcome break indeed.*

This was not an unhappy period of his life. He had an important job to do, which he did conscientiously, and with characteristic enthusiasm and good humour. He was proud of his companions, although increasingly depressed by their high casualty rate. It would appear that his concerns became known to the authorities. His Station Commander, Taafe, liked and appreciated him, but considered that the job was a poor use of Boothby's talents. Like Churchill in the First World War when he was in France, the political urge was very strong, and Boothby knew that Taafe was right.

Rainsford's version is that

when we were working under considerable pressure and training reports were a little behind, I turned to him somewhat crossly and said, 'Bob, the trouble with you is that your home is in Edinburgh, your constituency is in Aberdeen, and your heart is in the House of Commons.' Bob replied with that utterly disarming smile of his, 'Sir, I couldn't have put it better myself!' There was nothing more to be said, and I wasn't at all surprised when a little later Bob decided that after all his real work in wartime lay in Parliament, and I in no way disagreed, but we all missed him a great deal, and I have never known anyone from a political background who fitted so happily and so readily into Service life.

It is not quite clear when Boothby became involved with the Free French in London, but his closest friend in Charles de Gaulle's entourage was General Legentilhomme. Boothby had his reservations about de Gaulle personally – as did everyone – but he warmed to his cause and to Legentilhomme, who urged him to leave his RAF wilderness and to return to London to help him. Taafe entirely agreed that his right place was in the Commons and signed his release. Although there had been few grumblings in East Aberdeenshire, Boothby was also becoming concerned about the difficulties, almost an impossibility, of representing a constituency whilst on active service, but he left the RAF with very mixed emotions in 1942. He was glad that he had joined, but was relieved to be back on the political scene.

It was during this time that Boothby had fallen in love again.

Dorothy kept closely in touch with him, but the difficulties of wartime travelling and his duties meant that they saw rather less of each other than before, even though Macmillan was abroad in North Africa and the

* F. F. Rainsford, *Memoirs of an Accidental Airman*, pp. 67–9. His book was published in 1986. The Foreword, written by Boothby, was the last of Boothby's published writings.

Mediterranean, where his achievements made his reputation and marked him out, somewhat unexpectedly, as a potentially major political figure. As at this time they were physically separated, Boothby met a young woman of great attractiveness, sparkle and high intelligence. They were both lonely, and their mutual attraction was almost immediate. They gave each other, and received, much happiness, which was to be enduring. As in the case of Dorothy, Boothby later destroyed her letters to him, but was not entirely successful. By then, love had developed into a deep and affectionate friendship, which lasted all Boothby's life, and which was fully shared by her children, who were devoted to him, as their letters to him – which he carefully kept – demonstrate. He willingly helped them in many ways, and took a close interest in their lives and concerns.

This was considerably more than a wartime romance, and it is important in Boothby's life. His political career may have been saved from disaster, but was certainly severely checked. He pined to return to the parliamentary arena and the political aspects of the war, but felt that it was his duty to serve in the armed forces, even in bleak Lincolnshire and wartime East Anglia. The strains on him were considerable, and he was certainly far from his usual environment. Into this somewhat depressing period came someone who became, and remained, very special to him. They had the great capacity to make each other laugh, which was probably more important to Boothby than to her. She also knew all about Dorothy and Boothby's other romantic adventures, but her effect on his morale and happiness was beyond all calculation. He would not have wanted her name mentioned, or any hints to her identity given, but the episode was so important in the restoration of his cheerfulness and self-confidence that it cannot be ignored by his biographer, whereas other far more casual encounters can be.

Boothby's affections were consistently rather too easily aroused, and he was often outrageously indiscreet and weak, but there were four women in his life for whom he had particular feelings that made them special (although there were others who thought they were special); these were (in no particular order) Dorothy, Diana, his second wife Wanda, and this lady, who fully merits an honoured mention in the strange odyssey of Boothby's life. For, at that grim time, he had great need of comfort, kindness and happiness, which she gave him in full measure, and for which he was for ever grateful.

In March 1941 Boothby saw Weininger at his internment camp and wrote a detailed report to Herbert Morrison, who had succeeded Anderson as Home Secretary:

I found him in a very low state both physically and psychologically, and inclined to cry at the slightest provocation. He kept on saying, 'It is incredible, not understandable, I simply cannot grasp it.' He kept on repeating, 'Why didn't they arrest me until September 17th 1940? Why did they let me go to Holland and Belgium with you if I was such a dangerous character? Why did they never bother about my private files, but only about my business ones? I love England, and have never done anything against her. This law was only made for the purpose of dealing with people who are against England. I know I am the victim of persecution from some quarter.'

All he asked for was a proper court or tribunal with powers to try him – and that went for everyone else in his position. 'If I have done anything against this country there is no punishment severe enough to suit my taste. I would not plead for detention, but for forced labour. But if I am found innocent, I want my liberty, and my name restored.'

Boothby again wrote to Morrison on 15 April:

It seems to me to be a travesty of justice, and a negation of everything for which we are now fighting. As you can see from the attached note which I made of one conversation I had with Weininger, there is no more subtle form of torture to a sensitive and intelligent man than being deliberately kept in ignorance of the reason for his imprisonment.

Early in May Boothby's campaign against 18B, led by Sir Irving Albery and with a small group of MPs, which included the Labour MP Sydney Silverman, and which had prompted an exasperated Morrison to make it a resigning issue, bore some fruit in the release of Weininger. It was not done very gracefully, but Boothby's reward was a telegram: 'You taught us to believe in friendship. We are unable to express our feelings. Trude.'

Boothby was also campaigning on behalf of Youth, making a passionate plea in the House of Commons in March 1942:

We are no longer young. You have to go into the Royal Air Force to realise that you are, after all, an old buffer. It is a salutary, if somewhat painful, experience. I have watched at close quarters what we in the House would call boys, almost babies, easily and competently discharging responsibilities much more onerous, much more pressing, much more poignant, than those discharged by any Member of the House, even on the front bench. Let us face the truth. For twenty years the politicians of this country have been frightened of youth. It was not by youth, which was rigorously excluded from power for twenty years, that we were conducted to the brink of disaster. Now, as always, when the follies of politicians have landed us in war, we turn to youth to get us out of it. My plea is that not only while the tempest rages should youth be given a chance, but also after it is over.

On 2 March 1942 he drew the lessons of the naval disasters in the Far East and the escape of the *Scharnhorst* and *Gneisenau* from Brest, ridiculing Churchill's rather lame explanation that this had, in fact, been beneficial. 'In that case,' Boothby remarked, 'it seems to me that we should have escorted the ships.' While supporting the bombing offensive against Germany, as 'the only method available to us at present of striking directly against Germany', he called for naval construction to have the absolute priority. As the speech also contained advice to the First Lord of the Admiralty to 'deprive us of one of his weekend speeches and study the papers of Mahan, [from which] he would derive consolation as well as profit,' this contribution was not widely regarded as helpful.

Under the anonymity of 'Back Bencher' he had gone much further in the *New Statesman* on 23 February:

If Mr Churchill continues to ignore his parliamentary critics, and refuses to make the necessary changes, there will be a head-on clash between the executive and the legislature. And the legislature will win. . . . Mr Churchill has carried personal loyalty to mediocre subordinates to a point at which it has become a positive danger to the state. . . . Mr Churchill is the right, the inevitable Prime Minister. But it would be a dangerous mistake for him to assume that if, for any reason, he ceased to be Prime Minister we should lose the war. There is no lack of unity, or of purpose, amongst our people. It is up to Mr Churchill to give them increased heart, and a greater sense of urgency, by deeds as well as words.

This was a very widespread view. The euphoria of the arrival into the war on the Allied side of the Russians in June 1941 and the Americans in December, after the bombing of the American naval base in Pearl Harbor, had been followed by the disillusionment of defeat virtually everywhere. Churchill's imperfections were magnified by his critics, and he himself, unusually, was disconsolate. This was not surprising, as it was the darkest moment in the war.

By June 1942, with the British forces in defeat and disarray in North Africa and the Far East, the surrender of the garrison at Tobruk was the final event that brought together the critics of the Government. On 25 June Sir John Wardlaw-Milne, a senior and influential MP and Chairman of the all-Party Finance Committee, tabled a motion that read: 'That this House, while paying tribute to the heroism and endurance of the armed forces of the Crown in circumstances of exceptional difficulty, has no confidence in the central direction of the war.' To make matters even worse, it was announced that Sir Roger Keyes and Hore-Belisha would be prominent supporters of this motion of no confidence. Reactions abroad were primarily those of astonishment that, with Rommel almost at the gates of Cairo, such a motion should appear and be debated in the House of Commons. Churchill met the challenge robustly and arranged for the motion to be debated on 1 and 2 July.

Boothby was urgently summoned to attend the debate. He later related:

I lunched in the House of Commons. Churchill, whom I had not seen or heard from since my case, was sitting alone in a corner of the dining-room. To my amazement he beckoned to me to come over. It was the only time during the war that I saw him looking anxious. 'This', he said, 'is going to be a critical debate. Do you still support us?' I said that I did. Then: 'Do you still support me?' I said: 'I have no reason to, but there is no one else.' Then he said: 'Will you speak in the debate?' I replied that I had brought some notes. Whereupon he took me straight to the Speaker, and told him that he would like me to be called fifth in the debate.

Boothby's task was made immeasurably easier by the fact that Wardlaw-Milne wrecked what had been an impressive speech in a tense and full House by proposing that the Duke of Gloucester should be made Commander-in-Chief of all the British armed forces. Boothby's speech, the first major one since his disgrace, made a strong impression, Churchill himself describing it as 'powerful and helpful', the only reference to Boothby in that volume of his war memoirs. Boothby said:

When all is said and done, this is the Government, and this is the Prime Minister, who 'stood when earth's foundations fell'. . . . There is no reason for this House, or for the country, to lose spirit because of a tactical reverse in the North African desert.

There were also some characteristic asides – 'Committees are the curse of this country,' and 'The British Empire was not created by men who were miserable and melancholy. It was created by men who were merry, and I think that there are limits to the value of purposeless austerity,' which went down well.

The motion of censure was swept aside. Churchill asked Boothby to have a drink with him in the Smoking Room, where he proposed a toast to 'the Pegasus wings of Bob's oratory'. When Boothby returned to his station he found a telegram: 'I am so grateful. Winston.' As Boothby later wrote, 'and then he didn't speak to me again for a year. I had done my job.'

'The war is going beautifully, isn't it?' Boothby wrote to Compton Mackenzie. 'I could say a mouthful, but am frightened of censors. Made a speech in the H of C the other day, and the buggers cheered me when I got up, and again when I sat down, which was something.'

In August Boothby attended an experimental Scottish National Parliament meeting in Edinburgh, for which he received special leave, and took the opportunity of staying with Compton Mackenzie on Barra, which had its invariable restorative effect. Boothby wrote appreciatively:

Nowhere else in the world do I find a comparable happiness and – serenity is the only word I can think of. Now I return to God knows what like a giant refreshed. And no 'Retreat is necessary.'

The first meeting of the 'Scottish National Parliament' was a pretty dismal fiasco.

We were treated to a discourse on the distribution of whisky by Tom Johnston (I could have told him a thing or two about that), and some observations on the subject of Town Councillors by Lord Alness (who I thought was dead).

To the horrified dismay of all present, and particularly of Geordie Buchanan, a 'vote of thanks' was then moved; and we were told that, if we were good, we could see some 'educational' films next door. 'I like my films to have a love interest,' said Jock McEwen, as he hurriedly left the building, accompanied by yours truly. Not an auspicious start. But perhaps better than nothing.

It looks as if Stalingrad will fall tonight: alas! I have no Pol Roger 1928. I shall have to console myself by describing it to Leslie Hore-Belisha, while I show him how to fill his fountain pen.

During his period of exile, often miserable and on some occasions drinking too much, Boothby had brooded on how he could continue his rehabilitation. His relations with Churchill remained very distant, but he assumed, as did most other people, that Churchill would retire when the war ended and be succeeded by Eden, who, in spite of their very different temperaments, did not forget Boothby's staunchness in opposing appeasement and sympathised with his social and economic arguments. Eden also knew a great deal about matrimonial and emotional problems, and often took de Gaulle's side against Churchill. Boothby also assumed that the Old Guard that had so hated both himself and Eden – and still did – would fade away. Moreover, at that time he believed that the Conservatives would win the post-war general election, and that he would have a high claim for at least minor office.

These were perfectly reasonable assumptions, which were widely shared, and not least by Beaverbrook, with whom he kept closely in touch, and who was now equally disillusioned with Churchill. Unfortunately for Boothby, they turned out to be totally wrong in every respect.

When an active politician is down and depressed, this can take many courses. In Boothby's case, his temperament was such that his depression did not last long. His constituents, urged on by Gardie Duff, were totally staunch. His friends stood by him, and he by them. As has been related, he even went to see Mosley in prison. When this became known his enemies were abusive; others were impressed. All Mosley did was to rail against the unfairness of his incarceration until, on a prearranged signal of Boothby blowing his nose, the Governor ended the ordeal. There is a detailed report by the Prison Governor of this meeting: 'The visit then turned into a "public meeting" with Sir Oswald as the speaker – no, the orator – and Mr Boothby the audience.' It was typical of Boothby, and a gesture that the Mosleys never forgot. Nor did others, in a different sense.

When Churchill had been down in the post-1918 period, he had turned to writing to justify himself and his record, and had succeeded triumphantly. Lloyd George had not been so successful. For once, Boothby followed Churchill's example.

It was now generally recognised that he had been absolutely right on foreign affairs and defence, although this was accepted with considerable reluctance in some quarters. But Boothby believed, and with cause, that his record on economic matters had been equally important, and he was concerned that although Britain would probably have learnt its lesson on the perils of disarmament and isolation from Europe, there was no reason to believe that it had learnt the economic lessons. Richard Kahn of King's College, Cambridge, Roy Harrod of Christ Church, Oxford, and Thomas Balogh all urged him to write more on the subject, and offered their assistance and advice.

What Boothby envisaged was an economic tract with two purposes: to vindicate his own record, and to put forward compelling arguments for future Conservative policies. So he embarked on what became *The New Economy*.

Boothby's thesis was a familiar one. The root causes of the war were economic, and the follies of the 1920s had led to unnecessary hardship, deflation, mass unemployment and the rise of the dictators; as usual, the Bank of England and the Treasury were mercilessly assailed for their narrowness of view and faith in *laissez-faire*. 'The overthrow of Hitlerism will not restore the nineteenth-century capitalist system any more than the downfall of Napoleon restored feudalism.' He urged the nationalisation of the Bank of England and, more remarkably, 'the transformation of the banking system from a private profit-making concern into a public service', and controls over interest rates. Indeed, the whole thrust of his proposals was for a far greater degree of central government control than William Beveridge was proposing, or much of the Labour Party envisaged. Full employment was the objective. Of the servicemen he wrote:

What is it they want when they get back? Not pensions or doles or even homes for heroes; but, quite simply, jobs. THEY WANT TO BE WANTED. They do not want to be left to rot in idleness, and to be made to feel, as so many of them were made to feel before the war, that it is of no great consequence whether they are alive or dead.

Economists can debate Boothby's prescription and his proposed cures, but *The New Economy* aroused such interest and comment because his long-held views were now becoming widely more popular, and especially in the post-Beveridge debate. Also, although part of the purpose was self-justificatory, to which he was entitled, it was the thinking about the future that was attractive, particularly coming from a Conservative. It was also a major step in Boothby's return to the political scene, and important to the restoration of his self-confidence. Beaverbrook assisted the process with a kind note: 'A good friend always gives a good word at the right time – and you are it. Yours ever, Max.'

Many years later, in 1958, Boothby recorded the first occasion on which he met General de Gaulle, which was at a small private lunch with Sir Edward Louis Spears the day after he had flown over to Britain and delivered the broadcast to the French people which 'reverberated around the world':

The immediate impact of de Gaulle's personality was unforgettable and overwhelming. So far as I remember, there were only five of us at the luncheon table and he did not talk much: but every word he said counted.

He repeated, in crisp phrases and without any visible signs of emotion, what he had said over the radio – that France still had an Empire which could unite with that of Britain which held the seas and was continuing the struggle. He went on to elaborate, at no great length, upon this theme. But the dominant impression he made, which remains as vivid today as it was at the time, was one of singleness of purpose, total conviction and utter sincerity. It was difficult to believe that, at that moment of time, he stood almost alone.

At a later stage in the war I was closely associated with General Legentilhomme, de Gaulle's principal military adviser in London, and eventually Minister of War in the Free French Government at Algiers.

From this vantage-point it was possible to get a pretty close view of de Gaulle's wartime activities.

He was stubborn, aloof, intransigent, a thorn in everyone's flesh. .

He made no concessions because, as he truly said, he was not strong enough to make concessions. He fought with Roosevelt and with Churchill, to whom on occasion he said things that no one else would have dreamed of daring to say.

Above all, he fought for France, in whose greatness and glory he passionately believed. He remained always the incarnation of the soul of the French people: and, when the hour of deliverance arrived, he was accepted by them as their saviour.

Despite all he suffered at his hands (and suffer is the appropriate word) the final and characteristically generous verdict of Churchill's stands: 'I always admired his massive strength.'

Boothby was keen to assist de Gaulle and to offer practical help to the fledgling Free French Government in Exile.

Boothby's former secretary, Marjorie Brooks, had been widowed when her husband had been one of the victims of the pre-war disaster when the submarine *Thetis* had sunk on trials. She was not only a qualified secretary but spoke fluent French, so, at Boothby's suggestion, she went to work with the Free French; as they had no money she worked unpaid for the first year, but it was a sacrifice she willingly made, and which was to have momentous results for her and for Boothby.

Marjorie had remarried another naval officer and, as Marjorie Smith, introduced Legentilhomme to Boothby. Their mutual attraction was immediate and developed into close friendship.

General Paul Legentilhomme, who had served under Allenby in Palestine in the Great War, had refused to accept the 1940 armistice and had declared for de Gaulle. He was then commanding in East Africa but eventually, on de Gaulle's insistence, had reached London to join him.

Boothby later described Legentilhomme as 'one of the nicest and most intelligent generals I have ever known', and entirely agreed with his unfulfilled post-war ambition to withdraw French forces from Indo-China. Legentilhomme knew and liked Ho Chi Minh, and was convinced that a peaceful settlement was possible; he was ignored. He became Military Governor of Paris and was given an honorary knighthood by the British, but only de Gaulle listened to him about Vietnam. Churchill hardly listened to de Gaulle at all, but Legentilhomme told Boothby that at the end of a particularly difficult meeting Churchill asked, 'Am I to understand that you are prepared to make no concessions at all?', to which de Gaulle replied that 'At the moment, Prime Minister, I am too weak to make any concessions.' In Boothby's later account, 'Legentilhomme said that he then detected a glint of admiration in Churchill's eyes.' Boothby subsequently accused Churchill to his face of underestimating de Gaulle, saying that 'he is in your class, and that is where the historians will put him'. Churchill, according to Boothby, did not reply.

Whereas de Gaulle's relationships with Churchill and Roosevelt – and, indeed, most British and Americans – were at best bleak, and usually stormy, Legentilhomme, with his perfect English and deep respect for the British army, charmed everyone. De Gaulle saw no need to cultivate political friends in Britain, although he developed a high opinion of Eden, who supported him strongly and courageously, but Legentilhomme did.

Although Legentilhomme realised that Boothby's relationship with Churchill was virtually non-existent, and that his political fortunes were temporarily at a low point, he knew him to be a good friend of France; and, unlike others, regarded him as an important political personality. He asked Boothby to act in effect as an 'unpaid, informal and useful' friend of the Free French in Parliament, to which Boothby enthusiastically agreed.

What neither anticipated was that it was Boothby who successfully pressed for Legentilhomme to command the French forces in the 1944 Anglo-French recapture of Madagascar, or that Marjorie, whose second husband was killed in action in 1943, would marry Legentilhomme in 1947.

The frustrations of the Free French were well expressed in a letter from Legentilhomme to Boothby on 17 November 1942:

> On June 16th 1940, without worrying about what the other military leaders in the Empire were doing, not knowing anything about General De Gaulle, I telegraphed to the Foreign Office and to General Wavell, telling them that I would continue at Jibuti to fight side by side with Great Britain.
>
> What was my situation at that moment? I had 9,000 men under my command in Somaliland. In East Africa the Italians had 300,000 men, 47,000 of them already massed on the frontiers of French and British Somaliland ready to attack. In spite of that I made my decision to continue, since honour, and honour only, required it of me. I could not admit that France should disown her signature to Great Britain, who would now have to bear alone the weight of the war against Germany and Italy.
>
> And now what do we see?
>
> America negotiating with the traitors who covered themselves with dishonour in June 1940, with [Admiral] Darlan, who is twice a traitor, ready to betray for the third time if ever the Germans set foot again in North Africa, negotiating with [General] Noguès, [Yves] Chatel, [Admiral] Esteva, who in 1940 accepted that France should disown her signature, and who are now trying to save their skins and their situations under American protection.
>
> We see the amazing paradox of a Great Power calling itself Democratic, protecting in North Africa those who apply the Fascist regimes of Vichy. Do you think that the French people will accept that situation?
>
> What can they think, these Frenchmen in France and abroad when they see that the so-called 'United Nations' are ready to drop those who have never ceased to fight side by side with them, those who have always remained loyal to the democratic ideals? What can they think of the nations who are now ready to uphold those who betrayed them and who still remain faithful to their Fascist ideals?
>
> In whom can we have confidence?
>
> As far as I am concerned, so long as the situation is not made perfectly clear, I shall not go to Madagascar. I refuse to risk being forced, perhaps by a British General acting under the orders of his Government, or of the American Supreme Command, to accept to serve under the command of the traitor Darlan or of any other Quisling the Americans may have found. Having been named a rebel because at Jibuti I refused to obey the orders of Weygand and of Darlan (who at the beginning of July 1940 gave the order to attack British merchant and war ships whenever they were encountered)

... having twice been condemned to death, first by order of Laval's Government and afterwards by order of Darlan's, I will never accept their authority.

The Americans can easily find a Quisling who will be only too glad to continue to assure the Fascist Administration of Vichy, or of Darlan, at Madagascar, where I was given the mission of restoring the laws of the French Republic.

Nothing can astonish me any more, even to find myself one day in a British concentration camp for having never ceased to be loyal to Great Britain! And I can assure you that a certain anxiety is arising not only for a certainty amongst the French Fighting Forces, but also among the smaller Allied Powers who are beginning to fear that they themselves will one day be sacrificed in the same way to satisfy the politics of the Great Powers.

Munich has not yet been forgotten!

Finally it can easily be seen that it will be Stalin who will benefit from all this by forming around him when peace is declared the Communist Union of Europe.

To Legentilhomme's great satisfaction Darlan was assassinated not long afterwards, but the basic problems remained, not assisted by Roosevelt's invincible ignorance of European politics and detestation of de Gaulle. Legentilhomme and de Gaulle could not comprehend what British policy towards their country was, and these tensions were manifested graphically in Legentilhomme's letters to Boothby, who quickly changed from 'Dear Mr Boothby' to '*Mon cher ami*'. Boothby sympathised totally with him and de Gaulle, which did not endear him further to the British Government. In his own way de Gaulle – whom Boothby and Legentilhomme often referred to as 'De God', but not as irreverently as might appear, as they admired him deeply – was grateful. In 1960, when he was President of France, he wrote of Boothby to Legentilhomme that '*Je n'oublié pas l'amitié qu'il a si souvent manifesté à l'égard de la France* [I have never forgotten the friendship which he has so often expressed towards France]' He also once remarked to Legentilhomme, '*Votre ami Boothby est intelligent* [Your friend Boothby is intelligent]'; Marjorie related this to Boothby, writing, 'And that from de Gaulle is really something.' How de Gaulle and Legentilhomme repaid their debt of gratitude for Boothby's staunch support will be seen later.*

Boothby's role was to help the Free French by newspaper articles, speeches and questions in the Commons, and in conversations with ministers – particularly with Eden, by far the most sympathetic – putting forward the case for the de Gaulle Free French to be regarded as the legitimate government and voice of the French people. As relations

*See p. 351.

between de Gaulle, Churchill and Roosevelt became sulphurous, his endeavours did not commend themselves to Downing Street, but he persevered. Indeed, he found that the mere threat to table a parliamentary question often had the desired effect – as it did in the case of the Madagascar command. But his task was made immensely easier by the deep respect Legentilhomme enjoyed in the British military. Men who could not abide de Gaulle's imperial aloofness were entranced by Legentilhomme's good humour, courtesy and understanding of British problems; he was also, as they knew, a superb professional soldier.

For his part, Legentilhomme rated Boothby's role very highly, and was deeply appreciative of his kindness, friendship and devotion to the Free French cause. He knew all about Boothby's vicissitudes and deficiencies from Marjorie, and respected him all the more. Boothby liked and admired him intensely, and their correspondence has an exceptional warmth.*

Boothby's work for the Free French had its thankless aspects. Relations between Churchill and de Gaulle varied, but were usually strained, and Boothby invariably took the latter's side. After the successful landings in Normandy in June 1944, de Gaulle was refused permission by the British to go to France. Boothby was incensed and was given special permission by the Speaker to move the adjournment of the House of Commons to debate 'the refusal of His Majesty's Government to allow General de Gaulle to go to France'. So great was the sensation that Churchill was urgently summoned and arrived 'in a towering rage'. He said that if Boothby persisted, he would insist upon a secret session; Boothby accordingly withdrew his motion. A few days later de Gaulle was given permission to return to his country in triumph, and Churchill's fury against Boothby was so intense that the veteran Labour MP David Kirkwood

came up to me with an anxious look, put his arm round my shoulder and said: 'Bob, that man doesn't like you. Be careful. He could do you great harm.' I thanked him for his kindness and concern, but added, 'I don't think that, in the long run, he will.'

For his part, de Gaulle never thanked Boothby, and merely remarked coldly to Legentilhomme that 'I see your friend Boothby has been kicking up a fuss about me in the House of Commons!'

* * *

*In 1985, the year before his death, Boothby – by then a shadow of his former self – visited Marjorie at her flat in Villefranche-sur-Mer near Nice, where, on the promenade, there is a memorial to Legentilhomme. Boothby looked at it for a long time and then said, 'My God, I wish I could have been like him.'

The New Economy had impressed many people who were concerned with the post-war world, and Boothby was invited to attend a series of meetings in Oxford when Beveridge was preparing his second report on 'Full Employment in a Free Society', which Boothby considered more important than his first. He did not agree with all of its proposals, but wholeheartedly accepted – as he had urged for years – that the state has a responsibility for the employment of its citizens, and that full employment not only makes for a happier society but a more efficient one; this could only be achieved by a substantial increase in production by what Alexander Hamilton called 'the incitement and patronage of government'. Boothby did not consider that nationalisation, the Labour Party's traditional solution, was the answer at all. As he pointed out, Labour thinking on economic matters was curiously sterile, and there was no discernible strategy. But, with the exception of a few thinkers, notably people like R. A. Butler, Woolton and Boothby, much the same could be said of the Conservatives.

There was a dangerous feeling in Britain in 1943 and the first months of 1944 that the war was as good as won. North Africa had been swept clear of the Germans; the Italians had surrendered; the Battle of the Atlantic had – at terrible cost – been definitely won; Germany was being pounded virtually every night by the British and the Americans; and the Allies were firmly established in Italy. In the war against Japan, also, the tide had turned decisively, both in Burma and the Pacific. The pressure in Britain for 'A Second Front Now' was based on the entirely false popular assumption, fanned by Beaverbrook in particular, that the recapture of Europe would be a relatively easy affair. Churchill's warnings that there was still a very long way to go, and that the Germans and Japanese were far from defeated, were listened to with some impatience. Post-war planning was the major topic, whereas Churchill took the view that actually winning the war was the dominant priority. He was right, but this was not the national mood at that time, and gave rise to what became a widespread feeling that a great war leader is not necessarily suitable for peace; and the memories of life under the Conservatives in the inter-war years were, for millions of people, unhappy ones.

Boothby, deprived of any role in the conduct of the war apart from his assistance to the Free French, turned all his energies into producing a plan for a mixed economy that was based overwhelmingly on private enterprise, investment, and real incentives in the context of a national and international strategy. To do so in the context of a largely sluggish private sector and a trade-union movement that was narrow-minded, overpowerful, divided and selfish was not an easy task. 'Thus,' as Boothby wrote, 'the national economy is being forced to keep pace with the slowest. It is the negation of enterprise and progress; and, if it continues, we shall all be starving and freezing in perfect equality.' The increasing importance of the 'closed shop' was a case in point. Boothby warned against its evils, 'the path that leads direct to the totalitarian corporate state', but it was to take nearly forty years for a Conservative government to pluck up the courage to deal with this menace – which promptly collapsed with hardly a whimper, let alone a battle.

Boothby was careful, in calling for a centrally planned economy, that the mechanisms should be 'positive and creative, and not negative and restrictive . . . we are suffering at present from too much "planning" at the lower levels, and too little constructive planning at the highest level of all'.

Here were some of the national problems, but they could not be seen in isolation. Boothby, ever since 1928, had urged that some kind of European economic union was essential for European recovery. Also, the sterling area must be made into 'an economically interdependent group of nations pursuing a common economic policy', with London as its financial centre.

The foundations of his international approach were, therefore, the Empire and Western Europe. The trouble was that the United States had become the greatest single power and the greatest creditor nation. As Boothby discovered, when he returned to America in February 1945 as a journalist covering the United Nations meetings in Washington and San Francisco and as a lecturer, American politicians and economists were in some confusion about their country's role after the war, except for a large measure of agreement that it was not going to prop up 'British imperialism', about which most seemed obsessed. To Boothby's horror, the Bretton Woods Conference was concerned exclusively with monetary policy and the dominant role of gold. The International Monetary Fund was not only going to be based in Washington and be American-dominated, but this very dominance would be to the detriment of the sterling area and certainly would not assist Boothby's vision of European economic unity. Indeed, it would be disastrous for both. In spite of frequent assurances by ministers, on no occasion did the House of Commons debate Bretton Woods. Boothby wrote:

We have agreed, on paper, to hand over world economic power, and with it economic domination over every country outside the control of the Soviet Union, to the United States. In so doing, we have stabilized our own poverty, and rendered our recovery virtually impossible without further aid from, and dependence on, the United States. Out of £28 billion of monetary gold in the world, they now possess 23. There is nothing in this Agreement to lead one to suppose that their conception of international trade has got beyond that of a further exchange of goods for gold or debt.

It also made nonsense of all the talk in Britain of the merits of a planned economy because, as Boothby pointed out repeatedly, Bretton Woods meant tying the British economy to the largest deliberately unplanned economy in the world.

Boothby was one of the very few – certainly in the House of Commons – who realised the scale of what was at stake. In the summer and autumn of 1944, with British and American forces fighting together in Europe, with the Anglo-American air armada battering Germany, and with Roosevelt's presidential re-election campaign, the last thing the British Government desired was an argument with the Americans on the post-war international economic regime. Indeed, it did not want it even debated in Parliament. Frustrated, Boothby took up his pen to denounce the Bretton Woods negotiations, which he described as 'a calamity and a racket', and tried to rally powerful support both in Britain and in America. He had the burning conviction that he was, again, right. So he was, but, again, people had other preoccupations. It took the 1945 American Loan, which had to be spent exclusively on American goods, and the abrupt ending of Lend-Lease, to bring home to British politicians what the new realities were. By then, it was too late.

So vehement were Boothby's views on what was happening at Bretton Woods, which in effect was not only a return to the pre-war economic anarchy but one dominated by the Americans, with the level of monetary gold absurdly low – that of 1933 – that when early in 1945 he was invited to deliver a series of lectures in the United States, Eden gave him permission on the strict understanding that he would not speak about Bretton Woods.

Boothby sailed to New York in the great liner *Queen Mary* in her drab wartime grey, unescorted and travelling at great speed, with frequent changes of direction, and conveying thousands of wounded American servicemen home. There were only six other civilian passengers, but as they included Tommy Beecham and his wife Betty Humby, Malcolm Sargent and the American actress Katherine Cornell, Boothby was well content. So were they, as Boothby's mother had supplied him lavishly with whisky. 'This was much appreciated,' Boothby cabled her.

Boothby could never have enough of Beecham, who gave him access to his rehearsals and dined with him frequently. Beecham's rich personality, with his famous caustic comments on the abilities and otherwise of his musical colleagues, was attraction enough, but he was deeply serious about his profession and about music, one of the dominant fascinations of

Boothby's life. Although Beecham admired Sargent, especially as a choir-master, he liked to poke fun at him. When Boothby told him that Sargent had been in a convoy in Palestine that had been attacked by Arabs, Beecham's comment was, 'I had no idea that the Arabs were so musical.' Archie Newman's collected *Beecham Stories* and Neville Cardus' memoir were among Boothby's favourite reading, but were a poor substitute for the real thing. Beecham conducting Delius was, for Boothby, sheer perfection. 'Now that he is gone,' he wrote after Beecham's death, 'I don't think we shall ever hear the authentic voice of Delius again.' He particularly recalled a concert at the Edinburgh Festival when 'the ravishing sound reduced his Usher Hall audience to stricken silence'. The fact that Beecham admired Boothby's musical knowledge and dis-crimination was made plain when he proposed that he should become Chairman of the Royal Philharmonic Orchestra, which in due course Boothby did, to its immense advantage. This was an aspect of his life and character that often came as a considerable surprise to those who saw only the politician, journalist and media personality, but it was a supremely important one.

Boothby later related of the voyage:

The night before we got to New York, we had a brains' trust. I was the question master, and I put one of my own. 'To what extent was Richard Wagner responsible for the Nazi movement?' In all my life I have never heard two more brilliant speeches than those which were made by Beecham and Sargent. Needless to say, Wagner was completely exonerated. The packed audience of wounded American soldiers, most of whom had never heard of Wagner, sat spellbound.

When he reached New York the information he received from his friends about Bretton Woods – and particularly from Baruch and Bill Wasserman – so alarmed him that he wrote to the *New York Times* raising some very pertinent questions. His letter was not only published, but the paper came out strongly on Boothby's side in a major editorial. Boothby's opposition to what was going on was one thing; the hostility of the *New York Times* was serious. There was much fury at his conduct in London and in Washington.

Boothby realised that he had caused a furore when he received 'two long telegrams of anguish from our Ambassador in Washington, Lord Halifax. When, eventually, I reached Washington, I found that everyone was absolutely furious with me. . . . Distant rumbles swept across the Atlantic from Anderson, the Chancellor of the Exchequer, and from Eden.'

Boothby was summoned to see Halifax. Isaiah Berlin, who adorned the

British Embassy with his intellect, company and wit, told him that 'The first ten minutes will be very sticky, because he [Halifax] is as angry as he is capable of being – which isn't much. I know it will be difficult for you, but try to be humble. The signal that the tension has begun to relax will be when he asks his horrible little dog to jump into his lap.' Boothby's later account of his meeting with Halifax was:

When I was shown into his room he was sitting at his desk, looking both grave and sad. I began by saying: '*Peccavi*,' hoping to impress him with my knowledge of Latin. He replied: 'You have indeed.' But when, after about ten minutes, he asked his dog to jump into his lap, I burst out laughing. For this I received a well-deserved look of reproach.

Boothby was staying with Wasserman and his wife in Washington. Wasserman, who was also an old and valued friend of Weininger's – who was in the process of restoring his fortunes in America after his expulsion from Britain, where he had been declared a prohibited immigrant – invited the Vice-President, Henry Wallace, to lunch. He accepted, but then rang up to say that he had received instructions that he could not meet Boothby. According to Boothby, Berlin telephoned from the British Embassy to say that he could not be seen in public with Boothby, but that he knew of an excellent but small fish restaurant where no one would recognise them and where they could lunch together. Boothby's version of this allegedly clandestine meeting is hotly disputed by Berlin. 'I *don't* believe it,' he wrote indignantly to Boothby in 1978. 'I don't *wish* to believe it: too craven, even for me: moreover the fish restaurant, I remember it well, in Connecticut Av was the best-known establishment in the capital.' Boothby stuck by his version, and Berlin by his. On this occasion I do not accept Boothby's version.

Boothby's criticisms of the Americans, Keynes* and the whole Bretton Woods scheme had also caused a storm in London. Eden was indeed furious, and the *Daily Express* called for Boothby's immediate recall before he did more damage.

On 25 March, writing from Washington, Boothby gave Beaverbrook his most detailed description of the situation as it then was:

Personal
Dear Max
Your Mr. Maurice Webb was quite wrong when he wrote that, in view of my interest in Bretton Woods, I should come home. For the issue of Bretton Woods is being decided here. And, as far as I can see, we shall have little say in the matter, one way or the other.

---

* This was the only occasion on which they had a major disagreement.

I would like to give you a brief outline of the situation, from my point of view.

In order to give lectures in this country I had to obtain a special permit. It was therefore reasonable for Anthony Eden to ask, and for me to agree, that I should not lecture on the subject of Bretton Woods. I faithfully carried out this undertaking. In the twenty odd lectures I have now delivered I have never referred to it, even by implication.

Nor was there any great temptation to do so. In the middle west, interest in Bretton Woods is practically non-existent.

Not so in Washington. Here the administration is attempting to steam-roller the agreement through Congress, as a 'must' proposition, without amendment, and as quickly as possible.

The arguments advanced in favour of this course are (1) that it is a big step back along the road to an international gold standard and free multilateral trade; (2) that it is the first, and the most important, test of America's willingness to re-enter the international field; and (3) that as it was drawn up and signed by experts of forty-three countries, it would be necessary to call the whole bloody lot together again if a single comma was altered.

Contrast this with Keynes' assurances to us that it is the exact reverse of the gold standard, and that discriminatory trade agreements will be permissible: and with John Anderson's observation that the clarification of certain obscurities in the text is essential.

What clearly emerges is that, as agreement on certain fundamental objectives was not achieved, the FINAL ACT can only be put through at this juncture on the tacit understanding that it is differently interpreted in Great Britain and the USA.

Argue it as you will, these are dishonest tactics. And I don't believe that, in the long run, any good can come of them. Nor does Barney Baruch. He puts the blame on Keynes. I think they are all in it. And for this reason. I put some questions in a letter to the *New York Times*, to which I genuinely – if naïvely – thought some answers might be given which would, at least to some extent, clarify the positions. You can't imagine the heat that was then turned on. It came via the Embassy, but it came from the Treasury here. I have now had to promise to make no further comment on Bretton Woods, either orally or in writing, as long as I am in this country – on the ground that it is embarrassing both to the USG and to HMG. This goes for articles written for the press either here or at home! Of course Halifax is perfectly entitled to make this request, or any other – although it is a rather odd comment on democracy. But the fact that it *is* embarrassing to both Governments proves that the questions, which were of vital importance, cannot be answered. And I have since been told, privately, that this is the case.

Now for the politics of the business. Some of the opposition to Bretton Woods comes from Republicans as such, who will oppose anything put forward by this administration. Some of it comes from those who believe that any attempt at currency stabilisation is premature, that we in Great Britain have a special problem of our own to solve before we can hope to restore equilibrium in our balance of payments, and that the solution of that problem is an essential condition of ultimate world recovery. They genuinely want to help us solve it. For instance it has been suggested to me that the US treasury might place a credit of US five billion dollars at our disposal, which would bear no interest charge, in return for a sterling credit of an equal amount, to be used for the purpose of enabling American business to start new enterprises within the British Empire.

Those who support Bretton Woods are not at all so well disposed towards us. Listen to this, from Mr. Edward Brown, Chairman of the First National Bank of Chicago, and a likely American representative on the management committee of the fund:

'Since voting rights in the fund and control of its management are closely related to the quotas of various countries, and since the United States has the largest quota, *I think it can reasonably be assumed that the American viewpoint will dominate the management of the fund*. Furthermore, if, as is certain to be the case, the American dollar is the currency most in demand after the war, the knowledge on the part of other countries that the United States can withdraw if its viewpoint is flouted by the management *should practically ensure recognition of our views by the fund*.'

My own conviction is that they are frightened of three things – the ultimate fate of the gold hoard, the pulling power of our market, and the possibility of a revival of the sterling area. Now it is not open to argument or doubt that Bretton Woods puts gold right back on the map, accepts the bargaining power of export services as against that of markets, and prevents the re-establishment of a sterling area, which if it is anything, is a 'discriminatory currency arrangement'.

Indeed, it may well be too late. For what, in fact, is going to happen? Either the Bretton Woods agreement will be rejected by Congress, or passed as it stands. I have been told that the questions I asked, and Dr. White's inability to answer them, have influenced some of the Senators against it. I hope to God this is true. If the fund is postponed, which the opposition is asking, it will give us all a breathing space.

In any event, I don't regret having written my letter. Mercifully I have no political career to worry about. And at least it has convinced a number of people who matter, and who were unaware of it, that there is a British side to the case.

It isn't easy to contend against the cumulative power of two formidable administrations, with all the technique and apparatus of modern government at their command!

What is going to be the result?

Without even a say-so, we shall almost certainly find ourselves called upon to abrogate the final authority of Parliament over a wide sector of the economic field and hand it over to an international authority, situated in the United States, on which we shall be in a minority.

This authority will be governed by an infinitely complicated voting procedure: and subject to a set of rules which, in so far as they are intelligible, are capable of various interpretations. In addition the quotas, of the member countries, will bear little relationship to their credit requirements.

The tragedy of it is that, from the many conversations I have had with businessmen in New York and Congressmen so far here, I am absolutely convinced that we could have come to a good arrangement with the United States by direct and simple and straight-forward negotiation, either as the Great Britain they want to assist, or as the centre of a reconstituted sterling area. Then we should have known what we were doing, and built on solid ground.

As it is, we are being invited to plunge in the dark into a morass of 'multilateralism' and 'universalism'. And when this thing breaks down – as it is bound to do, for no international currency stabilisation fund can restore equilibrium to a shattered and distorted world – we shall find ourselves confused and bracketed in the mind of the American public with every little defaulting tuppenny-halfpenny country on earth.

One question I would like to ask you, in conclusion. How is the Tory party going to emerge from all this? I joined it, and have stayed in it, because I believed it stood for individual freedom, rational social reform, the strength and economic development of the British Empire, and a prosperous British agriculture. Admittedly it has pursued these objectives with a pretty faint spirit during the past twenty years. But no one else has shown any inclination to pursue them at all. What the hell it will stand for if Bretton Woods goes through, I don't know. If we want a prosperous agriculture, we shall have to exercise some form of control over the import of food. If we want a prosperous Empire (including Great Britain) we shall have to make reciprocal trade agreements in terms of money as well as goods. How do these things square with 'no member shall, without the approval of the fund, impose restrictions on the making of payments and transfers for current international transactions'?

We shall find that, in the opinion of the United States, they don't square.

In 1923 I stood as a Protectionist. I am still a Protectionist.

I believe that the uncontrolled interplay of supply and demand of unregulated international markets is no longer a practical proposition: and that a high degree of purposive direction of trade is essential, if chaos & periodic slumps are to be averted, and if depression in one country is to be prevented from spreading to others.

The demand of the workers for social security and reasonable wage standards involves not only a protected but also a planned economic system. In other words, the exercise by the State of a limited number of vital strategic controls over the national economy as a whole. I don't know if this is Socialism. I do know that, in the modern world, complete 'laissez-faire' capitalism means the complete control of the economic system by 'BIG BUSINESS'. A two months' tour of the USA is conclusive evidence of that. And I think that the small man is likely to fare better under the first alternative.

Without undue enthusiasm, I prefer the Treasury and the Board of Trade to a mysterious and complicated international fund, operating in secret and abroad – and to Baron Boel.

For one thing, you can ask them questions.

Yours ever
Bob

P.S. Since writing the above I have had a magnificent piece of news. The Federal Government have turned off the heat, and abandoned the attempt to 'railroad' Bretton Woods before San Francisco. I claim no special credit.

But two or three Senators, who I met privately at tea, said 'they were telling us that complete agreement had been reached on every detail, that the British government was pressing for ratification before San Francisco & regarded it as a test of our sincerity, and that the British public would consider it a breach of faith on our part if we failed to do it. Your letter blew all this sky-high, for the very good reason it isn't true. You rendered a great service. For we can never hope to come to a good agreement, on this or anything else, unless we are honest with ourselves, and with each other.'

Beaverbrook, very impressed and supportive, replied:

I am most grateful for this fascinating account of the Bretton Woods controversy in the United States.

It has given me a valuable insight into the various factors at work. And I hope you will allow me to congratulate you on a narrative which is as entertaining as it is enlightening.

The Americans did indeed have second thoughts. Unhappily, they went to the opposite extreme. As Boothby later wrote,

instead of doubling the price of monetary gold, as they should have done, the Americans went on, after the war, to demonetize it altogether. This, they said, was necessary because an increase in the price of bullion would be of benefit to South Africa and the Soviet Union. In fact it was a mortal blow to the western democracies. The dollar has proved to be no substitute for gold; and no alternative international measuring-rod has been found. As a result we have today no viable international monetary system in the free world.

Nor, he might have added, the sterling area, which, like the Empire Boothby wanted it to sustain, and Bretton Woods itself, have passed into the ashes of history.

Boothby's virtually lone stand against Bretton Woods may have made several people in Washington and London think again, and his mentor

Keynes – not destined to live the year – was uncomfortable, but it did nothing to improve his standing in Whitehall or in Downing Street. With the war approaching its triumphant conclusion, Hitler dead, a new President of the United States, and increasing anxiety about Stalin's rapacious advance into Europe, Churchill put if anything an even higher importance upon the Anglo-American alliance than ever. And now along came Boothby, causing trouble, as usual! Also, Boothby considered that his pledge to Eden not to mention Bretton Woods in his lectures, which he faithfully honoured, did not cover letters to the *New York Times* or newspaper articles and interviews. Eden took a totally different view and was enraged by his performance; he was exhausted by the strain of his wartime and personal burdens, and looked it, and his temper was notorious, but on this occasion his fury with Boothby was fully understandable. To this, Boothby responded that it was Eden who, among others, had given a personal pledge to the Commons that the Bretton Woods Final Act would be debated in the House before it was ratified, and had reneged on it. There was justice on both sides, but Churchill and Eden were in positions of mighty political power, and Boothby was not. The fact that he proved to have been absolutely right did not assist his cause at all.

Boothby then proceeded by train to San Francisco as a journalist to cover the negotiations over the Charter of the United Nations. It was a special train for the world's press. 'It was the most enjoyable journey I have ever had,' Boothby later related. 'We were all tight all the time. So much so that, when we reached Chicago, we were put in a siding in a stockyard and not allowed to get out.' When he arrived, he found an immensely hostile Eden, who cut him dead, but also Michael Foot, destined to be Boothby's favourite political and personal sparring-partner. Boothby greatly admired and liked the remarkable Foot family, the father Isaac, and the sons, Dingle, Michael and Hugh (later Lord Caradon), who on a memorable occasion did the *Brains Trust* programme together as a family. Foot, also in San Francisco as a journalist, asked Boothby, 'What are we doing here?' to which he replied, 'Reaping the bitter fruits of Yalta.' As the rapidly advancing Russians devoured huge quantities of Europe, the earnest discussions over the Charter had an increasing air of unreality, particularly when Molotov casually told Eden that the representative of the Polish Government who had gone to Moscow had been arrested and that another had been installed who was more amenable to the Soviet Union. Jan Masaryk, the Czech Foreign Minister, was distraught at this development. He and Boothby dined together, allegedly on 'aspirin and champagne', in Boothby's account. Boothby had long lost any faith in Beneš – he recognised that he was a victim of Munich, if a willing one, and to that extent was sympathetic to him, but always considered that he had capitulated too easily and feebly, particularly after all his fine words – but the Masaryks were made of stronger stuff, and, whatever others might have said and believed about the Czech assets affair, the Czechs themselves continued to regard Boothby as one of their best and most loyal friends. But Masaryk refused to accept Boothby's insistent advice not to return home after the war, replying that 'I love my country too much to do that.' Boothby was convinced that he would return to his death, which was indeed the case.

Boothby became increasingly convinced that the victorious Allies might well be in the process of throwing away the peace again, as they had in 1919. In his view Bretton Woods was a disaster, and now the political foundations of the new World Order were going wrong. In particular, there was no attempt to draw together the Western democracies in Europe into a regional union. In one of his articles he wrote of 'a dangerous and increasing sense of insecurity, and a return to the situation with which we are all horribly familiar'. These jarring notes were, again, not well received in the general euphoria of victory and peace in Europe, and the joys of an early return to British Party politics.

VE-Day was celebrated at the home of Sir Charles Mendl in his mansion in Los Angeles with a dinner and dance, attended by many famous actresses and wealthy well-jewelled ladies. Kingsley Martin had not been invited, but he asked Boothby if he and his host, 'an eminent American economist, who, like you, believes in economic expansion,' could be asked; Boothby gladly arranged this.

It was vaguely noticed at the party that the eminent economist was very eager to be close to the actresses and rich ladies, but in the general celebrations this was not regarded as particularly sinister, or even unusual. It was a good party.

Early the next morning Boothby and Martin travelled east by train, as both wanted to stop and see the Grand Canyon, and so missed the sensational end of the Mendl party, when it was discovered that most of the ladies had lost their jewellery and that other items of considerable value had vanished. The eminent economist had already left. He had, with remarkable skill and without anyone noticing, in effect stripped the ladies of their valuables while dancing or talking with them. Even the distraught victims were impressed by this aspect of the disaster.

When Boothby reached New York he had a telephone call from Lady Mendl to inform him of what had happened, and that the perpetrator was none other than Martin's host. He promptly telephoned Martin, who was in Chicago, to inform him of this interesting event. His unpublished account continues:

There was a stricken silence. He then said: 'This is appalling news. My reputation is at stake. I must go there immediately.' Soon afterwards I had another telephone call from Hollywood to say that they had found both the economist and the jewellery in San Francisco. I rang up Kingsley again to tell him the good news, but this brought him no consolation. He said: 'Did he take much?' I replied: 'Yes. Necklaces and bracelets – he nicked the lot.' Next day Kingsley rang me up again and said: 'I have telephoned to San Francisco and found that he is a known kleptomaniac, but hitherto has confined himself to books.' I said: 'Well, it's a pity he changed his mind that night but, anyway, they've got all the stuff back so there is nothing more to worry about.' He said: 'Nevertheless, in my position I feel I must go back to the West Coast in order to give an explanation.' I said: 'Don't be silly. After all, he was only putting his own policy of economic expansion to practical use.' He said: 'You're incorrigible,' and rang off.

On the flight back to London Martin approached Boothby and anxiously asked, 'I suppose that story is too good not to be repeated?', to which Boothby merrily replied, '*Much* too good, Kingsley. *Much* too good!' When Boothby returned to London he related this saga in White's to Evelyn Waugh, who was so delighted – Martin not being one of his favourite editors – that he took Boothby at once to see Nancy Mitford. She was also enchanted and told the Mosleys, now released. It became one of their favourite stories, and whenever they met Tom Mosley insisted that Boothby repeat it. But, when he came to write his memoirs, out of consideration for Martin, who had suffered enough ridicule in Los Angeles and London, he omitted it.

When Boothby returned from the United States, Churchill's wartime coalition had broken up on the insistence of Labour and a general election was imminent. He later claimed that 'I had no doubt that the Conservative Party was going to be heavily defeated.' This was wisdom after the event, but he ran a typically individualistic campaign which was based on his understanding of the concerns of East Aberdeenshire. He had his doubts as to whether he would win, but his faithful organiser, Archie Campbell, 'The Buchan Farmer', was confident. Boothby was less certain and was increasingly critical of Churchill's tactics, especially his radio broadcasts; however, he did expect a Tory victory, but not by as large a majority as most commentators anticipated, particularly in Scotland.

Boothby reported to Beaverbrook on 8 June from Beechwood:

Dear Max

Thanks for your letter, which reached me this morning, after chasing me round Great Britain.

I am bearing up – although it is a little hard to return to a General Election from a trip which was as exhausting as it was prolonged.

I know that, for once in my life, I did a good job. . . . But got no thanks from our people!

Only abuse for holding up Bretton Woods.

I think this election is going to be alright, and that the P.M. will pull it off. Without him I would not give the Tories two hundred seats.

The tide is running pretty strongly against us in Scotland at present: but may yet turn.

I feel that I still have a pretty strong personal hold in my own constituency. It takes many years to win the confidence of the Buchan farmers and fishermen. But once you have got them, they don't let go. And I have been fighting for them for twenty years.

I would give my soul to increase my majority this time. I made enough with my pen to pay all my election expenses, and am beholden to no man. If I win out, it will be the answer – to a lot.

After all, the democracy is the final court of appeal. There is no disputing that verdict.

I am standing, uncompromisingly, on my own policy – economic expansion, full employment, high wages, control of food imports, no deflation, no gold standard.

I am more convinced than ever that, if we accept Bretton Woods in its present form, we shall be doing a great disservice, not only to ourselves, but to the whole world.

To harness the world economy to static exchanges at this, of all, junctures, would surely be the ultimate height of folly.

No one has the foggiest idea what readjustments have to be made before anything approaching stability or equilibrium is achieved.

All we can be sure of is that they are bound to be tremendous.

If the exchange rates are arbitrarily fixed at rates which will almost certainly bear no relation to reality, then the *entire* readjustment will have to come through prices.

It won't take long for the strong creditor nations to gut the weaker of their gold and foreign assets – to no good purpose – and then to buy up their fixed assets, or stop trading altogether.

It is this passion for a premature 'universalism' that's going to get us all down, if we aren't careful. I can think of better uses for US dollars than to pour them down the sink of multilateral currency stabilisation – and I told them so.

Why can't we come to a direct agreement with the Americans?

There are many forms it could take.

They might well place five or ten billion dollars at our disposal, free of interest, provided we made an equivalent amount available to them in sterling, for industrial development within the sterling area. We could then agree to a de facto stabilisation of the dollar/sterling rate, subject to alteration on the part of either country, after due notice and consultation.

If we agree to the abolition of the sterling area, as Bretton Woods would have us do, how on earth can we ever hope [to] handle the problem of the sterling assets now blocked in London?

In the meantime the problems of rehabilitation & reconstruction ought to be dealt with in terms of the realities – i.e. goods and services – and apart altogether from purely monetary problems which, in present circumstances, are insoluble.

Yours ever
Bob

Boothby had the advantage that, at the start of his campaign, Labour had not appointed a candidate, and, again, the Liberals did not challenge him. Labour eventually chose Captain John Allan, a fine broadcaster, journalist and local farmer who had served in the army with great distinction throughout the war. This combination made him a very formidable and delightful candidate, as Boothby recognised.

Boothby's campaign was characteristic. While pledging support for Churchill, and urging national unity until the war against Japan had been won, on economic matters he reserved the right to take an entirely independent stand. He supported Beveridge '100 per cent', but was totally opposed to Bretton Woods. Challenged on his record, Boothby was on immensely strong ground, as Allan cheerfully admitted. 'It seems I cannot help being right!' Boothby declared, and relations between the two candidates were so good that Boothby publicly regretted that it was not a two-Member constituency.

There could have been a difficult moment when he was asked about a report in the *Daily Mirror* about his alleged engagement to Hitler's great admirer, Inga Arvad, a Danish lady whom Hitler had described as 'the perfect Nordic beauty'; Inga, who had married first a Hungarian film director and then an American actor, lived in California. The tricky part of the matter was that Boothby had had a curious on-and-off romance with this lady, and the story had truth in it. He was accused of conducting 'a whirlwind romance in an orange grove in California', to which he responded by asking whether any other candidate in the north of Scotland would be capable of a comparable feat. This went down well, and no more was heard of the matter, which was just as well.

This had been one of Boothby's madder adventures, made even worse when his letters to the lady found their way into an anti-British American newspaper and aroused much unwelcome public interest and comment, not least from the British Embassy in Washington. Boothby was supposed to be covering the United Nations conference, and his extra-curricular activities, so blaringly revealed, did not amuse his newspaper or the British Government. Boothby had no choice but to brazen it out, but the people of East Aberdeenshire did not consider it at all important, and were amused rather than censorious. But it had been an insane involvement, and Boothby was lucky to get out of it with so little injury. His friends could only groan once again, and his enemies gloat. But it was characteristic that he not only survived it in his constituency, but actually turned it to his advantage.*

None the less, Boothby found a political hostility in his audiences that he had not experienced since 1929, but, although his meetings were distinctly lively, he did not suffer the ordeal that other Conservative candidates endured. Some of the repeated questions, such as why he had voted for Chamberlain in May 1940 and voted against Beveridge, were so easy to rebut that one wonders whether they were asked by Tories. What worried Boothby, and rightly, was the Services' postal vote. It was overwhelmingly in favour of Labour, but he held on by 13,290 votes to 10,918, a majority of 2,372, which was, in the circumstances, a considerable achievement. Out of the seventy-one Scottish seats, the Conservatives held only twenty-four. Walter Elliot lost Kelvingrove by only eighty-eight votes, but, astonishingly, Sinclair lost his seat to the Conservatives in Caithness and Sutherland in one of the closest results in modern political history.†

Boothby had what was regarded by the local newspapers as 'a majority whose dimensions surprised friend and foe'. When asked for the reason, he replied, typically, that it was his personal hold on the goodwill of the people of East Aberdeenshire, and nothing to do with Conservative Party policy. 'That', the *Buchan Observer* commented, 'we believe to be the honest God-fearing truth of the matter. Without any pronounced press or other support, Mr Boothby has held East Aberdeenshire on his merits. He can afford to be a proud man today.'

Others, from White's Club, were less awed by his triumph:

> We all congratulate you most heartily, and are thankful that in the midst of the Red Ruin that remains you erect one pillar of sound Conservative Principle, of Prosperity, of Temperance, and of Morality. Duff Cooper, the Earl of Carlisle, Lord Stanley of Alderley, and the Earl of Birkenhead.

John Strachey had been returned for Dundee in the overwhelming Labour triumph, and he and a greatly relieved Boothby celebrated with champagne provided by Boothby on the sleeper to London.

Colin Coote wrote happily:

---

*Many years later Boothby's American friend Bill Wasserman revived the story in his draft memoirs; Boothby reacted with fury, writing to him that Inga had been introduced to him by Sir Charles Mendl, with whom he was staying in Los Angeles: 'We never had an affair. But we became good friends, and remain so to this day. Whenever she comes to London with one of her sons, she never fails to visit Wanda and myself, usually for a meal. I am very fond of her.'

†The figures were: Conservative 5,564; Labour 5,558; Liberal 5,503.

You are a bloody marvel, aren't you?. The saviour of England gets thrown out on his neck, but the Peter Pan of Hollywood gets triumphantly returned!

I have seldom been more pleased about anything in my life than I am about your victory. What fun you are going to have in the new House! And what lovely meat Dalton will be for your axe! (That is a damned silly appointment,* for there is *nothing* in Dalton – he is just vitriol in an old Etonian flask.)

This has been a vote against the Tory party and their records from 1920 to 1939. Moreover, I have seen ten elections, but never one conducted with more phenomenal imbecility than this. I am told Winston has at last parted brass rags with Beaverbrook: and high time too. He (B) cost the party *millions* of votes. He has already done his best to ruin my profession, and now has ruined the Tory party. An excellent candidate for disembowelling.

Give my love to your mother. I expect she realises the full glory of your ascent from the maelstrom.

Boothby did not take the overall result at all tragically. On 31 July Bruce Lockhart found him at a party given by the Radcliffes,

looking very fat and opulent in a new purple-blue suit. He tackled me afterwards on the election, informed me in a loud voice that he was the only Tory who had sung 'The Red Flag' in the House of Commons that day. He was violently critical of the flippant way in which the election was conducted and said that Brendan and Max were out for ever. . . . He almost exulted in the defeat of the Tories, and, like most other people, maintained that the Brendan–Max methods had cost the Tories a hundred seats.† He is an engaging but unreliable buccaneer.‡

---

* Hugh Dalton became Chancellor of the Exchequer. Bevin became Foreign Secretary.

† Bracken and Beaverbrook were strongly criticised for influencing Churchill to use the disastrous tactic of denouncing his opponents who had so recently been his colleagues. This struck exactly the wrong note from the beginning.

‡ Kenneth Young (ed.), *The Diaries of Sir Robert Bruce Lockhart*, pp. 477–8. Many would have ascribed the same description to Bruce Lockhart himself.

13

Post-War
1945–50

Boothby found a Party shocked to its core, and a very chastened Churchill. Among the large number of Conservatives who had lost their seats were Macmillan and Bracken (although both were shortly to find other and safer constituencies, and were not out of Parliament for long).*

Boothby had fought less as a Conservative than as Boothby, and the crash of so many of his enemies gave him pleasure. If he had expected office in a Conservative government, he now had the chance to shine in Opposition: he was asked to open for the Opposition on Dalton's first budget – and did so with considerable skill, speaking from the front bench for the first time since 1940.

After the election he had returned to Washington and came back more convinced than ever, as he told the Commons, that 'we cannot as the price of an American loan [to Britain] accept the economic dismemberment of the Empire and the disruption of the sterling area'. As the negotiations were still continuing, Dalton had to be non-committal in his genial reply, but Boothby's warning indicated that he was determined to retain his independence. One commentator remarked:

Whether Mr Boothby will ever again hold office I do not know, but should think it doubtful. But he will always have what even Ministers sometimes lack – a good Parliamentary audience. He is the man with the golden voice. But this speech was

---

* To Boothby's particular regret Harold Nicolson also lost his seat in Leicester. To the dismay and surprise of his friends he joined the Labour Party, blatantly in the hope of receiving a peerage, but proved a disastrously bad and unconvincing by-election candidate and wrecked what possibility there had been. He returned to literature, journalism and biography, and was knighted for his biography of King George V.

not mere honeyed words; it was a fine exposition of the economics of abundance which made a great impression on the House.

If Boothby had distressed one former mentor, Keynes, by his denunciation of Bretton Woods and the American Loan, he stood by another, Weizmann.

It had not been particularly easy for a Conservative MP in the 1930s to support Zionism and the Jewish National Home. In spite of the Nazi atrocities against the Jews in the war, British public opinion, and Conservative opinion, remained ambivalent, and when the fight against the British mandate began in earnest and British troops were killed, an ugly anti-Jewish backlash resulted. Bevin's sympathies were certainly not with the Jews, and although his biographer, Alan Bullock, has defended him valiantly against the charge of anti-Semitism, the tilt of British foreign policy became increasingly pro-Arab and anti-Zionist. Episodes such as the hanging of British sergeants and the blowing up of part of the King David Hotel in Jerusalem inflamed anti-Jewish feelings in Britain, and particularly in the Conservative Party, which at that time had remarkably few Jewish voters or Members of Parliament. The last period of the British mandate in Palestine is a miserable story, which conferred little lustre on either side and left bitter memories.

Boothby, who was vehemently opposed to Bevin's policies, formed a strong alliance with an old friend, Richard Crossman, former Oxford don and wartime innovator of psychological warfare, who had been elected Labour MP for Coventry East in the 1945 Labour triumph. Temperamentally they had much in common. Both tended to neglect the Commons – Crossman far more than Boothby – in favour of newspaper columns, radio and television, and political journalism. Both were nationally much better known than most ministers and parliamentary worthies. They were mavericks who outraged their own Parties. What made matters worse was that they were highly intelligent and articulate mavericks.

Crossman had also fallen under the spell of Weizmann, and was equally appalled by Bevin's attitudes. With admirable recklessness he took on his own Government, even moving a hostile amendment to the King's Speech in 1946. Attlee, for personal reasons, had always disliked and distrusted him, and Bevin's views on Crossman were venomous.

Like Boothby, Crossman was argumentative as well as independent. He was also very funny and a joyous companion, who liked Tories rather more than was thought decent and proper. He certainly relished Boothby, and the emotion was reciprocated. What was not adequately realised was that on this subject they were both deadly serious.

Boothby's difficulty was that while Churchill agreed with him, he was cautious in his statements and speeches, knowing that British opinion was deeply hostile to the Jewish attacks on British troops in Palestine and the assassination of the UN mediator, Count Bernadotte. This was very understandable, but Boothby felt that he had to take a more positive line, which he did, and he and Crossman became progressively more ostracised in the House of Commons as they battled for the Jewish cause. When the Labour Government abandoned the mandate and left the Jews to their fate, they were both outraged, but got little support, except from Churchill, who backed Boothby totally. Boothby later remarked that 'it was worse than Munich. Dick and I were being cut right, left, and centre in the Smoking Room.' They were also being roundly denounced elsewhere, but they stood their ground. When 'The Jews won their war of independence, to Bevin's discomfiture,' as Boothby observed, they felt vindicated. But few, outside the new State of Israel, applauded. Boothby doubted if he had a political future; Crossman was convinced that he had destroyed his. But both became regular and honoured visitors to the State of Israel.*

This marked a much-valued friendship. Crossman recorded in his diary a dinner party in February 1953 given by the liberal and hospitable Tory MP, Alec Spearman, where

We had superb food and drink and a really old-time conversation. . . . Bob, as usual, talking like a Socialist but finally admitting that the reason he was a Conservative was that he was a Cavalier, while all the real Socialists were Cromwellians.

This has a very authentic note, although a less Cromwellian personality than Crossman would have been difficult to find.

Boothby was an unusual British politician in many ways, but one thing that marked him out was his fervent Europeanism. In an age of insularity in British politics, which was to be depressingly long-lived, Boothby loved

---

* Many years later, after Weizmann's death, his widow wrote to Boothby:

My dear Bob

I can hardly tell you how I enjoyed seeing you the other day – reminiscences, your personality, your humanitarian touch to all the existing problems. I felt forty years younger; you need not feel younger; you are. . . . Best success and love from your devoted Vera.

Boothby was one of the founder members of the Anglo-Israel Association in 1949; he served on the Executive Committee until 1960, when he became Chairman of the Council. In 1962 he became its President. He resigned in July 1975, and from the Association in 1977, in protest at the actions of the Begin Government on the issue of Jewish settlements on the West Bank.

The team: Gardie Duff, Boothby and Archie Campbell,
East Aberdeenshire, 1940

Attending the Assembly of the Council of Europe, Strasbourg, 1949.
Left to right: Henry Hopkinson, Harold Macmillan, David Eccles, Winston Churchill,
John Foster, Sir Ronald Ross, Sir David Maxwell-Fyfe, Captain H. S. Vian-Smith, Boothby
and Brigadier Gerald Blunt.

The stars of *In the News*. Left to right: W. J. Brown, Boothby, Dingle and Michael Foot, and A. J. P. Taylor.

The last election campaign, 1955

'A very convivial Rector', St Andrews 1959

Engagement to Wanda, 19 August 1967

A note from Compton Mackenzie

In conversation with Somerset Maugham

Marriage, 30 August 1967

The last campaign on behalf of the fishermen, 1971

The East Aberdeenshire fishermen bid farewell to Boothby,
30 August 1986

and admired the countries and peoples of the Continent. Now, exhausted and devastated by the war, and with the East firmly under Soviet control, Western Europe looked, and was, forlorn. The miracle of its renaissance, one of the wonders of our century, was far distant in the dark days of 1946, but it was Churchill who saw the possibilities, and it was Boothby to whom he turned.

Churchill's vision of a United Europe was not new, and he had long advocated a 'United States of Europe' in speeches and articles in the inter-war years. When he returned to the theme at Zurich in a speech in 1946 which had an immense impact, he called for a partnership between France and Germany:

There can be no revival of Europe without a spiritually great France and a spiritually great Germany. The structure of the United States of Europe, if well and truly built, will be such as to make the material strength of a single state less important. Small nations will count as much as large ones and gain their honour by their contribution to the common cause.

Here was a cause to which Boothby could, and did, respond to with total enthusiasm. Churchill set up a small committee, and chaired the meetings. The other members included Duncan Sandys; Boothby's friend Edward Beddington-Behrens; and Joseph Retinger, a Pole who had been General Sikorski's political adviser.* Significantly, and ominously, Eden took no part, but with Churchill's leadership, oratory and matchless position, this did not seem to matter much at the time. The result of their campaigning was the convening of an international conference at The Hague in 1948, which led to the formation of the Council of Europe at Strasbourg in 1949.

The impetus towards a more European foreign policy was greatly assisted by momentous events. The United States had awoken from its short post-war euphoria. The Communist seizure of Czechoslovakia was followed by the murder of Jan Masaryk, which Boothby felt acutely. The Berlin airlift and other events fully justified Churchill's warning in Fulton, Missouri, that 'an Iron Curtain has fallen across Europe'.

Boothby's relations with Churchill remained complicated, although considerably warmer than they had been. General Ismay, the famous and often underestimated 'Pug', told Boothby at this time that 'you are one of the very few people he has ever been fond of. That is why he bothered.' Ismay also forecast that Churchill would take him up again if he thought that he would be of use to him, and then drop him again. Boothby had

---

* Sikorski's British liaison officer to the Polish Government in Exile had been Victor Cazalet; both were killed in 1943 when their aircraft crashed on take-off at Gibraltar.

come to the same conclusion, but it was clear that Churchill, against the advice of his wife and many of his colleagues, was determined to continue as leader and to become Prime Minister again. And, with the Conservative ranks so depleted, and not exactly brimming over with talent, Boothby's sheer ability and his skill at attracting publicity made the rapprochement essential for both. But it was never to be 'glad confident morning again', and both knew it.

The new arrangement – 'friendship' would be too strong a word for it – did not begin very well. Boothby felt passionately about the iniquities of Bretton Woods and the American Loan. Churchill, as always ill at ease in such areas, proposed that when the principle of the Loan was debated in the Commons in December 1945, the Opposition should not divide the House of Commons. Boothby took a totally different view, and when the debate took place on 5 December he made one of his most powerful speeches in denunciation of the Loan in a full House, to such effect that when he said that he was not proposing to take the time of the House any longer, there were cries from both sides of 'Go on', a very rare tribute indeed.

The American Loan was particularly beneficial to the American tobacco industry. Boothby was especially contemptuous of this aspect of the Loan, concluding his speech of denunciation of Dalton by declaring that 'You did not have a mandate to sell the British Empire for a packet of cigarettes'; he then threw one on to the floor of the House of Commons. It was not thrown at Dalton, but in his general direction, and caused the sensation Boothby had intended.

Describing the proposals as 'an economic Munich', Boothby announced that he would divide the House. So influential was his speech that a considerable number of Conservatives joined him in the No lobby. It was a real parliamentary triumph, but Churchill considered that his leadership had been challenged and was highly indignant; there were even dark mutterings about him resigning. Boothby's comments about returning to the gold standard also aroused certain unhappy memories which Churchill did not like being recalled. Boothby was totally unrepentant, and Churchill was angry.

But Boothby's consistency on the need for Western European unity, and even union, had made an impression upon Churchill, who not only agreed with him emotionally and historically, but saw that here was a political cause that separated the Conservatives from Labour, and had a real attraction. This was not cynicism, but political advantage from an issue was never far from Churchill's considerations. So Boothby was 'taken up' again.

An early example of their better relations arose over the situation in the

South Tyrol, which Boothby had visited often before the war, and for which he had a particular affection. It had been taken from Austria and became part of Italy in 1918, as part of the British strategy to bring Italy into the war on the Allied side. It had always been an uncomfortable situation, and Boothby now proposed that it should be returned to Austria. Boothby raised the matter in a special debate in the House, when he had an exceptionally sympathetic response. Churchill was impressed and gave Boothby's campaign his full support; indeed, their letters had much of the warmth of the old days, Churchill writing on 22 September 1946, 'I am very glad things have taken a more satisfactory turn about the Austrian Tyrol. I have no doubt that our debate in the House of Commons had a definite effect, *and the credit of it belongs to you.*' But Stalin would have none of it, and the Labour Government feebly dropped the matter.

Boothby's next campaign was to oppose strongly the Government's proposal to ban the manufacture of heroin in Britain. Boothby had consulted his medical friends, who were dismayed at a proposal that was clearly in the interests of the American pharmaceutical industry, and which could easily cause avoidable suffering. He tabled a motion to reject the Bill entirely on his own initiative. Churchill immediately summoned him to tell him that he fully supported this motion, and that he could tell the Minister of Health, Bevan, that he would certainly vote against the Bill, and possibly even speak against it as well. Remarkably, considering the huge parliamentary majority that Labour enjoyed, the Bill was promptly withdrawn, to Churchill's great satisfaction.

What neither Churchill nor Eden appreciated was Boothby's consistent hostility to Yalta: 'The peoples of Europe desperately want peace,' he said in a typical speech in 1945, 'and they are not getting it because of the intransigence of a handful of men in Moscow, and the failure of the Western democracies to agree upon a constructive policy of any kind.' This was true, but truth is seldom the most warmly received of the political gifts.

But with Churchill embarking on one of his greatest campaigns, to alert the United States in particular and the West in general to the real nature of the Soviet system and the dire threat it posed to democracy in Europe, he decided that a United Europe movement was essential and that the Conservatives should take the lead, with Boothby in a prominent position. The revival of Western Europe now became Boothby's dominant political concern, and was to remain so until disaster struck in 1952.

*   *   *

Boothby spent much of 1946 writing his first major book, greatly encouraged by Victor Gollancz and Compton Mackenzie. He had begun it at Honington, then put it aside for *The New Economy* and journalism. He was a remarkably fluent writer, but he worked hard at it, and this book was to be his personal assessment of why war had come, who was responsible, and how the post-war world could learn from the errors of the past. It was also important to him personally, as another step in the revival of his reputation and fortunes.

Nineteen forty-six also saw the beginning of Boothby's unexpected new career as a broadcaster as a member of the immensely popular *Brains Trust* programme. He had been on it on several occasions towards the end of the war, but now became a regular contributor. After six years of war there was in post-war Britain an immense hunger not only for sport but knowledge, and sales of the parliamentary *Hansard* rose spectacularly. Television was in its infancy, and radio was *the* medium, having proved its remarkable potency during the war. *The Brains Trust*, and then *Any Questions?*, had a huge following, and Boothby's unique voice, his natural wit and fluency, and intelligence became known to millions of people. It also made him a very attractive, and well-remunerated, popular journalist.

Boothby never bothered to learn to type. Everything he wrote he did by hand, and his beautiful handwriting was so clear that most of his work was delivered untyped and caused no difficulties. The other striking feature of his writing is that there are very few corrections; to a degree that any writer would envy, he got it right first time. And in 1946 he was writing – literally – his first major book, which eventually ran to over four hundred pages. It was, accordingly, a year of remarkable activity in the Commons, his constituency, on radio, in journalism and now on a major literary venture.

Politically, also, the tide seemed to have turned. Beaverbrook invited him for a weekend at Cherkley, and he was again a welcome lunch guest at Chartwell. But there are also many references in his engagement diaries to 'Lunch, D', 'Dinner with D at flat' and, once, 'to Brighton with D'. These were to feature regularly in his diaries until Dorothy Macmillan's death. Boothby probably exaggerated when he later said that they telephoned each other every day, but they were certainly in close and regular contact, although it is doubtful whether the relationship continued at the high level of passion it once had, and they were considerably more discreet. There were other women in Boothby's life, but no major attachments. His friendship with Diana, especially after the death of her husband in this year, remained strong and warm, so much so that their friends wondered why their marriage had been so disastrous, but Dorothy held him in thrall.

Boothby's nervousness about his book was increased when Strachey told him that Gollancz had become so obsessed by politics that he was neglecting his publishing business. There was, unfortunately, some truth in this. Gollancz had set such high standards of personal attention to his authors that they simply could not be maintained. 'I doubt if any non-professional author can have had less assistance, guidance, or encouragement from his publisher,' Boothby wrote in high indignation to Gollancz after discussing the situation with Strachey. In fact, although the general charge was justified, it was not so in Boothby's case and he withdrew his complaint, writing 'I now bite the dust.' But there is no doubt that the book merited more editing, and that the Gollancz of old would have done a far better job.

Having written the final version of his book at such remarkable speed, Boothby had difficulty with the title, not least because it was part-autobiography, part-political manifesto. His first choice was *To Live or Die?* A friend thought it too negative and suggested *I Choose to Live*. An unknown 'clerical friend' whom Boothby consulted commented rather stiffly that 'the choice in such matters is not given to mortals'. On one of the few occasions when Boothby accepted clerical advice, he saw the point. He then came up with *I Live to Fight*, which Harold Nicolson, among others, thought more suitable to the reminiscences of a prize-fighter than a politician. Boothby settled for *I Fight to Live*, which aroused one of his most bitter critics to comment that, of his generation, he had conspicuously failed to do so in two world wars, a jibe that was as unfair and inaccurate as it was cruel.

Other reactions were far more positive. Leo Amery praised the book enthusiastically, as did other reviewers, who included the ever-loyal Harold Nicolson and Malcolm Bullock. The Scottish reviewers particularly enjoyed his tilts at the English – 'The English had better take care! Their combination with the Scots has for so long been so felicitous that they are inclined to take it for granted. The truth is that they can no longer do without them' – and Richard Crossman shrewdly wrote that

Mr Boothby is that comparatively rare thing in England – a pure politician. He lives for the game, and, like the true gambler, he loves it whether he wins or loses. Mostly, as he reminds us, he has lost; but he retains his zest, and combines with it a streak of recklessness based on an inner despair.

The reviews were long and generally admiring, and the book swiftly went through four editions. Boothby had not received much in the way of praise for some time, and it was not vanity that made him keep every review and letter of delighted congratulations from friends and unknown readers. The royalties were very welcome, but the praise was the important thing. It was another crucial step in the fight back from oblivion. As it happened, the final title was exactly the right one.

I Fight to Live is not only autobiographical in the first part, but in the second – continuing the themes of *The New Economy* – it is a personal political and economic policy. This was perhaps a mistake, as the construction confused his readers, who were not sure whether it was an autobiography or a political tract. Also, more than four hundred closely printed pages were daunting. Harold Nicolson had severe reservations about this mish-mash, remarking characteristically of Boothby's *magnum opus* that 'It is like wearing a top-hat with shorts.' Boothby writhed, but took the point, although at the time he was cross with Nicolson. He was consoled by other much more favourable reviews and substantial sales.

He came out strongly in favour of regional economic and political union, and 'genuine co-operation between a democratic France and a democratic Federal Germany', but there were several personal statements:

I am, by nature, instinct and conviction a radical Tory. I could never accept the bleak puritanical rational dogmatic materialism of Liberalism or Socialism. There is a sharp distinction to be drawn between a liberal attitude towards life, and Liberalism in the party sense.

He quoted with warm approval Charles Masterman's dictum that 'The coldest of cold monsters is the State', and declared that 'I confess that I carry my detestation of personal power to the point of obsession.'

Relations with Churchill remained uneasy, but were notably warmer, although tinged with a mutual acerbity. One example may suffice. In August 1948 Boothby and Malcolm Bullock were on holiday in the South of France and were invited to join the Churchills at their hotel in Aix-en-Provence. It was a fairly extraordinary day, which Boothby vividly recorded immediately afterwards, with a skill and wit that makes his biographer once again lament the unwritten journal.

Much of the discussion was about the war, as Churchill was deep in his memoirs, but there were other diversions, as Boothby related:

Lunch was all right: langouste mayonnaise, soufflé, a couple of bottles of champagne on ice, and a bottle of Volnay, topped up with brandy.

'I find alcohol a great support in life,' he said. 'Sir Alexander Walker, who keeps me supplied with your native brew, told me that a friend of his, who died the other day, drank a bottle of whisky a day for the last ten years of his life. He was eighty-five.' 'If you ever give it up,' I replied, 'you'd die.' Silence.

Then: 'If I become Prime Minister again, I shall give up cigars. For there will be no smoking. We cannot afford it.' 'What,' I said, 'none at all?' 'Well, only a small ration for everyone. And then a black market in coupons, organised by the

Government, so that anyone who couldn't give it up would have to pay through the nose!' 'You'd better not say that before the election,' I said. 'I shan't,' he answered. . . .

I said that Vansittart had told me that, when he took the Secret Service reports to Baldwin, the latter said: 'Oh, take that stuff away. It gives me nightmares, I don't want to read it.' He had not heard this; and was appalled. 'You were on the right side then. How is your constituency? How are the herrings? You seem to have persuaded a reluctant public to eat them.'

I told him that my constituency had been turned into a safe seat under the new redistribution scheme. 'You deserve it,' he said. 'You have a great record there. They must love you very much. How long have you been there? Nearly a quarter of a century!'

I said that one of my troubles in life was that I was always right about public affairs, and always wrong about my private affairs. He thought for a moment, and then said: 'No. Sometimes wrong about public affairs, and sometimes right about private affairs. That would be a fairer statement of the case.' . . .

The conversation then turned to the Jews. I said that they were going to win hands down in Palestine, and get far more than they ever expected. 'Of course,' he said. 'The Arabs are no match for them. The Irgun people are the vilest gangsters. But, in backing the Zionists, these Labour people backed the winners; and then ran out on them. You were quite right to write to *The Times* protesting against the shelling of Jerusalem.' This brought Christopher Soames in.* He said that public opinion at home was pro-Arab and anti-Jew.

'Nonsense,' said Winston. 'I could put the case for the Jews in ten minutes. We have treated them shamefully. I will never forgive the Irgun terrorists. But we should never have stopped [Jewish] immigration before the war.'

He went on to say that he never saw Weizmann because he found him so fascinating that, if he did, he would spend too much of his time talking to him. 'Weizmann gives a very different reason,' I replied. 'What is that?' 'Last time I saw him he said that the reason you would not see him was because, for you, he was "Conscience".' Silence.

Then back to the war. . . .

The moment then arrived for departure to Les Baux, which he remembered from fifteen years ago, and where he thought he wanted to paint a picture. I said I could not, and would not, take my car unless they filled it up with petrol. This was accordingly done; and all the painting apparatus collected.

Winston then appeared in snake-skin shoes, and a Mexican sombrero hat; and off we set, before a wide-eyed crowd, in three cars. Winston and Clemmie and one detective in the first. The Soameses and another detective in the second. Malcolm and I in the third – mine – without a detective.

We told them they ought to see the ruins (Roman) of St Remy on the way. But they took the wrong road, so we got there first. Somewhat dazed by the

---

*He had married Mary Churchill in 1947. He never shared his father-in-law's enthusiasm for Israel or Zionism.

combination of tremendous heat and alcohol, I found a very nice niche in a beautiful Roman arch, where I curled myself up, and went fast asleep, dreaming of centurions. I thus missed the best scene of all.

On arrival, Winston clambered out of his car, gazed for a few seconds at the ruins, and said: 'How bloody. How absolutely bloody.' 'Look at Bob asleep,' said Malcolm, hoping to divert his attention. But all he said was: 'Bloody.' Clemmie and Mary thought it was quite lovely, and decided to stay for a while. Whereupon the old boy climbed back into his car, and drove off to Les Baux; alone, except for the chauffeur and detectives.

Clemmie and Mary then looked at the ruins from every angle. Christopher confided to me, when I woke up, that he hated sight-seeing; and thanked God that he and Mary were leaving the next day for a drive along the Riviera. He called it a 'pub crawl' but, if I know Mary, it won't be that. We all then set off for Les Baux – Clemmie, Malcolm and self in my car; Soameses following.

On arrival, the detective came up to me and said: 'There's a storm on. You'd better keep clear. It'll be over in ten minutes.' It then transpired that the painting tackle was all in the Soames' car, so he couldn't begin. He had gone off to the top of Les Baux, in a rage. The chauffeur and detectives seized the easel and paint-box and ran up the hill after him; while I looked for, and found, a *bistro*.

By this time all the sight-seers at Les Baux had turned out to see what the hell was going on.

Presently there was an uproar. I went out and found Winston striding down the street, with the chauffeur and detectives disconsolately following him, plus all the painting apparatus. 'There's nothing to paint here,' he shouted. 'There's beer to drink here,' I shouted back. So he came into the *bistro*, which was almost pitch dark, and sat down.

'Were you really asleep in that arch?' he asked. And then: 'Don't you think the Calais story [in 1940] is very dramatic?' By that time the beer had arrived. 'It is cool, but not cold,' he said, with truth. Two pails of ice immediately appeared. Clemmie ordered a lemonade. And peace was gradually restored. 'I hate the taste of beer,' Clemmie said. 'So do most people, to begin with,' he answered. 'It is, however, a prejudice that many have been able to overcome.' The bill was then demanded. Unthinkable, said the proprietress. It was the greatest honour they had ever had. Perhaps Monsieur Churchill would sign his name in the book? Monsieur Churchill would; and did. I went out with Malcolm, wondering whether I would ever be famous enough to pay bills with my signature. 'I think', I said, 'That we can now bugger off.' 'It's more than we can do,' said a detective, who was standing immediately behind me. I had not seen him.

The sombrero and the snake-shoes reappeared. 'Let us rendezvous at the hotel later.' But I was too tired to rendezvous any more. I killed a dog on the way back. And collapsed on to my bed, with a sty in my eye. Thus ended an astonishing afternoon.

* * *

Boothby now had a new home, a rented comfortable and sunny flat at 1 Eaton Square, where he installed his furniture, pictures and books. He was to live there for the rest of his life. When his mother died in 1949, he sold Beechwood for £19,000 – at that time not at all a derisory sum – and, having learnt some sense, profitably invested much of his inheritance and his income from his journalism in the firm of Mills and Allen, owned by his old friends the Mills brothers, Geoffrey, Bill and Sam, and Bill Allen. He had, at last, no financial problems. And he suddenly became a major national figure.

Post-war Europe offered the most exciting challenge of Boothby's life, and for once he found himself not only in the mainstream of Conservative thinking but in a position to lead and influence public opinion. The television age was only just beginning, but political radio – which had played such a major role in the 1945 general election – was becoming established, and Boothby proved himself an absolute master of both media.

Boothby's apprenticeship may have been at Oxford under Freddie Grisewood's guidance, but he had demonstrated from his very first election campaign a remarkable talent for spontaneous speaking and dealing with questions, hecklers and rowdy meetings. Compared with these – and the House of Commons – question-and-answer sessions on radio or television were easy meat, but it was the combination of his lovely voice, his sharpness and jovial good humour that made him an increasingly familiar figure. His true fame developed slowly, but no other politician, with the exception of Michael Foot, who became his regular sparring-partner, seized the opportunities that were suddenly provided for them. The important point was that Boothby enjoyed broadcasting and felt immensely at home in a television studio. For others this new environment was a cause of nervousness and, indeed, fear. Churchill hated it, as did Attlee. Few politicians were convincing on it. Boothby's innate fairness, independence of mind and thought, and amiability, gave people who were not naturally interested in politics immense pleasure. He was knowledgeable – and fun.

All this was being noted with mixed feelings by his colleagues, and was destined to cause immense difficulties, but at the time, with the Conservatives facing perhaps a decade of Opposition, Boothby was given a free rein on the air and in the House.

This was a very happy period for him, and not least because his emergence as a national figure made his journalism very rewarding, and the success of *I Fight to Live* was financial as well as personal and political. Also, the United Europe cause was one that was very dear to his heart, and into which he flung himself with gusto.

His basic credo was spelt out in many speeches, but perhaps the best of all was to the House of Commons on 5 May 1948:

It seems to me that the supreme object of our policy should surely be to build a democratic world order so strong that no state or combination of states would dare to challenge it. . . . Such a democratic world order can only be built up by the creation of a United States of Western Europe, in some form or other, in close association with the British Commonwealth, and with the United States of America, upon whose material strength the entire structure must in the first phase depend. . . . The process must be one of spiritual growth, as well as material progress; and the end must be a series of organic acts of union. I see no other way. The choice that confronts Hon. Members is fundamental. I do not think it is obscure. It is the choice between international anarchy and the rule of law; between the rebirth or the doom of our Western civilisation.

There were those in devastated Western Europe who shared Boothby's vision, especially Robert Schuman, whom Boothby greatly liked and admired. Churchill was idolised wherever he went in Europe, and his espousal of a United Europe fired multitudes with hope and excitement. In 1949 he led the Conservative delegation to the first meeting of the Consultative Assembly of the Council of Europe at Strasbourg. The other five delegates were Boothby, Macmillan, David Maxwell Fyfe, David Eccles and Ronald Ross, a Northern Unionist. Boothby later described this experience:

That summer I had been lent a lovely villa near Cadenabbia on the Lake of Como; and, as Churchill was himself in Italy at the time, he asked me to travel with him from Chiasso to Strasbourg. The journey lasted for most of the day. We had the usual sumptuous lunch, specially prepared for him, with plenty of champagne. To begin with we talked about the economic plight of Europe, and economic policy generally. After a while he said: 'You mustn't think that you know everything about economics, and that no one else knows anything.' I said: 'I sometimes do.' . . . On the way from Basel to Strasbourg I asked him what he really meant by 'a kind of United States of Europe'. He refused to be drawn. All he said was: 'We are not making a machine, we are growing a living plant.' And then, changing the metaphor, he added: 'We have lit a fire which will either blaze or go out; or perhaps the embers will die down and then, after a while, begin to glow again.'

Boothby's speech at the Assembly concentrated less on economics than on the need for an executive international political authority in addition to the necessary functional ones. He called for a co-ordinated monetary and fiscal policy, a European investment plan, and reciprocal trade and payment arrangements. 'From this speech Churchill did not dissent,' he later wrote.

None of this was noted with much favour in government circles, and the fact that it was so closely linked to Churchill's name and prestige did not help matters. Bevin was lukewarm; what was much more serious was that Eden had no time whatever for United Europe, and did not even join the delegation to Strasbourg. When Boothby urged him to reconsider, he replied, 'You are a European animal; I am an Atlantic one.' But as long as Churchill remained enthusiastic, Boothby believed that the impetus would be maintained, and that a Conservative Government would take the lead in the political, as well as the economic, unification of Europe. This was certainly the strong impression that Churchill made, especially in Western Europe.

Boothby was absolutely right when he later wrote that

in 1949 Britain could have had the leadership of a united Western Europe on her own terms. De Gaulle was not there to oppose it. They were clamouring for it. After all, we had at that time tremendous prestige, because we were the only one of the countries concerned which had not been conquered and occupied. What happened? Coldly and deliberately we set out to destroy the Council of Europe, and everything it stood for.

It is now obvious that the beginning of the greatest success story in post-war history was the Coal and Steel Community proposal that Robert Schuman devised. The British Government would have nothing to do with it, and only relatively few Conservatives – including Boothby and the young Edward Heath – saw the immense possibilities. Eden was hostile, and although Churchill protested at the refusal of the Government even to send an observer, let alone a delegation, to the talks that established the Community, he was then preoccupied by the Communist invasion of South Korea and other matters. Also, the European Movement itself was divided, with its federalists, constitutionalists and functionalists arguing among themselves, and the Conservative press – particularly the Beaverbrook newspapers – was almost universally hostile. Boothby was exasperated by them all, and particularly the federalists with their theories and proposals for which the Western nations were not ready. A memorandum he wrote in 1950 set out his apprehensions lucidly and strongly.*
His worst fears were to be fulfilled.

At the beginning of June 1949 Boothby resolved to keep his unhappily short-lived journal. It opened on the 2nd, when he received the formal letter from Attlee appointing him as a delegate to the Consultative Assembly of the Council of Europe. He wrote:

It is a reward for 2 years' hard work, and I am very pleased. The Council may come to nothing – or everything. But I am convinced it is the main – perhaps the only – hope of European civilisation.

* It is given in full as Appendix 2 to *Recollections of a Rebel*.

Together with my selection for the Parliamentary delegation to accompany the Speaker to Denmark for the celebration of the centenary of the Danish constitution, this marks my political rehabilitation, after nine years. If good enough for the Council of Europe, then, clearly, good enough for anything. The enemies know this, and will not be pleased. From all accounts they are, in fact, hopping mad.

There then came a detailed and lengthy account of a debate in the Oxford Union, accompanied by Sarah Macmillan. 'She is superlative company and the journey passed in a flash', preceded by 'Very bad food. Tepid white wine. There is really no need for this.' Perhaps this coloured his very low opinion of the standard of the speaking. A new young friend, Edward Boyle, was

distraught about his final exam, in the midst of which he was. In fact he could hardly speak – very different from the last time I saw him, when he was all gay and giggly. He said he had done a very bad paper in the morning, and must return at once to work for tomorrow's paper. A great mistake; but I could neither dissuade him nor brighten him. He remained sunk in gloom. Terrible things these exams. It is a delusion to suppose that you do not know how you have done. If you have done badly, you know it all too well. And if E. Boyle has done badly it will be a setback in what promises to be an interesting political career, because it will cause loss of confidence in himself and also in his friends.

Boyle's gloom was only too justified and he got a poor Third. But in October 1950 he became Conservative MP for Handsworth and achieved a national status with Boothby as a regular member of the *Any Questions?* panel. Twenty years later, after he had left politics to become a much-loved Vice-Chancellor of Leeds University, he joined Boothby in the Lords. However, Boothby's perception of his lack of self-confidence was a shrewd one.

The centenary events in Copenhagen proved a mixed privilege. Boothby's Oxford contemporary, Marcus Lipton, a controversial left-wing Labour MP, slept through the sermon and started to snore until Boothby prodded him awake – twice. The speeches were interminable.

The old tingling feeling which always accompanies acute boredom began to creep over me, resulting in fidgets. Then I looked at the King [of Denmark] and was at once consoled and soothed. Never have I seen a man in such a physical agony of boredom. With clenched hands and tortured expression he gazed fixedly at outstretched legs and boots. Not until the delegate from Greenland (half an Eskimo) began to speak in a language that was apparently unintelligible even to him did he relax, and then began to laugh uncontrollably. A very human monarch this; and my heart warmed to him.

Boothby was the speaker at the lunch in the town hall.

I sat next to a jolly Danish woman, who gave me a Danish toast with which to finish my speech to the assembled multitude gathered outside in the sunshine. With four schnapps and three beers inside me I found no difficulty in explaining my Danish origins, and the speech was a definite success. It is a gift, this extraordinary fluency on my feet. But I sometimes wonder whether it is altogether a desirable gift; and whether I wouldn't have done better work without it. Too late to change now.

He then went to Paris to negotiate the formation of a parliamentary group of the European Movement, which was eventually achieved, with considerable difficulty and bad feeling, particularly from the French. But, as Boothby remarked, 'The French may be difficult, but what the hell can you do without them?' He then stayed with the Duff Coopers in their lovely house in Chantilly, writing of Diana that 'She makes beauty exciting. What could be higher praise?'

Amongst others staying were Dean Acheson and his wife. Duff Cooper described the former as 'a nicer and more intelligent edition of Anthony Eden', which said rather more for his loathing of Eden than it did for his judgment.

On 23 June Boothby recorded in his journal:

Lunch to Winston at the Savoy. Sat between Malcolm Bullock and Willie Teeling,* and we drank 2 bottles of Pouilly Fuissé between us. Will Darling† opposite. A good and gay lunch. Winston did his stuff well enough, including the tears at the finish. Walked back to the House with Walter Elliot, slept in the smoking room, and eventually reached the Chamber in time to hear Dick Crossman make a wild and foolish speech. I had not intended to speak, but got up to answer this one, and Frank Bowles called me. I did fairly well, missing only one important point; and was deluged with congratulations afterwards. This is simply because hardly anyone attempts to debate nowadays. It was the novelty of hearing a speech answered that got them. However, it has done me good with the Party, and I am glad that Providence guided me to the debate at that particular moment.

Saw Aneurin in the smoking room, and told him that I had been asked to do an article about him for *Picture Post* for a large fee (£50), but had refused because if I said anything nice about him the Conservatives would not like it, and if I said anything nasty about him he would not like it. His comment: 'Why not tell the truth, and quarrel with your Party?'

After a hot day of golf and bridge with two very close friends, Boothby became reflective:

---

* Conservative MP for Brighton Pavilion.
† Unionist MP for Edinburgh and one of Boothby's favourite colleagues; the House of Commons loved him and mourned his death in 1955 with genuine sadness.

I hate living in London. For one thing, it is so frightfully dirty. But I do not see any alternative, so long as I remain in politics. And I do not think that I can leave politics at this juncture.

Oddly enough, this has been by far my most fruitful Parliament. . . . I sometimes wonder, now that my public rehabilitation is complete, I should not chuck the H of C (after celebrating my 25th anniversary), go and live in the country, and write. Political office has few attractions to offer to-day; and, at my stage, has lost any glamour it might once have possessed. I do not very much like my Conservative colleagues; and they certainly do not very much like each other.

And yet – I should probably be lonely. I should certainly have become a complete hedonist, like Duff [Cooper]. Duff looks, and I think up to a point is, happy. But his life seems to me to be pointless. Also, he is ten years older than me, and has had much better luck.

So, on the whole, I have come to the conclusion that I had better go on – at least over the next election, which means going on with the flat, and the dirt, for the time being.

After a dark period in Boothby's life and fortunes, the sun seemed to shine. Churchill did not have a Shadow Cabinet – a later innovation, introduced by Hugh Gaitskell – and his selection of front-bench speakers was somewhat arbitrary, but Boothby was a regular one. An opponent, J. P. W. Mallalieu, wrote of him in *Tribune* that

There is no one who has such an effective parliamentary style, with his skill at disarming an enemy, political or personal; none who has his assured assumption of diffidence, his half-laugh at himself, his passionate emotion, the trails of English – repeat, English – history which wisp about the Chamber long after he has left it. In his voice, his manner, his appearance, and sometimes even in what he says, he is the epitome of great Parliamentarians.

The twenty-fifth anniversary of his election to Parliament was celebrated in great style in the Aberdeen Music Hall, the largest venue available, and among the letters of congratulations was a special one from Harold Nicolson:

Congratulations on your semi-jubilee. It is a fine thing to have been 25 years in Parliament before the age of 50, and I don't wonder that you feel proud of it. But what you ought really to feel proud of is the strength of character which enabled you to emerge stronger than ever through an ordeal which would have shattered most people's courage. Being a cowardly man myself I admire courage almost more than any other quality, especially courage which entails not a momentary reaction to a sudden danger, but prolonged fortitude of will.

At Boothby's specific request the dress was informal. Gardie Duff was the chairman, and Walter Elliot the proposer of Boothby's health. Churchill sent a telegram: 'Every good wish to you my dear Bob on this auspicious occasion. Winston', and when Boothby rose to respond before an audience of over five hundred diners, 'Cheers rocked the hall', as the local press recorded.

Then, there came another very special honour. Boothby had no knowledge of the fact that several of his former Free French friends had recommended that he should be made an *Officier de la Légion d'honneur*. However, the authorities, including de Gaulle, who, although by his own choice out of office, had to give his approval as the leader of the Free French, did not consider that Boothby's services to France merited so high a recognition.

Boothby had inherited from his mother a remarkable portrait of Napoleon at the installation of *Chevaliers de la Légion d'honneur* at St Denis, which his great-grandfather had bought in Rio de Janeiro in 1820. Taking the view that his ancestor had probably stolen it, Boothby considered that it should return to the *Légion* at St Denis and offered it as a gift to the French people, which was willingly accepted. This generous gesture inspired Legentilhomme and General Dassault to renew the pressure and, to their delight, de Gaulle relented and gave his approval.

Boothby was en route to Strasbourg for a Council of Europe meeting, and it seemed an appropriate occasion to stop over in Paris to present the picture at St Denis. Knowing nothing of what his French friends had arranged, Boothby arrived at St Denis to be greeted by a large group of his friends and the press. Then, to his absolute astonishment, Dassault informed him that he was now an *Officier de la Légion d'honneur* and that the ceremony was about to begin. The award was given, the citation declaring: 'For services to the cause of France during the war, the ally he aided so gallantly in the darkest days of our common struggle.' The insignia was then bestowed on Boothby by Dassault, who ceremoniously kissed him on both cheeks amidst cheers to complete the occasion.

Marjorie Legentilhomme, who of course had been deeply involved in the plot with her husband, and who had known Boothby longer and better than almost anyone, has said that 'For the first – and probably only – occasion in his life Bob was utterly speechless. He just stood there, with tears streaming down his cheeks, while everyone cheered him.'

There was a sequel to this wonderful occasion, when in Strasbourg that evening Churchill noticed the rosette of the *Légion d'honneur* worn proudly in Boothby's buttonhole, and asked what it was. When Boothby explained,

> Churchill's face lit up, and he said with a smile: 'I've got something better than that.' He left the table, went to his bedroom, and came back wearing the *Médaille Militaire*. With him I always felt like a toy in the hands of a mischievous boy.

Boothby found this episode amusing and engaging; others were more doubtful.*

Thus, everything seemed to be going well. Boothby was happy and successful. His rehabilitation seemed complete. He was a regular participant on television and radio. His journalism had never been in greater demand, and few political stories seemed complete without a Boothby comment or quotation. He was also a popular and much-requested speaker on a variety of platforms. If not rich, he now had passed the period of his acute financial problems.

Boothby's generosity never ceased to amaze his friends. On one morning, feeling rich, he went out and bought four cars as presents for four particularly close friends. His accountant was, not surprisingly, concerned at this lavish largesse and remonstrated politely, but knew only too well that this was Boothby's nature. He loved making people happy, particularly children, and there were some very fortunate ones available. With no family of his own he created one, giving some the entirely false impression that he was fabulously wealthy. In fact, he was earning so much from his radio and television work and journalism that he could have been significantly well off if he could have kept away from the casinos and had not given so much money away. But in spite of those depredations, his portfolio of shares grew and prospered.

In the Commons, as so often happens, he was more appreciated on the Labour than the Conservative benches, and Aneurin Bevan repaid Boothby's friendship slyly on a memorable occasion in the House when, unusually, he was freed from his portfolios of Health and Housing and was permitted to speak in a general debate. He quoted the words Boothby had written about Churchill's 1925 decision on the Gold Standard: 'The best Mr Churchill can say about it is that we were shackled to reality.' Michael Foot, who was there, has described the sequel:

At that Bevan paused, looked round the House, and with a gesture of the head, and what looked like a wink to everyone else, dropped his voice to an incredulous whisper and repeated the words: '*shackled to reality*'. At once, all eyes turned upon the dishevelled, romantic, figure on the Tory front bench, and the whole place dissolved in one mighty gasp of good humour.†

The 'dishevelled, romantic, figure' was, of course, Boothby and not Churchill.

---

*Madame Legentilhomme and others have confirmed to me the truth of this story. Boothby was justifiably euphoric at the time and did not mind Churchill upstaging him at all.

†Michael Foot, *Aneurin Bevan*, vol. 2, p. 270.

Boothby found this episode amusing and engaging; others were more doubtful.*

Thus, everything seemed to be going well. Boothby was happy and successful. His rehabilitation seemed complete. He was a regular participant on television and radio. His journalism had never been in greater demand, and few political stories seemed complete without a Boothby comment or quotation. He was also a popular and much-requested speaker on a variety of platforms. If not rich, he now had passed the period of his acute financial problems.

Boothby's generosity never ceased to amaze his friends. On one morning, feeling rich, he went out and bought four cars as presents for four particularly close friends. His accountant was, not surprisingly, concerned at this lavish largesse and remonstrated politely, but knew only too well that this was Boothby's nature. He loved making people happy, particularly children, and there were some very fortunate ones available. With no family of his own he created one, giving some the entirely false impression that he was fabulously wealthy. In fact, he was earning so much from his radio and television work and journalism that he could have been significantly well off if he could have kept away from the casinos and had not given so much money away. But in spite of those depredations, his portfolio of shares grew and prospered.

In the Commons, as so often happens, he was more appreciated on the Labour than the Conservative benches, and Aneurin Bevan repaid Boothby's friendship slyly on a memorable occasion in the House when, unusually, he was freed from his portfolios of Health and Housing and was permitted to speak in a general debate. He quoted the words Boothby had written about Churchill's 1925 decision on the Gold Standard: 'The best Mr Churchill can say about it is that we were shackled to reality.' Michael Foot, who was there, has described the sequel:

At that Bevan paused, looked round the House, and with a gesture of the head, and what looked like a wink to everyone else, dropped his voice to an incredulous whisper and repeated the words: '*shackled to reality*'. At once, all eyes turned upon the dishevelled, romantic, figure on the Tory front bench, and the whole place dissolved in one mighty gasp of good humour.†

The 'dishevelled, romantic, figure' was, of course, Boothby and not Churchill.

---

* Madame Legentilhomme and others have confirmed to me the truth of this story. Boothby was justifiably euphoric at the time and did not mind Churchill upstaging him at all.

† Michael Foot, *Aneurin Bevan*, vol. 2, p. 270.

stand you take in the House. . . .I shall not forget your kindness at a time of trouble.' Belcher told Boothby that he intended to follow his example and return to active politics, but was unsuccessful. His mistake, as Boothby had warned him, was to resign from Parliament; there was to be no 'come-back' for him, but it is a good example of Boothby's warm-hearted consideration for those in misfortune.

14

Disappointments
1950–5

Although they had not won a single by-election from Labour since 1945, the Conservatives entered the 1950 election in high hopes. Boothby's opponent was a British Railways engineer, Gregor Mackenzie, who was twenty-three, and to whom I am indebted for his account of the contest:

I have fought – won and lost – seventeen elections, and can say that Bob Boothby was the ablest candidate I ever fought. He was also the most charming and considerate. He was very generous to me; I suppose some would say that with such a safe seat he could afford to be; I think that he was just a nice man. I particularly remember his speech after the count. After he had thanked the administration, the police, his agent and supporters, he went on to say that he thought that I was a very bright and enthusiastic candidate, and hoped most sincerely that I would soon be elected to Parliament, where he would welcome me warmly. I was very flattered. By the time I got to Parliament he was in the Lords, but true to his word in 1950 he came along and congratulated me in the warmest way.

During the campaign we often stayed in the same hotel and we would eat together. He gave me a lot of good advice, and I appreciated it. He told me that I'd be a junior minister one day and that I mustn't mind the hard slog (he had loathed it) and that I would become a fairly senior minister in time. Again, I was very flattered.

Apart from his wartime trouble with the Czech assets, I didn't think (nor did he) that he would ever become a senior minister. He did not enjoy his short spell in Government, for he was far too independent to be part of a team. He told me then that he would rather be a writer and broadcaster – or prime minister – than be a middle ranker. . . .

During the campaign we were both plagued by a man who kept asking about MP's pay. One night he got bored by this man, and when the question came up again Bob got to his feet and said, 'and a good thing too. Since I got the increase* I've bought myself a splendid new flat in the poshest part of London and a Rolls-Royce motor-car. I have caviar at breakfast and when I go to bed I retire with two bottles of the finest champagne and drink myself roaring rotten *fou* [drunk].' His reply brought the house down.

There were other details that Mackenzie noticed with admiration and interest. During the campaign the brave Fred Martin, Boothby's honourable and honoured former opponent, died, and Boothby cancelled all his engagements for a day in tribute to him. He also spoke most warmly of John Allan, remarking that he was too clever to be in Parliament, and throughout his own campaign he was very worried about how John Strachey was faring; indeed, it struck Mackenzie during the count that he was more concerned about Dundee than his own result.† As Boothby was scathing about Strachey's East African groundnuts scheme, now lost in the ancient histories of former political disasters which everyone has forgotten, this might appear odd, were it not for his deep personal affection for Strachey. What he genuinely opposed was Strachey's anti-Europeanism. But Boothby's closest personal friendship was not affected. Mackenzie was also very impressed by the obvious fact that Boothby's support came from people of all Parties, including his own. 'He certainly was very good for East Aberdeen – and beyond', was the verdict of his opponent, who also noted that at no point did Boothby even refer to his opponent's youth, remembering how young he had been when he had first stood for Orkney and Shetland.

The Conservatives nearly won the general election, but not quite. With a minuscule Labour majority, harassed ruthlessly by the Opposition, and with Boothby particularly prominent in a political war of attrition and exhaustion that brought little credit to Parliament and the Conservative Party, the Labour Government lived unhappily on borrowed time.

In July 1950 Boothby infuriated Beaverbrook by quoting in the House of Commons a private letter which Beaverbrook had written to him on 16 February 1928 praising his speech of 10 February on the coal, iron and steel industries. This, in a front-bench speech, caused great hilarity, but Beaverbrook was so irritated with this, and Boothby's fierce advocacy of the Schuman plan, that he sent up a reporter to the East Aberdeenshire constituency to test the waters. The report he received was as follows:

---

*From £400 to £600!
†Boothby's majority was 12,085.

I spent two days in the constituency testing opinion on Boothby's attitude to the Schuman plan. I saw local Conservative leaders, ministers, farmers, bankers, a doctor, shopkeepers – all people of weight.

They were all well aware of Boothby's advocacy of the plan. Their own views varied – some against the plan, some for it, a few anxious to see further discussion before coming to a decision.

But the overwhelming impression I got was of Boothby's unshakable popularity. Except for a Socialist banker, to a man they described him as a 'grand chief, a great MP'. There was affection as well as admiration. I cannot see his Schuman opinions hurting him in any way. Nobody will speak against him.

Sir Ian Forbes-Leith, President of the East Aberdeenshire Conservative Association, is a 'discuss Schuman further' advocate. He told me: 'No MP has done more, not only for his constituency but for Scotland as a whole than Mr Robert Boothby.'

Beaverbrook, impressed – and perhaps pleased – called his dogs off.

The Labour Government, deprived by death of Bevin and Cripps, deeply divided after the resignations of Aneurin Bevan, Harold Wilson and John Freeman – perhaps significantly, all close friends of Boothby – and with its tiny majority, limped towards the election, which duly came in October 1951.

Political television was in its infancy in the late 1940s, and there was even controversy within the BBC about whether it should cover the 1950 general election at all, but the result, although notably amateurish, was such a success that Norman Collins, the pioneering and controversial head of the television service, proposed a regular series of topical discussions by well-informed individuals. Edgar Lustgarten would be in charge, and the first broadcast of *In the News* was transmitted on 26 May 1950. The team consisted of Boothby, Michael Foot, W. J. Brown, an Independent MP of much spirit, and Donald McLachlan, then an assistant editor of the *Economist*.

Like all its successors, it was shown live and developed a certain ritual of its own. What was immediately apparent was that Boothby and Foot were perfectly suited for this novel programme, being astringent, good-humoured, witty and individualistic. By October it was established as a weekly programme with a regular team – Boothby, Foot, Brown and the historian A. J. P. Taylor.

In those far-off (and some would say happier) days a television set was a rarity, and there were less than 200,000 licences in the whole of Britain; radio, with its vast audience, remained the dominant medium, and *In the News*, although it ran for several years, never approximated to the fifteen million listeners to *Any Questions?*. But the impact on the favoured few of this remarkable programme was electrifying.

The arrangements for, and circumstances of, *In the News* were unusual. The four performers met at Lustgarten's Albany flat for sherry and a general discussion with him and the producer to give the programme an agreed pattern. This settled, there was then an excellent dinner in the wine cellar of the Ecu de France restaurant, when all discussion of the programme was absolutely barred. Tom Driberg was fascinated by how individuals differed before the ordeal. He wrote in his diary on 9 May 1952:

Bob Boothby is that unusual phenomenon, an extrovert and an introvert rolled into one ample person: sometimes he sits back watching us cynically through half-closed eyes, his only contribution an occasional deep, lascivious-sounding chuckle; sometimes the folly of some statesman, usually on his own side of the House, will have excited him to almost classically rotund and uninhibited invective. Michael Foot is as genial and twinkling in private as he is prickly in public.*

The excellent dinner consumed, the participants were driven in two hired Rolls-Royces to the television studios at Shepherd's Bush for somewhat prolonged technical preparations, after which Boothby invariably went to a nearby pub, usually accompanied by the others. With this additional fortification – the dinner had not been teetotal, either – they returned for the programme itself. Some found this drawn-out process not only tedious but frightening, but a few, including Boothby, loved the ritual. He was always happy and relaxed in a television studio, particularly when Michael Foot and Alan Taylor were his sparring partners. The programme had a remarkably large audience even then, and Boothby was one of the relatively few radio stars who succeeded triumphantly on television. He always believed, as did Foot, that *In the News* was the best of all the discussion programmes on television, especially when they were on it, and agreed heartily with Driberg's view that the BBC 'ought to show more courage in resisting pressure from the official Party machines'.

Most unfortunately Collins' unceasing battle for more resources, and more independence for television, caused one of those classic internal crises in the BBC, which resulted in his post as Controller being upgraded to Director. The appointment was awarded to George Barnes. Collins promptly resigned on 12 October, the first victim of *In the News*.†

The success of the programme had taken the two political Parties by

---

* Tom Driberg, *The Best of Both Worlds*, pp. 162–3.

† When Independent Television arrived, Collins revived the programme with the name of *Free Speech*, and with Boothby again a regular member of the team.

surprise, followed by real concern as its popularity increased, together with the mounting sales of television sets. They suddenly realised that there was a potentially invaluable political power which was entirely outside their control, and pressure was rapidly put upon Barnes, who had little political knowledge or even awareness.

The trouble with the programme's popularity and success in the eyes of the Party authorities was that neither Boothby nor Foot could be regarded as 'sound' representatives of their Parties, and even less so when Bevan resigned from the Government in April 1951, because Foot was not only an independent-minded firebrand but also an ardent Bevanite. Thus, the horror of both the Parties was greatly compounded. The very factors that made Boothby and Foot television stars – their intelligence, wit and honesty – caused the Party authorities special alarm. In this they made common cause, and heavy pressure was put upon Barnes to select rather more anodyne politicians for the programme, who could be relied upon to follow the Party line faithfully. Their purpose was to take over the programme, or to kill it off totally. As Barnes minuted, 'failure to use on occasions representatives of the main core of opinion in the two Parties will lead to interference and will endanger the programme. . . . Interference has begun and I must therefore insist that my directions are carried out.'*

The political pressures were specially alarming to the Governors of the BBC as Beveridge was conducting a major examination of the BBC's monopoly of radio and television; in the event, the majority report favoured its continuation, but there was an important minority report by Selwyn Lloyd, Conservative MP for The Wirral, advocating its abolition and the creation of independent television. With the Attlee Government barely hanging on to power, and the Conservatives firm favourites to win the next general election, the BBC was acutely aware of the reality of the threat to its cherished monopoly and independence.

The problem was made worse by the fact that *In the News* was the only television programme in which politicians regularly appeared. The days of Party Political Broadcasts and programmes such as *Panorama* or *Newsnight* were far away. There was even confusion over whether ministers could, legally, appear on television, and the problem of balancing the Parties had not yet been addressed. Thus, the only politicians seen weekly by an ever-growing audience were the three mavericks – Boothby, Foot and Brown. Party stalwarts in both camps writhed as Boothby and Foot happily pursued their individual lines, boosted by the knowledge that these were being greatly appreciated. If anything, Labour

---

* Quoted in Grace Wyndham Goldie's classic study, *Facing the Nation*.

ministers were even more outraged by Foot than the Conservatives were by Boothby, who was at least doing the Conservative image some good, whereas in their eyes Foot, the unashamed and articulate Bevanite, was doing Labour no good at all.* The pressures mounted.

Boothby suddenly became a famous face as well as a famous voice. He enjoyed his new stardom, and being stopped by enthusiastic strangers in the street seeking to shake his hand and to have his autograph. In the view of some of his friends it all went to his head for a time. One small, but revealing, example was glimpsed by Crossman when they attended the Madgalen Feast in March 1954. Crossman wrote in his diary:

Magdalen is a curious place. When we entered the Common Room nobody came forward to greet us and nobody took any trouble about us throughout the evening, which seriously upset Bob Boothby, who revealed himself for the first time to be a real prima donna. He only recovered his form next morning at the Baloghs', where we all had lunch.†

The Conservative hierarchy should have realised that here, most unexpectedly, was a major political asset. But, instead of encouraging and exploiting it, they worked assiduously and successfully to eliminate it. Most politicians at that time regarded television with at best distaste and many with fear. It was new, dangerous and inexplicable. The older generation, and especially Churchill and Attlee, disliked the new invention deeply, and there were to be strong feelings against televising the Queen's Coronation in 1953. As Boothby's fame and popularity outside Westminster rose, his colleagues increasingly resented it and him. When Churchill once rounded on him in the House of Commons and sneeringly referred to him as 'The Member for Television', this jibe was universally well received.

One person who admired Boothby's skills as a communicator without reservation was Arthur Salter, whose own abilities, which were considerable, were very different. He wrote to Boothby:

As a person with public fame, your power is not precariously based . . . it has as its foundation the memories of millions. It is usual too for 'screened' power to develop a kind of timidity that erodes character and pesonality. It is therefore with some touch of envy as much as admiration that I look at you. To be fiercely attacked and opposed – even for a time battered painfully – brings its own rewards, as the opposite experience does not.

---

* Boothby's friend, Noel Annan, the Provost of King's College, Cambridge, and no Conservative, wrote to tell him that his every appearance was worth a thousand votes for the Conservatives, whilst Michael Foot lost Labour a similar number. Boothby robustly replied that both calculations were a serious underestimate.

† Janet Morgan (ed.), *The Backbench Diaries of Richard Crossman*, p. 298.

Boothby was deeply moved: he valued the good opinion of Salter more than that of almost anyone after the death of Lloyd George, and this particular letter relieved him from his fears that his media fame would be transitory and swiftly forgotten. Nor was this just kindness. Salter thought the world of Boothby, and often startled colleagues and friends by saying so, when it was not at all a fashionable opinion, especially in the Conservative Party. Unhappily, there were not many Conservatives of Salter's perception, wisdom and human understanding.

The BBC was caught in a genuinely difficult dilemma. The trouble with *In the News* was its popularity, and much of this was based on the fact that it had a regular team. Barnes kept urging on Lustgarten the names of 'sound Party men' supplied by the political Parties, and Lustgarten – who was on a freelance contract – kept on resisting. As Mrs Goldie has written, 'It was almost more difficult to kill *In the News* than to keep it alive.' The issues of free speech and the independence of the BBC were at stake. But Barnes, entirely at sea in totally unknown waters, continued to see the Whips and to take their nominations.

In the end, the machine politicians won, as they usually do. The regular team became diluted by Party men so impeccably sound that *In the News* wholly lost its character and, thereby, its audience, and sadly faded into oblivion. It is a dismal story, and it did nothing to endear Boothby to his colleagues and Party officials, or them to him. They had deprived him of the ministerial office he considered he was entitled to; now they had deprived him of his new and exciting platform and career – and a not inconsiderable income, although he constantly complained of how niggardly was the BBC pay. But his fame as a major television personality had been made.

The best epitaph on this at first glorious, and finally inglorious, attempt by the BBC to make politics lively and interesting before its abject surrender came from Foot in a letter to Boothby on 15 November 1964:

Of course, you are absolutely right – any attempt to revive the glories of *In the News* are doomed. There will never be anything like it again, chiefly because all the participants, headed by yourself, (a) knew what they were talking about, (b) knew how to talk, and (c) did not give one single bugger for anybody, especially the organisations which happen to be presenting the programme. Then there was always the refreshing thought that the programme would keep wolves, worries, and much else from the door for the beginning of the week at least.

In the 1951 general election Boothby was opposed by a Mr Whipp, an able Aberdeen trade unionist and councillor, who had served in the Gordon

Highlanders in the First World War and subsequently in the Royal Horse Artillery, but the style of his campaign was unchanged.

Milton Shulman was dispatched to report on Boothby in action in East Aberdeenshire, and wrote a vignette that merits quotation:

Then, after a becoming mumble from the chairman, Mr Boothby takes a headlong and hearty dive into the welter of contemporary politics.

From the rich, parochial countryside of Aberdeenshire, Mr Boothby soon has the simple folk of Crimond floating on a magic carpet over Abadan and Cairo and Istanbul.

He concentrates on the split in the Socialist Party and foreign affairs. Smoothly, paternally, and with the authority of a man who took honours in history at Magdalen, Oxford, he tells them why the Tories will make a better job of handling foreigners than ever the Socialists did.

'Mr Bevan is an intimate acquaintance of mine,' he confides coyly. 'I might even say he is an intimate *friend* of mine. But he is not devoid of ambition. He thinks it would be a good idea if he were Prime Minister. I have even toyed with the same idea myself. But when this election is over, Mr Bevan will make his bid for power. And at this critical time it is important that this battle should be waged in Opposition,' he tells us in almost conspiratorial tones. 'Put them out to grass until this quarrel is settled,' he exclaims, right arm raised in an evangelical gesture. And then, with a reckless disregard for metaphors, 'Let the bulls gore each other in some grassy pasture until they have discovered a new faith or even souls, if they have any.' The good people of Crimond laugh politely and say nothing.

Then Mr Boothby presses on to exclaim that the 'fundamental issue of this campaign is foreign affairs'. He tells them of his trip to Istanbul as a delegate to the Inter-Parliamentary Union, of the benefits of Western Union, and the Schuman plan. Crimond remains silent. . . .

After a quiet orderly meeting with not a heckle to interrupt Mr Boothby's eloquent vistas of events in exotic places, the chairman asked for questions.

'Will ye no tell us, Mr Boothby,' asked a feminine voice near the front, 'why the new tea-room by the radar station has been given to a non-naturalised Italian?'

'That is a most difficult question,' answered Mr Boothby, coming down to earth with a thud. 'Write to me about it when the election is over.'

The Conservatives won the election with a majority of twenty-six over Labour, and sixteen overall, and Churchill returned to Downing Street. There was widespread expectation that Boothby would resume his ministerial career. He had re-established himself in Parliament and in the Party; his work on the Council of Europe had been widely noted and well publicised; he was regarded as one of the most effective Conservative speakers in the Commons, and outside he was a radio and television star; and he seemed to have completely restored his position with Churchill personally.

Boothby himself had no doubts. Returning to London, with a majority of 13,255, on the sleeper he gave hospitality and consolation to a defeated Liberal candidate, John Junor, who was taking up an appointment with Beaverbrook. Boothby told him that he would be Minister of Labour, which Junor thought an admirable idea. But when he reached Beaverbrook's house, and told him of this, Beaverbrook sadly shook his head. 'Look up *Hansard* of March 1938,' he said. 'There will be nothing for Boothby.' Nor was there. The shadow of Czech assets had won.

Boothby's disappointment was intense, and was fully justified. If his relations with Churchill had had their bad moments in the past, there had been better ones, and he had good reason for his optimism. His exclusion hurt Boothby deeply, and he blamed Churchill personally. Henceforth there was always a sharpness in his comments about Churchill that went beyond his previous reservations and criticisms. Also, frustrated and disappointed, he became even more of a maverick, more hostile than ever to the forces that had, in his interpretation, again deliberately thwarted his legitimate expectations. It was to prove another turning-point.

The post that Boothby had really wanted was that of Minister of State at the Foreign Office, with responsibilities for Western Europe. Given Eden's views that was out of the question, but immediately after the election there was an unprecedented debate at Strasbourg between representatives of the Assembly and the United States Congress. Boothby was invited by Churchill to represent the Conservative Party and, by strong implication, the new Government.

Boothby had very much in mind Churchill's call a year before in Strasbourg for a European army under a unified command, 'in which we should all bear a worthy and honourable part'. Boothby had strongly supported this initiative, but other reactions – notably American – had been cool, and Eden had conspicuously failed to support it. The disadvantages were considerably more apparent than the advantages, and, while in Opposition it is useful to throw out new ideas, things look very different in office. Thus it was on this occasion.

The new Home Secretary, David Maxwell Fyfe, came to Strasbourg to give a guarded semi-commitment to the concept, which seemed at the time to be rather more positive than it actually was. However, Eden, questioned that evening at a press conference in Rome, was emphatic that Britain would have nothing whatever to do with the European army or with the other suggestion for a European Defence Community. Maxwell Fyfe felt humiliated and the Consultative Assembly was thrown into confusion, particularly the British Conservatives, who sent an urgent appeal to Churchill 'to restore British prestige . . . and to show that His Majesty's Government mean to play their part in the military defence and economic development of a united Europe'. To this they received no reply.

Boothby wrote personally to Eden from Strasbourg on 30 November, in which he related the progress of the discussions and went on to say:

> I am disturbed and depressed by the present position here, which is approaching demoralisation. I know that you have always taken a dim view of the Council of Europe; and indeed it was designed, and has since developed, on lines which I myself have never fully approved. The fact remains that it exists; and its collapse, at this juncture, would I am convinced be a shattering blow to the morale of continental Europe. Moreover we have an accountable and inescapable moral responsibility. . . . In politics you can play with peoples' careers, and even with their lives; but you cannot, with impunity, play with their faiths. Today the youth of many continental countries in Europe believe passionately in the ideal of European union. That is their faith: and many of them have no other. I fear the consequence of disillusionment, especially in France and Germany. Far be it from me to offer any concrete solutions. But I do feel that it would be a good thing if the Consultative Assembly were given something to do, other than brooding introspectively over its present sense of frustration, and impending faith. From a personal point of view, I am now under sustained attack by the Beaverbrook press, which is likely to continue. I can only stand on the speeches I have made, which contain such coherent thought as I have been capable of during the past four years.

No reply exists in Boothby's papers.

Boothby dated the death of the Council of Europe from that moment, and, although personal relations were not affected, he never forgave Eden – indeed, he did not forgive the entire Government. But he persevered as Vice-Chairman of the Economic Committee, which produced a report heralding 'The Strasbourg Plan' for economic and monetary union in Western Europe. It was the genesis of the European Economic Community, building on Schuman. It was exceptionally far-sighted and prophetic, but was vetoed outright by the British Treasury. Others were to take up its ideas and proposals, and to create the greatest single triumph of the post-war era. Among ministers, Boothby's only sympathisers were Maxwell Fyfe, Macmillan and Sandys, but none had the seniority or weight to take on Eden, who, not only as Foreign Secretary but as heir-apparent, was in a dominant position. And Churchill, obsessed with nuclear matters and Big Three Summits, was not the Churchill of old.

But his renewed friendship with Boothby manifested itself in his support for the proposal by Paul-Henri Spaak and Jean Monnet to elect

Boothby as President of the Assembly. Somewhat to Boothby's surprise Eden also strongly backed his candidature. All would have been well except that the French delegation, with the exceptions of Paul Reynaud and Georges Bidault, wanted their own candidate, and, to general regret, Boothby was beaten. This was a heavy blow. He later wrote:

Reynaud said to me: 'Never mind, your turn will come.' But for the first and last time in my political life, I was inconsolable. That night I walked, as I often did, alone through the streets of Strasbourg. I came across a garden, and sat down on a bench in the moonlight under a lime tree. The scent was overpowering. All of a sudden I was reminded of Sachs in the second act of *Die Meistersinger*; of his soliloquy *'Wie duftet doch der Flieder'*; and then of the Night Watchman when, after the uproar, he comes on alone with his lantern and walks slowly up the silent, empty moonlit street to one of the loveliest melodies ever written. That is what Wagner did for Nuremberg. What had we done? Dropped bombs on it for a whole long night, for no conceivable military objective, and at colossal loss in Lancaster bombers and their crews. I found myself in tears.

Fortunately, on the following morning, a pretty girl who worked in the Secretariat consoled him by telling him that even if he had been elected he could have done nothing to save the organisation. 'I realised that she was telling me the truth; and, in one minute, she turned me from a miserable into a happy man. If I had dared, I would have kissed her. She is now Mrs Enoch Powell.'

Her forecast was absolutely right, and the creation of the fledgling European Economic Commission in 1956, with the British again standing aloofly apart, made the Council even less relevant. In 1957 Boothby gave up being a delegate, and not only for health reasons. His dream had been shattered. 'We missed the European tide, and are unlikely to see it at the flood again in our lifetime,' he later wrote, with understandable bitterness.

Beaverbrook kept urging Boothby to abandon his European policies and speeches, writing on 2 August 1952,

if only you would throw over this nonsense about Europe and give yourself to the consolidation of the British Empire you would get so much support and in such grateful measure, that even if you accomplish nothing you will be rewarded by the affection of your supporters.

Boothby robustly replied on 11 August:

The founders of the European movement, who have now become antagonists, have no moral right to lead the youth of Europe up the garden path if they meant to betray them at the end. . . .

It is as if you were now to turn round and say that the Empire is no good.

I shall never cease to believe that we might have had the leadership both of the United Empire and a United Western Europe.

Having thrown Western Europe to Germany, the consolidation of the Empire remains our only hope.

But what a struggle lies ahead! . . . Don't think of answering this outburst. I am angry and frustrated not because I have not got office, but because I have been taken for a ride and dropped in the snow.

The complex relationship with Churchill continued. One indication that Boothby was coming back into favour came when Churchill was in America with Eden in 1952, and Senator Green sang Boothby's praises, with which Churchill warmly agreed. Then, Boothby's long campaigns to get knighthoods for Lewis Namier and Compton Mackenzie were successful, as was a baronetcy for Gardie Duff – who, to Boothby's distress, died some months later. Ian Forbes-Leith took over from him with comparable style and loyalty, but Boothby felt Gardie's death acutely.

As Boothby informed Mackenzie,

Winston is such an incalculable and uncertain bugger that one could not be quite sure until the list was published, so I got up at 7 a.m. to listen to the News in the car. The ultimate test of friendship! When the Voice announced what I was waiting to hear, I went and got drunk on a cup of coffee. HOORAY! I am absolutely delighted.

Boothby organised a celebratory party for the Namiers and Mackenzies, which was an occasion of much jollity and happy memories, at the end of which Namier said: 'And now the two Knights must go home and do the washing up.' It was another example of one of Boothby's greatest qualities – his love of his friends, and theirs for him.

In December Boothby was invited to dine at Chartwell. While it is not strictly the case that 'it was the first time in nearly fifteen years that they had been together in close friendship', nor, sadly, that 'All was now reconciled',* Boothby was touched by the gesture. He wrote to Churchill on the 14th:

It took me back to the old care-free days when I was your Parliamentary Private Secretary, and there seemed to be no cloud on the horizon; and on to the fateful days when the cloud was no bigger than a man's hand, and there was still time to save the sum of things, and I do hope that I am not now the cause of embarrassment to you. I have had a long and hard struggle for survival, but I see light at the end of the tunnel; and, thanks to you, I have been able to do some work at Strasbourg which may one day bear fruit. I have no grievances.

* Martin Gilbert, *Winston S. Churchill: Never Despair*, p. 783.

Unhappily, this new reconciliation was not to be permanent. The gulf that had always existed between them in temperament remained too wide to be bridged. Churchill certainly made an effort, to which Boothby warmly responded, but too much had happened. Within a very short time new difficulties and misunderstandings were to arise, as they had so often in the past.

But Boothby's Christmas reconciliation with Churchill was again manifested in an act of real and typical Churchillian generosity. He may, or may not, have had feelings of guilt about the past, and the fact that Boothby, the best-known Conservative backbencher, had not received office, but, whatever the cause, it was his personal wish that Boothby should appear in the 1953 Coronation Honours List. He was offered a baronetcy, but Boothby disapproved of hereditary honours apart from the royal family, and chose to be a Knight of the British Empire, simply because it was the honour his father had received.

The announcement was greeted with great joy by his constituents, friends and his new army of television admirers. He was very moved by Churchill's magnanimous gesture, and the original *In the News* team gave a special dinner in his honour on 8 June, when Dingle Foot read out some lines he had written for the occasion, and which, mysteriously, appeared in the newspapers the following day.

> Since Britain first arose above the main
> Her Knights have been a-pricking on the plain.
> Not once nor twice in our rough Island's story
> The Knights have stood for honour – or for glory.
> The maidens at King Arthur's Court felt mad
> When paired for dinner with Sir Galahad,
> And murmured, when the table plan was seen,
> 'Of course she takes Sir L – God Save The Queen.'
>
> The spectacle our history affords
> Is one long line of knightly plumes and swords.
> The grand procession marches down the years,
> Hailed in each age by mixed guffaws and cheers.
> The great and the immortal, cheek by cheek,
> Sir Francis Drake, Sir Andrew Aguecheek.
> Across the sodden English fields they squelch,
> Sir Winston Churchill* and Sir Toby Belch!
>
> In this, the homeland of the brave and free,
> We do not take much stock in £SD,
> But hail the heroes of a thousand fights –

---

*Churchill and Eden were made Knights of the Garter in the Coronation Honours.

Those barefoot lads who end their days as Knights!
But now a new phenomenon is seen –
A Television Knight from Aberdeen!
Even the Tory Whips dare not refuse
The man who keeps their Party 'In the News'.
The cry goes up from several million hearts,
'With such a Knight, who gives a damn for Barts?'

Just listen while the Heralds' College gloats
– 'A herring rampant on a field of oats',
While listeners from the Danube to the Dee
Acclaim with shouts the latest KBE!
And in the Elysian fields, when shadows fall,
An old, fat man – the greatest Knight of all
– Says to Doll Tearsheet as he quaffs his sack,
Thank God, my sort of Knight is coming back!

Michael Foot also decided to enjoy himself. He wrote in his regular newspaper column:

For years he [Boothby] has been telling the Conservative Party exactly what he thinks of them in words which even they can understand. Now he gets a knighthood as an independent man – for services *not* rendered to the Tories. There has been nothing like it since that other buccaneer, Captain Harry Morgan, got the same title some 300 years ago. Pirates had a good time in the first Elizabethan age. Now Sir Robert gets a sword to hang beside his cutlass. I can hardly wait to see those faces on the Tory front bench when next he rises to direct one of them to walk the plank.

Noel Annan also took the 'buccaneer' line, comparing Boothby, amongst others, with Drake, Hawkins and Lovelace, adding that 'Your Knighthood is a slap in the face for the respectable, the grey, the dim, the bien-pensant, the fearful, the disenjoyers, and all to whom one wishes evil.' Boothby greatly relished this.

Frances Lloyd George sent a simple telegram which Boothby much cherished: 'My warm congratulations on recognition of your fearless and splendid record'; and Compton Mackenzie sang his praises with special warmth at a dinner in Aberdeen, where Boothby was presented with a bronze bust of his head by Lady Duff, Gardie's widow, as the gift of the Unionist Association, which, as Boothby remarked, bore 'a strong resemblance to the head of an Aberdeen Angus bull'. This was a great occasion, with over three hundred friends and constituents present, and with both Mackenzie and Boothby on top form.

One aspect of the press reactions, all very favourable, to Boothby's knighthood was that it gave some commentators the opportunity of praising his stand on homosexual law reform.

This was a remarkable triumph.

Boothby's standing in the Conservative ranks was not at all enhanced by this campaign, to which he had always been sympathetic but which he first seriously launched in a speech to the Hardwicke Society in February 1954. In it he denounced the 'iniquitous' law whereby homosexual relations between consenting adult males were a criminal offence. This was the notorious Labouchère amendment of 1886, passed by the Commons without discussion in the committee stage of an uncontentious piece of legislation. But it brought down Oscar Wilde and many others, and the fear that it engendered was widespread in the homosexual community. The speech was one of Boothby's finest and most courageous. The kernel of it was this memorable passage:

What has modern psychology got to teach us?

(1) That mature forms of sexuality are a composite protest in the formation of which primitive infantile elements, hereditary factors, upbringing and environment have all played their part;

(2) That sub-conscious bi-sexuality is a component part of all of us, and that the majority of males pass through a homosexual period at one period of their lives;

(3) That congenital homosexuals are seldom happy, but often endowed with creative or artistic gifts which can – within limits and in favourable circumstances – be directed into fruitful channels;

(4) That homosexuality should be regarded as a physical and mental disability which may sometimes be cured, and not as a crime which always must be punished. It is, in short, a biological and pathological condition for which the victim is only to a small degree responsible.

At that time, homosexuals received scant sympathy or understanding from the press, the police, the public and Parliament – and especially the Conservative Party. 'Queers' were the object of mockery, obscene jokes and persecution, often physical. In public life, Tom Driberg was the most notorious, and would have ended up in prison if Beaverbrook had not protected him (for which he was ill-rewarded by a hostile biography); Harold Nicolson was considerably more discreet. It was a taboo topic, except in the lower echelons of the popular press.

To take up this subject was, for a Conservative MP, an act of courage bordering on the suicidal. But, having started, Boothby persevered. He tabled parliamentary questions and saw the Home Secretary, David Maxwell Fyfe, who replied that 'I am not going down in history as the man who made sodomy legal.' But he was not totally dismissive, and at his request Boothby prepared a memorandum for him; Boothby also persuaded a group of his more eminent friends to sign a letter he wrote to *The Times*, and to support him in a special adjournment debate in the House of Commons. However, when during the campaign a number of prominent homosexuals advocated lowering the age of consent, Boothby strongly opposed them as he was vehemently against the practice of pederasty.

Although ministers, and most MPs, shrank from the issue, except for those who knew that denouncing homosexuals in constituency speeches guaranteed standing ovations, most privately recognised that the legal situation was insupportable, which was certainly the official view in the Home Office and among many lawyers. Also, the serious press and journals rallied to Boothby's crusade. In response to the adjournment debate, initiated by Boothby, Fyfe announced the appointment of a committee under the chairmanship of Sir John Wolfenden. Fyfe did not conceal his distaste for the matter, having a well-deserved reputation for being exceptionally unsympathetic towards homosexuals, but at least he chose a chairman and committee of high quality.

Michael Foot, who approved wholeheartedly of Boothby's campaign, described Boothby as a 'non-playing captain' of the homosexual team, but this was not the universal view. Indeed, the canard grew that Boothby's interest was very much a personal one, until many people, including many journalists, seriously believed that he was himself an active homosexual. From these privately expressed allegations the foundations were laid for a famous later episode in his life.*

He knew about these rumours, and knew that there would be a political price. But Wolfenden did not let him down, his committee's conclusions being exactly on the lines of Boothby's Hardwicke Society speech. Getting it approved by Parliament was to prove difficult, but the law was eventually changed, although not before a minister, Ian Harvey, had been ruined by it. Indeed, it was this case in particular that persuaded many that the then law was inhuman.

It was one of Boothby's great achievements, but it was not generally regarded as such at the time. Indeed, he was the recipient of much abuse and unpleasant comments from colleagues, and puzzled remarks from constituents. Wolfenden himself good-humouredly commented that Boothby's initiative had ensured that 'for the rest of my life, my name will be associated with homosexuality'.

Boothby's remark that 'the majority of males pass through a homosexual period at one period of their lives' was true in his case, but he was

*See pp. 414–21.

certainly not a 'congenital' homosexual, unlike several of his friends, notably Harold Nicolson, Tom Driberg, Maurice Bowra, Noël Coward and Somerset Maugham. His dominant strain was heterosexual, and while both he and I are very doubtful whether Sarah Macmillan was his daughter, there is little serious doubt that he was the father of other children. But there was a homosexual strain as well, which surfaced from time to time, and which made him sensitive to the concerns and difficulties of what he cheerfully called 'the buggers'. In this matter, as in others, Boothby was a complicated man.

Duff Cooper died on a sea voyage with Diana which had been undertaken to improve his poor health, on 1 January 1954, at the relatively early age of sixty-three. If his political career had tapered away disappointingly after his heroic stand over Munich, he had had a glorious late flowering as Ambassador in Paris and as an author, his autobiography *Old Men Forget* being immediately recognised as a classic of its kind.

Diana asked Boothby to deliver the address at her husband's memorial service in London. He was deeply flattered, but also acutely nervous, and went to great trouble over his tribute to his wayward but engaging friend. The several drafts remain in his papers. This nervousness was not at all apparent when he stood up to speak to the packed St Margaret's, Westminster, which consisted principally of Duff's political friends and colleagues, including Churchill. In front of this critical audience of several hundred professional speakers, Boothby delivered what many believe to have been his masterpiece:

I have been asked by Diana to say a few words about Duff. It is an almost impossible task, but one that could not be refused. I cannot claim to have been one of his most intimate friends. They belonged to that remarkable generation which met the full impact of the First World War; and hardly one survived it.

This left a deep imprint on the mind of Duff Cooper, as indeed it did upon the minds of all of us who were old enough to see the heroes of our youth consigned to that terrible furnace. Duff passed with great gallantry through it, but the experience struck to the very depths of his soul. He neither forgot nor forgave.

There are only two things that I want to say about him today. The first is that, in an age once described by the late Lord Baldwin as 'scorched and cynical', he was one of the comparatively few who felt deeply and passionately about public affairs. His sincerity was beyond dispute; and he was also fearless. This gave to his resignation speech that particular quality which will never be forgotten by those who heard it. In conversation he was a fine and intrepid talker, with a capacity for righteous fury which delighted his friends and dismayed only the pompous and the dull.

The second thing I want to mention was his gift, amounting almost to genius, for friendship. The late Charles Masterman gave to Arnold Bennett a great epitaph. When he was dying, he said to his wife: 'If you are in any difficulty or trouble – ever – go to Arnold. He's the man.' That was high praise, and it could be applied in equal measure to Duff. He was absolute for friendship; and at his best in the company of his friends. When he came into a room you felt a glow. You said to yourself: 'This is going to be stimulating and jolly' – and so, unfailingly, it was. Innumerable were the services which he rendered to his friends; and, in the main, unknown. They were not only given on the occasions of the major disasters of life. If any of them said a foolish thing, or wrote a foolish letter – and some of Duff's friends were sadly addicted to both – there was no trouble he would not take to extricate them. Whatever position he might have been holding, he always found time to go and see the man, or the men, or the committee involved, and soothe ruffled feelings and smooth over the difficulties. This cannot be said of everyone.

In his autobiography he referred more than once to autumn, his favourite period of the year.

> We will not weep that spring be past,
> And autumn shadows fall;
> These years shall be, although the last,
> The loveliest of all.

Thus he wrote in the dedication. The years were not vouchsafed, and this must be a matter for regret. But we should mourn, I think, nothing except our own loss. There is much to be thankful for. His marriage was a perfect thing. He wrote books that will live. He was a great ambassador – one of the very greatest. His political career will be remembered for an act of signal courage when most others are forgotten. Last, but not least, in the setting provided for him by Diana with such loving care, he led a full and rounded life and enjoyed much happiness – more, perhaps, than is given to most of us. For all this he was grateful, and said so; and when the summons came he was ready to go.

It only took a few minutes, and Boothby walked back to his place amid a stunned silence, with some gasps and sobs. Churchill himself was in tears. Seldom has a memorial address had such an electrifying effect upon an audience, and newspapers clamoured for the text, which was prominently published on the following day. Churchill sent a special message of admiration and gratitude. As the congregation emerged, many were asking each other how it was possible for an orator of that quality to be out of office.*

And yet, within a dispiritingly short time, he and Churchill were at each other's throats again.

*　　*　　*

* Most extraordinarily, neither the biographer of Duff Cooper, John Charmley, nor that of Diana Cooper, Philip Ziegler, refer to Boothby's tribute. Indeed, Ziegler states that it was delivered by Lord Salisbury; in fact, Salisbury read the Lesson.

When Churchill rose in the House of Commons to make his long-awaited speech on the hydrogen bomb in April, much of the press had turned against him, including the Americans, the *New York Times* being particular about noting his debility, describing him as 'only a shadow of the great figure of 1940'.

This speech gave his critics good cause to agree. On what was meant to be a great parliamentary occasion on the dominant issue of the time, Churchill chose to deliver a major assault on the role of the former Labour Government. It was universally considered to have been a disaster, an opinion Churchill himself later shared. The Conservatives were appalled and silent, the Opposition was enraged. Having lost the House, Churchill could only soldier on with his text, amidst increasing uproar. At this point, as Lord Moran noted, 'Sir Robert Boothby, white-faced, rose from the Tory benches and walked out of the Chamber. The Opposition cheered wildly this apparent mark of dissatisfaction with his leader.'*

Boothby's action was widely interpreted as an act of outrage against Churchill's speech, but the causes were more prosaic, as he explained to Beaverbrook:

Dear Max

I assure you it was no 'theatrical gesture' – though it may well have been dictated by emotion. I was in acute physical and mental pain. I had had a bit of my gum cut out at three-fifteen; I had come down to the House expecting an epoch-making speech from Winston and – like everyone else – I was keyed up.

By half-past four the anaesthetic had worn off, all I had got from the P.M. was an attack on Michael Foot, and the House was a bear-garden.

I hated the speech, the Labour Party, and my bleeding gum in about equal proportions. So I decided to go home to aspirin, and to bed, and went.

That's all there was to it.

Yours ever
Bob

In his diary account Crossman wrote that

Gradually the scene worked up to a fever, with all of us shouting 'Guttersnipe! Swine! Resign!' with Churchill standing there swaying slightly and trying to plough through his script. There came a terrible moment when Bob Boothby got up from his seat below the gangway, turned his back to Churchill and strode out beyond the Bar, stood there glowering and then disappeared. In the middle of the turmoil I suddenly detached myself from myself and thought how nauseating we

---

*Lord Moran, *Winston Churchill: The Struggle for Survival*, p. 536.

were, howling for the old bull's blood. I think we really would have lynched him if we could.

The Tory reaction to Boothby's action was very similar. When he rose at the 1922 Committee to speak on the issue of MPs' salaries he was shouted down, which not only angered him but genuinely surprised him. This was an instructive episode. A Select Committee of the House of Commons had recommended an increase in MPs' salaries from £1,000 to £1,500, and a non-contributory pension scheme. Churchill had said that it was 'inappropriate in present circumstances', and the Government proposed an alternative of allowances. This was rejected on a free vote in the House by 276 votes to 205, and the increase approved by 280 votes to 166. Boothby – and Walter Elliot – spoke and voted in the majority. Churchill, whose heart was not in the matter, proposed on 24 June that the motion be rejected; it was in fact passed, after much tumult, Boothby again being in the forefront of the opposition to the Government.

Boothby was almost physically assailed by his colleagues. 'There was a moment', he later recalled, 'when I hardly dared face the 1922 Committee, and addressed it with my hand on the door, in case immediate escape became necessary.' He described it as 'the roughest treatment I ever got from the Tory Party'. The glaring contrast with his immense public popularity and fame and the emotions of hateful resentment that he aroused in the Parliamentary Party was seldom so clearly exposed.

The Tory Party, with an election looming and Churchill's leadership and the succession still in doubt, was in a tetchy mood. Boothby got on their collective nerves, as he should have realised.

The *Express* newspapers made a particular point of abusing Boothby. When he protested to Beaverbrook, he received a characteristically genial reply on 4 June:

> . . . I am sorry that you think the *Daily Express* is giving you fair hell. But surely you are giving fair hell to the Tory Party. It may be hell all round.
>
> With good personal regards.
>
> > Yours ever,
> > Max

Boothby replied on the 9th:

> . . . I confess I felt a bit battered by the end of last week. Nevertheless, although I owe nothing to the Tory party, I shall continue to work – in the spirit of rare altruism – for the good of its soul.
>
> To you I owe belated congratulations on a birthday which I cannot believe is true. The operative figure must surely be six.
>
> You have supported, kicked, praised, cursed and stimulated me

throughout my political career – if such it can be called: and, for all of it, I am truly grateful.

In hell or heaven I remain, with warmest regards,

Yours ever,
Bob

The next day he sent a telegram to Beaverbrook; 'After that superlative and unattainable performance I have decided to chuck television and concentrate on politics so God help the Tory party, Bob.'

On 23 June, there came another memorable and unhappy clash between Churchill and Boothby over Europe. Boothby was speaking, and saying that the root cause of the difficulty which was taking the Prime Minister to Washington was a difference in the American administration as to whether war should be waged on China or whether it should be contained without war. Suddenly he found himself being shouted at by both front benches, what the *Daily Express* described as 'an unusual combination of Sir Winston Churchill and Mr Emmanuel Shinwell'.

Boothby shouted back that 'it is characteristic that the Socialist Executive should have come out flat in support of the EDC two days after it was buried'. He was startled to get an answer not from the Labour side but from Churchill.

The Prime Minister, looking grimly menacing, rose up and turned round on Sir Robert to say, 'Do you not think it is rather a fine thing on the part of members of a former government that they adhere to great acts of policy in which they have been concerned even after they cease to be responsible and even' – Sir Winston made a formidable bow to Sir Robert – 'even if there is no *popularity* to be got out of it?' Sir Robert braced himself. He reminded Sir Winston that it was the Prime Minister's first Strasbourg speech which originated the idea. In a placatory gesture he said to the Prime Minister, 'There was a time when you were violently attacked by both front benches and you stuck it out. I am going to stick it out too.'

Churchill glowered.

Boothby still had some admirers who followed his speeches with great respect, particularly on international and economic affairs, and had for several years. One was the influential American columnist Walter Lippmann, who had also become a friend, and who wrote to Boothby at this time that 'I don't know anyone speaking these days with whom I find myself agreeing so much or so often as with you.' This was pleasant information, but there were few of a similar view in the Government, with the odd exception of Eden, whose conduct of foreign affairs in 1954, the greatest single year of true achievement in his entire career, won Boothby's whole-hearted and publicly stated admiration. Eden was grateful for this, and said so, and their personal relations improved markedly, so much so that Boothby entertained hopes that he might have an opportunity for office in an Eden Government. He never understood that his love of being independent and speaking his own mind, and his television stardom, far from being assets in the eyes of his colleagues, were very much the reverse. His relations with Churchill continued their hot-and-cold pattern and with the Whips were very variable indeed. But he battled on, not without hope that his fortunes could be revived.

15

Transition
1955–60

Boothby viewed Churchill's retirement in April 1955 with mixed feelings. It was obvious that Churchill was only a part-time Prime Minister, and had been for some time, and in spite of his generosity in giving Boothby his knighthood, Boothby's opinion of him remained ambivalent for obvious reasons. Also, although Boothby and Eden had often been on the same side politically, they had never been more than friendly acquaintances since Oxford, and they had certainly been on opposite sides over Europe. They were antipathetic in their temperaments and attitudes to life, but there was no mutual hostility; Boothby had greatly admired Eden's handling of the 1954 Geneva conference on the Indo-China crisis, and in particular his courage in standing up to John Foster Dulles, which he had witnessed at first hand. 'I have never seen more political courage and patience, accompanied by greater diplomatic skill than he displayed,' Boothby wrote. 'For once glittering personal success, which had so often eluded him, was Eden's portion. This was his finest hour.' But he fully shared the doubts of Bracken, Beaverbrook and many others about Eden's capacity to move from the perpetual Number Two to Number One.

As Boothby always recognised, Eden did not lack personal or political courage, and, after a modest reshuffle of ministers in April, the most important seeming to be the appointment of Macmillan to succeed him as Foreign Secretary, he immediately called a general election, whose outcome was by no means certain. This time, Boothby realised that he had no expectation of office, and was amused rather than discomfited when he was told that Eden had said of him that 'This is not the

eighteenth century; I don't want Charles James Fox in my Government.'
But relations were friendly, and Boothby was genuinely touched to be
invited to lunch at 10 Downing Street; Eden was the first Prime Minister
to show him this hospitality, as not even Baldwin had done so. But on
Europe they remained as far apart as ever.

Eden's gamble was fully justified, and the Conservatives returned in
triumph, with 345 seats to Labour's 277, and six Liberals. The Conservatives did particularly well in Scotland, and after a typically good-
humoured contest in East Aberdeenshire, where there had been a major
boundary revision, Boothby's majority was 10,057. The *Daily Mirror* sent
its most famous commentator, 'Cassandra', William Connor, to report on
Boothby in action, and gave him a full page of virtually unstinted praise:

'We have the best cattle, the best men, the best women and the best fish in the
world,' said Sir Robert Boothby in the village hall at New Pitsligo.

The audience, as dour as they make them anywhere in North Scotland,
stamped its approval with its heavy boots on the bare wooden floor – the clapping
of hands is apparently considered a shade effeminate in these rugged parts. . . .
They like him, they admire him. He stands before them bulky as a hayrick in his
floppy tweeds, and there is no doubt of their approval for this ruddy, rosy man.

The one area in which Eden was expected to shine was in foreign
affairs, but his relationship with Macmillan, which had never been good,
worsened until Eden transferred him to the Treasury in December, to
Macmillan's intense displeasure, and replaced him with his former
Minister of State, Selwyn Lloyd, who could be expected to be more
amenable – and was.

Before this happened, however, Eden made a major speech at the
Mansion House in which, to Boothby's amazement and indignation, he
appeared to be urging a revision of the boundaries of Israel, and not to
Israel's advantage. Also, the Government's refusal to sell arms to Israel,
while selling them to its Arab enemies, notably the Egyptian leader,
Gamal Abdel Nasser, remained government policy. As the Middle East
situation deteriorated during the tense spring and summer of 1956, and
dominated all other issues, Boothby frequently raised this matter in the
Commons, and also advocated a defensive alliance with Israel, accompanied by a guarantee to the Arab countries against aggression, and with
the possibility of establishing a British base at Haifa. These suggestions
were rejected somewhat dismissively. Boothby remarked to John
Strachey that he had the same nasty feeling in his stomach that he had in
1938 that something awful was about to happen, and Strachey agreed.
When the explosion occurred at the end of July, after the Americans and
British withdrew the projected loan for the new Aswan Dam and Nasser

promptly 'nationalised' the Suez Canal by force and seized the assets of the Suez Canal Company, there was a frenzied outcry in both Britain and France, and a demand for military action, that was more reminiscent of 1939. But this time, Boothby was not on the side of the bellicose.

His mystification increased when, at the beginning of August, he returned to the question of arms supplies to Israel in the Commons. The Minister of State at the Foreign Office, Lord John Hope, declared that in spite of Nasser's actions there would be no change in British policy. With understandable astonishment Boothby asked,

Does my noble friend really mean to tell us that, in the light of the present situation, Her Majesty's Government are going to make no change in their policy of refusing certain classes of modern arms to Israel, at Israel's own request – that they do not recognise any difference in the situation which has arisen in the last few days?

Hope replied, somewhat feebly, 'I have tried to tell my Hon. friend what the Government's policy is.' Boothby's bewilderment increased.

I have described, in my biography of Anthony Eden, what was going on within the French and British Governments and between their military advisers. Boothby knew nothing of this, nor did the majority of the Government, but his Israeli contacts were exceptionally good, and he became fearful that, in the mood of fierce belligerency in Britain and France, grave errors, based on political expediency and emotion, rather than cold reason, would occur.

By September, British and French reserves had been called up and military preparations for the recapture of the Canal were proceeding, but in spite of much diplomatic activity nothing much seemed to be happening, and the Labour Party was moving rapidly away from Hugh Gaitskell's initial fierce denunciation of Nasser and support for military preparations. It was also becoming clear to Boothby and others that Dulles was simply engaged in a holding operation, and that real Anglo-American co-operation was minimal. What they did not know, and what was not known for many years, was the full extent of Eisenhower's total opposition to the use of force, nor the absolute clarity of his warnings to Eden. But Boothby knew enough from his own contacts to realise that the situation was bad, and getting worse.

The House of Commons met on 11 and 12 September, at the request of the Opposition, to debate the situation. Boothby spoke on the first day and, in one of his most effective speeches, denounced Nasser and his actions, and his conviction that 'shameless appeasement did not really pay'. Indeed, this part of the speech was so strong that it obscured his real

point, which was that the matter could only be resolved through negotiation, not through force, and by joint Anglo-American action. Eden had
been more impressed by Boothby's denunciation of Nasser and the
reference to the perils of appeasing dictators – which was his obsession,
also – and telephoned him the following morning to thank him. This call,
and the tone of some of the newspaper reports, alarmed Boothby, and he
arranged to write an article in the *News of the World* urging the role of the
United Nations Security Council, accepting economic sanctions against
Egypt, but giving as clear a warning about the use of force as he could.

Surely our course is clear. We must take care not to put ourselves in the wrong in
the eyes of world opinion. . . . Economic sanctions against Egypt are, in the
circumstances, fully justified. They have been used against us. But force should
only be used against force.

On 26 September he wrote to Eden at length on the situation. He
expressed his concern about the way matters were developing and
emphasised the need for bringing Nasser to negotiation. He went on to
say:

Our present objectives should not be the overthrow of Nasser himself, but
the establishment of certain basic principles in accordance with the
accepted doctrines of international law. In the final analysis the rights and
interests of the users can only be guaranteed by their own power and
influence, and this must be related to the amount of unity between them,
and the amount of support they are able to obtain from other countries.
The negotiations on this basis, whether their outcome is successful or not,
would bring Nasser down several pegs; and his subsequent overthrow
might only be a matter of time. We should, I think, be well advised to leave
his personal fate to the care of future events and of our American allies,
who are quite good at dealing with such matters when they are not fighting
Presidential elections. I don't think that, apart from essential military
precautionary measures, we can look beyond this at the moment. If Nasser
remains intransigent our moral position will be impregnable, but our
difficulties will be almost as great as his. Economic pressure, inadequately
or half-heartedly applied by the canal users, will be a long and costly
process; and you, more than any man alive, know just how ineffective
economic sanctions can be. On the other hand there is this difference
between the present situation and that which arose over Abyssinia. We then
had no real support from the United States, from France, or the League of
Nations. To-day we have massive support; and the political pressure on
Nasser from the oil-producing countries, and from India, who will see their
whole economic future in jeopardy, is bound to increase.
    The alternative – an ultimatum from ourselves and France – is now
pretty dire. If it came to that, I believe you would have a greater measure of

public support than many people think. You would certainly have all mine.*
But there is no denying the fact that public opinion has shifted in recent
weeks; or that there is an invincible reluctance on the part of many people in
this country to do anything which might smack of an attempt to pull French
chestnuts in Algiers out of the fire. Unfortunately, as I think, there is little
public sympathy here for the French predicaments in North Africa. And
this gives rise to an internal political problem which cannot be left out of
account.

I therefore come back to negotiation. Make him negotiate, if you possibly
can. If you succeed in doing this, I believe you can win a substantial victory.
At Geneva you faced an apparently impossible task when they all ran out on
you, and achieved it. Let's have a repetition!

To this Eden replied on 2 October:

My dear Bob

I agree with much of what you say. Of course what we have been and are
trying to do is to settle this matter by negotiation. But our American as well
as our French allies agree that the negotiations must be on our terms. It will
be disastrous if the result of negotiation was a settlement which strengthened Nasser's position and increased his prestige. We should then all be
finished in Asia and Africa, and in no long time either.

It seems to me, therefore, that we stand a chance of achieving our
objective by negotiation only if we share the greatest firmness and resolution but it is not more than a chance. I know that you agree with this and I
am especially grateful for what you write if the last resort of force is all that
is left to us.

The essential thing is that Nasser should not be judged by the world to
have got away with it. I found our French friends vigorous and firm. They
are young by our standards. I felt a doyen.

Yours ever
Anthony

'This was a disturbing letter,' Boothby wrote in his private account of
the crisis; 'it dramatised the situation to the point of absurdity, and
revealed no calm or steady view.' In contrast, Selwyn Lloyd, to whom
Boothby had sent a copy of his letter to Eden, wrote from New York to
him to say,

We certainly aim to bring Nasser to the conference table. That is what I am
now trying to do here; it is very difficult, however, to build up any sort
of pressure on the Egyptians when friend Foster keeps having Press
Conferences!

* As Boothby's letters and speeches made clear, this would only be acceptable and supportable if
the diplomatic means had been totally exhausted. His subsequent attitude was based on the fact that
he was not convinced that they had been. Nevertheless, this sentence – as Eden's subsequent letter to
him demonstrated – led to a major misunderstanding.

Early in October Boothby went on a parliamentary visit to the Middle East with three colleagues, as the guest of the British Petroleum Company. They visited Beirut, Tehran and Kuwait, and found genuine and widespread confusion about British Middle East policy. In one of his regular newspaper columns Boothby reported that all that was being achieved was the raising of Nasser's prestige in the area, and the time for the use of force was over. 'Now we have no alternative but to sweat it out – which does not mean total surrender to Nasser.' He urged 'a constructive policy with wisdom, coolness and determination'.

Boothby returned from his visit optimistic about the future supplies of oil – one of the key arguments for the recapture of the Canal – but increasingly worried about the position of the Government. The fervour of the end of July was evaporating, and the Conservative Party was becoming as restless as the reservists in Malta and Cyprus. There were ugly murmurings about Eden's alleged irresolution, and a general feeling that as the months passed Nasser had taken the initiative. When the French, who had been in close touch with the Israelis for some time, came to Eden at Chequers on 14 October with a new project, whereby Israel would attack Egypt in the Sinai and seize the Gulf of Hormuz – their real objective – and give the British and French their pretext for attacking Egypt and taking the Canal, he seized the opportunity. The Israelis would attack on the 29th; the British and French would issue an ultimatum to both Egypt and Israel on the 30th, on such terms that the Israelis would accept it and the Egyptians would not. The Anglo-French forces would then land and seize the Canal.

This collusion, so vigorously denied for many years, but now fully revealed, was of course unknown to Boothby, but he had strong suspicions of what had happened. He met Eden on 1 November in the Commons, after the Anglo-French ultimatum had been rejected by the Egyptians, the RAF was bombing Egypt and had destroyed the Egyptian air force, the Israelis were storming across the Sinai, and the House of Commons was in tumult. Boothby's account records:

He said: 'You have been very patient, and we might have played it your way; but I think this is better.' He then gave an explanation of what he was trying to do which left me completely bewildered; and John Strachey, who happened to be with me, equally so. All that was clear was that his mind was closed.

Also, as a dedicated friend of Israel, Boothby was pleased by the total defeat of Israel's bitterest enemy. But, unlike many other friends of Israel and opponents of Nasser, he condemned Eden's tactics and objectives, and particularly the failure to secure American complaisance. And then there came the Russians' brutal suppression of the Hungarian uprising. It was a terrible time, in which not many people in public life behaved very rationally. Boothby, although emotionally torn, was totally consistent. He believed that the crisis could be resolved without war. He may have been wrong, but that was his judgment. And he had lost all confidence in Eden.

Boothby was reluctant to say anything publicly while British troops were engaged, but when the operation had to be humiliatingly stopped on 6 November as a result of vehement pressure by the United States and in Britain, Macmillan leading the retreat, Boothby saw no reason why he should continue to support the Government. In 1971 he wrote to the Earl of Warwick, Eden's kinsman, that

> I never felt any personal animosity towards Anthony E; nor, I think, he for me. He is the only Prime Minister who ever asked me to lunch in Downing Street! I was against his anti-European policy, but he quite understood the reasons why. . . . I was against Suez because I could only see Doom. His hatred of Nasser was obsessive, and he wouldn't listen.

On 8 November the Commons debated the fiasco in an atmosphere of near-hysteria. The feeling within the Conservative Party outside Westminster was so intense that any Tory MP who was critical of the Government's action came under violent attack from the Tory press and his local Association. The emotions aroused had been unparalleled since Munich, and, once again, Boothby was standing against the tide in his own Party. He wrote to Eden to explain that he could not possibly support the Government and would continue to speak against its policy. Eden replied on 12 November:

> My dear Bob
>   Thank you for your letter. I am deeply sorry that you could not be with us the other night on national – as well as, of course, on personal – grounds.
>   Yours ever
>   Anthony

Boothby was later rather offhand about his abstention on the key Vote of Censure of 8 November. 'The truth is', he later said, 'that I never gave much thought to it, one way or the other, but went to the Smoking Room for a badly needed drink.' In fact, as I vividly remember, he was angry and contemptuous, still convinced that the issue could have been resolved by negotiation and better handling of the Americans, although, as he emphasised in the Commons, he was derisive about the sentimental pro-Arabism of people like T. E. Lawrence and Freya Stark.

There were, in the event, only eight courageous Conservatives who refused to support the Government in the lobby – Nigel Nicolson (Harold's son), Sir Frank Medlicott, Anthony Nutting (who had resigned from his Foreign Office post in protest), Cyril Banks, Edward Boyle (who had also resigned from the Government), J. J. Astor, William Yates – and Boothby. Only Boothby, Yates and Boyle survived politically.

But the uproar in the East Aberdeenshire Unionist Association genuinely astonished Boothby. He had been through severe difficulties before, especially over Munich and his resignation, but this was the worst experience of all. The Chairman, Ian Forbes-Leith, did his best, but the loss of Gardie Duff was a severe one. As in the cases of the other rebels, the Tory press was calling for their heads nationally and locally, and had a high success rate. What saved Boothby – although narrowly – were his enormous local popularity and the fact that he had, again, been totally consistent. Also, it was now dawning on his angry Association, as they looked at the post-Suez shambles, that he might well have been right. The storm was fierce, but it was very brief, and he emerged shaken but unscathed. But, as he frankly admitted, he had severely underestimated the intensity of feeling in his constituency and the bitterness of national humiliation. It was one of the rare occasions when he had misjudged the mood of his constituents. Perhaps he had become too complacent.

Eden's strained health then collapsed under the intense pressure, and his premiership languished sadly until it ended with his resignation early in January 1957. Macmillan unexpectedly succeeded him. In the new administration there was no place for Boothby, who was, not atypically, enjoying himself in Monte Carlo when the crisis broke.

Boothby had always enjoyed the good things of life, although never as excessively as he liked to pretend and claim – one thing he had in common with Churchill. The strength of his constitution never ceased to amaze his friends, and not least his ability to drink liberally and remain remarkably – although not invariably – sober and alert. Like his hero, Birkenhead, he regarded alcohol as necessary fuel, and if on occasion he did overdo things by no stretch of the word could he be described as an alcoholic. More seriously, he also loved good food, and plenty of it, and was seriously overweight.

In fact, he was considerably more concerned about his health than many realised, and was constantly complaining about one ailment or another. But this response was unusual. He had always worked hard and lived hard. Another unhelpful habit was his extraordinary attitude towards medicinal assistance. Friends would watch with astonishment and alarm as he dipped into glass jars filled with pills of all colours and types, and, admitting cheerfully that he had no idea what they were, consume them in the expectation that 'some of them might do me good'. The friends laughed nervously, in the hope that they were only vitamins and that this was 'another of Bob's jokes', but they were uneasy about whether this was just an act or something more seriously reckless. It was probably a mixture of the two. The combination of intermittent strenuous exercise, large meals, a formidable consumption of alcohol, much travelling, his constituency and Commons work, and the cumulative stress of his public life and television and radio appearances, was in itself a heavy burden on even the strongest of constitutions. A casual attitude to what he called his 'pep-pills' can hardly have assisted. This had always been the case, and although he was overweight, he had always enjoyed what his envious friends considered to be unfairly good health, and his mental and physical energies were formidable. But retribution was at hand.

Early one morning in July 1957 he telephoned his doctor, Stephen Blaikie, to complain of severe indigestion and pains in his arms. After remarking that 'you can't have indigestion in your arms', Blaikie came round immediately, realised that Boothby had had a heart attack and alerted the eminent heart specialist, Walter Somerville. Boothby denied that he had had a heart attack, 'because I haven't got one'. He was taken at once to the King Edward VII Hospital. While the doctors conferred over his case, Boothby watched Goodwood Races on television and telephoned his bookmaker. For once he was lucky and was able to win enough to pay off all his hospital expenses.

He was also lucky in his doctors and nurses, as he had two further minor attacks while in the hospital. When he was released five weeks later, he knew that he had received a very clear warning; now, he must not only amend his own lifestyle, but no longer continue to represent such a far-flung constituency.

The letters and telephone calls poured in. Jennie and Aneurin Bevan wrote:

> What a shock to give your friends! You ought not to do this to your contemporaries. It gives us the wrong ideas. Anyhow, you have a very large heart so there ought to be plenty of room to outmanoeuvre any kind of trouble. Here's wishing you a speedy and pleasant convalescence.

Michael Foot responded with characteristic cheerfulness:

> . . . I must have talked to at least two dozen people yesterday about it & you would have been pleased to hear how quickly-revealed, how obviously genuine & how widespread is the affection felt towards you.
>
> The House of Commons may be able to stagger along for a week or two, albeit in a minor key.
>
> The 1922 Committee, I'm told, is just able to muster a quorum.
>
> The European Movement gasps for breath, but is not actually dead.

A few brave herring fishermen still put out to sea.

No one will take a bet on the Common Market ever getting started, altho' the funeral oration has not yet been spoken.

A few disconsolate figures still assemble round the tables at Monte Carlo.

The doors at White's are not actually closed, but the secretary is deeply worried about the financial crisis.

According to the latest reports, the heavens have not yet fallen. Meteorological experts claim that the sun still keeps its course; but they are notoriously over-optimistic.

So: the world just manages to keep going without you. But FREE SPEECH can't.

So get better soon.

Yrs, Michael

In contrast, the Provost of Peterhead wrote:

Writing on behalf of the people of Peterhead let me say that they all feel as I do and we realise that the hard work you have put in for fishing and farming has been at least partly the cause of this collapse, so do be careful, and do exactly what the doctors tell you because we *need* and *want* you for a long time yet.

A particular girlfriend wrote from UNESCO:

How kind of you to have written, how kind of you to be better – and how very kind of you to lie! Of course it is *our* lunch and *my* company that killed you (almost only, Dieu Merci!) . . . Yet, there is no doubt that your heart works too much. John [Strachey] was right in saying that a 50% elimination process – as UNESCO would put it – should be imposed. He also says that I – in spite of my undeniable guilt in the present case – shall remain in the good half. But at present, do please *rest*, and *rest*, and *rest*. Please do that, however boring it can be, for your friends' sake. . . .

Clement Davies wrote on 23 July:

My dear Bob

How dare you frighten not only the wits (such as they are) out of me but as near as nothing frighten the very life out of me. I do not care a damn about the Imam of Muscat or the Sultan of Oman, but I approach the tape with the estimable object of seeing how the Glamorgan team are progressing – when! there it was 'Sir Robert Boothby taken ill'!!! Don't do that kind of thing again!! You are too fond of your friends (as they are of you) to send them into fits, jim-jams, and all the other awful evils that beset us.

Anyway, Rest, my lad, Rest, and get better, is the wish and prayer of all of us, & none more sincerely than,

Ever thine,
Clem

Beaverbrook, when he heard of the situation and that Boothby was thinking of retiring from politics, urged Boothby not to do so, following one of their frequent disagreements. Boothby had written to Beaverbrook on 25 January 1958:

Dear Max

Thanks for your letter.

I have no intention at all of being offensive to you. I am not, by nature, an offensive chap. But whenever I have dealings with those who exercise great power, something seems to go wrong; and I do, say, or write things which cause offence.

It happened with my uncle Walter Cunliffe, to a minor degree with Baldwin, and in a big way with Winston.

Now it seems to have happened with you.

I think there must be a muddy and rebellious imp in my subconscious who wants to squirt ink at great – and successful – men of action.

When I was doing my autobiography, my pen wrote: 'whenever I meet the man whose smile leads on to fame and fortune, whose frown causes the beholders to tremble, I have a secret desire to kill him'.

I was amazed when I read this sentence, because I had not consciously composed it.

But I let it go in, because I suppose it is true. . . .

Beaverbrook replied on 27 January:

My dear Bob

Unhappily you weren't brought up in the Presbyterian Church. You should have been. If fortune had led you into St Giles, instead of some Episcopalian institution foreign to your native land, you would have known more of the Bible.

So I now quote as my answer to your last letter a single text. 'A soft answer turneth away wrath.'

I still advise you to hold your seat. It was Tim Healey who told me a great many years ago: 'Don't resign: wait till you are fired.'

And as there is no chance of your faithful constituents rejecting you – even if Cross-Bencher asks the favour – I hope you will hold on and on during the next several elections.

You are an Institution in Parliament. You mean as much to the Chamber as the Speaker's Chair.

And with affectionate good wishes I am yours ever

Max

Beaverbrook kept trying to persuade him, writing:

. . . It is better to do like Churchill or, as in the song of your countryman, Harry Lauder, 'Keep right on to the end of the road'.

And when you reach it you will find me waiting at the gate along with Lloyd George and the other old boys who were such fun.

When the *Sunday Express* compared him with a buzzing bee, Boothby sent a postcard to Beaverbrook which simply reads, 'Yes – but a jolly bee, with a melodious buzz and no sting.'

Boothby, interviewed on radio after his release from hospital, cheerfully claimed that his doctor's recipe for a complete recovery was 'to drink like a fish'. Of course, it had been nothing of the sort, and Blaikie was more than irritated when his other patients eagerly telephoned him to check its veracity. Boothby had to issue a retraction, to the profound disappointment of all who had suffered a similar misfortune.

For once, he had to be realistic, and there was no shortage of friends and loved ones who urged him to be so. However, his vows of semi-abstinence and care do not appear to have been honoured very successfully. In January 1958 he attended one of Compton Mackenzie's more memorable Edinburgh parties. Boothby wrote gratefully:

> Your hospitality was Lucullus-like in choice, Carnegian in plenitude, your company a superb choice of pulchritude and erudition. I never saw your wine waiters with empty glasses, only full ones, a fact of extraordinary significance. I stopped counting after my 45th glass of champagne, slightly alarmed by the fact that that nice young waiter had begun to bring his twin brother with him. I discussed the Hereafter with Lady Cameron; the inadvisability of gin before breakfast with David Keir; the difficulty of having a baby after forty with a lady whose name I didn't exactly catch; I discussed English Litt with another lady whose brother-in-law I gathered would write the rest of us off the map if only he had the time. Dear Monty, your party was a tremendous experience, a liberal education. There will never be anything quite like it again, which I think is a splendid thought.

The uproar in East Aberdeenshire over Suez, with no Gardie Duff to man the barricades for him, had considerably shaken Boothby. Years later he still recalled it with a shudder. As the first life peerages were under consideration, he eventually wrote to Macmillan to ask that he should be considered. The letter was intercepted by Macmillan's faithful and witty unpaid private secretary and close friend, John Wyndham. Even Wyndham did not realise how complex the Boothby–Macmillan relationship was, and carried the letter in his pocket for several days before choosing the right moment to put what he thought was a bombshell before the Prime Minister. To his great surprise, Macmillan replied, 'Of course he must have it,' and asked Boothby to see him.* Dorothy Macmillan,

---

*Wyndham, by then Lord Egremont, described this incident vividly to me at Petworth in 1968, when Macmillan was another guest.

knowing how ill Boothby had been, added her voice to urge her husband to grant his wish. It is impossible to know how decisive her intervention was, but Macmillan did immediately agree to it. 'You can be the last of the old, or the first of the new,' he told Boothby. Neither had any doubt what the choice would be. Walter Elliot had recently died, very suddenly while on a walk, and the list of the first life peerages in 1958 included his widow, Kay, to Boothby's great pleasure.

Boothby had developed a warm friendship with Gaitskell over the years, almost as warm as that with Bevan, and they corresponded frequently. 'Three years of Tory rule = a higher interest rate than we have had since 1932,' Boothby wrote to him at this time. 'I must say, it takes a Conservative Chancellor to knock not merely the Stock Exchange but the whole national economy about.' Not remarkably, Gaitskell strongly agreed.

In October, two stones lighter in weight, Boothby made what was to be his last speech in the Commons, which he described as 'an economic sermon', deploring the Government's restrictive monetary and credit policies, and quoting at length from his speech of 2 November 1937:

Every sentence of that speech [he declared] applies exactly to the present situation. I find this a little disheartening. One bats away and does one's stuff, and everybody says 'Jolly good speech' and stands one a drink; but nothing happens. That is the depressing thing about politics. Here I am again, saying exactly the same thing. However I never give in, and I am not giving in now.

Together with the familiar plea for an expansionist policy and derision for 'the dear old Treasury', he harked back to the failure of the British response to the Strasbourg Plan and the need for an internationalist approach to the Commonwealth and Europe. In the post-Suez realism, and with Macmillan as Prime Minister, and with other committed pro-Europeans in senior positions – including the rapidly rising Edward Heath – the ministerial reception to his speech was notably warmer than it had been in the past. It was an appropriate note on which to end his Commons career.

The speech took a lot out of him, and it was clear from his appearance that he had some way to go before he could claim to have made a full recovery. He had no wish to die at fifty-seven. For once being sensible about himself, he realised that he simply could not do himself, the Commons and his constituents justice.

He consulted his aged aunt, Lady Cunliffe, who testily replied that after all the embarrassment he had caused the family, 'It will give you an opportunity to redeem yourself.' He also consulted others, among whom was Marjorie Legentilhomme, who was enthusiastic. '"Yes," he said, in his "black velvet" voice, "I *do* like the sound of *Lord Boothby*!"' And so it was decided. Macmillan wrote:

Dear Bob

Many thanks for your note, which I value very much. Life has, as you say, many ups and downs. I only hope that you will, as I believe you will, enjoy the platform that the other House will give you. It will enable you to put forward your contributions in a much better atmosphere than the House of Commons now has. We never seem to have anything except the great pressure of business and very few general debates. The other House is much better fitted for these.

It is curious, but true, that I think we have always agreed in politics. I hope you will believe me when I say how glad I am to have your good wishes.

Yours
Harold*

Maurice Macmillan, touchingly, also wrote:

My dear Bob

Those disciples who were doubtful about their own future resurrection must have viewed your Ascension with very mixed feelings, which as a marginal Member [for Halifax] I share to the full on reading the news of your impending move upwards. However I suppose we should be grateful that you will still be with us in the Palace of Westminster instead of in spirit only as would have happened if you had had to retire.

Katie and I were both delighted to read of your more than deserved honour. I must say that our pleasure was enhanced by the anticipation of your impact on their hereditary Lordships.

I hope you are pleased; I am sure that all your friends will be very glad that you have been honoured, that perhaps you will not do more than you should, and that you will still be there to tell them what to do.

There is nothing like having your cake and eating it.

Yours with affection
Maurice

Many constituents wrote, including Alexander Bell of Fraserburgh:

Dear Bob

My God – didn't we all here in Buchan get a pleasant surprise when

---

*Boothby and Macmillan continued to correspond and meet each other regularly. In a long letter on the economic situation, on 29 April 1960, Macmillan concluded:

Mr Grimond [the Liberal leader] rather plaintively observed that we seemed always to alternate between bust and boom, between the dangers of inflation and the troubles of deflation. This he seemed to think was the fault of the Government. Alas, as you and I know, it is the fault of an economy balanced like ours. Of course, if we succeeded in losing two wars, wrote off all our debts – instead of having nearly £30,000 millions in debt – got rid of our foreign obligations, and kept no forces overseas, then we might be as rich as the Germans. It makes one think a bit.

opening the morning paper to see you looking so well and intimated that you had been elected A LIFE PEER OF BRITAIN.

Grand – Bob man. I send you my most hearty congratulations and hope that you are long spared to wear this honour with DIGNITY AND RESPECT. I think you well deserve this recognition for the valuable work you have done for the good of your fellow men, specially in Buchan and East Aberdeenshire.

Personally Bob I am delighted to see you recognised in this way and wouldn't your father and mother have been pleased to know that you had become 'Baron Boothby of Buchan'. I am going to a party in the Alexandra Hotel Fraserburgh tonight and I will propose a toast to you – with great gusto.

If your ears are tingling you will understand I will be blowing you to the sky. You know damn well how I have stuck up for you ever since we first met thirty-five years ago.

Now dinner at Renoir and forget about your auld friends in Buchan. You could maybe still give us a good turn.

Don't you think this deserves a celebration!!! I certainly do – and intend setting the wheels in motion right away.

All good wishes, Bob Man.

I am so so pleased.

Yours sincerely
Alexander Bell

Charles Curran, Conservative MP for Uxbridge, commented that,

Putting you into the Lords is like putting a shark into a bowl of goldfish. I want to congratulate you most warmly, and to sympathise with them just as warmly. But it must be the biggest blow to Aberdeen since the invention of vegetarianism.

Among the many letters of congratulations, one in particular appealed to Boothby, from his old adversary, Arthur Christiansen, editor of the *Daily Express*:

Dear Bob

Now I suppose you are a life saint!

But it won't stop you from going to hell. So make the best of life as you have always done.

Your devoted
Chris

The announcement was greeted in East Aberdeenshire with a mixture of pleasure and sadness. 'Buchan is downright sorry to lose him,' declared the *Buchan Observer* in a glowing tribute to him, and there were many others. Dingle Foot picked up his pen again to hail the event:

Awake, my muse, and after five long years,
Attend Sir Robert to the House of Peers,
Where comes not rain nor hail nor any snow.
This is the place where all good rebels go,
First, in their flaming and tempestuous youth
They fight for freedom and campaign for truth,
And with unnervest and stiffest upper lips
Defy the lightning and annoy the Whips.
In eighty years with a discernment fine
They often take an independent line,
But the Establishment has its tit for tat,
It always knows a trick worth two of that,
For as at last their noble rage abates
For each of them the gilded chamber waits.
Some blessed by Venus, some approved by Mars,
The ermine covers all their glorious scars.
Sooner or later, you can take a bet,
Each crown of thorns becomes a coronet.

What moved Boothby most of all was that the Burghs of Peterhead, Fraserburgh, Turriff and Rosehearty, four Burghs of the constituency – after appropriate collusion – simultaneously offered him their Freedoms. The letters reached Boothby in the same post. Asked by a reporter how he felt, he roared back, 'Fancy, four Freedoms in one morning, isn't that wonderful? I'm jolly pleased. I value them much more than my barony. I am told that I cannot be arrested in any of the Burghs if I am drunk, whatever state I am in. I am just delighted.'

Boothby took his cousin Anne Carey as his guest at 'Freedom Week', which made an immense impression on her. For four days in December the lavish hospitality and generosity of the officials and people of East Aberdeenshire poured over them. Anne much enjoyed the reflected glory, and even being asked for her autograph; above all, she was extremely proud of the reception that Boothby had everywhere, including a triumphal visit to St Andrews. Even Boothby was surprised and overwhelmed by the warmth demonstrated towards 'Oor Bob'. Few, if any, Members of Parliament have ever received a comparable outpouring of affection and admiration from their former constituents. As Anne wrote to him, 'I liked the way the old chapter merged into the new one. So it should ever be.'

Michael Foot cheerfully told the *Daily Herald* that 'It's nice to see an old pirate established on the quarter-deck. He'd better be careful about the choice of title. Lord Boanerges of Bethnal Green should make the viewers sit up. I must try rolling it round my tongue.'

In fact, Boothby was having difficulties over his title and coat of arms. He wanted to be called Baron Boothby of Buchan and Rattray Head, and have a Scottish coat of arms with his supporters a Buchan farmer and a fisherman. Garter King of Arms opposed this, on the grounds that Boothby was English by origin. Lord Lyon took Boothby's side, claiming that he was de facto Scottish by his and his father's birth, that his mother had been definitely Scottish, and that he had represented a Scottish constituency for thirty-four years. Eventually Lyon and Boothby had their way.

On 20 May 1959 Boothby received another honour that he treasured, when he was presented with a silver tray by leading farmers in his constituency at the Station Hotel, Aberdeen. It was inscribed: 'To Bob from farmer friends in East Aberdeenshire who remember with gratitude and affection the long and fruitful furrow ploughed together.'

Boothby's sadness at leaving the Commons, and particularly East Aberdeenshire, was now resolved by an honour he coveted and appreciated greatly, the Rectorship of the University of St Andrews.

The Scottish custom of students democratically electing their Rectors, who hold their offices for three years has, unfortunately, never been imitated in England and Wales, where the tendency of Scottish students to elect popular and often controversial figures as Rectors, usually with little connection with academia, is viewed with disfavour, particularly among those who had known of the tumultuous and unseemly manner by which Prince Albert had been elected Chancellor of Cambridge in 1847. Scottish Rectorial elections had a reputation for being lively affairs, and on occasions youthful high spirits had been taken too far. But St Andrews had a tradition of good-humoured elections, and that of 1958 was no exception.

Having accepted the invitation from a delegation of students, Boothby was disconcerted to find that one opponent was his Conservative colleague, Sir Charles MacAndrew, Deputy Speaker of the Commons; another was the Communist poet, Hugh Macdiarmid, whose company Boothby greatly enjoyed, although not his politics; and the third was the former Arab League commander, General Sir John Glubb. MacAndrew was the official Conservative candidate, and Boothby was advised to stand as an independent. He consulted Macmillan, who suggested that he should do so. In the event he triumphed, with 723 votes, MacAndrew receiving 520, Glubb 428, and Macdiarmid, rather surprisingly, only 261. Isaiah Berlin telegraphed: 'Congratulations on joining my profession from the top.' Boothby was unashamedly delighted, and at once set to work on his Rectorial address; even more enjoyable was the fact that he had the right to bestow three honorary degrees at his installation, and from among the ranks of his many friends chose Maurice Bowra, Cyril (by now Lord) Radcliffe and Lord Brabazon. However, Boothby's election was not universally welcomed, an official of the Scottish Office muttering, somewhat loudly, that this proved that Scottish Rectorships should be abolished as an anachronism.

Boothby was never one to let slip a unique opportunity with a huge and friendly audience, and he did not intend to be uncontroversial in his Rectorial address. When he consulted A. J. P. Taylor, the historian mischievously replied, 'Barrie did Courage, and it did very well. Why not try Cowardice?' As Boothby remarked in his address,

I almost wish I had chosen it. I would at least have spoken from the heart. But in the end I decided in favour of Tolerance, for two reasons. First, because I believe that lack of tolerance is the root cause of the troubles which beset the world today – the main reason why our civilisation hovers uneasily on the brink of destruction. And second, because I believe it is the only virtue to which I can lay any claim.

Boothby's formal arrival at St Andrews for his installation has been vividly described by a junior administrator, D. P. Dorward, later the Secretary of Court and Clerk of Senate, in the graduate magazine of 1959:

On the Thursday morning the Rector was greeted at the West Port with a fanfare of trumpets by three students perched above the centre of the main archway, and after the usual exchange of greetings in near-perfect Latin the Rector was dragged through the streets in an open carriage propelled by a powerful team of blues and half-blues of the University. Lord Boothby was presented with a variety of objects, which included a lengthy knitted scarf, a pair of gold cuff-links, a glengarry, a pyjama case, a bottle of whisky, a University shield, a gramophone record, an outsize gold ball, a brick, and the jawbone of an ass. The symbolic import of the two last-mentioned objects is still being debated.

The Rector seemed to be enjoying the proceedings heartily and never lost command of the many diverse situations in which he found himself. . . . Lord Boothby is possibly the gayest and most ebullient Rector that the University has had for many years.

Boothby was also formally kidnapped by the students and then officially released after a drive in a woman undergraduate's car, fondly named 'Blissie'.

There was some concern that there might be serious student demonstrations as a result of the decision of the University Court and the Principal, Dr T. H. Knox, to divert a major science development scheme from St Andrews to Dundee. The Younger Graduation Hall was blazoned outside with a huge banner that read 'Irvine made St Andrews: I will make Dundee', and inside the hall fireworks were discharged, bells rung, and trumpets and whistles blown. The formal procession was followed by another one of students, led by a mace-bearer whose 'mace' was a science tripod carrying a mop topped by a wine bottle, a bunch of flowers and the words 'Dundee Unileversity', a somewhat unkind but very pointed reminder of Principal Knox's associations with Lord Lever-hulme. As the press reported, 'A terrific outburst of singing and cheers and cat-calls greeted the academic procession as it entered the hall, and these were renewed by the procession of students with their own mock version of an academic procession.' But there was an all-pervading atmosphere of goodwill, and the occasion was so popular that an overflow hall had to be arranged.

Then the Rector, who had already dismayed the Principal by omitting a sentence from the lesson at the University service from one of St Paul's epistles, 'because I didn't agree with him', rose to deliver his address.

After an opening blast against Marx and Communism, the Rector claimed that

in attempting to combine collective security and economic planning with social justice and personal liberty under the rule of law, the social democrats – in the widest sense of that term – are the real revolutionaries of the twentieth century; and tolerance is, in the long run, the most powerful weapon in their arsenal.

He then launched himself into considerably more controversial waters when he turned to the Reformation in Scotland, which

plunged Scotland into a long dark night, from which she was ultimately rescued by Robert Burns. Tolerance disappeared. How could it survive among those who saw life as a narrow path through the fires of hell? And with the disappearance of tolerance came, as was inevitable, the resurgence of dogma and its inseparable companions persecution, cruelty and tyranny. From this you may deduce that I am not a Knox man.

At this point the audience, seeing the discomfiture of the controversial Principal, erupted joyously, and it was some time before Boothby, eyes twinkling, could protest that he was not referring to the Principal at all but to John Knox, declaring that 'the Puritans of those days seem to me to be almost indistinguishable from the Communists of our own, and to have done just about as much harm to the world. If I said what I really thought about them, it would make you sit up. I dare not.' Boothby was given, in the detailed account in *The Citizen*, 'a close and attentive hearing', although other reports speak of frequent friendly interruptions and applause. One student was so dismayed by Boothby's assault on the

Puritans that he called out 'rubbish', upon which Boothby smilingly commented that he appeared to be one of those Puritans who needed tolerance. Amid roars of 'up, up, up,' the interrupter eventually rose and bowed his apology.

Then it was the turn of the Roman Catholic Church, although it got off rather lightly. Erasmus and Sir Thomas More, however, came in for high praise, John Foster Dulles for denunciation for his 'messianic obsession'. Not surprisingly, Charles James Fox was greatly lauded:

Here was a man after my own heart, who could lose £16,000 in one night, speak in the House of Commons on the Thirty-Nine Articles, sit up drinking for the rest of that night at White's, and win £6,000 before leaving for Newmarket; and who fiercely resented any interference with his private life.

This went down extremely well with the student audience, if considerably less so on the platform, but Boothby's point was that Fox was, in Edward Gibbon's words, 'perfectly exempt from any taint of malevolence', but when he added, 'We have not since known his equal', not only the moralists but the historians stirred uneasily. Burns was bad enough – but Fox!

Boothby then went on to praise eccentricity, citing Aubrey Herbert's custom of arriving at Parliament with two armed Albanian retainers, lamenting that 'Eccentricity is no longer tolerated, and even unorthodoxy is frowned upon. I have seen it drained from the House of Commons in my lifetime.' He dwelt, very presciently, on the menace in American politics of the power not only of television but of public-relations operators, 'whose sole object is to dilute truth with propaganda. . . . The lie on the lips then becomes the lie in the soul.' After championing humour – with another much-applauded swipe at Knox – and declaring that 'a humorous outlook on life is the greatest gift the gods have to offer', he defended Tolerance as a positive, and not a negative, quality, while emphasising that it should not be confused with Licence. He concluded with a message which was greeted with much greater enthusiasm by the students than it was by their elders:

My advice to you today, for what it is worth, is to make the most of life. It won't last long. As Robert Louis Stevenson said, we sail in leaky bottoms on great and perilous waters, we have heard the mermaidens singing, and know that we shall never see dry land again. 'Old and young, we are all on our last cruise. If there is a fill of tobacco among the crew, for God's sake pass it round, and let us have a pipe before we go!' Therefore I say to you, enjoy yourselves, and be gay. By doing so you will obey the will-to-live, and fulfil the only divine orders we know of. Beware of those who talk of salvation rather than happiness. What kind of a God is he that creates a world from which we have to be saved? Above all, beware of those who spend their time nosing out the alleged sins of other people, in order to punish them. They are mad, bad and dangerous to know.

There was a great deal of Boothby's philosophy of life in this memorable address, and the reactions were, as he had anticipated, very mixed indeed. A certain Reverend A. G. Stewart wrote an outraged letter to the *Scotsman*, and many others swiftly followed suit. Boothby supporters rallied to his defence, and Boothby himself willingly entered the fray with a further, and not wholly applauded, denunciation of the Churches for having betrayed the true message of Christ – adding, for good measure, 'all of them'.

Bernard Fergusson, who described himself as 'a Calvinist beast', and who rebuked Boothby for his 'eat, drink and be merry for tomorrow we die' philosophy, 'and I am still an adherent of the opening words of the shorter catechism', added,

> But seriously I congratulate you warmly on some lovely stuff which badly wants saying and deserves to be said as finely as you did it and enclose some minds. The Kirk was shocked at the things that were said by Lord Boothby of Buchan and Rattray Head. The more sonorous his wonderful handle the greater the row and the bigger the scandal and the more they would damn him by bell, book and candle, but Boothby of Buchan and Rattray Head will have the last word even after he's dead (at least Bernard thinks so, and so does Ed).

The ceremonies and celebrations continued, with a formal dinner given by the University Court and, perhaps more congenial, an uproarious greeting when he appeared at the Rectorial ball. On the following evening he attended the annual dinner of the Kate Kennedy Club, followed by the traditional torchlight procession, addressed briefly by the Rector before the customary bonfire. For Boothby, they had been three of the happiest days of his life. He later recorded:

The manses were ablaze, but I had my defenders, and much enjoyed an anonymous postcard from Argyllshire, written in red ink: 'With your love of the flesh-pots, and evident fear of death, you are easy meat for the Roman Catholic Church. I advise you to apply to Rome without delay. They will see you through – for a consideration.' Scotland alone could not have produced this.

Hume, Burns and Stevenson have exercised a dominant influence over me – there is an affinity between them that is essentially Scottish; and to them I am primarily indebted for the combination of scepticism, tolerance, and an invincible optimism which is the basis of my philosophy.

It was the opinion of one member of the Court, John Thompson, that Boothby had misjudged his audience and that his speech, while being amusing and eloquent, was inappropriate for the occasion. Of the reaction of the senior members of the University he commented that they 'thought that the young were hedonistic enough without the Rector acting as Silenus'. Knox was particularly incensed. He has been described as 'an able administrator but a man who was hopeless at human relationships, a man brought up in a narrow, non-conformist environment, and who plainly disapproved of everything Lord Boothby was, down to his cigar smoke'.

Boothby saw it as his major responsibility as Rector to represent the interests of the students, who were, after all, his electors and constituents, which he did with enthusiasm, real pleasure and zest. Thompson recalls one meeting of the Court when Boothby eloquently and forcefully urged the students' request that the traditional St Andrews Day holiday should be restored. He was also conscientious and efficient, 'at pains to read his papers and master the business of the day'. During Boothby's three-year tenure as Rector, the University expanded dramatically. Of Knox he wrote that 'we disapproved of each other. He was not very good with the students. I was. I loved their company. But one thing I will give him. When it came to the appointment of professors or lecturers he took infinite pains. He was quite unprejudiced, and he always chose the best.' But what impressed Thompson, and many others, most of all was Boothby's remarkable address at the 1961 St Andrews Burns Club dinner. Thompson relates the circumstances:

I went, curious to hear how he would dish up the usual mixture, and found a man far-stricken with flu – in a state in which any lesser man would have scribbled an apology, taken aspirins and whisky and gone to bed. He had a high temperature, was sweating profusely, but was determined to honour his engagement. We did *not* get the usual mixture. Instead he spoke at length about Burns as a prose writer in English, a scholarly piece of very well-informed literary criticism, and he did it so well that the members, who came from all walks of life, cheered him to the echo. He had obviously felt that the mixed company deserved his best and courageously gave it. It was a real loss to us all when he was compelled to leave after his speech, for his bonhomie would have gone out to ours and he would have found himself at home in the real world of St Andrews' men.*

Boothby's papers include a considerable amount of correspondence relating to St Andrews, of greater interest and value to the historian of the University than to his biographer, but which demonstrates the very keen personal interest Boothby took in the University's affairs. Among the beneficiaries to St Andrews was Harold Mitchell, Boothby's former

*I am most grateful to Sir John Carmichael, Mr Thompson and Mr Dorward for their assistance and recollections of Boothby's Rectorship.

parliamentary colleague and friend, a millionaire who resided in the Caribbean. He was a highly controversial figure, and some of Boothby's other friends strongly disapproved of this particular friendship, but at Boothby's personal request he endowed a special scholarship for students from the West Indies to go to the University. Another of Boothby's great interests was to establish a Chair of Russian Studies. Here, his close involvement with Israel and the Jewish community paid off handsomely, and the Chair was generously endowed by the Wolfson Foundation.

His Rectorship was shadowed by the bad feeling between St Andrews and its college in Dundee. At a time of massive expansion in higher education, Dundee Town Council, vehemently supported by the local press, campaigned for a separate University of Dundee. The first response by the Court was to work to eliminate duplication, but the campaign for separation was favoured by Knox. Boothby, who considered that 'it seems to me to be rather silly to have two separate Universities within fifteen miles of each other', was opposed to it. The separation eventually happened, and Boothby had to accept it, but very reluctantly.

Even Knox mellowed. When Boothby's Rectorship ended in November 1961, after three happy – if controversial – years, he wrote:

Dear Rector

Since this may be the last occasion on which I can so address you, I hope you will permit me to thank you, not only for renewed efforts with the Wolfson Foundation, but for all the help you have given to the University during your term of office.

Your portrait and Sir Harold Mitchell's benefaction will be permanent memorials of your work, but those of us who have seen you in action during the last three years will not forget the aid you gave us in crossing some difficult stiles.

On 10 November Boothby was 'dined out' by the St Andrews University Club of London, and in his speech of thanks said:

Tonight my Rectorship comes to an end. No one can say that it has been uneventful. It has coincided with the planning, and the start, of the greatest expansion the University of St Andrews has ever known, at a time when higher education is more important than it has ever been. To begin with the difficulties were many and great. There was a period of frustration when one simply could not see the way through. This has passed, I hope, for ever; and, without laying claim to personal credit which will be quite undeserved, it is naturally a source of intense gratification to me that all the difficulties have been surmounted.

Agreement has been reached, and concord achieved, between the University Court, the town councils of St Andrews and Dundee, the County Council of Fife, the Scottish Office, and the University Grants Committee. Let no one say that the age of miracles has passed.

Boothby was succeeded by his friend, C. P. Snow, a very different, but very capable, Rector. But so vivid were the memories of his Rectorship that when Snow's term of office was approaching its end in October 1963, Boothby received a letter on behalf of a large number of senior students both from Dundee and St Andrews to ask if he were willing to be nominated for the post of Rector again:

> It is perhaps unnecessary to say that your previous term of office was one of the most successful in living memory, and it would appear that a large number of students here would be more than delighted if you accepted . . . every student is, and will always quite rightly be, proud and eternally grateful for the immense work which you did on their behalf.

Boothby was naturally extremely touched by this kind invitation, but his long-standing objection to the split between St Andrews and Dundee prevented him from accepting:

> I cannot see what pleasure or satisfaction I could possibly derive from presiding over the necessary preparations for a development of which I strongly disapprove. In the circumstances, I fear I must definitely decline your invitation to accept nomination for a second term as Rector. But I should like to say how much I appreciated it, and how very proud this unexampled mark of confidence on the part of the students has made me.

Charles Snow was amongst others who begged Boothby to reconsider his position, but he was adamant. When Snow asked him why he would not return to St Andrews, Boothby replied, 'because I have read your books'. It was a good joke, but the real reason was that he did not believe in going back. The St Andrews chapter of his life was an immensely happy one, but it had closed, and he thought it unwise to reopen it. Unquestionably, he was right, but there were many, including those who had opposed his election and had reeled at his Rectorial address, who were genuinely sad at his decision. 'He brought us a lot of sunshine,' one has remarked, in tones reminiscent of East Aberdeenshire.

Boothby also became Chairman of a group applying for the North-East Scottish commercial television franchise, on which he placed very high hopes and urged Compton Mackenzie to join as a founder-member. 'As usual he was blowing bubbles that seemed as permanent as crystal balls,' the latter later wrote, sadly. Their application for what became Grampian TV failed.

Boothby and Mackenzie were convinced that the BBC had put an embargo on their appearing on television together, but in February 1959 both were invited, with Mark Bonham Carter, to take part in a *Brains' Trust* programme. Mackenzie recorded that

We were given a splendid dinner at Lime Grove. Gerald Beadle was the Head of TV and believed that a dinner in Lime Grove should be much better than a dinner in Broadcasting House. When we moved along to the studio Mark Bonham Carter had become completely de-Wykhamised by that splendid dinner and was prepared to take the questions as opportunities for laughter like Bob and myself. It was an enjoyable three-quarters of an hour and even the cameramen were all laughing. However, the eminences grises of the BBC were as little amused as Queen Victoria. I see now the expression of my cousin Leonard Miall as he observed on the way from the studio: 'Rather flippant?'*

Boothby wrote to him that 'I'm not surprised that they won't let us on together again. Someone wrote from the North of Scotland: "Sir Compton Mackenzie looked at you like a lioness inspecting her favourite cub."'

The House of Lords has, obviously, a significant political atmosphere, but it always has a considerable number of peers who have no interest in politics whatever, and relatively few who could be described as passionately partisan. Its very politeness is in itself an unnerving novelty to the person fresh from the hurly-burly of the Commons. Many who have had successful careers in the Commons – Eden being a classic example – have found the Lords a chilling audience, with no echo. Others find it a relief to have a remarkably well-informed, serious and thoughtful audience, and relish the contrast. Although, naturally, Boothby found it initially difficult to adjust to the new atmosphere, he quickly established himself, and some of his best speeches – particularly on economic and international affairs – were made in the Lords. Ever a clubbable man, he enjoyed his new club, while having the right, as an ex-Member of the Commons, to use the facilities of his old one, and particularly his beloved Smoking Room, where he continued to be a familiar figure. He missed the salary, which was by then £1,500 a year, and, above all, he missed East Aberdeenshire, but he had left it in a blaze of glory with his Four Freedoms in an atmosphere not short of adulation, and was always warmly welcomed back. Also, as he made it clear, he would continue to battle in the Lords for the fishermen and farmers of Scotland as vehemently as he had in the Commons, and was as good as his word.

Perhaps remembering his extreme youth when he had been adopted as their candidate, the East Aberdeenshire Unionists chose another twenty-three year old, Patrick Wolrige-Gordon. Boothby gave him his strong

*Compton Mackenzie, *Octave Ten*, p. 130.

support, but had his doubts about his maturity and suitability as his successor. Sadly, these proved to be justified. Wolrige-Gordon fell out badly with his Association, and there are some very unhappy letters from his former constituents in Boothby's papers. Initially Boothby kept well clear of the imbroglio, which was largely – although not wholly – caused by Wolrige-Gordon's espousal of Moral Rearmament when he fell in love with his future wife, the daughter of Boothby's one-time political journalist friend, Peter Howard, who had also embraced the Buchmanite cause. It is doubtful whether the electors of East Aberdeenshire knew much about the tenets of Moral Rearmament, but it all sounded rather odd, alien and cranky, and in alarming contrast to Boothby's cheerful agnosticism.

Eventually Boothby became seriously fed up with Wolrige-Gordon, who he thought was throwing the seat away and wrecking what he considered his greatest achievement in making East Aberdeenshire a safe Tory constituency. What made matters worse was that the popular press – including, unsurprisingly, the *Express* group – took up the matter as one of freedom of conscience, depicting the bewildered people of East Aberdeenshire as religious bigots. This was too much, and Boothby publicly denounced Wolrige-Gordon. It was wrong of him to have done so, but the Forbes-Leiths and others of his friends in the constituency had turned strongly against Wolrige-Gordon, and Boothby was genuinely angry, as I vividly recall, and exasperated beyond endurance. However, it was very unfair to a young man struggling for political survival; in the event he did survive, only to lose the seat, as Boothby had forecast, in 1974. Wolrige-Gordon may have made mistakes, but Boothby's public intervention in a local political row is very difficult to excuse.

An episode which occurred in the autumn of 1959 was particularly unpleasant, but as it was widely misunderstood at the time – and later – it must be related.

Boothby's generosity to Scots who were down and out in London was fabled, and lasted long after his death – indeed, to this day they arrive, at inconvenient hours, at 1 Eaton Square to seek assistance, which in his lifetime was never denied. If it was foolish, it was only too characteristic.

One young man, aged seventeen, and the son of two former constituents and friends, was given the job of occasional cleaning and odd jobs in Boothby's flat, to assist his butler, Gordon Goodfellow. One morning Boothby discovered that his valuable watch and chain were missing, and told the police; the young man was arrested, and Boothby's watch and chain were recovered.

Boothby wrote to him to say that he had no sense of grievance but was very disappointed in him, and suggested that he should co-operate fully with the magistrates. Somewhat eagerly interviewed by a journalist from the *Daily Express*, the young man said firmly, 'I have a very high opinion of Lord Boothby. He is not only generous, but he is a great character. I will always be grateful for his kindness to me.' But the interview led the *Sunday Express* to draw more sinister implications about their relationship, and Boothby protested strongly to the editor, John Junor, who was apologetic. However, Boothby wrote to him on 2 October:

> I am very surprised to hear that the boy attacked me in an interview, because I got him a job as a van-driver in Edinburgh; and have since had letters of almost piteous gratitude from him, and from his mother.
>
> However, as a great-aunt of mine used to say, all good deeds are punished.
>
> The fact remains that, to those who do not know that I would give half a bottle of champagne to a cat if it asked for it, the implications underlying John Gordon's paragraph – at least among the 'sophisticated' – was that I had rewarded him for services rendered. And I have had quite a rough time over it.
>
> However I don't really mind that. As an Air-Vice Marshal once remarked to Randolph [Churchill] in White's: 'I don't mind you calling me a bugger, because I know that I am not one. I *do* mind you calling me yellow.'
>
> What hurt like hell, and roused Aberdeenshire to a pitch of absolute fury, was that beastly remark about my 'punctured ego'. This was not 'verbal fisticuffs'. It was downright malice. And I can never quite forgive you for it, because we were old friends; and as I think I wrote at the time, you knew bloody well that I am not *that* kind of a shit.
>
> The hell with it all. We are growing old – I faster than you. I am out of party politics, God bless me, I am a Rector – and an LLD! If you are prepared to call it a day, so am I; and we might as well have a drink on it, for old times' sake.
>
> To-morrow, more's the pity.
>
> > *Away we both must hie*
> > *To air the ditty,*
> > *And to earth I.*
>
> > Yours ever,
> > Bob

Junor replied, apparently sincerely and contritely:

> My dear Bob
>   I am most distressed by your letter and in particular by your suggestion that we have been implying that you are a homosexual.

I do earnestly assure you that you are reading something into the
paragraph which was not in the mind of John Gordon when he wrote it.
And certainly was not, and never has been, in my mind. . . . Of one thing
you may be sure. There is no personal vendetta. There is instead a deep
personal admiration and a quite considerable affection.

Beaverbrook, to whom Boothby had also protested, wrote to him on 2
October:

I am sure that they have not been carrying any vendetta . . . the newspapers
with which I am connected will always give you a square deal.

Your many years of service in the House of Commons have given you a
prestige that has not often been excelled in the history of the House.

Yours ever
Max

But, in spite of these unequivocal disclaimers, an impression had been
created about Boothby's private life that was to surface more sensationally
in 1964.*

When Beecham's wish that Boothby should become Chairman of the
Royal Philharmonic Orchestra was made known to him, Boothby was
both flattered and delighted. But he soon found that the politics of music
are as convoluted and passionate as any other. First the financial situation
was bad, and then the Home Secretary, Henry Brooke, told the Commons that the orchestra had no right to call itself Royal. Boothby then had
a moment of pure inspiration. He had known the Queen Mother for a
long time, and was aware of her love of music and admiration for the
Philharmonic; he therefore wrote to ask if she would become its patron.
To his delight she accepted, and, in Boothby's words, 'she saved the
orchestra. Of all the manifold public services she has rendered to the
country, this is not the least.' Furthermore, the Queen, on the advice of
the then Home Secretary, Roy Jenkins, eventually restored the Royal title.
The orchestra flourished under Boothby's chairmanship and the Queen
Mother's keen patronage. Boothby took it on to honour Beecham's
memory and in gratitude for his long friendship; he found it hard going,
and often exasperating, but the fact that the orchestra not only survived its
financial and other crises, but developed into one of the greatest in the
world, was a very significant achievement, about which he was always very
modest, giving all the praise to others, and especially to the Queen

---

*And, very surprisingly, repeated in Sir John Junor's memoirs, published in 1990.

Mother. It was a good repayment of the debt he owed to music and musicians throughout his life.

Boothby was immensely attracted by the idea of a merger. The orchestra received no subsidies of any kind; concerts at the Albert Hall almost invariably lost money; and even a wholly successful tour of West Germany resulted in a loss. Thus, Boothby was very receptive when the Chairman of the Friends of Covent Garden, Sir Leon Bagrit, suggested that there might be 'some form of amalgamation or association'. As Boothby reported to the Queen Mother, early in 1963,

> It became clear, in the course of our talk, that his own ideas were extremely ambitious; and that what he envisaged was nothing less than an organisation on the lines of Vienna, where an orchestra of some 180 players gives concerts as the Vienna Philharmonic, and also plays in the State Opera House. It seemed to me that this opened up a new and hopeful line of advance for the whole future of music in London; and that we ought at least to have preliminary discussions with Covent Garden, with a view to subsequent negotiations if agreement in principle was reached. . . . The harsh fact remains that there are at present too many London orchestras pursuing too few concert halls.

No one else agreed with him. Glyndebourne would not co-operate; nor would the players; and the members of the Board of the Royal Philharmonic unanimously rejected the idea. Taking the somewhat portentous line 'No merger, No Boothby,' he resigned in March 1963. The public reason was the pressure of work and his numerous other commitments, and it was certainly true that his doctor had told him severely that after the age of sixty no one should pursue more than six professions simultaneously. But the real cause was the fact that he found himself in a minority of one on a major issue of strategy.

To return to 1958, John Freeman, whose political career appeared to have ended,* began one of the most famous series of interviews in British television, *Face to Face*, and chose the newly ennobled Boothby as his third interviewee. Boothby later related:

I was a little surprised when they told me that they wanted me to sit for a portrait by [Felix] Topolski. I was still more surprised when I reached the studio at Lime

---

*John Freeman had been Labour MP for Watford, 1945–55; Financial Secretary, War Office, 1946–7; Parliamentary Under-Secretary of State, War Office, 1947; and Parliamentary Secretary, Ministry of Supply, 1947–51. He resigned in 1951. He was assistant editor of *New Statesman*, 1951; deputy editor, 1958–60; and editor, 1961–5. From 1965 to 1968 he was High Commissioner in India, and from 1969 to 1971 British Ambassador to the United States. Later he became Chairman of London Weekend Television and Chairman of Independent Television News.

Grove and received a message: 'Mr Freeman thinks you will understand that he does not wish to see you before the programme.' I was then taken to a studio draped in jet black, with God knows how many cameras and lights. Then, suddenly, John appeared, and sat opposite to me with the cameras behind. And it began. I was not frightened, because I am always happy in a studio. But it was rather a daunting experience.

It was, in fact, a virtuoso performance by both men, and Freeman's friendship did not inhibit him at all from asking probing questions, including on the Czech assets affair, to which Boothby responded openly and engagingly. It was judged a sensational success, and there were widespread calls for it to be repeated. This was agreed to, and Freeman prepared an introduction which is as felicitous a portrait of the subject as has ever been attempted:

The programme that you are about to see is different in one important way from all the others we have done in *Face to Face*. Baron Boothby, of Buchan and Rattray Head – to give him his full title, which he rather enjoys – is a personal friend of long standing. That meant two things. First, that I already had very clear views about his character and personality. Secondly, that I had to ask myself whether I was tough enough to give a friend the full treatment, and not let him off lightly.

As to the first, many of you have your own opinions about Bob Boothby, but I will tell you how I see him. I think he is one of the most gifted and idealistic and truthful men anywhere in public life. He is also lazy and self-indulgent and over-generous. All these qualities mixed up together have resulted in the comparative failure of his public life, and the total success of his personal friendships. He has usually backed the right political horses; but when, in the end, they gallop home, Bob seldom shares the winnings. He is either in disgrace for having blurted out something indiscreet, or he is off playing baccarat at Deauville. Occasionally he amuses himself by trying, with perfect good humour, to deny these charges. You will be able to judge whether he does so in this programme – and whether I have succeeded in making them stick.

Boothby's outstanding personal virtue, in public and in private, was that while he could be very funny about others, he was never malicious, although a certain steel would enter his voice when Churchill's name arose – but, even on this sticky subject, there was far more admiration and praise than criticism. But, very unusually, he genuinely did not care what people thought of him; he was what he was, take it or leave it. It was this quality of total frankness and truthfulness about himself that had been largely responsible for his outstanding success on radio and television. The fact that all this was very un-English never seems to have occurred to him.

He was certainly determined to enjoy the House of Lords. He later claimed that it was Macmillan who suggested that he should be an

Independent peer and sit on the crossbenches, so that he would have greater freedom of action than if he took the Conservative Whip. As has been seen, Macmillan gave this advice regarding the Rectorship of St Andrews. Boothby took the advice, then and afterwards. He was delighted when I once told him that Selwyn Lloyd was alleged to have said when he became Speaker of the House of Commons, 'Thank God I no longer have to pretend I am a Conservative'; I rather got the impression that Boothby wished he had said it himself.

Thus, it was as an independent crossbencher that he sat in the Lords.

16

Twilight and Dusk
1960–86

*A*t its peak *Any Questions?* had an audience of over sixteen million listeners and the 'reply' programme for letters from the public, *Any Answers?*, which ran for half an hour, was also highly popular.

Radio, like television, and indeed most media, is very ephemeral, and it is difficult to convey to a later generation, in cold print, how enjoyable, what fun and how informative this programme was. My family listened to it religiously every week, and so, obviously, did many others. As in *In the News* and *Free Speech*, Boothby was absolutely at home in the programme, which he himself greatly enjoyed. It was another source of much jealousy on the part of his parliamentary colleagues and Conservative Central Office, which wanted other, no doubt more worthy, but far less amusing and interesting Conservatives on the programme to put the Party point of view with greater solemnity than Boothby could muster. As in the case of *In the News*, these hints – and rather more than hints – were initially firmly resisted by BBC radio.

Boothby's dedication to the programme was such that when he once fell and gashed his head rushing to catch a train at Paddington, injuring himself quite badly, he insisted on doing the programme, and was on his usual excellent form, until Grisewood led him to a waiting ambulance and he was taken to hospital. There was another awful occasion when he had a violent attack of hiccups during the programme – which was, of course, live – and on another he had a sudden and violent nosebleed. But each time the show went on, and no listener thought that anything was amiss. It was this sheer professionalism and reliability that made producers love him, and the actor *manqué* in him was given full rein.

Everyone who has been on the programme has stories about the experience. On one occasion Boothby drove Tom Driberg and Violet Bonham Carter down to Bristol. Driberg was drunk and in alcoholic tears; he had fallen violently in love with the American singer, Johnny Ray, but the latter had indignantly resisted his advances. He then remembered that it was Good Friday and, in lachrymose vein, asked Boothby to find a church when they got to Bristol. He reluctantly agreed, but his principal concern was how they were to sober Driberg up before the programme. Driberg then turned to Violet Bonham Carter, sitting primly in the back, and tearfully asked if she would come to church with him. 'I am not going to intervene between you and your Maker!' was the bleak reply. With the aid of much coffee and cold water they got Driberg on to the stage in reasonable order, and Grisewood, to whom this possibility was a recurrent nightmare, shielded him carefully.

Then disaster did strike. On 23 March 1962 the *Any Questions?* team of Grisewood, Boothby, Jack Longland, Mary Stocks and Ralph Wightman travelled to Liphook in Hampshire. The team dined well, as it was the 500th programme, and were in a relaxed mood, one of the topics of discussion being a very well-publicised recent remark of the Duke of Edinburgh that the *Daily Express* was 'a bloody awful newspaper, packed with lies'. This comment had occasioned a number of excellent cartoons, including a classic one by 'Giles' in the *Sunday Express* showing Beaverbrook arriving in chains at the Traitor's Gate at the Tower of London remarking, 'At least he reads it!', and harmless chaffing by the *Express*'s rivals. What none of the team seemed to have anticipated was that this would be raised in the programme, but it duly was by a Mrs Eastman. Boothby pounced on the question eagerly, strongly supported by Longland, but he did not leave matters with his excoriation of the *Daily Express* as a newspaper, but ploughed in deeper:

And, as for these Canadians, I have known them all – Morden, Borden, Beaverbrook, Dunn and Bennett. I would keep them all out of this country. I would throw in Roy Thomson as well. Keep them out. We have just passed an Immigration Bill to keep out the West Indians. My God, I would pass an Immigration Bill to keep out the Canadians. They have done nothing but damage to this country.

Many listeners were delighted, including Frances Lloyd George who wrote: 'I listened with sheer delight to your completely uninhibited broadcast in *Any Questions?* on Friday. I think I must have known Beaverbrook longer than you, but I hesitate to say what I really think of him because he has always been very kind to me.' So had he been to Boothby, but what the latter had considered to be jocular remarks were interpreted very differently by others. He awoke the following morning to find that, once again, he had got himself into very deep trouble.

The first shock was the announcement that the entire editorial staff of the *Daily Express* proposed to issue a writ for libel against the BBC, Boothby and Longland. This was bad enough, but it was only the beginning. Of the Canadians denounced by Boothby, only Thomson and Beaverbrook were alive, but Beaverbrook had been a close friend of Bennett and Dunn – whose widow was to be his second wife – and was a fierce protector of all Canadians. He was on holiday in the South of France when he was alerted not only by the *Express* but by an understandably irate Canadian High Commissioner. Fierce letters were dispatched to the Chairman of the Governors of the BBC and the Director-General demanding a total and abject public apology and damages, and expensive lawyers were swiftly marshalled.

The subsequent extensive correspondence between Beaverbrook's lawyers and the BBC centred on the degree of liability, if any, that the Corporation had for broadcasting a live programme over which it had no control and, therefore, it argued, no responsibility. Beaverbrook would have none of that and pursued the BBC tenaciously until it eventually tried to compromise with a full broadcast apology, but no damages. That, also, was rejected. Beaverbrook was not interested in the money – he chose a derisory figure of £5,000 damages – but in the principle, and his lawyers were urged on to final victory.

While these missives were flying around London, principally delivered by hand, the full horror of Boothby's position was now apparent to him. His first instinct was to write to Beaverbrook personally to apologise, but he was advised that this was legally quite improper in the circumstances, despite their long friendship. Legally, this advice was quite correct, but Boothby's silence irritated Beaverbrook further. Eventually, Boothby took up his pen.

Personal   May 11, 1962
Dear Max

    I have had your Solicitor's letter – and a lot of others!

    I am not concerned, at the moment, with the legal aspects. All I want you to know is that I very much regret what I said on that programme. As you were in the South of France at the time, you probably didn't hear it. It took place after a very good dinner to celebrate the 500th anniversay of 'Any Questions?'; and was, to say the least of it, light-hearted and gay. None of the questions were of a serious character; and I must confess that I took this one as a complete joke. It was loaded, in the sense that we were asked whether we agreed with the Duke of Edinburgh that the *Daily Express* was 'a bloody awful newspaper, packed with lies'. And our off-the-cuff answers were greeted by the audience in the spirit in which they were made – with ripples of merry laughter. No one listening could possibly have mistaken the mood; but I realise that in cold print they assume a very different character.

I am particularly vexed because, as your Solicitor rightly points out, we have been friends for 35 years; and I never forget that, in the darkest hour of my life, you were the staunchest friend I had in the seat of power. The letter which you sent me, at that time, is one of my most treasured possessions.

I can only claim, in extenuation, that I did subsequently say, in this actual programme, that you had rendered unparalleled service to Britain in the supreme crisis of fate; and flatly contradicted Mary Stocks when she said that you wanted a Peerage.

Well – there it is. You know well enough *how* it is when I am in a merry mood. And I can only say that I am sorry.

I had the greatest respect and admiration for Sir Robert Borden, who gave a splendid start to my political career when he much over-praised a speech which I made in Ottawa in the year 1925; and Sir James Dunn was always a good friend to me.

Altogether it is most unfortunate business, but my remarks were never intended to be taken seriously, and I can assure you that they sounded quite different from what they read.

I would still like to greet you at your birthday party; but, if you would rather I didn't, just let me know.

Yours ever
Bob

This put matters right at once. Beaverbrook had a very soft spot for Boothby and had no wish to pursue him; his real target was the BBC. He replied immediately that 'You may take it from me that as far as you are concerned I will not seek from you payment of any costs I may incur provided of course that I get an apology from you in open Court which has my approval,' to which Boothby fervently replied that 'You will indeed.' Beaverbrook instructed his solicitors 'to let Boothby off', especially when he learned that Boothby also had been having severe difficulties with the BBC about the terms of his apology, and which Boothby described to Beaverbrook as 'a parody of the bureaucracy upon which you trampled so successfully in 1940'. Then, the BBC offered £2,000 to Beaverbrook and claimed the full amount from Boothby.

Boothby wrote mournfully to Beaverbrook on 31 July:

I have had a long grilling over this and do not yet see the way out. It occurs to me that you might now be willing to call it a day, and withdraw both your Writs. Alternatively, if you wish to proceed against the BBC, that you might reduce the damages to a sum which is within my capacity to pay; because it now seems almost certain that I will have to pay them. But I am no lawyer; and your Solicitors are clearly in a better position to give an opinion than Yours ever Bob.

Beaverbrook was not going to have this, and the BBC lawyers were told emphatically that he demanded complete indemnity not only for his costs but for Boothby's as well. As an act of real kindness and magnanimity it was notable even by Beaverbrook's standards, and removed Boothby not only from an embarrassing but potentially very expensive situation. Boothby was not only relieved but sincerely grateful, and he wrote to Beaverbrook on 18 July that

> I have now cancelled all my radio and television contracts for the foreseeable future; and this letter is only to tell you that I think I have taken enough punishment, and to ask you to give me a break now – if only for old times' sake. I have made tentative plans to go in the autumn to look at your beloved Commonwealth. Please let me do this in some peace of mind.

Unhappily, having been extricated from a hopeless situation by Beaverbrook's friendship, Boothby now got himself into further trouble, to the despair of his friends – and of his biographer.

In the next episode of this unhappy saga, and after the BBC, Boothby and Longland had made a completely public apology, broadcast by the BBC and widely published elsewhere, strong objection was taken by Beaverbrook's lawyers to remarks made by Boothby in his *Dinner Time* programme on Independent Television.

The programme opened, inauspiciously, with Boothby apologising for remarks about the Royal Academy made in a previous programme, adding that 'I seem to spend most of my life these days making apologies in public. Whether this is a sign of rejuvenation or degeneration I am not sure.' Jo Grimond then remarked that politicians 'are getting extremely soft' about having to apologise for statements of opinion. Boothby warmly agreed – rather too warmly.

> It is true. We are mealy-mouthed. Terribly mealy-mouthed. And I think that the laws of libel are far too tough in this country. I have been afflicted by them lately by the press. But on the other hand I think they bear far more heavily on the press than they do on the individual. I think the libel laws of the United States are much better than they are in this country. They are much laxer. But why the devil should not you say almost anything you like?

To which Grimond commented that, 'If you are not careful, you are going to have another half hour [in Court] next week.'

This thoughtless idiocy nearly wrecked everything, but fortunately

Boothby had not named names and had condemned the law rather than the practitioners, and, mercifully, had defended the press. His own long-suffering lawyers took the firm view that his remarks, although unfortunate, were not actionable, and there the matter rested – until 1 December, when the editor of the *Sunday Express* received a letter from Boothby in which he accused Beaverbrook of 'supporting the filthy Nazi regime' and describing a recent tribute by him to Churchill as 'nauseating'. The full text was as follows:

> Sir
>
> Lord Beaverbrook's tribute to Sir Winston Churchill is moving. He has reason to be grateful to Churchill, who did him well.
>
> But who was the greatest champion and supporter of Neville Chamberlain before the last war? Beaverbrook. Who supported the shameful Munich agreement – against Churchill? Beaverbrook.
>
> Who supported the filthy Nazi regime? Beaverbrook.
>
> Who wrote, day after day, 'THERE WILL BE NO WAR'? Beaverbrook.
>
> So the tribute is not only moving, it is also nauseating.
>
> Boothby

It was not a letter intended for publication, nor was it published, but Beaverbrook was now seriously angry, and with good cause. It was decided not to issue a writ, but Boothby received a clear and strong warning that 'if you repeat these libels in a form which will enable our client to issue a writ against you, we will do so without further notice'.

Boothby's intemperate letter, of the kind to which he was all too addicted, was of course based upon his justifiable contempt for the position of the Beaverbrook newspapers towards the dictators before the war, a point on which Beaverbrook was understandably highly sensitive, but Boothby had, once again, gone too far, and more abject apologies were necessary. After this near-miss Boothby came to his senses and cordial relations were resumed, which lasted until Beaverbrook's death. Boothby's folly throughout almost defies belief, and he was fortunate that Beaverbrook, who comes out of the imbroglio with great credit for his tolerance, still retained his genuine affection and regard for him. He also understood that on the 1938–9 situation Boothby was irrational and obsessed. Both closed this lamentable episode with relief, but it did no good to Boothby's reputation, then or later, especially with the BBC, and marked a major event in the decline of his broadcasting and television careers, which were so crucial for his income.

Even more seriously, the lesson had been learnt the hard way that the BBC *was* legally responsible for what was said in live discussion groups, and that erratic and uncontrollable mavericks like Boothby could be an expensive form of public entertainment. The movement towards much safer, and much duller, participants had begun, and *Any Questions?* not only gradually lost its former zest and unpredictability but its huge listening audience. The price paid for Boothby's outburst after far too good a dinner (for which the BBC itself should have taken some responsibility) was a heavy one, and remains so. It was a melancholy milestone in the decline of perhaps the best regular radio programme ever put on by the BBC, and it was very ironical that it should have been Boothby who unwittingly but foolishly began the process.

But this controversy was nothing compared to the next major episode in his life.

The Macmillan Government had been rocked and grievously damaged by a series of scandals in 1962, culminating in that involving a senior minister, John Profumo, and the atmosphere in London was quite exceptionally poisonous, with wild and improbable allegations being made about the private lives and sexual habits of prominent people – the more prominent, the better. When Macmillan resigned the premiership in October 1963 it was for health reasons that were genuine, but the fevered atmosphere in Fleet Street continued. In 1964 Boothby became a victim of it.

In July 1964 Boothby was on holiday with Colin Coote in France in Vittel taking the cure when he became innocently embroiled in an episode that was bizarre even by the standards of his life, and which, although he later looked back upon it with amusement, was not funny at all at the time. Also, as it has been seriously misinterpreted, the full story must be related.

Writing to a new and valued friend, Wanda Sanna, he said that

> Like the Flying Dutchman, I wander about the world. I like to think that the cure here does me good. It is certainly very dull. Next week I return to London for a brief spell, and then move on to Canada and the United States. . . . I think that perhaps I should have been a film actor instead of a politician. Too late now. For that, and for everything except the life of a laughing rover. I wonder if we shall meet again? I hope so. I hope also that things are going well for you, and that you are happy.

This was written from the Grand Hotel on 16 July, on the eve of the storm that now engulfed him.

The *Sunday Mirror* had been conducting for some time a very worthy and timely investigation into protection rackets and brutal gangsterism in London, with which the names of the Kray brothers, although then not publicly known, have become inseparably linked. The *Sunday Mirror*, under the leadership of Cecil King and Hugh Cudlipp, was making a conscious and honourable attempt to distance itself from Sunday sensationalism, and had achieved a reputation for almost obsessive caution and being factually meticulous. It was, therefore, a genuine sensation when, on 11 July, under blaring headlines 'Peer and a Gangster: Yard Probe Public Men at Seaside Parties', it announced that 'a top-level Scotland Yard investigation into the alleged homosexual relationship between a prominent peer and a leading thug in the London underworld has been ordered by the Metropolitan Police Commissioner Sir Joseph Simpson'. The decision to publish the story was taken by the editor, Reginald Payne, in spite of the doubts of some of his colleagues, and without informing Cecil King or Hugh Cudlipp, who was on holiday on his yacht in the Mediterranean. It is possible that no one fully appreciated what a bombshell they had exploded. When the chief political correspondent, John Beavan, rang on the previous evening to ask if any political guidance was needed, nothing was said about the 'Peer and Thug' story, it being regarded simply as a crime story.

When Scotland Yard issued a strong denial that any such investigation was taking place, and that the story was a complete fabrication, the *Mirror* group found itself in a serious quandary. All that Monday's *Daily Mirror* could report was that rumours were buzzing, as indeed they were. In Vittel, Boothby and Coote speculated idly and amusedly about who the unnamed peer might be.

Also, no attempt was made to contact Boothby. What had happened was that some time before Ronald Kray had asked to see Boothby about a proposed business deal in Nigeria. Boothby had never heard of Kray – indeed, outside Scotland Yard and the East End criminal world, no one had – and invited him to his flat to discuss it. Kray had described the proposal, which Boothby, wisely for once, turned down. Kray had brought a photographer with him and asked if they could be photographed together, as he liked collecting pictures of himself with famous people. Boothby had agreed and thought no more about the matter. In fact, he had entirely forgotten about it.

On the Monday there arrived at the offices of the *Sunday Mirror*, without any letter or attachment, the photograph of Boothby in his flat sitting on his sofa next to Kray. Extraordinarily, this seemed to the editor as complete confirmation of the allegation, regardless of the Scotland Yard denial. On the following Sunday, under the blaring headline 'The Picture We Must Not Print', he published the photograph, describing it as 'of the highest significance and public concern'. Nor was this all, as the article linked the photograph with a new ruling that the Director of Public

Prosecutions had advised Chief Constables to refer any charges against homosexuals to him, with the clear implication that here was another Profumo-like cover-up. This was vehemently denied by the Attorney-General, Sir John Hobson, one of the most widely respected and honest men in public life, so the newspaper had printed another totally false story. Also, many were quick to note that the original story had stated that 'The peer concerned is a household name.'

When Boothby and Coote returned to London on the 17th, both were amazed to discover that not only was Boothby being widely named as the peer concerned but the rumours had greatly escalated. In a chance telephone conversation with Tom Driberg Boothby had asked who this famous peer was; there was an embarrassed silence, and then Driberg said, 'I'm sorry, Bob, it's you.' Boothby hurriedly got back copies of the newspapers and consulted friends, and was astonished to find that some actually believed the farrago of nonsense that was sweeping through London. Others, who did not, supplied him with the most lurid stories. In that post-Profumo atmosphere the degree of credulity about absurd rumours of men in public life had reached a level that was unprecedented and has, thankfully, never been reached since.

When Boothby realised the full scale of the allegations against him, as usual accompanied by happy sniggers among his enemies and the dismay of his friends, he resolved on direct action. Meanwhile, Cudlipp had returned from holiday and was appalled by the actions of his editor, which had taken his paper back to the kind of lurid and dangerous sensational-ism from which he and King had been working so hard to extricate their papers. Everything of substance in the stories had been strongly and publicly denied by the police and the Attorney-General; all that was left was a photograph! It says much for the mood of the time that so many people in public life seemed to accept that the charges must be true, while Cudlipp and King realised they were not.

Boothby's solicitor was abroad on holiday, so he telephoned his old friend, Gerald Gardiner, now an eminent QC and shortly to become Lord Chancellor, for his advice. It was agreed to meet the matter head on, and Gardiner prepared a draft letter before he, too, went on holiday in Italy. He also advised Boothby to entrust the negotiations to the solicitor Arnold Goodman, who had established a formidable reputation in these matters, but at that time was not well known outside his profession.

No friend could have done more to assist someone in a crisis. Never-theless, Gardiner and his advisers wanted to be quite clear, and con-vinced, of Boothby's total innocence of the allegations, and subjected him to strong interrogation. They emerged totally satisfied that he had been abominably libelled. Gardiner minuted on the notorious photograph that

'This sort of bad luck can happen to particularly polite people', which was absolutely true. Boothby took Gardiner's draft letter and added some personal embellishments of his own, and Goodman took up the matter of a suitably abject apology and a sum of money in lieu of damages with the Mirror Group's laywers. There was not much resistance, he discovered, and the negotiations were not prolonged. Goodman has modestly claimed that his role in the affair was a minor one, and that the principal credit for the outcome should be given to Gardiner; Boothby was eternally grateful to both of them.*

On 31 July Boothby delivered to *The Times* one of the most devastating letters of his life:

Sir,

On July 17th I returned to London from France and I found, to my amazement, that Parliament, Fleet Street and other informed quarters in London were seething with rumours that I have a homosexual relationship with a leading thug in the underworld involved in a West End protection racket; that I have been to 'all-male' Mayfair parties with him; that I have been photographed with him in a compromising position on a sofa; that a homosexual relationship exists between me, some East End gangsters and a number of clergymen in Brighton; that some people who know of these relationships are being blackmailed; and that Scotland Yard have for months been watching meetings between me and the underworld thug, and have investigated all these matters and reported on them to the Commissioner of the Metropolitan Police.

I have, for many years, appeared on radio and television programmes; and, for this reason alone, my name might reasonably be described as 'a household name', as it has been in the *Sunday Mirror*. On many occasions I have been photographed, at their request, with people who have claimed to be 'fans' of mine; and on one occasion I was photographed, with my full consent, in my flat (which is also my office) with a gentleman who came to see me, accompanied by two friends, in order to ask me to take an active part in a business venture which seemed to me to be of interest and importance. After careful consideration I turned down this request, on the ground that my existing commitments prevented me from taking on anything more, and my letter of refusal is in his possession.

I have since been told that some years ago the person concerned was convicted of a criminal offence; but I knew then, and know now, nothing of this. So far as I am concerned, anyone is welcome to see or to publish any photographs that have ever been taken of me.

I am satisfied that the source of all these sinister rumours is the *Sunday*

---

*I am most grateful to Lord Goodman for his kindness in showing me the papers on the case, particularly the correspondence with Gardiner, and his notes on the negotiations, and for discussing the matter with me.

Mirror and the *Daily Mirror*. I am not a homosexual. I have not been to a Mayfair party of any kind for more than 20 years. I have met the man who is alleged to be a 'king of the underworld' only three times, on business matters; and then by appointment in my flat, at his request, and in the company of other people.

I have never been to a party in Brighton with gangsters – still less clergymen. No one has ever tried to blackmail me. The police say that they have not watched any meetings, or conducted any investigations, or made any reports to the Home Secretary connected with me. In short, the whole affair is a tissue of atrocious lies.

I am not by nature thin-skinned; but this sort of thing makes a mockery of any decent kind of life, public or private, in what is still supposed to be a civilised country. It is, in my submission, intolerable that any man should be put into the cruel dilemma of having either to remain silent while such rumours spread, or considerably to increase the circulation of certain newspapers by publicly denying them. If either the *Sunday Mirror* or the *Daily Mirror* is in possession of a shred of evidence – documentary or photographic – against me, let them print it and take the consequences. I am sending a copy of this to both.

> Your obedient servant
> Boothby

The next day was a Saturday, and Boothby had already left London to stay with friends in Cambridge. If he had hoped to elude the press he was unsuccessful. All he could tell the reporters, 'clutching his glasses, his silver hair unruly, and unshaven,' the *Daily Express* noted, as though this was somewhat extraordinary early on a Sunday morning, was that he was consulting his lawyers on the following day and that 'it had to come out in the open'.

James Margach, the political correspondent of *The Times*, also tracked him down and wrote this vivid description:

Last night Lord Boothby, tired but ebullient, said 'I feel very happy. Thank God the letter has appeared. You can't imagine how relieved I am now that the lid has been blown off.'

He was in a country house expressly chosen for its seclusion. Croquet on the lawn, lavender and china dogs in the drawing-room reinforce the atmosphere of complete privacy. But a collage of daily newspapers strewn on the next chair – all of them with the name Boothby in headline black – was reminder that any severance from London was only temporary. When he went for a drink in a nearby pub, burly and hopelessly recognisable in weekend sports jacket and his inevitably faded Old Etonian tie, the silence was palpable enough to weigh by the pound. But ten minutes of Boothby's well-known telegenic personality thawed the tension.

Finally Lord Boothby returned for a dinner party. 'It's been quite a weekend,' he said.

The *Sunday Mirror* published the letter without comment, and in every newspaper it was a major item. Meanwhile the International Publishing Corporation now appreciated the full enormity of what its newspaper had done. To the great credit of King and Cudlipp they decided to take immediate action, rather than to place Boothby in the expensive business of issuing writs for libel, which, it was manifestly clear, he was fully entitled to do. What particularly horrified them both was that there was not a fragment of evidence to support, even faintly, the original charges, and they resolved to come to terms immediately and to settle the matter swiftly and generously. On 6 August IPC issued a complete apology signed by King himself 'to take all steps to clear Lord Boothby's reputation'; it declared that 'when a newspaper is wrong it should state so promptly and without equivocation', and that 'any imputation of an improper nature against Lord Boothby is completely unjustified'; it expressed 'the personal regret of myself and the directors of IPC that the story appeared', and said that IPC had paid Boothby £40,000 as compensation.

In 1964 £40,000 was a vast sum in compensation for libel, and reflected not only the legal advice submitted to IPC but the shame felt by King and Cudlipp over the whole affair. Boothby regarded it as 'dirty money' which he would not touch, although his finances were not in good shape. His first donation was to the King Edward VII Hospital, which had looked after him so well. The editor of the *Sunday Mirror* was summarily dismissed. Boothby wrote in gratitude to Gardiner in Italy, who replied on 10 August that

> I do realise that you must have had an awful 6 days and have felt that we were all being very tough with you, but that sort of thing requires a great deal of thought and some very careful handling. . . . We were lucky in having Mr. Goodman's help, as he is one of the shrewdest bargainers in the business. It is, I think, the fastest and largest settlement of the kind ever made. So it should have been.

One would have thought that this would be the end of the matter. When Ronald Kray was on trial in 1969 with his brothers, he excitedly claimed that he had many 'influential friends', including Boothby, the Earl of Effingham, Sophie Tucker and Judy Garland. 'Judy Garland – I would be having a drink with her now if I were out of here – Sophie Tucker and Lord Effingham. I've had drinks with all types of people, some of them quite distinguished,' he shouted into the microphone: 'Lord Boothby – I have had drinks with him.' This was true. At the famous photographed meeting Boothby had given him a gin and tonic; as he wearily told the press, 'My friends joke that Bob always offers his guests a gin and tonic.'

But astonishingly and lamentably, some of the mud stuck, and years later one still finds people linking Boothby's name with that of the infamous Krays. In his obituary in the *Daily Telegraph* it was written that 'When he was photographed in company with the Kray brothers, even the friendliest of eyebrows were raised.' He was never photographed 'in company with the Kray brothers', and the obituarist failed to mention the circumstances and the sequel.

Boothby's old friends rallied round strongly, Compton Mackenzie writing from France that 'I felt ten years younger' after he had read Boothby's letter. Arthur Salter wrote him a letter that he particularly treasured:

> Hickory Farm, Lee, Mass[achusetts]. Aug 4th.
>
> My dear Bob
>
> *The Times* of Saturday, with your letter in it, has just reached me here. I have read it with a combination of intense indignation, deep sympathy, & utter amazement such as I have rarely if ever before felt. I had of course seen rumours about 'a peer', but being away from England had not heard them connected with you, and your letter came as a staggering surprise. By the same post as *The Times* comes the *Sunday Times* of the 2nd, with its announcement that you intend to take legal action & I hope intensely that this will give you all that you wish from it.
>
> My mind has naturally gone back to the trivial technicality which, a quarter of a century ago, interrupted your political career – & I have been reflecting that since then no one in public life has, as one can see in retrospect, been so uniformly right on each of the great issues on which he has fought, or devoted such courage, ability and persistent effort in contending against those who took the opposite (and disastrously wrong) side at the time . . .
>
> Yours ever
> Arthur

Michael Foot wrote after the settlement was announced:

> I write to add my congratulations to the multitudes you must have received and deserved. You displayed great nerve and courage. But who would have expected otherwise?
>
> But I must add this one cautionary word. A non-playing captain who gets £40,000 in one slam runs a grave risk of losing his amateur status.

Boothby was almost swamped with congratulations, not only for the successful outcome but for the style with which he had handled the affair. He also had an outstandingly supportive and admiring response from the press. The *New Statesman* referred to it as 'one of the murkiest episodes in Fleet Street's recent history' and said that only two people emerge with credit from the Sunday Mirror/Boothby affair: Lord Boothby himself and Cecil King. Boothby has demonstrated for all the world to see that the right way to tackle a newspaper smear is to hit back hard and openly. Not all have his courage. Perhaps more will in the future as a result of his action.

The *Economist* commented that 'Everyone in Britain who has heard, half-believed, and maybe even done a bit to pass on with embroidery that latest bit of spicy nonsense can now feel thoroughly ashamed of himself. There should be a lot of red faces around Fleet Street, and around the Palace of Westminster, these days.'

The sequel contained some unusual happenings. The Krays, who had of course supplied the photograph to the *Sunday Mirror*, were so encouraged by Boothby's coup that they also attempted to sue the newspaper for libel, on the grounds that the phrase 'a leading thug in the underworld' was grossly defamatory of Ronald Kray's reputation and good name. But the Mirror group knew enough about the Krays to stand firm, and the impudent challenge faded away.

One very unfortunate consequence was that the Boothby case intimidated not only those journalists and newspapers which were hot on the trail of the Kray operations, but also the police. As John Pearson has written in his remarkable history of the Kray saga: 'They were entrenched now; nobody wanted to risk trouble from them. Four years of fraud and murder were to pass before the spell was broken.'*

Boothby proceeded to enjoy giving the 'dirty money' away, mainly in covenants to members of his family and the children of friends for their education. Characteristically, he was carried away and covenanted far more than the £40,000, as his second wife was to discover to her dismay. But the 'dirty money' was put to excellent use, and the matter closed in typical style and generosity.

Boothby never quite came to terms with Churchill, but he was astonished by the virulence with which Alan Brooke, Churchill's Chief of the Imperial Staff, spoke of his former master. He was by then Lord Alanbrooke, and even his carefully edited diaries – by Arthur Bryant – revealed his true feelings about Churchill. Even Boothby was startled, as he told Macmillan, who was not at all surprised. What Boothby had not appreciated was how much Macmillan had disliked Churchill as well. As so often happened, politically they were on the same side.

But Boothby's warm heart made him sad at Churchill's decline into

* John Pearson, *The Profession of Violence*, p. 125.

melancholy old age. He had known him for so long and, in spite of everything, totally acknowledged his greatness. The trouble was that whenever he did so he added a perfectly justified caveat. As Churchill had become a national icon, beyond all possible criticism, these reservations caused deep offence to the Churchillian faithful. What he knew was Churchill the man – brilliant, courageous, a marvellous writer, the greatest of modern orators, but fallible, egotistical and hard.

However, what Boothby also knew was that Churchill was a lonely man. Outside his family he had few friends left, and so Boothby would see him from time to time at Churchill's request, either in the House of Commons Smoking Room or at his London home at Hyde Park Gate.

Churchill did not stand at the 1964 general election (which the Labour Party narrowly won) and seemed to many to be in a terminal coma, which was not the case. He was just very old and very tired. But he wanted to see Boothby and invited him for dinner shortly before his death in January 1965. Boothby's account of this last meeting was in a letter to the eminent Oxford historian, Robert Blake:

> . . . One night he asked me to dine with him. His wife was ill in bed, so we were alone together. It was a difficult evening. He was pretty far gone. He didn't want to talk about the war. All he said was 'Historians are apt to judge War Ministers less by the victories achieved under their direction than by the political results that flowed from them. Judged by that standard, I am not sure that I will be held to have done very well.'
>
> I tried to arouse an interest by taking him back to the Battle of Jutland; but all he said was 'I used to know a lot about that, but now I have forgotten.' Finally he repeated something he had said to me many years before. 'The journey has been well worth making – once'. 'And then?' I said. 'A long sleep, I expect. I deserve it.' These were the last words he ever spoke to me.

Whenever Boothby was asked, by friends as well as journalists, why he had not remarried, his stock answer was that he was married to his constituency. The truth was that Dorothy Macmillan still exercised her remarkable influence over him, but even this was not the whole reason. He had what he himself called 'a psychological fixation . . . that the answer to my own life was marriage'. Maurice Bowra remarked that he had 'a jilt complex', and his habit of proposing marriage and then thinking better of it had caused considerable difficulties and embarrassments, and even one threat of an action for breach of promise.

There was also the sad memory of the failure of his marriage to Diana. They remained on excellent terms, and he was distressed for her when her husband died; he comforted her and took her on holiday with him and another close friend to help her at a very sad time. He certainly did not want to repeat the experience of a failed marriage, and there was no particular reason for him to marry again. His finances, thanks to wiser financial advice and his journalistic fame, were at last reasonably sound; he had his delightful flat in Eaton Square, where he was well looked after by his butler, Gordon; he had his host of friends, his books and unlimited foreign travel. Indeed, he was frankly envied by those struggling with the financial and other burdens of marriage and raising families. He was a devoted and much-loved godfather of several children, and honorary one of others, whose company he much enjoyed; if he was bored by London there were several families in England and Scotland who were delighted to have him as their guest. For once, his life had settled into a comfortable pattern.

But 'the psychological fixation' would not go away. Many years before his mother had said to him that she hoped he would marry an Italian girl. In 1956 he met Wanda Sanna.

Wanda's father, who was a Sardinian import-export wholesaler, died when she was nine. She found the atmosphere of the island stifling and limited, and went to the Spanish Convent in Rome until she was nineteen, and then studied languages at the Sorbonne. When she first met Boothby at the BBC in 1956 – not at Monte Carlo, as has sometimes been claimed – she had heard him on the radio and had been deeply impressed by his beautiful voice. She was twenty-three and Boothby fifty-six at this time; what is true is that they first got to know each other properly in Monte Carlo three years later, when she was working as a freelance interpreter for a French company and Boothby was 'nursing his bronchitis'. Her employer was a mutual friend and invited Boothby for a drink. A dinner invitation followed, during which Boothby distinguished himself by spilling soup on his dinner jacket and Wanda sponged him down. They met after that in France and London when her work took her there, but not often, and not too publicly, as Wanda was fearful of malicious gossip and was terrified by publicity of any kind. This was not fear of scandal, but being shy and introverted she hated the limelight that Boothby loved.

It was not long before Boothby proposed marriage. She suggested friendship instead, to which he replied, 'I don't need friends. I've got lots of friends. What I want is a wife.' But there were all the justified apprehensions of marrying a much older man, she knew about the ever-present Dorothy, and, although she increasingly found that they had much more in common than she had anticipated, including loneliness and the need for loving companionship, the disadvantages of marrying him loomed far greater than the possible pleasures. Whenever Boothby hit the headlines, which was still quite frequently, she shuddered and retreated. When Boothby became involved in the Kray brothers imbroglio, there were even vicious rumours that Wanda, because of her Sardinian background, was connected with the Mafia! As she had left the island as a young teenager, had hardly ever gone back, and had little connection with her family, this was somewhat improbable. But it was a mad, bad time of squalid rumour-mongering, and Wanda's 'Mafia connections' via the Krays thus did the rounds in certain circles. It was utterly preposterous and untrue, but, amazingly, there were some credulously stupid people who actually believed it.

She also realised that there could be no question of children. It would not be fair either on Boothby at his age or on the children. Nothing short of bankruptcy could budge him from 1 Eaton Square. So, until 1966, she hesitated and stalled him. She was strikingly beautiful, intelligent and a talented linguist.

Boothby was captivated and began to see her regularly. He constantly proposed, but Wanda always emphatically turned him down. The age difference in itself was a formidable obstacle, but she was right to have serious doubts as to Boothby's reliability as a husband. She was attracted by him, greatly enjoyed his company, and was impressed by his frankness and honesty. But marriage was an alarming venture, at which she quailed.

After one rejection, in April 1960, he wrote to her:

Darling Wanda

As I expected, I am sad and depressed. And to have had even the briefest glimpse of what might have been brought me no consolation.

Like my hero, Robert Burns, I have 'closed my eyes in misery and opened them without hope' since you left.

No. That is going too far. But, you see, although you may dread the future, at least you *have* a future. I have none. All I face is old age; and I cannot tell you how much I dislike it.

I once thought I would be able to grow old gracefully and even gaily, as a number of my friends have done. Not at all. I simply *hate* it.

Your flowers, which have now burst into a blaze of glory, bring me a little consolation. Also a day in the country, and in the sunshine, yesterday, with the first film of green coming over the woods, and the daffodils into full bloom. But spring no longer means much to me. I am more at home, and more content with autumn.

Now that I have finally made up my mind at least *how* to live, I am a bit easier in my mind. . . .

The great merit of London is that, although it is noisy and filthy, you can never be lonely – except in your heart.

This means, I hope, that we shall see each other more often – not that this will lead us anywhere. . . . It is a pity that you aren't thirty years older, and that we didn't meet over thirty years ago. The sparks would have flown then! Ecstasy would have been beautifully mingled with misery. But it would have been quite something.

Now we must wait for hell.

> Much love
> Bob

A major link with the past was broken when Dorothy Macmillan died suddenly of a heart attack on 22 May 1966. Among those who realised what this meant to Boothby was Mosley, who wrote at once:

> It is difficult at sad moments to say all we feel to friends, but as memory returns to many happy days I must send you all my sympathy in a tragic loss which means so much to you. I am so very sad for you.
>
> You know how much we should like at any time to have you here. Do come whenever you feel like it.

After Dorothy's death Boothby's family and friends became deeply worried about him. He seemed 'to go to pieces', as one has recorded. His drinking was no longer a joke, but a cause of much concern and embarrassment. One especially old friend rang him up one evening to be told in slurred tones that he never wanted to see her again in his life. Realising his condition she called on him the following morning, and he had no recollection of the conversation. Episodes like this, which were only too common, alarmed everyone, but another friend noticed with amazement one evening that Boothby, although hopelessly drunk, was writing an article in his perfect handwriting, and that the article itself was excellent.

It was one of the darkest and saddest periods of his life. He had his good days, when he was on his old form, but then would relapse dismally. Many friends were seriously, and justifiably, worried about there being a real scandal, unlike the Kray nonsense. Whether this was true or not, he was palpably in very bad shape physically and emotionally.

The fact was that he was suffering from grief. He had burned Dorothy's letters to him, but whenever the telephone rang he jumped to it, half-expecting to hear her voice. His only companion was Gordon. In his misery he took too many pills, did not eat enough and often drank himself into oblivion. His appearance itself was significant, usually scruffy and even slovenly. His condition was graphically shown in a letter from Bill Wasserman from New York on 17 April 1967:

> Dear Bob
>
> I have just returned from Jamaica, where I have learned that – according to your usual form – you have succeeded to make yourself notorious by getting drunk and falling down the stairs, and requiring seven stitches.
>
> I wonder whether you will grow up before you die.

Oh, Bob, the whole world loves you, but if you had just a few ounces of restraint and maturity at the right time your wonderful talents would have not been so wasted.

I know you have had a very good time out of life – and a very frustrating one. You have been so right all these years, so brilliant, so courageous – and such a damn fool!

I suppose we all look for our heroes to be perfect. The only trouble with your imperfections was that they stopped you from exerting an influence that, I think, might have changed the course of humanity to some degree.

If only the foresight that you and I had long before Bretton Woods – as far back as 1931 and 32, when part of the disaster that spewed Hitler and all his unholy works was due to stupid, outmoded economic and political thinking and which you and I opposed – you, with your eloquence and position, would have been put to good use then, you might have achieved the heights that could have imposed a different solution – had you been a little less reckless in your personal life. So I simply moan and cry over spilled milk! It is too late now, although I think, if you should come to America, your wisdom could be useful in Washington.

Let me hear from you.

Affectionately
Bill

Wanda's decision to succumb to Boothby's entreaties and to marry him earned her the admiration and gratitude of all who cared for him. One of his close friends, who did not particularly like Wanda, has said of her in total admiration that 'she gave him twenty years of life; without her, he would have been dead within a year'.

As Boothby's closest friends gradually realised, his feeling for Wanda was serious. For ten years he wrote to her regularly, took her out and pressed his cause, but without success. It seemed hopeless until Dorothy died in 1966, after which he tried again. His letters to Wanda, going back several years, had grown into those of hopeless love. 'If I had been twenty years younger,' he wrote in April 1965, '. . . but at sixty-five it is ludicrous. What have I got to offer? Only the remorseless approach of old age. I still love life, and will accept what is left of it with gratitude.' By April 1967 he was writing, 'I love you more than you can possibly imagine,' and he wrote her a beautifully formal proposal of marriage. This time he was successful, and the lengthy courtship ended in triumph and happiness in the Caxton Hall Registry Office on 30 August 1967.

It was a very jolly occasion. There was no formal reception, but Boothby invited the press – whom he had, of course, tipped off in advance, although he cheerfully denied it – to his flat for a drink. Nor was there an official honeymoon.

Boothby thus entered the only prolonged period of contentment and total happiness in his life. His family and friends initially had their doubts as to how it would work out – and so did Wanda – but it was to be a marriage which had its occasional storms, but was manifestly, and movingly, a truly loving partnership. Boothby's hospitality had always been generous, but after the amicable departure of Gordon – whom Boothby told should henceforth call him 'Bob' and not 'Your Lordship', as he was now a friend rather than a servant – Wanda's exceptional cooking became famous.

It is a cliché, which is seldom deserved, of a couple that 'they lived for each other', but in this case it was true. Wanda's prolonged grief after Boothby's death made a deep impression on those who know her. What they did not not know on their wedding day was that they were to have nearly twenty years of profound and real happiness. Boothby told no more than the truth in a note he wrote to her in December 1975:

My own darling Wanda
   This is just to let you know that I love you far more than anyone or anything else in this world: and that I am grateful, from the bottom of my heart, for what you have given me in return – the most unselfish love and devotion that I have ever known.
   You did what you set out to do. You saved my life, restored my position in public life, and brought me several more years of existence. You also enhanced the joy of living. I can never thank you enough.

Ever always your loving and grateful
Bob

Dingle Foot once again recorded a major event in his friend's life:

A novel form of union here is seen
Alliance between Sardinia and Aberdeen
Watch how our foremost television Peer
Now celebrates his sixty-seventh year.
Sometimes triumphant and sometimes rejected
He never fails to do the unexpected.
Beginning life as Churchill's PPS,
He followed Winston in the wilderness
And gave 'fondeur' in Parliamentary fights.
He gave his Whips a thousand sleepless nights
And then became, to their intense *chagrin*,
A master of the television screen.
Then, after one last Smoking-Room carouse,
He weaved his passage to the Upper House;
That place where Labour dogs and Tory vermin
Lose their identities beneath the ermine.
But still of one this never could be said –

The Lord of Buchan and of Rattray Head.
When libelled he, while obtaining just redress,
Took forty thousand smackers from the Press.
But, not content with victories like these,
He turns to other isles and other seas.
No Scottish lassie does he take to bed,
But now goes off to Wanda in the Med.

Among the shoals of letters of delight and congratulations there was a particularly warm one from Michael Foot:

What a boy! You continue to confound your enemies, delight your friends, & extract from the World much more than you deserve. Nobody contributes more to the gaiety of the nation, just by existing. It is a kind of genius.

Anyhow, I wish you the greatest happiness.

To your bride, I do not know what to wish – maybe, just that she should have as much pleasure from you as we have had, and Love.

Walter Somerville, to whom Boothby owed his life, wrote:

My dear Bob
  You have a great heart.
  Spiritually and anatomically.
  If you ever give a postgraduate course in *Living*, may I enrol?
  Please?
  My devotion, compliments, respect and affection to your lady and you.
  And multos annos.

Walter

In June 1967 Nasser, who, after his narrow escape in 1956 had successfully brought down the pro-Western Iraqi monarchy and Government and continued his policy of destabilisation in the Middle East, overreached himself by mobilising against Israel, ordering the removal of the United Nations forces, and closing the Gulf of Aqaba. The Israelis, faced with the combined threat of Syria and Jordan as well, wiped out the Egyptian air force on the ground before destroying the Arab armies and capturing the whole of Jerusalem, the Sinai up to the Suez Canal, the West Bank of the Jordan and the Golan Heights. Shattered by their overwhelming defeat in the Six Day War, the propaganda machines of the principal Arab states made wild and extravagant claims of Israeli brutality and the desperate state of Jerusalem, which were repeated in the British press and actually believed by many people. 'I thought I would go out and see for myself what was happening,' Boothby later related. 'I rang up El

Al, the Israeli airline, and asked them whether I could fly there. They said they had one plane going there that afternoon, but that it would be empty. I said that that suited me, and went.'

What he found in the immediate aftermath of the war was very different from the terrible reports to which *The Times*, amongst others, had given credence. He found an atmosphere of remarkable tranquillity, even serenity, with very little material damage, particularly in Jerusalem itself. What he did not like – and said so – was the Israeli encouragement to Arabs living on the West Bank to go to Jordan. He was also worried, and rightly, by the terrible conditions in the refugee camps in the Gaza Strip, and by clear indications of Israeli triumphalism. Although a lifelong Zionist, Boothby was greatly troubled by the predicament of the Arabs, especially the children, and did a radio broadcast before he left Jerusalem, ending with the words, 'Be kind, not cruel.'

When he returned to London he learned that the Lords were to debate the refugee problem on the following day, 28 June, and telephoned to put his name down for the debate, pointing out that he had just come back from Israel. He was called early to make what he later called 'the best speech I have ever made'. In it he described, simply and movingly, what the situation really was – nothing like as bad as was portayed in the British press, and in many respects immensely hopeful, but he was by no means uncritical of the Israelis. What worried him was that the Israelis might throw away a golden opportunity for a generous political offer to the Arab Palestinians on the West Bank and Gaza and a much better relationship with Egypt, Syria and Jordan. In this fear he was absolutely justified.

The House of Lords is an audience that is difficult to move emotionally, but this was a notable exception. Lord Longford, replying for the Government, described Boothby's speech as 'as good a speech as the noble Lord has ever made in this House, and more than that I cannot say'. What gratified Boothby more was that his speech had made a considerable impact upon Israeli official and political opinion, and resulted in a reversal of the policy of encouraging Arab emigration from the West Bank. Boothby cited this as one exception to the general rule that speeches rarely affect events; unhappily, his influence on Israeli attitudes and policies was limited to the refugee issue. He was to watch, with distress and almost despair, Israel isolating itself again and losing not only the political advantage but, in October 1973, almost its existence. But Boothby's reiterated warnings to his Israeli friends were politely ignored. Israel's new self-confidence developed into euphoria, followed by something suspiciously close to arrogance, for which it was to pay a very heavy price. Boothby did not foresee the exact course of events, but his instinctive judgment proved to have been right and wise.

Boothby was not the only non-Jewish friend and admirer of Israel who found the atmosphere of the country

rather oppressive. My religion is humour. As Maugham said in *The Summing Up*, it is man's only retort to the tragic absurdity of fate. This is not the strong suit of the Christian, Muslim, or Jewish religions – or indeed of any other, outside China. After a time the combination of prophets, commandments, sermons, wailing, kneeling, crucifixion, churches, mosques, synagogues, shrines, skullcaps, circumcision, Kosher food, chanting, candles, incense and souvenirs, all mixed up in a small space, gets me down.

But he always had a great taste for Jewish humour, much enjoying a remark of Weizmann's on a boring and lengthy speech by a rabbi that 'This is when all my latent anti-Semitism rises to the surface.' In a moving tribute to Weizmann at his former home at Rehovoth in 1960, he had quoted his last words to Meyer Weisgal: 'We are an impetuous people, and we spoil and sometimes destroy what has taken generations to build up.' Boothby was one of the best friends that the Jewish people have ever had in non-Jewish British politics; it was a pity that they did not listen to him more carefully.

In the spring of 1968 he fell seriously ill, but it was not another heart attack. He reported to Mosley on 26 April:

Dear Tom
    Thanks for your cards.
    The silly asses didn't get on to it in time. Too much alcohol was too easy an answer. The real trouble was an acute vitamin B deficiency; and they ought to have discovered this long before I began falling about and talking nonsense.
    Luckily they got on to it in time – I guess with about twenty-four hours to spare – and I am up and about; but will have to go carefully for a bit.
    We are going to Vittel at the end of May, returning on or about the weekend of June 22nd. It would be lovely to spend a night or even two with you, if you are to be there then. I want to show you – or rather you me, because we shall be carless – a picture of Napoleon inaugurating the Ecole de la Légionnaire d'Honneur, which I inherited, and gave to the French Govt.
    It is supposed to be the best portrait of him ever painted; and has been hung, appropriately enough, in the school at St. Denis.
    Love to D.

As ever
Bob

This project had to be cancelled as Boothby wrote to Mosley on 31 May: 'Alas the Vittel visit has had, inevitably, to be scrapped. Rottingdean (with memories of my private school) is a sad substitute.'

On the twentieth anniversary of the founding of the State of Israel Boothby left hospital to attend a huge celebration rally at the Albert Hall. He spoke to 6,000 Jews, and it was a triumph. Afterwards he and Wanda went to see Colin Coote, who was outside his house posting letters and who was amazed to see them. Boothby insisted that they all had an oyster dinner, after which he had to return to the hospital.

Boothby's finances were, at long last, in good hands and in better shape, thanks to Edward Beddington-Behrens, who had recently begun to look after his portfolio and to whom he wrote in September 1968:

> I don't take the pessimistic view that my friend the historian, Robert Rhodes James, took in a letter to me last week – that the United States (from which he has just returned) are on the brink of disintegration, and Europe on the brink of war.* But I am not very optimistic about this country. Oil is alright, shipping is alright, tanks are alright, Amblers are alright and so is Lyons. But we still have a very rough time ahead of us . . . and now, my dear Edward, 'operation BB' (Beddington-Behrens for the salvation of Bob Boothby) has been brought to a glorious conclusion. I am happily *frozen*; and shall not move again unless you tell me to buy something (and sell something to buy it with). So it only remains for me to thank you from the bottom of my heart, for all you have done for me.
>
> You have lighted the evening of my life, and given me a sense of security that I have never known. For this I can never hope adequately to express the gratitude I feel.

To which Beddington-Behrens replied on 11 September:

> I do appreciate your letter. As Renee says, you are the only one who has appreciated any help that I have tried to give them. Most of my other friends, for one of whom I have done so much more than in your case, accept this kind of thing and take it for granted, whilst, as you know, it takes quite a lot of worry and attention to try and do what I did originally, which is to back one's view against the majority. I do appreciate very deeply your heartfelt understanding of my very devoted intentions.

Tom Driberg (now Lord Bradwell) died in 1976. Boothby retained his affection for the old reprobate, who had claimed in a letter to him in 1968 that he was a reformed character – which Boothby read with some scepticism.

---

* We had just returned from the United States in turmoil over the Vietnam War, in a year that had included the downfall of President Johnson, the assassinations of Martin Luther King and Robert Kennedy, and the mayhem of the Democratic Convention in Chicago. The Warsaw Pact powers invaded Czechoslovakia in August. Hence my concern.

... If you are discussing 'that matter' with influential people, and disparaging remarks are made, you could say truthfully, that I no longer behave as I used to for years – *no* 'cruising', no casual promiscuity, only (very) occasional old friends.

Old age & prostatectomy, if not virtue, forbid more!

In October 1969 a group of Boothby's friends, including the Prime Minister, Harold Wilson, gave a dinner in his honour. Compton Mackenzie, then living in France, could not come, but sent a handwritten Toast regretting his absence and going on to say that 'on this occasion I also raise my glass to what will be the Golden Wedding next summer of a friendship which has been interrupted only by Bob's inability to keep awake after 10.30 p.m.! Blessings on you and Wanda, dear Bob, from your ancient friend Monty.' In another letter he wrote: 'What an unusual burst of common sense it was when you married dear Wanda!' When Mackenzie died in January 1973, Boothby gave the address at the Service of Thanksgiving at St Martin's in the Fields. 'His charm was equal to that of Lloyd George, his output to that of Churchill, his personality to that of Beecham. In versatility he perhaps excelled them all.'

Boothby then became involved in a posthumous operation to publicise the monstrous way in which Ealing Studios had treated Mackenzie over the film of *Whisky Galore*, particularly when he got wind of a hostile biographer who did not believe the story, and wrote to a mutual friend that Mackenzie 'never, if he could help it, told the truth about anything'. Sir Michael Balcon angrily denied the charge. But John Campbell, one of Mackenzie's executors, discovered the contract. He was paid £105 on signature of contract; £420 a month later, and twenty-five per cent of the producer's first receipts, to a sum not exceeding £1,050. Thereafter he would receive a flat sum of £525 every ten years. This was the total for a film that made a fortune for everyone else involved. Mackenzie was notoriously bad on money matters, but although Ealing were legally on firm ground, their moral position was very shaky indeed, as Boothby made very clear, in public as well as in private. There were veiled threats of libel actions, but, unsurprisingly, nothing happened. Boothby believed that his old friend had been naïve, but had been abominably treated by men who had become rich because of his work. Boothby remained Mackenzie's stalwart champion after death.

In January 1970 Wasserman wrote Boothby an immensely long letter about the current political situation in the United States and his detailed views on new developments in economic thinking, particularly praising Milton Friedman. His letter opens:

I was delighted to get your letter and to learn that at last you are willing to abandon the hurly-burly of life and seek contentment and tranquillity. I will believe it when I see it, but I think that ever since your marriage you have conducted your life with far more sagacity than ever before and I give credit for that worthy transition to the charming lady by your side. Bob, neither you nor I can ever find complete contentment too far away from the main arena.

In his equally long reply of 14 January, Boothby gave his own views of the current situation and only marginally disagreed with Wasserman.

So, you see, I am in rebellion against the whole economic establishment. Expansion is my slogan, and my prescription for a world which is starved not only of food but of capital equipment; and an abundance of liquidity, both the domestic and international use, in order to sustain it.

Of course I realise the danger of inflation, and the need for well-devised curbs and their judicious application. But the basic peril confronting the free world is not over-production. It is *under*production. Increased wage demands, if not matched by increased productivity, will of course result in a wage cost inflation, and rising prices. If the workers don't see this, they have to learn the hard way. But rising prices, provided they are kept under some kind of control, are infinitely better than continuous deflation culminating in recession, and an immense reduction of output.

In response Wasserman renewed his strong criticism of American economic policy and not least the extremely high cost of money. Comparing Nixon with Hoover, his letter ends: 'Keep in touch with me. You are one of the fairest and most stimulating minds I have ever encountered in a long life. I might add, dear Bob, I don't like growing old.'

In a footnote written in his own hand to a letter to Wasserman on 2 January 1971, Boothby complained:

P.S. I look out at the world, and do not like what I see. It seems to me that the desperate struggles of the present century have largely been in vain. The idiots in Vienna and Berlin who landed us in the first World War, and the cowards in London and Paris who landed us in the second, will bear a heavy responsibility before history. What have we got to show for it all? The division of Europe. The emergence of two super-powers in direct confrontation. A war-torn Middle East. Turmoil throughout Africa. The Vietnam follies. Liquidation of the British Empire – in my view an unmitigated disaster. A frustrated and drug-addicted youth. A feeling of hopelessness everywhere not to mention an almost universal tension, and growing pollution everywhere. If it were not for Wanda, whom I adore, I should be quite glad to be quit of it!

In November 1972 it was discovered that Wasserman had contracted cancer of the throat. In a warm letter of sympathy of 23 December

Boothby added that, 'Wanda looks after me like a baby, and I enjoy best the flat and the peace of this flat.'

In the last years of his life, suffused by much happiness in spite of declining health, Boothby's friendships meant everything to him.

When Diana became engaged to his old Oxford friend, Lord Gage, in October 1970, he wrote to her that

> I can't tell you how delighted I am with your news. I am very sure that you will make each other extremely happy, and that nothing better could have happened to you both. . . . After storms which would have wrecked most, we have both reached harbour. I hope we shall be there for a long time to come.

Diana replied: 'Do take care of yourself so you can have a long and happy life together. Even though you and I have not met this past year or so I am sure you know that I do not change, and always think of you with true affection.'

Boothby had kept in close touch with Richard Weininger and had pestered every Home Secretary to review his case and clear his name; he was eventually successful when Roy Jenkins called for the papers and came to the conclusion that Boothby had been right all along, and that there was nothing against Weininger.

Before this total exoneration, there was another footnote to the Czech assets affair, when in the summer of 1971 Jeremy Thorpe and Boothby gave a special lunch in the Palace of Westminster for the Weiningers, and the Serjeant at Arms who escorted them was the same man who, as a junior officer in 1940, had been responsible for Weininger when he gave evidence to the infamous Select Committee. It was a very happy occasion, Boothby reporting to Colin Coote that 'He is very old now, and pretty frail; and it gave him infinite pleasure to set foot once again on British soil – although God knows why.'

He also came to the assistance of another old acquaintance in 1973. Jack Webster of the *Scottish Daily Express* brought to Boothby's attention the fact that Putzi Hanfstaengl was prohibited from visiting this country. Boothby at once wrote to Robert Carr, then the Home Secretary, pointing out that he had broken with the Nazis during the war, had fled from Germany, and loved this country and 'would not hurt a fly if he could help it'. In fact, Webster's information was incorrect, and David Lane, the Junior Minister, replied that there was no objection whatever to his visiting this country, adding that the Home Office had agreed to his admission as long ago as 1957 when Randolph Churchill wrote on his behalf.

Boothby reported on his doings to Weininger on 10 August 1973:

Wanda and I went to Paris for a weekend to stay with the Mosleys. He is still marvellous company, and at seventy-seven still waiting for the call! The Duchess of Windsor came to dinner.

Had lunch at a bistro in Chartres, for four of us, cost over forty pounds! Travel is now far too expensive. But I am hoping to take W to Sardinia for a few days in September. My trouble is that more than half the modest fortune that Edward Beddington-Behrens made for me has vanished in the Stock Exchange slumps; and I don't know what to do.

Is the western world on the brink of some recovery, or of a most almighty crash? I wish I had more faith in Treasuries and central bankers. But I have been so right over the past fifty years, and they have been so wrong, that I have none left. . . . I am sorry to be so melancholy, but, for once in my life, I am very depressed. Is there any limit to the folly of mankind? Just look at Cambodia. Bombing, illegally, the wrong town! . . . Without Wanda, I could not hope to carry on. Like Edith [Weininger's daughter] was to you and Trude, she is my all and everything.

By the close of 1973 there was a massive miners' strike, and the beleaguered Heath Government was seriously considering calling a general election. Boothby, with mixed emotions, wrote to Wasserman on 16 December:

Baldwin once said to me 'the greatest ambition of my life is to prevent the class war from becoming a reality'. Heath has made it a reality. 'Confrontation' is the order of the day.

But can we, at this moment of time, give in to the outrageous demands of the miners and locomotive men without further demands from the other unions and a riproaring inflation? . . . As for you, despite Kissinger's heroic efforts, you will not have a credible government unless and until Nixon goes.

One of Wasserman's last letters to Boothby read:

It was good hearing from you. I am glad to know that old, fat, overindulged carcase of yours is still stirring. Of course, Marion and I would love to have you and Wanda to stay as long as you want. We would even increase our scanty liquor supply to give you an additional drink or two, and if you will send us a list we will be delighted to give you a dinner to include those people you would like to see. Unfortunately, Walter Lippmann died a few days ago and under these circumstances will not be available.

In November 1974, when Weininger realised that there was a real possibility that the Boothbys might have to give up their London flat, he wrote at once to say that if that eventuality ever arose they were to be in touch with him immediately so that he would come to their assistance. Boothby wrote back in gratitude on 29 November:

> I cannot tell you how relieved and happy she was to get your letter. I have never seen anything like it. She was getting pretty desperate – as indeed I am, and the feeling that she has a guardian behind her in case things get really bad makes all the difference to her. Meanwhile, thanks to you, the flat is saved; and for the time being I shall not have to change my abode.

Boothby's television appearances were now only occasional, but the old magic had not faded. He greatly appreciated this letter from Mr Desmond Wildsmith of Brighton on 15 February 1975:

> My Lord
>
> I am an old man, a relic of '98, and like many of my kind I spend a fair amount of time watching television. Much of it is very ordinary. But sometimes one sees and hears something quite delightful. Perhaps some lovely music, a nature film, or Mastermind or those very talented men, the Two Ronnies. You see my tastes are catholic.
>
> But last week there was really nothing to stir the pulse. Until its very end, the Parkinson programme. And after this young fellow had sparred rather unsuccessfully with two females – you came on.
>
> The next half hour was sheer delight for me. I hope you won't think me over-adulatory when I say that in these days, you are unique. You have everything that goes into what we call 'personality' – the voice, the appearance, the ready wit. But above all the ability to express in a few words what we lesser mortals couldn't present in a whole book. I can assure you that the whole time I watched you I was chuckling, and uttering heartfelt 'hear hears'.
>
> I won't go through it all again. But how true it was when you compared the public figures of today with those who strode before us in the days when you were first in Parliament. As you say, there were then perhaps twenty or more men there who could magnetise, and enthrall their audience! Nowadays we have some (usually) worthy men – but there is no magic coming out of them!
>
> And then there was your final utterance. Your greatest disappointment at not being sent to the Council of Europe. With British prestige as it then was, and Winston's backing, you would most assuredly have been its President. And the sad history of the Western world in the last three decades might have been changed.
>
> Well, I won't go on any further about what might have been. I'll just thank you for being yourself all your life – and letting us know you.
>
> So, my sincere good wishes to you Sir. May you continue to flourish and enjoy your life, blessed by all the things you so enjoy.
>
> Your sincere admirer

In recent years the British had got themselves into one of the most absurd international conflicts over fishing rights in Icelandic waters. Supported by an idiotically patriotic press, the Labour Government claimed that it had right on its side, to which it added might in the shape of the Royal Navy. The Icelandic fishermen and tiny gunboats responded with spirit. The 200-mile limit claimed by Iceland was very doubtful in international law, and the British fishermen had their livelihoods at stake as well, but matters should never have been allowed to reach this stage. Boothby, usually emphatically on the side of the fishermen, deplored and denounced 'the Cod War', and what he described as 'the bullying of Iceland', a NATO ally; he also believed that as conservation of fish stocks was an absolute priority, there should be an amicable agreement as soon as possible. Coming from that source, his Lords' intervention on 24 March 1975, followed up by others, had a significant impact. Saner counsels began to prevail, and the Cod War faded out and ended in an agreement on the lines Boothby had proposed. On this subject, at least, he was listened to almost with reverence.

Although it would not be entirely true to say that Boothby in the last decade of his life was always a model of sobriety, the contrast with his earlier days was very remarkable. He still enjoyed good food and good wine, but under Wanda's careful eye seldom any longer drank to excess except on special occasions. None the less, he could occasionally transgress, and on one occasion Wanda was so enraged that she gave him what was in effect an ultimatum. Boothby was so shaken that he sat down and wrote this letter to her on 31 May 1976:

> My own darling girl,
>   I can't tell you how lonely and sad I feel, or how sorry I am for all I have done to you.
>   I just sit here and cry. It hasn't been like this since I was at Rottingdean.
>   All I can say is that it has been a tremendous lesson, and that I have learnt it.
>   The doctors tell me I am getting better; but without you I don't care. I don't care about anything.
>   Please come back to me soon. *Please*. Without you I can do nothing. And I will be better.
>   Your very loving and very miserable Bob.
>   The doctors tell me I have been drinking too much lately, and must cut down on it. Oh, my darling, I love you so much; and miss you so desperately. I never thought that I could feel as I now do. Life is not worth living without you.

Of course, this wonderful letter made everything right. It speaks volumes for their love and trust, as everyone who saw them together realised.

One curious feature of Boothby's character was that he did not like animals, and was baffled by the obsession his friends – including Churchill – had with them. He loathed cats, which gave him 'the creeps', as he put it, and did not think much of dogs, either. One of Wanda's more notable triumphs was that she completely converted him to something approaching adoration for the small dogs she brought into his life, and which was reciprocated so intensely that one pined so miserably after his death that he did not long survive his master.

It would be wholly wrong to imply that Boothby had found serenity. He had certainly found happiness, but he was consistently physically unwell, and had his deeply moody spells. He remained difficult, although cheerful, but lived increasingly in the past. As he brooded, his feelings about Churchill became a topic of worry to those who loved him. And he became increasingly obsessed by the 'might have beens'. So, no doubt, will we all.

The difficulty with Boothby was that, in spite of the infirmities of old age, his mind remained sharp, but was being under-used. His journalism and literary reviewing not only brought in necessary money but kept him occupied; however, in Wanda's opinion this was not enough, and she dreaded that he might become bored and lapse into lassitude, which would have been depressing for them both.

It was she who suggested that he should write another book, and was the true originator of what became *Recollections of a Rebel*. Boothby had fascinated her with his accounts of people and events of which she had known nothing, and she was sure that people of her generation would be as well. Other friends gently pushed him in the same direction. He needed some persuading, but eventually wrote out in his own hand probably the best synopsis of an autobiography ever written, which greatly attracted a number of publishers. Hutchinsons was the successful one, and Boothby was given great assistance by Anthony Whittome. But it was very much his own book. He and Wanda talked about it for nearly two years, and then he sat down and wrote it in his own hand in less than three months, an astonishing achievement – physical as well as intellectual – for a sick man of seventy-eight. What was even more remarkable was that although he covered much of the same ground as in his previous books, there was a freshness and fun, as well as a seriousness and wisdom, and the standard of his writing was better than ever. Indeed, in the opinion of many, it was the best of all his books and fully deserved its immediate success.

It did, however, contain criticisms of Churchill, long simmering, which caused outrage, particularly this paragraph:

He would cry over the death of a swan or a cat. For human life he had little regard, least of all for his own. He enjoyed danger. But I have never disguised from myself the fact that this element of cruelty might have been essential for what he had to do. When he sacked or broke people, and he broke many, he never thanked and seldom saw them. He simply didn't care. And in some cases he did it with relish.

The reference to an 'element of cruelty' in Churchill's character caused the storm.

Jock Colville, whom Boothby detested, opened the assault in a letter to *The Times* on 19 October denying that Churchill had any emotions at all for Boothby, and that 'except for occasional meetings in the Smoking Room in the House of Commons, he seldom set eyes on him . . . and was not remotely interested in his views', which, of course, was nonsense. He also vehemently denied the charge of cruelty. Boothby retorted at length on 23 October, remarking that 'For many years Sir John Colville has been boasting and boring everyone in talk and print about his relationship with Sir Winston Churchill' and pointing out that what he had said was that Churchill had an 'element of cruelty' in his character. Mary Soames then came in strongly in defence of Colville, denying that her father had set out to destroy Boothby in 1941. Boothby retorted with his version of the affair. Alastair Forbes and Denis Kelly – the cataloguers of Churchill's papers – and Anthony Montague Brown, Churchill's last private secretary, intervened, Forbes supporting Boothby, but urging both of them to 'belt up' and pressing Mary Soames to get on with the biography of her mother.

This was all being followed with enormous interest and enjoyment as the exchange became more acrimonious, not only in the columns of *The Times* but in interviews with other newspapers; even Spike Milligan got into the act with an effective jab at Churchill's 'extreme cruelty' in the treatment of Dowding in 1940. Boothby's final letter of 28 October was generally reckoned to be a masterpiece, Paul Johnson writing that it was 'game, set and match'.

In his letter, whose character was good-humoured, Boothby quoted from his assessment of Churchill and accused him of cruelty to Dowding, Harris, Wavell and Cunningham, and said that he would follow Forbes' advice. To widespread regret the matter was closed, but Boothby was so incensed by Colville's action in denouncing him without having even read his book that he made the ultimate sacrifice by resigning from White's. Colville admitted that Churchill had made Boothby a KBE, adding waspishly, 'It was very decent of him. I don't know why he did it.' Johnson in the *Evening Standard* declared Boothby the winner against 'the entire

Churchill pack' and cited the bombing campaign against Germany as clear evidence of cruelty. This matter out of the way – and it had been carried at length in the *New York Times* in addition to the fascinated British press – the reviews themselves were warm and enthusiastic.

In June 1979 Boothby had a narrow escape when he was caught between the kerb and an oncoming car. He was walking to have his hair cut, looked left and did not see the car. Neither he, nor anyone else, had realised that he had a developing cataract in his left eye, and was virtually blind in it. He cracked and broke his leg in two places as well as tearing many muscles. He was unconscious for over a week, contracted pneumonia and was almost in a coma in the King Edward VII Hospital. It was thought that he was dying, but he made a rapid recovery. When he left the hospital, he insisted on hiring a Rolls-Royce to take him home.

In the last letter that Boothby wrote to Weininger before Weininger died, which is dated 4 July 1979, he finished up:

> I hope you won't mind exchanging a rather bright young thing for an elderly cripple. But once I get (literally) on my feet again, I am determined to be as cheerful as I possibly can, if only for Wanda's sake.

On the same day he wrote to Mosley:

> It was bad – two fractures of the left leg, and unconscious for a week. Everyone except myself thought I was gone. Then, suddenly, when they were reaching for the Bible, I took a turn for the better; and have since been slowly recovering. But it will be a long job; and I am afraid I shall be a cripple for the rest of my life. Wanda, I need hardly say, has been marvellous.

Boothby was indeed fortunate to survive. He wrote to Gladwyn Jebb, now Lord Gladwyn, on 19 July, when the crisis was over:

> Many thanks for your letter. I have had a rough time. Left leg broken in two places, followed by pneumonia; and unconscious for twelve days. The doctors told me that anyone of forty must have died, but that at seventy-nine you are indestructible, which must be a consolation for both of us. I am still in plaster, and shall be on two sticks for the rest of my days; but I do not mind much, as I view the modern world with increasing horror.

Although he was given a wheelchair, Boothby hated it and hardly ever used it. He struggled along on his sticks instead and even insisted on dressing himself, 'just to show I can do it'.

Wanda's English was not perfect. When asked by a journalist how her husband was, she replied that he was recovering, but was 'under heavy seduction'. When Boothby did recover, he was delighted.

One of Boothby's warmest and best friends was the broadcaster and writer, Arthur Marshall, who, to his own considerable surprise, had become, rather late in life, almost a cult figure through his humorous writing and cheerful television appearances – alas, on programmes that were often less than worthy of him – and who never failed to cheer Boothby up with his conversation and breezy letters. One example may suffice:

Dear Bob

Your splendid letter, for which so many thanks, has this very moment arrived. I could murder the BBC TV forwarding department. I have already written twice to tell them that I have not lived in Radnor Walk since 1970, but no notice is taken. I shall shortly send off a SNORTER. Meanwhile I have informed the owner of 6 Radnor Walk where I currently live. Life is too short for such silly stupid muddles.

Oh yes indeed, our COO-EEEE! brought back some fine memories of this and that, and of Genoa and Santa Margherita when you angelically fetched Dadie [Rylands] and me (still in deep mourning for the mater, if memory serves) from Le Touquet and drove us down, filling us with delicious food and endless bottles of The Boy ('I always think Krug's better' you constantly said). And then on we went to Monte C, where you gambled to great purpose and we kept meeting and trying to avoid that Irish M.P. who writes books on wonky subjects, and who had a distressing acne! . . .

The last time I made mention of your name was to the Queen Mum! Dorothy Dickson gave a little post-lunch gathering in Eaton Square and I was chatting to the Q.M. about various sidents. At the mention of your name, she gave a glad cry and said, '*Such* a jolly man!' And I AGREE!

Yours
Arthur

Boothby wrote to another friend in September 1977 envisaging a concert in honour of Thomas Beecham, 'with myself as footnote'.

If they do this, I would like them to begin with the overture to Die Meistersinger, go straight on to the Siegfried Idyll, then to Debussy's La Mer or L'Après Midi d'un Faune, and finally to Delius. Brigg Fair, In a Summer Garden, or the Walk Through the Paradise Garden it doesn't matter which. You will find no difficulty in discerning the thread which runs through all three composers. It is woven round one word – melody.

I would like it to be an emotional concert.

No Beethoven, no Mozart, certainly no Bach. In the second half a Brahms symphony, or perhaps Tchaikovsky's five or six. Or perhaps Yehudi Menuhin, a friend of mine, would come back to play Elgar's violin concerto which, when he was a boy, made his name and fame.

Finally, a lollipop – preferably the Sleigh Ride.

In short a typical Beecham concert of the music he loved most.

If you do this, I guarantee it will be a sell-out. It will be the last service I will render to the orchestra.

I still think I have a bit longer to go, but at my age you never know!

Boothby had quickly come to enjoy the Lords, which certainly gave him a public platform to pursue the causes that interested him most without the trammels of Whips or any kind of Party discipline. He did not abuse his position as a crossbencher, and tended to support the Government of the day unless he felt particularly strongly on an issue. One battle that he took from the Commons was over fishing, especially when the twelve-mile protection zone for British inshore fishing was imperilled by British entry into the EEC in 1972. Boothby had been advocating British entry for years, and it was a subject he spoke on repeatedly in the Lords, lamenting that Britain was 'in stagnant and almost impotent isolation', but on fishing he remained a total protectionist. On this occasion the Heath Government took his advice, to his delight, and in 1980 Peter Walker negotiated an even better arrangement which Boothby praised lavishly and warmly, declaring that Walker was the greatest Minister for Agriculture and Fisheries ever. There was much praise from all quarters – especially in Scotland – for the triumphant culmination of his almost lifelong championship of the industry.

Another old cause was homosexual law reform. In 1967 the Labour MP, Leo Abse, carried through the Commons the Sexual Offences Bill, which in effect implemented the recommendations of the Wolfenden Report and which received Government time and encouragement. Boothby welcomed it enthusiastically, but regretted that it did not apply to Scotland. The reason given for this curious omission was a technical one, based on the different laws relating to evidence, and the fact that a criminal prosecution for homosexual relations between consenting males was almost unknown in Scotland. These did not seem very valid reasons to Boothby, but as Abse had accepted the advice, he did not want to delay or jeopardise the Bill. However, he returned to the matter, and in 1977 he proposed a Bill in the Lords that would have extended the Act to Scotland. It was carried by a large majority in the Lords on a free vote, but did not make progress in the Commons. But Boothby's campaign succeeded totally in 1980, when an amendment to the Criminal Justice (Scotland) Bill was carried overwhelmingly in both Houses on free votes. Another long campaign had ended in success.

On foreign affairs he consistently supported Israel until 1977, constantly called for a strong navy, and felt vindicated when the 1982 Falklands campaign revealed not only the vital importance of sea power and a strong merchant marine, but also certain shortcomings in British naval design and constructions that had a familiar ring. Although he gave the 1964–70 Wilson Governments relatively friendly and sympathetic treatment, he was appalled by the decision to abandon British power East of Suez, particularly in the Persian Gulf, and – with greater foresight than perhaps he realised – the folly of withdrawing from Kuwait. 'Here is the richest oil-producing country in the world, and we have chucked it away!' he stormed. The Conservatives, now led by Edward Heath, pledged to reverse the policy, but when they came to power in 1970 it was too late.

Another issue on which he criticised the Wilson Government was Rhodesia. After Ian Smith's Unilateral Declaration of Independence in 1965, the Government imposed international economic sanctions, which caused a massive three-way split in the Conservative Party in the Commons which boded ill for its fortunes in the impending general election, which it lost heavily in 1966. Boothby liked Wilson personally, and his initial two Hungarian-born economic advisers, Tommy Balogh and Nicky Kaldor, were two particularly close and old friends, but after a visit to Rhodesia in 1968 he returned totally convinced that sanctions were futile and should be abandoned. He was right again, but the maintenance of sanctions was official Labour and Conservative policy, and was to remain so, but Boothby's warnings of their uselessness were to prove only too justified.

But it was on Europe – with the consistent urgings for British entry into the EEC, attempted unsuccessfully first by Macmillan and then, un- expectedly, by Wilson, and finally achieved by Heath – and on economic matters that he was most eloquent and fervent, and his reiteration of the need for gold as the basis of the international economy was so frequent that he was in danger of becoming a bore on the subject, as he cheerfully admitted. He saw little of merit in the policies of the Macmillan, Home and Wilson Governments in their economic policies, and in 1968 sum- marised to the Lords the post-war record:

We have been buoyant under Dalton; we have been austere with Sir Stafford Cripps; we have been rigorously controlled by Sir Stafford; we have watched the Prime Minister's 'bonfire' of controls when he was at the Board of Trade; we have seen the disastrous results of the premature removal of building controls; we have 'dashed for freedom' with Lord Butler; we have 'gone' with Mr Macmillan and Mr Maudling; we have 'stopped' with Lord Thorneycroft and Mr Selwyn Lloyd; we have both 'gone' and 'stopped' with Mr Jenkins, and now we have been devalued by him once again. My Lords, even the Hungarian Rhapsody, about which some of us had held such high hopes, has now ended on a somewhat discordant note. It is small wonder that all of us, whatever Party we may belong to, are feeling a bit dizzy.

On Europe he went far further than almost anyone else, not only urging entry into the EEC but also German reunification, the creation of a European central bank and a common European currency. Once again, his speeches on these subjects have an eerily prophetic ring. Again, he found himself almost the only prominent person in either House who declared that de Gaulle's vision of a united Europe was absolutely right, and he could well understand, from his own experience, why de Gaulle viewed the British and Americans with such suspicion and scepticism. Given their shabby treatment of him in the war this was not to be wondered at, he remarked, not to universal approbation.

His great disappointment was the economic performance of the 1970–4 Heath Government. It came into office in June 1970 with a free-market policy that looked ominously like *laissez-faire* to Boothby, but after the sudden death of the new Chancellor, Iain Macleod, there was an abrupt change of course. After much talk of not helping 'lame ducks', the Government announced substantial sums to rescue Rolls-Royce and Liverpool Docks. This was just the beginning. 'It simply does not add up,' Boothby told the Lords. '. . . It will not work.' Nor did it. He was dismayed by the ending of free school milk and the increases in dental and other medical charges and school meals, while at the same time reducing income tax by sixpence, a classic 'benefiting the rich' budget. He refused to support the Government on this package, and his fears about the gulf between the Government's previously declared policies and its actual performance proved to be vindicated. Only on the EEC entry, Heath's outstanding achievement, was he happy with that Government. Again, he wanted to go further, with a Federal Reserve Bank for Europe, but having achieved his point on the twelve-mile fishing limit – including a supportive visit to the fleet of trawlers which sailed down to London and then bucked up and down in the choppy seas off Brighton during the Conservative Party Conference – he welcomed the historic step.

The Government's industrial policies, and particularly its deteriorating relations with the trade unions, worried him deeply. The establishment of an Industrial Relations Court under a judge horrified him, and he forecast nothing but difficulty and confrontation, as his esteem for the legal profession was only marginally higher than that for the cursed Treasury. Events were to prove him right again, and it was the confrontation with the unions that was to result in the Government's miserable decline and eventual defeat.

Boothby admired Heath, but he became disenchanted with his combative approach, and on 19 December 1973 in the Lords, with a miners' strike raging, he compared Heath to Haig and called for 'peace, and nothing but peace'. When Heath lost the election very narrowly in the following February, he attempted a coalition with the Liberals; Boothby publicly declared that he should resign and advise the Queen to summon Wilson. After two embarrassing days he had to do this, but Boothby's advice displeased him. He was even less pleased when Boothby publicly urged him to resign the leadership of the Party 'before they throw him out, as they will. I know them.' Heath unwisely retorted that 'Lord Boothby knows nothing about politics; he is in the Lords.' After a second, and heavier, defeat in October 1974 Boothby's grim prophecy was fulfilled. Boothby may have been in his seventy-fifth year, but he knew something about politics, and a great deal about the Conservative Party.

Age was catching up on him, and his later speeches, like his conversation, increasingly dwelt upon the past, and were becoming repetitious, with too much self-justification for comfort. For example, in the spring of 1979, Iain Sproat saw Boothby in the Smoking Room in the House of Commons and asked whether he would like to speak for him in the forthcoming general election in Aberdeen. Boothby beamed at him, raised his glass of whisky and said, 'My boy, I will give you my finest and final speech.' Unfortunately, it was neither. Sproat records:

The first ten minutes were fine, but then he got on to the history of the herring industry, and lost the audience, until Wanda tugged him and he sat down. None the less, the first ten minutes was worth the trip and the experience.

On another occasion (23 March 1983) he admitted to being 'a crashing bore' on monetary policy and, although he still spoke good sense and was always entertaining, there was some truth in this. But he was still willing to take up causes, at the age of eighty-five denouncing corporal punishment in schools and supporting a European Commission directive to abolish it – successfully. Less happy, and unsuccessful, was his opposition to compulsory seat belts in cars, fulminating to the Lords about this further erosion of the liberty of the subject to do what he wanted to, including drinking and smoking himself to death if that was his desire. He was wrong, but the old libertarian flame still burned.

One minister in particular in the Thatcher Government aroused his ire, and that was the Secretary for Education, Sir Keith Joseph, particularly when he introduced sweeping changes in the universities. As these involved the Scottish universities, Boothby was angry, and as a former Rector he thought he knew something about the traditions and standards of the university system north of the border, whereas it seemed to him that Joseph knew absolutely nothing about it and was unwittingly causing havoc. As he well knew, the Scots were incensed at being dictated to by London on a particularly precious national source of pride. Boothby wrote a long letter to William Whitelaw setting out the situation and urging reconsideration. It may have been his unfortunate reference to

Joseph as 'a Jew from London', but all he received in reply was an acknowledgment so curt as to be offensive. He certainly took offence at it, and lost few opportunities of publicly defending the Scottish universities against English interference.

On 29 October 1984, on the sixtieth anniversary to the day when he was first elected to Parliament, the Lords of all Parties applauded his 'Diamond Jubilee'. Whenever Boothby complained of old age, which was often, Shinwell would merrily rebuke him for being so pessimistic. As he was over ten years older than Boothby, and remarkably spry, his example was a formidable one.

Shinwell was one of Boothby's many friends and former colleagues now in the Lords, and he and Gladwyn became a regular team whenever European matters arose. A less expected new friendship, and a very close one, was with Field Marshal Lord Montgomery, who, like him, enjoyed talking about the past. They had a considerable personal correspondence, mainly dealing with current events in Europe and complaints about the political weakness of NATO, but on one occasion, on 14 October 1970, Montgomery wrote a more detailed letter about events of the Second World War:

> The trouble in the 1939/45 war was that the Americans didn't understand the political side of wars. You go to war for political reasons and when it is clear you are going to win 'which was in 1943' it is essential to ensure you win with a political balance favourable to win the peace. We did not do so. Why? Because the Americans considered that all military action must be based on military factors, and politics come later. Once we had won the battle of Normandy I said we must go all out to get possession of the great political centres of central Europe – Berlin, Prague, Vienna. If we had fought the war properly we could have had the lot; we got none of them; Stalin got all three.
>
> Stalin was a great leader; he had vision. The Russians might well have left the war in the winter of 1940/41, but Stalin kept them in because he wanted to achieve his political object – which was to fasten his grip firmly and ever more firmly on Eastern Europe, which he did. He made practically no mistakes. Yalta was his greatest victory.
>
> We British have a good deal to answer for; we could have had the leadership of Western Europe after the war; we refused it. It is a fascinating subject and I would like to discuss it with you one day.
>
> Winston should never have become Prime Minister in 1951; he was an old and tired man. I have never had any use for Anthony Eden; he was a good number two, but failed when he became number one.
>
> If you are going to be a political leader, you must have vision and courage. Winston had both. Eisenhower did not understand the conduct of war.
>
> I would like to lunch with you one day in the House of Lords and have a good talk.

Alanbrooke also liked to reminisce, but his bitterness against Churchill had become even more intense than Boothby's, which was unhelpful.

On this subject Boothby was definitely becoming a bore, although not in public. One sad exception was an interview with the BBC's Radio Scotland, in which he was so vituperative that his comments were never broadcast, as the Corporation feared an outburst of indignation; they also reckoned it would do Boothby's standing no good at all, and they were right on both counts. It had become an obsession, and a tiresome one.

But he continued to go to the Lords and speak there, and he was astonishingly active up to the end, intervening frequently – and well – in the last months of his life, and even on his last day. Much though he enjoyed the 'club life' of the Lords, the Chamber was the place to be. He got much out of the Lords, but he gave it much, and if towards the end his speeches dwelt more and more on the past, and were rather too boastful and egotistical on occasion, he was forgiven, and he always had an attentive and interested audience. For the younger peers it was a shock to see this legendary burly figure so wizened and tiny, but although his speeches may have become old hat to the senior Lords they were new to a younger generation, who found his speeches, his company and his reminiscences fascinating.

He enjoyed the Lords and gave it some of his best speeches, and lived to see some of his most cherished objectives achieved. He reflected that perhaps he was not such a 'failure' after all.

Boothby and Macmillan continued to see each other and to write, although there was a certain despondency in this correspondence. Thus, Macmillan to Boothby on 26 March 1980: 'Yes, the twentieth century has certainly been a flop. Whether there is any hope of saving things now I am not sure. Still, one can only hope. Both you and I are too old to do much.' And then, again, on 30 January 1985:

> Dear Bob
>
> Certainly those inter-war years through which you and I had the misfortune to live without being able effectively to influence, sowed dragon's teeth [which] are now destroying us. But we must not give up hope.
>
> If we can only get our people to think about realities instead of dogmas and theories; in other words if we can make the Tory Party Tory, instead of Manchester school liberal, we might achieve something. But, alas, neither you nor I are young enough to be of much use.
>
> Yours ever
> Harold

When Mosley died in December 1980, the press, radio and television found difficulty in finding anyone to defend him. Boothby did so, and his widow wrote to him on 12 December:

> I was able to hear very well what you said about darling Kit on the wireless & it was perfect. Thank you, thank you. As you know, he really loved you. He so often spoke of you & your brilliance, he admired you, but it was much more than that, it was deep affection.

As in the case of many politicians, Boothby's attitude towards honours was ambivalent. He had been genuinely surprised and delighted when Churchill had offered him his knighthood; he had asked for his peerage, under the special circumstances of 1958, quite justifiably. In 1981, now that there was a Conservative Government, Boothby was hopeful of receiving the one major honour that had eluded him, membership of the Privy Council. He had heard from a mutual friend that Harold Wilson had recommended him twice, without success, and he now renewed his request. It fell to Christopher Soames to tell him that he had again been unsuccessful. 'I want you to know', he wrote, 'that both your desire, and the reasoning behind it, were known. It's one of those things.' Boothby replied on 24 February 1981, rather unconvincingly, that

> I do not really care a damn about the Privy Councillorship. It means nothing to the public, and does not even give me another title. . . . I do not even blame them [the Establishment]! After all, I have fought them for fifty years, and can hardly complain that they have no wish to do me a favour now. You gave me the honour I value most – the K.B.E. – and Harold my Peerage, both in their teeth. I am well content with that. It is more, perhaps, than I deserve.

But the fact was that he did want it, and was hurt.

That Boothby really did care about the matter was demonstrated when he wrote a very long letter to the Queen on 27 December 1983 describing his long political career in support of his claim. This could have caused embarrassment – and certainly does to his biographer – but he received a flattering and smooth reply from one of her private secretaries, which claimed that 'The Queen was very interested to read the account you gave her of your own political career. . . . As regards a Privy Councillorship, this is of course something which is given by the Queen on the advice of her Prime Minister.' No such advice was given.

Inevitably, perhaps, Boothby's mind was usually on the past and, in 1981, he participated in one last television tour de force, *Twentieth Century Remembered*, again on Wanda's suggestion. Interviewed by Andrew Boyle, a very much thinner and gaunter Boothby demonstrated once more his extraordinary talent as a performer, and the series still has a real historical value. He had a remarkable capacity to bring the past to life, as he did in a letter to the Queen Mother, in his own, now very crabbed, hand on 11 December 1985:

> I was thinking the other day of perhaps the most memorable week-end of my life at Trent Park long before the war. I stayed alone with Philip Sassoon on the Friday night.
>
> At six o'clock on Saturday morning I heard the sound of cart-wheels crunching on the avenue, and went out in pyjamas to see what was going on. I found the horse-drawn carts coming up the Avenue, filled with potted flowers of all kinds in full bloom, from Covent Garden, including lilies for the border round the swimming pool, and an army of gardeners to receive them. By lunch-time, when the guests arrived, including the Duke of York and yourself, they were all in; while peacocks and flamingoes, loosed from cages, strolled around the house.
>
> After lunch the Duke of York and I played a round of golf on the Home Course, and I shall never forget his delight when he holed a long putt on the 17th green to beat me by 2 and 1.
>
> When we got back we went for a flight over the grounds in Philip's private aeroplane. And then when we went into tea we found, amongst others, Bernard Shaw arguing with Winston Churchill over the tea-cups, Rex Whistler painting in the corner, Osbert Sitwell and Malcolm Bullock laughing in another corner, Kenneth Clark holding forth about pictures, and Heaven knows who else
>
> When we went up to change – into black tie – for dinner there was a cocktail and a carnation on every dressing-table. And dinner was served by a large fat butler whose name I forget, and six white-coated footmen. After dinner we watched a magnificent firework display on the lake. And finally Richard Tauber sang to us under the stars on the Terrace outside the house.
>
> Today it all seems like the dream of another world, now gone for ever. And so it is.
>
> We are exactly the same age, the main difference being that I tire very easily, and you never do.

In October 1985 the Conservative Government announced the results of further prolonged EEC negotiations on fishing agreements. Once again, Boothby was loud in his praises of the Minister concerned, Peter Walker, and in the Lords welcomed 'the best possible result we could have obtained and the best fisheries agreement we have ever had', adding that 'I never thought that I would live to see this day.' He also turned on Willie Ross (now Lord Ross of Marnock) who had quoted a typically curmudgeonly comment in the *Scotsman* saying that paper 'was talking absolute rubbish, and not for the first time,' glowering with such intensity at Ross that it was obvious to a delighted House that he was not talking about the *Scotsman* at all. It was a happy day.

In July 1983, immediately after the triumphant re-election of the Conservatives in a general election in which Boothby's old friend, Michael Foot, had led the Labour Party in a campaign of breathtaking ineptitude, one of the Government's first actions was to announce the closure of the Royal Naval Dockyard in Gibraltar. Boothby was incensed, pointing out in the Lords that 'If the Government have their way over this matter, there will be no permanent naval presence in the Mediterranean since the Tudors reigned over this country.' On another occasion he asked: 'Why choose this moment to harm the Gibraltarians, now happily British subjects, and still further to weaken British naval power?' But the Government pressed on, and Boothby, rather crossly, accepted the decision.

One of the pleasures of Boothby's old age was receiving letters from his former constituents, one of whom wrote to him in 1984: 'I had some Scottish friends here the other day, & we all agreed that you were so very highly respected & loved, that if you had been a communist, you would have still been a Member of Parliament representing Buchan.'

To the muted dismay of Wanda and his financial advisers, Boothby's generosity to his friends continued. One recipient wrote to him on 6 June 1985:

Darling Bob

Few people would think it worthwhile to give an old woman say, a hundred pounds, unless to pay for her funeral.

I am absolutely *delighted* to be given £200 and would certainly not waste it on a funeral (a sack into the sea is quite enough) & I am now thinking of all the lovely things I am going to do with it!

You have done a tremendously generous, kind & thoughtful thing – and I am more grateful & touched than I can possibly say.

Always my love, in such real gratitude.

Boothby's generosity to his godchildren and others, including friends like Frank Owen,* of whom there was little hope of return, was indeed remarkable, but he did expect results, and when one whom he had financed at Oxford failed even to get a degree he erupted with fury:

I am entitled to say that I think that this is an extremely bad show and I do say it.

Don't kid yourself that failure to get a degree after three years can do you any good in any sphere of life, or that it can be laughed off. It is a damned disgrace.

---

*Frank Owen had been a Liberal MP from 1929–31, and editor of the *Evening Standard*, 1938–41, and the *Daily Mail*, 1947–50.

I have often feared that you were wasting precious years at Oxford; but never became deeply alarmed until I heard you and your father discussing the possibility of an autumn pleasure cruise in the Piraeus. Then I began to wonder whether you would ever get down to it. If this doesn't shock you into taking hold of your life and making something of it, you will be sunk.

You have always thought that you could bluff your way through by charm, and tall talk unsupported by hard work and knowledge; and that you could make money the easy way. I suspect that you think that I owe such success as I have had in life to becoming secretary of the Canning Club and to speculation. You are quite wrong if you do. I have never done anything but lose money by gambling; and the only advantage I ever derived from it was that it acted as a stimulus to further and more intensive effort.

The truth is that success – and I don't mean mere worldly success, but the inner satisfaction that is derived from solid achievement – can only be obtained the hard way.

I worked like hell for the last thirty years. Worked and worked and worked. Hours and hours of concentrated reading; up, morning after morning, at five o-clock, and sometimes four when there is a job to be done. No one sees this. It looks quite easy when I 'throw off' an article or a speech. Let me assure you that it isn't. The position I have now won in public life is due to nothing but gruelling work, and the knowledge and experience that comes of it.

Now you have a chance, I think the last – to make good before it is too late. It will be a good idea to begin by realising that you have got to earn your living – the hard way.

Stop talking nonsense about 'going into politics', and making glib speeches and writing meretricious articles which you are not qualified to do. LEARN A TRADE. WORK.

And in the meantime don't try to persuade yourself that you have done anything, to date, except let your parents down, let me down, and let your uncle down.

I have stopped off here on my way from Italy to Strasbourg (here being Monte Carlo); and I wish that I had said all this, even more forcibly, two years ago. However, I dare say you had to have this knock – and it's a hell of a knock – to shake some sense into you. If it doesn't, it will be a knockout.

Yours ever,
Bob

The recipient of this fierce letter wrote some time later to him:

My dear Bob
. . . I sometimes wonder if I might have been a better or a more successful person if I had not had your £1500 to spend at Oxford – but it is a thought I always manage to dismiss. I shall always look back with unrelieved happiness on the many experiences and pleasures – both high and low – which your generosity made possible. . . .

With love.

So, all was well.

Boothby was, physically, a shadow of his former self. Now that the Lords were televised, viewers were shocked to see his emaciated figure, but his mind had not been affected. On 6 May 1986 he made his last intervention in the Lords. The issue was British entry into the Exchange Rate Mechanism of the European Monetary System. Christopher Soames, out of office, and also with the hand of death upon him, urged the Government, in the shape of Lord Young of Graffham, to take a positive decision in the lifetime of the Parliament to follow the universal advice to join the Exchange Rate Mechanism. The reply was negative, with the familiar dirge that 'We will be ready to join the Exchange Rate Mechanism as and when we judge the conditions are right for us to do so.' This did not go down well, particularly with Boothby. This was his last speech:

My Lords, may I ask the noble Lord whether he realises that for the last sixty years the whole world has suffered from recurrent economic depressions amounting to crises, causing much unemployment and poverty; and that the primary cause of these depressions in every case was the lack of an efficient and viable international monetary system? The noble Lord talks about keeping it under review. It has been kept under review for sixty years. The last serious attempt to tackle the problem was made at the Genoa Conference of 1922 by Mr Lloyd George, who unfortunately fell from power before he could carry it out. Does the noble Lord not think that the time has come for us to have another stab at it, by joining the EMS, and joining it now?

Lord Young responded as before, to Boothby's disgust. Boothby was, of course, once again absolutely right. Another superb opportunity was being permitted to slither away, as he realised, and with devastating consequences. Once again, and for the last time, his advice and his warnings were courteously ignored. His hated enemy The Treasury Mind had triumphed once more – and, once more, at dreadful cost. It was a highly appropriate note on which Boothby gave his final bow.

Boothby bore the tribulations of old age with fortitude, buoyed by Wanda's devoted care and the loyalty of his friends. 'For my part', he wrote to Ludovic Kennedy, 'I am *not* too good. And the main reason is that, instead of facing old age, I resent it and fight it. I am trying to reform, but fear it is too late!' He and Kennedy had had their differences in the past, but were now reconciled, and Boothby followed his career on television and his campaigns against injustices with growing admiration. Boothby wrote cheerfully to Kennedy on 25 March 1985:

As for me, I am now 85; and Parkinson's Disease has now joined Arthritis to torment me. My doctor went away the other day, and told his secretary to ring me up after a few days to find out how I was. I said: 'Tell him I am dying slowly and peacefully, with considerable courage and great dignity.' And that's about it.

The old wit had not gone. 'I used to think that euthanasia should be voluntary,' he wrote to Kennedy. 'I now think that it should be compulsory at eighty-five.' When he tried the same line on Marjorie Legentilhomme, however, he had a fierce response, as her beloved husband had lived happily and healthily until he was ninety-two. It was not one of his more tactful letters, but, as she has remarked, 'the old Bob had gone'. There were occasions when he could still hold court over a whisky in the Lords, but these became much fewer. But there was no whingeing, and he was deeply grateful for everything that was done to help him.

He claimed that 'I live on a diet of Complan and whisky, which isn't as bad as it sounds.' A taxi-driver asked if he was Lord Boothby, and when Boothby replied that he was, the driver said, 'Oh! God! I remember you as a fat jolly fellow on television. Now you look like Christ on the Cross.' 'This was overheard by that devout Catholic Lord Longford,' Boothby wrote to Kennedy, 'who now calls me Jesus!'

Arthritis had now severely affected his hands, and his beautiful handwriting became smaller, but still perfectly legible. Although he seldom went out for meals, he and Wanda continued to entertain their friends at Eaton Square and visit the Lords, where he saw his friends in the Peers' Guest Room. He had no expectations whatever of the afterlife, and was glad that he had been so careful to arrange that there would be no memorial service.

In May 1986, Peterhead Harbour decided that the new basin to be built in the harbour, the south basin, would be called Boothby Basin and, as the Clerk wrote to Boothby,

> It was felt that perhaps calling it Lord Boothby Basin was a bit of a mouthful!!! – hence the abbreviation, which we hope you wil not object to. We trust you are keeping well and we are arranging for a dram to be sent to you to toast the harbour's future prosperity.

Boothby was delighted. It was his last honour from his old constituency.

In June 1986 he paid his final visit to the Lords, terribly shrunken but beaming. A friend asked him how he was, and he replied, smiling, 'I'm dying, but too slowly.' His last known letter was to Marjorie Legentilhomme, which she received two days after he died.

The end came soon after, on 16 July. He had what was thought to be a mild heart attack and was taken to Westminster Hospital. He knew it was the end. He said to Wanda, 'I love you so much; look after the dogs', and peacefully died.

*   *   *

The public and private tributes were substantial and generous. Michael Foot described him as 'one of the most convivial men who ever lived – too intelligent, too humane, too warm-hearted, to be a real Tory'. Lord Gladwyn wrote a glowing tribute in *The Times* to his old friend: 'Impetuous, outspoken, generous, warm-hearted, artistic and forgiving, he had also, perhaps, the best instinctive judgment among the politicians of our time.' William Deedes wrote with real affection of a friend who 'simply could not resist drinking from brim to dregs every cup offered him. . . . He died of cardiac problems – and not for want of trying. There cracks a noble heart.' The tributes in the Scottish press had a special warmth, notably Jack Webster's memories in the *Glasgow Herald* of his appearance in his young life: 'Robert Boothby represented glamour on my childhood horizon, all-flowing hair, bow-ties, disarming smiles, and a voice of golden gravel – one of the finest orators and most rumbustious personalities this country has produced.'

Peter Strachan, editor of the *Buchan Observer*, wrote to Wanda:

> Dear Lady Boothby
>
> Always the gentleman – that's how I remember your man.
>
> Never out of humour, ever willing to oblige, courteous and sincere, and so anxious to do well by everybody.
>
> In Buchan he gave a lift to life 'on and off the record' for, in any company, he was the best of company. He gave so much of himself, and asked so little – as Bob, Sir Robert, and Lord Boothby.
>
> Thank you for being, as he himself did so, 'so wonderful'.
>
> Kindest regards
> Peter Strachan

Boothby had always had a special feeling for children and had helped them in various ways. Two wrote to Wanda, particularly movingly:

> Bob gave me my first fiver, huge, white and crinkly, in Wheelers when I was ten and a five pound note was riches! He was a fairy godfather to us children, immensely kind, funny, glamorous, generous, and wise. And how we looked forward to visiting One Eaton Square. His wisdom I came better to recognise and appreciate as I got older and read his articles (an excuse for a prurient youth to read the *News of the World*) and, later, books. Vision and common sense were uniquely combined. If he had had less of a sense of humour and had taken himself more seriously, he would have had more political impact, but the world would have been a much duller place, and Britain would now be a much less humane society. I think he made the right decisions.

And, another of his favourite children:

> Times when he used to visit us, endless lunches at One Eaton Square, treats, holidays – whenever he appeared there was always a feeling of

lightness, gaiety and affection in the air. He wasn't my godfather but it felt as though he was – and not just a godfather but a fairy godfather too!

Once he said to me (when I was eight years old and I had broken my arm on holiday), 'You can have whatever you like.' I said I would like a camera or a dog. He brought me the camera and look at the long-term effect! Here I am all these years later, busy photographing.

Another friend wrote:

I will never, I know, be able to enter your drawing-room without seeing him in his desk by the window, surrounded by newspapers, milk or whisky bottles, cigarettes and ashtray, yelling for Wanda. He is at peace now, but I bet St. Peter isn't – Bob will be yelling for him to fetch the newspapers to see what they have said about him.

He was cremated at Mortlake on 25 July with the minimum of ceremony, and on 30 August, in a fierce, wild sea, Wanda set off in the drifter *Starlight* from Peterhead, accompanied by his successor as MP for Buchan, Albert McQuarrie, who had made all the arrangements, Gilbert Buchan and other friends. One mile off Rattray Head Wanda and the skipper, Sandy Baird, scattered his ashes into the turbulent sea, followed by wreaths. Other boats had left Peterhead and Fraserburgh to be present at the brief service conducted by the Episcopal Bishop for Aberdeen and Orkney. As the wreaths were thrown, the fleet responded with a farewell blast on their sirens in tribute to 'The Fisherman's Friend'. Wanda used the ship's radio to speak to the skippers and crews of all the boats: 'This is Wanda Boothby. I wish to thank you all for helping me to carry out his wishes. North Sea fishermen and the farmers of this area were his first love, and his last.' Then the boats turned and headed for their respective ports through the heavy swell. Twelve boats had made the special journey for their farewell to their friend.

Boothby had never had any religious faith and was sceptical of those who did, especially those who tried to foist their bigotries on others. Burns and Fox were his favourites; the Calvinists were his implacable foes. 'For better or worse we are here,' he once wrote, quoting another. 'Involuntarily, I admit, and that alone is enough to damn the whole business.' In supporting Bertrand Russell in 1963 he wrote to the editor of the *Evening News*: 'The truth, Sir, is that life, as such, has no meaning or purpose. All we can hope to do is to make the best of it. And I hope you have the guts to print this letter.'

He liked to portray himself as a cheerful *bon viveur*, careless of life's fortunes and misfortunes. The reality was different. Many thought they knew him well, but few did. One who knew him really well throughout his life, and loved him very much, saw the seriousness in him. 'He never really enjoyed life,' she has told me, 'because he didn't know where he was going. He never saw anything before him.' She also, like many others, put down his ultimate failure and disillusionment to his love for Dorothy Macmillan, and its tragic consequences. 'That destroyed him. *She* destroyed him. But he truly loved her, and she truly loved him. Oh, my dear Bob, he was totally and utterly naïve in these matters. It was a tragedy.'

In 1965 Boothby was invited by George Unwin to contribute an essay to a sequel to *I Believe*, which had been published in 1940 and had had a phenomenal and enduring success. The new volume was entitled *What I Believe* and was published in 1966. Boothby began by remarking that

A better title for this essay would be 'What I do *not* believe'. For the truth is that, in the generally accepted sense of the term, I don't believe in much, beyond the undoubted existence of a life force which carries us, whether we like it or not, upon an irresistible tide. If I thought that the life force itself was eternal, I would try harder to deflect its course, or at least to divert it into more rewarding channels. But I know that it is not.

He took as his theme one of Arthur Balfour's more depressing passages, 'but which always brings to me a certain sense of exhilaration, similar to that of a frosty day'. For believers, whether genuine or hopeful, this was only the beginning of a particularly alarmingly fine essay in favour of nihilism. Jesus gets a very favourable mention, it is true, but, according to Boothby, Saint Paul wrecked everything by substituting

a religion of death for a religion of life, a religion of slavery to sin for a religion of emancipation from it, and a religion of suffering for a religion of joy. Calvin completed the grim process. . . . This is why the history of the Christian Churches has been one of such atrocious cruelty.

The afterlife is appropriately mocked ('Nothing is, or looks, more dead than a corpse. . . . The thought of a spiritual Boothby twanging a spiritual harp for eternity has, for me, limited attractions'), which delighted some reviewers and readers, but greatly shocked others, not least those who remembered his – to them – notorious Rectorial address. But, as in that denunciation, some sunshine is, inevitably, permitted to blaze through the clouds, and is Boothby's credo:

Courage and loving kindness are the infallible recipes for life – accompanied by a sense of humour which, as Maugham has said, is the only retort to the tragic absurdity of fate. I have found that compassion – the urge to diminish the sum of human suffering, and to help those who are in difficulty, trouble or distress – brings the most abiding personal happiness. And between compassion and cruelty there can be no compromise.

On that characteristic note, let us take farewell of him. Or is it adieu?

Notes on Sources

*T*he principal source for this biography has been the Boothby papers. These are substantial, starting with his childhood letters – the first at the age of four – and ending with a written parliamentary question in the House of Lords on the day that he died at the age of eighty-six. The letters are primarily concerned with Boothby's political interests and career, although there are correspondences with personal friends. From the age of twenty-three until almost the end of his life Boothby kept virtually every press cutting and article relating to himself and his constituency, and these volumes have been invaluable, not least because Boothby included items that were distinctly unfavourable to him, including his divorce and the comments on the Czech assets affair. Boothby kept a journal only for a short time in 1949, and his appointment diaries, although useful, are an inadequate substitute.

These papers have been collected and catalogued with great efficiency by his widow, and include copies of Boothby's correspondence with Churchill, Beaverbrook, the first Lady Mosley, Harold Macmillan, Oswald Mosley and Harold Nicolson. As we have seen, Boothby destroyed his lengthy correspondence with Lady Dorothy Macmillan, and her husband destroyed Boothby's letters to her. Boothby also destroyed other private correspondence, on the grounds that 'Letters intended for one pair of eyes only should not be seen by others'. Papers relating to his business affairs do not seem to have survived, with the exception of those relating to the Czech assets affair, most of which have been published as Appendices to *The Select Committee Report on the Conduct of a Member* in

January 1941. His letters to Compton Mackenzie are in the Mackenzie papers in the library of the University of Texas at Austin.

Boothby's own writings, broadcasts and television appearances, which provide exceptionally copious material for a modern biographer, have to be handled with some caution, particularly in Boothby's old age, but their quality and interest are considerable. His first publication was a joint venture with other Conservative MPs – including Harold Macmillan – in 1927 (*Industry and the State – A Conservative View*, Macmillan); *The New Economy* was published in 1943 by Secker and Warburg, and his first major work, *I Fight to Live*, by Gollancz in 1947; *My Yesterday, Your Tomorrow* (Hutchinson, 1962) is a collection of Boothby's articles and speeches, chosen by himself, and include his Rectorial address and his celebrated Burns Night speech, both delivered at St Andrews; *Recollections of a Rebel* (Hutchinson, 1978) may have caused a furore at the time of publication, but is both interesting and witty, and is one of the best of modern political autobiographies; like all such endeavours, it should be handled with some caution. Boothby's capacity to improve upon a good story was well known to his friends, but the basic story was almost invariably true.

Boothby features often in the diaries of Harold Nicolson, Chips Channon and Leo Amery, and Alastair Horne has related the Boothby–Dorothy Macmillan affair in the first volume of his biography of Harold Macmillan (Macmillan, 1987). On the basis of the papers and conversations I have seen and heard, my interpretation of this tragic relationship has been rather different, but the task of any biographer of Macmillan to penetrate his strange and immensely complex personality is a difficult one indeed. Maurice Bowra's caustic poetical view of the affair – *A Statesman's Tragedy* – has never been published and has been seen by only a few people, including me. For copyright reasons, it cannot be published yet. There are also references to the subject in the unpublished parts of the Channon diaries (Weidenfeld and Nicolson, 1967) which I, as editor, had deleted.

There is an admiring portrait of the young Boothby in Maurice Bowra's *Memories* (Weidenfeld and Nicolson, 1966) and a less flattering one in Ludovic Kennedy's *On My Way to the Club* (Collins, 1989). Both Nicholas Davenport (*Memoirs of a City Radical*, Weidenfeld and Nicolson, 1974) and Richard Weininger (*Exciting Years*, Exposition, 1978) contain lengthy accounts of two important periods of Boothby's life, and his own essay on his undergraduate period, in *My Oxford*, edited by Ann Thwaite (Robson Books, 1977), complements Bowra's and that of Hugh Thomas in his biography of John Strachey (Eyre Methuen, 1973). The Mosley relationship is dealt with in Mosley's own autobiography (*My Life*, Nelson, 1968) and in Robert Skidelsky's biography, *Oswald Mosley* (Macmillan, 1975). Boothby features in Colin Coote's *The Other Club* (Sidgwick and Jackson, 1971) and in Baffy Dugdale's diaries (Norman Rose (ed.), *Baffy – The Diaries of Blanche Dugdale, 1936–47* (Vallentine, Mitchell, 1973). There are some poisonous references to Boothby in James Stuart's *Within the Fringe* (Bodley Head, 1967) without actually naming him, and S. J. Hetherington is excellent on the Kinross and West Perthshire by-election of December 1938 (*Katherine Atholl – Against the Tide*, Aberdeen University Press, 1989), and an admirable counterweight to Stuart's grossly overrated memoirs. Charles Edward Lysaght's *Brendan Bracken* (Allen Lane, 1979) and A. J. P. Taylor's *Beaverbrook* (Hamish Hamilton, 1972) contain many references to Boothby, as do the companion volumes to Martin Gilbert's monumental biography of Churchill, although no reference is made to the Czech assets affair. Churchill's own war memoirs contain very few references to Boothby – a very clear sign of their changed relationship. F. F. Rainsford's *Memoirs of an Accidental Airman* (Harmsworth, 1986), with a Foreword by Boothby, refer to Boothby's wartime service in the RAF; Grace Wyndham Goldie's *Facing the Nation* (Bodley Head, 1977) describes how the political establishment neutered and then killed off the best political series in the history of British television, and of which Boothby was a conspicuous victim. Considering their long friendship there is surprisingly little about Boothby in Duff Cooper's *Old Men Forget* (Hart-Davis, 1953), but this is made up by John Charmley's *Duff Cooper* (Weidenfeld and Nicolson, 1986), although Boothby's memorial service address is not referred to.

Of books about the Munich period there seems no end, but Richard Cockett's *Twilight of Truth* (Weidenfeld and Nicolson, 1989) discloses how the Chamberlain Government manipulated and used the British press to deceive the British people in 1938 and 1939, and serves as a devastating corrective to the school of pro-Munich revisionists which has recently surfaced. As in Mrs Hetherington's biography of the Duchess of Atholl, it shows what Churchill and Boothby were up against (as does Stuart's book).

Boothby is often referred to in other memoirs and accounts, and I attempted a preliminary portrait of him in my *Churchill – A Study In Failure, 1900–39* (Weidenfeld and Nicolson, 1970).

Index

Note: il. in the index indicates a photograph of the subject.

The arrangement of subheadings in the index is chronological, with references to the character, relationships and writings of those indexed grouped at the end of the chronological sequences.

People are indexed by their names or titles at the time of the events described, with titles acquired subsequently added in brackets.

Abbreviations used:
RB   Robert Boothby, Baron Boothby of Buchan and Rattray Head
HC   House of Commons
MP   Member of Parliament
PM   Prime Minister
WWi   World War i
WWii   World War ii

461

More Autobiographical Non-Fiction from Headline:

—— WILLIAM WHITELAW ——
THE WHITELAW MEMOIRS

THE NUMBER ONE BESTSELLING AUTOBIOGRAPHY

'A delightful volume. Anyone reading it will quickly realise what a shrewd, good and lovable man the author is'
Sunday Telegraph

Member of Parliament for Penrith from 1955 until his elevation to a viscountcy in 1983, Lord Whitelaw has served in Government and in Opposition under Macmillan and Douglas-Home and as a Cabinet minister under Heath and Thatcher. His popularity among members of his own party is legendary; the respect he commands among his political opponents is both rare and remarkable.

The Whitelaw Memoirs are no dry, self-serving re-enactment of a life in politics. They are, instead, a thoughtful and concise recollection of the events and moods of the day in a political career which has spanned the posts of Leader of the House of Commons, Secretary of State for Northern Ireland, Chairman of the Conservative Party, Home Secretary and Leader of the House of Lords. For, while never courting controversy, Lord Whitelaw presided over such politically sensitive issues and events as the Iranian Embassy siege and the knife-edge complexities of the Northern Ireland situation of the 1970s.

The Whitelaw Memoirs tell the engaging lifestory of an outstanding family man who has come to embody for many such old-fashioned virtues as loyalty, fairness and political and personal decency. Most tellingly, they reveal – for the first time – the inner thoughts of a politician of consummate skill at the various crisis points of twenty-five years at the centre of British public life.

'The characteristically graceful memoir of a delightful, instinctively decent and – genuinely – popular public figure'
Guardian

'An eminently enjoyable, sometimes deceptively informal, personal story' *Evening Standard*

'Eagerly awaited . . . engagingly written' *Sunday Express*

'This excellent book' *The Times*

BIOGRAPHY/POLITICS   0 7472 3348 9

More Autobiographical Non-Fiction from Headline:

MY
MOUNTBATTEN
YEARS

IN THE SERVICE OF LORD LOUIS

WILLIAM EVANS

A six-year-old 'city urchin' evacuated during Hitler's war to the
Yorkshire Wolds in 1939, William Evans joined the Royal
Navy, due to conscription, in 1950. Rising to the rank of Chief
Petty Officer, he achieved his life's ambition when he was
appointed to the Royal Yacht *Britannia* in October 1959.
But he only managed one brief cruise of the Caribbean before
being whisked off by Lord Mountbatten, then Chief of the
UK Defence Staff, to head his Naval Retinue after
the death of Lady Louis in Burma.

There followed ten of the most hectic and exciting years of
William Evans' life. His duties took him to the four corners of
the world and gave him opportunities only dreamt of to rub
shoulders with kings and prime ministers, members of the lost
tribes, and eminent and distinguished people from the worlds
of business and entertainment. At the centre of it all, though,
was Lord Louis himself, one of this century's most charismatic
and intriguing statesmen. Evans served him selflessly and
devotedly, never taking a holiday, attending to his every
requirement, whether for a State visit, a military tour or a jolly
weekend with fellow Royals. Eventually, stress took its toll and
Evans left the service of Lord Louis, only to be reunited with
him, tragically, four days before he was killed by an IRA bomb
in his boat off Classiebawn Castle in August 1979.

Honest, simple and endearing, *My Mountbatten Years* is a book
to be read and treasured by all Lord Mountbatten's
many admirers.

NON-FICTION/AUTOBIOGRAPHY   0 7472 3417 5

More Political Non-Fiction from Headline:

THE
CHINESE
SECRET SERVICE

ROGER FALIGOT & RÉMI KAUFFER
TRANSLATED FROM THE FRENCH BY CHRISTINE DONOUGHER

'A racy story of naked ambition . . . The final message
is that China is still a poor country seething with suppressed
violence, where a minority political movement is using its
secret police and massive army to maintain power by
repression' *Sunday Times*

For the first time ever, the veil is truly lifted on the Chinese
secret service, the *Tewu*, and its shadowy founder, Kang
Sheng, who died – mourned publicly by millions, privately
by few – in 1975. The culmination of years of painstaking
research all over the Far East and Europe, *The Chinese
Secret Service* probes into the life of Kang Sheng and the
crucial role he and his secret services played in the
shaping of modern China.

Exploring every aspect of the Chinese secret service, from its
inception in Shanghai in the 1920s to its current role at
home and abroad, the authors lay bare a world of violence,
mystery and ruthless ambition: the merciless struggle
between Mao and Chiang Kai-shek, the incredible story of
the Chinese atom bomb, the turmoil of the Cultural
Revolution and beyond. By casting a cold and piercing light
on China's secret past, *The Chinese Secret Service* offers
vital historical illumination on the country's troubled
and confused existence today.

'An interesting new book' *Sunday Express*

'The book in its popular and vivid style serves to highlight
the treacherous, secretive, violent and factional nature
of the Chinese Communist Party and government'
The Times Educational Supplement

NON-FICTION/CURRENT AFFAIRS   0 7472 3368 3

A selection of bestsellers
from Headline

FICTION

DANCING ON THE RAINBOW	Frances Brown	£4.99 ☐
NEVER PICK UP HITCH-HIKERS!	Ellis Peters	£4.50 ☐
THE WOMEN'S CLUB	Margaret Bard	£5.99 ☐
A WOMAN SCORNED	M. R. O'Donnell	£4.99 ☐
THE FALL OF HYPERION	Dan Simmons	£5.99 ☐
SIRO	David Ignatius	£4.99 ☐
DARKNESS, TELL US	Richard Laymon	£4.99 ☐
THE BOTTOM LINE	John Harman	£5.99 ☐

NON-FICTION

ROD STEWART	Tim Ewbank & Stafford Hildred	£4.99 ☐
JOHN MAJOR	Bruce Anderson	£6.99 ☐
WHITE HEAT	Marco Pierre White	£5.99 ☐

SCIENCE FICTION AND FANTASY

LENS OF THE WORLD	R. A. MacAvoy	£4.50 ☐
DREAM FINDER	Roger Taylor	£5.99 ☐
VENGEANCE FOR A LONELY MAN	Simon R. Green	£4.50 ☐

All Headline books are available at your local bookshop or newsagent, or can be ordered direct from the publisher. Just tick the titles you want and fill in the form below. Prices and availability subject to change without notice.

Headline Book Publishing PLC, Cash Sales Department, PO Box 11, Falmouth, Cornwall, TR10 9EN, England.

Please enclose a cheque or postal order to the value of the cover price and allow the following for postage and packing:
UK & BFPO: £1.00 for the first book, 50p for the second book and 30p for each additional book ordered up to a maximum charge of £3.00.
OVERSEAS & EIRE: £2.00 for the first book, £1.00 for the second book and 50p for each additional book.

Name ....

Address ....

....

....